INTERNATIONAL SURVEY OF FAMILY LAW

Published on behalf of the International Society of Family Law

INTERNATIONAL
SOCIETY OF FAMILY
LAW

ISFL

INTERNATIONAL SURVEY OF FAMILY LAW

2022 Edition

Edited by
Robin Fretwell Wilson
June Carbone

In collaboration with
Luyi Song
Parker von Sternberg

INTERSENTIA
Cambridge – Antwerp – Chicago

Intersentia Ltd
8 Wellington Mews
Wellington Street | Cambridge
CB1 1HW | United Kingdom
Tel: +44 1223 736 170
Email: mail@intersentia.co.uk
www.intersentia.com | www.intersentia.co.uk

Distribution for the UK and
Rest of the World (incl. Eastern Europe)
NBN International
1 Deltic Avenue, Rooksley
Milton Keynes MK13 8LD
United Kingdom
Tel: +44 1752 202 301 | Fax: +44 1752 202 331
Email: orders@nbninternational.com

Distribution for Europe
Lefebvre Sarrut Belgium NV
Hoogstraat 139/6
1000 Brussels
Belgium
Tel: +32 (0)800 39 067
Email: mail@intersentia.be

Distribution for the USA and Canada
Independent Publishers Group
Order Department
814 North Franklin Street
Chicago, IL 60610
USA
Tel: +1 800 888 4741 (toll free) | Fax: +1 312 337 5985
Email: orders@ipgbook.com

International Survey of Family Law. 2022 Edition

ISBN 978-1-83970-264-8
D/2022/7849/132
NUR 828

British Library Cataloguing in Publication Data. A catalogue record for this book is available from the British Library.

PREFACE

With the 2022 edition, we mark a passing from Margaret Brinig's many years of effort overseeing the International Survey of Family Law as General Editor, to our assumption of the responsibilities. We hope to live up to the example Professor Brinig has set.

This year's edition comes as we begin to resume in person activities and, over the next year, we will mark the International Society of Family Law's golden jubilee. As the world recovers from COVID-19, this edition will mark the developments across the globe and examines some of the innovations that have arisen in the context of the disease and how these innovations have been integrated into family law practice.

An extraordinarily broad review of developments from around the world is included in the 2022 Survey. The volume examines the growing inclusion – and continuing limitations – of LGBT families into family law adjudication, chronicling developments in China, Ireland, and South Africa. It considers the status of de facto relationships in the Czech Republic, and the challenges of determining parenthood in the context of assisted reproduction and surrogacy in Belgium and France. A number of contributions report on the incorporation of international treaties into domestic law, particularly in Norway, Hong Kong and Australia, whilst others explore the challenges of managing cross-border issues involving the enforcement of foreign judgments and migration in France, Sweden, and Chile. Articles address the fragmentation of family law in Australia's federal system and the role of artificial intelligence in family law adjudication in Italy. In addition, this volume reports on grandchild adoption in South Korea, the decision-making capacity of the disabled in Poland, abortion in England and Wales, grounds for divorce in the Seychelles, the impact of COVID 19 on Slovenian custody adjudication, spousal support developments in the United States, and the impact of demographic changes on spousal support in China.

Our thanks go to Christine Bidaud and the Family Law Center of the Université Jean Moulin Lyon 3, who have provided the French translations for the contributions. This year's volume was produced in collaboration with the research team of Luyi Song and Parker von Sternberg. We are grateful to

Aylin Cakan and Pamela Melton for their assistance with the preparation of the Survey.

The next two volumes will celebrate the Society's fiftieth anniversary.

June Carbone, Minnesota
Robin Fretwell Wilson, Illinois
September 2022

CONTENTS

LIST OF CONTRIBUTORS

Zaahirah America
LLB Graduate, Faculty of Law, University of the Western Cape (UWC), South Africa

Massilia Amzal
PhD Student, Family Law Center, Université Jean Moulin Lyon 3, France

Małgorzata Balwicka-Szczyrba
Associate Professor of Law, Faculty of Law and Administration, Department of Commercial Law, University of Gdańsk, Poland

Bastien Baret
Associate Professor, Research Team Confluence, Sciences and Humanities – EA 1598, Lyon Catholic University, France

Christine Bidaud
Professor and Co-Director of the Family Law Center, Research Team Louis Josserand, Université Jean Moulin Lyon 3, France

Claire Brunerie
PhD Student, International Private Law Center, Université Jean Moulin Lyon 3, France

Aurore Camuzat
PhD Student, Family Law Center, Research Team Louis Josserand, Université Jean Moulin Lyon 3, France

June Carbone
Robina Chair of Law, Science and Technology, University of Minnesota, United States of America

Siyuan Dong
Postdoctoral Fellow, East China University of Political Science and Law, Shanghai, China

Michelle Fernando
Senior Lecturer in Law, University of South Australia, Australia

Isabella Ferrari
Professor in Comparative Private Law and Law & New Technologies, Department of Engineering 'Enzo Ferrari', University of Studies of Modena and Reggio Emilia, Italy

Éric Fongaro
Professor, Deputy Director of IRDAP, Co-Director of the Master 2 Law and Estate Management and Head of the Comparative Private Law course, University of Bordeaux, France

Katrine K. Fredwall
Associate Professor, Institute of Private Law, Faculty of Law, University of Oslo, Norway

Hugues Fulchiron
Professor, Co-Director of the Family Law Center, Research Team Louis Josserand, Université Jean Moulin Lyon 3, France; Judge at the Cour de cassation

Elise Goossens
Assistant Professor of Civil Law in Context, Faculty of Law, University of Antwerp; Assistant Professor of Family Law, Faculty of Law and Criminology, Free University of Brussels; Research Fellow, KU Leuven, Belgium

Maebh Harding
Assistant Professor, UCD Sutherland School of Law, University College Dublin, Ireland

Guillaume Kessler
Associate Professor, Research Law Center Antoine Favre, Université de Savoie Mont Blanc, France

Zdeňka Králíčková
Professor, Faculty of Law, Masaryk University, Brno, Czech Republic

Suzana Kraljić
Full Professor, Faculty of Law, University of Maribor, Slovenia

Dongjin Lee
Professor, School of Law, Seoul National University, South Korea

Xia Li
Professor, Law School, East China University of Political Science and Law, Shanghai, China

Guillaume Millerioux
PhD Student, Temporary Research and Teaching Assistant, Family Law Center, Research Team Louis Josserand, Université Jean Moulin Lyon 3, France

Alexis Mondaca
Professor of Civil Law, University of Talca, Chile

Najma Moosa
Senior Professor, Department of Private Law, Faculty of Law, University of the Western Cape (UWC), South Africa

Taylène Moreira De Sá
PhD Student, Family Law Center, Research Team Louis Josserand, Université Jean Moulin Lyon 3, France and University of São Paulo, Brazil; Lawyer and Member of the Brazilian Institute of Family Law (IBDFAM)

Mathilde Mosiek-Brasset
PhD Student, Family Law Center, Research Team Louis Josserand, Université Jean Moulin Lyon 3, France

Jamil Ddamulira Mujuzi
Professor of Law, Faculty of Law, University of the Western Cape, South Africa

Margot Musson
PhD Student, Family Law Center, Research Team Louis Josserand, Université Jean Moulin Lyon 3, France

J. Thomas Oldham
John H. Freeman Professor of Law, University of Houston Law Center, Texas, United States of America

Anna Parker
Judge, Federal Circuit and Family Court of Australia (Division 2), Australia

Elizabeth S. Perry
Senior Lecturer, Faculty of Law, Uppsala University, Sweden; Adjunct Lecturer, Department of Law, Umeå University, Sweden

Anja Pich
Masters Student and Lecturer in Law, University of South Australia, Australia

Marie Pincet
PhD Student, Family Law Center, Research Team Louis Josserand, Université Jean Moulin Lyon 3, France

Grant T. Riethmuller
Judge, Federal Circuit and Family Court of Australia (Division 1), Australia

Anne Scully-Johnson
Associate Professor (Adjunct), Faculty of Law, The Chinese University of Hong Kong

Frederik Swennen
Full Professor of Family Law and Kinship Studies at, and Dean of, the Faculty of Law, University of Antwerp, Belgium; Member of the Executive Council of the International Society of Family Law

Anna Sylwestrzak
Associate Professor of Law, Faculty of Law and Administration, Department of Civil Law, University of Gdańsk, Poland

Mary Welstead
CAP Fellow, Harvard Law School, Harvard University, Massachusetts, United States of America; Visiting Professor in Family Law, University of Buckingham, United Kingdom

Robin Fretwell Wilson
Mildred Van Voorhis Chair in Law, University of Illinois College of Law and the Director of the Institute of Government and Public Affairs, University of Illinois System, United States of America

Mingmei Xiang
PhD Student, Law School, East China University of Political Science and Law, Shanghai, China

AUSTRALIA
DEFRAGMENTING THE EVER-GROWING FAMILY LAW SYSTEM

Grant T. Riethmuller* and Anna Parker

Résumé

Le système juridique fédéral de l'Australie a adopté diverses lois (parfois incohérentes) relatives à la réglementation des relations familiales, promulguées

---

* I am indebted to my Legal Associate, Jessica Faulder, for her assistance in preparing this chapter.

à la fois par le Commonwealth et par les gouvernements des États et des territoires. Au cours des dernières décennies, le gouvernement du Commonwealth a pris un certain nombre de mesures visant à remédier à cette fragmentation juridique. Dans la même période, une tendance à qualifier l'ensemble des lois relatives à la famille et aux questions connexes de « système de droit de la famille » s'est de plus en plus développée, ce qui a suscité de plus grandes attentes et une pression croissante pour améliorer l'homogénéité et la cohérence entre ces lois, les tribunaux et autres organismes qui les administrent. Cet article montre de quelle manière la défragmentation et l'harmonisation des lois relatives à la famille et aux questions connexes ont été réalisées en Australie, notamment la récente fusion des tribunaux fédéraux de droit de la famille.

1. INTRODUCTION

The law of marriage was first administered in Australia by the various states, which were then British colonies, prior to federation. The law was that brought from England, based upon a mixture of common law traditions,[1] English legislation and the traditions of the Ecclesiastical Courts. Throughout the 1800s, there was a variety of state and territory marriage legislation.[2]

Following federation in 1901, jurisdiction to make laws with respect to marriage and matrimonial causes was conferred upon the federal government, although this jurisdiction was barely exercised prior to 1959 when the Commonwealth passed the Matrimonial Causes Act 1959 (Cth). However, from federation in 1901 until 1961 when the Commonwealth passed the Marriage Act 1961 (Cth), each state and territory remained responsible for regulating marriage, resulting in the legal requirements for marriage varying from border to border.[3]

Whilst the Commonwealth government has slowly been addressing the deeply fragmented laws relating to marriage and matrimonial causes, steady social change has broadened the difficulties faced by the Commonwealth. Over the last 100 years, 'family law' has emerged as a far broader concept than the original concept of matrimonial causes, as a result of two significant social changes. First, there has been a significant shift in family formations and what is understood as constituting 'family', including a steady rise in the number of both heterosexual and same-sex de facto relationships. This has led to far more

1 Social Policy and Legal Affairs Committee, *Inquiry into the Marriage Equality Amendment Bill 2012 and the Marriage Amendment Bill 2012*, 2012, para. 2.4.

2 See e.g. Matrimonial Causes Act 1899 (NSW), Matrimonial Causes Act 1858 (SA), and Divorce and Matrimonial Causes Act 1857 (Vic).

3 Australian Law Reform Commission, *Review of the Family Law System*, 2019, para. 2.5.

litigation as remedies with respect to personal relationships have become more accessible. Second, as broader understandings of what constitutes family have developed, there has been an increasing tendency on the part of those seeking reforms to refer to the broad area of law relating to families and the courts and other agencies that implement them as the 'family law system'. Of course, what makes up the modern idea of 'family law' is simply a loose category of laws that impact upon families, and until recent times was never conceptualised as a 'system'.

Neither the Commonwealth nor the states have exclusive legislative power with respect to all matters relevant to what is now encompassed by the broad category of 'family law'.[4] Matters relating to the area of law now described as 'family law' but not sufficiently connected to the concepts of 'marriage' or 'matrimonial causes' fall within the legislative remit of the states, at least until the states refer the relevant legislative powers to the Commonwealth. This had the consequence, until relatively recently, that spouses who were or had been married[5] had their disputes as to settlement of property, care arrangements for their children, and other associated matters dealt with in the federal family law system, whilst unmarried couples and sole parents were subject to state laws and legal systems, which differed from state to state and varied in the extent to which they mirrored the laws of the Commonwealth.

The fragmented nature of Australia's 'family law system' has been the subject of sustained criticism and calls for reform for many years. In 2003, a major parliamentary inquiry identified 'gaps and duplication' in the system.[6] A Productivity Commission report published in 2014 described the system as 'complex and fragmented'.[7] Similar observations have been made in a number of other inquiries and reviews in recent decades.[8] In this chapter we briefly

---

4 Australian Law Reform Commission, *Family Violence – A National Legal Response*, 2010, para. 2.43.

5 Which, until 9 December 2017, did not include same-sex couples.

6 House of Representatives Standing Committee on Family and Community Affairs, *Every Picture Tells a Story: Report on the Inquiry into Child Custody Arrangements in the Event of Family Separation*, 2003, para. 4.27.

7 Productivity Commission, *Access to Justice Arrangements*, Inquiry Report No. 72, Vol. 2, 2014, p. 846.

8 See e.g. Family Law Pathways Advisory Group, *Out of the Maze: Pathways to the Future for Families Experiencing Separation*, 2001, p. 5; Family Law Council, *The Best Interests of the Child? The Interaction of Public and Private Law in Australia*, 2000, para. 2.4; Family Law Pathways Advisory Group, *Out of the Maze: Pathways to the Future Family Law Council, Improving the Family Law System for Clients from Culturally and Linguistically Diverse Backgrounds*, 2012, para. 1.3; House of Representatives Standing Committee on Social Policy and Legal Affairs, *A Better Family Law System to Support and Protect those Affected by Family Violence*, 2017, pp. 75–78; Government of Victoria, *Royal Commission into Family Violence*, 2019, p. 19. For academic discussion of this issue, also see F. Kelly and B. Fehlberg, 'Australia's Fragmented Family Law System: Jurisdictional Overlap in the Area of Child Protection' (2002) 16 *International Journal of Law, Policy and the*

recount the steps that have been taken to defragment laws and legal processes relating to the family in Australia and identify further areas that remain in need of reform.

2. THE PROBLEM OF THE FEDERAL CONSTITUTIONAL STRUCTURE

The Commonwealth of Australia is a federation, made up of six states and two major territories. In addition to the federal government, each of the states and one of the two major territories has its own parliament and separate system of government.[9] Residents of each state are subject to the laws both of their state and of the Commonwealth, and lawmaking power is divided between the two levels of government in complex and sometimes overlapping ways. The federal government is limited in the matters in relation to which it can legislate by those powers bestowed on it by Australia's Constitution. However, many powers remain with both levels of government until the federal government makes laws in the particular area, at which point the federal laws prevail if there is any inconsistency.[10] Once the federal government has 'covered the field', there remains no room for valid state laws.

When the Constitution was drafted, lawmaking powers with respect to private individual rights and obligations were generally left to the states, but consideration was given to the need to achieve uniformity and avoid varied and conflicting laws as between the states in the areas of marriage and divorce.[11] As a result, specific constitutional powers were conferred upon the Commonwealth in a number of areas. The constitutional power upon which the federal government may rely to make family laws rests primarily upon the powers to make laws with respect to marriage,[12] and with respect to 'divorce and matrimonial causes, and in relation thereto, parental rights, and the custody and guardianship of infants.'[13]

Family 38; H. Astor and R. Croucher, 'Fractured Families, Fragmented Responsibilities: Responding to Family Violence in a Federal System' (2010) 33(3) *University of New South Wales Law Journal* 854; S. Peel and R. Croucher, 'Mind(ing) the Gap: Law Reform Recommendations Reporting to Child Protection in a Federal System' (2011) 89 *Family Matters* 21.

9 The intricacies of Australia's system of government as it applies to territories is beyond the scope of this chapter, but many of the limitations imposed on the family law system as a result of the federal structure apply in similar ways to the territories as they do to the various states.

10 Australian Constitution s. 106.

11 J. Quick and R. Garran, *Annotated Constitution of the Commonwealth of Australia*, Legal Books, 1976 (reprint of 1901 ed.), p. 610.

12 Australian Constitution s. 51(xxi).

13 Australian Constitution s. 51(xxii).

Whilst the concept of 'matrimonial causes' is not defined in the Constitution, it was considered at the time of federation to cover matters 'subsidiary and consequential to marriage and divorce', including 'probably maintenance of wives and children, and marriage settlements'.[14]

Powers not specifically granted to the Commonwealth by the Constitution may be referred by the states and become federal powers if the referral is accepted by the federal government.[15] The federal government may decline to legislate in an area within its powers for a variety of reasons. The most common reason for the Commonwealth to decline to exercise lawmaking jurisdiction is the cost of administering laws in various areas, of which child protection is a pertinent example. In other areas the Commonwealth simply does not have the existing infrastructure to administer laws, for example laws relating to protection from 'apprehended domestic violence' (the statutory phrase for fear of future violence), which rely heavily upon the state-based police forces as the Australian Federal Police has a relatively small presence in Australian communities. The more cynical may point to the reality that there is little that can be done in areas like child protection that is likely to garner significant voter support for the government of the day.

3. THE COMMONWEALTH GOVERNMENT ENTRY INTO THE FIELD OF FAMILY LAW

The Commonwealth did not pass any substantive legislation with respect to marriage, divorce or matrimonial causes for nearly 60 years after the Constitution was enacted.[16] The Commonwealth's first major legislation with respect to marriage, divorce and related matters combined was by way of the Matrimonial Causes Act 1959 (Cth), under which jurisdiction was vested in the Supreme Court of each state and territory.[17] The Matrimonial Causes Act 1959 (Cth) was the first unified law regarding divorce and matrimonial causes. Later, in 1961, the Commonwealth Parliament passed the Marriage Act, which unified the regulation of marriages throughout Australia. Combined, the Matrimonial Causes Act 1959 (Cth) and the Marriage Act exercised the Commonwealth jurisdiction in relation to both divorce and marriage for the first time.

The most significant change to family law was brought about by the enactment of the Family Law Act 1975 (Cth), which remains the primary

14 Quick and Garran, above n. 11, at p. 611.
15 Australian Constitution s. 51(xxxvii).
16 Marriage Act 1961 (Cth); Matrimonial Causes Act 1959 (Cth).
17 A. Dickey, *Family Law*, Thomson Reuters, 6th ed., 2013, p. 109.

legislation governing family law in Australia, although it has been amended numerous times over the intervening years, extending the scope of its coverage of family law issues. The definition of 'matrimonial cause' used in the Family Law Act has evolved and expanded over the years since the Commonwealth first legislated in this area. The present definition[18] is lengthy and includes proceedings relating to a range of matters including divorce, nullity, property, maintenance, injunctions, financial agreements and enforcement; including certain matters involving third parties, bankruptcy trustees of bankrupt parties and legal personal representatives of deceased parties where there is a sufficient connection with the matrimonial cause.[19]

It is apparent that the Commonwealth has long since travelled beyond the limits of the constitutional powers conferred at federation, relying more recently upon referrals of state powers and administrative changes to continue the movement toward defragmenting Australia's family laws.

3.1. EARLY STEPS TOWARDS DEFRAGMENTATION

Prior to 1959, the Commonwealth introduced legislation that addressed limited issues relating to matrimonial causes, marriage or divorce. In 1919, after World War I, the Commonwealth enacted the Matrimonial Causes (Expeditionary Forces) Act 1919 (Cth) in order to extend England's Matrimonial Causes (Dominion Troops) Act 1919 to Australian military forces. In 1945, the Commonwealth enacted the Matrimonial Causes Act 1945 (Cth), which was the first federal legislation concerning divorces.[20] The Matrimonial Causes Act 1945 (Cth) increased the jurisdiction of the states' and territories' Supreme Courts to facilitate the hearing of proceedings in matrimonial causes under state and territorial law where issues concerning domicile were otherwise problematic. The Commonwealth later enacted the Marriage (Overseas) Act 1955 (Cth), which solemnised the marriage of Australian citizens overseas. These limited legislative forays can be seen as, in substance, addressing the interstate and intercountry movements of Australians since the time of the First World War.

---

18 Family Law Act 1975 (Cth).

19 For detailed consideration of the limits of the jurisdiction conferred on the Commonwealth by the marriage and divorce and matrimonial causes powers, see *Russell v. Russell; Farrelly v. Farrelly* [1976] HCA 23; (1976) 134 CLR 495; *Dowal v. Murray* [1978] HCA 53; (1978) 143 CLR 410; *Vitzdamm-Jones v. Vitzdamm-Jones; St Clair v. Nicholson* [1981] HCA 8; (1981) 148 CLR 383; *Fountain v. Alexander* [1982] HCA 16; (1982) 150 CLR 615; *Re F; Ex parte F* [1986] HCA 41; (1986) 161 CLR 376.

20 Australian Law Reform Commission, above n. 3, at para. 2.5.

3.2. FIRST MAJOR STEPS TO ADDRESS FRAGMENTATION

The first real step toward defragmenting family law in Australia was the introduction of the uniform divorce laws by the Commonwealth with the passage, in 1959, of the Matrimonial Causes Act 1959 (Cth). The legislation provided uniform divorce laws together with uniform laws for property settlements, maintenance proceedings and children's orders with respect to married spouses. Whilst the Matrimonial Causes Act 1959 (Cth) unified divorce law, it was still administered by the state Supreme Courts as the Commonwealth did not have a federal court structure suitable for the determination of matrimonial causes in place at that time. In 1961, the Marriage Act superseded the disparate state laws and provided a uniform Commonwealth law addressing marriage.[21] The most significant change to substantive family law was brought by the Family Law Act, which heralded the introduction of a federal family law court together with no-fault divorce.

3.3. THE COMMONWEALTH FAMILY COURT

At the time of commencement of the Family Law Act 1975, the Commonwealth was constrained by practical and political pressures, primarily because it did not have an established matrimonial court structure to hear cases under the Family Law Act. Upon commencement of the Family Law Act in January 1976, Commonwealth jurisdiction in relation to matrimonial causes was exercised by the Supreme Courts of each state and territory.[22]

Section 21 of the Family Law Act established the Family Court of Australia. The concurrent exercise of Commonwealth jurisdiction by the Supreme Courts of the states continued until such time as both the Family Law Act and the new Commonwealth court were established and entirely operational, after which new proceedings needed to be commenced in the Family Court of Australia (except in the Northern Territory and Western Australia).[23] In the Northern Territory, Commonwealth jurisdiction under the Family Law Act still remains concurrent between the Supreme Court of the Northern Territory and the federal family law courts.[24]

Section 41 of the Family Law Act also provided for the establishment of Family Courts by the individual states, and conferred jurisdiction under the

---

21 Ibid, at para. 2.47.

22 Ibid.

23 Ibid.

24 Family Law Act 1975 (Cth) s. 39; Governor-General of the Commonwealth of Australia, Proclamation, 23 November 1983.

Act upon such courts. In the period of over four decades since its enactment, only Western Australia has taken up this option.[25] The existence of the separate Family Court of Western Australia has meant that some of the issues of fragmentation experienced in the other states have been avoided, as the same court can exercise jurisdiction in relation to both the federal and state matters arising in relation to an individual family in that state. The existence of that separate state court also represents continued fragmentation, with litigants in one state engaging with a separate court system from that which is in operation in the rest of the nation, leading to some unique forms of fragmentation.[26]

4. GROWTH OF DE FACTO RELATIONSHIPS

Since the 1970s, the marriage rate has fallen significantly in Australia, and the number of ex-nuptial children has greatly increased, leading to a shift in what is generally understood as constituting 'family'. The result of these social forces highlighted two major problems: first, that ex-nuptial children were outside the ambit of the Commonwealth's matrimonial causes powers, and thus a prime example of the problem of fragmentation in what has, in recent times, become understood as the 'family law system'; and secondly, that there was no uniform system of laws allowing for de facto spouses to seek financial relief on the breakdown of their relationships.

4.1. CHILDREN BORN OUTSIDE OF MARRIAGE

It was not until 1986 that the states began referring power to the Commonwealth with respect to ex-nuptial children. For instance, New South Wales referred state power to the Commonwealth through the enactment of the Commonwealth Powers (Family Law – Children) Act 1986 (NSW) with respect to 'guardianship, custody, maintenance and access' of ex-nuptial children; this legislation is

---

25 Family Court Act 1975 (WA); subsequently replaced by the Family Court Act 1997 (WA).

26 For example, the ability to have superannuation (a matter in relation to which legislative power is conferred by the Constitution on the Commonwealth: Australian Constitution s. 51(xxiii)) split between parties to relationships that have broken down is presently available in all states except Western Australia, with the consequence that there is fragmentation both as between married and unmarried couples in that state, and as between de facto couples in Western Australia and the rest of the nation. The relevant power has been referred by Western Australia to the Commonwealth (Commonwealth Powers (De Facto Relationships) Act 2006 (WA)), and federal legislation to rectify this (Family Law Amendment (Western Australia De Facto Superannuation Splitting and Bankruptcy) Act 2020 (Cth)) has been passed but has not yet commenced.

mirrored in each state, except Western Australia.[27] The legislation did not, however, refer state powers in relation to adoption or child protection. Although in 1996 the Family Law Act was amended to include a child 'welfare power',[28] it is necessary to note that this 'welfare power' is narrow when compared to state legislation addressing child welfare.[29] The 'welfare power' conferred on a court in the Family Law Act, as expressed by the Full Court of the Family Court, enables the court to provide any relief necessary for the protection of children, such as protecting a child from abuse (subject to any statutory provisions to the contrary set out in section 69ZK).[30] Whilst the Family Court may have a 'welfare power', this is not sufficient to give it jurisdiction to hear applications by child protection agencies (which are state-based) nor even to force such agencies to participate in proceedings.[31]

4.2. CHILD MAINTENANCE

Prior to 1989, separated parents usually sought the assistance of the state courts at the local or magistrates' level for awards of child maintenance because, although these matters were dealt with pursuant to the Family Law Act, the amounts were generally too low to warrant the cost of making an application to the Family Court. Accessing child maintenance through the courts presented many issues for separated parents, including the expense of obtaining court orders, the difficulty in updating court orders to account for changes, including inflation and an increase in a parent's capacity to pay, the difficulty of enforcing child maintenance orders, and the making of orders which required low-level maintenance payments which were not necessarily indicative of a parent's capacity to provide financial support to their child. The issues became more pressing for the Commonwealth government (which administers the social security system) as the rapid increase in the divorce rate increased the number of parents obtaining government benefits.[32] As a means of addressing these issues, the Child Support Scheme was established in 1988 with the enactment of the Child Support (Registration and Collection) Act 1988 (Cth) and the Child Support

[27] See Commonwealth Powers (Family Law – Children) Act 1986 (NSW); Commonwealth Powers (Family Law – Children) Act 1986 (Vic); Commonwealth Powers (Family Law – Children) Act 1990 (Qld); Commonwealth Powers (Family Law) Act 1986 (SA); Commonwealth Powers (Family Law) Act 1987 (Tas).

[28] Family Law Reform Act 1995 (Cth), introducing a new Part VII.

[29] Australian Law Reform Commission, above n. 4, at para. 2.51.

[30] *Re Z* [1996] FLC 92-694 at 83, 231, 265.

[31] *Secretary of the Department of Health and Human Services & Rollinson & Cheeseman & Ors* [2010] FamCAFC 258.

[32] Australian Government, *Guides to Social Policy Law – Child Support Guide*, 2022, para. 1.1.2.

(Assessment) Act 1989 (Cth).[33] The benefits of the scheme for children and their carers ultimately overcame arguments as to states' rights, which delayed the referral of powers with respect to ex-nuptial children in some states to the Commonwealth for inclusion in the scheme.

The Child Support Assessment Act provides for a national scheme for the administrative assessment of the amount of child support payable, calculated in accordance with a statutory formula.[34] This formula accounts for both parents' income, the number of dependent children, and the care arrangements (nights of care) of the children.[35] As child support is managed by an independent Commonwealth Child Support Agency, separated parents are able to access child support for their children in a manner which alleviates the issues that arose when it was managed at the court level.

4.3. PROPERTY SETTLEMENT RIGHTS FOR DE FACTO SPOUSES

From 1986 until 2008, unmarried couples were required to seek resolution from two different courts in the event that their relationship broke down, namely a state court for property and/or maintenance disputes, and the federal Family Court (and federal administrative child support system) for parenting and child support issues.[36] In order to address this fragmentation, the states (other than Western Australia) referred their powers in relation to property and maintenance disputes to the Commonwealth. As a result, the Family Law Amendment (De Facto Financial Matters and Other Measures) Act 2008 (Cth) was enacted, which, since 2009, provides both married and de facto couples with substantially the same remedies upon separation for spousal maintenance and property settlement orders pursuant to the Commonwealth Family Law Act.

The result of the various state referrals of power is that the Commonwealth family law courts have jurisdiction to hear matters concerning marriage and divorce, and disputes in relation to parenting and property after relationship breakdown. The states, however, maintain jurisdiction over adoption law and child protection, as well as family violence and other related criminal matters that may be relevant to Commonwealth family law proceedings and may constitute

---

33 Australian Law Reform Commission, *Family Violence and Commonwealth Laws – Child Support and Family Assistance*, 2011, para. 12.

34 Ibid, at para. 13.

35 Ibid.

36 Australian Law Reform Commission, above n. 4, at para. 2.57; also see B. Fehlberg and J. Behrens, *Australian Family Law: The Contemporary Context*, Oxford University Press (Australia), 2008, pp. 34–35 (providing a general summary).

part of what is now characterised as the 'family law system'.[37] Adoptions are largely administered by the same government agencies that deal with child welfare and protection.

5. FAMILY LAW BEYOND THE JURISDICTION OF THE COMMONWEALTH

The fragmentation of family law originally meant that like cases were treated differently depending on the marital status of the parties and their place of residence. While this has been addressed to a significant extent by the developments we have outlined, it remains the case that even where parties have been married, there are aspects of the consequences of breakdown of their marriages which have remained within the various state systems. These areas include family violence protection orders (often known as restraining orders), public child protection matters, and laws as to adoption, parentage, the status of children, and the recognition of parent–child relationships. This has meant that the same family or former couple have often been required to engage with two courts or legal systems[38] and that their legal issues have been regulated by multiple different (and sometimes conflicting) laws, leading not only to confusion and duplicated expense, but sometimes to inconsistent findings and outcomes (for example, a finding in a state court that family violence of a particular kind had occurred (or that particular conduct did or did not constitute family violence), accompanied by a contrary finding in family law proceedings).[39] The difficulties this presents are compounded by the potential for lack of clarity surrounding the issue of whether causes of action arising between parties to marriages fall within state or federal jurisdiction.[40] The practical difficulty facing the Commonwealth with respect to the two significant areas of child protection and family violence is not merely the requirement to have the states refer their relevant powers, but also the need for significant administrative infrastructure if these functions are to be administered by the Commonwealth.

Areas of law not directly within the rubric of 'family law', but having an impact on family law matters also vary from state to state, with the consequence that even to the extent that the content of family law is itself consistent as

---

37 Australian Law Reform Commission, above n. 4, at para. 2.53.

38 In some cases, potentially three legal systems, if the parties live in different states and have proceedings pending in each state and a federal court.

39 Often the results differed as the tests to be applied differed or further evidence was available at the family law hearing that had not been presented when seeking a domestic violence protection order.

40 See e.g. *Re LSH; Ex parte RTF* [1987] HCA 53; (1987) 164 CLR 91; *Emerald & Emerald* [2018] FamCAFC 217; (2018) FLC 93-870.

between the states, local laws can affect the manner in which the federal law is applied. Examples of this, which have emerged over the years, include different laws relating to property ownership, the legality of use of recording and surveillance devices and freedom of information processes. The consequence of these circumstances has often been a further basis for arguments that the 'family law system' is fragmented across state and federal lines.

The Australian Law Reform Commission commented on the issue of 'jurisdictional fragmentation' in a comprehensive review of the Australian family law system, which concluded in 2019 (ALRC Report).[41] The ALRC Report identified 'enormous pressures on courts exercising family law jurisdiction, including structural pressures, caused by the jurisdictional intersection of the federal family law system and the state and territory child protection systems'[42] and 'structural and systemic difficulties'[43] arising from the 'bifurcated model, which requires parties to navigate multiple courts across jurisdictions'.[44] The review noted that the jurisdictional conflicts 'create confusion, duplication, wasted resources, and barriers to access to justice.'[45]

The ALRC expressed a view that 'the resolution of family law disputes which involve complex matters of both state and federal law' required 'the development of a more holistic approach to what might properly be considered to fall within the scope of a modern family law system, particularly regarding modern notions of parents and families, and different cultural understandings of family.'[46] The ALRC's ultimate recommendation, like those of prior reports, was for a comprehensive overhaul of the entire 'system' at state and federal levels.[47] Such an overhaul, however, is beyond the individual constitutional or legislative powers of governments at either level. Nonetheless, initiatives have continued to be undertaken, at both state and federal levels, to address the issue of fragmentation.

6. THE BURDEN OF THE FAMILY LAW CASE LOAD AND CREATION OF THE FEDERAL MAGISRATES COURT

With the continuous rise in the number of cases being litigated in the Commonwealth Family Court driven not only by increasing divorce rates but by expanding notions of 'family', it appeared unsustainable and unnecessary

41 Australian Law Reform Commission, above n. 3.
42 Ibid, at para. 1.2.
43 Ibid, at para. 1.7.
44 Ibid.
45 Ibid, at para. 2.11.
46 Ibid, at para. 2.12.
47 Ibid, at para. 1.29.

to have every family law case determined by a superior court judge. Thus, in the late 1990s policy-makers turned to consider alternative structures, such as delegating powers to registrars or the creation of a new court at a lower level.

In 1999 another tier was added to the family court structure when the Federal Magistrates Court was established. The Federal Magistrates Court was to relieve the Family Court from the voluminous routine and shorter matters that it was otherwise required to deal with, leaving the Family Court to focus primarily on complex hearings. In this context, it is important to recognise that the Family Court was established as a superior court of record with equal standing with the Federal Court and the state Supreme Courts, making it inappropriate for that court to be hearing a high volume of routine and less difficult cases. However, the jurisdiction of both the Federal Magistrates Court and Family Courts overlapped to a substantial degree[48] as the subject matter of family law does not admit of an easy definition of complexity that may be applied at the time of filing proceedings. The filings in the Federal Magistrates Court grew rapidly and soon comprised the overwhelming majority of family law filings (particularly if one considers only disputed parenting and property claims rather than including uncontested processes such as consent order approvals and divorces). In 2013, in recognition of the volume and complexity of the work being undertaken by its judicial officers, the Federal Magistrates Court was renamed the Federal Circuit Court of Australia.[49]

Around the time the Federal Magistrates Court was established, the then shadow Attorney-General, and now Deputy Chief Justice McClelland, was opposed to the creation of a second federal court for family law. The opposition to the establishment of the Federal Magistrates Court arose from concerns relating to funding and the way in which the resources of the Federal Court and the Family Court of Australia were to be redistributed to facilitate and aid in the funding the operation of the new Federal Magistrates Court.[50] The shadow Attorney-General was opposed to the lack of separate funding and resources of the Federal Magistrates Court, and was concerned that rural and regional Australians would be impacted by the Family Court's resources being wound back in those areas, where the Federal Magistrates Court would be unable to fill that void to an acceptable level due to resourcing limitations.[51] In this regard, there were concerns that the creation of the Federal Magistrates Court would in turn limit access to justice for persons living in rural and regional Australia.[52]

48 Dickey, above n. 17, at p. 109.

49 Ibid.

50 Commonwealth, *Parliamentary Debates*, House of Representatives, 26 September 2001, 31472–73 (Robert McClelland, Shadow Attorney-General).

51 Commonwealth, *Parliamentary Debates*, House of Representatives, 26 September 2001, 31473 (Robert McClelland, Shadow Attorney-General).

52 Ibid.

As it transpired, the services provided by the Federal Magistrates Court to non-metropolitan areas were so significant that its subsequent name of Federal Circuit Court was chosen to reflect that aspect of its work.

7. CRITICISMS OF THE DUAL COURT STRUCTURE

In 2008, the Attorney-General's Department released the report *Future Governance Options for Federal Family Law Courts in Australia: Striking the Right Balance*,[53] which reviewed the structure and operation of the federal family courts. The review concluded that there was a 'significant level of duplication of administrative structures and corporate services' across the Family Court and the Federal Magistrates Court, and that the duplication 'is not financially sustainable and utilises resources that could be directed more effectively to assisting litigants'.[54] It was said that the duplication was not only inefficient and costly in administration, but it also caused confusion for litigants in relation to determining the court in which to file when commencing proceedings. The review noted that the Family Court attempted to formulate a system which would filter matters based on the complexity of a matter (with more complex cases being heard by that court),[55] although the vast majority of cases were, by then, being heard in the Federal Magistrates Court. Not only was the jurisdiction of the Family Court to hear proceedings that relate to family breakdown not exclusive, but litigants were said to be confused by the different rules and different forms in operation between the Family Court and Federal Magistrates Court,[56] which had rules adapted to the smaller and less complex cases primarily heard in that court. There was much focus in the reports and critiques which followed upon the efficiencies that could be obtained by merging court structures, with one consultant suggesting that a merger alone could result in up to 8,000 more cases being determined each year.[57]

8. SOME SMALLER STEPS TOWARDS REFORM

Ensuring an ease of information flow between the federal family law courts and state/territory courts is a necessary step in addressing fragmentation in

---

53 Attorney-Generals' Department, *Future Governance Options for Federal Family Law Courts in Australia: Striking the Right Balance*, August 2018.

54 Ibid, at p. 5.

55 R. Missingham, 'Budget Review 2009 10: Legal issues and the Attorney-General's Portfolio – Courts', Research Paper No. 33, Parliamentary Library, Parliament of Australia, 2009.

56 Ibid.

57 PricewaterhouseCoopersAustralia, 'Review of Efficiency of the Operation of the Federal Courts', Report, April 2018, p. 8.

the administration of family laws. As state courts have broad jurisdiction in relation to child welfare, and deal with family violence and issue protection orders, an information flow between the state and federal family courts is necessary to ensure that the family law courts have access to all relevant information that may be crucial to the making of family and parenting orders.[58] It is also necessary to ensure that orders made by the federal family law courts are not inconsistent with orders made by the state courts in relation to family violence and protection to ensure the safety of victims of family violence and their children.[59] For example, the federal family law courts need to be aware of any Apprehended Domestic Violence Orders (ADVOs) which may be in place to protect a party. The flow of information between state and federal family courts is also necessary for the effective functioning of child welfare authorities and the police.

A major hurdle in addressing this information flow has been privacy laws that restrict the sharing of information between government agencies and the private sector. The Privacy Act 1988 (Cth) applies to all government and private sector organisations, including federal courts.[60] However, each state and territory has enacted child protection laws which secure the privacy of parents and children, whilst permitting information-sharing between police, child protection agencies, and other prescribed bodies.[61] For example, in 1998, New South Wales introduced the Children and Young Persons (Care and Protection) Act 1998 (NSW) which enabled information-sharing in relation to the safety, welfare and well-being of a child between state organisations such as New South Wales Police, government agencies, schools and hospitals, and some Commonwealth agencies, including the family law courts.[62] However, the Children and Young Persons (Care and Protection) Act 1998 (NSW) stipulates that these information-sharing provisions override any other law, including the Privacy Act 1988 (Cth).[63]

The more recent introduction of state- and territory-based care and protection legislation has permitted the sharing of information and provided courts with family law jurisdiction with the ability to gain access to relevant and necessary information from child protection agencies and to access other information in relation to family violence and child welfare. Access to, and

58 Australian Law Reform Commission, *Information Sharing between agencies*, 2010, para. 30.126.
59 Ibid.
60 Privacy Act 1988 (Cth) s. 6.
61 See e.g. Children and Young People Act 2008 (ACT) ch. 25; Care and Protection of Children Act 2007 (NT) ss. 34, 38; Child Protection Act 1999 (Qld) Part 4; Children, Young Persons and Their Families Act 1997 (Tas) Part 5A.
62 Children and Young Persons (Care and Protection) Act 1998 (NSW) s. 248(6).
63 Ibid, s. 245D(3).

the sharing of, this information is often crucial to family law proceedings. Access by the family law courts to information is also aided by the issuing of subpoenas and by legislative provisions enshrining mechanisms for the provision of relevant information to the family law courts by state and territory agencies.[64]

More recently, in 2019 to 2020, the Family Court of Australia and the Federal Circuit Court sought to harmonise their own processes in order to recast the family law jurisdiction and create a clear and consistent pathway for litigants.[65] In early 2020, the first Joint Practice Direction, *Joint Practice Direction 1 of 2020 – Core Principles in the Case Management of Family Law Matters*, was issued by the Chief Justice of the Family Court, who was also the Chief Judge of the Federal Circuit Court, seeking to reconcile the management procedures between the two courts.[66] The Joint Practice Direction[67] outlined ten core principles of the family law jurisdiction across both courts, such as prioritising safety, and achieving the overarching purpose of the Family Law Act for just, safe, efficient and timely resolution of matters.

Between 2019 and 2020, the family law courts began the process of drafting a single, harmonised set of rules which would apply to both courts, and would rectify previous issues litigants had experienced where each the Family Law Court and the Federal Circuit Court had their own family law rules.[68] The harmonisation process undertaken within the family law courts also focused on creating a singular case management pathway and a consistent set of forms for use across the two family law courts.[69] Harmonisation of these aspects of family law jurisdiction was achieved in 2021. This step appears to reflect a policy decision that consistency of processes (based upon the processes required for more complex cases) should be favoured over processes adapted to the nature of the underlying cases.

9. THE MERGER OF THE COURT ADMINISTRATIONS

In May 2018, the Commonwealth government announced plans to address the identified difficulties associated with having federal family law jurisdiction exercised by two separate courts by way of a merger or amalgamation of the

64 See e.g. Family Law Act 1975 (Cth) ss. 67Z, 69ZW.

65 Family Court of Australia, *Annual Report 2019–2020*, p. 4.

66 Ibid.

67 Family Court of Australia and Federal Circuit Court of Australia, *Joint Practice Direction 1 of 2020 – Core Principles in the Case Management of Family Law Matters.*

68 Family Law Rules 2004 (Cth); Federal Circuit Court Rules 2001 (Cth).

69 Family Court of Australia, above n. 65, at p. 4.

Family Court and the Federal Circuit Court. The Federal Circuit and Family Court of Australia Bill 2018, which was designed to implement the proposed merger, was introduced. However, some aspects of the proposed reforms, including a proposal to remove the appellate jurisdiction held by the Family Court of Australia from the new structure and to cease appointments to the court formerly known as the Family Court of Australia, proved controversial, and the Bill ultimately lapsed.

On 5 December 2019, the Federal Circuit and Family Court of Australia Bill 2019 was introduced. The new Bill included many key features of the earlier Bill but did not include the aspects which had proven most controversial. On 1 September 2021, the Federal Circuit and Family Court of Australia Act 2021 (FCFCoA Act) took effect. The Family Court of Australia and the Federal Circuit Court of Australia were moved into a single court structure known as the Federal Circuit and Family Court of Australia (FCFCoA). The Family Court was renamed the Federal Circuit and Family Court of Australia (Division 1) and the Federal Circuit Court was renamed the Federal Circuit and Family Court of Australia (Division 2). The Explanatory Memorandum to the Bill outlined that the intentions of the proposed reforms included creating a consistent pathway for Australian families in having their family law disputes dealt with in the federal courts, improving the efficiency of the federal court system, and ensuring outcomes for Australian families are resolved in the most timely, informed and cost-effective manner possible.[70]

Although the two courts remain legally distinct, it is intended that the experience of litigants and litigators will become more consolidated and streamlined than was the case prior to the enactment of the FCFCoA Act. While the FCFCoA Act has not (and could not) address the identified difficulties with fragmentation across state and federal jurisdictions, the placement of the two courts into a single administrative structure is intended to go a considerable way towards addressing many of the issues with fragmentation at the federal level which arose upon the creation of the Federal Magistrates Court.

The FCFCoA Act establishes a single point of entry, such that all new proceedings are commenced in Division 2, with cases suitable for determination in Division 1 (generally cases with greater complexity, those likely to consume significant periods of time or those suitable to specialist Division 1 lists) transferred to that Division prior to final hearing. This means that those litigants who were formerly uncertain as to which court was most suitable for their matters no longer have a choice as to where to file. The decision as to whether a case is heard in Division 1 is now largely made by registrars of the court. Somewhat ironically, the Federal Circuit and Family Court of Australia

70 Explanatory Memorandum, *Federal Circuit and Family Court of Australia Bill 2019*, para. 8.

(Division 1) (formerly the Family Court of Australia) no longer has original jurisdiction under the Family Law Act 1975, receiving jurisdiction only in individual cases upon their transfer from the Federal Circuit and Family Court of Australia (Division 2).

The two courts now feature a single case management pathway largely managed by the registrars under the direction of the court administration through the 'National Assessment Team'. This is intended to avoid the risks of confusion, repetition, inconsistency and delay which were associated with the previous system, when matters were transferred between the two courts, which had different case management procedures, sometimes more than once. If a matter is transferred to the Division 1 court, it can continue at the same point in the case management pathway with minimal disruption. Once a matter is transferred from the Division 2 to the Division 1 court, the likelihood of a transfer of a case back to the Division 2 court is limited, because the FCFCoA Act confers the power to transfer matters from Division 1 to Division 2 on the Chief Justice alone.[71]

The consolidated FCFCoA case management pathway has been designed with the aim of streamlining court processes, by focusing on early triage and risk assessment, dispute resolution and efficient court processes. In summary, upon commencement of proceedings in Division 2, the first court event is a hearing presided over by a judicial registrar, who will undertake triage, risk assessment and issues assessment, before making such directions as are required to facilitate the progression of the matter to the next phase. Any required interlocutory hearing will follow, after which the parties, subject to safety concerns, are required to undertake a dispute resolution process. For matters that remain unresolved following dispute resolution, there will be a compliance and readiness hearing, at which a judge will assess whether all orders and directions have been complied with and ensure that a genuine attempt at dispute resolution has been undertaken, before matters will proceed to a final hearing. This structure is similar to the previous Family Court of Australia structure, save that the registrars are now largely under the direction of the National Assessment Team. The structure is a radical change from that which had been used in the Federal Magistrates (Federal Circuit) Court of judicial docket management with little involvement of registrars.

A new set of Rules of Court, forms and practice directions, including a central case management practice direction, have accompanied the commencement of the FCFCoA. Each of these measures applies across both courts. This is a notable departure from the previous system, under which the rules and procedures varied between the two courts, sometimes in significant respects. Although, as

71 Federal Circuit and Family Court of Australia Act 2021 (Cth) s. 52.

with all standardisation processes, compromises must be made: for example, more relaxed rules enabling substituted service and the automatic release of subpoenaed documents in the Federal Circuit Court have been replaced with the more stringent versions of the substituted service rules from the Family Court and the requirements for greater engagement with the court with respect to subpoenas.

The FCFCoA Act enshrines the universally desired and aspirational overarching purpose of facilitating the just resolution of disputes according to law and as quickly, inexpensively and efficiently as possible;[72] and imposes statutory obligations on parties and lawyers to conduct proceedings and negotiations in a way that is consistent with the overarching purpose.[73]

The FCFCoA structure, and key features of the harmonisation between the processes formerly operating in the two courts, reflect the recommendations of several key reports into the family law system which have been undertaken in recent years, and which have, in part, been aimed at addressing the concerns about fragmentation as identified earlier in this chapter. These include the ALRC report,[74] which recommended the introduction of a joint practice note for case management outlining a consistent case management system and clarifying the responsibilities of parties, practitioners and the courts in achieving just and efficient outcomes; and the second interim report of the Joint Select Committee on Australia's Family Law System,[75] which recommended an expanded role for registrars to alleviate the burden on judges and harmonisation of the Rules and processes of the federal family law courts with the aim of providing consistency and clarity for court users.

The FCFCoA (Division 1) retains appellate jurisdiction, but unlike the previous structure, there is no longer a separate appeals division, and all of the judges of Division 1 are now eligible to hear and determine appeals. The earlier proposed reform model, which included removal of the appellate jurisdiction to the Federal Court of Australia,[76] which does not presently hold jurisdiction under the Family Law Act, would arguably have introduced a new form of fragmentation within the federal system.

The model ultimately introduced, however, may be seen as adding to the cohesiveness of the system by retaining family law appellate jurisdiction within

72 Federal Circuit and Family Court of Australia Act 2021 (Cth) ss. 67(1), 190(1).

73 Ibid, ss. 68, 191.

74 Australian Law Reform Commission, *Family Law for the Future: An Inquiry into the Family Law System*, ALRC Report 135, 2019.

75 Joint Select Committee on Australia's Family Law System, Second Interim Report, 2021.

76 Federal Circuit and Family Court of Australia (Consequential Amendments and Transitional Provisions) Bill 2018 (Cth) Schedule 1.

the specialist family law courts and ensuring that it is exercised by judges who now also regularly hear family law trials. However, the enormous funding increases that came with the new Act[77] may indicate that the efficiencies arguments previously raised were not considered realistic by policy-makers in government.

10. CONCLUSIONS

Wide-reaching social change, particularly change with respect to family formations, and accompanying development of the law, have expanded the concept of 'family law' far beyond the limited confines of marriage, divorce and ancillary matters within which it was conceptualised by early lawmakers. This, together with the constitutional structure within which Australian family law necessarily operates, has resulted in the development of fragmented and disjointed legal frameworks for the determination of legal issues arising from the breakdown of family relationships. The result is now being judged against a concept of a coherent family law 'system'. Unsurprisingly, in this context, the variety of law, courts and administrative processes that impact upon families have been criticised for being unwieldy, confusing and inconsistent.

In this chapter, we have explored the extent to which, in the face of these considerable systemic and other challenges, the governments of the Commonwealth and the various states have taken gradual but steady steps towards defragmentation and harmonisation of laws affecting families. Some of these measures have taken the form of substantial legal developments, while others have been in the form of administrative changes. As we have seen, the major legal and structural developments in this area have been bolstered by smaller changes designed to harmonise the processes with which family law litigants engage and alleviate the difficulties associated with the fragmentation which remains. Most recently, the amalgamation of the federal family law courts into a single, consolidated court structure with harmonised case management processes represents a significant development in the process of addressing fragmentation at the federal level.

The challenge remaining is to find creative and innovative ways of addressing the residual fragmentation of laws within the penumbra of the growing breadth of the concept of 'family law'. Whilst the increased focus now seen at the federal level can be expected to bring further improvements, wholesale changes to the broader fragmentation of what is now understood as

[77] Federal Budget Overview 2021–2022, p. 34.

'family law' is beyond the power of any individual government and may only be brought about through collaboration between governments at all levels. Some of the intergovernmental initiatives described in this chapter represent significant and promising developments, and it is to be hoped that the general trend towards cohesion and defragmentation will continue into the future.

AUSTRALIA

RECOGNITION OF CHILDREN'S RIGHTS AND THE HIGH COURT OF AUSTRALIA

Michelle FERNANDO and Anja PICH

Résumé

Cet article étudie la prise en compte des droits de l'enfant dans les jugements relatifs aux affaires familiales rendus par la High Court of Australia, la plus haute juridiction australienne. Nous analysons l'impact qu'aurait une approche substantielle des droits de l'enfant, basée sur les valeurs et les principes de la Convention des Nations Unies relative aux droits de l'enfant, sur les jugements et les décisions. En se concentrant sur les deux seuls jugements en matière de droit de la famille rendus au cours de la dernière décennie, et en s'appuyant sur des affaires plus anciennes, les auteurs observent que la High Court n'a pas réussi à adopter une approche substantielle des droits de l'enfant. En ce qui concerne les deux affaires les plus récentes, l'approche de la High Court en matière de droits de l'enfant était inexistante, dans la mesure où elle n'a pas du tout abordé le concept de droits de l'enfant. Les auteurs affirment que cette attitude ne permet pas de considérer les enfants comme des détenteurs de droits à part entière et qu'elle contrevient aux obligations internationales de l'Australie. Nous soutenons qu'une approche substantielle des droits de l'enfant devrait être adoptée pour garantir que l'Australie respecte ses obligations envers les enfants et le droit international, pour faciliter le développement de la common law et la promotion des droits de l'Homme, et pour que les décisions prises soient meilleures.

1. INTRODUCTION

Internationally, judicial decisions increasingly frame legal issues concerning children in terms of children's rights.[1] Courts in many countries expressly reference the United Nations Convention on the Rights of the Child (UNCRC),[2] discuss the importance of upholding the rights of children where it is within the power of the court to do so, and give rights-based considerations substantial weight in their decisions. This trend has extended to courts of appeal and, in some jurisdictions, the very highest courts.[3] However, family law judgments in recent cases decided by the High Court of Australia, Australia's highest court, suggest that Australia is out of step in its lack of acknowledgement and recognition of children's rights.

This chapter explores what it means to take a children's rights approach to judicial decision-making. It discusses the operation of children's rights in Australia and how the concept of children's rights applies to family law. The chapter then examines judgments of the High Court of Australia involving children in family law matters, focusing on the only two judgments delivered in the past decade. We observe that, in relation to these two judgments, the court failed to engage with the concept of children's rights at all. We note some older cases where children's rights were more visible. However, overall, the High Court has failed to take a substantive rights-based approach to family law decision-making since Australia's ratification of the UNCRC. We discuss the implications of this and argue that the High Court, as Australia's highest

1 J. Tobin, 'Judging the Judges: Are They Adopting the Rights Approach in Matters Involving Children?' (2009) 33 *Melbourne University Law Review* 579, 583.

2 Opened for signature 20 November 1989, 1577 UNTS 3 (entered into force 2 September 1990); E. Sutherland, 'Making Scotland "the Best Place in the World to Grow Up"?' in M. Brinig (ed.), *The International Survey of Family Law*, Intersentia Publishing, 1st ed., 2020, p. 219; Tobin, above n. 1, 597.

3 See e.g. *Williamson v. Secretary of State for Education and Employment* [2005] 2 AC 246 (House of Lords); *In the matter of D (A Child)* [2019] UKSC 42; *ZH (Tanzania) v. Secretary of State for the Home Department* [2011] UKSC 4; *Re McLaughlin* [2018] UKSC 48; *DV v. Lord Advocate* [2020] HCJAC 33; *BJG v. DLG* 2010 YKSC 44; *Office of the Children's Lawyer v. Balev* [2018] 1 SCR 398.

court, has a responsibility to ensure that the internationally recognised rights of children are visible, recognised and influential in family law decision-making. This is a responsibility the court owes to children, but also to the administration of justice in ensuring that the best possible decisions are made.

This chapter only examines the High Court's approach in family law judgments concerning children. It should not be taken as a comment about how the High Court treats human rights generally, or how it treats children's rights in cases that do not involve family law.

2. THE OPERATION OF CHILDREN'S RIGHTS IN AUSTRALIA

The UNCRC, adopted by the UN General Assembly in 1989, 'marked the full transformation, and complete emergence of the idea of children as rights bearers at the international level.'[4] The UNCRC grants a wide range of rights to all children under the age of 18 years in ratifying countries.

Rights that are relevant to family law include that the best interests of the child be 'a primary consideration' in all actions concerning them (Article 3(1)), care and protection (Article 3(2)), respect for the responsibilities, rights and duties of parents (Article 5), the right to maintain relationships with both parents (Article 9(3)), the right to express views and have them be given due weight (Article 12), common parental responsibilities (Article 18) and protection from harm from abuse or neglect (Article 19(1)).

Australia ratified the UNCRC in December 1990. In doing so, it agreed to undertake all legislative, administrative and other measures to implement the rights therein.[5] Nevertheless, this has not been the case. Some principles of the UNCRC were present in the Family Law Act 1975 (Cth) (FLA) prior to Australia's ratification of the treaty, and others were implemented as a result of the ratification. However, there are many principles of the UNCRC which have not been legislated. The most notable is the right of children to express their views, despite ongoing entreaties from the UN Committee on the Rights of the Child for Australia to give children this statutory right.[6]

Article 3(1) is reflected, and indeed expanded, by section 60CA of the FLA, which requires the court, in children's matters, to regard the best interests of

---

4 J. Tobin, 'The Development of Children's Rights' in G. Monahan and L. Young (eds.), *Children and the Law in Australia*, LexisNexis, 2nd ed., 2008, p. 26.

5 United Nations Convention on the Rights of the Child, opened for signature 20 November 1989, 1577 UNTS 3 (entered into force 2 September 1990) (UNCRC), Art. 4.

6 United Nations Committee on the Rights of the Child, *Concluding Observations on the Combined Fifth and Sixth Periodic Reports of Australia*, CRC/C/AUS/CO/5-6, 2019, para. 22(a).

the child as 'the paramount consideration'. Two 'objects and principles' in section 60B(1) and 'primary considerations' in section 60CC(2), which emphasise the benefit to children of having a meaningful relationship with both parents and the need to protect children from harm, are reflective of Articles 9(3) and 19(1) respectively. Article 18(1) is reflected in the acknowledgement in section 61C that each parent has parental responsibility for a child. Article 12 is somewhat acknowledged in section 60CC(3)(a), which requires a court to take account of any views expressed by a child, but does not go so far as to give children a right to be heard. As we will discuss below, the High Court recently held that section 60CC(3)(a) also does not require the court to ascertain the views of the child, which appears to contravene Article 12(2).[7] Section 43 states that, in exercising jurisdiction under the FLA, a court must have regard to 'the need to protect the rights of children and to promote their welfare'. Section 60B(4), inserted in 2011, states than an additional 'object' is to give effect to the UNCRC. However, these provisions do not give the UNCRC the force of law, and only reinforce the common law position of the effect of international treaties on domestic law.[8]

A ratified treaty is binding on Australia in international law. However, the treaty does not become part of Australian domestic law unless it is given the force of law by statute.[9] Australia has not given the force of law to any of the seven international human rights conventions it has ratified, and remains the only modern liberal democracy in the world without a national statement of rights.[10] As Tobin wrote:

> Australia has remained obstinate in its refusal to implement the [UN]CRC. This is not to say that children do not have human rights in Australia ... or that articles under the [UN]CRC have not informed, or are incompatible with, discrete aspects of legislation and policy within some jurisdictions in Australia. On balance, however, there has been no deliberate or concerted effort to use the [UN]CRC and the notion of children as rights bearers as the benchmark against which to develop, implement and monitor laws and policies affecting children.[11]

Without the force of law, treaties are used as an aid to interpret domestic legislation. Where there is ambiguity in legislation, the courts have held that an interpretation of the legislation which complies with an international instrument

7 *Bondelmonte v. Bondelmonte* (2017) 259 CLR 662.

8 M. Fernando, 'Express Recognition of the UN Convention on the Rights of the Child in the Family Law Act: What Impact for Children's Rights to be Heard?' (2013) 36(1) *University of New South Wales Law Journal* 88.

9 *Minister of State for Immigration and Ethnic Affairs v. Teoh* (1995) 183 CLR 273 (*Teoh*).

10 J. Bessant and R. Watts, 'Children and the Law: An Historical Overview' in G. Monahan and L. Young (eds.), *Children and the Law in Australia*, LexisNexis, 2nd ed., 2008, p. 21.

11 Tobin, above n. 4, at p. 24.

should be adopted.[12] Further, principles contained within international instruments can be used in exercising judicial discretion and as a guide to developing the common law.[13] If there is any contradiction or inconsistency between an international treaty and domestic law or policy, however, the domestic law will prevail.[14]

In relation to aspects of the UNCRC that have been implemented into Australian family law legislation, it can be taken that a court, in following the law, will uphold those principles. However, this is different from taking a children's rights approach. Even where articles of the UNCRC have not been implemented into the FLA, in the absence of specific incompatibility with existing legal frameworks, there is scope for Australian courts to incorporate elements of a substantive children's rights approach in their decision-making.[15] Children's rights have been specifically acknowledged in numerous Australian family law cases.[16] In ratifying the UNCRC, Australia made commitments at an international level and held out a promise to Australian children that they will be treated in accordance with their human rights entitlements.[17]

3. TAKING A CHILDREN'S RIGHTS APPROACH TO DECISION-MAKING

In considering how a children's rights approach should be incorporated into decision-making, we have adopted the approach to children's rights expounded by Tobin and others.[18] This approach is grounded in the UNCRC. There are several core values and principles of the UNCRC that are of particular relevance to judges and the way they adjudicate disputes concerning children.[19]

A children's rights approach to decision-making requires that children be recognised as rights-bearers and 'not merely as objects of protection,

---

12 *Teoh*, above n. 9, at p. 287 (Mason C.J. and Deane J.).

13 *Mabo v. Qld (No. 2)* (1991) 175 CLR 1, 40 (Brennan J.); *Teoh*, above n. 9, at p. 288 (Mason C.J. and Deane J.).

14 *Polites v. Commonwealth* (1945) 70 CLR 60.

15 Tobin, above n. 1, 583.

16 See e.g. *Harrison v. Woollard* (1995) 18 Fam LR 788; *Director General, Department of Community Services v. De Lewinski* (1996) FLC 92-674 (Nicholson C.J.); *N v. N* (2000) 27 Fam LR 284; *ZN v. YH and Another* (2002) 29 Fam LR 20; *Re Jamie* (2013) 50 FamLR 369 (Bryant C.J.); *Karamalis v. Karamalis* [2018] FamCA 312.

17 Australian Law Reform Commission and Human Rights and Equal Opportunity Commission, *Seen and Heard: Priority for Children in the Legal Process*, Report No. 84 (1997), para. 3.18.

18 See e.g. H. Stalford, K. Hollingsworth and S. Gilmore (eds.), *Rewriting Children's Judgments: From Academic Vision to New Practice*, Hart Publishing, 2017; L. Lundy and L. McEvoy, 'Childhood, the United Nations Convention on the Rights of the Child, and Research: What Constitutes a "Rights-Based" Approach?' in M. Freeman (ed.), *Law and Childhood Studies: Current Legal Issues Volume 14*, Oxford University Press, 2012.

19 Tobin, above n. 1, 585.

beneficence or charity'.[20] Children's rights must be actively considered, and not subsumed within the rights or interests of other parties, such as their parents.[21] This recognises children as independent human beings with their own personality and ability to participate in society.[22] Article 3(1) advances a requirement that children's rights be considered in all matters concerning them, and specifically includes actions by 'courts of law'. A children's rights approach therefore requires courts to interpret and apply the law in a way that explicitly or implicitly recognises children's rights, and routinely consider the impact of their decisions on those rights.[23] The model offered under the UNCRC recognises that the children's rights are usually situated within the context of a family unit. Parental responsibility therefore has a great role to play in the realisation of those rights, which must also accommodate and recognise a child's evolving capacity.[24]

Another feature of the vision for children's rights articulated by the UNCRC is that a child's best interests are not the paramount consideration but only a 'primary' consideration.[25] In the context of Australian family law proceedings, this principle is elevated in the FLA to the 'paramount consideration'.[26] However, prioritising the child's best interests does not automatically equate with upholding children's rights.[27] The 'best interests' principle in the UNCRC must be informed by other rights. In particular, a children's rights approach includes a requirement to 'avoid a subjective and speculative assessment of a child's best interests and to ensure appropriate consideration is given to the views of a child.'[28]

The 'best interests' principle, if applied without reference to other rights of children, runs the risk of subscribing to the 'dark side' of the traditional welfare of children model, including the paternalism inherent in a situation where those with decision-making power determine what the interests of the vulnerable are.[29] The approach of the UNCRC is to recognise children's evolving capacity to exercise their rights autonomously as they mature and develop.

---

20 Ibid, 586.

21 M. Freeman, 'Why it Remains Important to Take Children's Rights Seriously' (2007) 15 *International Journal of Children's Rights* 5, 11.

22 L. Lundy, '"Voice" is not enough: conceptualising Article 12 of the United Nations Convention on the Rights of the Child' (2007) 33(6) *British Educational Research Journal* 927, 928.

23 Tobin, above n. 1, 588.

24 Ibid, 587.

25 UNCRC Art. 3(1).

26 Family Law Act 1975 (Cth) s. 60CA (FLA).

27 H. Stalford and K. Hollingsworth, 'Judging Children's Rights: Tendencies, Tensions, Constraints and Opportunities' in Stalford, Hollingsworth and Gilmore (eds.), above n. 18, at p. 35.

28 Tobin, above n. 1, 589.

29 Tobin, above n. 1, 590, citing J. Eekelaar, *Family Law and Personal Life*, Oxford University Press, 1st ed., 2006, p. 13.

It also recognises that capacity is not a prerequisite for an entitlement to human rights.[30] As Tobin said, '[c]hildren may lack capacity to exercise their rights but they do not lack interests, and it is their interests, not their capacity, which form the foundation of rights'.[31]

Article 12 mandates that children's views be given due weight and that children must be given the opportunity to be heard. These views, while they may not be determinative, represent a 'critical ingredient' in undertaking an assessment of a child's best interests.[32] Children's participatory rights are integral to any elaboration of children's rights, and distinguish a rights-based approach from traditional welfare approaches.[33] Children's *right* to demand that their best interests are a primary consideration means that children must play an active role in the determination of their best interests.[34] A best interests assessment in accordance with this approach therefore involves consideration of the child's wishes, the relevance of any other rights under the UNCRC, the particular circumstances of the child, and any available empirical evidence that may be of relevance.[35]

Judicial decision-making that is consistent with these principles is described by Tobin as taking a 'substantive' rights approach to matters concerning children.[36] Tobin identified four areas which are necessary to manifest that approach in judicial decision-making.[37] We have refined these in the context of family law judgments. The four areas are conceptualisation, procedures, content and reasoning.

Conceptualisation requires judges to acknowledge that children's rights exist and that they are relevant to the proceedings. This requires judges to be aware of how children's rights are impacted in cases which may otherwise

30 M. Freeman, 'The Human Rights of Children' (2010) 63(1) *Current Legal Problems* 1, 13–14.

31 J. Tobin, 'Justifying Children's Rights' (2013) 21 *International Journal of Children's Rights* 395, 403.

32 Tobin, above n. 1, 590; Stalford and Hollingsworth, above n. 27, at p. 78.

33 Eekelaar, above n. 29, at pp. 160–62; Tobin, above n. 31, 416.

34 Tobin, above n. 1, 591; Stalford and Hollingsworth, above n. 27, at p. 67; J. Fortin, 'Accommodating Children's Rights in a Post *Human Rights Act* Era' (2006) 69 *Modern Law Review* 299, 318.

35 Tobin, above n. 1, 592.

36 Ibid, 593.

37 Ibid, 603. Note that these areas are consistent with Stalford, Hollingsworth and Gilmore (eds.), above n. 18, at ch. 3: five markers of a children's rights judgment: (i) the utilisation of formal legal tools including the CRC in domestic proceedings and the cross-pollination potential of children's rights sources to inform judicial decision-making in the supranational courts; (ii) the use of scholarship to inform key concepts and tensions (such as the child's best interests and child autonomy); (iii) the endorsement of child-friendly procedures to maximise children's participation in legal processes; (iv) the centralisation of the child's voice and experience in the narrative of the judgment; and (v) the communication of the judgment in a child-friendly way.

be framed as disputes between parents.[38] However, conceptualisation entails more than just recognising the existence of rights. It requires a thorough analysis determining what the rights are, the content of them and how judicial reasoning can be considerate of those rights.

A court's *procedures* should also be conducted in a manner which is considerate of the child's rights and ensures that his or her interests are represented independently from those of their parents.[39] Examples include engaging an independent legal representative for the child. While an Independent Children's Lawyer (ICL) in Australia is not obligated to act on a child's instructions, they can advance the child's interests independently of the parents' preferences.[40] Judges may also choose to meet with a child to discuss the proceedings, confirm the child's views and answer questions.[41] Fostering the active participation of children in legal proceedings which affect them is a major feature of a children's rights approach to judicial decision-making.[42] It 'reinforces the child's dignity, autonomy and status as rights-holder.'[43] It also provides the judge with the benefit of the child's genuine views and experiences, promoting decisions which are arguably better informed and more effective.[44] It is part of a judge's role to ensure that the method and manner in which children's participation is facilitated is appropriate in the circumstances.[45] It should also be noted that children should not be compelled to express their views,[46] and they are entitled to choose not to exercise their right to be heard.[47]

A judge must determine the *content* of children's rights by interpreting the meaning of these rights based on a child's circumstances. This goes beyond *conceptualisation* to ensure that the rights that are recognised are interpreted in a way which reflects the particular vulnerabilities, perspectives

---

38 Tobin, above n. 1, 588.

39 Tobin, above n. 1, 606–609; Australian Law Reform Commission and Human Rights and Equal Opportunity Commission, above n. 17, at paras. 4.4–4.9.

40 N. Taylor, 'Involving Children and Young People in Family Law Decision Making' (2006) 20(2) *Australian Journal of Family Law* 154, 167.

41 M. Fernando, 'Conversations Between Judges and Children: An Argument in Favour of Judicial Conferences in Contested Children's Matters' (2009) 23 *Australian Journal of Family Law* 48.

42 N. Thomas, 'Towards a Theory of Children's Participation' in M. Freeman (ed.), *Children's Rights: Progress and Perspectives: Essays from the International Journal of Children's Rights*, Brill Publishing, 2011, p. 48.

43 Stalford and Hollingsworth, above n. 27, at p. 76.

44 Ibid, at p. 76; Fernando, above n. 41, 55–56.

45 See M. Fernando, 'Children's Voices in Family Law Proceedings in Australia, the United Kingdom, Canada and New Zealand' in M. Breger (ed.), *Exploring Norms and Family Laws Across the Globe*, Lexington Books, 2022, ch. 11.

46 In Australia this is legislated in FLA s. 60CE.

47 United Nations Committee on the Rights of the Child, General Comment No. 12, *The Right of the Child to be Heard*, CRC/C/GC/12, 2009, para. 16.

and experiences of children.[48] 'Regarding best interests (and by implication, welfare) as a right thus demands more than passing reference to the principle or a presumption that its component parts are understood; it necessitates transparent, rigorous, systematic, even forensic, deliberations of the various factors that have comprised that assessment.'[49]

Further, a children's rights approach should be evident in the way a court approaches its *reasoning*. Judgments must include a clear explanation of the reasons for the decision delivered in a manner which the child can understand,[50] demonstrate that the child's views have been considered adequately and show how competing rights have been balanced. Regardless of whether a decision is consistent with the child's views, a children's rights approach requires the judge to 'explain the extent of the consideration given to the views of the child and the consequences for the child.'[51]

> A children's rights judgment should therefore seek to understand and persuade from the child, not adult, perspective. In this way, the crafting of judgments – as well as the reasoning, outcomes and proceedings – can become a vehicle for the child's right to be heard and for recognising her as an active, rights-bearing agent.[52]

Finally, the reasoning in a children's rights judgment requires a court to expressly balance competing rights and interests.[53] This may entail balancing the conflicting rights of the individual child,[54] competing rights of children generally[55] or the rights of the child with the rights of other parties, such as their parents or the State.[56] While family law matters should generally be resolved

---

48 Tobin, above n. 1, 611.

49 Stalford and Hollingsworth, above n. 27, at p. 65.

50 See generally Stalford, Hollingsworth and Gilmore (eds.), above n. 18; *Re A (Letter to a Young Person)* [2017] EWFC 48 where Jackson J. delivered his judgment in the form of a letter to a 14-year-old boy.

51 J. Doek, 'Child Participation' in J. Todres and S.M. King (eds.), *The Oxford Handbook of Children's Rights Law*, Oxford University Press, 2020, pp. 268–270; United Nations Committee on the Rights of the Child, General Comment No. 12, *The Right of the Child to be Heard*, CRC/C/GC/12, 2009, para. 33.

52 Stalford and Hollingsworth, above n. 27, at p. 81.

53 D. Archard and M. Skivenes, 'Balancing a Child's Best Interests and a Child's Views' (2009) 17 *International Journal of Children's Rights* 1, 2; Tobin, above n. 1, 612.

54 See e.g. *Re T (paternity: ordering blood tests)* [2001] 2 FLR 1190 where a purported biological father's application for a DNA test required the court to balance the child's right to respect for his private life with the child's right to know his identity and paternity.

55 See e.g. *R (Begum) v. Governors of Denbigh High School* [2007] 1 AC 100 where a primary school hijab ban required the court to balance the rights of all children attending the school with the rights of one child claiming violation of freedom of religion.

56 See e.g. *Williamson v. Secretary of State for Education and Employment* [2005] 2 AC 246 where a ban on corporal punishment in schools required the court to balance the religious beliefs of parents and teachers who asserted their 'right' to have children physically disciplined in schools with the children's right to protection from the State.

by applying the best interests principle,[57] this is not the only consideration and other rights and interests may be relevant.[58] The court's reasoning should explain which competing rights were considered and how they were balanced in order to reach the outcome. While such an approach to judicial reasoning can be complex, 'the advantage of such a strategy is that it might produce a deeper analysis of the child's own position.'[59]

4. THE HIGH COURT'S APPROACH TO CHILDREN'S RIGHTS

In this section we analyse the Australian High Court's approach to children's rights in the only two family law cases involving children decided in the past 18 years. We make observations about the court's approach in these cases, and in older cases where children's rights may have been more visible. In all instances we observe that the High Court has failed to take a substantive children's rights approach according to the principles of the UNCRC and the areas for consideration as outlined by Tobin.

4.1. *BONDELMONTE v. BONDELMONTE* (2017) 259 CLR 662

This case concerned an appeal against orders requiring the return of two older children, boys aged 15 and 17, from New York, where they had remained after a holiday with their father, in breach of parenting orders. It also concerned the interim living arrangements ordered for the children upon their return to Australia.

The parties separated in 2010 and had equal shared parental responsibility for their three children. The mother agreed to the father taking the two boys for a holiday in New York in January 2016. The younger daughter was not included in the plans and remained in Australia with the mother. During the holiday, the father informed the mother that he intended to stay in New York and that the boys would remain with him. The mother filed an application in the Family Court to secure the return of the boys.

The main issue was the ascertainment and treatment of the boys' views. At the interim hearing Watts J. accepted evidence from the father that the boys

---

57 Note that the best interests of an individual child are not paramount in cases involving principles of the Hague Convention on the Civil Aspects of International Child Abduction, opened for signature 25 October 1980, 1343 UNTS 89 (entered into force 1 December 1983).

58 R. Chisholm, '"The Paramount Consideration": Children's Interests in Family Law' (2002) 16 *Australian Journal of Family Law* 87.

59 Fortin, above n. 34, 313.

wished to remain in New York and that neither wanted to return to Australia or to live with the mother. This was based on conversations the father had had with the children and text messages that one of the boys had sent to the mother. Watts J. did not order a 'wishes' report, which would involve the boys expressing their views to an independent expert in New York, because he did not expect those views to be any different to what the father had reported.[60] Watts J. accepted that the children's views were genuine. However, the weight that may have otherwise been attached to those views was 'weakened by the circumstances which have been contrived by the father.'[61] Watts J. determined that it was in the best interests of the children to return to Australia pending a determination about whether, in the long term, they would live in Australia or the USA.

The matter was further complicated because the father refused to indicate that he would return to Australia if the children were ordered to return. The relationship between the mother and the boys being strained, Watts J. accepted that it was possible that one or both boys would refuse to live with the mother in Australia. He therefore made orders that, should the father not return and the children refuse to live with the mother, the boys live either in supervised accommodation paid for by the father or that each boy live with a particular family friend, which had been arranged by the mother.[62] This would require them to be separated. The children were not consulted about these arrangements.

The decision was unsuccessfully appealed to the Full Court and then to the High Court. The unanimous High Court (Kiefel, Bell, Keane, Nettle and Gordon JJ.) confirmed that the views of a child 'are but one consideration of a number to be taken into account in the overall assessment of a child's best interests.'[63] In particular, Watts J. had considered that there were other matters about which the children had not appeared to give any thought, such as the effect of separation from their sister and mother on those relationships in the future.[64]

The father also argued that the court was obliged to seek the children's views about their proposed living arrangements in Australia. However, the High Court said that section 60CC(3)(a) of the FLA (which requires the court to consider 'any views expressed by a child') does not expressly or impliedly require the court to seek the views of a child. It only requires that the views that have been 'expressed' are considered.[65]

60 *Bondelmonte v. Bondelmonte* (2017) 259 CLR 662, paras. 22–23.
61 Ibid, at para. 23.
62 Ibid, at para. 15.
63 Ibid, at para. 34.
64 Ibid, at para. 36.
65 Ibid, at para. 43.

The High Court's judgment, when viewed from a children's rights perspective, is disappointing. There was no consideration of a child's right to express their views in matters concerning them, nor a court's obligation to give children an opportunity to be heard. Indeed, the High Court stated the opposite: that a court is under no obligation to seek the views of children. This view was based solely on section 60CC(3)(a) of the FLA, and apparently overrules earlier Full Court authority to the effect that children's views should ordinarily be ascertained, with the court then having discretion as to the weight to be given to those views, based on the child's age and maturity and the circumstances of the case.[66] The High Court's view clearly contravenes the rights provided by Article 12 of the UNCRC. Hollingsworth and Stalford described the judicial discretion to ensure children's views are heard and considered in line with Article 12 as 'an essential pre-requisite to a children's rights judgment.'[67] Here the High Court failed to either expressly or impliedly conceptualise the issues in the case in terms of children's rights.

The High Court's approval of Watts J.'s reliance on the children's apparent failure to consider the future of their relationships with their sister and mother (which was based on the content of the younger child's text messages) disregards the fact that the children were not consulted for the purposes of these proceedings, and it was therefore not possible to know whether they *had* given those matters any thought. Part of a children's rights approach is to ensure that procedures are in place to enable children to be active participants, and to enable their genuine views to be heard so that the best decisions are made.

The context of this case was an interim hearing, which often does not allow for full consideration of the issues. However, these were complex circumstances, involving trans-Atlantic relocation, uncertain and potentially unstable living arrangements and significant change to almost every aspect of the children's lives. The children were not given an opportunity to express their views to the court, either directly or indirectly (such as through an expert report). Particularly given their advanced ages, and the drastic changes to their living arrangements proposed, it was a violation of their rights and contrary to their best interests that their views on these matters were not sought.

Reithmuller commented that the case could be seen to reflect 'an underlying narrative centred upon the rights, interests and behaviours of parents and the demands of the court to have orders respected',[68] in particular the actions of the father in unilaterally relocating with the children in breach of court orders and his refusal to return in any circumstances. The best interests of children are

66 *Joannou v. Joannou* (1985) FLC 91-642; *Harrison v. Woollard* (1995) 18 Fam LR 788.

67 Stalford and Hollingsworth, above n. 27, at p. 78.

68 G. Reithmuller, 'Greater Recognition of Adults as Individuals' in M. Brinig (ed.), *The International Survey of Family Law*, Intersentia Publishing, 1st ed., 2018, p. 80.

the paramount but not the sole consideration in parenting cases, and the court is entitled to consider other factors in its reasoning. However, as Reithmuller noted, these kinds of considerations must be overtly expressed and given proper weight, and the court must explain how they were balanced against the interests of the child. The ability for a court to articulate in its reasons how children's rights have been considered and weighed against other interests is one of the indicators of a substantive children's rights approach. Here those considerations were not articulated. The court also failed to interpret children's rights based on the age, perspectives and experiences of the children involved. Reithmuller noted that as the eldest child was nearly at the age of majority, the orders would be unenforceable in relation to him in any event. It would therefore be difficult to argue that children's rights were construed from his perspective or that the outcome was focused on his interests.[69] From a children's rights approach, it is extraordinary that the practicalities of this decision for a 17-year-old child were not considered. Making orders which undermined his autonomy without expressly considering the fact they could not be enforced could not be said to be in his best interests.

4.2. *RCB v. THE HONOURABLE JUSTICE FORREST AND ORS* (2012) 247 CLR 304

In 2010, an Australian mother living in Italy brought her four Italian daughters to Australia, ostensibly for a one-month holiday. They refused to return to Italy and the father sought their return through the regulations which implement the Hague Child Abduction Convention in Australia.[70] The children were aged 14, 12, 9 and 8 years at the time of the first hearing, and the mother raised various defences, including that the children objected to returning.

The primary judge, Forrest J., received evidence of the children's views through the written reports of two experts who had spoken with the children. The children were not represented by a lawyer and had no opportunity to express their views directly to the court or otherwise participate in the proceedings. Forrest J. did not accept that the children objected in the sense required by the regulations because, while all four wished to remain living in Australia with their mother, they missed aspects of their lives in Italy. Each accepted the prospect of return if their mother would return with them and they could live predominantly with her.[71] In addition, Forrest J. agreed with the family

69 Ibid, at p. 80.
70 Family Law (Child Abduction Convention) Regulations 1986 (Cth) (Regulations).
71 *Department of Communities (Child Safety Services) v. Garning* [2011] FamCA 485 (23 June 2011), paras. 117–118.

consultant (court-appointed expert) that the children's ability for abstract thought and future forecasting was not fully formed and that they lacked the ability to truly predict the impact of their choices on their future relationship with their father.[72] He ordered that they be returned.

Following numerous court events and incidents, the children's maternal great-aunt, as litigation guardian for the children, made application to the High Court on grounds that Forrest J. had failed to afford the children an opportunity to have separate and independent representation, had failed to take their interests into account, and had otherwise acted contrary to the rules and principles of natural justice with respect to the children. The application was unanimously dismissed and, in doing so, the High Court made some important comments about the relevance of children's views to cases involving the Hague Convention on the Civil Aspects of International Child Abduction (Hague Convention).[73]

The plurality[74] noted that the interests and views of a child may be relevant to the existence of Australia's obligation to return the child when a defence is raised.[75] Where there is evidence suggesting that children object to being returned, the court must assess the strength of the objections and whether the children are of sufficient age and maturity that it is appropriate to take account of their views.[76] This then presents a practical issue of how the court is to be sufficiently and fairly apprised of that information. The plurality determined that this can be met by the appointment of a family consultant. Being an officer of the court and skilled in advising about these kinds of issues, a family consultant can hear and assess a child's views and report back to the court and the parties.[77]

The plurality rejected any suggestion that a child who objects needs to be directly represented by a lawyer in every case, stating that this wrongly assumed that a child whose maturity is at issue can nonetheless instruct a lawyer and that only a lawyer could sufficiently and fairly determine the child's views and transmit them to the court. The children had made no application to intervene as parties in the primary proceedings, so no practical unfairness had resulted.[78] Further, there was no allegation that Forrest J. should have made an order appointing an ICL because there were no circumstances at the initial hearing which the court might properly have characterised as 'exceptional'.[79]

---

72 Ibid, at para. 120.

73 Opened for signature 25 October 1980, 1343 UNTS 89 (entered into force 1 December 1983).

74 French C.J., Hayne, Crennan, Kiefel and Bell JJ.

75 *RCB v. The Honourable Justice Forrest and Ors* (2012) 247 CLR 304, paras. 22–23 (*RCB*).

76 Ibid, at para. 43; Regulations reg. 16(3)(c).

77 *RCB*, above n. 75, at paras. 44–45.

78 Ibid, at paras. 46–47.

79 Ibid, at para. 36.

In Australia, exceptional circumstances are a prerequisite for the appointment of an ICL in Hague abduction cases.[80]

As Fernando and Ross wrote:

> [T]he language used by Australia's highest court set a low bar for the treatment of children and their views in Hague Convention matters. The judgment made no mention of a child's right to express their views or to be given an opportunity to be heard, and indeed the judgment did not mention children's rights at all. The language used by the High Court suggested that the only purpose of hearing children's views is to undertake the forensic exercise described.[81]

RCB was selected as the only Australian judgment to be rewritten as part of the Children's Rights Judgments Project.[82] Schuz's critique of the original judgment noted its 'invisible approach' to children's rights.[83] She wrote that the judgment 'indicate[s] a complete lack of awareness of children's right to participate and to have their interests properly represented.'[84] The plurality's view that ensuring procedural fairness for the children was essentially a practical question of informing the court of the information on which to base its findings about the child's objection and maturity 'ignores the fact that the child's right to be heard is not purely an instrumental right. Rather, participation recognises that a child is a moral and social actor in his own right and empowers him.'[85] A court's ability to define and interpret children's rights based on the child's experiences, rather than merely as a practical matter for the court to address, is consistent with a substantive rights approach. Schuz described as a 'fallacy' the view that the nature of Hague abduction proceedings, as a procedural tool for allocating jurisdiction and enforcing foreign court orders, means that children's rights are not relevant.[86] Numerous scholars[87] have explained the various ways in which children's rights are engaged in Hague proceedings, '*inter alia*, because

---

80 FLA s. 68L(2A).

81 M. Fernando and N. Ross, 'Stifled Voices: Hearing Children's Objections in Hague Child Abduction Convention Cases in Australia' (2018) 32(1) *International Journal of Law, Policy and the Family* 93.

82 Published in Stalford, Hollingsworth and Gilmore (eds.), above n. 18.

83 R. Schuz, 'Commentary on RCB as Litigation Guardian of EKV, CEV, CIV and LRV v The Honourable Justice Colin James Forrest' in Stalford, Hollingsworth and Gilmore (eds.), above n. 18, at p. 499.

84 Ibid, at p. 499.

85 Ibid, at p. 499.

86 Ibid, at p. 496.

87 See e.g. C. Fenton-Glynn, 'Participation and Natural Justice: Children's Rights and Interests in Hague Abduction Proceedings' (2014) 9 *Journal of Comparative Law* 129; L. Elrod, 'Please Let Me Stay: Hearing the Voice of the Child in Hague Abduction Cases' (2011) 63 *Oklahoma Law Review* 663; R. Schuz, *The Hague Child Abduction Convention: A Critical Analysis*, Hart Publishing, 2013; T. Boezaart, 'Listening to the Child's Objection' (2013) *New Zealand Law Review* 357.

of the fateful implications such proceedings may have for the lives of children both in the short term and often also in the long term.'[88]

In his rewritten judgment of *RCB*, Simpson noted the problems with presuming that a family consultant's report is a sufficient method of presenting the court with evidence of children's objections and maturity. Opinions in reports about the needs and interests of children can be affected by various biases in the report writer.[89] Simpson was particularly critical of the family consultant's view that the children lacked maturity because their ability for abstract thought and 'future forecasting' was not fully formed. 'To the extent that [future forecasting] implies being able to see into the future, I doubt that this is an attribute that many adults possess (if any). Nor am I convinced that a fully formed ability for abstract thought is something that all mature adults possess let alone children.'[90]

Given the requirements for a particularly strong feeling and age and degree of maturity that need to be satisfied before a child's objection can be taken into account in Hague matters,[91] a family consultant's evidence should be closely examined, including through thorough cross-examination.[92]

An independent lawyer appointed to represent the interests of the children would be an appropriate person to take that role. Simpson noted that, once the child's objections are raised as a real issue in the case, there would appear to be sufficient grounds to justify the 'exceptional circumstances' that would allow the appointment of an ICL.[93] Schuz dismissed the plurality's comment that the primary judge had not been asked to appoint a lawyer as ignoring 'the duty of the state to provide the child with an opportunity to be heard in proceedings concerning him and to ensure that he has proper representation.'[94] Under a substantive children's rights approach, the court has an obligation to ensure that the court's procedures enable the child's rights and interests to be independently (and accurately) represented.

An ICL in Australia is a best interests representative, and not a direct advocate for the child. This may be viewed as problematic from a substantive rights approach because the appointment of an ICL does not ensure that the child's views will be expressed to the court in a truly independent way.[95] Nevertheless, both Simpson and Schuz noted that the role of an ICL is not

88 Schuz, above n. 83, at p. 497.
89 B. Simpson, 'RCB as Litigation Guardian of EKV, CEV, CIV and LRV v The Honourable Justice Colin James Forrest' in Stalford, Hollingsworth and Gilmore (eds.), above n. 18, at p. 509.
90 Ibid, at p. 510.
91 Regulations reg. 16(3)(c).
92 Simpson, above n. 89, at p. 508.
93 Ibid, at p. 508.
94 Schuz, above n. 83, at p. 499.
95 Tobin, above n. 1, 608.

necessarily limited in that regard. While an ICL is 'not obliged to act on the child's instructions',[96] there is nothing preventing an ICL from acting in accordance with the views of a mature child.[97] Simpson observed that an ICL cannot establish the child's best interests without ascertaining his or her views, and preventing an ICL from advocating the child's views 'would make a mockery of the "best interests of the child" principle as there must be many cases where the child's views reflect his or her best interests'.[98] Further, Schuz observed that the benefit to children of having an ICL extends beyond that person's role in enabling the child's voice to be heard. It is also a method of ensuring that the child's case is presented to the court in a persuasive and professional manner.[99] The right to be represented in legal proceedings is universally recognised as a basic human right.[100] It allows the child's position to be put forward 'in any equal manner to the others involved in the case, who are usually represented by professional lawyers.'[101]

4.3. OLDER CASES

In neither of the High Court cases discussed above was a children's rights approach taken. The court's approach to children's rights was instead, as coined by Tobin, 'invisible'. None of the four areas for consideration of children's rights were adhered to, and the *real* interests of children, including their interests as rights-bearers, were not considered. It is open to the court to consider the rights and perspectives of others, such as parental rights and behaviours, or the global interests involved in having children who are taken from their home countries without permission returned. However, a court must articulate those rights and interests and weigh them properly against children's rights.

The High Court's approach to children's rights has not always been 'invisible'. In *De L v. Director General, NSW Department of Community Services and Anor (De L)*,[102] for example, the High Court arguably upheld the rights of children to procedural fairness and to express their views. Like *RCB*, the case also concerned an application under the regulations implementing the Hague Convention to return children unlawfully retained in Australia to their home country. The primary judge had erroneously directed the family consultant to 'ascertain the wishes of the children and their maturity to express those wishes',

96 FLA s. 68LA(4).
97 Simpson, above n. 89, at p. 507; Schuz, above n. 83, at p. 501.
98 Simpson, above n. 89, at p. 508.
99 Schuz, above n. 83, at p. 496.
100 Ibid, at p. 495.
101 Ibid, at p. 496.
102 (1996) 187 CLR 640 (*De L*).

rather than to ascertain whether the children 'objected' to being returned, which is the standard required by the Convention, and the regulations at that time.[103]

Given evidence by the children's mother that they did not want to return to the USA, and the primary judge's significant reliance on the family consultant's report, which had not been directed to the correct issue, the plurality of the High Court[104] acknowledged the practical difficulties confronting the mother in establishing whether or not the children objected in the relevant sense and found that 'procedural fairness requires that there be a rehearing of the matter to determine whether, in fact, [the children] do object to that course.'[105] While the right to procedural fairness was framed as a right of the mother, and not of the children, the implication was that children must be given an opportunity to express their views in a way that is relevant and potentially influential to the issue being decided. In rejecting the Full Court majority's view that a return order could be made on the basis that there was no evidence that the children 'objected' in the relevant sense, the High Court impliedly upheld a right of children to express their views and have them properly considered, where this inquiry is relevant to proceedings.

The plurality in *De L* made two other comments that could be said to be supportive of children's right to be heard. First, it said that where children object to being returned, and are of a sufficient age and maturity that their views would appropriately be taken into account, 'there ordinarily should be separate representation.'[106] Second, the plurality cited with approval a comment made by Nicholson C.J. in the Full Court that the policy of the Convention is not compromised by hearing what children have to say.[107] Again, the High Court did not mention children's rights explicitly, but relied heavily on Nicholson C.J.'s reasoning throughout the judgment, which did expressly emphasise the court's obligation to give children a proper opportunity to be heard under the UNCRC.[108] Nevertheless, it cannot be said that the High Court took a 'substantive' children's rights approach in this case, and the decision has been criticised as focusing on the rights of the adults involved instead of the children.[109]

---

103 In 2004 the Regulations reg. 16(3)(c) was amended to also require that the child's objection 'shows a strength of feeling beyond the mere expression of a preference or of ordinary wishes.'

104 Brennan C.J., Dawson, Toohey, Gaudron, McHugh and Gummow JJ.

105 (1996) 187 CLR 640, 659.

106 Ibid, 660. It is noted that this comment was made prior to a legislative amendment which allows an order for children to be separately represented in Hague Convention matters only in 'exceptional circumstances': FLA s. 68L(3).

107 (1996) 187 CLR 640, 657.

108 *Director General, Department of Community Services v. De Lewinski* (1996) FLC 92-706 at 83,015–83,016.

109 Schuz, above n. 83, at p. 502.

Former High Court Justice Michael Kirby referenced the UNCRC in several minority judgments in family law matters, making clear that the UNCRC is relevant to child-related proceedings under the FLA.[110] In *Re JJT and Ors; Ex Parte Victoria Legal Aid*, Kirby J. made specific the links between the FLA and the rights afforded to children under the UNCRC, noting that a court is required '[b]oth by Australian law and by international law' to make decisions affecting children in accordance with their best interests.[111] His Honour noted that '[t]he [FLA] affords a wide range of protections for children which reflect a parliamentary recognition of their separate identity and rights'.[112] Kirby J. also observed the benefit of separate representation for children in assisting the court to determine the best interests of children as distinct from the positions of their parents, which are 'often coloured by their own interests and perspectives'.[113]

Kirby J. also referred to children's rights in *Minister for Immigration and Multicultural and Indigenous Affairs v. B (MIMIA v. B)*.[114] The issue in the case was whether the Family Court's jurisdiction to make orders for the 'welfare of children' in section 67ZC extended to a power to make orders releasing children from immigration detention. The majority of the Full Court held that the welfare jurisdiction did extend to releasing children from immigration detention and that the indefinite detention of children was unlawful.[115] The Full Court's decision was overturned by a unanimous High Court. The High Court's judgment largely focused on a statutory construction of the Family Court's welfare jurisdiction. However, Kirby J.'s minority judgment engaged with the UNCRC, particularly Article 37(b), which provides that the detention of children is a 'measure of last resort'.[116] Kirby J. ultimately concluded that, in this case, the children's detention was nevertheless lawful as the relevant provisions of the Migration Act 1958 (Cth) were constitutionally valid, and the detention of the children was not 'indefinite' as it was linked to their parents' voluntary decision to leave Australia, or a successful outcome in legal proceedings.[117]

Tobin criticised Kirby J.'s reasoning in *MIMIA v. B* as taking a 'selective' rights approach because his Honour identified children's rights, but did not conceptualise them.[118] Kirby J.'s reasoning subsumed the rights of the children

110 *Northern Territory v. GPAO* (1998) 196 CLR 553, paras. 224–233 (dissenting); *Re JJT; Ex Parte Victoria Legal Aid* (1998) 195 CLR 184, paras. 15–45 (*Re JJT*); *Minister for Immigration and Multicultural and Indigenous Affairs v. B* (2004) 219 CLR 365, paras. 144–173.

111 *Re JJT*, above n. 110, at para. 15.

112 Ibid, at para. 42.

113 Ibid, at para. 43.

114 (2004) 219 CLR 365, paras. 144–173 (*MIMIA v. B*).

115 *B & B* [2003] 30 Fam LR 181, 243–244 (Nicholson C.J. and O'Ryan J.; Ellis J. dissenting).

116 *MIMIA v. B*, above n. 114, at paras. 166–169.

117 Ibid, at para. 172 (Kirby J.).

118 Tobin, above n. 1, 599.

within the parents' rights and their 'voluntary choice' to leave Australia (and therefore leave immigration detention) rather than considering the rights of the children independently from their parents and determining how the children's detention impacted their rights. In contrast, Tobin observed that the Full Court took a 'substantive' rights approach which recognised that 'children are entitled to be treated as individuals and not as the property or appendages of their parents.'[119]

Interestingly, Kirby J. was the minority judge in *De L*. His Honour did acknowledge children's rights under the UNCRC, including the right to be heard in Article 12. However, his Honour prioritised the principles of the Hague Convention, including children's collective rights to be protected from the harmful effects of abduction[120] and the need to return children swiftly so that abducting parents cannot benefit from delay and the laws in other countries are respected.[121]

Fortin observed that courts often adopt an entirely different approach when dealing with applications brought on behalf of children themselves.[122] This can be said to be true for cases involving medical decisions for children such as *Secretary of the Department of Health and Community Services v. JWB and SMB (Re Marion)*,[123] where the High Court confirmed that parental responsibility did not extend to the power to authorise non-therapeutic sterilisation of a 14-year-old intellectually and physically disabled girl. The High Court held that such an 'invasive, irreversible and major surgery'[124] required court authorisation, and that the child's best interests are paramount in deciding whether to order a sterilisation procedure.[125] The High Court judgment made several observations which are consistent with a children's rights approach. While the Court recognised that such complex decisions will inherently involve the interests of other family members, such as caregivers and parents, the child's interests prevail in the event of any conflict.[126] This may result in a court refusing to order a sterilisation procedure if the child's best interests do not coincide with the parents' wishes.[127] The High Court recognised the potentially conflicting rights of children and their parents, but demonstrated a substantive rights approach by conceptualising and interpreting children's rights based on the perspective and experiences of the child, rather than the parents. However,

---

119 *B & B*, above n. 115, 243 (Nicholson C.J. and O'Ryan J.); Tobin, above n. 1, 599.
120 *De L*, above n. 102, at paras. 447–448 (Kirby J.).
121 Ibid, at para. 437 (Kirby J.).
122 Fortin, above n. 34, 304.
123 (1992) 175 CLR 218 (*Re Marion*).
124 Ibid, 250.
125 Ibid, 259.
126 Ibid, 306.
127 Ibid, 315.

Fortin's observation does not ring true for *RCB*, discussed above, where the case was nominally brought on behalf of the children themselves but a children's rights approach was not taken. This is probably because the case was essentially framed by the court as advancing the interests of the mother, who had previously unsuccessfully contested the original return order through several court applications and appeals.

5. DISCUSSION

While there are some older cases which at least superficially promote children's rights, such as *De L*, the High Court judgments do not take a substantive approach to children's rights. Even in situations where the High Court has recognised or conceptualised children's rights, it has not engaged with those rights based on the perspectives and experiences of the child. The High Court's reasoning does not sufficiently demonstrate how children's rights have been considered and balanced against other competing rights or interests, or explain the decision in a manner which the child is capable of understanding.

Our case analysis revealed that the High Court seems inclined to prioritise the rights and interests of parents over those of children. It also indicated that the High Court may be more receptive to children's rights in cases involving medical decision-making and parental authority, such as in *Re Marion*. Where the focus is on the rights of parents and others, at least in recent times, the High Court's approach to children's rights has been 'invisible', with the rights and interests of children unarticulated. This is despite the fact that all of these cases have a tremendous impact on children, and in all of them children's rights should be acknowledged as separate from the rights of their parents.

In failing to take a substantive children's rights approach to decision-making, the High Court is excluding the benefits such an approach offers. These include benefits for children, both individually and collectively, for development of the common law, for better judicial decision-making and for the recognition of Australia's international obligations and human rights generally.

A children's rights approach to judgments 'increase[s] visibility of children within the law by ensuring that their status as rights-holders is recognised, that their voices are heard and that their interests are identified and factored into judicial decision-making.'[128] This acknowledges that children are not simply extensions of their parents, but individuals with their own views, interests and rights which should be respected. In the context of judicial decision-making, it is particularly important to take a children's rights approach as children are often denied a legal voice in other processes, such as parliamentary legislative

128 Stalford and Hollingsworth, above n. 27, at p. 73.

drafting and elections.[129] This makes children politically vulnerable as many decisions are made which directly affect children, and yet effectively subsume their interests with those of adults.[130] In some instances, children's social, economic, political and legal rights are entirely dependent on the ability and willingness of an adult to promote these rights.[131] A children's rights approach to judgments entails an element of moral reasoning which is beneficial for children not just in the context of legal proceedings they are involved in, but also because it demonstrates respect, and encourages development of children's rights more widely.[132] It also promotes the judiciary's role in developing the common law. Advancing children's rights is an important aspect of this.[133] A children's rights approach will generally result in decisions which are consistent with a child's welfare and best interests,[134] meaning that better decisions are made.

A children's rights approach is particularly necessary in Australia. Due to a lack of constitutional or legislative protection of children's rights and human rights generally, individuals rely on the common law to protect and uphold their rights.[135] The extent to which the UNCRC is domestically applied depends heavily on judicial discretion.[136] In the absence of a legislative or constitutional human rights framework, it is important that our highest court is receptive to protecting and upholding children's rights. The High Court's role in promoting human rights generally has been recognised extensively,[137] and in the context of children's rights such an approach would be consistent with

129 Stalford and Hollingsworth, above n. 27, at p. 44; B. Byrne and L. Lundy, 'Children's Rights-based Childhood Policy: a six-P Framework' (2019) 23(3) *The International Journal of Human Rights* 357; Thomas, above n. 42, at p. 62.

130 H. Stalford, K. Hollingsworth and S. Gilmore, 'Introducing Children's Rights Judgments' in Stalford, Hollingsworth and Gilmore (eds.), above n. 18, at p. 5; A. Nolan, 'The Child as "Democratic Citizen" – Challenging the "Participation Gap"' (2010) 4 *Public Law* 767.

131 Stalford and Hollingsworth, above n. 27, at p. 63; P. Alderson, 'Common Criticisms of Children's Rights and 25 Years of the IJCR' in M. Freeman (ed.), *Children's Rights: New Issues, New Themes, New Perspectives*, Brill Publishing, 2017, p. 42.

132 Tobin, above n. 1, 431.

133 M. Hedley, *The Modern Judge – Power, Responsibility and Society's Expectations*, LexisNexis, 2016; A. Nolan, *Children's Socio-Economic Rights, Democracy and the Courts*, Hart Publishing, 2011; J. Eekelaar, 'The Role of the Best Interests Principle in Decisions Affecting Children and Decisions about Children' (2015) 23 *International Journal of Children's Rights* 3.

134 Fortin, above n. 34, 311.

135 *Al-Kateb v. Godwin* (2004) 219 CLR 562, paras. 150, 168 and 176 (Kirby J.) (dissenting).

136 Stalford and Hollingsworth, above n. 27, at p. 76.

137 See e.g. *Thomas v. Mowbray* (2007) 233 CLR 307, para. 17 (Gleeson C.J.) and para. 111 (Gummow and Crennan JJ.); *Al-Kateb v. Godwin* (2004) 219 CLR 562, para. 19 (Gleeson C.J.) (dissenting) and paras. 180–183 (Kirby J.) (dissenting); *Coco v. The Queen* (1994) 179 CLR 427, para. 17 (Mason C.J., Brennan, Gaudron and McHugh JJ.); G. Williams, 'The High Court, the Constitution and Human Rights' (2015) 21(1) *Australian Journal of Human Rights* 1; F.E. Johns, 'Human Rights in the High Court of Australia, 1976–2003: The Righting of Australian Law?' (2005) 33(2) *Federal Law Review* 287.

the UN Committee on the Rights of the Child calling for all judicial bodies to systematically consider 'how children's rights and interests are or will be affected by their decisions and actions.'[138] It also provides an opportunity for the High Court to fulfil its obligations, at both an international and a domestic level, to demonstrate compliance with international instruments.[139] As Australia's highest court, the High Court has a responsibility both internationally and in developing the common law to acknowledge children as independent rights-bearers and to promote greater recognition of human rights generally. It also owes that responsibility to children as citizens.

Further, taking a children's rights approach can benefit judicial understanding and reasoning: for example, by informing a judge's assessment of a child's best interests.[140] It allows judges to both understand and explain how a particular decision promotes children's rights.[141] A substantive rights approach ensures that judges consistently and fairly engage with children's rights and facilitates a 'sturdier foundation for judicial decision-making'.[142] It provides scope to

> achieve more informed, reasoned and accountable decision-making by: recognising best interests as a right; articulating clearly that right – informed by the wider rights of children including their right to be heard; giving appropriate weight to the child's interests (underpinned by the justifications set out in the previous section); ensuring other agenda do not displace the child's best interests; and being open to alternative ways of conceptualising best interests for example using a relational approach.[143]

This is beneficial, not just for the individual child, or children as a collective with rights, but also for the coherence of judicial decision-making more widely. A children's rights approach to judgments ensures the active recognition and application of children's rights in a substantive manner – which is lacking in other political, social and legal procedures – and promotes persuasive, structured and analytical judicial decision-making.[144] This improves the quality of judgments and development of precedents.[145]

---

138 United Nations Committee on the Rights of the Child, General Comment No. 5, *General Measures of Implementation of the Convention on the Rights of the Child (arts. 4, 42 and 44, para. 6)*, CRC/GC/5, 2003, p. 4.

139 Tobin, above n. 1, 580.

140 See e.g. *Re Alex: Hormonal Treatment for Gender Dysphoria* (2004) 31 Fam LR 503, paras. 41 and 208–209 (Nicholson C.J.).

141 Stalford and Hollingsworth, above n. 27, at p. 65.

142 Ibid, at p. 85.

143 Ibid, at p. 69.

144 Fortin, above n. 34, 326.

145 Fenton-Glynn, above n. 87, 134.

6. CONCLUSION

The High Court of Australia has often failed to recognise the importance of conceptualising children's rights in the context of a family law dispute. Its treatment of children's rights in recent cases has been 'invisible'. A substantive rights approach to family law judgments by the High Court would be in the best interests of children who are involved in judicial proceedings and of children as a collective. Failing to do so risks treating children as 'objects of concern' or property of their parents, instead of independent rights-bearers.[146] This approach also has wider legal and policy advantages as it facilitates development of the common law in a manner which fulfils international obligations and promotes human rights. It also leads to better, fairer and more consistent judicial decision-making. Taking a substantive rights approach gives judges the opportunity to facilitate real change by actively engaging with children's rights rather than routinely applying the law without considering the moral, social and political complexities which underpin legal issues involving children.[147]

We acknowledge that 'the adoption of a substantive rights approach begins with the capacity to conceptualise a dispute through the eyes of a child – a task which, for judges and lawyers, can often prove difficult.'[148] While the shift to a children's rights-based approach is not an easy task given existing conventions and norms of judicial decision-making,[149] it is a change which is worth making.

---

146 Stalford and Hollingsworth, above n. 27, at p. 70.
147 Tobin, above n. 1, 623, 625.
148 Ibid, 625.
149 Stalford and Hollingsworth, above n. 27, at p. 85.

BELGIUM
WHAT IS A PARENT?
Answers and Questions

Frederik SWENNEN and Elise GOOSSENS

Résumé

Qu'est-ce qu'un parent ? La réponse à cette question est devenue complexe ces derniers temps. L'émergence de nouvelles constellations familiales a incité de nombreuses juridictions à reconsidérer prudemment le concept même de parent(alit)é. En Belgique, la catégorie de la parenté légale est devenue plus inclusive au cours des dernières décennies : les conséquences du changement de la désignation légale du sexe ont été réglementées ; la co-maternité a été introduite à la suite de l'introduction du mariage entre personnes de même sexe et de l'adoption par des personnes de même sexe \; en cas de procréation médicalement assistée, la parenté est attribuée au(x) parent(s) intentionnel(s) et non au(x) donneur(s).

Néanmoins, le droit de la parenté en Belgique reste largement inspiré du modèle de la 'Famille Sexuelle'. Le législateur l'a même renforcé en incluant de nouvelles constellations de parenté sous les labels déjà existants, comme celle des personnes trans, des co-mères et des autres parents intentionnels dans le cadre de la loi sur la procréation médicalement assistée. Dans le même temps, les responsabilités parentales restent réservées aux parents légaux ou aux adoptants, avec une exception pour les accueillants familiaux. En outre, il n'existe actuellement aucun cadre juridique pour la gestation pour autrui ou la parenté multiple.

Nous suggérons deux modulations de la loi belge afin de répondre aux besoins de toutes les familles. Premièrement, le législateur pourrait envisager d'introduire la parenté sans responsabilités parentales, et les responsabilités parentales sans parenté. Deuxièmement, la parenté et la parentalité multiple pourraient remplacer l'approche dyadique actuelle envers ces deux institutions. Malheureusement, le législateur n'a actuellement pas prévu de telles réformes.

1. INTRODUCTION

What is a parent? The answer to this question has become much more complex in recent times. Many jurisdictions, including Belgium, are struggling to incorporate non-conventional family formations into family law. The emergence of new family formations gives rise to a cautious reconceptualisation of parenthood, away from more traditional kinship categories. However, jurisdictions address this ongoing shift in different ways and at a different pace.

In a comparative project, Claire Fenton-Glynn brings together scholars from around the world to discuss the ways in which parenthood is determined in their countries, as well as how the law is responding to new and emerging issues.[1] This chapter presents the authors' contribution to that project on the law of parenthood in Belgium.

The Belgian law of parenthood reflects the status approach typical of civil law jurisdictions. In these jurisdictions, legal parenthood in principle is an exclusive container category for an indivisible set of parental rights, obligations and prohibitions.[2] Upon the establishment of their legal parenthood, all parental functions are bestowed upon the parents *ex lege*: passing on their name(s), parental responsibilities, maintenance obligations, inheritance rights for the children,

1 C. Fenton-Glynn, *The Law of Parenthood*, Intersentia, forthcoming 2023.

2 F. Swennen and M. Croce, 'Family (Law) Assemblages: New Modes of Being (Legal)' (2017) 44 *Journal of Law and Society* 532, 536.

parental civil liability and certain (incest) prohibitions.[3] The establishment of legal parenthood – or adoption – is both a sufficient and necessary condition for the bestowal of parental responsibilities and all other parental functions. Legal parenthood and parental responsibilities hence are almost fully interdependent institutions in Belgian law.

We will explain in this chapter how the category of legal parenthood has become somewhat more inclusive over recent decades (in addition to the relaxation of the conditions for adoption, a discussion of which is beyond the scope of this chapter). By contrast, parental responsibilities remain reserved for the legal parents or adopters, with an exception only for foster carers. No imminent reforms are to be expected.

2. HISTORICAL BACKGROUND

It took the Belgian legislature until the Parenthood Act 1987[4] to abandon the distinction between 'legitimate' (born from the marriage between their parents) and 'illegitimate' (born outside a marital relationship or from an adulterous relationship of (one of) the parents) children regarding the establishment of legal parenthood that the European Court of Human Rights (ECtHR) found to violate Articles 8 and 14 of European Convention on Human Rights (ECHR) in the *Marckx v. Belgium* case.[5] The (opposite-sex) marital family model, however, survived up until a 1995 reform[6] regarding the exercise of parental responsibilities.

Currently, whether a child's parents are or have been engaged in an adult union with each other and the type of adult union are irrelevant for the establishment of legal parenthood – except in the context of assisted reproduction (see below, section 5) – and for the conferral of parental functions.

The legislature recognises three methods of establishing parenthood: through marriage, parental acknowledgment, and judicial declaration. Limited reforms between 2006 and 2018[7] have streamlined the conditions between these

---

3 M. Godelier, *Métamorphoses de la parenté*, Fayard, 2004, pp. 240–243; E. Goody, *Parenthood and Social Reproduction. Fostering and Occupational Roles in West Africa*, Cambridge University Press, 2007, p. 6.

4 Act of 31 March 1987 amending certain provisions on parenthood, *Moniteur belge* 27 May 1987.

5 *Marckx v. Belgium*, 13 June 1979, Series A no. 31.

6 Act of 13 April 1995 concerning the joint exercise of parental responsibilities, *Moniteur belge* 24 May 1995.

7 Act of 1 July 2006 amending the provisions of the Civil Code relating to the establishment of parenthood and its consequences, *Moniteur belge* 29 December 2006; Act of 6 July 2007 on medically assisted reproduction and the destination of surplus embryos and gametes, *Moniteur belge* 17 July 2017; Act of 18 June 2018 containing various provisions on civil law …, *Moniteur belge* 2 July 2018.

methods, and between mothers, fathers and co-mothers who establish their parenthood by these methods. Furthermore, the consequences of the change of legal sex designation for legal parenthood have been regulated (2007,[8] 2017[9] – see below, section 3) and co-motherhood has been introduced (2014[10] – see below, section 4.3) following the introduction of same-sex marriage in 2003[11] and same-sex adoption in 2006.[12]

Those reforms notwithstanding, the law on parenthood in Belgium remains by and large inspired by the model of the 'Sexual Family'.[13]

Religion has played no role in the development of the law of parenthood in Belgium. However, many of the above reforms were made possible during the 1999–2007 window of two ethically liberal Purple coalitions, from which the Christian Democrat party had been excluded.

3. 'MOTHERS', 'FATHERS' AND 'PARENTS'

The Civil Code[14] separately regulates the establishment of two parental roles: 'motherhood' on the one hand, and either 'fatherhood' or 'co-motherhood' on the other. The conditions for the establishment of each parental role were streamlined in the 2006 and 2014 reforms (see above, section 2).

The 'mother' and either the 'father' or the 'co-mother' are recorded, under those labels, on the child's birth certificate (Article 44 old Civil Code). Belgian law also uses 'parent' as an umbrella term to cover all parents, for example in the context of child support (Article 203 ff. old Civil Code) or parental responsibilities (Article 372 ff. old Civil Code). The term 'parent', as opposed to 'mother' or 'father', is not used in official records, however.

8 Act of 10 May 2007 concerning transsexuality, *Moniteur belge* 11 July 2007.

9 Act reforming regulations on transgender persons as regards the registration of the legal sex reassignment in civil status records and its consequences, *Moniteur belge* 10 July 2017.

10 Act of 5 May 2014 concerning the establishment of co-motherhood, *Moniteur belge* 7 July 2014.

11 Act of 12 May 2003 opening marriage to persons of the same sex, *Moniteur belge* 28 February 2003.

12 Act of 18 May 2006 amending certain provisions of the Civil Code to allow adoption by persons of the same sex, *Moniteur belge* 20 June 2006.

13 M.A. Fineman, *The Neutered Mother, the Sexual Family and Other Twentieth Century Tragedies*, Routledge, 1995, pp. 1–2, 143, 152.

14 In the context of a long-term legislative project, the books of the 1804 Civil Code are being replaced with new books. Rather than labelling the new set of books as the New Civil Code, the legislature has opted to rename the remainder of the 1804 Civil Code, awaiting the introduction of the remaining new books, as the 'old Civil Code'. This includes the family law provisions. See Art. 2 of the Act of 13 April 2019 to establish a Civil Code and to insert Book 8 'Evidence' into it, *Moniteur belge* 14 May 2019.

The establishment of co-motherhood is by and large calqued on that of fatherhood. There is no similar parental status of co-fatherhood for the father's male partner – only adoption is possible, for example in the case of surrogacy (see below, section 6). According to the legislature, the more intensive involvement of a surrogate vis-à-vis that of a sperm donor justifies the difference between the positions of a co-father and a co-mother.[15]

Furthermore, a 2017 reform has better accommodated parenthood of trans persons. A 2007 reform had already confirmed that upon legal sex reassignment, the original parental role was upheld for the children born *before* the reassignment. However, both the legal sex and the dead name of the trans parent are changed on their children's birth certificate to the new legal sex and current name.[16] Until 2017, legal sex reassignment was made dependent on prior gender reassignment surgery and permanent infertility/sterility, by which issues related to parenthood over children born *after* the reassignment were avoided. In keeping with the case law of the ECtHR,[17] the 2017 Act has abandoned the conditions of gender reassignment surgery and infertility/sterility. Therefore, provision also had to be made regarding the parental role over children born after legal sex reassignment (Article 135/2 old Civil Code):

- in the event that a trans man gives birth to a child after legal sex reassignment, he will be recorded as the mother (*mater semper certa est* – see below, section 4.1);
- in the event that a trans woman conceives a child by natural reproduction, or consents to medically assisted reproduction, her parenthood will be established according to the rules on fatherhood, but she will be recorded on the birth certificate as the co-mother. The legislature thus bridges the fact that a cis woman cannot (yet) conceive a child by natural reproduction, whilst a trans woman can.

These reforms hence have left the Belgian law of parenthood somewhat entangled in its old premises. On the one hand, the law on parenthood remains rooted in the Sexual Family model. The birth certificate records the 'mother',

15 On this, G. Seghers and F. Swennen, 'Meemoederschap zonder adoptie – de wet van 5 mei 2014 tot vaststelling van de afstamming van de meemoeder' (2014) *Tijdschrift voor Belgisch Burgerlijk Recht* 480, 482.

16 G. Verschelden, 'De privaatrechtelijke positie van transgender personen in België' (2019) *Tijdschrift voor Privaatrecht* 1211, 1250.

17 E.g. *YY v. Turkey*, 10 March 2015, ECLI:CE:ECHR:2015:0310JUD001479308, paras. 110, 116 and 121. For the international context, see E. Brems, P. Cannoot and T. Moonen (eds.), *Protecting Trans Rights in the Age of Gender Self-Determination*, Intersentia, 2020, and J.M. Scherpe (ed.), *The Legal Status of Transsexual and Transgender Persons*, Intersentia, 2015.

and either the 'father' or the 'co-mother', with no opportunity for another designation, such as 'parents' – leaving aside recognition and registration of foreign certificates or judgments. When developing a parental regime for co-mothers and trans persons, the legislature chose to fit these new constellations into the existing binary mother/father framework, rather than reconceptualising the law of parenthood. On the other hand, this approach has arguably reached its limits, as the accommodation of trans persons' parenthood demonstrates. The question arises as to whether the gendered approach to parental roles should be abandoned altogether – as indirectly suggested in a recent judgment of the Constitutional Court.[18] The answer is not a straightforward yes, however, particularly from the perspective of trans parents themselves.[19]

4. NATURAL REPRODUCTION

4.1. MOTHER

The mother is the fe/male person who gave birth to the child (Articles 312, section 1, 135/2 and 44, 2° old Civil Code). This premise reflects the *mater semper certa est* adage, which applies in Belgium.[20] The mother is always recorded on the birth certificate; anonymous or discreet birth is not (yet) possible in Belgium. The recorded motherhood can be challenged on the basis that the mother has not given birth to the child (see also below, section 4.4).

In the event that motherhood has not been established at birth, for example in the case of anonymous birth abroad or abandonment of a new-born child, it can be acknowledged at the municipal civil registration service (Articles 313 and 327 old Civil Code). Acknowledgment can also be challenged afterwards, on the basis that the mother has not given birth to the child.

In the event that motherhood has not been (correctly) recorded at birth or been acknowledged, it can be judicially declared, too (Articles 314 and 332*quinquies* old Civil Code).

---

18 Constitutional Court 19 July 2019, no. 99/2019, available at: <www.const-court.be>, last accessed 04.01.2022. On this, P. Cannoot, 'The Limits to Gender Self-Determination in a Stereotyped Legal System: Lessons from the Belgian Gender Recognition Act' in E. Brems, P. Cannoot and T. Moonen (eds.), *Protecting Trans Rights in the Age of Gender Self-Determination*, Intersentia, 2020, pp. 50–51.

19 A. Margaria, 'Trans men giving birth and reflections on fatherhood: what to expect?' (2020) 34(3) *International Journal of Law, Policy and the Family* 225.

20 F. Swennen, 'The changing concept of "family" and challenges for family law in the Benelux countries' in J.M. Scherpe (ed.), *European Family Law*, Vol. II, Edward Elgar Publishing, 2016, p. 14.

4.2. FATHER

As per the presumption of paternity, the mother's male spouse (husband) is designated as the father of the child born during the marriage or within 300 days after the dissolution or annulment of the marriage (Article 315 old Civil Code). The recorded fatherhood may be challenged on the basis that there is no genetic link between the father and the child, except where the former has consented to natural or artificial donor conception from which the child is likely to have been born (Article 318, section 4 old Civil Code; see also below, section 4.4). If applicable, the previous husband will be designated as the father in cases where the fatherhood of the current or last husband has successfully been challenged (Article 317 old Civil Code). The presumption of paternity only applies within marriage, not within other adult unions. Virtually all Belgian legal scholars advocate extending the presumption to (at least) the mother's registered partner (in Belgium this is called 'legal cohabitation'), but this has not yet been acted upon by the legislature.[21]

In the event that fatherhood has not been established on the basis of the presumption of paternity, it can be acknowledged by any man, with the consent, if applicable, of the mother and the child aged over 12. No proof of a genetic tie is required. Acknowledgment is not possible if a prohibited degree of kinship exists between the mother and the intended father. The parental acknowledgment can be challenged on the basis that there is no genetic link between the father and the child. Standing is limited to the child('s representative), the mother and the (contended) father, excluding the father if he had knowingly and wilfully acknowledged a non-genetically related child, and the mother or child if either of them had knowingly and wilfully consented to such 'mendacious acknowledgment.'

If fatherhood has not been established on the basis either of the presumption of paternity or of acknowledgment, it can be judicially declared on the basis of a genetic tie between the alleged father and the child. This is possible even if a prohibited degree of kinship exists between the mother and the intended father, as long as the court finds that the declaration of paternity would not run counter the best interests of the child.

There is no obligation (on the part of the mother) to register the father, nor for the State to ascertain information in that regard. It is perfectly lawful to have only one legal parent (see also Article 44 old Civil Code). The father may, of course, try to acknowledge the child, or have his paternity declared judicially. The mother and the child aged over 12 cannot veto the initiative by the father, but the court may refuse to establish fatherhood if any of the parties concerned

[21] On this, L. De Schrijver, *Evaluatie en toekomstperspectieven van de wettelijke samenwoning*, Wolters Kluwer, 2021, pp. 142–148.

prove that doing so would be contrary to the best interest of the child. The courts rarely accept such an argument.[22]

4.3. CO-MOTHER

As mentioned above, the legislature has copied and pasted the rules on fatherhood to co-motherhood in female same-sex marriages (Article 325/2 old Civil Code). While this can hardly be considered to be 'natural reproduction', this is a textbook example of the performativity of the Sexual Family model.[23]

Co-motherhood, in the end, is based on the consent of the co-mother to a joint parental project with the mother under the 2007 Act on Medically Assisted Reproduction or, in the case of a spouse, any other joint parental project, for example self-insemination with a friend's sperm. Put otherwise, co-motherhood can only be challenged upon proof that the child cannot be born from such a project. This framework leaves unanswered many questions regarding the allocation of co-motherhood in cases of non-medically assisted reproduction outside the context of marriage.

4.4. COMMON RULES

Motherhood, fatherhood and co-motherhood can be challenged under comparable conditions, that is, *by and large* comparable conditions, the differences having resulted in a messy and probably discriminatory statutory framework.[24]

Applications to challenge parenthood are limited to those persons who are directly involved with the child: the (intended) mother, the (intended) father, the (intended) co-mother, and the child.

Applications should be made within strict time limits of, in principle, one year after the (biological) truth is discovered, and up to the age of 22 for an application by the child. The court should determine when the applicant discovered the truth, for example upon receiving the result of a voluntary DNA test.[25] Regarding those strict limits, the Constitutional Court has ruled that

---

22 On this, T. Wuyts, 'Biologisch ouderschap en de rol van het belang van het kind bij de vestiging van een afstammingsband' (2021) *Tijdschrift voor Jeugd en Kinderrechten* 71.

23 F. Swennen and M. Croce, 'The Symbolic Power of Legal Kinship Terminology: An Analysis of "Co-motherhood" and "Duo-motherhood" in Belgium and the Netherlands' (2016) 25(2) *Social and Legal Studies* 181, 192.

24 F. Swennen, *Het personen- en familierecht. Een benadering in context*, Intersentia, 2021, pp. 451–478.

25 Constitutional Court 17 October 2013, no. 139/2013; Constitutional Court 29 January 2014, no. 16/2014; Constitutional Court 2 June 2016, no. 87/2016, available at: <www.const-court.be>, last accessed 04.01.2022.

any applicant should have a practical and effective, rather than only theoretical and illusory, opportunity to challenge. For instance, if a man knows that he has conceived a child, and another man acknowledges the child more than one year later, the former would not have had the opportunity to challenge the latter's fatherhood within the one-year period following the child's birth.[26] Furthermore, the strict time limits have been found to violate the (adult) child's right to know his parents in many Constitutional Court judgments.[27]

But what concerns practitioners the most is the inadmissibility in principle of a challenge to a parental role that is already confirmed de facto by continuous, but not necessarily current, 'possession of status'. Possession of status is interpreted differently by different courts and is to be proved by facts which collectively or separately demonstrate the parental relationship, such as: (1) that the child has always borne the name of the alleged parent (*nomen*); (2) that the alleged parent has treated the child as his or her own or vice versa (*tractatus*); and (3) that the child is recognised as such by the family and in society (*fama* – see Article 331*nonies* old Civil Code). More importantly, the Constitutional Court[28] and the Court of Cassation[29] have determined that courts may exempt an applicant from the inadmissibility of their petition on the basis of possession of status if a balancing of interests so commands. The Constitutional Court leaves little room for consideration of interests other than the legal confirmation of the biological bond, however.[30]

Taken together, the applicable rules – on the strict time limits, on the concept of possession of status, on the exemptions – offer too little legal certainty as a whole.

5. ASSISTED REPRODUCTION

5.1. MEDICALLY ASSISTED REPRODUCTION

5.1.1. Access to Medically Assisted Reproduction

The 2007 Act on Medically Assisted Reproduction explicitly regulates medical assistance with artificial (donor) insemination, and with *in vitro* fertilisation,

---

26 Constitutional Court 6 April 2011, no. 54/2011, available at: <www.const-court.be>, last accessed 04.01.2022.

27 E.g. Constitutional Court 3 February 2016, no. 18/2016, available at: <www.const-court.be>, last accessed 04.01.2022.

28 E.g. Constitutional Court 3 February 2016, no. 18/2016, available at: <www.const-court.be>, last accessed 04.01.2022.

29 Court of Cassation 7 April 2017 (2018) *Rechtskundig Weekblad* 941.

30 Constitutional Court 3 February 2016, no. 18/2016, available at: <www.const-court.be>, last accessed 04.01.2022.

including gamete or embryo donation, pre-implantation diagnostics and intracytoplasmic sperm injection. The 2003 Act on Research on Embryos *in vitro* explicitly prohibits legal cloning.[31]

The 2007 Act defines an intended parent as 'any person who has decided to become a parent through medically assisted reproduction, whether or not with their own gametes or embryos' (Article 2, paragraph f of the 2007 Act). Both single and multiple parental projects are accommodated, but the Act implies that the latter concern a 'couple' (Articles 2, paragraphs r and s, and 7 of the 2007 Act), whereby any couple qualifies: married or not, cohabiting or not, opposite-sex or not.[32]

Furthermore, legal restrictions apply to the female donor and the intended mother: they must ordinarily have reached majority[33] and be younger than 46 years (for the removal of gametes or at the time of applying for the implantation of embryos or the insemination of gametes) or 48 years (for the actual implantation of embryos or insemination of gametes; Article 4 of the 2007 Act).

Post-mortem implantation of a cryopreserved embryo and post-mortem insemination of cryopreserved gametes is permitted in Belgium if the intended mother's partner has stipulated thus in the contract with the fertility centre. It may be executed at the earliest six months after the death and at the latest two years after (Articles 2, paragraphs r and s, 16 and 45 of the 2007 Act). Post-mortem gamete retrieval is not explicitly regulated, and some scholarship claims that it can be stipulated by contract.[34]

For the remainder, every fertility centre has developed its own protocol, including medical and conscientious restrictions, on eligibility for medically assisted reproduction (Article 5 of the 2007 Act), for example with a view to refusing apparently unfit parents.[35] Article 5 consolidates the practice as it existed in 2007, which left a wide margin of discretion to fertility centres.[36] This leaves some intended parents in legal uncertainty and, potentially, scope

---

31 Art. 6 of the Act of 11 May 2003 on research on embryos in vitro, *Moniteur belge* 28 May 2003.

32 M.-N. Derèse and G. Willems, 'La loi du 6 juillet 2007 relative à la procréation médicalement assistée et à la destination des embryons surnuméraires et des gamètes' (2008) *Revue trimestrielle de droit familial* 279, 300.

33 The removal of gametes, surplus embryos, gonads or fragments of gonads from a minor for the purpose of cryopreservation may be performed on medical grounds, e.g. prior to medical treatment likely to cause infertility.

34 L. Oplinus, *Juridische analyse van het Belgische regelgevende kader met betrekking tot medische hulp bij de voortplanting*, PhD thesis, KU Leuven, 2021, pp. 237–238.

35 V. Vanderhulst, 'Medisch begeleide voortplanting en draagmoederschap' in T. Vansweevelt and F. Dewallens (eds.), *Handboek Gezondheidsrecht*, Vol. II, Intersentia, 2014, p. 36.

36 T. Wuyts, 'Medisch begeleide voortplanting: de kloof tussen recht en realiteit anno 2021' in E. Alofs, K. Byttebier, E. Goossens and J. Van Doninck (eds.), *Redelijk eigenzinning. Liber amicorum Eric Brewaeys, Philippe Colle, Erna Guldix en Bruno Maes*, Knops Publishing, forthcoming 2022.

for arbitrary private actor decisions on what, in the end, is a human right.[37] This is all the more discomforting since the 2007 legislature wanted to abstain from dogmatism and to demonstrate ethical pluralism.[38]

Compared to adoption, the 2007 Act caters for a somewhat broader group of intended parents. Adoption is accessible for single adopters, and for opposite- and same-sex couples, but only in so far as they have been married, in a registered partnership or in a permanent and affectionate (viz. conjugal) cohabitation for at least three years (Article 342, section 1, paragraph a old Civil Code). Adoptive projects can be further executed after the couple's separation in some cases. The Constitutional Court has, however, stretched the condition of conjugality for joint adoptive projects to include the adoption by an uncle or an aunt respectively who cohabited with the child and its single parent.[39] Likewise, some fertility centres accommodate platonic (non-conjugal) parental projects within the legal confinements of the maximum of two legal parents. Overall, the condition of conjugality for joint parental projects under the 2007 Act and for adoption seems anomalous vis-à-vis natural reproduction, where no condition of conjugality between the child's parents is required. The law, we think, should also accommodate platonic parental projects under the 2007 Act and adoption.[40]

A further difference between the 2007 Act and adoption is the assessment of the intended parents' capability and suitability as parents. Far more stringent legal requirements apply to intended adopters (Article 346 old Civil Code) than to intended parents under the 2007 Act. Fertility centres' broad discretion may, however, result in access to medically assisted reproduction for intended parents who would be ineligible to adopt, and vice versa. That is not so say that the same requirements should apply to such different parental projects.

5.1.2. Donated Gametes

Both sperm and egg donation, including double donation of sperm and eggs,[41] and donation of surplus embryos[42] are permitted, as Belgian law does not require a genetic link with (either of) the intended parent(s).

---

37 *SH and Others v. Austria*, 3 November 2011, ECLI:CE:ECHR:2011:1103JUD005781300.

38 M.-N. Derèse and G. Willems, 'La loi du 6 juillet 2007 relative à la procréation médicalement assistée et à la destination des embryons surnuméraires et des gamètes' (2008) *Revue trimestrielle de droit familial* 279, 301.

39 Constitutional Court 16 February 2017, no. 25/2017; Constitutional Court 13 July 2017, no. 95/2017, available at: <www.const-court.be>, last accessed 04.01.2022.

40 F. Swennen, 'The Public in Family Law: Should the Law Channel Parents towards Coupledom?' in Y. Emerich and L. Saint-Pierre Harvey (eds.), *Le public en droit privé*, Éditions Yvon Blais, 2019, pp. 137–138.

41 Double insemination of sperm (from different donors) is explicitly prohibited in Art. 54 2007 Act.

42 Embryos created in the context of medically assisted reproduction but not implanted into a woman (Art. 1, para. d, 2007 Act).

Only free donation of embryos and of gametes is permitted in Belgium and trading human embryos or gametes is prohibited. Only donors of gametes can receive an allowance covering their travel expenses, loss of income and, for egg donors, hospitalisation costs related to the removal of eggs (Articles 22 and 51 of the 2007 Act).

Only anonymous donation of surplus embryos is permitted. Donation of gametes is anonymous in principle, but non-anonymous donation is permitted if consented to by both the donor and the receiver(s) (Articles 2, paragraph i, 22 and 57 of the 2007 Act). Access to the donor's identity is never directly possible for the child, and vice versa.

In the case of anonymous donation, fertility centres are obliged to make confidential any data that could lead to the identification of the donor (Articles 28 and 57 of the 2007 Act). Medical information related to the donor that may be important for the healthy development of the (unborn) child may be released to the intended parents to assist with their decision-making, and to the primary care physician of the child or the receiver(s) (Articles 36 and 65 of the 2007 Act).

The anonymity of donation is currently a hotly debated issue in Belgium. The legal doctrine unanimously advocates abolishing the blind preference for donor anonymity and proposes to accommodate the child's right to know their origins.[43] Less is written on the anonymity of the child towards the donor.[44] The legislature of the Flemish federated entity recently established a Parentage Centre, which helps people with questions related to their genetic relatives and offers counselling and psychological support.[45] However, the principle of anonymous donation results from federal law and remains unchanged.

---

43 E.g. I. Boone and E. Decorte, 'Hoelang nog blijft België het recht van donorkinderen op informatie over hun genetische afkomst negeren?' (2021) *Rechtskundig Weekblad* 190; E. Decorte, 'Een kinderrechtenconforme benadering van toegang tot afstammingsinformatie voor donorkinderen' (2021) *Tijdschrift voor Jeugd en Kinderrechten* 7; G. Mathieu, *Le secret des origins en droit de la filiation*, Wolters Kluwer, 2014, L. Oplinus, *Juridische analyse van het Belgische regelgevende kader met betrekking tot medische hulp bij de voortplanting*, PhD thesis, KU Leuven, 2021, pp. 421 ff.; T. Wuyts, 'Het recht op identiteit in de Belgische rechtsorde' (2015) *Tijdschrift voor Familierecht* 60.

44 L. Oplinus, *Juridische analyse van het Belgische regelgevende kader met betrekking tot medische hulp bij de voortplanting*, PhD thesis, KU Leuven, 2021, p. 426; F. Swennen, *Het personen- en familierecht. Een benadering in context*, Intersentia, 2021, pp. 424–425.

45 <https://afstammingscentrum.be/>, last accessed 28.02.2022. On this, E. Decorte, 'De zoektocht naar roots: het decreet van 26 april 2019 houdende oprichting van een afstammingscentrum en een DNA-databank' (2020) *Rechtskundig Weekblad* 522; J. Ryngaert, 'Vlaams afstammingscentrum en DNA-databank: een bescheiden maar belangrijke stap vooruit vanuit kinderrechtenperspectief' (2019) *Tijdschrift voor Familierecht* 110.

5.1.3. *Allocation of Parenthood*

In the case of medically assisted reproduction, parenthood is assigned to the intended parent(s) and not the donor(s). The parental project hence takes precedence over the genetic ties.

The statutory wording of that principle has caused some legal uncertainties regarding the intended parents, however. Articles 27 and 56 of the 2007 Act stipulate that the Civil Code provisions on parentage are to be applied in favour of the intended parent(s). As mentioned in section 4.2 above, judicial declaration of paternity is possible upon proof of a genetic tie between the child and the alleged father (Article 332*quinquies* old Civil Code). The question has arisen as to whether this provision allows judicial declaration of the paternity of an intended father in the case of medically assisted reproduction with donor sperm, where there is no genetic tie with the intended father. It seems nonsensical to read Articles 27 and 56 of the 2007 Act otherwise than to confirm that the intended father is to be declared the legal father in such cases. And that is also how the Constitutional Court has interpreted Article 332*quinquies* old Civil Code.[46] In the same vein, it is not permitted to challenge the parenthood of the mother's husband (i.e. the father) or wife (i.e. the co-mother) in a case where they had consented to the use of donor sperm, be it through artificial or natural reproduction techniques, to conceive the child (Articles 318, section 4 and 325/2 old Civil Code).

Furthermore, Articles 27 and 56 of the 2007 Act block the donor(s), the intended parent(s) and the child(ren) from bringing any legal action to establish the parenthood of the donor and from pursuing monetary claims against the donor(s) based on parenthood.

5.2. NON-MEDICALLY ASSISTED REPRODUCTION

The 2007 Act and its rules on the assignment of parenthood only apply in the case of medically assisted reproduction. In the case of non-medically assisted reproduction, for example natural reproduction or artificial insemination with the assistance of a friend or an online donor, the default rules on natural

46 Constitutional Court 7 February 2019, no. 19/2019, B.7.3, available at: <www.const-court.be>, last accessed 04.01.2022. Also see I. Boone, 'Recente ontwikkelingen in het afstammingsrecht en het naamrecht (2017–2019)' in I. Boone and C. Declerck (eds.), *Themis 111 – Personen- en familierecht*, die Keure, 2020, p. 24; L. Oplinus, *Juridische analyse van het Belgische regelgevende kader met betrekking tot medische hulp bij de voortplanting*, PhD thesis, KU Leuven, 2021, pp. 398–405.

reproduction apply. A court hence allowed the acknowledgement as father of the man with whom the intended mother had connected as a donor on an online platform.[47] As mentioned in sections 4.2 and 4.3 above, the Civil Code only accommodates parental projects where the mother's spouse is an intended parent and consents to heterologous insemination. The spouse will be considered the father or co-mother respectively, to the exclusion of the donor (Articles 318, section 4 and 325/2 old Civil Code).

5.2.1. Surrogacy

Surrogacy is neither explicitly regulated, nor explicitly prohibited in Belgium. Since 2005, many unsuccessful parliamentary attempts have been made at regulating domestic surrogacy arrangements. Awaiting regulation, some of the (academic) fertility centres assist intended parents with non-commercial (gestational) surrogacy arrangements in the shadow of the law, within the confines of their own ethics protocol. In such cases, the default rules apply to the allocation of parenthood (see above, section 4): the person who gives birth will be registered as the mother (and their spouse as father/co-mother) of the child. Trying to register a supposititious child is a criminal offence for the intended parents (Article 363 Criminal Code); the child's birth certificate will also be rectified in that case (Article 314 old Civil Code). The intended father can usually establish their paternity via parental acknowledgment or judicial declaration of paternity. While there is no statutory requirement of a genetic link, such a connection seems relevant in view of the case law of the European Court of Human Rights.[48] The intended mother, co-mother and 'co-father' can only adopt the child, to which the birth mother needs to consent, as she was appointed as the legal mother in the first place. It is disputed to what extent, if at all, the family court may consider the conflict of a (commercial) surrogacy agreement with public policy when deciding on the adoption.[49]

Default private international law rules apply to the recognition of legal parenthood arising from international surrogacy arrangements. Legal parenthood established in a foreign judgment can be more easily recognised than parenthood established by a foreign birth certificate. In the latter scenario, a choice of laws check is conducted (Articles 22 and 27 Code of International

---

47 Family Court Antwerp 4 January 2021 (2021) *Rechtskundig Weekblad* 561.

48 See the factsheet available at: <https://www.echr.coe.int/Documents/FS_Surrogacy_eng.pdf>, last accessed 22.04.2022.

49 L. Cohen, 'L'adoption simple ou plénière de l'enfant issu d'une gestation pour autrui par le co- parent de même sexe' (2019) *Revue trimestrielle de droit familial*, 845, 852–854.

Private International Law). In both cases, evasion of the law and the public policy exception might prevent the family court from recognising the foreign judgment or certificate. However, family courts have adopted a flexible approach in that regard, in view of protecting the child's best interests.[50] As Belgian birth certificates only provide for the entry of one mother and either a father or a co-mother, the recognition of foreign birth certificates or judgments with two fathers is often an administrative Calvary, yet always with the entry of two fathers as the result.[51]

5.2.2. *Multiple Parenthood*

Neither simultaneous recognition of more than two parents nor simultaneous allocation of parental responsibilities to more than two persons is currently possible in Belgium, with two *quasi*-exceptions. As a rule, parenthood hence remains dyadic with a dyadic assignment of parental responsibilities of the parents.[52]

The first *quasi*-exception is simple adoption. Simple adoption establishes a parent–child relationship between the adopter(s) and the adoptee, without severing the first parents' legal parenthood. However, most of the legal parent's parental functions are suspended in favour of the adopter(s), for example regarding parental responsibilities (Articles 353–8 to 353-10 and 354-2 old Civil Code), or are referred to the second line vis-à-vis the adopter(s), for example as fallback maintenance obligations in the event of insolvency of the adopter(s) (Article 353-14 old Civil Code). In the case of simple step-parent adoption, only the parent whose partner adopts retains their parental functions (Articles 353–9 and 353-14 old Civil Code); triple allocation of parental functions is not possible in such cases. And only one parent's partner can adopt the child, too; step-parent adoption by both parents' partners is not (yet) legally accommodated, unfortunately.[53]

---

50 P. Wautelet, 'Draagmoederschap in ipr-land: over onbeantwoorde vragen en onduidelijke parameters' (2021) *Tijdschrift voor Familierecht* 150, 156.

51 S. Eggermont, 'Draagmoederschap: één tegen allen, allen tegen één' (2021) *Tijdschrift voor Familierecht* 166. Also see European Court of Justice case C-490/20, *VMA v. Stolichna obshtina, rayon 'Pancharevo'*, ECLI:EU:C:2021:1008 (birth certificate recording two mothers).

52 N. Cammu, 'How Should We Name the Parents? The Challenges of Plus-Two-Parent Families for Legal Kinship Terminology' (2017) 31 *International Journal of Law, Policy and The Family* 328; N. Cammu, '"Legal Multi-parenthood" in Context: Experiences of Parents in Light of the Dutch Proposed Family Law Reforms' (2019) *Family & Law* July 2019, DOI: 10.5553/FenR/.000042; N. Cammu '"We Are Three Parents, but Legally Two": Absent Legality, Present Display' (2021) 42(5) *Journal of Family Issues* 1007; F. Swennen 'Motherhoods and the Law' in H. Willekens, K. Scheiwe, T. Richarz and E. Schumann (eds.), *Motherhood and the Law*, Universitätsverlag Göttingen, 2019, p. 101.

53 F. Swennen, 'Wat is ouderschap?' (2016) 53 *Tijdschrift voor Privaatrecht* 11, 77.

The second *quasi*-exception is the *ex lege* or voluntary transfer of parental responsibilities to foster carers. In the case of a full transfer, parental responsibilities will be exercised exclusively by the foster carer(s). In the case of a partial transfer, the foster carer(s) and the parent(s) will each (jointly) exercise part of the parental responsibilities exclusively (Articles 387*quinquies* and 387*septies* old Civil Code).

5.2.3. *Social Parenthood*

Absent statutory protection, the courts have accommodated various forms of social parenthood to a limited extent.

Informal foster caretakers of the child, such as grandparents, have a so-called 'blocking right' against the return of the child to their parents. The Court of Cassation has ruled that a court may bestow the so-called precarious physical custody of the child upon non-parents with whom the child resides, in the event that it finds that the termination of that arrangement at the request of the parents would run counter the best interests of the child.[54] The ruling of the Court of Cassation predates the formal, statutory regulation of foster care, and it is disputable to what extent the allocation of precarious physical custody would be in accordance with the rights of the parents under the current statutory framework.[55]

Non-parents who informally take up parental responsibilities together with a parent or the parents – such as de facto co-mothers before the statutory regulation of adoption by the mother's female partner (2006) and co-motherhood (2014), or step-parents – cannot claim legal recognition of their role. They might refer to a tacit mandate by the parent(s), but only as long as their joint involvement with the parent(s) has not ended due to divorce or other reasons. Courts have been benevolent towards those informal caregivers upon termination of their joint involvement with the parent(s). Article 375*bis* old Civil Code provides for a right to personal relations and contact with a child with whom the applicant has a special affective bond. Personal relations and contact have been interpreted flexibly, so as to establish de facto joint parental responsibilities on the basis of this provision.[56] Already in 2003, the Belgian Constitutional Court had

---

54 Court of Cassation 19 December 1975 (1976) *Arr.Cass.* 492.

55 A. De Wolf and F. Aps, 'Rechtsbescherming bij materiële bewaring van een kind door een derde' (2004) *Echtscheidingsjournaal* 54.

56 F. Swennen, *Het personen- en familierecht. Een benadering in context*, Intersentia, 2021, p. 558.

appealed to the legislature to regulate social parenthood.[57] As of 2021, only co-motherhood and foster care have however been codified.

Furthermore, a parent's spouse or registered partner is legally obliged to contribute to, and is liable for, the household expenses, including those for the children of whom they are not the parent (Articles 221, 222 and 1477, sections 3–4 old Civil Code).

6. CONCLUSIONS AND EVALUATION

At the legal-technical level, the path-dependent development of the Belgian law of parenthood over the past 30 years has allowed the legislature to reconcile legal certainty with flexibility to a decreasing degree (section 4.4).

Typical of civil law jurisdictions, the law of parenthood had been laid down in statutory provisions with an ample margin of discretion for the courts. The legislature has remained within this register even when the ECtHR and the Belgian Constitutional Court stressed the need to allow the courts to acknowledge intended ('water') and social ('milk') parents, besides the biological ('blood') parents, on an ad hoc basis.[58]

This evolution causes a lag between the law in the books ('ink') and the law in action, for example when courts apply the admissibility conditions for legal actions challenging parenthood (section 4.4), interpret the role of intent in the 2007 Act on Medically Assisted Reproduction (section 5.1.3), accommodate intended parents in domestic and international surrogacy arrangements (section 6) or create a *quasi*-status for step-parents (section 8). Chiming with Sally Engle Merry's analysis of women's rights,[59] one could see this as *vernacularisation* of the legal provisions on parenthood. Precisely because this movement is still ongoing, the legislature thinks it premature to clamp the fluid law in action in an updated static legal framework.

Further path-dependent development is to be expected in the course of the next few years, with the insertion of the provisions on the allocation of parenthood in cases of medically assisted reproduction into the Civil Code[60] and

---

57 Constitutional Court 8 October 2003, no. 134/2003, available at: <www.const-court.be>, last accessed 04.01.2022.

58 On ink, blood, milk and water: F. Swennen, 'The changing concept of "family" and challenges for family law in the Benelux countries' in J.M. Scherpe (ed.), *European Family Law*, Vol. II, Edward Elgar Publishing, 2016, pp. 17–18.

59 S.E. Merry, *Human Rights and Gender Violence: Translating International Law into Local Justice*, University of Chicago Press, 2006, p. 219.

60 See the proposals by L. Oplinus, *Juridische analyse van het Belgische regelgevende kader met betrekking tot medische hulp bij de voortplanting*, PhD thesis, KU Leuven, 2021, part 8.

with the creation of a legal framework for domestic and international surrogacy arrangements.[61]

At a more abstract level, path-dependence is also at work when the legislature in fact reproduces and even reinforces the Sexual Family model by including non-normative forms of parenthood under the existing labels, such as that of trans persons (section 3), co-mothers (section 4.3)[62] and other intended parents under the 2007 Act on Medically Assisted Reproduction (section 5.1.1).[63] The performative effect of this strategy risks reducing the variety and pluralism of parenthood practices.[64] One should, however, not too easily abandon the current gendered approach to parenthood, for this could result in an unjust politics of sameness, too.[65]

Rather than keeping the same register of 'law's families', a modulation is needed to capture the future 'families we live with'.[66]

First, the interdependence in principle of parenthood and parental responsibilities seems obsolete. In particular, intent (water) has become more important as a substrate for parenthood, with a view to letting the intended parents exercise parental functions.[67] At the same time, the right of the child to know his or her (genetic) origins makes it difficult to abandon blood as the foundation in principle for the establishment of parenthood, even if the exercise of parental functions by genetic parents would not be desired or desirable. The legislature might, therefore, consider introducing parenthood without parental responsibilities, for example for donors, and parental responsibilities without parenthood, for example for step-parents.[68]

---

61 Several proposals are pending in Parliament, and the government is expected to propose a bill soon.

62 F. Swennen and M. Croce, 'The Symbolic Power of Legal Kinship Terminology: An Analysis of 'Co-motherhood' and 'Duo-motherhood' in Belgium and the Netherlands' (2016) 25(2) *Social and Legal Studies* 181, 192.

63 Also see J. McCandless and S. Sheldon, 'The Human Fertilisation and Embryology Act (2008) and the Tenacity of the Sexual Family Form' (2010) 73(2) *The Modern Law Review* 175.

64 F. Swennen 'Motherhoods and the Law' in H. Willekens, K. Scheiwe, T. Richarz and E. Schumann (eds.), *Motherhood and the Law*, Universitätsverlag Göttingen, 2019, p. 106.

65 M.A. Fineman, *The Neutered Mother, the Sexual Family and Other Twentieth Century Tragedies*, Routledge, 1995, pp. 34, 67–68, 70; A. Diduck, '"If only we can find the appropriate terms to use the issue will be solved": Law, identity and parenthood' (2007) 19 *Child and Family Law Quarterly* 458; and more generally V. Vendetti, *The Law and Politics of Inclusion. From Rights to Practices of Disidentification*, Routledge, 2019.

66 A. Diduck, *Law's Families*, Cambridge University Press, 2003, p. 20.

67 N. Cammu, 'Intent to parent is what makes a parent? A comparative analysis of the role of intent in multi-parenthood recognition' (2019) 32(2) *Canadian Journal of Family Law* 281.

68 See, regarding motherhood, F. Swennen 'Motherhoods and the Law' in H. Willekens, K. Scheiwe, T. Richarz and E. Schumann (eds.), *Motherhood and the Law*, Universitätsverlag Göttingen, 2019, pp 101 ff.

Second, multiple parenthood and multiple parental responsibilities could replace the current dyadic approach to both institutions. Multiple parenthood has recently been suggested as a desirable avenue towards open (inter-country) adoption.[69] And the framework on parental responsibilities for foster parents could be extended towards other social (milk) parents.[70]

Unfortunately, however, the legislature has currently not scheduled such modulations.

---

69 Communication to the Flemish Government of 17 September 2021 on inter-country adoption, VR 2021 1709 MED. 0315/1, available at: <http://.beslissingenvlaamseregering.vlaanderen.be>, last accessed 05.01.2022, p. 1.

70 For a detailed proposal, see U. Cerulus, *Een statuut voor de zorgouder in het licht van de grondrechtenbescherming*, die Keure, 2019 (PhD thesis, UHasselt).

CHILE

COMMENTS ON THE REGULATION OF THE 'FIRST WELCOME' IN THE PROTOCOL OF THE INTERINSTITUTIONAL TECHNICAL TABLE OF CHILE

Alexis MONDACA*

Résumé

Le Chili a été surpris par le flot d'immigrés qui est entré sur son territoire. Cette situation a suscité l'inquiétude d'un certain nombre d'institutions que la présente contribution relate. Les conditions que doivent remplir les enfants et les adolescents immigrés pour être accueillis au Chili lorsqu'ils sont arrivés sur le territoire sans être accompagnés d'adultes, et qui constituent un groupe particulièrement vulnérable, sont expliquées dans cet article. L'article est rédigé au prisme du principe de l'intérêt supérieur de l'enfant qui exige de ne pas faire de distinctions fondées sur le lieu de résidence des enfants et des adolescents.

* alexis.mondaca@utalca.cl.

1. INTRODUCTION

Since the last decades of the twentieth century, Chile has experienced a significant increase in the number of immigrants,[1] a phenomenon that has surprised Chilean society as a whole and that has led to the inevitable conclusion that the Chilean State did not have the right conditions to receive a large number of immigrants. This situation explains all the problems that migration is currently causing in Chile.

In a more specific way, the migratory crisis was evident on the northern border of Chile, particularly the part that borders Peru and Bolivia. In this area, the precarious conditions in which foreigners were arriving could be seen, including children and adolescents (henceforth, unaccompanied minors) who were notoriously lacking food and water and, in many cases, had inadequate clothes to withstand the inclemency (temperature changes) of the desert climate which is typical of the area.[2]

The situation motivated a group of organisations to start working together to efficiently address various challenges generated by the migratory crisis. Thus, the following institutions joined forces: the Carabineros de Chile (law enforcement police), the Chilean Investigative Police, the Office of the Ombudsman for Children, the Ministry of Justice and Human Rights, the Undersecretary for Children, the National Service for Specialised Protection of Children and Adolescence (Better Childhood), the United Nations Children's Fund (UNICEF), the United Nations Refugee Agency (UNHCR), and the Office of the United Nations High Commissioner for Human Rights (OHCHR).

The result of the work of the aforementioned institutions was the drafting of the Protocol of the Inter-institutional Technical Committee of Chile for the protection of unaccompanied and separated children in the context of migration and/or in need of international protection (the Protocol).[3] This text analyses, among other matters, a series of principles (including the best interests of unaccompanied minors, non-discrimination, comprehensive protection of childhood and adolescence, and family reunion), the judicial treatment that must be given to immigrant unaccompanied minors, the monitoring and follow-up mechanisms for the implementation of the Protocol, and – what constitutes the focus of this chapter – the first welcome that must be offered to children and adolescents who have arrived alone on the territory of Chile.

---

1 L. Oyarzún, G. Aranda and N. Gissi, 'Migración internacional y política migratoria en Chile: tensiones entre la soberanía estatal y las ciudadanías emergentes' (2021) 106 *Colombia Internacional* 91.

2 R. Vásquez, 'Impacto de las migraciones en Chile. Nuevos retos para el pediatra' (2009) 80 *Revista Chilena de Pediatría* 164.

3 See <https://www.pjud.cl/prensa-y-comunicaciones/noticias-del-poder-judicial/66359>, last accessed 09.08.2022.

The initial reception that must be provided to all unaccompanied minors who have emigrated without the company of adults or who have been separated from them must meet, according to the Protocol, the following conditions: the reception must take place in a suitable space, language that is characterised by being clear and simple must be used, translators must be available and the presence of officials duly trained for the work of reception must be present.[4] Next, we will briefly discuss each of these conditions.

2. THE WELCOME MUST TAKE PLACE IN A SUITABLE SPACE

This first condition is aimed mainly at members of the Chilean State police, that is, the Investigative Police and Carabineros de Chile. This becomes clear when we consider that, usually, the first contact between immigrants and the State of Chile takes place through interactions with officials of the aforementioned police forces, especially with detectives of the Investigative Police, since they carry out, among other functions, migration control tasks.

Unaccompanied minors are most likely to enter Chile by crossing the northern border, especially in the vicinity of a small town called Colchane. They generally enter Chilean territory by land (since they lack the necessary resources to buy plane tickets) after travelling many kilometres in desert conditions. Unaccompanied minors in the north tend to be the most vulnerable migrants.

Many of the unaccompanied minors discussed in this chapter enter Chilean territory via unauthorised border crossings, so, from the point of view of Chilean immigration law, their status is classified as 'irregular' or 'illegal'. Considering this, and fearing being detected by the competent authorities, they try to avoid any contact with the Chilean State, which eventually ends up increasing their vulnerability.

Notwithstanding this, both those children and adolescents who enter through official border crossings and those who are detected entering irregularly by the Chilean authorities must be received in suitable places. However, it is no surprise that the Chilean police stations were not designed or built to meet the needs of immigrant children.

The Protocol governing these encounters states that: 'In the case of the Carabineros de Chile, the service provided by officials of this institution will be conducted in the family rooms or intrafamily violence office, preferably by the official in charge of that unit.' The Protocol adds that in the event that the police

4 Protocol, pp. 22–23.

does not have these facilities, a space 'differentiated from the guard modules' shall be enabled. In this way, the Protocol is concerned with the physical space in which immigrant children first interact with State authorities, an important factor in creating an environment that allows an adequate communication process between State agents and immigrants.

3. USE OF CLEAR AND SIMPLE LANGUAGE

In light of the special conditions that characterise immigrant children and adolescents who find themselves without the company of adults, it makes sense that they experience fear and feel great mistrust towards the State authorities of the destination State of their migratory movements. Said fear and mistrust are understandable, given that immigrants, especially those who have entered via irregular border crossings, including those who have not yet reached the age of majority, live in constant fear of being expelled in the event of being detected by State officials.[5]

As a result of this, it is necessary to use language that is not abstract and that enables authentic communication between immigrants and State officials. In this sense, it is expressed in the Protocol that:

> when it is necessary to talk about complex concepts, it will be convenient to use drawings or manipulable objects such as play dough, markers and paper sheets to show what is transmitted with drawings or diagrams. In addition, it is useful to build the information together. It is possible to have a sheet of paper and write words or schemes with symbols when necessary information is being built, such as their migratory path, the notion of refuge and what it implies. Use simplified language, avoiding the use of terms that are not of public knowledge or difficult for children to understand, according to their age and maturity.[6]

This is especially relevant considering the urgency of avoiding new violations of the rights of children and adolescents. Regarding the latter, we will briefly discuss sexual offences and the right to health. Regarding the former, many immigrant children have been victims of sexual offences. Often it is the case that unaccompanied minors have entered Chile accompanied by adults, but it has not been possible to quickly prove the corresponding ties of kinship or the nature of guardianship of these adults. This is influenced by the fact that many immigrants do not have any official documentation from their respective

---

5 The expulsion of immigrants, many of whom have formed family ties in Chile, has generated a strong debate that has divided society.

6 Protocol, p. 22.

countries of origin. The aforementioned circumstance conspires against the detection and subsequent punishment of crimes against immigrant children and adolescents.[7]

As for the right to health, State officials must make immigrant children and adolescents understand that they are entitled to a series of rights enshrined both in international instruments (for example, in the Convention on the Rights of the Child) and in the Chilean legal system (the Law of Guarantees and Integral Protection of the Rights of Children and Adolescents and the Law on Migration and Immigration). Among such rights, we want to specifically highlight the right to health because of its obvious link with the survival of every individual.

Consequently, it would be very advantageous for immigrant children and adolescents to know that, regardless of their immigration status, the State of Chile guarantees them access to and care in the facilities that make up the public health system.[8] In this respect, they are considered to lack resources, so they are classified as belonging to the so-called 'Level A', which guarantees them free medical care. However, in practice, it can be seen that the standard of the services provided to those who are in 'Level A' is far from high.

In addition to the above, a first-order right regarding the situation of immigrant children and adolescents is the right to family reunification, which will be the subject of a particular study in a later section.

4. AVAILABILITY OF TRANSLATORS

The official language of Chile is Spanish, and almost everyone in Chile speaks Spanish, even though Chile guarantees protection of the languages of the ancestral peoples that, before the arrival of the Spanish, occupied the country. Therefore, from what has been said, a foreigner who can make himself understood in Spanish, in principle, does not suffer from any problem of communication with the local population.

As we have already indicated, the main migratory movements received by Chile are from South American countries (Colombia, Venezuela, Peru and Bolivia).[9] In these countries the official language is Spanish, so the Chilean population does not need the intervention of any interpreter to communicate

[7] C. Galaz, I. Pávez and L. Magalhães, 'Polivictimización de niños/niñas migrantes en Iquique (Chile)' (2021) 21 *Si Somos Americanos. Revista de Estudios Fronterizos* 133.

[8] N. Liberona and M. Mansilla, 'Pacientes ilegítimos: acceso a la salud de los inmigrantes indocumentados en Chile' (2017) 13 *Salud Colectiva* 509.

[9] D. Rojas and T. Avilés, 'Actitudes hacia dialectos del español usados por inmigrantes en Santiago de Chile' (2013) 2 *Boletín de Filología* 101.

with immigrants from such countries. The situation of immigrants from Haiti is different, however.[10]

Indeed, in Haiti there are two official languages: French and Creole. The elite speak French, while the majority of the Haitian population communicates in various dialects of Creole. In Chile, practically nobody speaks Creole, nor there is any interest in learning that language, except for rare initiatives that aim to increase the knowledge of Creole.[11] For this reason, the isolation which Haitian immigrants living in Chile experience can be understood, which has had deadly consequences.[12]

On the point in question, the Protocol correctly indicates the following: To guarantee the right of the unaccompanied minor to be assisted free of charge by a translator and/or interpreter, in the event that they do not understand or speak the Spanish language or have a hearing disability,[13] the pertinent inter-institutional coordination will be carried out to observe the provision of said service.'[14]

However, the problem of the lack of communication between Chileans and immigrants cannot be analysed in its entirety without including in the analysis the xenophobia and discrimination that exist in Chile, especially against certain groups of foreigners, even if they speak Spanish. Indeed, the most discriminated-against immigrants are of African descent, especially Caribbean women under 40 years of age, who, moreover, are seen as sexualised objects.[15] Thus, a fundamental part of the fight against the lack of communication to which several immigrants are subjected is the eradication of xenophobia and racism. In this task, a key role is played by inclusive education aimed at the next generations, founded on equality and the rejection of all kinds of arbitrary discrimination.

---

10 Instituto Nacional de Estadísticas de Chile, 'Población extranjera residente en Chile llegó a 1.462.103 personas en 2020, un 0,8% más que en 2019', available at <https://www.ine.cl/prensa/2021/07/29/población-extranjera-residente-en-chile-llegó-a-1.462.103-personas-en-2020-un-0-8-más-que-en-2019>, last accessed 23.09.2022.

11 V. Sumonte, 'Desarrollo de la competencia comunicativa intercultural en un programa de adquisición de la lengua criollo haitiana en Chile' (2020) 25 *Íkala* 159.

12 The death of a young mother caused public shock since she was arrested and died in a police station in the capital of Chile, Santiago. She was accused of allegedly abandoning her minor daughter, in circumstances that she was chasing a criminal who had stolen her bag. It was later shown that such abandonment never happened. Unfortunately, the lack of a translator was a contributing factor in her death, since she could not communicate with her captors. A. Valle, '10 irregularidades que marcan la investigación de la injusta muerte de la haitiana Joane Florvil', *Diario El Mostrador*, 15 October 2017.

13 The Protocol also refers to children and adolescents who have a hearing disability that may cause communication problems. The foregoing is a sample of the application in Chile of the Convention on the Rights of Persons with Disabilities, adopted in New York in 2006 and which has been a mandatory rule in Chile since 17 September 2008.

14 Protocol, pp. 22–23.

15 M. Echeverri, 'Tredad racializada en la migración forzada de afrocolombianos a Antofagasta (Chile)' (2016) 45 *Nómadas* 96.

5. PRESENCE OF DULY TRAINED OFFICIALS FOR RECEPTION WORK

The members of the Chilean police have as one of their main objectives, along with controlling the entry and exit of both people and merchandise, the fight against drug trafficking. The illicit trafficking of drugs and narcotic substances constitutes one of the greatest scourges that Chilean society currently has to face.[16] Given this state of affairs, it makes sense that police-officer training has not traditionally included providing immigrants with a good reception. On the contrary, officers are instructed in physical activity, intelligence work, self-defence, handling of firearms, detection of prohibited substances and the capture of potential offenders.

Only in recent decades have subjects such as the respect for essential rights without incurring in arbitrary discrimination, such as those based on nationality or foreign status, regardless of whether or not immigrants have a regularised immigration status, become part of the police training curriculum.

Considering what has been said in the preceding sections, and taking into account that nothing allows us to presume that the migratory movements in the direction of Chile will cease, the Protocol indicates that: 'The police officers who carry out the first welcome reception must have training in human mobility, the rights of children and adolescents in general and the rights of unaccompanied and separated children and adolescents in particular and the international protection needs that may arise, as well as on the adequate implementation of this protocol.'[17] In this respect, the Protocol, following the experience of other countries, has considered the importance of providing proper comprehensive training (which goes beyond strictly police aspects), based on human rights and ethics, to police officers, including the Carabineros de Chile and the Investigative Police.[18]

In addition to what has been indicated above, it is pertinent to highlight as a particularly positive aspect of the Protocol that it has been established that the training of the officers who will be in charge of the initial reception of immigrant children should not be carried out exclusively by police training schools. On the contrary, the other organisations that have been involved in the creation and signing of the Protocol will also participate in the aforementioned

---

16 Chilean society looks with fear on the attempts of foreign cartels (from Mexico and Colombia) to start operations in Chile. V. García, 'Territorios fronterizos. Agenda de seguridad y narcotráfico en Chile: el Plan Frontera Norte' (2015) 181 *Estudios Internacionales* 73.

17 Protocol, p. 23.

18 M. Bernal, 'La función policial desde la perspectiva de los derechos humanos y la ética pública' (2019) 13 *IUS* 255.

training, those that have vast experience in the defence of human rights. With this in mind, the following is made explicit in the Protocol:

> The institutions that sign this Protocol and that make up the Inter-Institutional Technical Table for its implementation, detailed in chapter VII of this instrument, will collaborate in the training activities necessary for the specialisation of the police officers of the Carabineros de Chile and the Chilean Investigative Police who perform tasks of the first welcome reception of unaccompanied and separated migrant children and adolescents in the context of mobility.[19]

6. WHAT DO WE DO WITH IMMIGRANT CHILDREN NOT ACCOMPANIED BY AN ADULT? FAMILY REUNIFICATION?

The reality of the problem generated by immigrant children who have arrived on Chilean territory without the company of adults cannot be made invisible. Without disregarding the aforementioned characteristics of the 'initial reception', we must recognise that it is only a first step that, by definition, does not solve the underlying problem. It must be followed by a definitive solution that is to the greatest extent possible respectful of the right of children and adolescents to live in a family.[20]

Without prejudice to other measures, such as recourse to foster families, adoption or internment in State residential facilities[21] reunification with members of the family themselves is presented as a very favourable option, except in extraordinary situations, in light of the requirements arising from the principle of the best interests of the child.

In Chilean domestic law, there was no explicit recognition of the right to family reunification. However, Chile has ratified various treaties and conventions that refer to such a right. The landscape described has recently changed with Law No. 21,325, the new Immigration and Aliens Law.[22] In effect Article 19(1) of the Law holds as follows:

> Residents may request family reunification with their spouse or with that person who maintains a relationship that, in accordance with the applicable law, produces

---

19 Protocol, p. 23.

20 M. Pérez, 'El entorno familiar y los derechos de las niñas, los niños y los adolescentes: una aproximación' (2013) 138 *Boletín Mexicano de Derecho Comparado* 1158.

21 Unfortunately, such facilities have been the object of strong, albeit justified, criticism due to the serious rights violations suffered by the unaccompanied minors interned in them, which have caused, on more than one occasion, the death of unaccompanied minors. M. Gallegos, C. Jarpa and D. Opazo, 'Derechos del niño y sistemas residenciales en Chile: representaciones sociales de adultos cuidadores' (2018) 17 *Psicoperspectivas* 3.

22 Law No. 21,325, 20 April 2021, *Diario Oficial*.

effects equivalent to marriage, parents, minor children, children with disabilities, single children under 24 years of age who are studying and minors who are under their personal care or guardianship, and the State must promote the protection of the unit of the family.

Although it is true that the express regulation of the right to family reunification represents an undeniable step forward on the path that leads to respect for immigrants' rights, Law No. 21,325 suffers from an obvious flaw. In effect, it employs the expression 'residents'. This expression must be understood as including, in accordance with the provisions of Article 1(17) of Law No. 21,325, the '[f]oreign beneficiary of a temporary, official or definitive residence permit'.

In other words, those immigrants who have not been able to regularise their immigration status have been left out of the right to family reunification. Therefore, the immigrants who most frequently and intensely suffer from discrimination and violations of their rights will not be able to reunite with their families on Chilean soil. This differentiation between immigrants who have some type of visa and those who do not have a regularised administrative situation is one of the most striking characteristics of the new Immigration and Aliens Law.[23]

In paragraph 2 of the aforementioned article, it is established, regarding immigrant children and adolescents, that: 'Applications for family reunification of children and adolescents with resident foreigners will be processed as a priority.' As the reader will be able to notice, Law No. 21,325 does not provide for family reunification for children and adolescent migrants in Chile who wish to reunite with family members who do not have a regularised immigration status in Chile. This is a case in which the principle of the best interests of unaccompanied minors is not acknowledge as a primary consideration, contrary to what is established in Article 3 of the Convention on the Rights of the Child.

7. THE PROTOCOL AS A MANIFESTATION OF A GENUINE CONCERN FOR THE BEST INTERESTS OF IMMIGRANT CHILDREN

In the main bodies that made up the old Chilean Immigration Law, there was no greater concern for the protection of the rights of immigrant children and adolescents than for other immigrants. Indeed, the old Chilean Immigration

---

23 A. Mondaca, 'La reunificación familiar' in I. Ravetllat and L. Bobadilla (eds.), *Niñez, familia, migración y derechos*, Tirant lo Blanch, 2022, pp. 229–260.

Law was based on the doctrine of national security; consequently, within a Manichean vision of society, which divides the world between the good and the bad, many immigrants were included on the side of the bad guys. Hence, the immigration regulations were concerned only with controlling the entry and exit of immigrants into and out of the country, but not with their integration and even less with their inclusion.[24]

Unlike what has been done in the past, the new regulation of immigration and foreigners declares that it wishes to harmonise Chilean law with the requirements emanating from various instruments that make up the increasingly powerful international human rights law. Although we have already stated that Law No. 21,325 does not protect all immigrants, but discriminates in relation to the enjoyment of rights on the basis of their legal immigration status, it cannot be ignored that it represents progress.

Indeed, the aforementioned legislation refers in explicit terms to the principle of the best interests of the child, equality and the elimination of all arbitrary discrimination. Additionally, on the thorny issue of expulsions, Article 129 indicates a series of factors that must be taken into account by the administrative bodies when the time comes to decide on the issuance of an act ordering the forced departure of an immigrant from Chilean territory. Among these factors are family ties formed abroad.

Ultimately, Law No. 21,325, although it does not fully protect all immigrants, brings us closer to a more inclusive society. The pending challenge is to grant greater protection to the groups of foreigners who are most invisible in terms of ownership of a series of rights held by all of us who are part of the human species (health, education, housing, family life, etc.), i.e. immigrants who have not obtained some type of visa. The Protocol that we have commented on is on this path, a text that does not grant its protection exclusively to children and adolescents who have obtained some type of visa, but, on the contrary, does not make any distinction based on that criterion. In short, it should be noted that the Protocol respects the requirements of the principle of best interests more strongly than the Chilean immigration regulations.

We hope that in the future Chilean law, when the time comes to continue granting protection to immigrant children and adolescents, chooses to deepen what is established in the Protocol and does not continue to differentiate between unaccompanied minors based on immigration status.

8. CONCLUSIONS

Based on the discussion above, we can conclude, first of all, that the State of Chile and its society was surprised by the explosive increase in the number of

---

[24] N. Rojas, *El contrato de trabajo para extranjeros*, Ius Civile, 2017, p. 27.

immigrants entering its territory. In addition, it has become clear that the level of vulnerability of many immigrants, when we take into account considerations of a humanitarian nature, required a State reaction aimed at guaranteeing the enjoyment and exercise of fundamental rights, especially with respect to children and adolescents who arrived without adult company. In line with the above, and clearly applying the principle of the best interests of unaccompanied minors, the Protocol that we have analysed has been concerned, among other aspects, with the conditions in which the initial reception given to such immigrants must take place. Thus, the aforementioned document has become a concrete example (and, therefore, has not been relegated to the limits of mere theory) of what is required in the scenario described, i.e. real respect for the famous best interests principle.

CHINA

RESEARCH ON THE NECESSITY AND FEASIBILITY OF RECOGNISING SAME-SEX COUPLES' STATUS UNDER CIVIL LAW IN CHINA

Siyuan DONG*

* The author thanks Dr Darius Longarino, Researcher at Paul Tsai China Center at Yale Law School, and Peng Yanhui, visiting scholar at Yale University, for editing this chapter.

Résumé

Actuellement, le mariage entre personnes de même sexe n'est pas prévu au sein du chapitre « Mariage et famille » du Code civil chinois. La Chine n'a pas non plus légiféré sur les partenariats civils ou les cohabitations hors mariage afin de protéger les droits et intérêts des couples de même sexe. En 2020, l'auteur a aidé un réseau d'organisations communautaires LGBT en Chine à mener, à titre bénévole, une enquête auprès des minorités sexuelles de ce pays sur leur opinion à l'égard de la reconnaissance des relations homosexuelles. La plupart des personnes interrogées ont déclaré qu'elles souhaitaient épouser leur partenaire de même sexe en Chine. Toutefois, certaines personnes interrogées ont déclaré avoir dissimulé leur orientation sexuelle et avoir contracté des mariages entre personnes n'ayant pas la même orientation sexuelle. D'autres ont expliqué avoir contracté des « mariages contractuels » (i.e. des mariages entre une femme lesbienne et un homme gay qui ont pour but de donner l'apparence extérieure d'une relation conjugale hétéronormée).

Le rapport accompagnant l'enquête affirme que certains fondements ont été posés pour que la Chine reconnaisse le statut des couples de même sexe. La Chine a déjà dépénalisé l'homosexualité et ne la considère plus comme une pathologie. Au-delà, la légalisation du statut civil des couples de même sexe bénéficie d'un certain soutien public. La plupart des départements judiciaires adoptent une attitude tolérante envers les groupes LGBT, et des avancées ont été faites en termes de valeurs culturelles. En 2019, Taiwan, en Chine, a légalisé le mariage entre personnes de même sexe. Le rapport recommande de promulguer une loi sur le partenariat civil ou la cohabitation non-maritale pour reconnaître le statut des couples de même sexe en droit civil et ainsi mieux protéger leurs droits et intérêts légitimes.

1. INTRODUCTION

On 28 May 2020, the Third Session of the Thirteenth National People's Congress passed the Civil Code of the People's Republic of China (Civil Code). Article 1041 of the Civil Code's chapter on Marriage and Family stipulates: '[T]he principles of the marriage system include the freedom of marriage, monogamy, and equality between men and women'. The Code's Marriage and Family chapter does not recognise same-sex marriage. China also does not have laws on civil partnership or cohabitation to protect the legal rights and interests of same-sex couples. Currently, same-sex couples can only create legal instruments like contracts, voluntary guardianship agreements, living wills and wills to arrange the personal and property affairs of both parties in a same-sex relationship. In China, legal recognition of same-sex relationships still has a long way to go, but such recognition is feasible and necessary.

2. THE NECESSITY OF RECOGNISING THE LEGAL STATUS OF SAME-SEX COUPLES IN CHINA

In 2019, many thousands of citizens submitted comments to lawmakers calling for legalising same-sex marriage in China's first-ever Civil Code. Months later, Huang Wei, director of the Civil Law Office of the Legal Affairs Commission of the Standing Committee of the National People's Congress, said that: '[W]e found the letters were the same. The content was the same – just copied and pasted'.

Since the letters sent to lawmakers may not objectively reflect the LGBTQI+ community's demand for same-sex marriage, the Chinese LGBT NGO China Marriage Equality Advocacy Network undertook a survey to better understand the needs of the community and the challenges they face with regard to relationship recognition. The survey ran from June 2020 to June 2021,[1] and the author participated in conducting it as a volunteer.

A total of 11,427 questionnaires were collected, of which 10,702 were valid questionnaires, resulting in an effectiveness rate of 93.66 per cent. The respondents were LGBTQI+ sexual minorities who were in a relationship at the time or who had been in a relationship. 70.09 per cent of respondents were between the ages of 19 and 30 (7,501). 19.62 per cent of respondents were between the ages of 31 and 40 (2,100). Regarding the respondents' assigned gender at birth or the gender marker on their government-issued national identification card, 52.06 per cent of respondents had a female marker (5,571) and 47.94 per cent had a male marker (5,131). 48.15 per cent of respondents identified as women (5,153), 49.71 per cent identified as men (5,320), and 2.14 per cent identified as the so-called 'TA' gender (229).[2] 83.7 per cent of respondents identified as homosexual (8,958) (the target population of the survey), 12.47 per cent as bisexual (1,335), 1.74 per cent as pansexual (186), 1.14 per cent as transgender heterosexuals (122), 0.35 per cent as asexual (37), and 0.6 per cent as 'other' (64).

Nearly 90 per cent of the respondents said they had fallen in love one to five times.[3] 12 per cent had a same-sex partnership that was ongoing or had lasted for more than half a year but less than a year, 31.78 per cent for one to three years, 28.88 per cent for three to seven years, and 11.37 per cent for more than seven years. A stable partner relationship provides a realistic basis for the desire to marry. In this survey, more than 80 per cent of the respondents have

1 It should be noted that the term 'partner' here refers to an intimate relationship that includes emotional, economic and sexual elements recognised by both parties, so relationship models such as unrequited love, one-night stands and concealing one's sexual orientation and getting married to a heterosexual person are excluded.

2 TA stands for gender identity other than male and female.

3 Once: 24.29%; twice: 21.36%; three times: 21.83%; four times: 11.61%; five times: 9.11%.

had or are currently in a stable same-sex relationship of over six months. The desire to attain civil status is not a whim, but is based on the real needs of a stable partnership. The following data illustrate the necessity of recognising the civil law status of same-sex couples in China.

2.1. SOME RESPONDENTS SAID THEY CONCEALED THEIR SEXUAL ORIENTATION TO ENTER INTO MIXED-ORIENTATION MARRIAGES

In China, some sexual minorities choose to conceal their sexual orientation and enter into a mixed-orientation marriage with a heterosexual due to social and family pressure.[4] *Tongqi* usually refers to a straight woman unwittingly married to a non-straight man in China.[5] *Tongfu* (straight husbands of lesbian women) exist but do not speak up as much nor receive as much attention, and thus are not widely considered a 'social problem' in China. Chinese law does not expressly address the issue of mixed-orientation marriages. However, according to Article 1091 of the Civil Code, if the divorce is due to one of the following circumstances, the non-fault party has the right to claim compensation for damages: (1) bigamy; (2) cohabitation with others; (3) domestic violence; (4) abuse or abandonment by family members; and (5) other major faults. The Marriage Law, which the Civil Code replaced in 2021, did not contain a clause for 'other faults'. This new clause raises the possibility that a *tongqi* could claim compensation when divorcing her gay husband who concealed his sexual orientation in order to enter into the marriage. In the first year that the Civil Code came into force, a court supported a *tongqi* who made such a claim.[6]

---

4 Such marriages are often referred to as 'deceptive marriages' or 'mixed-orientation marriages'.

5 Y. Zhou, H. Xie and C. Song, 'I Married a Gay Man: Tongqi's Agency in Marital Decisions' (2021) *British Journal of Social Work* 1.

6 The court of first instance held that the husband's concealment of his sexual orientation before marriage deprived his wife of her right to make prudent judgements and rational choices, based on a comprehensive understanding of his true situation, about whether to marry him. He also violated the duty of loyalty between husband and wife by repeatedly having improper relationships with many people of the same sex. This severely impacted the wife's emotions, which were based on traditional values. The husband's behaviour seriously damaged the emotional foundation of mutual honesty, mutual trust and mutual respect between husband and wife. This constituted a major fault on his behalf that caused a complete breakdown of the relationship between the two parties and resulted in divorce. The court ruled that the deceived party has the right to file a claim for compensation. According to the extent of the defendant's fault, the court of first instance determined the amount of compensation to be 30,000 RMB.

The vast majority of respondents (87.73 per cent) in our survey said that they did not conceal their sexual orientation to enter into a mixed-orientation marriage and they did not want to do so. Another 6.73 per cent said that although they had not concealed their sexual orientation to enter into a mixed-orientation marriage, they want to do so. 3.54 per cent had concealed their sexual orientation and entered into a mixed-orientation marriage, but were divorced before participating in the survey. Two per cent of respondents were in a mixed-orientation marriage when they participated in the survey.

Nearly 90 per cent of respondents were 19 to 40 years old at the time of the survey. The Civil Code stipulates that the legal marrying age is 22 for men and 20 for women. Most of the respondents were of legal marrying age. China has a strong tradition of pressuring people to marry and rear children, but most respondents believed that they should resist such pressure from the elders and that gays and lesbians should not conceal their sexuality in order to enter into a mixed-orientation marriage. However, 5.54 per cent of respondents have or, at the time of the survey, were concealing their sexual orientation in order to enter into a mixed-orientation marriage, and 6.73 per cent were planning or wanting to do so. The proportion is not high, but 'a grain of ash of the times, falling on an individual's head, is a mountain'.[7] The consequences of same-sex couples not being recognised by civil law are borne by the spouses in mixed-orientation marriages. The tragedy of a *tongqi* committing suicide after finding out her husband is gay is common.[8] Changhui Song, a PhD of Gender and Development Studies at the Asia Institute of Technology, believes that recognition of the civil law status of same-sex couples in China will help solve the problem of *tongqi*. It is helpful, after all, for LGBT people to have the option to marry a person of their choice. However, to fundamentally solve the *tongqi* issue, apart from recognising the civil law status of same-sex couples, it is also necessary to reduce the overall social pressure to marry and rear children.

---

7 See <http://www.chinawriter.com.cn/2013/2013-08-21/171603.html>, last accessed 26.04.2022.

8 In June 2012, Luo, a female teacher at a university in Chengdu, jumped to her death in anger when she found out that her husband was gay and had been cheating on her. Luo's parents claimed 630,000 yuan from the man. The court of first instance held that whether Luo and her husband knew about the other party or both parties had homosexual tendencies before marriage would not affect the legal effect of the voluntary marriage registration. Luo's parents believed that the man had concealed his sexuality when entering into the marriage, but the court did not support this view. Luo committing suicide by jumping off a building was not the only way to deal with her husband's homosexuality, and whether the man had comforted or looked after his wife, or could have prevented the tragedy, does not result in a change or transfer of the subject of legal responsibility. Therefore, there was insufficient evidence for the assertion that the man's actions have a causal relationship to Luo's death, and the court did not support Luo's parents claims.

2.2. SOME RESPONDENTS HAD ENTERED INTO 'CONTRACT MARRIAGES'

Internalised homophobia often drives individuals to conform to the expectations of heterosexual orthodoxy, whether consciously or unconsciously. To appear 'normal', some sexual minorities often suppress themselves and deliberately display behaviours that conform to heterosexual norms. Sexual minorities may be actively replicating and maintaining the influence and control of heterosexual orthodoxy over everyday life.[9] Sexual minorities concealing their sexual orientation to enter into mixed-orientation marriages is the manifestation of internalised homophobia and heterosexual orthodoxy.

Some gays and lesbians enter into 'contract marriages',[10] in which they pretend to be in a heterosexual relationship. A 'contract marriage' only has the form of marriage (such as registration, the appearance of monogamy, no kinship between spouses, etc.). It does not have the essence of marriage – love and emotion. The standard for litigation for divorce is that 'the relationship between husband and wife has been broken'.[11] But for gays and lesbians who enter into contract marriages, marriage is only a tool to cover up their true sexuality, and the emotional basis of marriage never existed in the first place.

In the survey conducted by the China Marriage Equality Advocacy Network, 94.57 per cent of respondents had not ever entered into a contract marriage. 80.15 per cent of these respondents did not want to enter into a contract marriage, while 10.77 per cent were somewhat interested in entering into a contract marriage. 3.64 per cent wanted to enter into a contract marriage very much. 2.8 per cent of respondents were once in a contract marriage but had later divorced. 2.63 per cent of respondents were in a 'contract marriage' at the time of the survey.

Contract marriages help the parties conceal their sexual orientation, but such marriages will likely require that the parties fabricate even more lies to sustain the concealment of their sexual orientations. Whether the secret can be kept depends on a lot of factors that are difficult to maintain. In addition, the 'husband and wife' relationship is fragile, and both parties must use contractual rules to manage issues in the relationship, such as who will bear the cost of the wedding and whether or not they will have children. According to the author's

---

9 W. Wei, 'Perception of Same-Sex Marriage from Within: The Impact of Internalized Heteronormativity over Chinese Tongzhi' (2010) 4 *Journal of East China University of Science and Technology (Social Science Edition)* 39.

10 Contract marriage refers to a marriage between a gay man and a lesbian pretending to be a heterosexual couple in order to resist the pressure from their families and society; registered contracted marriages have the same legal effect as traditional heterosexual marriages.

11 Cf. Civil Code Art. 1079.

observations as a volunteer at a LGBT NGO for many years, contract marriages often end in divorce, with the parties deep in dispute and physically and mentally exhausted. If civil law were to recognise same-sex relationships, gays and lesbians would no longer have to disguise themselves as heterosexuals to enter into 'performative' contract marriages. Instead, they could use their time and energy to maintain healthy interpersonal relationships that are conducive to social and family harmony.

2.3. THE VAST MAJORITY OF RESPONDENTS WANTED TO MARRY THEIR SAME-SEX PARTNER IN CHINA

The vast majority of respondents (89.25 per cent) wanted to marry their same-sex partner in China. 2.49 per cent did not have this desire and 8.25 per cent said that it did not matter. 34.09 per cent of respondents indicated that they were immigrating or considering immigrating to countries or regions that had legalised same-sex marriage,[12] and 1.11 per cent had already immigrated to such countries. The widespread desire among respondents to marry is not surprising. China has a strong tradition of family and clan. Common adages illustrate these values, such as 'having no posterity is the greatest of the three unfilial acts'. Marriage has long not been a 'choice' but a 'must', not a private matter but a 'family affair'. In China, the choice of marriage partners, the conclusion of the marriage and the relationship of the couple are considered a family or even public affair.[13] The law should give same-sex couples the right to marry both because it is highly desired among sexual minorities and because it will help prevent a drain of talent from China.

2.4. FEW LAWS ADDRESS DISPUTES INVOLVING SAME-SEX COUPLES

Some respondents reported that they and their partners had experienced legal difficulties due to the lack of legal recognition of their relationship. Such difficulties included statements that 'one party cannot sign the surgery agreement when the other party needs surgery', and 'one party has no right to inherit property when the other party passes away'.

---

12 It must be noted that the willingness to immigrate does not mean the ability to immigrate.

13 X. Fei, *Earthbound China, Reproductive System, Earthbound Reconstruction*, Commercial Press, 2019, p. 167.

In recent years, there have been many cases involving disputes among same-sex couples. There are two similar cases in Beijing and Xiamen: one of the lesbian partners provided eggs and the other provided the uterus to conceive a child. After the breakup of the same-sex partnership, dispute arose over establishing paternity/maternity over the child, and both parties competed for the eligibility for guardianship and support of the children. These two cases have triggered a big discussion in academic circles in China on whether to adopt the 'gene theory', tying parental status to the genetic relationship, or the 'childbirth theory', giving greater weight in determining parental status to the birth mother's gestational role. No laws or case precedents directly address this issue, but judges in China cannot refuse to judge a case because of a lack of relevant laws. In the Xiamen case, the Court of First Instance ruled that in the absence of clear legal provisions, the legal parent–child relationship cannot be confirmed or established based on genetic information alone. According to the court, under Chinese traditions and morality, the establishment of the mother–child relationship is not based on biological genes, but on the gestation process and the emotional connection brought about through labour pains – this is why the Medical Certificate of Birth records the mother who gave birth.[14] Therefore the court in Xiamen used the 'childbirth theory', ruling that the 'gene theory does not conform to basic public morality'.[15] It did not examine the relationship between the parties and the children or the ability of each party to raise the children. At present, another such custody case is pending in Beijing.

The law should be interpreted to clarify that courts should not rely solely on the 'gene theory' or the 'childbirth theory', but instead should give primacy to 'the best interest of the child theory'.[16]

---

14 See <https://mp.weixin.qq.com/s/eaVO6cZj6W6sBGFAvp-N3A>, last accessed 26.04.2022.

15 According to Article 39 of the Interpretation of the Supreme People's Court on the Application of the Marriage and Family Section of the Civil Code of the People's Republic of China (1), where the father or mother files a lawsuit in the people's court for the denial of the parent–child relationship, and has provided the necessary evidence to prove it, and the other party refuses to do a paternity test without evidence to the contrary, the people's court may determine that the claim of the party denying the parent–child relationship is valid. Where the father or mother and the adult child file a lawsuit requesting confirmation of the parent–child relationship, and provide the necessary evidence to prove it, and the other party refuses to do a paternity test without evidence to the contrary, the people's court may determine that the claim of the party confirming the parent–child relationship is valid. Article 39 is considered to be the legal basis for China to adopt the 'gene theory' for the determination of a parent–child relationship.

16 The theory of the best interests of the child abandons the idea that there can only be one father or one mother, and takes the best interests of the child as the principle, examines the economic, emotional, health and other aspects of both parties, and makes a decision that is most beneficial to the child.

3. THE FEASIBILITY OF RECOGNISING THE CIVIL LAW STATUS OF SAME-SEX COUPLES IN CHINA

3.1. CHINA HAS DECRIMINALISED AND DEPATHOLOGISED HOMOSEXUALITY

In 1997, China's Criminal Law was revised, and the crime of 'hooliganism' that was used to punish same-sex sexual behaviour was abolished. In 2001, the Psychiatry Branch of the Chinese Medical Association approved the Chinese Classification and Diagnostic Criteria of Mental Disorders, Third Edition (CCMD-3). The document revised the diagnostic provisions on homosexuality and no longer identified homosexuality as a mental disorder or a morbid mentality. However, 'self-discordant homosexuality' remained classified as a sexual orientation disorder. 'Self-discordant homosexuality' is when an individual's homosexuality catalyses anxiety, depression or other such conditions. Since the CCMD-3 no longer classified homosexuality itself as a mental illness, this change is often considered to mark the depathologisation of homosexuality in China.

However, the fact that the CCMD-3 still retained the word 'homosexuality' and seems to deliberately link homosexuality to mental illness (if the core of the disorder is the 'self-discordant' aspect of the condition, why is homosexuality specifically mentioned in the CCMD-3?). This has created confusion and has caused some psychiatrists to believe incorrectly that homosexuality is still a form of mental disorder in China. On 25 May 2019, the 72nd World Health Assembly held in Geneva, Switzerland reviewed and approved the International Classification of Diseases, the 11th revision (ICD-11), which entered into force on 1 January 2022. In the same year, the National Health Commission of the People's Republic of China issued the Chinese version of the ICD-11, actively requesting the full use of the ICD-11 and requiring all the health administrative departments at all levels to increase publicity, implementation, supervision and guidance of the new classifications. ICD-11 does not specify a classification of diseases related to 'homosexuality', which is a step further than the CCMD-3.

In 2016, the United Nations Human Rights Council adopted Resolution 32/2 on the Prevention of Violence and Discrimination Based on Sexual Orientation and Gender Identity, which made recommendations on LGBT+ issues for all UN Member States. The resolution sets out phased goals for LGBT+ equality, summarised as follows:

1. decriminalise same-sex sexual behaviour and repeal other discriminatory legislation;

2. protect the LGBT+ community from violence and inhumane treatment (including prohibiting conversion therapy, properly training the police, and taking positive measures to punish crimes against LGBT+ people);
3. repeal 'prohibition of the promotion of homosexuality' laws;
4. implement anti-discrimination legislation to clarify the basic rights of LGBT+ people (including the rights to health, employment, education, housing, property and inheritance), rectify the phenomenon of discrimination, and provide institutional support for transgender and intersex people;
5. allow same-sex couples to have a civil union relationship to ensure their right to adopt and form a family; and
6. allow same-sex couples to marry.

These goals are sequential. The latter goals are premised on achieving the earlier goals. Of course, there are real-world exceptions. For example, Taiwan, China, legalised same-sex marriage without first passing legislation on civil unions. Professor Geya Wang believes the legalisation of same-sex has helped move China closer to legalising same-sex marriage. The State's adopting of a more rational and scientific attitude toward sexual minorities has laid a foundation for sexual minorities to pursue legal status. The arrival of this period has brought people's serious re-examination and tolerance of homosexuality, and also brought about the legal appeal of homosexuals' marriage rights.[17]

3.2. THE LEGALISATION OF SAME-SEX MARRIAGE IN CHINA HAS A BASIS IN PUBLIC OPINION

Our survey asked respondents about how passers-by reacted when they engaged in public displays of same-sex affection, such as holding hands, hugging, kissing on the face and mouth, wearing couples' accessories or couples' clothes, and making a marriage proposal. 5.9 per cent of respondents said that passers-by responses were very friendly; 13.1 per cent said somewhat friendly; 7.7 per cent said not very friendly; and 0.5 per cent said very unfriendly. 72.7 per cent of respondents said passers-by had no response. Thus, more than 90 per cent of passers-by had no reaction or even expressed friendly support for the intimacy of same-sex couples. Only less than 10 per cent of passers-by had an unfriendly response. Recognising the civil law status of same-sex couples and increasing the visibility of same-sex couples will likely not lead to a lot of conflict

[17] G. Wang, 'Research on the Legal Regulation of the Marriage Rights of Homosexuals' (2008) 1 *Gansu Social Sciences* 33, 33–34.

between same-sex couples and passers-by in public places. Professor Yinhe Li believes that there is no extreme oppression and hatred against sexual minorities by Western religions in China. Many people in China hold a moderate attitude towards homosexuality, while the US public's views are more polarised. This difference might be related to the difference in the two countries' traditional cultural attitudes towards homosexuality.[18]

In December 2019, the Beijing News, a prominent Chinese newspaper, launched a public opinion survey on ifeng.com[19] asking 'do you support the legalisation of same-sex marriage in the Civil Code?' Nearly 10 million netizens participated in the survey. 67.34 per cent of participants (6,673,066) voted in support, 30.46 per cent (3,018,812) voted in opposition, and 1.75 per cent (173,710) voted neither for nor against. 0.44 per cent (43,908) of participants indicated that same-sex marriage has nothing to do with them. Although this survey is not necessarily representative of public opinion, it is at least indicative of netizen attitudes. Coincidentally, on 3 July 2018, the Comparative Law and Public Law Research Centre of the Faculty of Law of the University of Hong Kong published a survey on public attitudes towards same-sex marriage conducted between 12 May and 6 June 2017. Of 1,437 respondents, 50.4 per cent said they supported same-sex marriage. This is significantly higher than the results of the Centre's 2013 survey, in which only 38 per cent of respondents said they supported same-sex marriage. The support rate for hospital visits and inheritance had also increased.[20] The existing survey data suggest growing public support for China's civil law to recognise the status of same-sex couples.

3.3. SOME JUDICIAL DEPARTMENTS HAVE AN INCLUSIVE AND TOLERANT ATTITUDE TOWARD LGBT PEOPLE

In China, LGBT people are still sometimes treated unfairly due to their sexual orientation or gender identity or expression, such as suffering workplace discrimination or conversion therapy. In recent years, more and more LGBT people have sought to safeguard their legal rights and interests through litigation or arbitration.

Some of these cases were lost, such as:

- the first gay employment discrimination case (2015);
- *Qiubai v. Ministry of Education* (2014–2017);

[18] Y. Li, *My Social Observation*, China Federation of Industry and Commerce Press, 2014, pp. 90–112.

[19] A web platform available throughout China.

[20] See <https://mp.weixin.qq.com/s/ZCKn6LLcJ_6VZqZlbrPbFA>, last accessed 26.04.2022.

- the first same-sex marriage registration case (2015–2016);
- Xixi's case against homophobic textbooks (2017–2021);
- the SARFT General Rules for Reviewing the Contents of Online Audiovisual Programs case (2018–2019);
- the transgender equal employment rights case (2019–2020);
- the China Southern Airlines employment discrimination case (2020–present) (lost in arbitration, litigation in progress).

As for cases that were won, these include:

- *Fan Popo v. National Radio and Television Administration* (2015);
- the first transgender employment discrimination case (2016) (won on 'illegal termination' grounds, but lost on discrimination claim);
- the Guangdong HIV employment discrimination case (2016);
- the case of a Zhumadian gay man being forcibly confined to a mental hospital (2017);
- the Sichuan HIV employment discrimination case (2018);
- the gay kindergarten teacher employment discrimination case (2018).

Cases involving LGBT rights protection have mixed outcomes. In the written verdicts for these cases, some courts upheld a fair attitude towards LGBT people and based their decisions on the facts and the law. A few courts even clearly expressed a respectful and inclusive attitude towards the LGBT community. In the *Dangdang Discrimination Against Transgender Employees* case, the judges wrote:

> [M]odern society presents a trend of increasing diversity. We always find a lot of new things around us, and we will learn to accept these new things gradually, unless they threaten the interests of others, the collective, the country or society. Perhaps it is our tolerance for many new things that has laid the foundation for the long-term development of civilisation and the great progress of society. We are accustomed to understanding society according to our knowledge of biological gender, but there are still some people who need to express their gender identities according to their own life experiences. We often need to re-examine and recognise this kind of persistent social expression. This re-examination and recognition may require a very long process. But it is true that more and more people choose to be tolerant, and it is indeed necessary for us to gradually change our attitude. Because only when we tolerate diverse ways of living can we have richer cultural concepts and lay a cultural foundation of tolerance for a society ruled by law. This may be the logic of some scholars who pointed out that social tolerance is the blessing of the rule of law.[21]

---

21 See <https://baijiahao.baidu.com/s?id=1686017369441528527&wfr=spider&for=pc>, last accessed 26.04.2022.

This judgment reflects the judiciary's compassion for the LGBT community in China.

3.4. BREAKTHROUGHS IN CULTURAL VALUES

On 6 November 2018, the third round of China's Universal Periodic Review was held in Geneva. The Chinese delegation responded positively to the 'LGBT+ rights issue' for the first time at this meeting, and explained China's basic position: 'our country has always respected the right to health of LGBT+ groups, and provided them with equal social security to protect the right to undergo gender reassignment surgery'. The delegation nonetheless added, '[a]t the current stage, our country's refusal to give LGBT+ people the right to marry someone of the same sex is not because of discrimination. This policy is determined by our country's historical and cultural values'.[22] However, as Professor Xia Li said, the meaning and forms of marriage are in the process of continuous development. Traditionally, marriage was restricted to two people of the opposite sex, but the reasons for doing so are no longer sufficient. The argument that 'it is stipulated by law' only appeals to the coercive power of the State and is unconvincing.[23] Tradition should not be an obstacle to the reform of marriage. If it was, Denmark would not have been the first country to pass the Registered Partnerships Act in 1989 to protect the legal rights and interests of same-sex couples, and the Netherlands would not have been the first country in the world to achieve same-sex marriage in 2001. In *Obergefell v. Hodges*, which legalised same-sex marriage in the United States, the US Supreme Court said that the question of whether the historical and cultural traditions of marriage can be transcended was under debate.[24] The majority opinion written by Justice Kennedy held that history and tradition guide and discipline this inquiry, but they do not set its outer boundaries.[25] Remarking that society had long regarded interracial and inter-class marriages as being prohibited, the Court reasoned that the definition of marriage is subject to revision again by popular opinion.[26]

---

22 'Here Comes the Video, China Responds to LGBT Issues at UN for the First Time', China Development Brief, 13 November 2018, available at: <http://www.chinadevelopmentbrief.org.cn/customer/details.html?id=22194&type=>, last accessed 26.04.2022.

23 X. Li, 'Research on the Legalization of Same-Sex Marriage' (2008) 3 *Hebei Law Science* 101, 102–103.

24 See *Obergefell v. Hodges*, 576 U.S. 644, 656–663 (2015).

25 Ibid.

26 Ibid.

3.5. LEGALISATION OF SAME-SEX MARRIAGE IN TAIWAN, CHINA

In 2015, Jiawei Qi asked the Taiwan Alliance to Promote Civil Partnership Rights lawyer group to bring a same-sex couple registration case to Taiwan's Constitutional Court. In 2017, the justices held that it is unconstitutional for the current Civil Law in Taiwan not to protect same-sex marriage. The Court asked the legislature to amend the Civil Law within two years of the decision. In May 2019, the Taiwanese legislature passed the Judicial Yuan Shi Zi No. 748 Interpretation and Implementation Law allowing same-sex couples in Taiwan to legally register their marriage. Judicial Yuan Shi Zi No. 748 Interpretation and Implementation Law is a law that specifically allows same-sex couples to establish a same-sex marriage relationship. The law applies civil law provisions on property regimes, child custody after divorce and legal inheritance to same-sex couples who seek legal recognition, extending to these couples most of the rights enjoyed by opposite-sex married couples. However, the law distinguishes opposite-sex couples from same-sex couples in terms of name, content and form. Although same-sex couples can 'register for marriage', they are still far from achieving substantial equality. The main differences are discussed below.

3.5.1. *Transnational Same-Sex Marriages*

Taiwan recognises or allows registration of same-sex marriage only if both parties of the same sex are from countries or regions where same-sex marriage is legal. If one or both parties are from countries or regions that do not recognise same-sex marriage, then only the household registration system can be applied, not the same-sex marriage law. The turning point occurred in a case in August 2021.[27] The plaintiffs in this case were a same-sex couple – Taiwanese Zeyan Ding and Macanese Zhanhui Liang. The two went to the household registration office in 2019 to apply for marriage registration and were rejected. The lawsuit was filed in October and the couple won. On 13 August 2021, the two officially registered their marriage. This is the first case of same-sex marriage registration involving a Taiwanese citizen and a Macau citizen, but regrettably Taiwan has not removed the limitation, allowing recognition only if both parties are from regions where same-sex marriage is allowed. Therefore, this case is only relevant for cross-border marriage of same-sex couples from Taiwan and Macau. Nonetheless, it marks a step forward in Taiwan's protection of gay rights.

---

27 See <https://mp.weixin.qq.com/s/lQRJAiXcP_vaMmq53XclOQ>, last accessed 26.04.2022.

3.5.2. *The Parent–Child Relationship*

In Taiwan, same-sex partners can adopt each other party's biological children, but they cannot jointly adopt other children. Nor can one party adopt the children the other party adopted before their marriage. The law does not presume that children born in a same-sex partnership have a legal relationship to each parent, so the non-consanguineous party needs to adopt the child to establish a parent–child relationship under the law. Although surrogacy is not legal in Taiwan, Taiwanese law allows heterosexual couples to have children by using donated sperm or eggs. Until recently, this had not available to same-sex couples.

The turning point occurred in a 2022 case. A gay couple in Taiwan wanted to adopt a child together, but only one of them could adopt the child as a 'single' father. They filed a lawsuit in a Kaohsiung court. On 4 January 2022, the court issued a ruling allowing the two to jointly adopt a daughter by invoking the Convention on the Rights of the Child to protect the best interests of the child. On 13 January 2022, the two went to Taipei Xinyi Household Registration Office for adoption registration with the court judgment. This is the first instance of joint gay-parent adoption in Taiwan. The case also became the first in Taiwan, China and even in Asia to allow both partners of a same-sex couple to have parental rights for non-consanguineous children.[28]

3.5.3. *Other Issues*

The Judicial Yuan Shi Zi No. 748 Interpretation and Implementation Law does not expressly affirm that a same-sex partnership is a 'marriage relationship'. It only stipulates that two people of the same sex can 'register'. If the relationship is to be terminated, it is called a 'termination of marriage registration', not a 'divorce'. The term 'permitted' is used for related rights and obligations of heterosexual couples, and there is no heterosexual 'affinity relationship'. This distinction shows that the status of same-sex couples and opposite-sex couples in Taiwan is still unequal in civil law.

Mainland China and Taiwan have close geographical ties and share the historical and cultural traditions of the Chinese legal system. The fact that same-sex marriage can be legal and implemented in Taiwan indicates that there is no insurmountable cultural barrier to the recognition of the civil law status of same-sex couples in mainland China.

---

[28] R. Dai, 'Marriage and adoption can only choose one? Comment on the first legal approval case of gay family adoption in Asia', available at: <https://mp.weixin.qq.com/s/Cw72cU3Z0jzBm3t1S0GDBg>, last accessed 26.04.2022.

4. CONCLUSION

To sum up, it is necessary and feasible for mainland China to recognise the civil law status of same-sex couples. However, the Civil Code has just been passed, so immediate revision of the Civil Code is not realistic. Unlike in Taiwan, there is no constitutional review (judicial review) mechanism in mainland China. Therefore, it is impossible to legalise same-sex marriage through a legal interpretation of the Supreme People's Court. Therefore, the most appropriate and realistic approach is to recognise the civil law status of same-sex couples and protect their legal rights by promulgating laws such as the Cohabitation Law and the Civil Partnership Law. This is also in line with the order of the phased goals of LGBT+ equal rights in the UN Resolution on the Prevention of Violence Based on Sexual Orientation and Gender Identity and Discrimination.

It is difficult to estimate the specific number of sexual minorities in China, as there is no unified definition of sexual minority. According to an estimate by sociologist Yinhe Li many years ago, homosexuals accounted for 3–4 per cent of the total population of China.[29] Although the proportion is small, they are also descendants of the Chinese nation. As Professor Dayuan Han has said, even if only one person chooses such a way of life, the country and society should fully guarantee it. We cannot only have the concept of the group without the concept of the individual. Our obstacle is one of ideas. In promoting the spirit of the Constitution, we should respect the uniqueness of individuals and push forward the tolerance of society.[30]

---

29 Y. Li, *Subculture of Homosexuality*, China Friendship Publishing Company, 2002, p. 6.

30 See D. Han, 'Lecture on Constitutional Protection of Transgender Rights in My Country', Lecture on Renmin University of China–Yale Project, available at: <https://mp.weixin.qq.com/s/2PA1W7Q-8I_7YDEvyoiCCA>, last accessed 26.04.2022.

CHINA

THE PROTECTION OF PROPERTY RIGHTS AND INTERESTS OF DIVORCED FEMALE FAMILY CAREGIVERS

Xia Li and Mingmei Xiang

Résumé

Jusqu'à présent, la protection des droits patrimoniaux et des intérêts des femmes divorcées en charge du foyer familial a été négligée par le Code civil et la loi de la République populaire de Chine sur la protection des droits et intérêts des femmes. La loi chinoise devrait élargir le champ des biens susceptibles d'être divisés, en reconnaissant que, sous certaines conditions, les diplômes professionnels, les droits à pension et les avantages acquis pendant le mariage sont des biens qu'il est possible de partager au moment du divorce. Elle devrait également préciser que les pensions qu'il est possible de partager ne se limitent pas à l'assurance retraite de base versée sur des comptes individuels, mais incluent également l'assurance retraite fournie par les employeurs. La loi chinoise devrait aussi ajouter un système de pension alimentaire après divorce.

1. THE PROBLEM

The provisions of the Civil Code and the Law on the Protection of Women's Rights and Interests still have shortcomings in terms of the scope of division of property, the time limit for exercising the right to request compensation upon divorce and post-divorce support for divorced female family caregivers. These provisions do not adequately take into account the protection of property rights and interests of the family caregiver during and after divorce. Article 47 of the Law on the Protection of Women's Rights and Interests still limits the protection of property rights and interests of family caregivers on the basis of the premise of a 'separate property regime',[1] and Article 1088 of the Civil Code is no longer limited to the property regime adopted during the marriage.[2] However, an analysis of the legal provisions related to family care and judicial cases[3] after the entry into force of the Civil Code shows that the protection of the property rights of divorced female family caregivers is in need of revision.

2. JUSTIFICATION OF PROPERTY RIGHTS AND INTERESTS OF FEMALE FAMILY CAREGIVERS

Family caregiving is labour intensive, requiring emotional support and care in addition to the actual work, which is not easily perceived and often taken

1 Art. 47 reads: 'The spouses agree in writing that the property acquired during the marriage belongs to each of them, and that the woman who has assumed more obligations for raising children, caring for the elderly and assisting the man in his work has the right to request compensation from the man during the divorce'.

2 Art. 1088 reads: 'Where one spouse is burdened with additional duties for raising children, looking after the elderly, or assisting the other spouse in his work, the said spouse has the right to request for compensation upon divorce against the other party, and the other party shall make due compensation. The specific arrangements for making such compensation shall be determined by the spouses through agreement, or adjudicated by the people's court where no such an agreement is reached'.

3 See <https://baijiahao.baidu.com/s?id=1692011462315325035&wfr=spider&for=pc>, last accessed 23.04.2022. The Beijing Fangshan District Court ruled that 'for the compensation requested by Ms. Wang, since Ms. Wang had more obligations in raising the children, the

for granted. Family caregiving means addressing the needs and dependencies of family members and providing physical, financial, emotional and nursing care. Family caregiving is not limited to children, the disabled and those with physical and mental impairments that are temporary or persistent due to illness or accidental injury. With the development of society, family care has expanded to include one spouse moving with the other because of the other spouse's career or professional development needs, one spouse earning money and providing financial support for the other spouse to complete education or training or to obtain other qualifications to improve their career or income, etc.[4]

The negative effects of caregiving responsibilities on family caregivers include:

- Stress and pressure: caregiving often causes caregivers physical, psychological, social and financial stress;
- The caregiver's experience and feelings: social alienation due to caring for a sick family member, doing hard work but facing difficulties and criticism from the elderly and other family members;
- The impact of caregiving on employment: caregivers may withdraw from paid employment altogether, partially change their work patterns or retire early;
- Economic dependence and poverty: in addition to physical fatigue and psychological stress, family caregivers experience de facto inequality because they are unable to work outside the home and are weaker than their spouses in financial and household decisions.[5]

Historically and in the present day, it is usually the female role – wife, mother, grandmother, grandmother, daughter, daughter-in-law – who takes on the responsibilities of caregiving in the family. The rhetoric used in Article 47 of the Law on the Protection of Women's Rights and Interests seems to tacitly acknowledge that the woman in fact assumes more caregiving responsibilities.

---

application of the Civil Code is more conducive to protecting Ms. Wang's legitimate rights and interests, so Ms. Wang's request for compensation from Mr. Chen is justified; for the amount of compensation, the court took into account the length of their marriage and the living conditions described by both parties. The court ruled that Mr. Chen should pay Ms. Wang 50,000 yuan in compensation for household chores.' The article 'A full-time wife in Shandong was awarded 930,000 "housework compensation" for divorce after the relationship between husband and wife broke down', published by Shandong High Court on 7 April 2021, did not directly confirm the value of housework, but was mixed up with property division.

4 R. Thompson, 'Spousal Support Eh: Sorry, Not Your American Alimony' (2019) 41 *Houston Journal of International Law* 641.

5 H. Hong, M. Liao and Y. Xie, 'Fairness in the Distribution of Care Assignment: A Preliminary review of the social care system in Taiwan' (2012) 11 *Journal of Social Development Research*. 46.

Article 1088 of the Civil Code expresses the burden of domestic work as being 'on the part of the spouses', and although it has been de-gendered, what we can see is that family law incorporates a formal equality into an unequal situation. The formal model of equality actually aggravates historical inequalities, as it does not take into account the reality of the weight of 'mothering' in the family, especially by ignoring the difference in the ability of a woman who has given birth to compete in the marketplace/workplace with a man who does not take on caregiving responsibilities.[6] Several studies have shown that in the conflict between professional work and domestic work, the burden of domestic work has a negative effect on women's earnings, an effect known as 'the penalty effect of domestic work'. Gender differences in household work, especially in the amount of time put into household work, are the main cause of the earnings gap between men and women.[7] According to Judge Posner, 'the family is an important unit of production, and the most important input to this production process is not market goods at all, but the time among family members, especially the time of the wife in the traditional home.'[8]

A 2019 ILO report titled 'A Quantum Leap for Gender Equality: Creating a Better Future for All' concludes that 'the causes of gender inequality in the workplace are complex, with women bearing the brunt of household chores'.[9] The report goes on to note that between 2005 and 2012, the average time women spent on household chores decreased by 15 minutes per day, but for men it increased by only eight minutes.[10] Women's caregiving responsibilities often prevent them from advancing in the workplace or marketplace, and many caregiving responsibilities are not appropriate to delegate to others, so the primary caregiving responsibilities remain within the family and are primarily carried out by women.

Because female family caregivers devote their time and energy to family caregiving, their human capital in the workplace is inevitably lower than that of their husbands during marriage and after divorce. This effect will continue until both parties choose a spouse again, with the female family caregiver suffering far greater losses than the husband, while the husband with a job is almost unaffected by the divorce. In the context of China's current 'three-child' policy, which allows a couple to have up to three children, the social costs of family caregiving are further magnified. Although the value of family caregiving is recognised in the Civil Code and the Law on the Protection of Women's Rights and Interests,

6 M.A. Farman, *The Myth of Autonomy: A Theory of Dependency*, trans. by X. Li, China University of Political Science and Law Press, 2014.

7 J. Xiao, 'The impact of domestic work on gender income gap-an analysis based on the data of the Third China Women's Social Status Survey' (2017) 6 *Women's Studies Series*.

8 R.A. Posner, *The Economic Analysis of Law*, China Encyclopaedia Press, 1997.

9 See <https://politics.gmw.cn/2019-03/08/content_32615209.htm>, last accessed 23.04.2022.

10 See <http://www.humanrights.cn/html/2019/2_0308/42563.html>, last accessed 21.09.2022.

it is not universally and fairly used, which inevitably has the following effects on female family caregivers. First, women have become more reluctant to have children, with overall fertility falling in recent years. In addition, women who do have children have become more likely to rely on elderly family members for childcare so that they can focus on study or professional development. Second, some family caregivers who devote themselves full-time to family care and do not have income from employment dare not file for divorce when the couple's relationship becomes unhappy, which prevents women from asserting their right to divorce.

What is particularly thought-provoking is that the newly amended Population and Family Planning Law of the People's Republic of China has formally incorporated the 'three-child' policy into law, and the burden of family care is bound to increase significantly. However, if women continue to bear the primary responsibilities for family care and this structural historical inequality is not radically changed, women will simultaneously face the challenges of having to compete in the workplace and of taking primary responsibility for the care of three children within the family, including pregnancy, childbirth, upbringing and education, which require a lot of time, energy and emotion. They are thus caught in a 'motherhood dilemma', which is mainly characterised by a high childcare load and motherhood penalties. According to the 2014 China Family Dynamics Tracking Survey (CFRS), although grandparental support is common, 58.9 per cent of children under the age of three are mainly cared for by their mothers during the day, and 74.1 per cent at night.[11] On the other hand, when women become mothers, they need to divide their energy between work and family, which inevitably leads to career interruptions and reduced opportunities for career development. With the inclusion of the 'three-child' policy in law, the Law on the Protection of Women's Rights and Interests should provide systematic support for female family caregivers who take care of young children.

3. THE CURRENT LEGAL STATUS OF THE PROTECTION OF PROPERTY RIGHTS AND INTERESTS OF FAMILY CAREGIVERS

The value of family care is not explicitly recognised in the Law on the Protection of Women's Rights and Interests. The Civil Code recognises the value of family

[11] See W. Fan, 'The Causes and Solutions of the Motherhood Difficulties: A Discussion of the Three-Child Support Policy', speech at 'Interpreting the Three-Child Birth Policy and Promoting the Construction of Inclusive Support Measures', an academic forum organised by the Editorial Department of Women's Studies Series, Institute for Women's Studies, All-China Women's Federation, 19 June 2021.

care, but only very coarsely. Examining current cases before the courts shows that there is a gap between the value of family caregiving in the legislation and in society. In the current legal system, the protection of the property rights and interests of female family caregivers is not fair in substance, as shown in the following sections.

3.1. PROPERTY AVAILABLE FOR DIVISION IN DIVORCE DOES NOT INCLUDE DEFERRED GAIN PROPERTY

Article 1062 of the Civil Code defines the scope of the community property of the spouses as 'real property' acquired at the time of divorce.[12] The Law on the Protection of Women's Rights and Interests lacks a definition of the scope of the community property of the spouses and only vaguely provides in Article 47 that 'women shall have equal rights to possess, use, benefit and dispose of the community property of the spouses in accordance with the law, regardless of the income status of the spouses'. However, both laws omit the two most important types of deferred property – professional degrees and pensions.

3.1.1. Professional Degrees Acquired During Marriage Fall Under the Property Category

Does a professional degree obtained during marriage count as divisible property in the event of divorce? The answer is yes, because a degree is the end product of a family's joint effort. Both spouses plan their family life around the activity of one spouse obtaining a degree, and principles of fairness require that the spouse who did not obtain an advanced degree should be compensated when the advanced degree (of the other spouse) is the result of a joint family investment. The degree holder has made a tremendous effort, not only for his or her own sake, but also for the sake of the entire family. The other spouse, in turn, has made efforts and contributed in other ways in this regard.

The exception to the rule that professional degrees are not property is found in several cases in the United States from New York, including *O'Brien v. O'Brien* and *McSparron v. McSparron*, as well as in the language in

---

[12] Art. 1062 reads: 'The following property acquired by the spouses during their marriage constitutes community property and are jointly owned by the spouses: (1) salaries and wages as well as bonuses and other remuneration received from services rendered; (2) proceeds obtained from production, business operation, and investment; (3) proceeds arising from intellectual property rights; (4) except as otherwise provided in Subparagraph (3) of Article 1063 of this Code, property acquired from inheritance or given as a gift; and (5) other property that shall be jointly owned by the spouses. Husband and wife have equal rights when disposing of the community property.'

Woodworth v. Woodworth.[13] One interesting case involving valuation of a medical degree is that of *In re Marriage of Francis.*[14] The expert testified to the difference between a college graduate and a doctor's income over the expected length of practice and then reduced this amount to the present value. His testimony was based on the assumption that 70 per cent of most medical firms' income is due to the labour (or future efforts of the doctor), leaving 30 per cent to the capital investment made during his education. This amount accordingly was split based on the relative contributions of the spouses.[15]

3.1.2. Pension Benefits as Property

China's pension insurance is composed of three pillars: basic pension insurance, supplementary pension insurance and individual savings pension insurance. The condition for receiving pension insurance is that the accumulated contributions have been made for 15 years by the legal retirement age. Although pension insurance coverage is now almost universal, women who are full-time or part-time family caregivers do not receive the same basic pension benefits as those who have a stable career. For husbands who have a job, pensions include the basic employee pension insurance and the employer's supplementary pension insurance. The basic employee pension insurance benefits and the supplementary pension insurance benefits provide them with an 80 per cent replacement rate pension, ensuring that they maintain a standard of living after retirement that is no less than what they had when they were employed.[16]

Although pension insurance is not recognised as community property by the Civil Code, according to Article 25 of the Interpretation (I) of the Marriage and Family Section of the Civil Code, 'the basic pension and bankruptcy settlement compensation that both spouses have actually obtained or should obtain shall be recognised as other property that should be jointly owned'. At the same time, according to the provisions of Article 80 of the aforementioned Judicial Interpretation,[17] the time and scope of pension acquisition are limited:

---

13 See e.g. *O'Brien v. O'Brien*, 489 N.E.2d 712 (N.Y. 1985); see also *McSparron v. McSparron*, 662 N.E.2d 745 (N.Y. 1995); and *Woodworth v. Woodworth*, 337 N.W.2d 332 (Mich. App. 1983).

14 See *In re Marriage of Francis*, 442 N.W.2d 59 (Iowa 1989).

15 M.F. Brinig, 'Marital Property: An American Perspective' in B. Atkin (ed.), *The International Survey of Family Law*, Jordan Publishing, 2016.

16 R. Zhang, 'A New Type of Community Property for Spouses – Pension Rights During Marriage' (2018) 2 *Law Review*, 67.

17 Art. 80 of the Marriage and Family Section of the Civil Code Judicial Interpretation reads: 'If one of the spouses has not retired at the time of divorce and does not meet the conditions for receiving the basic pension, and the other spouse requests to divide the basic pension according to the community property of the spouses, the people's court shall not support it; if the basic pension insurance premiums are paid by the community property of the spouses after marriage, and one of the spouses claims to divide the part of the pension account actually

in terms of time, the individual should be retired and eligible for the basic pension, and in terms of the scope, the actual individual part of the basic pension insurance premiums paid by the married couple's community property and the interest can be divided as the community property of the couple, excluding the supplementary pension insurance provided by the employee's employer. Under this system, even if the family caregiver and the husband with a job have also worked for the family, the husband's basic pension cannot be divided because he had not retired at the time of divorce, and even if the husband retires upon divorce, only the part of the husband's personal account contributions can be divided, excluding the part of the basic pension insurance paid by the husband's employer. In Shanghai's current pension insurance system, for example, the family unit contribution to the pension insurance rate accounts for 20 per cent, which is much higher than the husband's personal contribution of 8 per cent. Yet, if the husband retires after the divorce, the wife will receive no portion of this amount.

In contrast, pensions are usually considered marital property in foreign countries. Section 407(a) of Title 42 of the US Code provides legal procedures to protect social security benefits from division, i.e. they are not subject to any form of garnishment in divorce proceedings, except for alimony or child raising. If pensions are unpaid at the time of divorce, they are usually deferred until they are actually received, but there is also the possibility of being discounted to cover risks and awarded in a lump sum payment at divorce. To avoid creating speculative attributes, they are usually distributed for payment at the time the pension is actually paid.[18]

In Germany, former spouses who have been married for ten years and meet the necessary age requirements have the right to federal social security benefits according to the Family Section of the German Civil Code. In addition, in a related constitutional lawsuit in Germany in 1980, the distribution obligor argued that the system of distribution of old-age benefits and pensions unlawfully interfered with his or her property rights by including the expectancy rights of his or her statutory annuity insurance in the distribution of the remainder of the couple's property upon divorce. In its decision, the Federal Constitutional Court recognised the property rights of the social security annuitant by setting three criteria: personal disposability, previous payments by the individual, and the survival of the rightholder, and held that the system was designed to implement equal rights in marriage.[19] According to the German Civil Code, the pensions included in the division of marital property include: (1) statutory annuity insurance; and (2) other social insurance benefits: civil

---

paid by the individual during the marriage and the interest as the community property of the spouses at the time of divorce, the people's court shall support it.'

18 See Brinig, above n. 15.

19 N. Sun, 'Divorce Annuity Rights Distribution System: German law as a reference' (2008) 25 *Journal of National Chung Cheng University* 14.

service insurance, old-age disability annuity insurance paid by specialised professionals, corporate annuity insurance, and private commercial insurance contracts for the elderly or disabled, all of which can be requested to be distributed upon divorce.[20]

3.2. THE LIMITATION PERIOD FOR THE EXERCISE OF CLAIMS FOR COMPENSATION AFTER DIVORCE

How long is the limitation period on the right to claim divorce compensation? Article 1088 of the Civil Code and Article 47 of the Law on the Protection of Women's Rights and Interests both stipulate that the right to claim is limited to the 'time of divorce', which means that the right to claim is not available after the divorce. This imposes severe conditions on the exercise of this right by family caregivers, even more severe than the three-year ordinary statute of limitations provided for in the Civil Procedure Law, and does not allow for a fair assessment of the value of family care and the compensation to be paid to family caregivers.

In Swiss law, on the other hand, the right to claim compensation is granted to the spouse of the family caregiver during the marriage as usual. For example, according to Articles 164, 165 and 175 of the Swiss Civil Code (amended as of 1 January 2016), during the marriage, the family caregiver may request the other spouse to pay an appropriate amount of money on a regular schedule for him or her to use as he or she sees fit and if the family caregiver significantly exceeds his or her contribution to the family's livelihood, he or she may request the other spouse to pay appropriate compensation; in the event of separation or lack of possibility of living together, the court may be requested to determine the amount of money to be paid by one spouse to the other.

4. PROPOSAL TO PROTECT THE PROPERTY RIGHTS OF DIVORCED FEMALE FAMILY CAREGIVERS

4.1. EXPLICITLY STIPULATE FAIRNESS AS A PRINCIPLE FOR DIVIDING PROPERTY IN DIVORCE

The Civil Code and the Law on the Protection of Women's Rights and Interests should establish fairness as the basic principle for the division of community property for the following reasons.

---

20 For details of the legal provisions, see the German Civil Code, compiled by the School of Law, National Taiwan University and the NTU Law Foundation, Peking University Press, 3rd printing, May 2020, Art. 1587.

The premise of the principle of fairness is equality, since the domestic work of the family caregiver and the social work of the party involved in the market work have equal value to the family. Both parties in a marriage have equal legal status, and based on the premise of equality, the family caregiver should be compensated, which is the natural way of achieving substantive equality. The 'fairness' in the principle of equitable division means 'justice' or substantive equality, which extends to both the contribution and the needs of the family caregiver.

4.1.1. Contribution

Contribution here is roughly the same as the scope of family care, but requires consideration of the contribution of the family caregiver during the marriage, in addition to the contribution of the family caregiver after the divorce, primarily for child-rearing and education. The duration of the marital relationship also needs to be considered. The longer the marriage lasts, the greater the family caregiver's contribution is. In the early no-fault divorce states in the US, household contributions should be conceived as a factor in measuring entitlement to property or contributions in community property equitable distribution states.[21] In addition, according to Article 307 of the US Uniform Marriage and Divorce Act, when dividing marital property, the court shall consider the following factors: the contribution of either party to the acquisition of the community property, including the contribution of one spouse by way of household chores, etc., and the factors to be considered in the division mainly reflect the requirements of equitable division.

4.1.2. The Practical Needs Rule

The rule of need has two components. First, the division of property in divorce takes into account the family caregiver's care of children during the marriage, compensating the caregiver for the lost earning capacity associated with that care. Second, the primary family caregiver (most commonly the mother) typically receives more custody of the minor children, while the father is responsible for financial provision and visitation. This further increases the caregiver's need after the divorce. Under the current 'three-child' policy, the woman with more direct custody of the children will have a dramatically increased caregiving burden, and bringing up the children will require new inputs and financial changes that may arise at any time, such as changes in the children's medical or educational environment. Thus, the needs of the children of whom the family caregiver has

---

21 Brinig, above n. 15.

sole custody after the divorce must be a consideration in the divorce. Depending on financial ability, the financial needs are divided into actual financial needs and foreseeable future financial needs, which include: (1) the family caregiver's current assets; (2) the family caregiver's education, practical skills, work experience and time away from the workplace; and (3) the family caregiver's future earning capacity. The standard for 'need' is reasonableness, which consists of two levels: the first level is to meet the basic needs of the family caregiver, and the second level is to meet the needs of the family caregiver's actual situation. 'As marriage should be regarded as a joint endeavour, the longer the relationship endures, the closer the economic union, the greater the presumptive claim to equal standards of living will be upon its dissolution.'[22]

Article 47 of the Law on the Protection of Women's Rights and Interests stipulates that community property is based on the Civil Code and related judicial interpretations, while according to the current judicial interpretation of the Civil Code, the pension insurance is the 'basic pension actually obtained or that should be obtained'. This not only limits the scope of the couple's community property, but also denies the fact that pensions are property, which is unfair in terms of protecting the property rights of full-time family caregivers. It is recommended that the scope of community property be expanded to include professional degrees and pensions obtained during marriage, not just the real property of the common house. The reasons for this are as follows.

First, pensions and pension insurance interests are community property. In China, the pension insurance benefits that can be divided upon divorce are only the basic pension paid by the individual account with the community property, leaving out the pension insurance supplied by the employer. Although this part is not paid directly by the individual, it is also the consideration of the employee's labour, and the unit of one spouse will not pay out part of his or her labour remuneration but will keep and save it, which obviously belongs to the deferred salary.[23] Both the basic pension and the supplementary pension are earned by the man with a job during the marriage, or the consideration for their work, including the contribution of the female family caregiver.

There is no necessary connection between the community property accumulated during the marriage and the time of receipt. Under the community marital regime, the factor to be considered in determining whether property is community marital property is whether the property was acquired during the marriage; whether the property was actually received during the marriage does not affect the nature of the property. Unlike professional degrees, pension rights and interests are expected and attainable, and although the amount

22 *Moge v. Moge* [1992] 3 SCR 813 (Can.), para. 84

23 Z. Xu, 'Research on the mechanism and effect of pension insurance in regulating income distribution – an analysis of urban workers' basic pension insurance as the main body' (2014) *Southwest University of Finance and Economics* 45.

is unpredictable when the conditions are not met, this is not a legal basis for excluding pension rights and interests from community property. Since the concept that household work has the same value as socially productive work has been recognised, the pension expectancy benefits accumulated by one spouse during the marriage should be shared by the other spouse. According to the spirit advocated by the relevant UN literature, both spouses should share equally all the property rights acquired during the marriage.[24] The recognition of pension rights and interests as community property affirms the value of women in family care. Housewives should have the same economic value as the male working outside the home, highlighting the attribute of equality in marriage and family life, as well as realising the freedom of divorce and the protection of the rights and interests of the weak.

Second, professional degrees acquired during marriage are community property. In the current knowledge-based economy, the assets owned by most couples are human capital rather than tangible houses and cars. Human capital can bring economic benefits, such as the increased earning capacity that comes with the greater knowledge and skill associated with practising certificates and professional degrees. The value of the family caregiver is also implied by the fact that the family caregiver takes on the burden of caregiving, which frees up the other party's energy and time and even the family's community property to use as tuition to obtain a professional degree. The value of a degree is reflected in its gradual appreciation in the future, while women are more likely to become 'vulnerable workers', at a disadvantage in terms of human capital and the need to bear the cost of childbirth, which adds a certain amount of irreplaceable family caregiving responsibilities, resulting in less time in the workplace. Husbands who have a job, on the other hand, accumulate and add value to their human capital and can generate greater gains or value in the future compared to family caregivers. The result is that the wife's human capital suffers when the marriage breaks up, and she may also be responsible for raising the children, reducing her standard of living during the marriage.

4.2. ADDITIONS TO THE POST-DIVORCE SUPPORT RELIEF SYSTEM

The post-divorce support relief system is not provided for in the Civil Code or the Law on the Protection of Women's Rights and Interests, which is obviously particularly unfair to the party who directly raises multiple children after divorce,

[24] W. Wang, 'On the Treatment of Pension Insurance Expectancy Benefits in Divorce – Article 13 of Interpretation (III) of the Marriage Law as the Center' (2016) 2 *Journal of Dalian University of Technology (Social Science Edition)* 110.

and to elderly full-time family caregivers. A post-divorce support relief system should be added, specifically by drawing on the thrust of the German Civil Code, the Swiss Civil Code, and Article 308 of the Uniform Marriage and Divorce Act of the United States. The post-divorce support relief system for childcare, old age, disability or invalidity, unemployment, and compensation for human capital should be included in the post-divorce support relief system, and the eligible party should be able to request support from the other party, based on a lack of sufficient assets to meet his or her reasonable needs and the inability to support him- or herself, raise children through suitable employment or work away from home due to childcare. In addition, the factors to be considered in calculating the amount and duration of support include: (1) the financial resources of the spouse claiming support, including the shared community property, the ability to independently satisfy needs, and expenses concerning raising children living with one of the parties; (2) that spouse's need to obtain sufficient education or training to be able to find suitable gainful employment; (3) the standard of living enjoyed during the marriage; (4) the duration of the marriage; (5) the age and physical and mental condition of the spouse claiming support; (6) the ability of the spouse claiming support to meet his or her own needs while meeting the other party's ability to pay; and (7) when a professional degree is not counted as marital property at the time of divorce.

In summary, the current provisions of the Civil Code and the Law on the Protection of Women's Rights and Interests in China are not equal in substance with respect to the scope of property that can be divided among female family caregivers in the event of divorce, and in terms of the principles of division of property, and they are unjust to female family caregivers.

CZECH REPUBLIC

ON COUPLES IN DE FACTO UNIONS IN THE CZECH REPUBLIC

Zdeňka Králíčková*

Résumé

L'article est relatif aux couples de concubins, notamment ceux formés par un homme et une femme. Il cherche à montrer les différences entre les droits et devoirs des concubins et ceux des époux ou encore des couples de même sexe liés par un partenariat enregistré. Les conventions entre concubins étant rares, l'article s'attache à étudier l'applicabilité aux couples de concubins des règles juridiques inscrites dans les différentes parties du code civil tchèque pendant leur relation, après la rupture de la concubinage ou encore lors du décès de l'un d'eux. L'article insiste sur l'absence de différence entre les enfants nés hors mariage et ceux nés dans le cadre du mariage. Dès lors que la filiation est juridiquement établie, il n'y a aucune discrimination des mères et pères non mariées vis-à-vis de leurs enfants. Ils sont tous titulaires de l'autorité parentale. En outre, il existe des dispositions spéciales qui protègent la partie la plus faible: la mère non mariée peut obtenir un droit sur les biens du père de l'enfant pendant une période raisonnable et dans des limites adéquates. Toutefois, la protection de la partie dite faible dans les unions de fait est beaucoup plus limitée que celle existant dans les couples mariés et de partenaires enregistrés.

* zdenka.kralickova@law.muni.cz.

1. INTRODUCTION

In 2022 the Czech Republic will be reaching the tenth anniversary of the passing of the new Civil Code in 2012. When it came into effect in 2014, the *International Survey of Family Law* published a comprehensive study on the starting points, values and most important changes of the new main legal source of Czech family law.[1] It was also stressed there that all kinds of families are protected by the legal order of the Czech Republic, mainly thanks to the Convention for the Protection of Human Rights and Freedoms, as these human rights are guaranteed by the right to respect for private and family life,[2] and thanks to the Czech Charter, which automatically provides protection for all families, for example it protects both families established under statutory provisions and de facto (Article 32(1) Charter).[3]

However, the current Civil Code, similarly to previous acts, only provides for marriage for people of the opposite sex in its Book Two (Family Law).[4] Besides that, there are general principles set out in Book One (General Part), where it is stressed that 'family, parenthood and marriage enjoy special legal protection.'[5]

Regarding other legal sources of Czech family law, there is the Act on Registered Partnership from 2006, which regulates the relationship status between same-sex partners.[6] For political reasons, registered partnership was

---

1 See Z. Králíčková, 'New Family Law in the Czech Republic: Back to Traditions and Towards Modern Trends' in B. Atkin (ed.). *The International Survey of Family Law*, Jordan Publishing, 2014, pp. 71–95.

2 See the Convention for the Protection of Human Rights and Freedoms, published as Communication No. 209/1992 Sb. in the Czech Republic, Art. 8.

3 See the Charter of Fundamental Rights and Freedoms, Constitutional Act No. 2/1993 Sb., Art. 32(1), as amended.

4 Act No. 89/2012 Sb., Civil Code (CC), as amended. An English translation of original text is available at: <http://obcanskyzakonik.justice.cz/index.php/home/zakony-a-stanoviska/preklady>, last accessed 10.12.2021 (even though the Civil Code has been amended, the amendments are not relevant to the issue in question). As for transsexuals, the new Civil Code regulates that the change of sex of a person occurs at the time of the surgical operation disabling the reproduction functions and changing the sex organs (see s. 29 CC). It is presumed that the day of the change of sex is the day recorded in the certificate issued by the provider of health services. The change of sex does not affect the personal status of a man/woman or their personal and property situation; their marriage or registered partnership ceases to exist, however. Details are included in Act No. 373/2011 Sb., on Specific Health Services, as amended. There was also a pending draft before the elections in 2021 aiming to introduce an administrative change of gender.

5 Compare with s. 3(2)(b) CC.

6 Act No. 115/2006 Sb., on Registered Partnership, as amended.

not included in the new Civil Code, although it had been planned and drawn up by the main creators of the new Civil Code.[7] Despite the enactment of the Civil Code, the Czech approach to family recognition remains a matter of intense debate. The fact that two 'opposite' drafts were introduced in the Parliament of the Czech Republic in 2021 illustrates the continuing clash of values.

The first pending draft may be seen by some as progressive and modern, while others will view it as a step undermining traditional family values. According to this pending draft lodged by a group of members of Parliament, the concept of marriage as regulated by the Civil Code should be changed radically.[8] It is stated currently that '[m]arriage is a permanent union of a man and a woman formed in a manner provided by this Act.'[9] Should the pending draft be passed, the relevant section would state: '[m]arriage is a permanent union of two people formed in a manner provided by this Act.'[10]

The second pending draft lodged by a different group of members of Parliament suggested an amendment to the Charter of Fundamental Rights and Freedoms[11] with the aim of strengthening the position of the family based on traditional marriages. As was generally mentioned above, the Charter provides that '[p]arenthood and the family are under the protection of the law.'[12] According to the draft amendment, the new version should state that '[p]arenthood, the family and marriage as a union of a man and a woman are under the protection of the law.' If this amendment were to be passed, it would probably ban any future changes to the Civil Code along the lines proposed in the first pending draft. In other words, marriage would remain as 'the traditional concept'.

The question is whether there will be the political will to pass one of the above-mentioned proposed bills after the recent election in autumn 2021.

---

7 See K. Eliáš and M. Zuklínová, *Návrh občanského zákoníku* (Draft for the Civil Code), Ministry of Justice, Spring 2005; and K. Eliáš and M. Zuklínová, *Principy a východiska nového kodexu soukromého práva* (Principles and Starting Points of the New Code of Private Law), Linde, 2001.

8 Parliament of the Czech Republic, Chamber of Deputies, Parliamentary Term No. VIII, Draft No. 201/0.

9 S. 655 CC.

10 The pending draft did not intend to change the current regulation on affiliation.

11 Parliament of the Czech Republic, Chamber of Deputies, Parliamentary Term No. VIII, Draft No. 211/0.

12 Art. 32(1) Charter.

With regard to de facto unions, there is no special regulation of them in the Czech legal order. This issue has not ever been discussed seriously and there have not been any pending drafts to 'improve' the situation of de facto cohabitees since the passing of the new Civil Code. Moreover, couples living in de facto unions enjoy less protection than under previous regulations in some respects.

A relevant statistical picture of de facto unions does not exist. Census figures provide the best available data, but the reports may not be accurate or complete. The question is how significant the figures from the census actually are. The census from 2011 showed quite a small number of people living in de facto cohabitation. The last census, which was conducted in 2021, showed an increase in de facto unions.[13]

However, the statistics on the proportion of children born outside of marriage are more reliable. There are many of them in the Czech Republic these days: almost a half of all births.[14] The following chart by the Czech Statistical Office shows the increasing proportion of children born out of wedlock after the fall of the old political regime in 1989.[15] Again, it is difficult to rely on such statistical data for a full picture. The chart below does not say anything about the parents of these children. Some of them have both legal parents, but some of them do not: fatherhood has not legally been established. It is generally known that some children born out of wedlock live with both parents and some live only with one of them – very often with their mothers.

---

13 See Census Course, *Census 2021*, available at: <https://www.scitani.cz/csu/scitani2021/recent-news>, last accessed 28.11.2021 (noting that '[t]he Census began at midnight on March 26–27, 2021.' According to the webpage of the Czech Statistical Office, 'the Census is a traditional component of the statistics in each country. It has been held in our territory since 1869 and takes place every 10 years, as in most other countries. Thanks to this, the results make it possible to compare the current state of our country with the past as well as the rest of the world … In combination with data on education, housing or household composition, the results make it possible to analyse the situation of recent graduates, single people … or people without income for example').

14 It might be interesting that during 'communist times', former Czechoslovakia used to have quite a low rate of children born out of wedlock (only 5–8%) and there were a lot of marriages. Cohabitation without marriage as a family model was used mainly by divorced or widowed people. For relevant data and previous family law see M. Hrušáková, *The International Encyclopaedia of Laws*, Kluwer Law International, 2002, and M. Hrušáková and L. Westphalová, *The International Encyclopaedia of Laws*, Kluwer Law International, 2nd ed., 2011.

15 See Czech Statistical Office, *Proportion of Live Births Outside Marriage*, available at: <https://www.czso.cz/csu/czso/proportion-of-live-births-outside-marriage-1950-2019>, last accessed 28.11.2021.

Figure 1. Proportion of live births outside marriage, 1950–2019

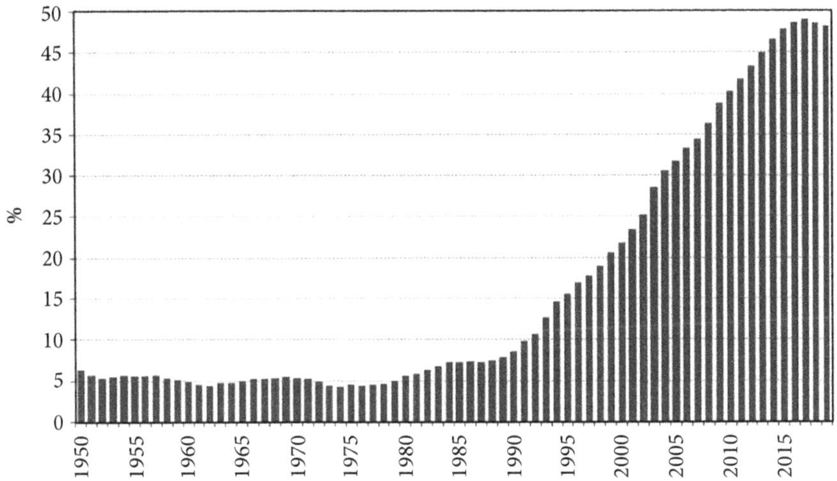

Source: Czech Statistical Office, *Proportion of Live Births Outside Marriage*, available at: <https://www.czso.cz/csu/czso/proportion-of-live-births-outside-marriage-1950-2019>, last accessed 28.11.2021.

One does not have to have a degree in sociology to know that living in cohabitation has become more popular than marriage among the youngest couples nowadays. Due to the considerable changes over the past decades, the portrait of the family has been changing, which is, of course, reflected in the legal orders of different countries.[16]

The Czech Republic is influenced by European developments. However, there are many questions which should be answered by demographers, sociologists and other professionals, including lawyers. One of those questions is whether the laws of the Czech Republic adequately reflect the changes in the family and whether there should be more legal innovations in the future in the light of, for instance, the Principles of European Family Law regarding the Property, Maintenance and Succession Rights and Duties of Couples in de facto Unions[17]

---

16 See M. Antokolskaia (ed.), *Convergence and Divergence of Family Law in Europe*, Intersentia, 2007; G. Douglas and N. Lowe, *The Continuing Evolution of Family Law*, Jordan Publishing Limited, 2009; C. McGlynn, *Families and European Union. Law, Politics and Pluralism*, Cambridge University Press, 2006; and J.M. Scherpe (ed.), *European Family Law*, Vols. I–IV, Edward Elgar Publishing, 2016.

17 See K. Boele-Woelki et al., *Principles of European Family Law regarding the Property, Maintenance and Succession Rights and Duties of Couples in de facto Unions*, Intersentia, 2019.

of the Commission on European Family Law (CEFL).[18] It should be noted that these Principles are the fourth project by the CEFL, following the Principles of European Family Law regarding Divorce and Maintenance Between Former Spouses, the Principles regarding Parental Responsibilities, and the Principles regarding Property Relations Between Spouses.[19]

Despite the fact that the new Civil Code expressly protects the family established by marriage, it should be observed that informal unions of a man and a woman, or anyone, also enjoy protection in connection with the above-mentioned constitutional basis of the legal order. Besides that, there are some provisions set out in the new Civil Code that are applicable to de facto couples. The rest of the chapter is devoted to a discussion of all the Books of the new Civil Code, especially to the provisions which can be used by people living in de facto unions during their relationship, after the breakdown of the cohabitation or upon the death of one of the cohabitees.[20]

2. BOOK ONE: GENERAL PART

As was stressed in the introduction, the new Civil Code expressly protects the family established by marriage. But there are two important sections that should be mentioned concerning cohabitees. First of all, there is the 'concept of close persons' based on three definitions.[21] According to that law:

1. a close person is a relative in the direct line, sibling and spouse or a partner under the Act of Registered Partnership;
2. other persons in a familial or similar relationship shall, in relation to each other, be considered to be close persons if the harm suffered by one of them is perceived as his or her own harm by the other;
3. persons related by affinity and persons permanently living together are also presumed to be close persons.

---

18 See Commission on European Family Law available at: <http://ceflonline.net/>, last accessed 12.11.2021.

19 See K. Boele-Woelki et al., *Principles of European Family Law regarding Divorce and Maintenance Between Former Spouses*, Intersentia, 2004; K. Boele-Woelki et al., *Principles of European Family Law regarding Parental Responsibilities*, Intersentia, 2007; and K. Boele-Woelki et al., *Principles of European Family Law regarding Property Relations between Spouses*, Intersentia, 2013.

20 For the first version see Z. Králíčková, 'The Missing Concept of Cohabitation of the Opposite Sex in de facto Unions in the Czech Republic', Paper presented at the conference 'Cohabitation in European Context' held at the Faculty of Law, Masaryk University, Brno, Czech Republic, in April 2021.

21 S. 22 CC.

The 'concept of close persons' is rather 'traditional'. There were similar definitions in previous legal regulations, both the Civil Codes from 1950 and 1964. This 'concept of close persons' is important for the whole legal order, for instance for penal law, administrative law, state benefits law, tax law, etc.

However, the 'concept of close persons' should be distinguished from the 'concept of persons sharing the same household', which is relevant for instance in housing law and succession law. There are many points of contact between the two legal concepts, which means that a close person is very often a person living with another in one household. In the other words, a cohabitee in a de facto union can enjoy rights from both areas of law.

Secondly, it is worth mentioning the provisions regulating 'running of a limitation period'.[22] The new Civil Code provides that between spouses a limitation period neither commences nor runs while the marriage lasts. This is 'traditional' wording. However, the new Civil Code provides as a novelty that this concept applies, by analogy, to mutual rights of 'persons sharing the same household',[23] which is rather revolutionary, but still is not widely known and is rarely used by cohabitees.

3. BOOK TWO: FAMILY LAW

Due to the quite limited concept of family as being based on marriage regulated in the new Civil Code, there are no articles there that would establish mutual rights and duties between the cohabitees; for example, there is no duty to help each other, no community property, no protection of the family dwelling, no concept of common household goods and no mutual maintenance duty by operation of law. Unfortunately, there are not often property contracts between cohabitees, which causes a lot of problems for the so-called weaker party upon dissolution of the de facto relationship.

However, as there is no discrimination against children born out of wedlock, the rights and duties of the parents of any child are equal. It should be mentioned that if an unmarried man and an unmarried woman have a child together, they are both principal holders of parental responsibility by operation of law without being discriminated against by comparison with married parents of a minor child. However, parenthood must be legally established. There are no differences between the children at all in neither the personal nor property spheres in the Czech legal order.

---

22 S. 646 CC.

23 Besides, this provision extends the rules on a person represented and his or her legal representative, on a ward and his or her guardian and on a person under tutorship and his or her tutor.

Czech family law traditionally protects property claims of an unmarried mother of a child against the child's father or presumed father. There were always relevant provisions in previous Family Law Codes from 1949 and 1963, and even in one from 1811.[24] The new Civil Code regulates '[m]aintenance and support, and provision for the payment of certain costs for an unmarried mother.'[25] It provides that if the child's mother is not married to the child's father, the child's father shall provide her with maintenance for two years from the birth of the child and with a reasonable contribution to cover the costs associated with pregnancy and childbirth.[26] Besides that a court may, on the application of a pregnant woman, order the man whose paternity is presumed to provide her with an amount needed for her maintenance and a contribution to cover the costs associated with pregnancy and childbirth in advance. And in addition, a court may, on the application of a pregnant woman, also order the man whose paternity is presumed to provide in advance an amount needed for the maintenance of the child for the period in which the woman would be entitled to maternity leave as an employee under another legal regulation. This would be 28 weeks, and in the case of siblings or more children, 37 weeks.[27] It should be added that cohabitees cannot adopt their partners' children nor can cohabitees jointly adopt another child. Cohabitees also cannot become foster parents. On the other hand, in terms of the law against domestic violence, 'anybody' can seek protection. Cohabitees are thus not excluded from the regulation.[28]

4. BOOK THREE: PROPERTY RIGHTS AND SUCCESSION

As was mentioned in the introduction, there is no community property between people in de facto unions, no protection of family dwellings and no concept of common household goods in comparison with married couples. If people in a de facto union acquire a property together, there can only be co-ownership with shares on the same terms as non-cohabitants. Provided they have not agreed otherwise, the new Civil Code states that the shares of the cohabitees are equal.[29]

---

24 See above n. 14.

25 See s. 920 CC.

26 See ss. 910 ff. CC (holding that regarding maintenance towards the child, both of the child's parents have a duty to provide maintenance and the child has the right to the same living standard as his or her parents until he or she reaches the capacity to provide maintenance for himself or herself).

27 See s. 195(1) of Act No 262/2006 Sb., Labour Code, as amended.

28 See ss. 751 ff. and 3021 CC; see also Act No. 292/2013 Sb., on Special Civil Proceedings, ss. 400 ff. (interim proceedings on protection against domestic violence).

29 See s. 1122(3) CC.

Regarding the rights of a surviving cohabitee, his or her situation is in practice rather weak as there is seldom a will or an inheritance contract. The rights of the surviving person are protected only by the 'concept of persons sharing the same household'. It must be stressed that anybody can be such a person. The new Civil Code mentions 'persons sharing the same household' in two provisions defining heirs of the second and the third class. Cohabitees can never be an heir of the first class, where only spouses and children can inherit. If there is a child in a cohabitation relationship, he or she 'takes all'.[30]

Regarding the second class of heirs, the law stipulates that if the decedent's descendants do not inherit, this class includes the spouse, the decedent's parents, and 'those who lived with the decedent in the common household' for at least one year before his or her death and, as a result, cared for the common household or were dependent for maintenance on the decedent.[31] The second class of heirs inherit equally. However, the spouse shall always inherit at least half of the decedent's estate. The surviving cohabitee can never be the only heir in the second class of heirs. He or she falls to the third class.

The law regulating the third class of heirs provides that if neither the spouse nor any of the parents inherit, the decedent's siblings and 'those who lived with the decedent in the common household' for at least one year before his or her death and, as a result, cared for the common household or were dependent for maintenance on the decedent inherit equally in the third class of heirs.[32]

To summarise, in order to inherit the surviving cohabitee must prove many details from his or her shared life with the decedent during the succession proceedings, mainly regarding the existence and duration of the de facto union, etc.

Additionally there is the concept of a 'forced heir' – someone who inherits even though the decedent left a will that did not provide for that person. Forced heirs include the decedent's children and, if they do not inherit, their descendants, for example the grandchildren, etc. If a forced heir is a minor, he or she must inherit at least three-quarters of his or her statutory inheritance share. If a forced heir is an adult, he or she must inherit at least a quarter of his or her statutory inheritance share.[33]

However, for couples living in de facto unions, another new provision might be useful. The new Civil Code provides that a surviving pregnant cohabitee has the right to limited maintenance from the inheritance; the mother of the decedent's child for six weeks postpartum has the same rights.[34] The protection

30 See s. 1635 CC.
31 See s. 1636 CC.
32 See s. 1637(1) CC.
33 See s. 1643 CC.
34 See s. 1666(1) CC.

of cohabitees in this field is the same as the protection of a surviving spouse, who has the right to fair maintenance from the decedent's estate for six weeks after the death of his or her spouse; if a widow is pregnant, she has the right to fair maintenance until the end of the sixth week postpartum.[35]

Additionally, it is provided that if a surviving spouse has been denied statutory inheritance or his or her statutory inheritance has been reduced, the surviving spouse is entitled to the necessary provision for life until he or she remarries, provided that he or she otherwise lacks such provision and is unable to provide for himself or herself; in this manner, however, he or she may not get more from the decedent's estate than what half of his or her statutory inheritance share would have been.[36] However, a spouse who, without serious reasons, did not share the family household with the decedent, a spouse lacking the capacity to be an heir, or a spouse who renounced or refused inheritance is not entitled to the necessary provision for life.

5. BOOK FOUR: OBLIGATIONS

The new Civil Code recognises private autonomy, in particular the freedom to contract. The partners in de facto unions may in principle conclude any agreements before and during their cohabitation and after the separation. There are almost no limits and no provision for any authority to scrutinise the agreement. As mentioned before, unfortunately, there are seldom property contracts between the cohabitees, which causes a lot of problems for the so-called weaker party upon dissolution of the de facto relationship.

Regarding family dwellings, there are no special provisions that would protect the situation of a surviving partner living in a de facto union in a flat rented by the deceased lessee. The new Civil Code provides rather limited general rules in provisions titled 'Consequences of the Death of a Lessee'.[37] It holds that if a lessee dies and there is no joint lease for the apartment, the lease passes to 'a member of the lessee's household' who lived in the apartment on the day of the lessee's death and has no apartment of his or her own. If that person is a cohabitee, the lease passes to him or her only if the lessor consents to that. Here we can see a big problem for cohabitees due to a lower level of protection than under previous regulations. It must be mentioned that the law also provides that, after its passage, the lease for an apartment shall end no later than two years from the date of the passage of the lease. This does not apply if the person to whom the lease passed has reached the age of 70 by the date of passage

35 Ibid.

36 S. 1666(2) CC.

37 See s. 2279 CC.

of the lease. Likewise, this does not apply if the person to whom the lease passed has not reached the age of 18 on the date of passage of the lease; in such a case, the lease shall end no later than the date on which the person reaches the age of 20, unless the lessee and the lessor agree otherwise.

6. CONCLUSION

People of the opposite sex can enter into marriage and enjoy the 'standard' catalogue of rights married couples are entitled to. People of the same sex can enter into a registered partnership and receive more limited protection under the law, especially in the case of the death of one of the partners. De facto couples are not allowed to enjoy either statutory personal rights or property rights like spouses or registered partners. As there is almost no regulation of the rights and duties of cohabitees, the situation of the so-called weaker party is rather difficult. There is a lack of legal certainty, especially in families with minor children, when the de facto unit breaks down.

However, it is not easy to strike a fair balance between the private autonomy of those who form a de facto union and between the protection of the so-called weaker party and the welfare of families not based on marriage. Should the legislature respect the autonomy of the persons who 'refuse' 'official and formal' marital or registered partnership status, or should the lawmaker associate substantial legal consequences with de facto unmarried unions? There are rarely property agreements, inheritance contracts and wills between unmarried persons, which is to the detriment of the so-called weaker party, i.e. in particular those who, following the de facto separation or death of the 'main breadwinner', were taking care of minor children and therefore do not have sufficient independent sources of livelihood and the possibility of supporting themselves.

It is generally known that the legal orders of European states are very different. Only optimists can speak about European standards in this field. However, we can see the first steps towards spontaneous harmonisation of the rules regulating the situation of couples living in de facto unions, taken mainly thanks to the case law of the European Court of Human Rights and the Principles of European Family Law created by the academics involved in the project of the Commission on European Family Law.[38] It is uncertain how Czech legislators will respond to unmarried cohabitation. One can agree with the view that the new Civil Code should cover in principle all private law matters, including family law, as

[38] For more see Z. Králíčková, 'Changes in Czech Family Law in Light of the Principles of European Family Law' (2021) 1(1) *Law, Identity and Values* 85–98.

it is customary everywhere in countries with comparable legal environments.[39] On the other hand, the autonomy of the will of the free person must be respected. In private law, the balance between values, harmony, the protection of the so-called weaker party and the interests of the family as a whole, whatever form it may take, must always be sought.

In my view, the Czech lawmaker should rethink the concept of protection of families not based on marriage and 'improve' at least the provisions regarding family dwellings in the Civil Code, especially to strengthen the right of a surviving cohabitee as 'a member of the lessee's household' to make passing on a lease more favourable. The stability of the new Civil Code is undoubtedly valuable; however, the standard of protection of couples in de facto unions in the Czech Republic is in some respects even weaker than in the previous legislation, the Civil Code from 1964.

[39] See M. Zuklínová, 'Budoucí občanský zákoník a rodinné parvo' (The Future Civil Code and the Family Law) (2003) 1/2 *Acta Universitatis Carolinae, Iuridica* 141 (addressing theoretical questions and starting points).

ENGLAND AND WALES

ABORTION IN ENGLAND AND WALES

The Ethical Challenge

Mary Welstead

Résumé

Dans le cadre de l'enquête internationale de l'ISFL de cette année, j'ai choisi d'examiner sept affaires qui illustrent le fait que, malgré la facilité d'obtenir un avortement en Angleterre et au Pays de Galles, il existe toujours un débat, dans les tribunaux et en-dehors, sur les questions éthiques complexes qui sont en jeu.

Dans ce débat, les termes « fœtus », « enfant » ou « enfant à naître » ont tous été utilisés de manière interchangeable pour désigner l'être *in utero*. Le choix du terme utilisé peut refléter la position éthique d'une personne sur l'avortement ou indiquer qu'avant la naissance, la loi actuelle ne reconnaît pas le fœtus comme une personne juridique. Compte tenu de cette absence de reconnaissance juridique, et dans le souci de rester neutre sur la question de l'interruption volontaire de grossesse, j'ai utilisé le terme « fœtus » tout au long de cet article, excepté lorsqu'une autre expression a été utilisée dans les cas étudiés.

In this year's International Survey, I have chosen to examine seven cases which illustrate that, in spite of the ease with which an abortion may be obtained in England and Wales, there remains an ongoing debate, both in and outside of the courts, on the complex ethical issues involved.[1]

In this debate, the terms foetus, child or unborn child have all been used interchangeably to refer to the being in utero. The term used may reflect a person's ethical stance on abortion or may be indicative of the fact that prior to birth the current law does not recognise the foetus as a legal being. Given this lack of legal recognition, and in an effort to remain neutral on the issue of abortion, I have used the term foetus throughout this chapter except where an alternative expression has been used in the cases under consideration.

1. THE LAW: ABORTION REMAINS A CRIME

In spite of the generous provisions of the Abortion Act 1967 (see below), the Offences against the Person Act 1861, sections 58 and 59 remain in force and provide, respectively, that it is a criminal offence to procure an abortion by way of drugs or other means, or to procure drugs, or other means, to bring about an abortion. It is, however, rare for criminal proceedings to be brought under these provisions.

The Infant Life (Preservation) Act 1929 provides that any person:

> who with intent to destroy the life of a child capable of being born alive, by any wilful act causes a child to die before it has an existence independent of its mother, shall be guilty of felony, to wit, of child destruction, and shall be liable on conviction thereof on indictment to penal servitude for life.

---

1 See L. Ewbank and D. Maguire, 'Understanding Trends in Use of Abortion Services in England: An Exploratory Briefing', *The Kings Fund*, September 2021; see also <https://www.gov.uk/government/statistics/abortion-statistics-for-england-and-wales-2020/guide-to-abortion-statistics-england-and-wales-2020>, last accessed 25.04.2022.

No offence will be committed if the act which caused the child's death was done in good faith to save the mother's life. For the purposes of the Act, any woman whose pregnancy lasted for 28 weeks or more is considered to be pregnant with a child who is capable of being born alive.

Section 1(1) of the Abortion Act 1967 (the 1967 Act), as amended by the Human Fertilisation and Embryology Act 1990 (HFEA 1990), provides that no offence will be committed when a pregnancy is terminated by a registered medical practitioner following the opinion of two registered medical practitioners that:

(a) … the pregnancy has not exceeded its twenty-fourth week[2] and that the continuance of the pregnancy would involve risk, greater than if the pregnancy were terminated, of injury to the physical or mental health of the pregnant woman or any existing children of her family; or
(b) that the termination is necessary to prevent grave permanent injury to the physical or mental health of the pregnant woman; or
(c) that the continuance of the pregnancy would involve risk to the life of the pregnant woman, greater than if the pregnancy were terminated; or
(d) that there is a substantial risk that if the child were born it would suffer from such physical or mental abnormalities as to be seriously handicapped.

It is worthy of note that section 1(1)(a) and (b) makes no provision to take into account the effect of the pregnancy on the physical or mental health of the prospective father of the child, or on the prospective child who falls within the ambit of section 1(1)(d).

Section 4 of the 1967 Act provides a conscientious objection clause which allows a doctor to refuse to participate in any aspect of abortion except where the mother's life is in danger, or she is likely to suffer a grave injury. Doctors who object to treating a woman who wishes to have an abortion must explain to her their objection and make arrangements for her to see a colleague who has no such objections.[3]

2. THE RIGHT TO ABORT A PREGNANCY: COERCIVE BEHAVIOUR

Under the law of the jurisdiction, only the pregnant woman has a right to make the decision to undergo an abortion, provided a woman is able to meet

---

2 Amended from 28 weeks by the HFEA 1990; for a discussion of the precise meaning of the 24-week rule, see *R (on the application of British Pregnancy Advisory Service) v. The Secretary of State for Health and Social Care* [2020] EWCA Civ 355.

3 See the advice of the British Medical Association, available at: <https://www.bma.org.uk/advice-and-support/ethics/personal-ethics/expressing-your-personal-beliefs-as-a-doctor>, last accessed 25.04.2022.

requirements of the 1967 Act and is deemed to have mental capacity to consent to an abortion. The legislation makes no provision for the prospective father to demand that the woman has the pregnancy terminated or continues to full term.

In 2015, a new offence of controlling or coercive behaviour in an intimate or family relationship came into being under section 76(1) of the Serious Crime Act 2015 (the 2015 Act). Coercive behaviour is defined as conduct in which one person forces or compels another, with whom he or she is in an intimate relationship, to do or not to do something or to act or not to act in a certain way. It may involve violence, threats and intimidation. The behaviour must be either continuous or repeated and carried out by the defendant who knew or ought to have known that it would have a serious effect on the victim's everyday life by causing fear, alarm or distress.

The new offence may prove to be helpful to victims where an attempt is made to force them to abort or not abort a pregnancy.[4] The offence was discussed in *F v. M* (2021),[5] a fact-finding decision. F was a young woman from a British Hindu family who had a relationship with a young Muslim man, M, by whom she became pregnant. He did not want her to abort the pregnancy because he wished to marry her for the purpose of obtaining British citizenship and believed that she would be more likely to agree to marriage if they had a child together. He contacted the police and gave false information that the woman, who had returned home to stay with her family, was in danger of an honour-based killing by her parents. The police accepted the accuracy of this information and visited the family. Hayden J. commented: 'It is alarming how readily this appears to have been accepted as a genuine concern by the police and others. It is entirely groundless.' F returned to M and decided not to have an abortion and gave birth. She did not wish to have a second child soon after the birth of her first one but M using sexual coercion succeeded in impregnating F. She went ahead and gave birth once more but left M and returned to her parents. F awaits a decision on his application to have contact with both children.

In *R v. Chilvers (Rev. 1)* (2021),[6] a man tried to coerce his girlfriend into having an abortion when she became pregnant for a second time after they had both agreed that the first pregnancy should be terminated. The woman refused to abort the second pregnancy and the man finally accepted her decision and she went ahead and gave birth. When she became pregnant for the third time, she made secret arrangements to terminate the pregnancy. She cancelled her

---

4 See *AK (A Child) (Fact Finding)* [2021] EWFC B73, which illustrates that coercive behaviour claims are not easily proven.

5 See *F v. M* [2021] EWFC 4.

6 See *R v. Chilvers* [2021] EWCA Crim 1311.

initial appointment at the clinic after the man became aware of her plans but eventually went ahead and underwent a termination. When the man discovered what she had done, he became very angry and abused her sexually, physically and verbally. The woman killed their two-year-old child and attempted to hang herself. She was diagnosed with dissociative disorder and amnesia and subsequently pleaded guilty to the manslaughter of the child on the grounds of diminished responsibility. She received a prison sentence of 15 years. The man was found guilty of coercive behaviour throughout the relationship and received a prison sentence of 18 months.

3. PREGNANT CHILDREN AND ABORTION

3.1. GILLICK COMPETENT

In *Gillick v. West Norfolk and Wisbech AHA (1985)*,[7] the House of Lords, in a majority judgment, held that minor children below the age of 16 could consent to medical treatment if they understood fully the treatment proposed, and their parents could not object to their decision.[8] Such children are generally referred to as being 'Gillick competent' and may consent to having an abortion.[9]

3.2. THE FACTS IN *X (A CHILD)* (2014)[10]

Sir James Munby, the President of the Family Division at that time, heard an urgent application to terminate the pregnancy of a girl who was 13 years old and mentally impaired. She was about 14 weeks pregnant and, at first, said that she did not want to have an abortion. The prospective father was aged 14.

---

7 See *Gillick v. West Norfolk and Wisbech AHA* [1985] UKHL 7.

8 See *A (A Child)* [2014] EWHC 1445 (Fam), in which Mostyn J. held that a 13-year-old had sufficient understanding and intelligence to decide whether or not to have an abortion. Were she to decide not to, he expected that her family and Social Services would give her considerable support. Should she go through with a termination, her family would need to assist her 'after what is inevitably going to be an unpleasant and traumatic experience.'

9 Under patient confidentiality rules, once a Gillick competent child has made a decision, parents may not be involved in it without the child's consent although a child will be encouraged to speak with their parents and seek their cooperation. Children over the age of 16 years are permitted to give their consent to, or to refuse to consent to, medical treatment. The Family Law Reform Act 1969 s. 8(1) provides that: 'The consent of a minor who has attained the age of sixteen years to any surgical, medical or dental treatment which, in the absence of consent, would constitute a trespass to his person, shall be as effective as it would be if he were of full age; and where a minor has by virtue of this section given an effective consent to any treatment it shall not be necessary to obtain any consent for it from his parent or guardian.'

10 See *Re X* [2014] EWHC 1871 (Fam); see also *A (A Child)* [2014] EWHC 1445 (Fam).

3.3. THE JUDGMENT

The President pointed out that although two doctors were satisfied that the girl met the requirements of the 1967 Act, it was for the court to decide whether it would be in her best interests to authorise an abortion to be carried out against her wishes. The court, in the exercise of its inherent jurisdiction, had the power to order the use of restraint and physical force to compel the girl to undergo an abortion.[11] However, only the most compelling of arguments, such as a clear risk to the mother's life at that time, or her long-term health, could justify such an order contrary to the girl's wishes. The girl was mentally incapable of giving her consent in a legal sense, but the President maintained that her agreement, in a colloquial sense, was required. The President suggested that the term '*accepting*' of the termination captured what he believed to be required of the girl if the procedure were to go ahead.

The girl had an IQ of 54, the comprehension of a seven-year-old, and the vocabulary of a six-year-old. The psychiatrist described her as damaged and impaired and, for a good part of the time, out of control. Although healthy, the girl was physically immature. The psychiatrist was of the opinion that although the girl understood that an abortion would mean the death of her baby, she did not fully understand pregnancy and the process of giving birth. Her understanding of the actual responsibilities involved in having a child was very limited. The psychiatrist believed that if the pregnancy were to be ended, it would cause considerable harm to the girl. She would view it as an assault and a continuation of the pregnancy might have a less detrimental effect on her. The consultant obstetrician recommended that the abortion be carried out surgically under a general anaesthetic.

By the end of the hearing, the girl had expressed a wish, which had endured for two days, to have an abortion. The President made an order that she did not have the capacity to give a legal consent and, subject to her compliance and acceptance of the procedure, an abortion should be carried out.[12]

The President appeared to align his decision with respect to X's best interests with the requirements of the 1967 Act, stating that there had to be a compelling reason for him to order an abortion, against the girl's wishes, such as a clear risk to her life or health. Given the President's acceptance that the girl lacked the capacity to consent, her best interests could well have embraced a wider range of factors.[13] It would be interesting to speculate what compelling reason

[11] See *Re C (Detention: Medical Treatment)* [1997] 2 FLR 180; *Re PS (Incapacitated or Vulnerable Adult)* [2007] 2 FLR 1083.

[12] See also *Re X (A Child) (No. 2) An NHS Trust v. X* [2021] EWHC 65 (Fam); *A London NHS Trust v. KB & Anor* [2020] EWCOP 59.

[13] See e.g. *Aintree University Hospitals NHS Foundation Trust v. James* [2013] UKSC 67.

the President would have accepted in order to order the abortion had the girl not given her agreement in a 'colloquial sense'.

4. MENTALLY INCAPACITATED ADULTS

4.1. *RE AB* (TERMINATION OF PREGNANCY) (2019)[14]

In *Re AB* (2019), Lieven J. granted a National Health Service (NHS) Trust's application for an order to terminate the pregnancy of a mentally incapacitous woman on the ground that it was in her best interests to do so. Some two weeks later, the Court of Appeal overturned Lieven J.'s decision.[15]

4.1.1. The Facts

AB, a 24-year-old Nigerian woman, had been adopted soon after her birth by a midwife, CD, who worked in London. CD's sister lived in Nigeria and AB was left in her care. Twice a year, CD visited her sister and AB. At the age of 12, AB moved to London, where she lived primarily with her grandmother; CD spent significant periods of time with them. AB was developmentally retarded from birth and had a very low IQ, estimated to be between 35 and 49; she was educated in special schools. Her mental age was that of a six- to nine-year-old. AB's considerable behavioural difficulties had to be controlled by medication.

In 2017, on the death of her grandmother, AB was very distressed and went to live with CD, who arranged for her to be taken to Nigeria for five months. On her return to the UK, AB was found to be between 10 and 12 weeks pregnant but was unaware of the fact. Following psychiatric and social assessments, the professionals responsible for AB's antenatal care concluded that it would be in her best interests to undergo an abortion. The NHS Trust was concerned because AB's medication had had to be discontinued during the pregnancy. Furthermore, if the pregnancy went ahead, the local authority planned to apply for a care order prior to the birth and, at birth, the baby would be immediately removed from AB. Although AB had expressed a wish to have the baby, her social worker explained that her attitude to the pregnancy fluctuated: she had no understanding of the birth process or what would happen afterwards. She had no idea that she would be unable to live with the baby. She was also unaware of

14 See *Re AB* [2019] EWCOP 26.
15 See *Re AB* [2019] EWCA Civ 1215.

the potential impact on her mental health or the emotional and psychological consequence of having a baby, which for her was rather like having a nice doll.

Given AB's incapacity to consent, an application for the termination had to be made to the court.

CD was totally opposed to abortion and when AB was around 16 weeks pregnant, she took her daughter and her possessions to hospital. CD told those in charge that she was leaving AB in their care because she felt she could no longer look after her if the abortion were to go ahead; it would be against her beliefs. AB was placed in a residential unit by the authorities.

By the time the NHS Trust's application came before Lieven J., AB was almost 23 weeks pregnant, and close to the cut-off point of 24 weeks in section 1(1)(a) of the 1967 Act. CD told the judge that she would not have AB back to live with her if an order were to be made to terminate the pregnancy. Lieven J. deplored the fact that the application was being made so late in the day when the NHS Trust had been aware of the situation for two months. The judge acknowledged that the termination would be highly invasive and bewildering for AB because it would be carried out by caesarean under a general anaesthetic. However, she made the necessary order for AB to have her pregnancy terminated.

CD decided to appeal the decision with the support of the Official Solicitor who represented AB.

4.1.2. The Appeal

Counsel for CD maintained that in her analysis of AB's best interests, Lieven J.:

- had placed too great a weight on the fact that if the pregnancy were to continue, the local authority would remove the child immediately after the birth;
- had failed to carry out a detailed balancing exercise to determine AB's best interests by ignoring the requirement that there must be significant evidence that her life or her long-term health would be put at serious risk if the pregnancy were to continue; and
- had failed to have full regard to AB's wishes and feelings and/or her right to respect for her private and family life, under Article 8 of the European Convention on Human Rights 1950 (the Convention).[16]

The NHS Trust opposed the appeal.

---

[16] Counsel for CD had relied on the comment of Munby J. (as he then was) in *Re X* (2014), above n. 10, at p. 3, that in many cases, only the most compelling of arguments could justify terminating a pregnancy against a woman's will. Counsel interpreted this to mean that to order a termination without AB's consent, unless the stricter provisions of s. 1(1)(b) of the 1967 Act were met, would be a profound invasion of her Art. 8 rights.

4.1.3. *The Judgment*

The Court of Appeal heard the appeal urgently because of the 24-week cut-off point. It held that if the pregnancy of an incapacitated person was ordered to be terminated in accordance with the provisions of the 1967 Act, it would be a legitimate and proportionate interference with her Article 8(1) rights under the Convention. Article 8(2) of the Convention permits such an interference where it is for the protection of a person's health.[17]

A court's task in determining whether to grant an order for termination overlapped with the duty of the two doctors who had to decide whether a woman's circumstances fell within the provisions of the 1967 Act. However, the tasks were not identical; it remained the task of the court to decide whether the termination would be in the woman's best interests.[18]

4.1.3.1. The Mental Capacity Act 2005: The Best Interests Test

The Court of Appeal centred its decision on the provisions of section 4 of the Mental Capacity Act 2005 (MCA 2005), which provides guidance, albeit limited, on how a court should determine a person's best interests. The section states, inter alia, that in so far as is reasonably possible, the court must take into account: the incapacitated person's past and present wishes; her feelings and the beliefs and values that would be likely to influence her if she had capacity; any other factors that she would be likely to consider were she able to do so; and the views expressed by any person caring for the incapacitated person or who is interested in her welfare.[19]

In *Aintree University Hospitals NHS Foundation Trust v. James*,[20] Lady Hale explained that the advantage of the best interests test was that it placed the focus on the patient as an individual, rather than on the views of the medical experts alone. The court had to take into account all the circumstances of the patient, both medical and non-medical, and, although the test contained a strong element of substituted judgment by the court, it was not a substituted judgment test.

---

17 See *SB (a patient; capacity to consent to termination)* [2013] EWHC 1417 (COP).

18 See *Re X* (2014), above n. 10.

19 The MCA 2005 Code of Practice s. 5 provides further and rather confusing general guidance: 'Not all factors in the checklist will be relevant to all types of decisions or actions, and in many cases other factors will have to be considered as well, even though some of them may then not be found to be relevant.'

20 See *Aintree University Hospitals NHS Foundation Trust v. James* [2013] UKSC 67.

The Court of Appeal stressed that only the best interests of AB were under consideration and not those of the foetus.[21] However, the Court added, rather confusingly, that this did not mean that it should be unaware of the fact that the NHS Trust's application sought to end an otherwise viable pregnancy. An order for termination should only be granted if there was clear evidence that it would be in AB's best interests and not on a 'fine balance of uncertainties'.

4.1.3.2. The Evidence of the Professionals

The Court of Appeal accepted that Lieven J. had been entitled to take into account the evidence of the Trust's medical experts who were responsible for AB. They were all in agreement that, on balance, termination of AB's pregnancy was the right course of action. If the pregnancy went ahead, the baby would be removed at birth because AB was incapable of caring for a child. There was also a small risk of postpartum psychosis occurring, which would be a very serious mental illness. AB would require emergency psychiatric inpatient care for weeks or even months. This could trigger lifelong problems for her. Most of those who had experienced the condition remained very frightened and traumatised.

The Court held that Lieven J. had jumped to premature conclusions about the effects of a post-birth separation on AB. The judge had stated that were the pregnancy to continue and the baby removed immediately after the birth, it might result in a double trauma for AB. If the baby were handed into the care of CD by the local authority, AB would lose not only her baby but also her home with CD because in the light of her behavioural difficulties, it would be too high a risk to allow AB to live in the same home as the baby. According to the Court of Appeal, this latter eventuality remained most uncertain. The local authority and the police were in the process of investigating how AB had become pregnant and any assessment of CD as a carer for the baby would involve a close look at her behaviour in caring for AB. In particular, CD's conduct in handing AB over to the hospital, without any preparation for such a distressing event, would be a relevant factor in such an assessment.

4.1.3.3. AB's Wishes and Feelings

The Court of Appeal was critical of Lieven J.'s finding that AB's likely reaction to a termination was 'one of the real unknowns in the case'. CD, who knew AB best, had stated that she believed AB would be very upset at the loss of

21 See *Vo v. France* (2005) 10 EHRR 12; *Paton v. British Pregnancy Advisory Service Trustees* [1979] QB 276; *Paton v. United Kingdom* (1980) 3 EHRR 408.

her baby. AB's social worker, in spite of her views on AB's ability to cope with the pregnancy, supported her in her wish to have a baby, as did the Official Solicitor.

The Court of Appeal stated that the fact that Lieven J. was unable to give AB's views a great deal of weight did not mean that they should be disregarded, and it was a significant omission on the judge's part to do so. In *Wye Valley NHS Trust v. B* (2015),[22] Peter Jackson J. (as he then was) maintained that as the MCA 2005 and the Convention made clear:

> a conclusion that a person lacks decision-making capacity is not an 'off-switch' for his rights and freedoms. To state the obvious, the wishes and feelings, beliefs, and values of people with a mental disability are as important to them as they are to anyone else and may even be more important. It would therefore be wrong in principle to apply any automatic discount to their point of view.

4.1.3.4. Beliefs and Values

The Court of Appeal held that it would be mere speculation to consider the beliefs and values which would have been likely to influence AB had she been mentally capacitous. AB had been brought up in a community strongly opposed to abortion and, in the right circumstances, that could have been a significant factor in assessing AB's best interests. However, because AB had never been capacitous, there was no direct evidence about her actual beliefs and values. It was impossible to say, had she been capacitous, whether she might have lost her faith or rebelled against her community by the time she became an adult. The Court held that Lieven J.'s judgment could not be criticised for failing to mention such matters.

4.1.3.5. Consultation with Others

Apart from the professionals, the only other person who was consulted about AB was CD. Lieven J. had referred to the fact that CD was a devout Roman Catholic who was completely opposed to abortion. CD maintained that it was not spoken about in her community and there was a stigma attached to those who had had a termination. However, the Court of Appeal, rather surprisingly, viewed CD's evidence as more focused on AB's interests than on her own religious views. She believed that AB would be very upset were she to have a termination and did not know what had happened to the baby.

---

22 See *Wye Valley NHS Trust v. B* [2015] EWCOP 60.

4.1.3.6. The Court of Appeal's Criticism of Lieven J.'s Conclusions about AB's Best Interests

Lieven J. had stated that her task was to focus on AB's best interests as an individual and not on:

> societal views on termination, the rights of disabled people in general (including as set out in the United Nations Convention on the Rights of Persons with Disabilities) or some concept of the benefits of having a genetic child and being a biological mother.[23]

The judge had found it impossible to assess accurately the risks to AB if the pregnancy continued, or the emotional and psychological risks of termination. There was a real danger of everyone imposing their own moral or philosophical views about abortion onto AB, whom Lieven J. suspected was unable to understand concepts of choice, guilt and cultural norms.

The Court of Appeal stressed the importance of the underlying ethos of the MCA 2005, which demands that those making decisions on behalf of incapacitous persons must respect and maximise their individuality and autonomy where possible. Viewed objectively, it might be regarded as an unwise choice for AB to give birth to a baby with whom she would not be allowed to interact. However, in so far as AB was able to understand her situation, she wanted to give birth to the baby; those who knew her best believed that to be in her best interests.

AB's feelings were important and unique to her. Lieven J. should have factored them into her balancing exercise rather than concentrating on the views of the medical experts, which were based upon uncertainties. Their conclusions were insufficient to justify what would be a profound invasion of AB's rights by terminating such an advanced pregnancy against her wishes.

In granting the appeal, the Court acknowledged Lieven J.'s very difficult position in that she had to make the decision after hearing oral evidence, and produce a written judgment, which was careful and well thought out, with the utmost urgency.

The consultation of those responsible for AB on her wishes and feelings must also be questioned. Their responses appeared to be more indicative of their beliefs and values than AB's wishes and feelings. CD had shown minimal concern for her daughter during her childhood. She had abandoned her to the care of the hospital during her pregnancy without any preparation for such a disturbing move, yet she was consulted about AB's wishes. AB's social worker

23 *Re AB* [2019] EWCOP 26, para. 51.

believed that AB had almost no understanding of pregnancy and birth and would be unable to play a part in the child's future. For AB, the idea of a baby resembled being given a doll which could be thrown on one side. Yet the social worker too maintained that AB wished to have the baby. The detailed attendance note prepared by the Official Solicitor's Agent shows a frightening lack of understanding by AB of pregnancy, birth and childcare, as well as confusion about her feelings with respect to termination; it is worthy of reading.[24] Yet the Court of Appeal took into account the views of these three people rather than those of the medical experts responsible for AB's physical and mental health. In fact, the Court appeared to underplay the effect on AB's health of a continuance of the pregnancy. Minimal attention was paid to the fact that AB's medication to control her behaviour had had to be discontinued because of the effect it might have on the foetus. There was no discussion of the effect of this discontinuation or how AB might cope with the remainder of her pregnancy, which was likely to be a very frightening experience for her.

4.2. A FINAL QUESTION

One must question how big a part the fact that AB was almost 24 weeks pregnant played, albeit *sub silentio*, in the Court of Appeal's decision. Eleanor King L.J. hinted that it did. She stated that although the foetus was not the concern of the Court, this did not mean that the judges should not be aware that the NHS Trust's application sought to end an otherwise viable pregnancy. The Court of Appeal was critical of the fact that the case had reached the courts so close to the 24-week deadline in the Abortion Act. It might well be that the Court was reluctant to order a termination at a stage where babies have been born alive.[25]

5. FOETAL ABNORMALITY: SECTION 1(1)(D) 1967 ACT

5.1. AN ETHICAL CHALLENGE

In *R (on the application of Crowter and others) v. Secretary of State for Health and Social Care* (2021) (*Crowter* (2021)),[26] Lord Justice Singh and

24 See para. 27 of Lieven J.'s judgment in *Re AB* [2019] EWCOP 26.

25 <https://www.tommys.org/pregnancy-information/premature-birth/premature-birth-statistics>, last accessed 25.04.2022.

26 *R (on the application of Crowter and others) v. Secretary of State for Health and Social Care* [2021] EWHC 2536 (Admin).

Mrs. Justice Lieven commented that there was little doubt that claims relating to abortion involved highly sensitive and sometimes controversial issues which:

> generate strong feelings, on all sides of the debate, including sincere differences of view about ethical and religious matters. This Court cannot enter into those controversies; it must decide the case only in accordance with the law.[27]

The case of *Crowter* (2021) did, indeed, involve sensitive and controversial issues. However, in spite of the judges' firm belief that they could not enter into the world of ethics, the case illustrates the thin dividing line which the court attempts to tread between law and ethics in the context of abortion. At the centre of any consideration of abortion is the ethical dilemma which Lady Hale recognised must, inevitably, be addressed by the court because:

> the community undoubtedly does have a moral interest in protecting the life, health, and welfare of the unborn. ... But the community also has an interest in protecting the life, health, and welfare of the pregnant woman. ... The question, therefore, is how the balance is to be struck between the two.[28]

5.2. THE FACTS IN *CROWTER* (2021)

The first claimant, Heidi Crowter, was a 26-year-old woman who had been born with a comparatively mild form of Down's syndrome (DS). She lived independently, was employed and had recently married a man who also had DS. Heidi was a DS activist who wished to change people's attitudes towards people like her and her husband; she wished to see section 1(1)(d) of the 1967 Act reformed because she believed it to be discriminatory and disrespectful to those born with DS.

The second claimant was the mother of the third claimant, a boy born with DS who was aged two at the time of the court hearing. He had met all the developmental milestones for a child of his age.

5.3. DOWN'S SYNDROME

Babies born with DS (trisomy 21) have a third copy of chromosome 21. As a consequence, they have developmental disabilities, which may range from

---

27 Ibid, at para. 5.

28 See *Re the Northern Ireland Human Rights Commission for Judicial Review* [2018] UKSC 27, para. 21.

mild to severe. Some DS pregnancies end in a stillbirth and some children with DS do not survive for long. However, the majority of children with DS are likely to live for between 50 and 60 years.

Screening for DS can be carried out between 10 and 14 weeks of gestation, but diagnostic tests undertaken between 15 and 20 weeks are more accurate.

In 2018, a little over 50 per cent of women diagnosed with DS opted to have their pregnancy aborted. Only a minority of those abortions were carried out after 24 weeks of gestation.[29]

5.4. THE NEED FOR COUNSELLING AND SUPPORT

The Royal College of Gynaecologists has emphasised that pregnant women should receive counselling and support if they were considering having a late abortion. However, the second claimant maintained that she had been made to feel guilty when she chose to continue her pregnancy having been advised not to do so. The implied message from the medical professionals was that children with DS were of no value.

5.5. THE CONVENTION AND ABORTION

The European Court of Human Rights (ECtHR) has recognised the consensus amongst a substantial majority of Member States with respect to abortion, whilst there was a significant diversity of views on the status of the foetus and the gestational limits for abortion.[30] Member States have tended to favour the mother's rights in resolving the ethical dilemma of the status of the foetus.

5.6. THE CLAIM

All three claimants contended that section 1(1)(d) of the 1967 Act was incompatible with their rights under Articles 2, 3, 8 and 14 of the Convention

---

29 See *Crowter* (2021), above n. 26, at para. 11. The 90% termination rate in the National Down's Syndrome Cytogenetic Register (NDSCR) report in 2018 refers to prenatal diagnosis of Down's syndrome. However, not all children with Down's syndrome in England and Wales are diagnosed prenatally. The 2010 report of the NDSCR states that: 'In 2010, 1,868 Down's syndrome diagnoses were made, 1,188 (64%) prenatally and 680 (36%) postnatally. In the 2010 report, of the 680 cases where Down syndrome was diagnosed postnatally, there were 651 live births and 29 still births/foetal deaths. Out of those diagnosed prenatally 942 pregnancies were terminated; there were 63 live births; 37 still births/miscarriage; and 195 with an "unknown outcome".'

30 See *RR v. Poland* (2011) 53 EHRR 31. The European Group on Ethics at Community level has explained that 'it would be inappropriate to impose one exclusive moral code.'

(the right to life, the right to not be subjected to torture or to inhuman or degrading treatment or punishment, the right to respect for private and family life, and the right to enjoy Convention rights without discrimination, respectively). They sought declarations under section 4 of the Human Rights Act 1998 (HRA 1998) that the legislation infringed their Convention rights in that it allowed late abortions of pregnancies where there was a substantial risk that the resultant child would be seriously handicapped. Those pregnancies where there was no such risk could only be terminated up to 24 weeks of gestation (see section 1(1) of the 1967 Act), unless they fell within the ambit of section 1(1)(b) or (c), when they could be aborted after 24 weeks.

The terms 'substantial risk' and 'seriously handicapped' in section 1(1)(d) are not defined in the Act.[31] In *Jepson v. Chief Constable of West Mercia Police* (2003),[32] the court held that clinicians had significant freedom to determine whether there was a substantial risk of a serious handicap, provided that the handicap concerned was neither trivial nor easy to correct or would be merely disadvantageous to the child.

5.7. COUNSEL FOR THE CLAIMANTS

5.7.1. *Article 2 of the Convention: The Right to Life*

Counsel for the claimants maintained that section 1(1)(d) of the Abortion Act 1967 was incompatible with Article 2 of the Convention because the provision endangered the life of a disabled unborn child at a time when it was both viable and sentient. Referring to domestic law, which was relevant to the meaning of Article 2, counsel maintained that in *A-G's Reference*

31 The Royal College of Obstetricians and Gynaecologists was commissioned by the Department of Health and Social Care to give guidance on s. 1(1)(d), and its report, *Termination of Pregnancy for Foetal Abnormality in England, Scotland, and Wales*, was published in 2010. 'Substantial risk' was not defined in the report; whether a risk was to be regarded as substantial would depend upon clinicians weighing up a number of factors such as:

- the possibility of effective treatment for the disability either *in utero* or following birth;
- the degree of the child's likely awareness of the handicap;
- the likelihood of the child being able to communicate;
- the potential suffering of the child;
- the probability of the child being able to live independently as an adult;
- the extent to which a person would have to rely on others for acts essential for their health; and
- the nature and severity of the abnormality, the timing of the diagnosis, and the likelihood of the handicap occurring.

32 See *Jepson v. Chief Constable of West Merica Police* [2003] EWHC 3318 (Admin).

(No. 3 of 1994) (1998),[33] the House of Lords had declared that the foetus was 'a unique organism to which existing principles could not necessarily be applied.'[34]

Counsel also argued that as the Infant Life (Preservation) Act 1929 was equivalent to the law relating to murder and the Act referred to 'a child which is capable of being born alive',[35] there was a clear recognition that a viable being *in utero* was worthy of protection.

The Congenital Disabilities (Civil Liability) Act 1976 recognised that duties were owed to an unborn child (who had correlative rights) which were expressly, or impliedly, based upon the foetus having, or having the potential for, human life.[36]

5.7.2. Protection of the Foetus and Abortion

Giving a viable unborn child the protection of Article 2 would not make abortion unavailable on the grounds outlined in *R v. Bourne* (1939),[37] nor would it prevent abortions permitted under sections 1(1)(b) and (c) of the Abortion Act 1967. Furthermore, abortion on the grounds of fatal foetal abnormality would not be affected; in such a case the foetus would not be viable and there would be no life outside the womb to protect.[38]

5.7.3. A Rejection of Counsel's Arguments

The court rejected all of counsel's arguments. The ECtHR had never decided that a foetus, even a viable one, had Convention rights. The controversial and difficult issue of when life begins had been left to the margin of appreciation of Member States. The recognition, by both the domestic legislation and its courts and the ECtHR, that there might be circumstances in which the foetus had interests which the State was entitled to protect did not mean that the foetus enjoyed Article 2 rights.[39]

---

33 See *A-G's Reference (No. 3 of 1994)* [1998] AC 245.

34 Ibid.

35 Infant Life (Preservation) Act 1929 s. 1(1).

36 See s. 1 of the Act.

37 See *R v. Bourne* [1939] 1 KB 687.

38 See *Re Northern Ireland Human Rights Commission's Application for Judicial Review* [2018] UKSC 27, para. 371.

39 There was no jurisprudence from the Strasbourg institutions to dispute that view (see e.g. *Paton v. United Kingdom* (1981) 3 EHRR 408; *Boso* (Application No. 50490/99) [2002] ECHR 846). The European Commission of Human Rights, in *Reeve v. UK* (Application No. 24844/94), stated that the UK prohibition of a claim for damages for wrongful life was based on public policy considerations. Such a claim would violate 'the sanctity of human life', and the aim of the prohibition was to protect the right to life of the foetus. The judgment in *Vo v. France* (2004) 40 EHRR 12 stated that it was not desirable or possible to answer the question in the

Lord Mance in the Supreme Court in 2018 stated that:

> there is in law no question of a balance being struck between the interests of two different living persons. The unborn foetus is not in law a person, although its potential must be respected. In addition, the current legislation already recognises important limitations on the interests and protection of the unborn foetus. It permits abortion of a healthy foetus in circumstances where the mother's life would be at risk or where she would suffer serious long-term damage to her physical or psychological health.[40]

The fact that the domestic law of murder did not protect the life of the unborn child was significant, and although the Infant Life (Preservation) Act 1929 might protect a viable foetus, the courts had a discretion over sentencing which was not so with respect to murder.

Parliament had reached a view on these nuanced issues, and it was a matter for Parliament and not the court to decide whether the law relating to the protection of a viable foetus should be changed.

5.7.4. Article 3 of the Convention: No One Shall be Subjected to Torture or to Inhuman or Degrading Treatment or Punishment

Counsel for the claimants focused on the fact that a viable unborn child immediately before birth would be sentient and would suffer pain during the abortion procedure. Expert evidence maintained that a foetus would be sentient and aware of pain from 24 weeks' gestation onwards. Foetal anaesthesia was standard practice when *in utero* surgery was performed after 18 weeks. Counsel maintained that it was both surprising and disturbing that anaesthesia was not, as a rule, administered to an unborn child when an abortion was carried out. It was a violation of human dignity and incompatible with Article 3. The third claimant had been born at 36 weeks of gestation as a fully developed, sentient being. To have permitted an abortion at that stage would have been a breach of his rights under Article 3.[41]

The court dismissed all of the challenges under Article 3; there was no positive decision of the ECtHR (or even the former Commission) which

abstract whether the unborn child was a person for the purposes of Art. 2 of the Convention. Counsel for the claimants in *Crowter* (2021) maintained he was not indulging in an abstract challenge to Art. 2 but was focusing on the position of a viable unborn child immediately prior to full-term birth which, arguably, was protected by domestic legislation.

40 Ibid, at para. 119.

41 In *H v. Norway* (Application No. 17004/90) (1992), the European Commission of Human Rights had dismissed a complaint relating to an abortion based on Art. 3 but claimed counsel, only on the grounds of lack of evidence of foetal pain.

decided that a foetus was protected by Convention rights, including in particular Article 3.[42]

5.7.5. *Private Life*

Counsel for the claimants argued that the regulation of abortion came within the sphere of private life. The ECtHR has failed to decide whether the term 'others' in Article 8(2) includes the foetus. However, it had reiterated on a number of occasions that, in balancing any interference in a pregnant woman's Article 8 rights and the protection of any public interest in the life of an unborn child, the Member State has a wide margin of appreciation.[43]

5.7.6. *Stigmatisation and Illogicality*

Attention has been drawn to the illogicality of protecting children born with disabilities whilst legalising selective abortions to prevent the birth of such children. Lord Shinkwin, a Conservative peer, in his witness statement to the court explained:

> For me, as a severely disabled person, section 1(1)(d) drives a coach and horses through everything Parliament professes to believe in concerning disability equality. Its continued application and indeed active promotion stigmatise disabled human beings before we are even born because its specific purpose is precisely to prevent us from being born ... We are life unworthy of life.[44]

5.7.7. *Assertion of Pre-Birth Rights Post-Birth*

Finally, counsel relied on the fact that the domestic law recognised that an unborn child had rights and interests under Article 8 which could be asserted after birth by a person such as the third claimant who now enjoyed Convention rights.[45]

5.8. THE COURT'S VIEW OF ARTICLE 8

The court accepted that abortion came within the scope of Article 8(1) but only in the context of the rights of the pregnant woman and not the rights of such

42 See *Crowter* (2021), at para. 80.

43 See *A, B and C v. Ireland* (2011) 53 EHRR 13.

44 See *Crowter* (2021), at para. 34.

45 See the Congenital Disabilities (Civil Liability) Act 1976; *Burton v. Islington Health Authority; de Martell v. Merton and Sutton Health Authority* [1993] QB 204.

persons as the first and third claimants. It concluded that there had been no interference with the claimants' rights under Article 8(1) and that the circumstances did not fall within the ambit of Article 8 for the purposes of Article 14.[46]

5.8.1. *Article 8(2)*

Given the court's decision that there was no infringement of Article 8, it was also unnecessary for it to consider the plaintiffs' claim under Article 8(2). However, the court decided that, in case its decision was wrong, it would hear the claimants' arguments with respect to Article 8(2).[47]

5.8.2. *The Remedies Sought by the Claimants*

As the court had rejected the claim of incompatibility, no declarations under sections 3, 4 and 7 of the HRA 1998 were possible. However, the court acknowledged that had it found in favour of the claimants, the only possible declaration was one of incompatibility under section 4 of the HRA 1998.[48]

5.9. A FINAL WORD

Perhaps the final word on abortion in the context of an abnormal foetus should be left to Lord Shinkwin in a speech to the House of Lords:

> So, I say to colleagues, especially those with responsibility for women and equalities issues: do not patronise us by making it easier for non-disabled people to kill us simply for the crime of being diagnosed with a disability before birth, and then claiming it is all about equality. If equality has become so distorted that it now justifies a stronger group of human beings condemning another, weaker group to death for disability, right up to birth, we really are in trouble. I believe that this distortion of equality is the single biggest challenge we face because the statistics show that our very survival is under threat.[49]

---

46 Given this conclusion, there was no need for the court to consider the matter of discrimination. Nevertheless, it decided that in case it was wrong, it would address the issue (see *Crowter* (2021), at para. 136 ff.).

47 Ibid, at para. 108 ff.

48 A reading down of s. 1(1)(d) under s. 3 of the HRA 1998 would have amounted to judicial legislation rather than interpretation (see *Ghaidan v. Godin-Mendoza* [2004] UKHL 30). A declaration under s. 7 of the Act that it would be unlawful for the Secretary of State to fund abortions carried out under s. 1(1)(d) would be impossible to make because of the application of s. 6 of the Act.

49 Hansard Vol. 792: 28 June 2018.

6. RELIGIOUS OBJECTIONS TO ABORTION

6.1. THE USE OF ADMINISTRATIVE LAW TO ACHIEVE AN ETHICAL AIM

In 2020, Singh L.J. observed that:

> The issue of abortion raises questions of ethics and social policy on which many people have strongly held views, which are sometimes diametrically opposed and irreconcilable. Those questions are not for the courts to determine. The role of this Court, as always in judicial review proceedings, is to determine the lawfulness of the Secretary of State's decision, nothing else.[50]

In two recent cases, recourse has been made to administrative law by anti-abortion activists in an attempt to overturn the current law.

6.2. *R (ON THE APPLICATION OF CHRISTIAN CONCERN) v. SECRETARY OF STATE FOR HEALTH AND SOCIAL CARE* (2020)[51]

When, in March 2020, England was placed under lockdown because of the COVID-19 pandemic, the Secretary of State for Health and Social Care made an Approval that medical abortions could be carried out in women's homes for the duration of the pandemic.[52] The Approval was to be limited in duration and would come to an end when the Coronavirus Act 2020 expired or, at the latest, by 30 March 2022.[53]

---

50 See *R (on the application of Christian Concern) v. Secretary of State for Health and Social Care* [2020] EWHC 1546 (Admin), para. 4.

51 *R (on the application of Christian Concern) v. Secretary of State for Health and Social Care* [2020] EWCA Civ 1239.

52 See s. 1(3A) of the 1967 Act; the Secretary of State had already made an earlier Approval in 2018 which permitted women to take Misoprostol at home if they had first taken Mifepristone at a clinic and they were less than ten weeks pregnant

53 On 23 February 2022, the Health Minister, Maggie Throup, stated that medical early abortions at home would end at midnight on 29 August 2022. Pre-pandemic rules would return, and women would have to take the first abortion medication in a clinic or hospital but would be able take the second one at home. The minister maintained that it would ensure the well-being and safety of pregnant women. The Royal College of Obstetricians and Gynaecologists, the Royal College of Midwives and the British Medical Association amongst other medical organisations objected to the decision. They expressed concern that the decision would force women to use unregulated providers of abortion medication. In a letter to the Prime Minister, they wrote: 'To remove this service, despite the scientific and medical support it carries, would indicate a deep mistrust of women and an institutional disregard for their reproductive rights.' Over 125,000 women have accessed abortion medication since the 2020 Approval was made. Anti-abortionists have welcomed the Minister's decision to revert to the pre-2020 situation (see A. O'Dowd 'Medical abortion: Clinicians oppose government plan to

A medical abortion involves the administration of two types of medication. The first of these, Mifepristone, brings pregnancy to an end by blocking the body's production of progesterone. The second medication, Misoprostol, is normally taken within 24–28 hours of Mifepristone and causes contractions which expel the foetus.

The new Approval meant that a registered medical practitioner was allowed to prescribe the medications from his or her home following a remote consultation[54] with the pregnant woman whose pregnancy was no more than ten weeks in duration.[55] Women were thus able to have medical abortions without having had any examination in person by a medical professional.

Christian Concern (CC), an Anglican evangelical advocacy organisation opposed to abortion, made a claim for judicial review of the Approval. The Divisional Court declined the claim and CC made an application for permission to appeal the decision.

6.2.1. CC's Arguments

CC maintained that section 1 of the 1967 Act contained two distinct requirements that had to be satisfied for an abortion to be lawful: the pregnancy had to be terminated by a registered medical practitioner and carried out in a hospital or a place approved by the Secretary of State (see section 1(3) and (3A)). The Secretary of State's 2020 Approval, in allowing a pregnant woman to self-administer medication that had been posted to her home, did not fulfil those requirements. The medical practitioner would not be able to make all the material decisions and remain in control of the procedure. Furthermore, the gestational stage of the pregnancy would not have been checked to ensure it fell within the ten-week rule for medical terminations of early-stage pregnancies.

---

end home based arrangements', *BMJ*, 25 February 2022, <https://www.bmj.com/content/376/bmj.o501>, last accessed 26.09.2022). The Department of Health and Social Care announced that from 30 August 2022, the provisions for at home early medical abortions would become permanent. The Minister for Public Health, Maggie Throup stated that the wellbeing and safety of women requiring access to abortion services was paramount. The extension of the provisions would allow women to have more choice in how and where they access abortion services, while ensuring robust data is collected to ensure their continued safety (see the Abortion (Amendment) Regulations 2022).

54 Remote consultations were already happening. See the National Institute for Health and Care Excellence (NICE) Report, January 2021, p. 1: 'Providing assessments by phone or video call can be particularly beneficial for women living in remote areas; women experiencing domestic violence, abuse or coercion from their partner or family; and women experiencing cultural barriers to accessing abortion services. Providers should, however, ensure that safeguarding procedures are in place for all women, including those accessing the service remotely. Providing a choice of assessment by phone, video call or face to face ensures that women can access abortion services in the way that best suits their personal circumstances.'

55 Medical abortions may take place at a later stage of pregnancy, even after 24 weeks, if the woman fulfils the provisions of s. 1(1)(b), (c) or (d) of the 1967 Act but the abortion will take place in a hospital.

According to CC, the 2020 Approval was contrary to the legislative purpose of the 1967 Act and the Secretary of State's discretion under section 1(3A) of the Act to grant Approvals had to be carried out with the purpose of the Act in mind. The Secretary of State was free to approve a class of places which were safe, but he could not approve unregulated places such as women's homes, which might well be unsafe and where the women might be under pressure to undergo, or refrain from undergoing, an abortion. In extreme cases, the Approval might have the effect of legalising abortions in not dissimilar conditions to those illegal back street abortions which had taken place with considerable frequency prior to the 1967 Act.

6.2.2. *The Secretary of State's Response*

The Secretary of State maintained that the legality of the 2020 Approval was supported by case law. The House of Lords in *Royal College of Nursing v. Department of Health and Social Security* (1981)[56] had accepted that the abortion procedure was undertaken as a team effort. A medical practitioner would be in charge and responsible for all those involved in the treatment of a woman undergoing an abortion. He or she would give specific instructions to those carrying out that part of the treatment appropriate to their roles.[57]

6.2.3. *The Expert Evidence*

Dr. Imogen Stephens, an obstetrician, gynaecologist and public health medicine consultant, explained that the aim of the temporary changes in the 2020 Approval was to enable women to have early medical abortions, which were time-sensitive, during the pandemic. Since March 2020, abortion services had been cut back, and in some areas had been withdrawn completely; clinic staff had been transferred to hospitals in order to deal with patients who had COVID-19. Had the Approval not been made by the Secretary of State, women would have had to travel to a clinic to take the abortion medication, which would have increased the risk of spreading the virus. Those women who could not access a clinic because of difficulties in finding childcare, or who could not leave home because of an abusive relationship, would have missed the ten-week deadline. Some of them might have resorted to unsafe illegal abortions. Such dangers would far outweigh any risk to women who took the medication at home following a remote consultation with a medical practitioner.

Dr. Stephens stated that teleconsultations had already become a regular feature of medical abortion procedures. Women were given information about aftercare,

---

56 See *Royal College of Nursing v. Department of Health and Social Security* [1981] AC 800.

57 Ibid; see also *SPUC Pro-Life Scotland v. Scottish Ministers* [2019] CSIH 31; *British Pregnancy Advisory Service v. Secretary of State for Health* [2011] EWHC 235.

access to a 24-hour helpline and information about the nearest emergency centre should they require it. If concerns were identified during remote consultations, the woman would be required to attend a face-to-face meeting.

6.2.4. *The Court of Appeal's Conclusion*

The Court of Appeal stated that one of the reasons for providing the Secretary of State with the power to make an Approval under the 1967 Act was to deal with a change in circumstances and, thereby, fulfil the purpose of the 1967 Act, which was to ensure that women had access to safe and legal abortion.

The Court denied CC permission to appeal the Divisional Court's decision. The pre-pandemic Approval in 2018 had never been legally challenged in England and Wales. The only material difference between it and the 2020 Approval was that the latter allowed women to take both Mifepristone and Misoprostol at home, whilst the 2018 Approval only permitted Misoprostol to be taken at home. The Court of Appeal found that there was no good evidence to distinguish between the nature and effect of the medications to find it unsafe for them to be taken at home.

CC had sought permission to present further evidence to the Court of Appeal. The Court refused permission and stated that it considered that CC's application was only to advance its views on the ethics of abortion rather than to argue the issue of the legality of the Secretary of State's Approval.

6.3. *DULGHERIU & ANOR v. THE LONDON BOROUGH OF EALING* (2019)[58]

6.3.1. *The Facts*

In *Dulgheriu & Anor v. The London Borough of Ealing* (2019) (*Dulgheriu* (2019)), anti-abortion activists who were affiliated with a Christian group called the Good Counsel Network challenged the validity of a 2018 Public Spaces Protection Order (the Order), which the London Borough of Ealing (the Local Authority) had made under section 59 of the Anti-social Behaviour, Crime and Policing Act 2014 (the 2014 Act). The objective of such Orders was to protect those who were victims of anti-social behaviour. The Local Authority was most concerned about the anti-abortion demonstrations in front of the Marie Stopes Centre, which provided abortion and family planning services and wished to bring the demonstrations to a halt.

The activists' aim was clearly to deter women who sought to undergo abortions at the Centre. Over a long period of time, they had gathered in front

[58] See *Dulgheriu & Anor v. The London Borough of Ealing* [2019] EWCA Civ 1490.

of the Centre, displaying posters of foetuses at various stages of gestation, and handing out leaflets. They had also carried life-like foetus dolls and had held prayer vigils. The women visiting the Centre, whom the appellants called 'Mum', were threatened with hell fire for seeking an abortion, and photos were taken of them. Rosary beads were given to the women and to other members of the public who passed by. These anti-abortion activities were opposed by pro-choice protestors who attempted to occupy the same space as the anti-abortionists; they played loud music and chanted in support of the women.

The Local Authority maintained that the demonstrations by both the anti-abortionists and those who were pro-choice had been, or would be, detrimental to the quality of life of those who lived or worked in the locality or who were visiting it. The demonstrations were persistent and unreasonable; the imposition of a ban on all abortion-related protests close to the Centre would, therefore, be justifiable. A limited number of demonstrations would be permitted in an area some 100 metres away from the entrance to the Centre.

The anti-abortionists challenged the Local Authority's power to make an Order where the activity complained of affected only, or mainly, occasional visitors to the area and not those who lived or worked there or who visited it regularly. They also questioned whether the restrictions imposed by the Order infringed rights, under the European Convention on Human Rights (the Convention), relating to freedom of religion, expression and assembly under Articles 9, 10 and 11 respectively.

The lower court judge rejected the challenge and the anti-abortionists appealed.

6.3.2. *The Appeal*

In their appeal, the appellants maintained that the lower court judge had erred in holding that the phrase 'those in the locality' in section 59(2)(a) of the 2014 Act applied to the women who visited the clinic, who were only occasional visitors.

They also claimed that he was wrong to hold that the Article 8 rights of the women were engaged. The activities of the appellants were carried out on a public highway and there could be no expectation on the part of the women who visited the clinic that they would not be challenged by them. Abortion was a topic of public importance and was controversial and the women would have been aware that there would be anti-abortionists objecting to their wishing to take advantage of the Centre's services. No recording or publication of the reason why the women were visiting the clinic had been made.

In the appellants' view, the judge had given too little weight to their rights under the Convention, when considering whether the Local Authority's Order was necessary in a democratic society and whether its terms could have been less restrictive.

6.3.3. *The Appeal Court's Judgment*

The Court held that the terms of the 2014 Act made clear that Parliament had decided not to limit the meaning of 'those in the locality' in section 59 to those who lived and worked in the area.[59] The interpretation of the Act would all depend on the nature of the locality. In the circumstances confronting the Local Authority, it covered not only residents and regular visitors to, or people who worked in, the locality but also others and a ban on the appellants would be justifiable. To accept the strict interpretation of section 59 put forward by the latter would be impractical. That interpretation would affect patients in hospitals and hospices, and other medical facilities, as well as their visitors. It would have the potential to produce uncertainty about the legality of any Order imposed by a local authority. It was unlikely to have been Parliament's intention to have the provision of the 2014 Act interpreted in such a way.

Given that the lower court had found that some visitors to the abortion clinic had been seriously damaged both psychologically and emotionally by virtue of the anti-abortionists' conduct,[60] the Local Authority had been correct to interpret the expression 'those in the locality' broadly.

The Court rejected the appellants' arguments, which denied that the Article 8 rights of the women attending the Centre were engaged. In 2018, Lady Hale had stated that for women

> who become pregnant, or who are obliged to carry a pregnancy to term, against their will there can be few greater invasions of their autonomy and bodily integrity and the decisions whether to have an abortion or not was a private and sensitive matter for a woman which clearly fell within Article 8.[61]

The Court held that the activities of the appellants clearly engaged the Article 8 rights of those visiting the clinic. They had infringed the women's rights to decide to undergo an abortion. The women's desire that their visit would be as private as was possible was a reasonable one and they had a legitimate expectation that it would be respected.

Although the appellants had a right to express their religious or other beliefs under Article 9 of the Convention, the judge below had balanced that right with the other relevant articles of the Convention. The Local Authority

---

59 The appellants had relied upon *Summers v. London Borough of Richmond Upon Thames* [2018] EWHC 782 (Admin), for their rigid view of s. 59 of the 2014 Act.

60 See *Dulgheriu & Anor v. The London Borough of Ealing* [2018] EWHC 1667 (Admin).

61 This has been repeatedly confirmed both by local courts and the ECtHR (*P v. Poland* [2012] ECHR 1853). In *Re Northern Ireland's Human Rights Commission's Application for Judicial Review* [2018] UKSC 27; [2019] 1 All ER 173, para. 6.

was also under a duty, by virtue of section 72 of the 2014 Act, to undertake a balancing of Convention rights when deciding to make the Order restricting the protestors' activities and had done so.

6.3.4. *The Decision*

The Court of Appeal concluded that the judge below had been entitled to find that the Article 8 rights of the women visiting the clinic outweighed the rights of the appellants under Articles 9, 10 and 11 of the Convention and that the terms of the order were proportionate.[62]

7. A CRITIQUE OF THE CURRENT LAW

7.1. THE STATUS OF THE FOETUS v. THE PREGNANT WOMAN

The case law considered in this chapter draws attention to the problematic nature of the current law. The majority of the provisions of the Abortion Act 1967 were based on a political compromise between differing views on the status of the foetus. There were those who viewed the foetus as an unborn child, deserving of a right to be protected from destruction. The only exception was in the most extreme of circumstances, such as where a pregnant woman's life or health was at serious risk or where the pregnancy would result in the birth of a severely handicapped child or one who might even die at birth. Others accepted that until a foetus reached a stage of development where it would be possible for a woman to give birth to a child who had a chance of survival, abortion should be possible but only if the continuance of the pregnancy would affect the woman's physical or mental health or that of her children. Since the 1967 Act came into force, a third group has come to the fore. Its supporters believe that pregnant women have a right to bodily autonomy and that they should have the right to decide for themselves whether to have an abortion, possibly even up to the moment of birth.

7.2. THE VIEWS OF THE MENTALLY IMPAIRED

These differing standpoints continue to affect judicial decisions. In the case of *X (A Child) (2014)*,[63] Sir James Munby purported to make a decision

62 In March 2020, the Supreme Court refused the appellants' application for permission to appeal.

63 See *Re X* (2014), above n. 10.

on the basis of the best interests of a pregnant severely mentally impaired 13-year-old who was incapable of giving consent. He appeared to ignore the best interests of the child. Rather he regarded abortion as such an important issue that the court should not make an order for it to be carried out without the most compelling of reasons, such as a clear risk to the girl's life or long-term health. So concerned was the judge that that he went to the extreme of 'inventing' the term 'agreement in a colloquial sense'. If the girl could show such an agreement, he would permit the abortion to go ahead (the girl seemingly did, but how her agreement manifested itself, we are not told). It would be interesting to speculate what decision the President would have made had he found that even an agreement in this nebulous sense was not forthcoming.

The case of *Re AB (Termination of Pregnancy) (2019)*[64] illustrates the clash between Lieven J.'s approach in the Court of Protection and that of the Court of Appeal. Lieven J. stressed the need to consider the best interests of AB as an individual rather than focus on societal views on the ethics of abortion, or the rights of disabled people in general or the benefit of becoming a biological mother. In AB's case it was highly unlikely that she would have been able to enjoy the benefits of motherhood. The Court of Appeal, by contrast, was more concerned to avoid imposing an order for abortion on an adult mentally impaired woman whose pregnancy was close to the 24-week limit laid down in section 1(1)(a) of the 1967 Act.

It may be laudable that the Mental Capacity Act 2005 emphasises the importance of hearing the views of an incapacitated person. However, those views may be difficult to take into account when the complex issue of decision-making about an abortion is involved. The cases of *Re X (2014)* and *Re AB (2019)* illustrate the difficulties of a best interests test for the mentally challenged. The test was formulated for resolving issues far removed from abortion, which continues to raise the ethical dilemma of the conflict between the foetus and the pregnant woman.

The Court of Appeal in *Re AB* (2019) accepted that there was no direct evidence about AB's actual beliefs and values about abortion and that it would be mere speculation to consider them. Yet the Court was prepared to infer her wishes and feelings from evidence which showed her to be totally confused and, at times, incomprehensible. The courts pay lip service to the principle that substituted judgment has no part to play in decision-making for the incapacitous. Yet the reality is that courts do exactly that when it is not possible to assess the wishes of an incapacitated person like AB or X who have never had capacity.

---

64 *Re AB* (2019) in the Court of Appeal, above n. 15.

7.3. FACING THE ETHICAL CHALLENGE

The judgment in *Crowter* (2021) demonstrates that no matter how hard the judiciary try to avoid entering into the ethical debate about late abortions, the 1967 Act hauls them back in. The Administrative Court, although perhaps an inappropriate forum to consider such a matter as human rights and the foetus, determined that the being in embryo was not protected by the Convention. It has been said that:

> There can be no doubt as to the acute sensitivity of the moral and ethical issues raised by the question of abortion or as to the importance of the public interest at stake.[65]

Such a view is reflected in *Crowter* (2021), which, throughout the hearing, was dominated by the permanent ethical conundrum inherent in pitting the variable and unpredictable status of the foetus against the rights and interests of the pregnant woman. The foetus in *Crowter* (2021) was variously described as having no rights, a being which was a unique organism and deserving of protection and respect, an unborn, and an unborn child.

Any move towards a satisfactory resolution of this conundrum and a reform of the current abortion law requires an ethical decision to be made about the starting point of life and a determination of the status of the foetus. There is a persuasive view that, regardless of its status, the foetus will always come second to the rights and interests of the woman carrying it. This view, however, does not diminish the need to attempt to reach a consensus about the status of the foetus. If such a consensus recognises that a foetus is worthy of some respect and protection, the question must be asked and answered about the practical consequences of such recognition.

The reaching of a consensus may encourage the development of further diagnostic tools to reveal, and where possible treat, foetal abnormalities as early as possible in a pregnancy to reduce the need for late abortions. Such abortions, particularly when undertaken very close to birth, cannot be a good experience for women or the clinicians who must carry them out or, indeed, for the foetuses, which according to counsel for the plaintiffs in *Crowter (2021)* can be aborted late in pregnancy without being anaesthetised. This revelation is particularly shocking given that animals used for research purposes must be killed humanely when the research comes to an end.

The use of administrative law to achieve the ethical aims of anti-abortionists in the cases of *CC* (2020) and *Dulgheriu* (2019)[66] also illustrates the need to

---

65 See *A, B and C v. Ireland* (2011) 53 EHRR 13, para. 233.

66 See above n. 60.

find a compromise between the aims of religious groups and the broader, more liberal views of the pro-abortionists. Administrative law is not an appropriate forum for those who are opposed to abortion to argue their ethical stance. The democratic political process is available to them, as it is for all pressure groups who wish to put forward their views on reform of the law to which they are opposed. They must be allowed to play a part in any discussion which precedes law reform in this field.

8. REFORM

It is 31 years since Parliament last considered reform of abortion law when it amended the 1967 Act.[67] Since then, the abortion debate has been concerned with a number of overlapping matters, such as: the status of the foetus; the increase in the survival rate of babies born before the current 24-week limit of gestation;[68] the advance in treatment of some disabling foetal conditions; the change in a positive direction of societal attitudes towards disability; the continued criminalisation of abortion; early medical abortion at home; abortion for the mentally disabled; the need for two doctors to certify that a woman has met the requirements of the 1967 Act; and whether medical professionals should be allowed to opt out of treating women for abortion.

In *Crowter* (2021), the Court was resolute in its view that the issue of late abortion was for Parliament to decide and not for judicial law reform. Parliament had the ability to obtain wider information from expert bodies, which could advise it on reform of the law, and from public consultation, in which many differing views could be put forward by members of the public. Parliament also had the benefit of democratic legitimacy, which allowed it to intervene in areas of difficult or controversial social policy. The courts had no such authority.[69] It should now use these resources to revisit the law relating to abortion and consider how it should be reformed in a way which is in line with the ethics and scientific advances of the twenty-first century.

---

67 See Human Fertilisation Act 1990 s. 37.

68 See *R (on the application of British Pregnancy Advisory Service) v. The Secretary of State for Health and Social Care* [2020] EWCA Civ 355.

69 See *Crowter* (2021), at paras. 81 and 82.

FRANCE

A CHRONICLE OF FRENCH FAMILY LAW: 2021

Christine BIDAUD (Dir.),
Hugues FULCHIRON, Massilia AMZAL, Bastien BARET, Claire BRUNERIE,
Aurore CAMUZAT, Éric FONGARO, Guillaume KESSLER,
Guillaume MILLERIOUX, Taylène MOREIRA DE SÁ,
Mathilde MOSIEK-BRASSET (Coord.), Margot MUSSON and Marie PINCET

Résumé

Le droit français de la famille a cette année été marqué par l'entrée en vigueur de plusieurs nouvelles lois dans des domaines très différents. Une loi du 24 août 2021 appelée « loi confortant les principes de la République » a renforcé le principe de la réserve héréditaire lors d'une succession internationale en rétablissant une possibilité de droit de prélèvement sur les biens situés en France dans certains cas (1). Un Code spécialement consacré à la justice pénale des mineurs est également entré en vigueur (2). Quant à la loi bioéthique, elle a enfin été adoptée le 2 août 2021. Elle a mis fin à l'anonymat des donneurs de gamètes (3) et elle a autorisé l'accès à la procréation médicalement assistée aux couples de femmes et aux femmes seules (4). Elle a également modifié l'article 47 du Code civil français relatif à la force probante des actes de l'état civil étrangers dans le but d'obliger la Cour de cassation à modifier sa jurisprudence en matière de transcription des actes de naissance des enfants nés à l'étranger avec l'assistance d'une mère porteuse (5). En matière de filiation, il faut également relever une jurisprudence ayant permis à un homme transsexuel d'être inscrit comme mère de son enfant biologique qu'il avait eu avec son épouse (6). Les questions de prise en compte du genre ont également fait l'objet d'une circulaire à destination des personnels travaillant en milieu scolaire (7). L'évolution de la jurisprudence française s'est particulièrement manifestée quant au contenu de l'ordre public français en matière internationale. La Cour de cassation française a, d'une part, modifié sa position sur la reconnaissance des jugements de divorce inégalitaire étrangers (8) et, d'autre part, jugé qu'une décision étrangère refusant de tenir compte d'un contrat de mariage français était conforme à l'ordre public français en matière internationale (9). La Cour de cassation a, en revanche, maintenu sa position antérieure sur la question des tests osseux pour déterminer l'âge des personnes se prétendant mineures (10) ainsi que sur les conditions dans lesquelles un juge peut refuser d'entendre un mineur qui en fait la demande (11). La Cour a également été confrontée à la question de savoir si la liberté d'expression allait jusqu'à permettre à un site de rencontres extra-conjugales de faire de la publicité par voie d'affichage dans des lieux publics (12). Enfin, les conclusions finales du Comité sur le droit des personnes handicapées sur la législation française relative aux personnes vulnérables appellent quelques observations (13).

French family law has been marked this year by the entry into force of several new laws in very different areas. A law of 24 August 2021 called the 'Law Consolidating the Principles of the Republic' strengthened the principle of the reserve portion of the estate in an international succession by re-establishing the possibility of a right of levy on property located in France in certain cases (section 1). A special code on juvenile criminal justice has also come into force (section 2). The Bioethics Law was finally adopted on 2 August 2021. It put an end to the anonymity of gamete donors (section 3) and authorised access to medically assisted procreation for female couples and single women (section 4). It also amended Article 47 of the French Civil Code on the probative value of foreign civil status records to force the Cour de Cassation to change its jurisprudence on the transcription of birth certificates of children born abroad by surrogacy (section 5). Regarding parenthood, another case should be noted that allowed a transsexual man to be registered as the mother of the biological child he had had with his wife (section 6). The question of taking gender into account was also the subject of a circular aimed at staff working in schools (section 7). The evolution of French case law is particularly marked regarding the content of French public policy in international matters. On the one hand, the French Cour de Cassation has modified its position on the recognition of foreign unequal divorce judgments (section 8) and, on the other hand, has ruled that a foreign decision refusing to take account of a French prenuptial agreement was in conformity with French public policy in international matters (section 9). The Cour de Cassation, however, maintained its previous position on the question of bone tests to determine the age of persons claiming to be minors (section 10) and on the conditions under which a judge may refuse to hear a minor who requests such a test (section 11). The Court was also confronted with the question of whether freedom of expression went so far as to allow an extramarital dating website to advertise using posters in public places (section 12). The final conclusions of the Committee on the Rights of Persons with Disabilities on French legislation relating to vulnerable persons call for some observations (section 13).

1. THE CONFLICT OVER THE INHERITANCE RESERVE[1]

For several years, the reserved portion of inheritance provided by the French Civil Code in favour of the children and spouse of the deceased was in turmoil. There were three opposing camps: those who, attached to the principles of freedom, equality and solidarity, defended the traditional reserve; those who, in the name of individual freedom and economic liberalism, called for the disappearance of an institution considered archaic; and those who, sensitive to contemporary political, social and economic developments, proposed rebuilding the family's protective mechanisms around the principles of solidarity and responsibility across generations.[2]

---

1 Hugues Fulchiron, Professor, Judge at the Cour de Cassation, Co-director of the Family Law Center, Research team Louis Josserand of University Jean Moulin Lyon 3. The term 'inheritance reserve' is a French legal concept not known in English law, translated as 'reserved portion of an estate'.

2 On these debates, see the Report of the Working Group on the Reserved Portion, C. Peres and P. Potentier (eds.), Ministry of Justice, December 2019.

In two rulings, *Jarre* and *Colombier* of 2017,[3] the French Cour de Cassation stated that 'a foreign law designated by the conflict rule which ignores the reserved portion is not in itself contrary to French international public policy and can only be set aside if its concrete application, in the case in question, leads to a situation incompatible with the principles of French law considered to be essential.' The Cour de Cassation emphasised that in this case it was not claimed that the children set aside were in a situation of economic precariousness or in need. A high-profile case, that of the succession of the singer Johnny Halliday, brought the issue into the public arena and showed the attachment of some of the population to the intra-family transmission of property.[4]

The law of 24 August 2021, a law strengthening the principles of the Republic, does not directly reassert the public order nature of the reserve. According to the new Article 913 para. 2 of the Civil Code:

> [W]here the deceased or at least one of his children is, at the time of death, a national of a Member State of the European Union or habitually lives there, and where the foreign law applicable to the succession does not allow for any reserve mechanism to protect the children, each child or his heirs or successors may make a compensatory deduction from the property existing in France on the day of the death, so as to be re-established in the reserve rights that they are granted under French law, within the limit of those rights.

The former 'right to levy', which was abolished ten years ago because of its discriminatory nature, since it was reserved, at the time, for French nationals, has therefore been resurrected.[5]

In order to avoid a new censure by the French Constitutional Council and to avoid being condemned by the Court of Justice of the European Union, the legislator has given the new right of levy an excessive scope of application: it is granted to each child or to his or her heirs or successors if 'the deceased or at least one of his children is, at the time of death, a national of a Member State of the European Union or habitually lives there, and if the foreign law applicable to the succession does not allow for any mechanism of reservation to protect the children'.

For example, suppose there is a United States citizen with most of his assets located in the US, who also owns a building in France. He is survived

3 Civ. 1re, 27 September 2017, n° 16-17.198 and n° 16-13.151.

4 The singer and his family had moved to California. The singer, who spent part of his life there, had set up various trusts whose beneficiaries were his new wife and the children adopted with her, which deprived his children from a first marriage of their rights. The case ended up before the French courts, which considered that the singer had his habitual residence in France and that French law was applicable.

5 Cons. const., 5 August 2011, n° 2011-159 QPC D. 2012, 1228.

by four children, all of whom are US citizens. Under the rules of private international law, the succession, from the French point of view, is governed by American law (more precisely, the law of the state of the United States in which the deceased had his habitual residence at the time of his death), which does not recognise the reserve. But further suppose that one of his children happens to live in Ireland. Under the new Article 913 of the Civil Code, not only this child, but also any of his brothers and sisters, even if they are residents of the United States, may claim the share of the property located in France that is due to them by virtue of the reserve as provided for under French law, even though the law applicable to the succession is American law. No 'fraud' or manoeuvre is to be suspected on the part of the deceased and the only 'European' connection in this case is via a State, Ireland, which does not recognise the reserved portion of the estate.

Furthermore, the text raises sensitive issues of implementation. On the one hand, the right of levy is called into effect 'when the foreign law that applies to the succession does not allow any reservatory mechanism that protects the children.' However, in addition to mechanisms of the reservatory type, there are, in the Anglo-Saxon countries and certain northern European countries, 'functional equivalents' which make it possible to protect children, particularly when they might otherwise be in need. Will the right of levy come into effect when there is no mechanism for reserving rights in the strict sense, even though the heirs could implement, under the foreign law normally applied, mechanisms which would give them rights equivalent to, or even greater than, those given to them by French law in their capacity as reserving persons?

On the other hand, the right to levy is only possible when the foreign law applicable to the succession 'does not allow any mechanism of reservation that protects the children'. What if, like some Spanish civil law systems, the reserve is reduced to an almost symbolic share? Under the text, the protection will not apply. It is therefore better to be deprived of all rights than of some of them.

In any case, the protective mechanism only applies if the person concerned (still) has property in France.

2. THE ENTRY INTO FORCE OF THE FRENCH PENAL CODE FOR MINORS[6]

For quite some time, French authors, lawyers and judges had been calling for a reform of the criminal law for minors, to adapt the Order of 2 February 1945 to the major developments and reforms it was followed by. This text was quite revolutionary at the time, for it established the principles on which criminal

[6] Margot Musson, PhD student at University Jean Moulin Lyon 3, Family Law Center, Research team Louis Josserand.

law for minors has been built for decades, including measures and procedures adapted to the age of the child, the creation of specialised jurisdictions, and the pursuit of education and rehabilitation of the child. It is based on the principle of discernment, which states that only a child able to distinguish good from evil and to understand the seriousness of their actions can be brought before the courts.

Thus, an Act was promulgated in 2019 and led to an Order in the autumn of 2019 and two implementation decrees in 2021. The French Penal Code for Minors finally came into force on 30 September 2021. Some of its goals, which can be found in the preliminary article, are to simplify, accelerate and better adapt the procedures and measures for juvenile perpetrators. With these general guidelines and a Code specifically devoted to criminal law for minors, this law has been found to apply independently of the rest of the French Penal Code for certain matters. Some examples of the Code's provisions help to demonstrate these specificities.

First of all, the measures will differ depending on the juvenile perpetrator's age. Until the age of ten, only educative measures can be pronounced, i.e. measures that provide for the child's protection, assistance, education, social inclusion, and access to health care through individualised support. Such measures may include the child's removal from his or her home and placement in an appropriate setting, a warning or probation. Between the ages of 10 and 13, these measures can be complemented by educative sanctions, such as a prohibition on meeting the victim or accomplice, a reparation measure, or a civil training course. Finally, from the age of 13, adapted penal sentences – such as probation, social-judicial follow-up, jail time or community service – can be pronounced taking into consideration the child's personality and the circumstances. These sentences are tailored to the age of the child, and they cannot exceed half of the maximum penalty that may be imposed on adult offenders. However, this reduced penalty can be rejected by the judge in light of the child's personality and the offence, or by the law under specific circumstances.

In addition, it should also be stressed that the Code establishes a presumption of discernment when the child is over 13 years old, even though this presumption may be overturned. Before the entry into force of the French Penal Code for Minors, the question of criminal liability rested in the hands of the judge, who had the sovereign power to decide whether or not the child presented to him or her could understand his or her actions. This innovation was greatly inspired by France's international engagements, in particular by the United Nations Convention on the Rights of the Child, Article 40 of which indicates that States should try to establish 'a minimum age below which children shall be presumed not to have the capacity to infringe the penal law'.

To conclude, this reform has been largely welcomed by authors and legal practitioners. Nonetheless, some are still worried about the adequacy of the material resources given to practitioners to enable them to enforce the law and protect the best interests of the child.

3. FRANCE'S SHIFT ON DONOR ANONYMITY: THE IMPACT OF THE 2021 BIOETHICS LAW[7]

Over the past 40 years, the legal landscape of gamete donation has evolved considerably. Legal changes in this area have been punctuated by numerous public and political debates on the right of children to know their origins. As a result, in Sweden, Germany, Austria, the United Kingdom, the Netherlands, Switzerland and Finland, the donation of identifiable sperm and eggs is now mandatory. The legislative situation in France is interesting on this matter. After a comprehensive legal review in 2011 of the social and political challenges of donor anonymity, the shift finally took place through the Bioethics Law approved by a vote on 2 August 2021.[8]

The French Bioethics Law brings changes in many areas. At the same time opening up access to medically assisted procreation to single women and female couples, the law removes the anonymity of the gamete donor. Therefore, consent to the communication of non-identifying information and to the identity of the donor becomes a condition of donation. Under the new legislation, the medical team will have to inform the couple or the woman applying for medically assisted procreation with a third-party donor of the child's ability to have access to such information. Non-identifying information includes the donor's age, physical characteristics, family and professional status, and motivation for donation.[9] This data will be centralised by the Biomedicine Agency.[10]

Children born through medically assisted procreation with a third-party donor will, once they have reached the age of 18, be able to apply to a new commission – the Commission for Access to Non-identifying Data and to the Identity of the Third-party Donor – to obtain the donor's identity, non-identifying data or both. In addition, the new legislation clarifies that gametes from anonymous donations can still be used, until a date set by decree (not yet announced). On the eve of this date, the storage of embryos and gametes from anonymous donations will be terminated. As for children born under the

[7] Massilia Amzal, PhD student at University Jean Moulin Lyon 3, Family Law Center, Research team Louis Josserand.

[8] Law No. 2021-1017 of 2 August 2021 on bioethics.

[9] Art. L. 2143-I of the Public health Code.

[10] The Agence de la biomédecine is a public agency created in 2004. It carries out its missions in the fields of organ, tissue and cell removal and transplantation, as well as in the fields of procreation, embryology and human genetics.

previous system, the new commission will contact the donors and ask for their consent to the communication of non-identifying data and of their identity.

While this represents notable progress, as the new law abandons the model of secrecy around donation, the effectiveness of having the right to access one's origins remains debatable. Despite the general transition towards donor identifiability, both in European countries and beyond, the requirement of disclosure of the use of donation has not translated into high disclosure rates. Indeed, in Sweden, the first country to ever lift anonymity in 1985, research shows that after the introduction of identifiable donation, no evidence was found that parents using identifiable donors were more likely to disclose this information to the child.[11] Likewise, in the United Kingdom, there has been no significant increase in disclosure rates following the introduction of legislation mandating identifiable donation in 2005.[12]

France is likely to face similar challenges when it comes to effective disclosure of third-party involvement. This raises the question of what measures could be put in place to ensure that children have access to their origins. Could it be provision of a multidisciplinary medical team counselling the prospective parents on the advantages of disclosure, providing advice about how and when to provide such information to the child, and offering ongoing support for the parents after the child is born? Is a more direct measure acceptable, for instance by automatically sending information to the child when the child reaches 18 years of age?

Regardless of the path chosen in the long run, it remains fundamental to continue reflecting on the avenues envisaged to guarantee an effective right of access to one's origins.

4. THE OPENING UP OF MEDICALLY ASSISTED PROCREATION TO ALL WOMEN[13]

After many twists and turns, detailed in the two previous chronicles,[14] the Law on Bioethics was adopted on 2 August 2021.[15]

---

11 K. Nikos, M. Doumergue and S. Zadeh, 'Sperm donor regulation and disclosure intentions: results from a nationwide multi-centre study in France' (2018) 5 *Reproductive Biomedicine & Society Online* 38–45.

12 Ibid.

13 Aurore Camuzat, PhD student at University Jean Moulin Lyon 3, Family Law Center, Research team Louis Josserand.

14 See A. Camuzat, 'The Opening-up of Medically Assisted Procreation to All Women, A Chronicle of French Family Law: 2019' in M. Brinig (ed.), *The International Survey of Family Law*, Intersentia, 2020, p. 130; and M. Mosiek, 'The Opening-up of Medically Assisted Procreation to All Women, A Chronicle of French Family Law: 2020' in M. Brinig (ed.), *The International Survey of Family Law*, Intersentia, 2021, p. 197.

15 Law No. 2021-1017 of 2 August 2021 on bioethics.

One of the major changes brought about by the law of 2 August 2021 is the abandonment of the four pillars on which medically assisted procreation was based. These were the existence of a couple, the heterosexuality of the parental couple, the existence of medical causes and the anonymity of the third-party donor. According to Article 1 of the Law on Bioethics, which reforms Article L. 2141-2 of the Public Health Code, 'medically assisted procreation is intended to respond to a parental project. Any couple formed by a man and a woman or two women or any unmarried woman has access to medically assisted procreation'. The new law remarkably strengthens the right to become a parent by expressly opening up recourse to medically assisted procreation to single (unmarried) women and to female couples and by replacing, for all its beneficiaries, the condition of medical sterility with that of a parental project.

The Law on Bioethics of 2 August 2021 constitutes a considerable turning point in the evolution of family law since it goes so far as to modify the very definition of parentage. Faced with the opening up of medically assisted procreation to female couples, the legislator had to address the consequences. Several choices were open to it: to use adoption procedures, to create an *ad hoc* method of establishing parentage or to completely overhaul French parentage law.

The Law on Bioethics created a new type of parentage, based on participation in a parental project. For female couples, a specific form of parentage for medically assisted procreation has been introduced, without modifying the whole law of parentage. This means that the parentage of a child resulting from medically assisted procreation in a heterosexual couple or for an unmarried woman remains subject to ordinary law. Married heterosexual couples will be able to use the presumptions of maternity[16] and paternity.[17] Unmarried heterosexual couples will be able to establish a parent–child relationship through an act of recognition.[18] For single women, parentage may be established through the presumption of maternity. According to this presumption, the mother is the woman who gives birth.

A special regime has been developed for children born as a result of medically assisted procreation in a female couple.[19] The new provisions allow for the establishment of the mother of intention of the child's parentage by providing for an early joint recognition of the child by both women before a notary at the time of consent to medically assisted procreation. The real change lies in the establishment of parentage with regard to the intended mother. Previously, only the woman who had given birth could establish her parentage in relation to the

16 Art. 311-25 French Civil Code.
17 Art. 312 French Civil Code.
18 Art. 316 French Civil Code.
19 Art. 342-9 to 342-12 French Civil Code.

child, according to the adage *mater semper certa est* (presumption of maternity). Now, the basis for establishing parentage for female couples is the existence of a common parental project, made concrete by recourse to medically assisted procreation.

Finally, the law of 2 August 2021 offered the possibility for couples who have already had recourse to medically assisted procreation abroad to carry out a joint recognition, before a notary, in order to establish a link of parentage between the child and the mother of intention. This possibility is open to them for three years, i.e. until 4 August 2024.

Whether it is a question of early joint recognition or joint recognition of the child simply conceived, this is the first time that double maternal parentage can be established outside the framework of adoption. It is possible to see here the abandonment of the model of carnal parentage, which is nevertheless dominant in the common law of parentage. Moreover, this situation seems to indicate an evolution of the legal qualification of 'mother' in French law. Although the Law of 2 August 2021 raises many questions, one main question remains: why not completely overhaul the French law on parentage?

5. THE PARENTAGE OF CHILDREN BORN ABROAD BY SURROGACY: THE LEGISLATURE'S TIME[20]

Readers of this column have been able to follow year on year the developments and procrastinations of France in the way it deals with surrogate motherhood. As a reminder, this practice is prohibited in France. Since the beginning of the 2010s, the French and European courts have been interacting to find a solution that respects the fundamental rights of children while preserving the national ban. The latest case law on this subject was presented in this review last year. It is only necessary to add a decision of the Cour de Cassation, delivered on 13 January 2021, which confirms the position taken. Thus, the transcription of birth certificates of children born abroad as a result of surrogate motherhood must be carried out for all intended parents.

We had mentioned a potential legislative delayed, delayed because of the pandemic situation. This development has finally taken place, with the adoption of the Bioethics Law on 2 August 2021. The main innovation is the opening up of medically assisted procreation to female couples.[21]

[20] Bastien Baret, Ass. Professor at Lyon Catholic University, Research Team Confluence, Sciences et Humanités – EA 1598.

[21] A. Camuzat, 'The Opening-up of Medically Assisted Procreation to All Women', section 4 above.

This law also introduced a change in the area of surrogate motherhood. The legislature affirmed its position on the subject, which had long been requested. It added a paragraph to an article relating to the reception of civil status documents performed abroad. Article 47 of the Civil Code provides that records made abroad are presumed to be valid, except in the case of non-compliance with the rules of form provided for by local law, irregularity, falsification or fraud. Fraud is defined as the discrepancy between the facts mentioned in the document and reality, such as when it is stated in a document that a person was born in 1990 when in fact he or she was born in 2010. The notion of reality addressed by this article was classically a factual reality, not a legal one. The legislature intervened to add a clarification, according to which this reality 'is assessed in the light of French law'.

This means that a record which designates as the mother a woman who has not given birth to the child is not in accordance with reality as defined by French law, which provides that the mother is the woman who gives birth. The aim is clearly to regulate the case law of the Cour de Cassation on the subject, in order to limit the transcription of the records to the intended father alone. For the other parent, recourse to adoption remains open.

This development makes it possible to clarify the parliament's position on the subject. However, it calls for various reflections, which we will briefly address.[22]

First of all, the language chosen is very general. During the parliamentary debates, another text was proposed, specific to the issue of surrogate pregnancies. The solution adopted is different. Although motivated by the desire to reduce the scope of the case law of the Cour de Cassation, the new provision is supposed to apply to all acts that are subject to the control of Article 47. By this logic, there is the potential for confusion or even contradiction within this article itself when it is used in litigation that is not related to surrogate motherhood.

Secondly, the very context of the adoption of this law raises doubts about the interpretation that will be given by the courts to the 'reality' of the notion of mother in French law. As Aurore Camuzat has written, the opening up of medically assisted procreation to female couples and the introduction of a new method of establishing filiation reserved for women who do not gestate in this situation may indicate an evolution in the legal qualification of mother in French law.[23]

Finally, this law contradicts the latest position of the Cour de Cassation, which leads us to question once again the reasons for the evolution of this court's

---

22 For an in-depth treatment of this issue, see C. Bidaud, 'La force probante des actes de l'état civil étrangers modifiée par la loi bioéthique: du sens à donner à l'exigence de conformité des faits à la réalité "appréciée au regard de la loi française" …' (2022) 1 *Rev. crit. DIP* 529.

23 A. Camuzat, 'The Opening-up of Medically Assisted Procreation to All Women', section 4 above.

position. It had opted for 'transcription for all', basing its decision in particular on respect for fundamental rights in the *Mennesson* case and then, to generalise its solution, on equality. Could such arguments be used to avoid actually complying with the legislative injunction? No decision has yet been handed down on the subject, but it is possible to think that the Cour de Cassation will be able to use the *in concreto* proportionality review that it has been using since 2013 to apply this new rule, while having the possibility of setting it aside from time to time when it does not sufficiently respect the rights and freedoms of individuals, particularly when adoption is difficult to implement.

The legislative intervention was awaited, and it has finally come. The very general wording allows the legislature not to mention too directly the legal consequences of surrogate pregnancies carried out abroad in the Code, which facilitates both the political aspect of this evolution and potential future modifications. This choice also allows the Cour de Cassation to keep a certain margin of manoeuvre, which could avoid a potential condemnation by the European Court of Human Rights. However, this choice leads to uncertainties in the other areas affected by this very general provision, without these issues necessarily having been anticipated.

6. DENIAL OF VISITATION RIGHTS FOR THE MOTHER'S EX-WIFE[24]

The decision rendered by the Cour de Cassation on 7 July 2021,[25] a little more than a month before the final vote on the bioethics reform, illustrates the difficulties that the wife or partner of the biological mother have encountered in the case of separation. The absence of a status recognised by the law in the absence of adoption obliged them to claim a visitation right as a third party, as provided for by Article 371-4 of the Civil Code. Jurisprudence has occasionally recognised the rights of social parents,[26] but those rights remained very fragile. The Paris Court of Appeals refused all visitation rights to a mother's ex-partner who had taken parental leave to take care of the child for four years, until the couple separated. The judges based their decision on the passionate and unreasonable conflict existing between the two ex-partners and on the frank hostility of the child and its somatic manifestations, which had occurred since

---

24 Guillaume Kessler, Ass. Professor at Savoie Mont Blanc University, Research Law Center Antoine Favre.

25 Cass. 1re civ., 7 July 2021, n° 19-25.515, Droit de la famille 2021, comm. 142, obs. V. Egéa.

26 See e.g. CA Besançon, 1 September 2016, n° 15/99916, Droit de la famille 2016, comm. 252, obs. S. Tétard.

the implementation of the right of access and accommodation.[27] The Court of Appeal of Rouen, on the other hand, based its decision to grant such a right on the existence of a common parental project.[28] The Cour de Cassation subsequently validated this case-by-case assessment on the basis that the rights of same-sex couples and those of opposite-sex couples were assessed in the same way in this context. Consequently, it rejected the referral to the European Court of Human Rights for an opinion.[29] This argument is both fair and questionable. If the situation of the ex-spouse or partner is indeed considered in the same way from the point of view of Article 371-4, fathers, in the case of opposite-sex couples, have a possibility which was until now denied to second mothers: the possibility of having their status as a parent established and not being considered a mere third party.

The decision rendered on 7 July 2021 retains the same position. Even though in this case the social mother was married to the biological mother, the Court confirmed the decision of the Court of Appeal, which had denied her any right of access on the basis that the separation had occurred when the child was still very young, that no emotional bond had been able to develop with the child, who was now six and a half years old, and that the conflict with the mother, who was now living with a new partner with whom she had had a child, had not subsided. While recognising that the birth was undoubtedly the result of a joint project, the judges concluded that the establishment of visitation rights would be contrary to the interests of the child.

If the social mother had been recognised from the beginning as the child's second legal mother, such a situation could not have occurred. The delay in resolution would not have been so long. Her parental rights would have been secured through the establishment of visitation rights much earlier and the bonding could have been established as it should have been. Being considered a third party and having to rely on Article 371-4 of the Civil Code allows the biological mother to obstruct the creation of the relationship and to let time pass until it becomes impossible. This is how much the new dual maternal recognition system (under Article 342-10 of the Civil Code) will improve the situation for non-biological mothers.

Not all the problems will be solved because nothing has been foreseen in the case of at-home insemination, a practice that will undoubtedly continue given the risk of sperm shortages in the context of medically assisted procreation. The work on LGBT+ parenthood is thus far from being completed in France.

---

27 CA Paris, 5 June 2014, n° 14/01098, JCP G 2014, 931, obs. G. Kessler.

28 CA Rouen, 3 April 2014, n° 13/03333, Droit de la famille 2014, comm. 99, obs. C. Neirinck.

29 Cass. 1re civ., 24 June 2020, n° 19-15.198, Procédures 2020, comm. 148, obs. M. Douchy-Oudot.

7. THE CHALLENGES OF DEALING WITH GENDER IDENTITY IN THE CONTEXT OF SCHOOL[30]

Gender identity issues are sometimes raised in the school environment. In order to provide the tools for the national educational personnel to be able to respond to such issues, the French Ministry of Education published a circular on 29 September 2021 that pursues the following objective of 'a better consideration of the questions relating to gender identity in the school environment.'

It should be made clear that a circular, except in the case of a regulatory one, has no legal force and simply guides the actions of public servants and agents in the application of laws and prescriptions. In seeking to ensure equal access to education for all, the circular considered the integration of all pupils to be necessary for the success of the educational objectives.

This is achieved in particular through the special attention that must be accorded to transgender pupils or those who are questioning their gender identity. It should be noted that, as a circular, it has no binding force and is only intended to guide the administration's action. To this end, it is addressed to all educational staff in order to review the terms of the subject, identify and anticipate the questions that are likely to arise, and propose ways of responding to them.

Immediately, the circular dispels certain preconceived ideas that are no longer valid in light of the latest developments in French positive law. In fact, the circular reminds us that the congruency between the sex assigned at birth and the one which an individual claims to be must be considered an event specific to each person and his or her intimate feelings, and is not to be confused with a psychological disorder or a pathology. It then describes the different stages through which such students are likely to progress and underlines the singular nature of each situation, which must be handled on a case-by-case basis. The text recommends that teachers guide these pupils and show them the greatest possible degree of respect.

Subsequently, the circular outlines three key principles: listening, support and protection for pupils who find themselves in such a situation. First of all, it seeks to create a dialogue with the pupil, who will then be able to ask questions. It also anticipates several scenarios that may arise with regard to the family background of the child and recommends counselling or even mediation with the child's family.

Once the dialogue has been established, the circular considers the different ways of accommodating the transgender student. It first considers the use of the

---

30 Mathilde Mosiek, PhD student at University Jean Moulin Lyon 3, Family Law Center, Research team Louis Josserand.

usual forename that the child wishes to bear so that it corresponds to the gender which he or she claims to be. The difficulties that may arise from the opposition of those who have parental authority over the child are also considered. Dialogue is again a path favoured by the circular. As the gender with which the child identifies can also be expressed, the circular recommends the prevention of any situation of discrimination or harassment. The issue of the use of private spaces is also considered: the circular sets out several options in order to best respond to the pupil's concerns, from authorising access to individual toilets or toilets that match his or her gender identity to introducing modified timetables for the use of changing rooms or communal showers.

Listening to and supporting the pupil does not go without also protecting him or her against all forms of discrimination or harassment of which he or she could be a victim. For this reason, the circular makes the prevention of transphobia a collective and partnership approach in which the educational team must be trained to support transgender pupils. Approved or contracted associations could also help raise awareness of these issues among pupils. Above all, this prevention must involve a coherent school policy to combat all forms of gender-based violence.

8. THE EFFECTS OF UNEQUAL FOREIGN DIVORCE JUDGMENTS IN FRANCE: EVOLUTION OF THE CASE LAW[31]

Since 2004,[32] all foreign unequal divorce judgments (repudiation, cases of gendered divorce that only the man or the woman can use, etc.) have not been able to produce any effect in France. The difference in treatment between men and women in access to divorce proceedings or in the effects of divorce was systematically considered contrary to French public policy in international matters.

The French Cour de Cassation changed its jurisprudence by a decision of 17 March 2021.[33] In this case, a woman of French–Algerian nationality and a man of Algerian nationality were married in Algeria, where they established their first marital home. The wife had bought a house in France on her own in 2009. On 4 July 2017, the spouses were divorced by an Algerian judge at the request of the wife. She then requested the expulsion of her ex-husband from the house in France based on this Algerian divorce decision. The husband contested

[31] Christine Bidaud, Professor at University Jean Moulin Lyon 3, Co-director of the Family Law Center, Research team Louis Josserand.

[32] Cass. 1re civ., 17 February 2004, five decisions, see especially decision n° 02-11.618 and n° 01-11.549.

[33] Cass. 1re civ., 17 March 2021, n° 20-14.506.

the recognition in France of the Algerian divorce decision that served as the basis for the expulsion proceedings. According to the husband, the Algerian judgment based on Article 54 of the Algerian Family Code was contrary to the principle of equality of spouses and could not, therefore, be recognised in France. This provision relates to divorce by compensation (*Khol'a*), which allows divorce on the unilateral wishes of the wife, without the agreement of the husband, through the payment of a sum of money by the wife to her husband. The Cour de Cassation rejected the argument, stating that:

> [W]here a divorce decision has been pronounced abroad in the application of a law which does not grant one of the spouses, because of his or her membership of one sex or the other, equal access to divorce, its recognition is not contrary to international public policy, provided that it is invoked by the spouse for whom the less favourable rules are provided, that the procedure followed was not vitiated by fraud and that the other spouse was able to assert his or her rights.

According to the Cour de Cassation, divorce by *Khol'a* should therefore not be considered as a repudiation: 'the former pronounced on the wife's initiative, is subject to the payment of a sum of money, whereas the latter that is the result of the sole will of the husband, who can only be required to pay pecuniary reparation in the event of recognition by the judge of an abuse of rights.'

This solution may legitimately raise questions about the equal access of spouses to various divorce proceedings. It cannot be denied that the result of the decision allows a foreign divorce decision based on a 'sexualisation' of divorce proceedings to produce effects recognised in France. However, in some cases, the consequences of a lack of recognition may be just as serious as recognition. If the foreign divorce decision is not recognised, the wife has to start the divorce proceedings again in France. The French judge must already have jurisdiction over the divorce and then the French decision will never be recognised in the country of origin of the spouses because the foreign judges will base their decisions on their own divorce judgment. If the French decision provides for financial compensation, the wife will never be able to obtain it when the husband resides abroad. Therefore, when the recognition of the unequal divorce is requested by the less well-treated spouse, it is acceptable that the foreign judgment can be recognised in France. However, this does not mean that all unequal divorces pronounced abroad will be recognised in France. When this recognition is requested by the spouse who has benefited from the more favourable rules, and especially when it concerns a repudiation without the wife even having been heard, the decision will have no effect on French territory. The Cour de Cassation recalled this in a decision handed down the same day.[34]

[34] Cass. 1re civ., 17 March 2021, n° 19-26.071.

9. EXEQUATUR OF A FOREIGN DECISION REFUSING TO GIVE EFFECT TO A MARRIAGE CONTRACT DRAWN UP IN FRANCE[35]

In a decision of 2 December 2020 (no. 18-20691), the Cour de Cassation granted exequatur to an American judgment that refused to give effect to a marriage contract drawn up by a French notary.

A man of French nationality and a woman of Russian and American nationality married in 1991 under a separate property regime, pursuant to the terms of a marriage contract drawn up by a notary in France. They then moved to the United States.

In 2001, the wife filed a petition for divorce in a US court. In 2002, a judge issued a decision and order dismissing the husband's claim that the French marriage contract was valid and enforceable and dismissing the application of the contract. In 2003, a second judge issued a trial decision, followed by a judgment of divorce in 2004, which pronounced the divorce against the husband and, among other consequences of the disunion, ruled on the liquidation of the spouses' property interests by refusing to give effect to the marriage contract registered in France.

In 2005, the ex-wife applied to the Tribunal de Grande Instance de Paris for an exequatur of the 2003 and 2004 American decisions. As a counterclaim, the ex-husband asked that the 2002 judgment be declared unenforceable in France.

According to the ex-husband,

> a foreign judgment which sets aside, without any reason, a French authentic instrument, registered by a French public officer in the name of the French Republic, is necessarily contrary to French international public policy, since the position of the French legal order, embodied in the authentic instrument, was a basis for the parties' expectations, which are perfectly legitimate since the authentic instrument is valid in France.

Further on, it was argued that 'the freedom of the spouses to choose the law applicable to their matrimonial regime, and hence their matrimonial regime, is a component of French international public policy by guaranteeing legal certainty and respect for the legitimate expectations of the spouses.'

Considering the effects of a foreign decision in France, even if public policy, in this case, could not be conceived in its full effect but only in its

[35] Eric Fongaro, University Professor, Deputy Director of IRDAP, Co-director of the Master Law and Estate Management, Head of the Comparative Private Law course.

attenuated effect, the answer given by the judges of the Cour de Cassation is reminiscent of the method followed in the *Jarre* and *Colombier* cases relating to the conformity with international public policy of a foreign law that ignores the reserved portion of inheritance.[36] According to the Première Chambre civile, 'a decision rendered by a foreign court which, by application of its national law, refuses to give effect to a marriage contract received in France is not in itself contrary to French substantive public policy.' However, this solution is immediately tempered. The foreign decision would be deprived of effect if it enshrined 'in a concrete manner, in the case in question, a situation incompatible with principles of French law considered to be essential.' It is thus rightly recalled that the infringement of international public policy must be assessed *in concreto*. It remains to be seen which essential principles of French law could be invoked against a foreign decision refusing to give effect to a marriage contract registered in France. On this point, the decision lacks clarity and seems to be based on a rather casuistic approach. The court emphasises that the American judge proceeded to liquidate the property interests of the spouses according to the principle of 'equitable distribution', taking into account the income and expenses of the parties, the consequences of the joint choices made during the marriage, and the constant elements of the spouses' lifestyle. It is also stated that the effect of the decisions rendered was not disproportionate to the reality of the financial and property situation of the ex-husband. The Cour de Cassation also pointed out that the dispute had many points of contact with the United States, where the spouses had settled after the marriage and where they continued to reside, where their children were born, where the husband obtained diplomas and carried out various professional activities and where the couple's real estate assets were located on the day of the divorce application. The Première Chambre civile thus once again makes use, as in the *Jarre* and *Colombier* cases, of a public policy of proximity, the implementation of which, in other cases, is not certain to be the easiest.

In the end, neither the principle of freedom of matrimonial agreements, which is a matter of public policy in domestic law, nor the objectives of legal certainty and foreseeability that were invoked, could, in this case, be an obstacle to the recognition in France of American decisions.

If there is one lesson to be learned from this judgment, it is that a marriage contract drawn up in France, even if valid, will not necessarily be recognised in common law countries.

---

36 Cass. 1re civ., 27 September 2017, n° 16-17198 and Cass. 1re civ., 27 September 2017, n° 16-13151.

10. BONE TESTING AND THE STRICT APPLICATION OF ARTICLE 388 OF THE CIVIL CODE[37]

In France, Article 388 of the Civil Code, introduced by Law No. 216-297 of 14 March 2016, specifies the conditions under which a bone test, which has the purpose of determining a person's age, may be ordered. As a reminder, these examinations can only be ordered 'in the absence of valid identity documents and when the alleged age is not likely.'[38] Moreover, the examination must be ordered by a decision of the judicial authority and the consent of the person is totally required. Paragraph 3 of this article specifies that the bone test findings alone cannot determine whether the person is a minor. The margins of error of these conclusions must be specified and if there is any doubt as to whether the individual is a minor, doubt must benefit him. Questioned by the Cour de Cassation on the constitutionality of this provision, the Constitutional Council reaffirmed, on 21 March 2019, the constitutionality of bone X-ray examinations for the purpose of determining age.

On 12 January 2022, the Cour de Cassation was confronted with a question relating to the application of this article.[39] In this case, a person born in Guinea, claiming to be born in 2004, wished to obtain the benefit of the educational assistance procedure, a measure for minors only. In order to prove his age, the individual had in his possession an extract from the civil status register, his passport and a supplementary judgment. The person concerned was entrusted, by the public prosecutor, to the child welfare service and had, at the same time, requested three types of expert reports: an expert report on the authenticity of the extract from the civil status records and the supplementary judgment that the individual had produced, a social expert report and a bone test. The documentary expertise highlighted the falsified nature of the documents transmitted. As for the social expert report, it noted that the behavioural traits of the person could reveal an age between 16 and 17 years. On the other hand, the bone test found that the individual could be between 18 and 20 years old.

The Paris Court of Appeal, in a decision dated 17 January 2020, noted the disparity of the ages invoked by the various expert reports and by the individual himself. Since there was no evidence of the reality of the individual's minority, it concluded that the individual could not benefit from the protective measure he requested. The latter therefore appealed to the Cour de Cassation, arguing that, among all the documents, there was a doubt as to his minority which should

---

37 Claire Brunerie, PhD student at University Jean Moulin Lyon 3, International Private Law Center (CREDIP).

38 Art. 388 French Civil Code.

39 Cass. 1re civ., 12 January 2022, n° 20-17.343.

have benefited him. He criticised the Court of Appeal for not having noted the absence of a margin of error in the results of the bone test.

The Cour de Cassation had to answer the question of how to assess the existence of a doubt when faced with contradictory documents.[40] In the end, it applied Article 388 of the Civil Code strictly – and in our opinion, rightly so. It overturned the decision of the Court of Appeal, noting that only the bone examinations had led to a determination of the majority of the person concerned. It is worth noting the attachment of the counsellors to the strict application of Article 388 of the Civil Code and the objective assessment of the doubt.[41]

This decision is to be commended in that it preserves the best interests of the child.[42] The unreliability of bone tests obliges the legislature to use them with caution. Indeed, there is a significant margin of error, from six months to three years. This margin is amplified when the tests are performed on teenagers of about 16–18 years old, who are the majority of the people who request educational assistance.[43] More than with any other technique, the doubt must benefit the person concerned.

11. THE RIGHT OF THE CHILD TO BE HEARD[44]

In a decision of 14 April 2021,[45] the French Cour de Cassation reminded us that the decision to refuse to hear a minor is not appealable and such a refusal based on the minor's lack of discernment (the ability to form his or her own views) must be justified by the judges.

In this case, after the separation of a couple, a parental conflict arose over the exercise of parental authority and more specifically over decisions relating to the health of the child. The lower court allowed the mother to make medical decisions concerning the child, then aged nine, on her own. The father appealed the court's judgment and the child asked to be heard at that time. The Court of Appeal of Lyon affirmed the court ruling and rejected the minor's request on two grounds: his lack of discernment and the need to protect him from parental conflict. For information, the child was then 11 years old. As a result, the father

---

40 E. Supiot, 'Tests osseux : doute et intérêt supérieur de l'enfant', *Dalloz actu*, 26 January 2022.

41 Ibid.

42 Ibid.

43 C. Bidaud, 'L'utilisation des preuves scientifiques dans le droit des migrants' in *La famille du migrant*, LexisNexis, 2020, p. 277.

44 Marie Pincet, PhD student at University Jean Moulin Lyon 3, Family Law Center, Research team Louis Josserand.

45 Cass. 1re civ., 14 January 2021, n° 18-26.707.

objected to the Court of Appeal for having rejected his child's request for a hearing and for having made such a ruling on decisions relating to his health without having heard him first.

The French Cour de Cassation relied on Article 388-1 of the French Civil Code and Articles 338-4 and 338-5 of the French Civil Procedure Code to reach its resolution. After recalling that the decision to refuse to hear a minor could not be appealed, the Cour de Cassation quashed the appeal court's judgment by ruling that, when a minor asks to be heard, this is his right, and that the mere fact of referring to the minor's lack of discernment is an inadequate justification for refusing to hear the child. In other words, the judges should have demonstrated why the child was not capable of discernment to reject his request for a hearing.

In French law, pursuant to Article 338-5 of the Civil Procedure Code, 'the decision ruling on the request for a hearing made by the minor is not subject to appeal'. Thus, the court's ruling, a literal application of the text, is hardly unexpected on this point. The following is perhaps more enlightening, as the notion of the child's discernment, which came to us from the Convention on the Rights of the Child,[46] may have caused difficulties for French judges. Only two grounds are legally accepted for refusing to hear the minor when he or she has requested it: lack of discernment and the fact that he or she is not interested in the proceedings.[47] Contrary to the age standard, the subjective notion of discernment is necessarily subject to interpretation. While there are undoubtedly advantages to the use of this notion in French texts without giving it a definition, there is also the potential for abuse. The use of lack of discernment to justify the refusal of a hearing, without the need to explain why, is one example. Fortunately, this decision shows us that the Cour de Cassation ensures that this very vague notion will not become an 'easy excuse' to override the right to be heard.

By requiring judges to explain why the minor whose request for a hearing has been refused is not capable of discernment, the French Cour de Cassation once again[48] shows its intention to protect the effectiveness of the child's right to express his or her views on all matters and decisions that affect him or her.[49]

---

46 Art. 12 Convention on the Rights of the Child, translated into French: 'Les Etats parties garantissent à l'enfant qui est capable de discernement le droit d'exprimer librement son opinion sur toute question l'intéressant'.

47 Art. 338-4 Civil Procedure Code.

48 The Cour de Cassation regularly shows the importance of the child's right to be heard (see, to that effect, Cass. 1re civ., 18 March 2015, n° 14-11.392).

49 This right is enshrined in the Art. 12 Convention on the Rights of the Child.

12. WEBSITE FOR EXTRAMARITAL DATING IS NOT A VIOLATION OF THE FIDELITY OBLIGATION IN MARRIAGE[50]

Blackdivine LLC is an American company and the publisher of Gleeden (www.gleeden.com), a website created to promote extramarital dating. In 2015, this company posted ads on buses in Paris with the slogan: 'the first website for extramarital dateing.' On 22 January 2015, the National Confederation of Catholic Families' Associations (CNAFC) sued Blackdivine LLC. The Confederation's requests were basically to invalidate the contracts between the website and the users because of their illegal 'cause', to forbid such advertisements and to order the company to pay an indemnity. On 9 February 2017, the judge declined the Confederation's requests and so did the Court of Appeal.

The Confederation has filed an appeal with the French Cour de Cassation against the Court of Appeal's sentence. The appeal was only about the advertisements and the indemnity requests. The Confederation argued that Article 212 of the French Civil Code (about the fidelity obligation in marriage) had been violated, as well as Articles 1 and 4 of the Code of the International Commercial Chambre about the advertising practices. According to the Confederation, freedom of speech must be limited by the fidelity obligation in marriage.

There are two questions to consider: does the advertising violate the fidelity obligation of married couples? And is it possible to limit freedom of speech in this case?

Before answering the first question, the Court considered that the Code of the International Commercial Chambre does not have the same value as other legal instruments: it is only a reference. The Court also noted that the tort of adultery only concerns the couple. This means that there is no tort outside of the spouse's relationship to each other; generally, this tort is only alleged in divorce proceedings.

This analysis brings us to the second question about freedom of expression. Article 10 of the European Convention on Human Rights mentions freedom of expression and its limitations. As the fidelity obligation is restricted to the couple, according to the answer to the first question, the Court concluded that forbidding the advertising would not be proportional to the freedom of expression.

The Court also understood that the advertisement was not using indecent images and that its slogans were ambiguous, so they were not inappropriate for

[50] Taylene Moreira De Sá, PhD student at University Jean Moulin Lyon 3 and University of São Paulo, lawyer and member of the Brazilian Institute of Family Law (IBDFAM).

children, which was another reason to conclude that the freedom of expression could not be limited in this case.

13. CONCLUDING OBSERVATIONS OF THE COMMITTEE ON THE RIGHTS OF PERSONS WITH DISABILITIES ABOUT FRENCH LEGAL MEASURES OF PROTECTION[51]

After a first Report of the Special Rapporteur on the rights of persons with disabilities (the Special Rapporteur),[52] it is now the Committee on the Rights of Persons with Disabilities (the Committee) which has expressed concerns about the French civil law's compliance with Article 12 (equal recognition before the law) of the Convention on the Rights of Persons with Disabilities (CRPD).[53]

Since the publication of the General Comment No. 1 on Article 12, the Committee has defended the notion of legal capacity based on human rights and has adopted a strong position on States parties' obligations. Among other things, the Committee states that 'perceived or actual deficits in mental capacity must not be used as justification for denying legal capacity.'[54] In other words, mental capacity and legal capacity should be clearly distinguished. Regarding States parties' obligations, these notably have 'to replace substitute decision-making regimes by supported decision-making[, which] requires both the abolition of substitute decision-making regimes and the development of supported decision-making alternatives.'[55]

In its concluding observations on the initial report of France, the Committee notes with concern that deprivation of legal capacity is based on medical assessments of the person's mental capacity. The Committee also reports 'the absence of supported decision-making mechanisms compatible with the Convention, and measures that perpetuate substituted decision-making and fail to recognize the will and preferences of persons with disabilities.'[56] Hence, the Committee urges France to 'review its understanding of legal protection measures' and 'redirect organizational and financial resources from substituted

51 Guillaume Millerioux, PhD, University Jean Moulin Lyon 3, Family Law Center, Research team Louis Josserand.

52 Special Rapporteur on the rights of persons with disabilities, *Report on her visit to France*, A/HRC/40/54/Add.1, 8 January 2019.

53 Committee on the Rights of Persons with Disabilities, *Concluding observations on the initial report of France*, CRPD/C/FRA/CO/1, 4 October 2021.

54 Committee on the Rights of Persons with Disabilities, *General Comment No. 1 on Article 12: Equal recognition before the law*, CRPD/C/GC/1, 19 May 2014, para. 13, p. 3.

55 Ibid, para. 28, p. 8.

56 Committee on the Rights of Persons with Disabilities, above n. 53, para. 25, p. 7.

decision-making to develop supported decision-making mechanisms that respect the dignity, autonomy, will and preferences of persons with disabilities'.[57] However, these alarming observations must be tempered. Limitation of legal capacity is justified when an adult cannot express his or her wishes, meaning that he or she cannot provide for his or her interests.[58] Making limitation of legal capacity conditional on the absence of will is closely tied to the notion of legal capacity as the ability to express a wish (to conclude legal transactions). Will and legal capacity cannot be separated from each other. But it is true that limitation of legal capacity should not entirely be based on a medical certification. A medical-social evaluation of the adult's situation should be enshrined to correctly individualise the legal response to his or her needs.[59]

It can be maintained that legal measures of protection, especially guardianship and curatorship, are not, per se, incompatible with Article 12. It all depends on the way they are applied in practice. Indeed, a legal measure of protection becomes a substituted decision-making regime when any decision 'is based on what is believed to be in the objective "best interests" of the person concerned, as opposed to being based on the person's own will and preferences.'[60] Rather than abolishing guardianship or curatorship, France should find solutions to guarantee the consideration of the wishes and preferences of adults, unless special circumstances require otherwise. Eventually, a compromise should be found between the status quo and the unwise Committee's recommendations.[61]

---

57 Ibid, para. 26, p. 7.

58 Art. 425 French Civil Code.

59 For now, a medico-social evaluation is mandatory only when the legal measure of protection is requested by the prosecutor (Art. 431 French Civil Code). It should be extended to all requests. See, in that sense, A. Caron-Déglise, *The Evolution of Legal Protection of Adult*, Report of Inter-ministerial Mission, 2018, pp. 30 ff.

60 Committee on the Rights of Persons with Disabilities, above n. 53, para. 27, p. 6.

61 For further information, see G. Millerioux, *La capacité juridique des majeurs vulnérables* (Legal capacity of vulnerable adults), thesis, Lyon, 2021 (only in French).

HONG KONG

HELLO, CAN YOU HEAR ME? IMPLEMENTING ARTICLE 12 OF THE UNCRC IN THE HONG KONG LEGAL SETTING

Anne Scully-Johnson

Résumé

Cet article est un extrait de la recherche menée pour le Comité des droits de l'enfant de Hong Kong (HKCCR) qui examine la mise en œuvre à Hong Kong du droit des enfants d'être entendus dans les procédures les concernant, garanti par l'article 12 de la CIDE. Alors que les recherches commandées par le HKCCR s'étendent à de multiples domaines, de l'éducation et la santé à l'élaboration de politiques constitutionnelles, ainsi qu'aux loisirs et à la culture notamment, cet article propose une analyse critique de la manière dont la voix des enfants est entendue dans le cadre juridique existant à Hong Kong. Les résultats de la recherche laissent penser que, bien que la législation relative au droit de l'enfant d'être entendu en vigueur à Hong Kong soit à bien des égards meilleure que dans d'autres États dont la législation a été examinée dans l'étude de la HKCCR, l'avis de des enfants est au mieux consultatif et, au pire, n'existe que dans les textes et non dans la pratique. Après avoir identifié les éléments qui font obstacle à une meilleure participation des enfants, cet article propose des recommandations afin d'améliorer la situation.

1. INTRODUCTION

This chapter will present the findings of research into how Article 12 of the United Nations Convention on the Rights of the Child (UNCRC) has been implemented in Hong Kong's legal sector. This research is part of a wider project commissioned by the Hong Kong Committee on Children's Rights (HKCCR), a non-governmental organisation originally formed in 1992 to promote, advance and ensure the rights of the child in Hong Kong. The aim of the wider project was to establish an independent baseline study of the implementation of Article 12 across all relevant sectors in Hong Kong, from constitutional and high-level policy-making to health and education to matters of leisure, culture and built environment, amongst others.[1] This baseline could then be used to identify existing gaps in the implementation of Article 12, as well as providing a yardstick to measure future progress. The HKCCR has kindly given permission to share here the section of the study that looks at the child's right to participate in legal proceedings and in legal settings where decisions will be made which affect them.[2] The full study can be found on the HKCCR's website.[3]

---

1 A vital limb to this research project, in which children are invited through their schools and clubs to share their views on child participation, is currently on hold given the impact in recent years of civil rights protests and the COVID-19 pandemic on the suspension of children's school attendance and club activities. It is expected that once schools and clubs are functioning normally again, this research will be resumed.

2 The section has been edited to fit the format for this chapter.

3 Available at: <http://v2.childrenrights.org.hk/v2/archive/04concerns/BaselineStudyImlementationArticle12HK.pdf>, last accessed 31.07.2022.

2. BACKGROUND

Hong Kong became a party to the UNCRC in 1994 and, as such, the Hong Kong Government is committed to respect and implement those rights of the child enshrined in the Convention. Since the Convention came into being in 1989, the UN Committee on the Rights of the Child has identified four aspects of the Convention which it designates as the 'general principles' of the Convention: the Article 2 principle of non-discrimination; the Article 3 best interests principle; the Article 6 right of the child to life, survival and development; and the Article 12 right of the child to express their views and to have those views taken into account.[4] The Committee has explained that these four principal articles guide the interpretation and implementation of all other rights under the Convention. So, not only is Article 12 an important right in itself but it is also a 'gateway' right. As a gateway right, implementing Article 12 facilitates the exercise of other Convention rights.

Article 12 requires specifically that:

> 1. States Parties shall assure to the child who is capable of forming his or her own views the right to express those views freely in all matters affecting the child, the views of the child being given due weight in accordance with the age and maturity of the child.
> 2. For this purpose, the child shall in particular be provided the opportunity to be heard in any judicial and administrative proceedings affecting the child, either directly, or through a representative or an appropriate body, in a manner consistent with the procedural rules of national law.

Article 12 itself does not feature the word 'participation' but it is often referred to as the child's right to participate. Indeed, the UN Committee on the Rights of the Child has acknowledged Article 12 as being synonymous with the child's right to participate, stating:

> A widespread practice has emerged in recent years, which has been broadly conceptualized as 'participation', although this term itself does not appear in the text of article 12. This term has evolved and is now widely used to describe ongoing processes, which include information-sharing and dialogue between children and adults based on mutual respect, and in which children can learn how their views and those of adults are taken into account and shape the outcome of such processes.[5]

---

[4] See UN Committee on the Rights of the Child, Convention on the Rights of the Child, 20 November 1989, available at: <https://www.ohchr.org/en/instruments-mechanisms/instruments/convention-rights-child>, last accessed 31.07.2022.

[5] UN Committee on the Rights of the Child, General Comment No. 12, *The Right of the Child to be Heard*, CRC/C/GC/12 (12 May 2009), p. 3, para. 3, available at: <https://www2.ohchr.org/english/bodies/crc/docs/advanceversions/crc-c-gc-12.pdf>, last accessed 31.07.2022.

3. UNPACKING ARTICLE 12

3.1. THE MEANING OF ARTICLE 12

A key stage in this study was to build a framework by which to understand the meaning and scope of Article 12 and thereby assess the degree and manner of implementation thus far in Hong Kong. The first step in building this framework was to look at Article 12 itself. There is today a widespread literature concerning Article 12 and its informal synonym, child participation. However, one of the richest sources of elaboration of the content and scope of Article 12 is to be found in the United Nations Committee on the Rights of the Child's General Comment No. 12 (2009): *The Right of the Child to be Heard* (GC12).[6]

The first part of Article 12 requires that States Parties

> *assure* to the child who is *capable of forming his or her own views* the right to *express those views freely* in *all matters affecting the child*, the views of the child being *given due weight* in accordance with *the age and maturity* of the child.[7]

'*Assure*', as noted in GC12, connotes 'a legal term of special strength, which leaves no leeway for States Parties' discretion. Accordingly, States Parties are under strict obligation to undertake appropriate measures to fully implement this right for all children.'[8]

Further in GC12, '*capable of forming his or her own views*' 'should not be seen as a limitation, but rather as an obligation for States Parties to assess the capacity of the child to form an autonomous opinion to the greatest extent possible … it is not up to the child to first prove her or his capacity.'[9] This can also be linked to the Articles 13 and 17 requirement to provide a child with appropriate information necessary to form a view.

That the child can '*express those views freely*' requires that the child can choose whether or not to express a view, and moreover that the child must not be manipulated or coerced in any way to express a view. This, it has been suggested, requires that '[i]f children are to be able to express their views, it is necessary for adults to create the opportunities for children to do so.'[10]

---

6 Ibid.
7 Ibid (emphasis added).
8 Ibid, p. 8 (emphasis added).
9 Ibid, p. 9.
10 G. Lansdown, 'Promoting Children's Participation in Democratic Decision-Making' (2001) 6 *Innocenti Insights* 2.

The right arises in '*all matters affecting the child*', which GC12 notes means a fairly broad approach is acceptable in interpreting the range of matters which affect the child. In practice this has been taken not to go so far as to give a general political mandate to children but does extend to cover matters affecting a child, not just personally, as an individual, but also a child as member of a group of children, or even as 'children as a constituency'.[11]

The requirement that the child's views are '*given due weight*' has been subject to debate. Some commentators see this as a potential limitation when linked to the child's age and maturity. However, GC12 makes it clear that there is a minimum threshold of consideration which the child's views must be accorded: 'simply listening to the child is insufficient; the views of the child have to be seriously considered when the child is capable of forming her or his own views.'[12] It has been suggested that this threshold consequently requires that the child should be given some feedback on the impact or consequences of their views.[13]

The double requirement to consider the '*age and maturity*' of the child means that the weight given to the child's views 'needs to reflect their level of understanding of the issues involved. This does not mean that young children's views will automatically be given less weight.'[14] This also links to Article 5 on the evolving capacities of the child and the need for parents and other relevant persons to have respect for those. Age alone is not a sufficient indicator of the weight to be given to the views of the child.

So, as Gerison Lansdown has noted:

> It is important to understand clearly what Article 12 does and does not say. It does not give children the right to autonomy. It does not give children the right to control over all decisions irrespective of their implications either for themselves or others. It does not give children the right to ride roughshod over the rights of their parents. However, it does introduce a radical and profound challenge to traditional attitudes, which assume that children should be seen and not heard.[15]

The second part of Article 12 is more specific:

> For this purpose the child shall in particular be provided the opportunity to be heard in *any judicial and administrative proceedings affecting the child*, either *directly, or*

11 Ibid.
12 GC12, at para. 28.
13 A. Parkes, *Children and International Human Rights Law: The Right of the Child to be Heard*, Routledge-Cavendish, 2013.
14 Lansdown, above n. 10.
15 Ibid.

> *through a representative* or an appropriate body, in a manner consistent with the procedural rules of national law.[16]

The application of the child's right in '*any judicial and administrative proceedings affecting the child*' is intended to be without limitation and holds irrespective of who initiates the proceedings. Moreover, the UN Committee reads this provision as implicitly requiring States Parties to create an environment in which the child can exercise this right in a way that is accessible, not intimidating and child-appropriate. This is also linked to Articles 13 and 15, which require the child to have access to appropriate information.

Where the child chooses to be heard, then there must be the possibility for a child either to be heard *directly* or if heard '*through a representative*', then the 'representative must be aware that she or he represents exclusively the interests of the child and not the interests of other persons (parent(s)), institutions or bodies (e.g. residential home, administration or society). Codes of conduct should be developed for representatives who are appointed to represent the child's views.'[17]

So, the child's capacity to form and express a view freely, should the child wish, is presumptive, as is the fact that their view will be demonstrably considered. Further steps must be taken to facilitate the child's wish, in an appropriate manner, on a case-by-case basis. However, the child's view is not automatically determinative of the matter at hand.

3.2. THE NATURE OF CHILD PARTICIPATION

Article 12 has evolved to encompass the concept of 'child participation', which Hart defines as 'the process of sharing decisions which affect one's life and the life of the community in which one lives.'[18] Hart identifies several ways in which a child may participate and ranks these as steps upwards on a ladder from non-participation to five increasing degrees of participation.

Hart's lowest levels of what might be claimed to be 'child participation' include any engagement of children which is either manipulated, decorative or tokenistic and are therefore deemed to be 'non-participation'. On manipulation, Hart says '[i]f children have no understanding of the issues and hence do not understand their actions, then this is manipulation … Another example of manipulation is a situation where children are consulted but given no feedback at all.'[19]

16 UNCRC, above n. 4.

17 GC12, at para. 37.

18 R. Hart 'Children's Participation: From Tokenism to Citizenship' (1992) 4 *Innocenti Insights* 5.

19 Ibid, 9.

Children's participation as decoration occurs when children are included and presented as part of the process but have no idea why they are there, provide no input on the issues and are simply there to be 'decorative'. Tokenism is only mildly better, being 'those instances in which children are apparently given a voice, but in fact have little or no choice about the subject or the style of communicating it, and little or no opportunity to formulate their own opinions.'[20]

Moving up Hart's ladder, more authentic participation begins when child participation is 'assigned but informed': '[t]he children understand the intentions of the project … They know who made the decisions concerning their involvement and why … They have a meaningful (rather than "decorative") role … They volunteer for the project after the project was made clear to them.'[21] Slightly better participation is when child participants are 'consulted and informed': '[t]he project is designed and run by adults, but children understand the process and their opinions are treated seriously.'[22] Better still is when children participate in projects initiated by adults, but the decision-making is shared with children. Hart calls this '[a]dult-initiated, shared decisions with children.'[23]

The two forms of participation Hart considers to be the most engaged forms of child participation are where participation is child-initiated and child-led, or greater still, child-initiated and decisions shared with adults. Hart locates the latter at the top of the scale of child participation because not only do the children take the initiative and responsibility for their participation but because they also incorporate adults' support into their participation as a resource which can enhance their own participation on their own terms.

Whilst Hart's 'Ladder of Participation' presents a useful mapping of the possibilities for child participation, it has been criticised for presenting a seemingly incremental view of child participation: that each rung of the ladder builds upon, and subsumes, the previous step; this view may not reflect the reality of children's participation, which may be less cohesive and more 'patchy' than Hart suggests. Further criticism of Hart's ladder is that it implies a 'hierarchy of values', which may lead to participatory activities being unfairly and misleadingly judged as failing to meet a high standard.[24] Sometimes, though, a less 'intense' form of child participation might be the better option when,[25] for example, intensive participation may detract from other ways a child would wish to spend their time. For instance, for a child for whom sports are important, participating

---

20 Ibid.
21 Ibid, 11.
22 Ibid, 12.
23 Ibid.
24 J. Hart, J. Newman, L. Ackerman and T. Feeney, *Children Changing their World: Understanding and Evaluating Children's Participation in Development*, Plan International, 2004, p. 48.
25 Ibid.

on a Children's Legislative Council is time-consuming and may leave no time for playing a favourite sport, while participating in a policy-making survey and receiving feedback on their input would still leave time to play sport. Treseder addresses this criticism by positing a non-hierarchical alternative which arranges the top five levels from Hart's ladder in a circle, demonstrating that they are different, but equal, forms of good participation.[26]

For the EU's 'Evaluation of legislation, policy and practice of child participation in the European Union' report, the research team took as their working definition of child participation: '[t]he democratic action and involvement of individual children and groups of children in matters affecting them.'[27] They adopted the Framework for Monitoring and Evaluating Children's Participation developed by Lansdown,[28] and took a non-hierarchical view of three main types of participation: consultative, collaborative and child-led. Lansdown defines consultative forms of participation as adult-initiated, adult-led and managed. Children have no control over the outcomes, although they may be provided with opportunities for 'organizing together, acquiring skills and confidence and contributing towards influencing outcomes.'[29] Collaborative processes are initiated by adults. They involve collaboration with children and the creation of structures through which children can challenge or influence outcomes. They will usually involve children taking 'self-directed action once the project is underway.'[30] Lastly, child-led processes, or self-advocacy processes as Lansdown terms them, are where the issues of concern are identified by children themselves, and the role of adults is to facilitate, not lead. The process is controlled by the children.[31]

3.3. THE QUALITY OF CHILD PARTICIPATION

The nature of child participation is significant but must be viewed alongside the quality of that participation too. GC12 states that all child participation processes must demonstrate these qualities:

- *Transparent and informative* – children must be provided with full, accessible, diversity-sensitive and age-appropriate information about their rights.

---

26 P. Treseder, 'Empowering Children and Young People', Save the Children, 1997.

27 European Commission, Directorate-General for Justice and Consumers, T. Young, L. Day, J. Ronicle et al., *Evaluation of legislation, policy and practice of child participation in the European Union (EU): final report*, Publications Office, 2015, p. 2, available at: <https://data.europa.eu/doi/10.2838/45596>, last accessed 31.07.2022.

28 Lansdown, above n. 10.

29 Ibid, 16.

30 Ibid, 21.

31 Ibid, 26.

- *Voluntary* – participation must not be coerced and children can withdraw participation at any time.
- *Respectful* – children's views have to be treated with respect and they should be provided with opportunities to initiate ideas and activities.
- *Relevant* – the issues on which children have the right to express their views must be of real relevance to their lives.
- *Child-friendly* – environments and working methods should be adapted to children's capacities.
- *Inclusive* – participation must be inclusive, avoid existing patterns of discrimination, and encourage opportunities for marginalised children, including both girls and boys, to be involved.
- *Supported by training* – adults need preparation, skills and support to facilitate children's participation effectively.
- *Safe and sensitive to risk* – in certain situations, expression of views may involve risks. Adults have a responsibility towards the children with whom they work and must take every precaution to minimise the risk to children of violence, exploitation or any other negative consequence of their participation.
- *Accountable* – a commitment to follow-up and evaluation is essential.[32]

Post-analysis review of the data gathered for the HKCCR baseline study suggested that three further qualities were also important: participation should not be limited to ad hoc, one-off opportunities for participation; children's participation should not be limited to a sectoral interest but should be combined with macro-level children's rights capacity-building processes; and participation should be understood not only as an exercise of rights but also as an exercise of responsibilities. As Hart says: '[t]he Convention, being more concerned with protection, does not emphasize the responsibilities which go along with rights. Children need to learn that with the rights of citizenship come responsibilities.'[33] Ideally children's participation will balance rights and responsibilities in a child- and context-appropriate manner.

3.4. THE CHILD PARTICIPATION MATRIX

Having considered the meaning and scope of Article 12, the nature, quality and settings of child participation, a working Child Participation Matrix was adopted for the baseline study. Using this matrix, the nature of child

---

32 GC12, at para. 134. See also M. Skivenes and A. Strandbu, 'A child's perspective and children's participation' (2006) 16(2) *Children, Youth and Environments* 10 for an earlier guideline on quality of child participation.

33 Hart, above n. 18, 7.

participation as implemented in Hong Kong would be evaluated as falling within one of four categories: inauthentic; consultative; collaborative; or child-led. The presumption would be that child-led participation was better than collaborative participation and collaborative participation more authentic than consultative participation. However, bearing in mind the criticism of the hierarchical nature of Hart's 'ladder', this presumption would be rebuttable, depending upon the context in which the child participation was conducted and the specificity of the children involved. The success or otherwise of the implementation of child participation in Hong Kong would further be assessed by how far opportunities for participation embodied the qualities outlined in GC12, supplemented by three further qualities: participation should be iterative wherever possible, embedded in general children's rights capacity-building processes rather than merely sectoral, and the exercise of participation rights should be balanced in a child-appropriate manner with responsibilities.

4. METHODOLOGY

Following a two-stage literature review, the empirical research for the baseline study entailed data collection using requests for information from Article 12 duty-bearers and potential duty-bearers. The Hong Kong Administration has instituted an 'Access to Information Code'[34] and this was employed to make formal requests to government departments and bureaux covered by the Code. Where duty-bearers were not covered by the Code, they were contacted with information about this study and asked to complete the same questionnaire as that sent to bodies covered by the Code. In total 31 requests for information were made: 16 to government departments and bureaux and 15 to statutory bodies. 31 responses were received, of which 30 made material responses to the questionnaire. Next, semi-structured interviews were conducted with stakeholders across the 'hotspot' settings for child participation identified in the literature review.

In total 32 invitations to interview were issued and 21 interviews were conducted, with a total number of 24 interviewees. Interviewees were representatives from: (1) international and domestic NGOs; (2) statutory bodies (3) academia; (4) the Legislative Council; and (5) individual professional experts working with child rights in sectors including law, social work, education and health. From the data gathered, this chapter will focus on the findings on the nature and quality of child participation in the legal setting in Hong Kong.

---

[34] Code on Access to Information, available at: <https://www.access.gov.hk/en/home/index.html>, last accessed 22.09.2022.

5. LAW, MECHANISMS AND STRUCTURES FOR CHILD PARTICIPATION IN LEGAL PROCEEDINGS

Children may be involved in legal proceedings in myriad ways. In criminal proceedings they may be victims, witnesses or defendants.[35] In non-criminal cases, meaning civil proceedings, a child has no 'standing'. This means that, because they are a minor, they are deemed by Hong Kong law to be a 'person under disability' who cannot represent themselves but must conduct civil proceedings through a 'next friend' or guardian.[36] This means that they cannot initiate proceedings directly as a party to protect their legal rights and interests, no matter their maturity or capacity. Children might also be affected by legal proceedings concerning their welfare where the child's parents divorce or separate, where the child needs care or protection or the child is to be adopted.

5.1. LEGISLATION AND CHILD PARTICIPATION

Despite no general incorporation of Article 12 into domestic law in Hong Kong, Article 12 and child participation are nonetheless incorporated into certain aspects of domestic legislation. Specifically, children's participation in legal proceedings which affect them is provided for in domestic legislation in several instances. The Guardianship of Minors Ordinance (Cap. 13) (GMO) section 3[37] requires that, in any proceedings before any court relating to the custody or upbringing of a minor or the property of a minor, the best interests of the child will be the first and paramount consideration and due consideration should be given to the views of the minor where it is practical to do so having regard to the minor's age and understanding and to available information from the Director of Social Welfare. In its original incarnation, section 3 referred not to the 'views' of the child but to the 'wishes' of the child. This was amended in 2012 purely to better reflect the language of the UNCRC.

The requirement to hear the views of the child is confirmed and underscored in section 7A(3)(b) of the Domestic & Cohabitation Relationships Violence Ordinance (Cap. 189) (DCRVO), which states that, in circumstances of domestic violence, where a court is contemplating the variation of an existing child custody order, the court should give due consideration to the wishes of the

---

35 The age of criminal responsibility in Hong Kong is ten years of age. Before this age a child is deemed to be incapable of legal culpability (*doli incapax*). Several years ago a campaign to raise the age of child criminal responsibility to 14 years of age, in conformity with many jurisdictions globally, was unsuccessful.

36 Rules of the High Court (Cap. 4) s. 54, Order 80.

37 Guardianship of Minors Ordinance (Cap. 13) s. 3.

minor if, having regard to the age and understanding of the minor and to the circumstances of the case, it is practicable to do so.[38]

Turning to legal guardianship of children, the GMO section 6(5) requires that where, to come into effect on their own death, a parent or guardian wishes to appoint a guardian for the child, the parent or guardian of the minor is required to take into account the views of the minor as far as practicable having regard to the minor's age and understanding.

Where a child is to be adopted, the Adoption Ordinance (Cap. 290) (AO) section 8 requires due consideration to be given to the wishes and opinions of the infant, having regard to the age and understanding of the infant.[39] Here, infant means anyone under 18 years of age unless now or previously married. Where care and control of an infant is to be passed to another person with a view to the infant being adopted, the court is also required to give due consideration to the wishes of the infant.[40]

The child's participation in the adoption process is guided by both 'broad brush' legislation and more detailed regulatory provisions[41] to the effect that

> the adoption order if made will be in the interest of the infant, due consideration being for the purpose given to the wishes and opinion of the infant, having regard to the age and understanding of the infant; having regard to the age and degree of maturity of the child … he or she must be counselled and duly informed of the effects of the adoption and of his or her consent to the adoption, where such consent is required; the infant/child's consent to the adoption, where such consent is required, has been given freely, in the required legal form, and expressed or evidenced in writing. To achieve due consideration of the infant's views, a social worker will understand the infant's view to adoption as appropriate to his/her age and maturity. A thorough discussion regarding an infant's views to adoption should also be made as far as possible and he/she should be reassured that they can voice their views and feelings freely.

Social workers are reported to receive training to achieve this degree of child participation in the adoption process.

The Child Abduction and Custody Ordinance (Cap. 512) (CACO) gives effect in Hong Kong law to the Hague Convention on the Civil Aspects of International Child Abduction. Schedule 1, Article 13 states that, when considering whether to return a child abducted from their lawful custodian, the

---

38 Domestic & Cohabitation Relationships Violence Ordinance (Cap. 189) s. 7A(3)(b).

39 Adoption Ordinance (Cap. 290) s. 8.

40 Ibid, s. 23B(2)(b).

41 Details of the statutory requirements are stipulated in s. 8(1)(b), s. 23B(2)(b), Schedule 3 'Relevant Provisions of Protection of Children and Co-operation In Respect of Intercountry Adoption' Arts. 4(d) and 21(1) and (2) of the Adoption Ordinance (Cap. 290); and Schedule 2 Part II point 11 of the Adoption Rules (Cap. 290A).

judicial or administrative authority may also refuse to order the return of the child if it finds that the child objects to being returned and has attained an age and degree of maturity at which it is appropriate to take account of their views.

The Protection of Children and Juveniles Ordinance (Cap. 213), which governs the application for and making of court orders for the assessment and detention of children deemed in need of care or protection, makes no reference to the child's views.

The Juvenile Offenders Ordinance (Cap. 226) section 8 provides for the child to engage in the Juvenile Court trial procedure, if they wish, by putting questions to witnesses, making statements or giving evidence. This may be done directly or via a parent or guardian.

The legislative provisions requiring the child's views to be heard are largely given effect in Social Investigation Reports (SIRs) compiled for the courts by a Social Welfare Officer. The Social Welfare Department (SWD) reported that it has compiled and disseminated Guidelines on the social worker's role in relation to these reports. In custody cases specifically, the SWD views its role in compiling these reports as part of an evaluative process in which children's views and preferences about post-divorce arrangement are presented to the court. The Social Welfare Officers now refer to Guidelines on Custody Evaluation, which 'have been updated to highlight important judicial developments, which allow greater opportunities for children's voices to be heard in family law proceedings affecting their interests and raise colleagues' awareness of children's right to participation.'[42]

As a channel to present the child's views to the court, the SIR is not without criticism. Inconsistency in the approach taken to compiling SIRs was a recurring theme in the stakeholder interviews for this study: 'the first line of response is always the social worker, and as I said, every social welfare officer deals with it slightly differently.'[43] One interviewee from the legal setting went further, taking the view that the reports were 'very patchy. It depends on which social welfare officer you get. Sometimes they change over the course of proceedings. Often they change because one of the parents becomes so enraged about them that eventually they bully the Social Welfare Department or the Court into saying there must be a new person.'[44]

The reasons offered for inconsistency of approach were varied and ranged from lack of uniform training or standards,[45] insufficient training on the legal context and proper scope of the SIR[46] and the inherently difficult nature of

[42] Questionnaire response from the SWD.
[43] Interview No. 5.
[44] Interview No. 6.
[45] Interview No. 3.
[46] Interview No. 1.

child participation work. One interviewee from the legal setting noted that representing the child's views to the court required highly developed skills to understand the motivation for the child's stated views, whether that was immaturity, naivety, fear of hurting either parent or fear of punishment for saying 'the wrong thing'. Another interviewee noted that in some cases cultural barriers might impact negatively on the ability of the welfare officer to accurately represent the children's views.[47]

5.2. THE JUDICIARY AND CHILD PARTICIPATION

The Hong Kong Judiciary, in response to a request for information for this study, reported that it has itself issued three Practice Guidance Notes to enable the child's right to participation in legal proceedings. These stand in addition to legislation and guidance created by the Legislature and the Administration respectively.

The first is PDSL5 Guidance on (Judges) Meeting Children. This Guidance explicitly references Article 12 and provides that direct communication between the judge and the child in a case can be requested by either the child or the judge. The child's consent to meeting the judge will be taken as an indication of whether the meeting is in best interests of the child. If the judge refuses the child's request to meet, the judge should explain their reasons to the child.[48]

The second is PDSL6 Guidance on Separate Representation for Children in Matrimonial and Family Proceedings. This also explicitly references Article 12. It provides that where it is considered to be in the best interests of the child, and particularly where a child of mature years is expressing strong views on the proceedings affecting them, the court may appoint either the Official Solicitor to represent the child or a guardian *ad litem* will stand as party to the proceedings on the child's behalf. The guardian *ad litem* may then instruct a lawyer to represent the child.[49]

The final, and most recent, Guidance Note is PDSL10.1 Guidance on Child Arrangements: Domestic Violence. This PDSL came into force on 1 February 2019, and while it does not explicitly reference the UNCRC, it references PDSL6, which does in turn refer to UNCRC Article 12. The Guidance Note makes provision for

47 Interview No. 5.

48 Practice Direction – PDSL5 Guidance on Meeting Children, available at: <https://legalref.judiciary.hk/lrs/common/pd/pdcontent.jsp?pdn=PDSL5.htm&lang=EN>, last accessed 22.09.2022.

49 Practice Direction – PDSL6 Guidance on Separate Representation for Children in Matrimonial and Family Proceedings, available at: <https://legalref.judiciary.hk/lrs/common/pd/pdcontent.jsp?pdn=PDSL6.htm&lang=EN>, last accessed 22.09.2022.

separate representation of a child where there is reason to believe the child has been subjected to or exposed to domestic violence or where there is a risk of such violence occurring in the future.[50]

It is not clear from the Judiciary's response how often judges take the opportunity to hear from the child directly under either PDSL5 or PDSL10.1. One interviewee from the legal setting expressed the view that it was still relatively unusual for judges to meet with children directly, saying 'I think that the resistance to it is just because it is so new and alien and nobody really knows, and they are worried about a mis-step because you have taken the wrong role. Partly it is also that paternalistic history we have, don't involve the children, don't involve the children.'[51] Another interviewee expressed the view that some judges were more likely than others to meet children directly and that this could be attributed to personality or background.[52]

Naturally, an absence of robust training in how to conduct a meeting with a child would serve to compound any personal inherent reticence or concerns about breaching the common law requirement of fairness between the adult parties to the case by hearing the child in private. The Judiciary's response to the questionnaire did not include information on training. However, a judicial interviewee confirmed that judges are given training, although it was not clear whether this was on a voluntary or mandatory basis.[53]

One interviewee from the legal setting took the view that in fact judges rarely met with children and that, in a culture where children are seen as holding an inferior position hierarchically to adults, there was the possibility that judges may, without taking up specialist, mandatory training, inadvertently bring this background into any meeting with children.[54] The view was also expressed that, unless handled by a properly trained judge, the meeting may not result in a child freely expressing their views:

> I think now what happens is that a judge sees the child and there is a record taken and [then] the judge hopefully makes clear to the child that the judge will listen to them, what they say will be told to the parents and ultimately it is for the judge to make the decision and not the children ... But of course, one of the difficulties with children is if there is anxiety, then they may not tell the judge [their true views] because they have been told that the judge is going to tell the parents.[55]

---

50 Practice Direction – PDSL10.1 Guidance – Child Arrangements: Domestic Violence, available at: <https://legalref.judiciary.hk/lrs/common/pd/pdcontent.jsp?pdn=PDSL10.1.htm&lang=EN>, last accessed 22.09.2022.

51 Interview No. 5.

52 Interview No. 1.

53 Interview No. 20.

54 Interview No. 1.

55 Ibid.

Looking at separate representation for children under PDSL6, two interviewees from the legal sector stated that they had experienced separate representation to be very powerful as a means of conveying the child's views.[56] One, however, noted that the current process for appointing separate representation can be onerous and costly if not undertaken by the Official Solicitor's Office and this may be one reason why it does not happen more often,[57] while the other noted that representing children requires great skill and some training other than legal training.[58] More information on separate representation for children was provided by the Office of the Official Solicitor.

5.3. THE OFFICE OF THE OFFICIAL SOLICITOR AND CHILD PARTICIPATION

The Office of the Official Solicitor (OSO) is located in an independently operated government unit, separated from the other sections of its 'home' department, the Legal Aid Department (LAD).[59] The OSO was approached in a follow-up enquiry for further information regarding separate representation of children after the LAD did not refer to the OSO in the survey responses the LAD provided. It was apparent that the OSO had the potential for promotion of child participation given the Judiciary's PDSL6 Guidance on Separate Representation for Children.

In its response, the OSO stated that:

> OSO is not a bureau/department responsible for formulating or overseeing policies relating to Article 12 of UNCRC. OSO receives referrals from courts when it appears to a court that any child ought to be separately represented. When OSO represents the child, he/she will be interviewed to ascertain that he/she can express his/her views freely. Such views will be respected and included in the report prepared by OSO and presented to the requesting court.

Nothing was said about how personnel interviewing children are trained to elicit effective child participation. In terms of disseminating knowledge to relevant children and adults, the OSO said that 'OSO provides pamphlets at its office counter as well as softcopy of information leaflet on its web site describing its work concerning minors.' The OSO is also a member of the current Family Court Proceedings Users Committee, another avenue for sharing information about its work with children.

---

[56] Interview Nos. 1 and 18.

[57] Interview No. 18.

[58] Interview No. 1.

[59] See below for information on the Legal Aid Department's response on child participation.

The number of cases each year in which the OSO represents children fluctuates considerably. In 2015 there were nine cases; in 2016, 14 cases; in 2017, four cases; and in 2018, 12 cases. Without knowing the overall number of cases in which children had a significant interest, it is impossible to know whether this is an 'active' response to facilitating child participation in legal proceedings or not. However, in the case *R v. N* in 2009, on an application for separate representation of the children by the Official Solicitor, the judge noted that '[Counsel] has submitted that there have been many cases in Hong Kong where the Official Solicitor has been appointed to represent the children. I have to confess that I am not aware of that many. So far in my Court, there has been only one in the past five or six years.'[60]

Whilst the Official Solicitor may provide an avenue for child participation in legal proceedings, one interviewee expressed concern about the quality of that representation in terms of transparency and respect for the child: 'Official Solicitors sometimes, or even often, play a dual role which I think is actually sometimes in conflict because one role might be to represent the child's voice whereas the other is to advocate the child's best interests and they might not necessarily be aligned. And I always think that is a bit of a difficult situation.'[61]

5.4. CHILD PARTICIPATION IN CRIMINAL OR CARE PROCEEDINGS

As the government department responsible for criminal prosecutions, the Department of Justice (DoJ) was asked to provide information on policies and mechanisms in place to promote child participation. The DoJ responded with reference to (1) children as witnesses in criminal proceedings and (2) children as defendants. Where children are participating in criminal proceedings as witnesses, and in some instances will also have been the victim of the crime being prosecuted, the Department has not adopted child-specific policies. Children would be included in the general categories of victim, witness and vulnerable witness under the relevant Statement, Charter and Prosecution Code. These provisions include references to being kept informed and being able to express views to a prosecutor, or where relevant, to the court.

Where children are defendants in a prosecution, there are specific provisions for the prosecution of children under 16 years. These are given in paragraph 15 of the Prosecution Code. However, this paragraph does not make mention of the juvenile's right to participate or to express their views in decision-making about

60 *R v. N* [2009] HKEC 2622.

61 Interview No. 5.

mode of prosecution. Most juveniles will be prosecuted in a specialist Juvenile Court unless an alternative non-judicial method is possible. The Department did not give any information on training for prosecutors in relation to child participation. Nor has the Judiciary provided information on proceedings in Juvenile Court.

In terms of the disposition of criminal prosecutions against juvenile offenders, the SWD provides community-based statutory supervision and guidance for offenders through several channels: the Probation Service, the Community Service Orders Scheme, and a residential training and aftercare service where cases are referred to them by court. Upon receiving a referral from the court, the probation officer, a registered social worker, will prepare the social inquiry report on the offender, make recommendations and provide statutory supervision and guidance for a period as ordered by the court so that the offender may be rehabilitated within the community. The offender's views will be considered throughout the process of their rehabilitation. Before making such an order, the court shall explain, or cause to be explained to the offender, in a language understood by them, the effect of the order.

In addition to the core work of the Department, the DoJ also reported that it sought to promote child participation by hosting secondary school student visits. These visits are designed to promote children's understanding of the work of the Department and strengthen career and life planning education. Further special outreach events are organised by the Prosecutions Division to raise awareness of criminal law amongst school students.

The Duty Lawyer Service (DLS) is a separate government office which provides representation for those appearing in Juvenile Courts. Since 2013, to fulfil the obligations under Article 37(d) of the UNCRC, the Government has commissioned the DLS to operate the Legal Representation Scheme (LRS) to provide legal representation for children and juveniles who appear in the Juvenile Court for either criminal prosecution or as the subject of a 'Care or Protection' hearing and to provide children with an opportunity to be heard in judicial proceedings affecting them. The LRS aims to ensure that every child deprived of their liberty shall have the right to prompt access to legal and other appropriate assistance. No information is available about training for lawyers working with juveniles.

Where children are either victims of crimes or witnesses to crimes committed against others, their participation in the legal process may be sought by the police. In response to a request for information concerning policies regarding child participation, the police stated that all officers employed with the Child Abuse Investigation Unit receive specialised training to equip officers to engage with abused children and to support appropriate child participation in the investigation of child abuse cases. Further, police officers engage with SWD policies to have support persons accompany child witnesses who are participating in the criminal justice process by giving evidence. Child witnesses are encouraged to participate as witnesses by special measures to allow them to give evidence by video link. By policy, the child should be kept the informed of any developments and be told the outcome of the case. Lastly, police officers participate in public education and awareness programmes to inform children of the law and thereby enhance their self-protection abilities. No information was given on complaints received or how children's views were given due weight in these processes.

Children in 'Care or Protection' legal proceedings will come into contact with social workers. The SWD has disseminated guidelines which refer to enabling child participation: according to the Procedural Guide for Handling Child Abuse Cases (Revised 2015),[62] the children's participation is encouraged and their voices will be heard at different stages in handling suspected child abuse cases, including the application to court for a Care or Protection Order. Their wishes and feelings will be explored and attended to in formulating follow up welfare plans. Social workers will brief and prepare the child according to the child's maturity or how much the child understands.

One interviewee made the point that there is no specialist Bar to represent children in criminal proceedings or in 'Care or Protection' proceedings (both sets of proceedings being heard in the Juvenile Court) and consequently there is no standard set for training those lawyers who represent children in the Juvenile Court. Furthermore, Juvenile Court proceedings can appear to be similar to adult legal proceedings:

> Generally speaking, there are very few barristers with experience and primarily their expertise is in Criminal proceedings, and rarely in child protection. You could practically say there is no child protection bar in Hong Kong … to say that it is a proper well-formed group of advocates who do that on a regular basis is just a falsehood … No one is paying anyone to do it and no one is asking anyone to do it. The primary forum for child protection work is the Juvenile Court dealing with care and protection orders but they are asking the DLS to arrange Barristers and the result is that all of the lawyers, including the Magistrate, their primary focus is on criminal procedure, criminal aspects … to the point where … they normally refer to the child as a defendant in care or protection proceedings, the magistrate often refers to the child as the defendant, which may be indicative of a paradigm problem, without being critical of anyone. There is a reason why the Juvenile Court was separated from the rest of the criminal court, it was supposed to represent a different ethos, a different paradigm but even then, the juvenile criminal proceedings should be separate from child protection proceedings. And you often basically have presiding over the cases people who 99% of the time are doing criminal practice and the lawyers who are appearing for the child are almost always also appearing for the parent. The duty

62 This Guideline has since been further updated in 2020: <https://www.swd.gov.hk/en/textonly/site_pubsvc/page_family/sub_fcwprocedure/id_1447/>, last accessed 31.07.2022.

lawyer treats them as the same group which results in an amalgamation of interests and sometimes a conflict of interest.[63]

5.5. FUNDING CHILD PARTICIPATION IN LEGAL PROCEEDINGS: THE LEGAL AID DEPARTMENT

When approached for information regarding policies to promote child participation, the LAD's response was that there are no child-specific policies or measures in relation to applications for LAD's services. This may be because representation in Juvenile Court is provided by the DLS and children will be unlikely to have standing directly in other proceedings. Nonetheless, it is conceivable that legal aid would be necessary to fund proceedings brought on behalf of a child and therefore some degree of child participation, even if limited to access to child-appropriate information, is conceivable. Underlying all of this is the convention that children do not have standing to initiate legal proceedings directly themselves but must do so through an adult representative, usually referred to as a 'next friend' or 'guardian *ad litem*'.

More broadly, information is provided for children on the work of the Department in another sense: in 2017–2018 the LAD arranged eight visits to the Department by children to promote children's understanding of the work and services of LAD and to enhance students' career and life planning education.

5.6. ALTERNATIVE DISPUTE RESOLUTION (ADR): CHILD PARTICIPATION IN FAMILY MEDIATION

Increasingly, as legal proceedings become more costly and time-consuming, parties are turning to alternative forms of dispute resolution. This is particularly true in divorce or separation cases involving children. Family mediation provides a forum in which separating couples can come to an agreement about the future upbringing of their children. The dominant form of family mediation used in Hong Kong is child-focused mediation, where children are not involved in the mediation process directly, but the mediator will keep the children's best interests at the forefront of their parents' minds. However, children can participate actively, in a child-appropriate manner, in child-inclusive mediation. In this process, children speak privately to a qualified child consultant who will, if appropriate, elicit their views about their family situation. With the children's agreement, the child consultant will separately feedback the child's chosen message, if any, to the mediator and the parents.

---

[63] Interview No. 6.

Interviewees from the legal sector found this process to be a positive example of child participation in a matter directly affecting them:

> I think most people mistake, or wrongly interpret child-inclusive to mean the children come into the room and negotiate with the parents. But it is actually just an avenue for feeding in how the children feel or think or maybe give a recommendation that the parents haven't thought about ... or simply sometimes give some insight to the parents of the impact their conflict has on the child, it makes them rethink what they are doing. So, I remember one was, they had to trace the child's body ... and one had a big knife on her head and said my head hurts every time I see my parents fight ... So, this is why I think this is a wake-up call to jolt [the parents] out of their polarised positions in the conflict. ... You are dealing with something that is going to impact the children for life and it has a profound effect so why on earth would they not be entitled to a voice? It does not have to be a deciding voice but for God's sake hear them.[64]

Nonetheless, when asked, interviewees from the legal sector responded that to their knowledge there were very few mediators practising child-inclusive mediation and that there was a need for more qualified child consultants who could take on the role of talking to the child and feeding back to the parents.[65]

Proper training is necessary because, where there are no child consultants available and mediators themselves are not properly trained in the skills and protocols specific to child-inclusive mediation, there is a risk that the inclusive mediation process will harm rather than empower the child. Recent research on family mediation in Hong Kong reported that: 'One child said that the mediator was caring and patient, and the mediator explained the mediation process in great detail. This child felt relaxed when attending the meetings. Another child's experience was relatively negative because the mediator asked her to state her living arrangement preference in front of her parents.'[66] In this latter instance, this cannot be said to be child participation which protects the child from the risks of participation, as required under the GC12 quality statement.

6. EVALUATING THE IMPLEMENTATION OF CHILD PARTICIPATION IN THE LEGAL SETTING

The legal setting is certainly a 'hotspot' setting for child participation. Article 12 is not incorporated into Hong Kong law generally, but it is reflected

64 Interview No. 5.

65 Interviews Nos. 1 and 5.

66 Central Policy Unit, The Government of the Hong Kong Special Administrative Region, *A Study On Family Mediation Services In Hong Kong*, 2017, p. 115.

in several legislative provisions relating to how children's views impact on legal proceedings. Further, existing laws have been amended to incorporate the language of the UNCRC. However, to what extent does the practical application of these provisions afford good-quality, meaningful child participation?

Looking first at the *elements* of Article 12, the relevant legal provisions and judicial practice guidelines provide for voluntary participation with weight given to children's views based largely on age combined with maturity. The child can directly express their views, specifically to the judge, or indirectly as relayed through a representative of the child, usually a social worker, legal representative, or during child-inclusive mediation. Problems regarding the *elements* of Article 12 arise in relation to the extent to which these opportunities to be heard happen in practice or in the competence and training of those who indirectly represent the child's views to the court. Lastly, where one professional, usually a social worker or the Official Solicitor, represents both the child's views and the child's best interests, this may present conflicts of interest or distract from the clarity and strength of the child's view.

Turning to the *forms* of child participation, and utilising the categories of participation adopted for the Child Participation Matrix – inauthentic, consultative, collaborative and child-led – we see that most of the provisions enabling the child's views to be heard fall within the consultative participation category. In the context of legal proceedings, where it is only the court that has the power to decide an outcome, this may therefore be the most appropriate form of child participation.

Nonetheless, separate legal representation for children and the participation of children in child-inclusive mediation present real opportunities for children to participate collaboratively in matters which affect them. Separate representation allows children to collaborate in the definition and presentation of their 'case' to the court. Child-inclusive mediation allows the child a chance to influence the agreement reached by their parents at the outcome of the mediation. However, in both instances there appears to be a lack of properly trained personnel to take on the roles of specialist lawyers representing children, child-inclusive mediators and child consultants.

Good-quality child participation in the legal setting must be participation that fits with the GC12 attributes: respectful of the child, transparent, informative, child-friendly and so on, as well as iterative and rights-focused. However, without sufficient properly trained personnel and adequate follow-up, child participation in legal proceedings cannot be deemed good-quality child participation.

There are several specific areas in which the quality of the child participation is problematic. First, much of the child participation in legal proceedings takes place via the SIR process, yet this presents several issues: (1) in terms of respect for the child, the SIR fulfils two potentially conflicting roles: representing the child's views and the child's best interests; (2) in terms of accountability, there seems to be no prescribed follow-up for the children or opportunity for the child to check the social worker has accurately understood and reported the child's views; and (3) regarding training to support the adults facilitating child participation, concerns raised in interviews suggest that the quality of the SIR can be 'patchy'. This suggests better training is needed to accurately represent the views of the child.

Second, where the consultation is directly between the child and the judge, concerns raised in interviews suggest that this option is not used frequently by the Judiciary and that this reticence may, in part, be due to insufficient training for judges in how to talk to children and elicit their views in an appropriate manner.

Third, in terms of proceedings in the Juvenile Court, the quality of child participation must be diminished by the absence of a specialist Bar from which the DLS can call on appropriately trained lawyers to represent children who are in trouble or at risk. It is also of concern whether, when a child must agree to express certain views, such as being remorseful, in order to avoid custodial sentences, the child can be said to be participating freely.

Looking at other opportunities for child participation reported by government bodies in the legal setting, the visits arranged by government departments are valuable as educational opportunities, but they are not necessarily instances of authentic child participation. That these events have been reported as child participation suggests a misconception of what child participation entails. However, if the children are asked to give feedback on their experience and that feedback is reflected or acted upon by the Departments in arranging future visits, and the children are informed of this, then this would form valuable consultative participation for the children in an educational matter, but not a legal matter.

Overall, legislatively and in terms of judicial guidance, there is a documentary framework for child participation in legal proceedings. However, the extent of child participation and the quality of that participation are dependent on having sufficient numbers of expert personnel, trained appropriately, consistently employing universally accepted standards of practice. There is certainly room for improvement in this regard.

7. CONCLUSION

It is evident that laws, policies and structures are in place to facilitate child participation in the legal setting. While few of these innovations referenced the UNCRC or the *elements* of Article 12 directly, many and varied policies and mechanisms for child participation were reported by duty-bearers for this study.

With regard to the *form* of child participation, a significant proportion of policies and measures reported provide for 'consultative' participation by children. The value of consultation may vary depending on the stage of decision-making at which the consultation takes place; however, given the specific characteristics of the legal setting it may be that consultative child participation is the most appropriate form of child participation for this setting. That said, one glaring exception is the child's inability to initiate proceedings themselves, without an adult nominally leading the action.

Turning to the *quality* of the participation opportunities reported, few of the examples of consultative participation mechanisms encompassed systematic provisions for, and actualisation of, accountability in the form of follow-up with children on the impact of their participation. In addition to a lack of systematic follow-up with child participants, there is, in general, a low level of good-*quality* training for adults who work with child participation and a low level of child-friendly information for child participants. Other GC12 attributes of good-quality participation are similarly scarce in the reported opportunities for child participation. The overall impression is that child participation is delivered in a fragmented and somewhat ad hoc manner. Whilst some duty-bearers have instituted innovative child participation policies on paper, experience shows that these do not necessarily deliver meaningful child participation in practice. For example, children in legal proceedings theoretically have multiple avenues by which to express their views. In practice, stakeholders' feedback suggests these avenues are either rarely utilised, or where the child's view is sought in a more routine manner, usually by social workers for the SIR, the quality of this process can be 'patchy'.

8. RECOMMENDATIONS

It is not possible to present all of the recommendations arising from the study here. However, significant recommendations for reform would include changes to general policy-making, education, training and capacity-building and data collection with a view to mainstreaming good-quality child participation in legal proceedings and alternative dispute resolution processes.

In relation to children who are either involved directly in legal proceedings or whose families are so involved, to promote good-quality child participation, children should be provided with child-friendly information for court proceedings, including information on matters such as separate representation, meetings with judges and remedies. Where a court order is made which affects the child, a child-friendly version should be delivered to the child, and, where appropriate, the same for judgments.

For each child whose parents are engaged in divorce or custody proceedings, in the interests of transparency, which is itself an element of good-quality child participation, the child should be provided with the contact details of either a named individual or a hotline to answer any questions or concerns they have about the legal proceedings and associated issues so that they are informed about the proceedings and can thereby raise questions or concerns if they wish.

To support active collaborative participation for children, the Department of Justice, the Judiciary and the legal professional bodies should review the Official Solicitor and guardian *ad litem* systems of separate representation. As part of this review, essential consideration should also be given to how to improve information for children about their options for separate representation in an age/maturity-appropriate and child-friendly manner.

To ensure good-quality child participation by those children who find themselves before the Juvenile Court, the Department of Justice, the Judiciary and the legal professional bodies should review generally the Juvenile Court jurisdiction, setting and processes. Particular consideration should be given to specialist training for those adults working with children in the Juvenile Court and to the aptness of the environment in which the Juvenile Court functions in terms of whether it is a child-appropriate space. This is not to detract from the gravity of criminal proceedings at the Juvenile Court, but is instead an opportunity to balance, as Hart recommends, children's rights with children's responsibilities in a way which can be meaningful for the children involved. One further consideration, to ensure good-quality participation, might be to look at whether to take 'Care or Protection' work out of the Juvenile Court jurisdiction, away from the Court's emphasis on criminal proceedings, and to locate it within its own specialist forum where child participation can be addressed in a context-specific manner.

Hong Kong is in the course of developing a new Family Court venue. This would be an ideal opportunity to create an environment which not only serves its adult participants but which also promotes and facilitates child participation as widely as possible where relevant. The inclusion of special suites for judges to meet with children and special suites for child consultants or specialist legal representatives to meet with children would be a positive innovation, as would establishing a child-friendly resource centre, to mirror the unrepresented litigants resource centre located at the High Court. To consider bringing family mediation services within the same venue could maximise available resources for meaningful child participation so that the child's voice can be heard across the family law processes.

Fundamentally, the data shows an absence of training for personnel for delivery and review of meaningful child participation in the sector. Whilst opportunities for child participation may exist 'on the books', they are less evident in practice. It is recommended that the relevant legal professional bodies and the Department of Justice take steps to build the competence and capacity of professionals to work with children's participation. Additionally, the Judiciary may welcome expert assistance and training for Judges hearing child-related proceedings at all levels of the court hierarchy. This training would include guidance on how to facilitate meaningful child participation, particularly in relation to meeting with children or separate representation for children. This training could also extend to guidance and support for judges on when and how to write child-appropriate judgments and court orders. Data collection on when judges meet with children directly, and with what outcome, would enable a system of periodic review to identify any issues which indicate that opportunities for child participation could be improved.

To address the need for more specialists, it is suggested that the relevant bodies promote the development of an accredited pool of barristers, solicitors, mediators and consultants who can deliver effective, collaborative or even, where apt, child-led participation for children caught up in legal matters. With regards to the specialist Bar, membership of this specialist Bar should be a requirement for eligibility to work with children under the Duty Lawyer Service and for the Official Solicitor's Office.

Turning to the other professionals whom a child may encounter during the course of legal proceedings, the data suggests that it is incumbent upon the Department of Justice, the Judiciary and the legal professional bodies to review how social workers and expert witnesses are currently employed to gather the child's views. This would entail a reconsideration of the boundaries to their roles and the qualifications deemed necessary for those social workers and expert witnesses to be engaged in legal proceedings. The aim is to ensure good-quality child participation which accurately represents the child's views and does not add to the trauma children may experience when their lives are touched by legal proceedings. Ideally, the system could move away from a position whereby one person both reports the child's views *and* makes an evaluation of what is in the best interests of the child.

Turning to alternative dispute resolution, the Social Welfare Department and the Department of Justice could work together, along with the Judiciary, to promote the development of child-inclusive mediation. This would entail the development of training programmes for child-inclusive mediators and child consultants, and the introduction of professional accreditation for child-inclusive mediators and child consultants, with the requirement for continuing professional development to maintain good practice and to address formation of bad habits over time. To underpin the necessity of good-quality work with child participation in mediation, allowing for feedback from children on their experience of the process and to ensure children receive feedback on their input to the process, it is recommended that a binding code of conduct for child-inclusive mediators and consultants be established. Mediators and consultants would not be permitted to hold themselves out as able to practise child-inclusive mediation until they had completed the relevant training, received accreditation and maintained an ongoing adherence to the code of conduct and continuing professional development requirements.

If even a small proportion of these recommendations are acted upon, the standard of implementation of Article 12 of the UNCRC in Hong Kong's legal setting would be substantially improved and children afforded meaningful avenues to express their views on matters which impact greatly on their lives and well-being.

IRELAND

LGBT+ FAMILY RIGHTS IN IRELAND

Stretching Traditional Conceptions of Parenthood

Maebh HARDING

Résumé

Cet article présente et analyse de manière critique le traitement des familles LGBT+ dans le droit irlandais. Si les récents changements apportés au droit irlandais par l'entrée en vigueur de la deuxième partie de la loi de 2015 sur les enfants et les relations familiales permettent désormais d'accorder le statut de parent aux personnes qui ont utilisé des formes particulières d'assistance médicale à la procréation, ces nouvelles voies d'accès à la parentalité sont très restreintes. Les familles LGBT+ continuent de se heurter à des obstacles juridiques pour la reconnaissance de leur lien entre parents et enfants. Le traitement inégal de la relation parent-enfant au sein des familles LGBT+ dans le droit irlandais résulte à la fois d'une réforme inadéquate et d'une incohérence fondamentale quant à l'utilité réelle du statut de parent légal.

1. INTRODUCTION

Irish law has accepted LGBT+ families in principle, but legislation falls far short of an inclusive practical framework. Following the commencement of Part 2 of the Children and Family Relationships Act 2015 on 4 May 2020, Irish law now recognises that children conceived through assisted reproductive technology (ART) may have two mothers. Part 4 of the Act (which also commenced on 4 May 2020) extends the categories of people who may apply for legal guardianship. This is helpful in facilitating joint decision-making by parents in LGBT+ families who are not recognised by law as parents. However, legal recognition of the parent–child dependencies within LGBT+ families remains patchy and limited. Such families continue to face significant practical problems. While there have been numerous calls for the Children and Family Relationships Act 2015 to be extended to cover a wider range of ART scenarios,[1] and for Ireland to legislate to regulate the legal consequences of surrogacy,[2] this chapter argues that a more fundamental conceptual shift in the legal understanding of parentage is required to achieve equality for all families.

This chapter will critically assess the law relating to the recognition of LGBT+ families in Ireland. It will examine the limits of available 'work-arounds' to address common practical problems encountered by such families. Finally, it will argue that the failures of Irish law stem from an incoherent view of what matters in according the status of legal parent and an engrained (yet often unexamined) attachment to the heterosexual nuclear family model.

---

1 L. Bracken, *Same Sex Parenting and the Best Interests Principle,* Cambridge University Press, 2020, ch. 5; L. Bracken, 'In the Best Interests of the Child? The Regulation of DAHR in Ireland' (2016) 23 *European Journal of Health Law* 291; C. O'Mahony, *A Review of Children's Rights and Best Interests in the Context of Donor-Assisted Human Reproduction and Surrogacy in Irish Law*, 2020, available at: <https://www.gov.ie/en/publication/3e601-a-review-of-childrens-rights-and-best-interests-in-the-context-of-donorassisted-human-reproa-review-of-childrens-rights-and-best-interests-in-the-context-of-donor-assisted-human-reproduction-and-surrogacy-in-irish-law-duction-and-surrogacy-in-irish-law/>, last accessed 08.03.2022; B. Tobin, 'Assisted Reproductive Techniques and Irish Law: No Child Left Behind?' (2020) 64 *The Irish Jurist* 138.

2 L. Bracken, 'The Assisted Reproduction Bill 2017: An Analysis of Proposals to Regulate Surrogacy in Ireland' (2017) 68 *Northern Ireland Legal Quarterly* 577; B. Tobin, 'An appraisal of Ireland's current legislative proposals for regulating domestic surrogacy arrangements' (2019) 41 *Journal of Social Welfare and Family Law* 205; D. Madden, 'Assisted Reproduction in Ireland – Time to legislate' (2011) 17 *Medico-Legal Journal of Ireland* 3; M. Harding, 'Ireland and Cross Border Surrogacy' in K. Trimmings and P. Beaumont (eds.), *International Recognition of Cross Border Surrogacy Arrangements*, Hart, 2013, pp. 219–230.

2. EQUAL RECOGNITION OF ADULT COMMITMENT

In 2015, the Irish people voted for marriage equality, changing the definition of marriage in the Irish Constitution to include spouses of the same sex.[3] This was a fundamentally important cultural shift for the recognition of LGBT+ families in Ireland.

The Irish Constitution recognises only one form of the family, the marital family.[4] Married families are the State-preferred paradigm and families that are not based on marriage are not given constitutionally protected status.[5] While legislative recognition is given to other types of family ties, marriage equality was the only way in which LGBT+ families could be given equal recognition as families under Irish constitutional law.

Irish law had previously made legislative provision for the recognition of same-sex adult partnerships under the Civil Partnership and Certain Rights and Obligations of Cohabitants Act 2010. This created the 'marriage-like' institution of civil partnership, which carried with it many, but not all, of the legal consequences of marriage.[6] Most importantly, mere legislative recognition meant that civil partners were not given constitutional recognition as a family unit.

Civil partnership has been prospectively abolished since the passing of the Marriage Act 2015.[7] The Civil Partnership and Certain Rights and Obligations of Cohabitants Act 2010 also created a limited safety net for financially dependent cohabitants who may petition the court for financial redress at the end of their cohabiting relationship.[8] This scheme is open to both same-sex and different-sex partners.

LGBT+ families now have equal status when it comes to legal recognition of adult commitment. Marriage is open to all, and the safety net of the cohabitation redress scheme is accessible to all adults in intimate dyadic relationships who satisfy the qualifying conditions. However, as will be examined, the recognition and protection of parent–child dependencies in LGBT+ families is not so straightforward.

---

3 The Thirty-fourth Amendment of the Constitution (Marriage Equality) Act 2015 was approved by referendum on 22 May 2015 by 65% of voters.

4 Constitution of Ireland 1937 Art. 41; *HAH v. SAA* [2017] 1 IR 372, 129.

5 F. Ryan, 'Out of the Shadow of the Constitution; Civil Partnership, Cohabitation and the Constitutional Family' (2012) 48 *The Irish Jurist* 201.

6 Marriage Equality, *Missing Pieces Report*, 2011, available at: <https://gaylawnet.com/ezine/family/missing_pieces.pdf>, last accessed 29.07.2022.

7 Marriage Act 2015 s. 8.

8 Civil Partnership and Certain Rights and Obligations of Cohabitants Act 2010 Part 15.

3. RECOGNISING PARENT–CHILD LINKS IN LGBT+ FAMILIES

Two recent changes to Irish law have improved the legal recognition of the parent–child links within LGBT+ families. Part 2 of the Children and Family Relationship Act 2015 extends the recognition of legal parenthood to intentional parents where donor-assisted human reproduction (DAHR) is used. Part 4 of the Children and Family Relationship Act 2015 now allows non-parents to apply to the court to be recognised as guardians, giving them some decision-making powers and responsibilities towards a child. However, such laws inadequately cater for many LGBT+ families because the automatic rules of legal parenthood are very narrow in scope. While guardianship is broader, it requires a court application and provides only limited recognition of the parent–child dependency. This section will also examine the limited usefulness of adoption as a remedial mechanism for recognising such relationships within LGBT+ families.

3.1. LEGAL PARENTHOOD

Ireland's longstanding traditional rules ascribing legal parenthood rely on assumptions about the heteronormative marital family. Developed from principles of the common law, Irish law assumes that the father of a child is the mother's husband[9] and, where the mother is unmarried, birth registration (which requires the father to acknowledge the child) is prima facie evidence of legal fatherhood.[10] These rules supported a presumption of legitimacy for children born to married mothers. This was important in preserving the stability of family life and spared children from the real legal stigma of illegitimacy, which was not abolished until the enactment of the Status of Children Act 1987.[11] These presumptions can now be rebutted by applying to court for a declaration of parentage,[12] which allows the birth to be re-registered on the basis of genetic evidence of biological parentage.[13] The usual standard of proof in Irish civil litigation (the balance of probabilities) applies. Parentage is thus assumed from the status of marriage and, where challenged, established by biological evidence.

Assisted reproductive technology (ART) severs adult intentions about parenthood from genetics and challenges the operation of the traditional rules.

---

9 Status of Children Act 1987 s. 46(1).

10 Ibid, s. 46(3).

11 Ibid, s. 2 (although legal differential treatment of marital and non-marital families continues to exist due to the constitutional preference for the marital family).

12 Ibid, s. 35.

13 Ibid, s. 38 (as amended).

Irish law contained no legal definition of motherhood, presuming it to be obvious. However, the DNA test-based declaration of parentage mechanism under the Status of Children Act 1987 was designed to be used to prove maternity as well as paternity,[14] which initially suggested that genetics might be the determining factor for parenthood.

In *MR v. An t-Ard Chláraitheoir*,[15] the Supreme Court ruled that the default Irish definition of motherhood was based on gestation and not genetics. This was a case of altruistic domestic surrogacy where a woman had given birth to her sister's genetic child. Irish law does not prohibit surrogacy, but there is no legislation in place to regulate the consequences of surrogacy. The court therefore had to consider how the general rules of determining maternity would apply to this situation. While the child's genetic father was easily registered as the father on the child's birth certificate, the genetic mother could not be registered because she was not also the gestational mother. Despite this decision, genetic testing continues to be used to establish maternity in immigration cases.[16] In this context, gestation is assumed where a genetic link is proven, and no evidence of surrogacy is introduced.

Women who conceive through ART are thus recognised as mothers under Irish law and their husbands can rely on the presumption that they are the legal parent of children born to the marriage even where no genetic link exists. However, the same presumption does not apply to female spouses[17] and has no application to male same-sex married couples because neither spouse can give birth. Irish law does not apply specialised legal rules to surrogacy situations. So while the traditional presumptions can give effect to the intentions of heterosexual married families who use ART, the same is not true for same-sex married couples.

For unmarried couples, the traditional rules will ultimately recognise the gestational mother and the genetic father as the legal parents of any children conceived through IVF. This excludes unmarried fathers where donor sperm is used. Female second parents cannot be recognised at all under the traditional rules even if they have a genetic link to the child.

3.1.1. Children Conceived through DAHR

The Children and Family Relationships Act 2015 now bases parenthood on declared adult intentions for children conceived through a particularly prescribed form of ART known as donor-assisted human reproduction (DAHR)

14 The Law Reform Commission, *Report on Illegitimacy*, LRC 4 – 1982, p. 105.
15 *MR v. An t-Ard Chláraitheoir* [2014] 3 IR 533.
16 See e.g. *MH and SH v. Minister for Justice and Equality* [2020] IEHC 360; and *FB v. Minister for Justice and Equality* [2020] IECA 89.
17 Status of Children Act 1987 s. 46 (refers only to husbands and fathers).

after 4 May 2020. This allows parenthood to be separated from genetics, but gestation still remains vital. The best interests of the child are only taken into account when awarding legal parenthood in some retrospective transitional measures,[18] which will be discussed below.

DAHR must occur in Ireland in a clinical setting and the couple must use either donor gametes or a donated embryo.[19] It excludes children conceived outside Ireland and children conceived in non-clinical settings from its remit. The narrow scope of the Act was deliberate and expressly acknowledged by the Irish government, which warned that the majority of anonymously donated sperm and eggs in storage in Irish fertility clinics could not be used in a DAHR procedure unless the new consent provisions were complied with or if a transitional provision applied.[20]

For children born following DAHR, section 5 provides that the child's legal parents will be the woman who gave birth to the child (the legal mother) and her spouse, civil partner or cohabitant (the second legal parent). The Act is very clear that anyone who has donated genetic material as a donor under the Act will not have any parental rights nor be the child's legal parent.[21] But these rules apply only where there has been full compliance with the required written consent procedure by intending parents[22] and the gamete or embryo donor. In cases of full compliance, the intended parents are automatically registered as the child's legal parents on their birth certificate.[23]

The consent process required by the Children and Family Relationships Act is similar for mothers, second parents and donors and is intended to protect the right to identity of donor-conceived children. Adult intention of parentage must be clear and in writing. The mother must consent to her spouse or cohabitant being the second parent.[24] The mother and intended second parent must consent in writing to being parents,[25] and express their understanding that the donors will have no rights as parent. Donors[26] must declare that they are aware that they are not the legal parent of any child born.[27] The consent of donors will not be valid where it is given in exchange for financial compensation in excess of 'reasonable expenses'.[28]

---

18 Children and Family Relationships Act 2015 ss. 21 and 22.

19 Ibid, s. 4.

20 Department of Health, *Children and Family Relationships Act 2015 Publication*, 2 March 2020, available at: <https://www.gov.ie/en/publication/e2bd0a-children-and-family-relationships-act-2015/>, last accessed 08.03.2022.

21 Children and Family Relationships Act ss. 6 and 26.

22 Ibid, s. 5(8).

23 Civil Registration Act 2004 s. 19A (as amended).

24 Ibid, s. 9

25 Ibid, ss. 9 and 11.

26 Ibid, ss. 6, 14 and 16.

27 Ibid, s. 6.

28 Ibid, s. 19.

Intending parents and donors must also declare that they consent to their information being recorded for the National Donor-Conceived Person Register, agree to provide the required information for the Register and declare understanding that the Register may be accessed by any resulting child who may seek to contact genetic donors and confirm that they have received all relevant information from the clinic.[29]

Maintaining the integrity of the National Donor-Conceived Person Register is the central regulatory priority of this part of the Children and Family Relationships Act. The underlying policy goal is to ensure that the identity rights of children conceived through DAHR are protected. However, it is argued that the legislative focus on ensuring the integrity of the Register, without exception, is unrealistic and undermines the rights to identity of children who are conceived through ART processes that are not fully compliant with the Act.

The National Donor-Conceived Person Register contains information relating to every child born through DAHR, including the date and place where the DAHR procedure was carried out, the names, addresses and contact details of intending parents,[30] and the name, address, date of birth, nationality and contact details of any donor, along with details of the date and place of gamete donation.[31] Non-identifying information recorded on the Register can be easily accessed by the adult child and also by the child's parents before the child turn 18.[32] When children turn 18, they may request identifying information and contact details of any relevant donor. Identifying information is not automatically given to the adult child. The Minister for Health will inform the relevant donor of the request and may refuse to release the information where the donor makes representations to the Minister as to why the safety of the donor or child requires the information not to be released.[33] There is also a process for adult children to request identifying information and contact details for any genetic siblings they might have, but this requires active mutual consent from donor-conceived siblings to such matching.[34]

The National Donor-Conceived Person Register is linked to the Register of Births.[35] Where an adult donor-conceived child requests a copy of his or her birth certificate they will be informed that further information relating to them is available from the Register.[36] This measure is designed to ensure that donor-conceived children will have access to the information, even where they did not know that they were donor conceived. It remains to see how effective this will be.

---

29 Ibid, s. 13 for intending parents, s. 7 for donors.
30 Ibid, s. 25.
31 Ibid, s. 24.
32 Ibid, s. 34.
33 Ibid, s. 35.
34 Ibid, s. 37.
35 Ibid, s. 39.
36 Ibid, s. 39.

Birth certificates are provided to parents after birth registration and many adults have no occasion to request new copies of their birth certificate.

The integrity of the National Donor-Conceived Person Register is ensured by placing express legal obligations on the DAHR facilities, to ensure that appropriate consents and declarations are given[37] and to collect identifying information about all parties involved to be recorded on the National Donor-Conceived Person Register.[38] Carrying out procedures without obtaining appropriate consents is expressly forbidden by statute. Non-compliance may eventually result in the prohibition of future DAHR procedures taking place at a DAHR facility, but the primary enforcement mechanism is for a court order to be issued to require the facility to comply with their legal obligations.[39] This leaves room for DAHR facilities to remain operating for months without ensuring full compliance.

Intending parents are incentivised to fully comply with the Act because where appropriate consents are not given, and the required information is not collected, the situation will fall outside the scope of the Act. There is no mechanism within the Act for approving or waiving situations of minor non-compliance which occur after 4 May 2020.[40] In such cases, it may be impossible for a same-sex parent to be recognised as the child's second legal parent.

Determining parental status when clinics have not complied with statutory requirements is an issue that has troubled the English High Court for some years and generated a high level of case law, as up to 46 per cent of clinics found anomalies within their records.[41] The English High Court must review each case on its facts to see that the substance of the statutory requirements has been complied with. This is not an area of law in which the English High Court can exercise discretion by emphasising the best interests of the child,[42] but it has taken a pragmatic approach to statutory interpretation so that errors in record-keeping will not affect parental status if the substance of informed consent can be proved.[43] It remains to be seen if Irish courts will be required to exercise the same sort of pragmatic creativity.

---

37 Ibid, ss. 25 and 26.

38 Ibid, s. 28.

39 Ibid, s. 32.

40 Such parents would have to apply to court for a declaration of parentage under s. 35 of the Status of Children Act 1987 to determine the significance of the non-compliance on their legal status of parent.

41 See *In the matter of HFEA 2008 (Cases A, B, C, D, E, F, G and H Declaration of Parentage)* [2015] EWHC 2602 (Fam), paras. 6–8.

42 The best interests principle only applies to judicial decision-making in relation to parental orders under s. 58 of the HFEA 2008. Human Fertilisation and Embryology (Parental Orders) Regulations 2010 (SI 2010/95).

43 See e.g. *Re AD & Others Human Fertilisation and Embryology Act 2008* [2017] EWHC 1026 (Fam).

The Children and Family Relationships Act 2015 provides for (slightly) more flexible transitional measures which can retrospectively determine the legal parentage for children who were conceived using ART before 4 May 2020.[44] Sections 21 and 22 allow the Circuit Court and District Court to award the status of legal parent to intending parents by declaration.[45] Such declarations can be made where children were conceived through anonymous gamete donation either within Ireland or outside Ireland. No declaration can be made where a 'known donor' was used, where fertility treatment occurred in a non-clinical setting or where the child was born outside Ireland. 18 per cent of respondents in Bracken's study on LGBTI+ families who conceived children through ART before 4 May 2020 were not eligible to apply for a retrospective declaration of parentage because 40 per cent of the ineligible had used a known donor and 60 per cent had conceived through non-clinical insemination.[46]

In order for a retrospective declaration to be made, it must be shown to the court's satisfaction that the gamete donor was unknown to the mother of the child and any other intending parent and was not themselves an intending parent of the child.[47] Moreover, this person must remain unknown to the intended parents at the time of the application.[48] The legislation does not address legal procedures to protect the rights of the donor where the conception occurred outside Ireland. The process cannot be used if a second parent has already been recorded as the other parent of the child on the Irish Register of Births.[49] The intention behind this restriction has nothing to do with the rights of children to know their identity and is instead designed to exclude open co-parenting situations. Following the high-profile case of *JMcD v. PL*,[50] it was felt that such situations could result in conflict between the known sperm donor/father and the intending parent couple.[51] The restriction also includes known egg donors, even though such women are not recognised as having any parental rights in Irish law.

This author agrees with O'Mahony that there is no justification for requiring the donor to be unknown. The rule cannot prevent conflict between known donors and parenting couples and merely discriminates between different

---

44 Children and Family Relationships Act 2015 s. 20.

45 Ibid, s. 23.

46 L. Bracken, *LGBTI+ Parent Families in Ireland: Legal Recognition of Parent-Child Relationships*, University of Limerick, 2021, p. 24, available at: <https://lgbt.ie/wp-content/uploads/2021/11/LGBTI-Parent-Families-Report.pdf>, last accessed 29.07.2022.

47 Above n. 44, at s. 20(d).

48 Ibid, s. 20(e).

49 Ibid, s. 20(f).

50 *JMcD v. PL* [2007] IESC 28.

51 G. Shannon, *Tenth Report of the Special Rapporteur on Child Protection*, 2016, pp. 149–150, available at: <https://assets.gov.ie/27443/7fbed34559d44634a31593372e47882c.pdf>, last accessed 08.03.2022.

groups of children born following similar ART procedures.[52] As O'Mahony suggests, the right of the known donor to be considered as a parent could be protected by giving them an opportunity to object to the order being made.[53] Such donors could also sign retrospective consents similar to those required of new donors under the 2015 Act.

Joint applications by the mother and intended second parent are brought to the District Court,[54] whereas the Circuit Court hears contested applications, which can be made by the mother, the intended second parent or the child.[55] In all cases the child must be joined as a party to proceedings[56] and the declaration is only binding on the State where the Attorney General is a party to proceedings.[57]

For District Court applications, each applicant must swear affidavits and the intended parent must consent to the making of the application.[58] In deciding whether or not to make the declaration, the court must be satisfied that it is in the child's best interests to do so[59] and must give the child an opportunity to make his or her views known to the extent possible given the child's age and understanding.[60] This is the only place in Irish law where the best interests of the child determine legal parentage.[61]

For Circuit Court applications, evidence is required in addition to affidavits.[62] For such applications, the Circuit Court will make the declaration where it is proven on the balance of probabilities that the child was conceived through DAHR and that a relevant person was their intended parent.[63] Best interests have a different place in the decision-making process here; the court can refuse to make the declaration if it would not be the best interests of the child concerned or would be contrary to the interests of justice.[64]

These transitional measures give recognition to LGBT+ families who went ahead with ART in the absence of long-promised legal regulation. However, the measures are limited, onerous and involve potentially expensive litigation.

---

52 C. O'Mahony, *A Review of Children's Rights and Best Interests in the Context of Donor-Assisted Human Reproduction and Surrogacy in Irish Law*, 2020, p. 41.

53 Ibid, p. 42.

54 Children and Family Relationships Act 2015 s. 21(2).

55 Ibid, s. 22(2).

56 Ibid, ss. 21(3) and 22(3).

57 Ibid, ss. 21(10) and 22(8).

58 Ibid, s. 21(4).

59 Ibid, s. 21(9).

60 Ibid, s. 21(8).

61 In contrast, while the English High Court must only consider the best interests of the child when making parental orders following surrogacy under s. 54 of the Human Fertilisation and Embryology Act 2008 and even then, it is an overriding principle and not an express statutory condition that must be satisfied.

62 Ibid, s. 22(5).

63 Ibid, s. 22(6).

64 Ibid, s. 22(7).

LGBT+ families have been vocal about the distress caused to them by the delays in enacting the Children and Family Relationships Act 2015 and the requirement on them to take court proceedings to gain recognition for their families.[65] Respondents to Bracken's study found having to go through the court system for retrospective declarations of legal parenthood very onerous.[66]

3.1.2. Children Conceived through Surrogacy

Surrogacy takes place in Ireland, and Irish families also make use of international surrogacy services, but Irish law contains no legislative provision to recognise the parentage of children born through surrogacy. The surrogate mother is recognised as the legal mother in Irish law. Where there is a genetic link with a male parent, the parentage of the genetic father can be recognised under the traditional rules.

It is currently not possible for two men to be recognised as the legal parents of a child born through surrogacy unless adoption has been used.[67] The 13 per cent of the participants in Bracken's study who had used surrogacy were all male with male partners. 92 per cent had used surrogacy services outside Ireland and most had been issued with a birth certificate recording them as joint legal parents. None of these families were recognised by Irish law as having joint legal parents.[68]

However, recent developments in this area mean that surrogacy may soon become a legally recognised path for the creation and recognition of LGBT+ families.

As O'Mahony[69] notes, Ireland's failure to regulate the parental consequence of surrogacy leaves Ireland out of line with the recommendation of the

---

65 J. Wilson, 'Same-sex couple both recognized as parents of their children after lengthy campaign', *The Irish Times*, 20 October 2021, available at: <https://www.irishtimes.com/news/ireland/irish-news/same-sex-couple-both-recognised-as-parents-of-their-children-after-lengthy-campaign-1.4706046> accessed 08.03.2022.

66 L. Bracken, *LGBTI+ Parent Families in Ireland: Legal Recognition of Parent-Child Relationships*, University of Limerick, 2021, p. 28, available at: <https://www.ul.ie/research/lgbti-parent-families-ireland-legal-recognition-parent-child-relationships>, last accessed 08.03.2022.

67 The likelihood of adoption being used in this way is explored in the next section.

68 L. Bracken, *LGBTI+ Parent Families in Ireland: Legal Recognition of Parent-Child Relationships*, University of Limerick, 2021, p. 28, available at: <https://www.ul.ie/research/lgbti-parent-families-ireland-legal-recognition-parent-child-relationships>, last accessed 08.03.2022.

69 C. O'Mahony, *A Review of Children's Rights and Best Interests in the Context of Donor-Assisted Human Reproduction and Surrogacy in Irish Law*, 2020, available at: <https://www.gov.ie/en/publication/3e601-a-review-of-childrens-rights-and-best-interests-in-the-context-of-donorassisted-human-reproa-review-of-childrens-rights-and-best-interests-in-the-context-of-donor-assisted-human-reproduction-and-surrogacy-in-irish-law-duction-and-surrogacy-in-irish-law/>, last accessed 08.03.2022.

UN Special Rapporteur on the sale and sexual exploitation of children[70] and the requirements of Article 8 of the ECHR as interpreted in *Mennesson v. France*.[71]

The regulation of surrogacy has been the subject of proposed legal reform since 2005,[72] but up until now there has been very little practical progress. In 2017, the government proposed a General Scheme for an Assisted Human Reproduction Bill[73] and approval for the publication of the amended scheme as the Health (Assisted Human Reproduction) Bill 2022 had just been granted by cabinet at the time of writing.[74] The central idea behind the Bill is to create a governing body for assisted human reproduction to regulate service providers. Part 6 of the published general scheme provides for altruistic surrogacy to take place in Ireland. At least one of the intending parents must be genetically related to the child and the surrogate mother cannot be genetically related to the child.[75] On enactment, any other forms of non-compliant surrogacy, including commercial surrogacy will be prohibited in Ireland and it will become an offence to engage in such surrogacy.[76]

The general scheme is open to couples and individuals regardless of gender, but they must prove that they are either unable to gestate a pregnancy or that it would be harmful to a woman's health to do so.[77] One of the intended parents must also be genetically related to the child. In 2019, the Joint Committee on Health expressed concern that the need for a genetic link between one of the parents and the child could exclude couples who cannot produce gametes from using surrogacy and prioritised genetics over other ways of becoming a legal parent.[78]

The model for ascribing parentage following this limited form of surrogacy has three compulsory stages. First, treatment must be pre-authorised by the

---

70 *Report of the UN Special Rapporteur on the sale and sexual exploitation of children*, A/74/162, 15 July 2019, para. 20.

71 *Mennesson v. France* (Application No. 65192/11), paras. 99–102 (requiring States Parties to recognise the parent–child relationships arising from international surrogacy arrangements in all cases involving a genetic link between the child and the parents); L. Bracken, 'The ECtHR first advisory opinion: Implications for cross-border surrogacy involving male intended parents' (2021) 21 *Medical Law International* 3.

72 Commission on Assisted Human Reproduction, *Report of the Commission on Assisted Human Reproduction*, 2005.

73 Department of Health, *General Scheme of the Assisted Human Reproduction Bill 2017*, available at: <https://www.gov.ie/en/publication/4ac72d-general-scheme-of-the-assisted-human-reproduction-bill-2017/>, last accessed 08.03.2022.

74 Department of Health, *Cabinet approval for publication of Health (Assisted Human Reproduction) Bill 2022*, available at: <https://www.gov.ie/en/press-release/5377c-cabinet-approval-for-publication-of-health-assisted-human-reproduction-bill-2022/>, last accessed 08.03.2022.

75 Health (Assisted Human Reproduction) Bill 2022 s. 36(1).

76 Ibid, s. 36(2) and (4).

77 Ibid, s. 39.

78 Joint Committee on Health, *Report on Pre-Legislative Scrutiny of the General Scheme of the Assisted Human Reproduction Bill*, July 2019, p. 20.

regulation authority, which will scrutinise a written 'surrogacy agreement' demonstrating that consent has been obtained from all parties and that the personal details of the parents, surrogate and donor will be recorded on a newly created National Surrogacy Register. Then following birth, the surrogate must give new written and informed consent for the child to live with the intended parents.[79] Finally, the intended parents must apply to court for a parental order within six months following the birth of the child.[80] The court must ensure that the surrogacy agreement falls within the limits of the regulatory scheme and that there is consent from the surrogate and each intending person. The consent of the surrogate can be waived.[81] In addition, the parental order must be in the best interests of the child involved.[82] Only when an order has been made by the court will the surrogate cease to be considered as the child's legal mother.[83] Counselling and legal advice must be provided to the surrogate and each intending parent at all three stages of the process.[84] All relevant information will be maintained in a National Surrogacy Register and will be accessible to the child on the same basis as the National Donor-Conceived Person Register even if the parental order is never made.[85]

The general scheme mirrors the DAHR provisions of the Children and Family Relationships Act 2015 in the narrowness of its scope and onerous procedural requirements. O'Mahony has argued in favour of streamlining domestic surrogacy to incentivise its use and giving powers to the Irish High Court to grant parentage and parental responsibility to intending parents and nationality and citizenship to a child following international surrogacy arrangements.[86] Tobin[87] has argued in favour of a fully pre-birth approval model in order to facilitate domestic surrogacy.

The 2019 Joint Health Committee[88] recommended supporting further international collaboration in this area, such as the Hague Conference's ongoing project on Parentage/Surrogacy.[89] In July 2022, the Special Joint Oireachtas Committee on International Surrogacy recommended extending a

79 Above n. 75, at s. 46.
80 Ibid, s. 47.
81 Ibid, s. 48(2).
82 Ibid, s. 48.
83 Ibid, s. 49.
84 Ibid, s. 43.
85 Ibid, ss. 50 and 51.
86 C. O'Mahony, *A Review of Children's Rights and Best Interests in the Context of Donor-Assisted Human Reproduction and Surrogacy in Irish Law*, 2020, p. 39.
87 B. Tobin, 'An appraisal of Ireland's current legislative proposals for regulating domestic surrogacy arrangements' (2019) 41 *Journal of Social Welfare and Family Law* 205.
88 Joint Committee on Health, *Report on Pre-Legislative Scrutiny of the General Scheme of the Assisted Human Reproduction Bill*, July 2019, p. 22.
89 <https://www.hcch.net/en/projects/legislative-projects/parentage-surrogacy> last accessed 08.03.2022.

more flexible, post-birth, parental order system to children born as a result of international surrogacy agreements.[90] Intending parents would be obliged to provide evidence that they had complied with all the proposed information and consent requirements of the Health (Assisted Human Reproduction) Bill 2022 but there would be an overriding judicial discretion in exceptional circumstances.[91] They recommended that intending parents should be able to apply for a pre-authorisation certificate from the proposed new governing body for assisted reproduction service providers, in order to streamline the process.[92] The Committee felt that a genetic link between one intending parent and the child, proved to the court through DNA testing, should be required to obtain a parental order in cases of international surrogacy but suggested that a domestic scheme could be more flexible.[93] They also suggested that international surrogacy agreements should be fairly and ethically compensated.[94] The Committee called for immediate legislative action by amending the Health (Assisted Human Reproduction) Bill 2022.[95] The proposals have been welcomed by activist groups and the Ombudsman for Children. The recommendations of the Committee will be debated when the Irish Parliament returns from its summer recess in September 2022.

3.2. THE RECENT EXTENSION OF GUARDIANSHIP RIGHTS

Part 4 of the Children and Family Relationships Act 2015 makes changes to the law of guardianship, extending the category of adults who can acquire decision-making powers and responsibilities for children. Guardianship gives adults long-term decision-making powers for children, including the right to decide where a child should live or how they will be educated, the right to consent to medical treatment and the right to decide a child's religious upbringing.[96] Guardians have also have prima facie rights of custody as against non-guardians.[97] Guardianship can sometimes work for LGBT+ families, allowing them to 'work around' some of the issues they encounter because both partners

90 Joint Committee on International Surrogacy, *Final Report*, July 2022, p. 30. available at: <https://data.oireachtas.ie/ie/oireachtas/committee/dail/33/joint_committee_on_international_surrogacy/reports/2022/2022-07-06_final-report-of-the-joint-committee-on-international-surrogacy_en.pdf/>, last accessed 29.07.2022.

91 Ibid, p. 33.

92 Ibid, pp. 38–39.

93 Ibid, p. 33.

94 Ibid, p. 31.

95 Ibid, p. 51.

96 Some of these rights and responsibilities are now outlined in s. 6E(11) of the Guardianship of Infants Act 1964, but this is not exhaustive.

97 Guardianship of Infants Act 1964 s. 10(2)(a).

are not recognised as joint legal parents. The inadequacy of guardianship as a 'work around' will be addressed in the next section.

The Irish rules for awarding guardianship rights are mother-centric and marital status remains very important. Mothers are automatically legal guardians of their children in all circumstances.[98] Heterosexual married couples are automatically joint legal guardians of their children.[99] From 4 May 2020, the spouse of a woman who gives birth following a DAHR procedure will have automatic guardianship as long the consent requirements outlined above are complied with.[100] Irish law makes assumptions about the second parent's commitment to their child from the existence of a marriage.

For second parents who are not married to the mothers of their children,[101] guardianship is not automatic, and positive action must be taken to secure the status. Guardianship rights will arise where the parent marries the mother following the birth,[102] where the couple have been cohabiting for a minimum of 12 months, including three consecutive months after the birth,[103] by agreement with the mother that is recorded in the form of a statutory declaration,[104] or where guardian rights are granted by court order.[105] Such guardianship rights are not as permanent as the automatic guardianship rights that are given to spouses[106] and can be stripped by the court where the guardian fails in their duties towards the child.[107]

For the first time, section 6C of the Children and Family Relationships Act 2015 allows non-parents to apply to court directly for guardianship.[108] There are two classes of potential applicants: step-parents or cohabitants who have lived with a parent of the child for at least three years and shared day-to-day responsibility for the child for at least two years,[109] and foster parents or people acting *in loco parentis* who have provided for the child's day-to-day care for a continuous period of more than 12 months where the child has no existing parent or guardian who is willing or able to exercise the rights and

---

98 Ibid, s. 6.

99 Ibid.

100 Ibid, s. 6B(1).

101 Unmarried female partners recognised as second female parents following DAHR are now treated in the same way as unmarried fathers.

102 Guardianship of Infants Act 1964 s. 6B(1).

103 Ibid, ss. 2(4A) or 6B(2)(b).

104 Ibid, ss. 2(4) or 6B(4).

105 Ibid, s. 6A.

106 Which can only be removed in the case of legal adoption.

107 Guardianship of Infants Act 1964, s. 8(7) (where it is in the best interests of the child to do so and the guardian is unable to act or has failed in their duties).

108 Prior to changes made by the Children and Family Relationships Act, it was only possible for non-parents to be appointed guardian in the case of testamentary guardianship or where the child had no living guardian; Guardianship of Infants Act 1964, ss. 7 and 8.

109 Above n. 102, at s. 6C.

responsibilities of guardianship. For LGBT+ families where one of the intended parents is not recognised as a legal parent, this mechanism allows that person to apply to court to be recognised as the child's guardian two years after the child's birth. Where the child has been left entirely in the care of a non-parent, this mechanism allows the situation to be regularised by court order after 12 months. This is designed for informal foster parent situations, but is also helpful where an LGBT+ family separates before the two-year requirement for cohabitation is fulfilled and the child remains with the non-parent.

Non-parent applications for guardianship are made with notice to existing parents or guardians.[110] Guardianship cannot be awarded without the permission of all guardians, although the court can dispense with consent of a guardian if is unreasonably withheld and it is in the best interests of the child to make the order.[111]

When deciding to grant non-parent guardianship rights, the court applies the best interests of the child principle and in addition must ensure that the child has an opportunity to be heard and have their views taken into account.[112] The court must also address the number of guardians and the degree to which they are involved in the upbringing of the child.[113]

Non-parent guardians work alongside parent guardians. Their powers can be limited by the court[114] and they can also be stripped of guardianship rights by the court.[115] Guardianship ceases when the child turns 18, so it does not create a life-long legal connection between a social parent and a child.[116]

O'Mahony suggests that awarding guardianship is enough to satisfy Ireland's bare minimum international human rights obligations to recognise intended parent–children relationships for children born through ART[117] and surrogacy.[118] He suggests that it is, in principle, justifiable to give intended parents the functional but lesser status of guardianship where they do not comply with requirements of DAHR as this discourages non-compliance and ensures the integrity of the National Donor-Conceived Person Register.[119] However, he argues that in such cases the standard two-year wait for guardianship should be removed.[120] This author argues that even without the wait, guardianship is not

110 Ibid, s. 6C(3).
111 Ibid, s. 6C(6) and (7).
112 Ibid, s. 6C(8).
113 Ibid.
114 Ibid, s. 6C(9).
115 Children and Family Relationships Act 2015 s. 114.
116 Guardianship of Infants Act 1964 s. 8A.
117 C. O'Mahony, *A Review of Children's Rights and Best Interests in the Context of Donor-Assisted Human Reproduction and Surrogacy in Irish Law*, 2020, p. 12.
118 Ibid, p. 39.
119 Ibid, pp. 12–13.
120 Ibid, p. 14.

an equivalent recognition of the life-long dependency created between parent and child and has real long-term disadvantages for parent and child as compared to legal parenthood. It is inappropriate to conclusively determine the nature of a child's legal kinship ties based on policy approval or disapproval of their parent's level of compliance with preferred legal pathways.

3.3. ADOPTION

The Adoption (Amendment) Act 2017 has extended the class of people eligible to adopt to include married couples, civil partners, cohabiting couples and individuals.[121] Now, under the Adoption Act 2010 as amended, LGBT+ people can access domestic adoption and intercountry adoption on the same terms as heterosexual people. All eligible adopters must be assessed by the TUSLA (the Child and Family Agency) and deemed suitable to adopt.[122]

Domestic adoption is not a route commonly used by LGBT+ families. In Bracken's recent study, only 10 per cent of participants had engaged in adoption, and all adoptions had occurred outside Ireland.[123] This is not surprising as only 728 domestic adoption orders were made in Ireland between 2010 and 2020.[124] There are fewer than ten adoptions of children by strangers per year and the vast majority of domestic orders are for step-parent adoptions.

Prior to the 2017 Act, adoption was the only mechanism available to grant a step-parent guardianship rights over a child while their parent remained alive. The child's parent and step-parent adopted the child jointly as a married couple. Since 2017, there is no longer any need for a birth parent to adopt their own child in such circumstances. The step-parent can apply to adopt the child and the child is then deemed to be the child of the step-parent and their birth parent.[125] The definition of step-parent has also been extended to include civil partners and cohabiting couples.[126]

The consequence of step-parent adoption is that the child is considered in law to be the child of the birth parent and the birth parent's new partner. All legal recognition of the relationship between the child and the other birth parent

---

121 Adoption Act 2010 s. 33 (as amended by Adoption (Amendment) Act 2017, s. 16).

122 Ibid, s. 34.

123 L. Bracken, *LGBTI+ Parent Families in Ireland: Legal Recognition of Parent-Child Relationships*, University of Limerick, 2021, p. 32, available at: <https://www.ul.ie/research/lgbti-parent-families-ireland-legal-recognition-parent-child-relationships>, last accessed 08.03.2022.

124 Adoption Authority of Ireland, *Celebrating 10 years of the Adoption Authority of Ireland 2010–2020*, 2020, available at: <https://aai.gov.ie/images/Celebrating_10_Years_of_the_Adoption_Authority_of_Ireland.pdf>, last accessed 08.03.2022.

125 Adoption Act 2010 s. 58A (as amended).

126 Ibid, s. 37(5).

is severed. Step-parent adoption is most commonly used where one of the birth parents has died or where the father has never been involved in the child's life. Where the birth parent has guardianship rights, they must consent to the step-parent adoption.[127] Where the birth parent is a non-guardian, they must be consulted, but their permission is not required.[128]

The eligibility criteria for step-parent adoption are slightly less onerous than those for step-parent guardianship.[129] The child must have lived with the step-parent and the birth parent for a continuous period of two years, but there is no requirement for the relationship between the birth parent and their partner to have lasted any particular period of time.[130]

This author suggests that step-parent guardianship is a now more appropriate mechanism to give step-parents decision-making rights as it preserves the child's legal links to their entire birth family. However, step-parent adoption could be used as an appropriate 'work-around' for surrogacy situations, allowing a genetic father to adopt with his partner or spouse and severing all legal links to the gestational surrogacy mother. O'Mahony suggests domestic adoption for situations where legal parenthood cannot be granted under the Children and Family Relationships Act 2015.[131] However, Freedom of Information responses suggest that the Adoption Authority of Ireland is refusing to process adoption applications relating to surrogacy or DAHR until there is legislative change.[132]

4. THE LIMITS OF 'WORK-AROUNDS' AND PRESSING PRACTICAL PROBLEMS

Bracken's recent study on the legal recognition of parent–child relationships casts light on the scale of disadvantage faced by LGBTI+ families who are excluded from legal recognition as parents in Ireland.[133] Her self-administered, anonymous online survey captured the experiences of 99 parents who self-identified as LGBTI+. These parents had used different pathways

127 Ibid, s. 40(3).

128 Ibid, s. 30.

129 Examined above.

130 Adoption Act 2010 s. 37(5)(b).

131 C. O'Mahony, *A Review of Children's Rights and Best Interests in the Context of Donor-Assisted Human Reproduction and Surrogacy in Irish Law*, 2020, p. 13.

132 A. Conneely, 'Legal Rights Call for Children Born Through Surrogacy', *The Irish Times* 10 June 2021, available at: <https://www.rte.ie/news/ireland/2021/0610/1227220-surrogacy/>, last accessed 08.03.2022.

133 L. Bracken, *LGBTI+ Parent Families in Ireland: Legal Recognition of Parent-Child Relationships*, University of Limerick, 2021, p. 24, available at: <https://www.ul.ie/research/lgbti-parent-families-ireland-legal-recognition-parent-child-relationships>, last accessed 08.03.2022.

to parenthood – 67 per cent had used DAHR (as defined on the form), 10 per cent had used adoption, 13 per cent had used surrogacy and 10 per cent had used another route to parenthood. Most respondents were co-parenting[134] female[135] parents. The study showed that in 53 per cent of the two parent families captured by the survey, both parents were not recognised as legal parents of all their children.[136] Moreover, in 47 per cent of such families, both parents did not have legal guardianship. As Bracken observes, the findings reflect the current Irish reality that a significant portion of LGBTI+ families are not fully recognised under Irish law.[137]

Bracken's sample was mainly made up of highly invested, committed LGBT+ parents who were actively seeking legal recognition as a family. Such families highlighted the practical, day-to-day problems they encountered in caring for their children caused by rigid administrative systems. Same-sex partners faced problems in being accepted as a parent and being recognised as eligible to give parental consent in child-care settings and medical settings.[138] Irish law's failure to properly recognise the parent–child dependency in all LGBT+ families makes these highly committed families feel like second-class citizens. Moreover, where the family has been less proactive and adult relationships break down, parents and children are left in vulnerable situations, disadvantaging such children in the longer term.

O'Mahony suggests that a swift path to guardianship would be enough to satisfy Ireland's international human rights obligations in recognising parent–child relationships for children born through ART and surrogacy.[139] However, recognition of the parent–child dependency through guardianship does not achieve equality of recognition for such families.

Guardianship simply cannot act as an appropriate substitute for legal parenthood in many areas of law where rights are determined by legal kinship links and not parental decision-making powers. Nationality is one such area.

Brexit has triggered legal challenges to the definition of legal parenthood for the purposes of Irish nationality where LGBT+ families living in Britain have sought EU citizenship for their children through Irish citizenship based on the parent–child link. Section 7(1) of the Irish Nationality and Citizenship Act 1956 states that '[a] person is an Irish citizen from birth if at the time of his or her birth either parent was an Irish citizen or would if alive have been an Irish citizen'. In 2017, the Irish Passport Office denied Katie Gallagher and

134 90%.
135 79%.
136 Above n. 133, at p. 17.
137 Ibid, at p. 18.
138 Ibid, at p. 21.
139 C. O'Mahony, *A Review of Children's Rights and Best Interests in the Context of Donor-Assisted Human Reproduction and Surrogacy in Irish Law*, 2020, p. 39.

Holly Groombridge a passport for their 11-week-old son. The child had been conceived through reciprocal IVF using donor sperm and born in the UK.[140] Katie, an Irish citizen, was the genetic mother while her wife, Holly, was the gestational mother. The passport was denied because the Passport Office did not consider the child to have an Irish parent according to Irish law. However, if Katie had been a man, she would have been recognised as the child's prima facie legal parent under the marital presumption. This family's situation cannot be remedied by the transitional measure of the Children and Family Relationship Act 2015 because the birth of the child occurred abroad.

However, very recently, the Irish High Court has taken a different view of legal parenthood for the purposes of nationality. In *A, B and C v. Minister for Foreign Affairs and Trade*,[141] Barrett J. recognised the parental status of two male parents under common law principles of Irish private international law, holding that parental status is determined by the law of the domicile and not by Irish law. In this case both parents were domiciled in England, they had a child through surrogacy and were recognised as legal parents following a parental order from the English High Court. The genetic father was British and the second legal parent was Irish. Barrett J. held that the order of the English court should be recognised[142] and further held that section 7(1) must be interpreted to mean that a child is an Irish citizen if, at the time of his or her birth, the person who would become his or her parent was an Irish citizen, as opposed to limiting the section to people who were actually recognised as parents at the time of birth. He justified this interpretation as required to ensure compliance with obligations under the ECHR following the decision in *Mennesson*.[143]

While the decision in *ABC* is to be welcomed, it is in direct contradiction with the policy of the Department of Foreign Affairs, which insists that in cases of surrogacy, Irish authorities are required to apply Irish law and may not recognise foreign birth certificates or foreign court orders.[144] The Department of Foreign Affairs usually requires DNA evidence to prove a genetic link between the child and an Irish genetic father in order to establish a parent–child link for the purposes of granting the child a passport. Moreover, such passports cannot be granted unless the consent of all of the child's guardians is given or where

---

140 L. Walsh, '11-week old baby refused Irish passport because his UK-based mum is not his dad', *The Meath Chronicle*, 6 November 2017, available at: <https://www.meathchronicle.ie/2017/11/06/11-week-old-baby-refused-irish-passport-because-his-uk-based-mum-is-not-his-dad/>, last accessed 08.03.2022.

141 [2021] IEHC 785.

142 Ibid, at para. 6.

143 Ibid, at para. 33.

144 Department of Foreign Affairs, *Citizenship, Parentage, Guardianship and Travel Document Issues in Relation to Children Born as a Result of Surrogacy Arrangements Entered into Outside the State*, available at: <https://www.dfa.ie/media/dfa/alldfawebsitemedia/childrens-issues-surrogacy-guidance-document.pdf>, last accessed 09.03.2022.

consent is dispensed with by a court.[145] Russia's violent invasion of Ukraine has caused particular problems for 14 Irish families who were due to have babies using surrogacy services in Ukraine between February and May.[146] The Department of Foreign Affairs has fast-tracked emergency travel document to help these couples bring the children into the State more quickly.[147] This high-profile crisis has increased pressure on the Irish government to provide appropriate legal mechanisms to recognise the parent–child relationships created by surrogacy.

Legal parenthood is a vital component in establishing financial obligations between parents and children. Irish inheritance law is still based entirely on legal parenthood.[148] On intestacy, the deceased person's estate is distributed to their spouse and 'issue', i.e. legally recognised children.[149] Where a will is made, such children have a right to apply for a discretionary statutory share where their parent has failed to make 'proper provision' in accordance with his means.[150] While it is possible for LGBT+ families to obviate this problem by making wills to provide for their children, their bequests will be subject to much higher rates of inheritance tax, where their children are not legally recognised as their children.[151] Where they are not so proactive, such children simply do not have a right to inheritance or a right to seek proper provision from a will.

Maintenance obligations are imposed on a broader basis than legal parenthood alone, but legal parenthood still affects when obligations arise and how long they endure. Where parents are married, spouses are liable to support children of the other spouse and any child for whom the other spouse acted *in loco parentis*, as long as they have treated the child as a member of the family, knowing that they are not the parent of that child.[152] So for married LGBT+ families, child maintenance can be imposed regardless of parental status, where the family have lived together as a family. For unmarried families the situation is slightly more complicated. Where parents are unmarried but have cohabited, each is liable for their legal children,[153] and for any child for whom

145 Passports Act 2008 s. 14 (as amended).

146 S. Carswell, 'Irish couples awaiting surrogacy births in Ukraine face "daily horror"', *The Irish Times*, 27 February 2022, available at: <https://www.irishtimes.com/news/ireland/irish-news/irish-couples-awaiting-surrogacy-births-in-ukraine-face-daily-horror-1.4813301>, last accessed 08.03.2022.

147 S. Carswell, 'Travel documents for Irish surrogacy babies in Ukraine to be fast-tracked', *The Irish Times*, 15 February 2022, available at: <https://www.irishtimes.com/news/ireland/irish-news/travel-documents-for-irish-surrogacy-babies-in-ukraine-to-be-fast-tracked-1.4803462>, last accessed 08.03.2022.

148 Succession Act 1965 s. 4A (as amended by the Children and Family Relationships Act 2015).

149 Ibid, s. 67.

150 Ibid, s. 117.

151 Capital Acquisitions Tax Consolidation Act 2003 Schedule 2, Part 1.

152 Family Law 1976 s. 3.

153 Ibid, s. 5B.

they have acted *in loco parentis*, but only if they are the child's legal guardian.[154] An unmarried parent is thus required to proactively make a formal legal commitment to a legally unrelated child before the obligation of maintenance is imposed. This maintenance obligation ends with guardianship when the child turns 18. In all other circumstances, maintenance would be payable until the child turns 23 where they are in full-time education (or would have been in full-time education where maintenance had been paid) or indefinitely in the case of children with mental and physical disabilities where it is not reasonably possible for them to maintain themselves fully.[155]

Irish State welfare payments and benefits for families are more squarely based on social parentage; people caring for dependent children qualify as long as they satisfy the other requirements of the particular scheme.[156] Parents leave and parental benefit (which together provide five weeks' paid leave for new parents in the first two years of their child's life) are open to parents or the spouse/cohabitant of a parent of a child.[157] However, the contractual parental leave benefits of many employers may not be so inclusive in their understanding of 'parent'.

While guardianship may provide a functional equivalent for committed LGBT+ families who seek recognition to make decisions for their small children, it falls very short of the lifetime recognition of the parent–child link that legal parenthood provides.

5. CONCLUSION: THE INCOHERENCE OF IRISH LEGAL PARENTHOOD

This author argues that the unequal treatment of the parent–child dependency within LGBT+ families goes deeper than the inadequacies in the current legislative framework and is rooted in conceptual incoherence as to what legal parenthood should be about, which is replicated in new forms of legislation. In some situations, social ties and parental intention are enough for legal parenthood; for fatherhood a genetic link is often crucial, whereas for mothers genes are irrelevant if gestation can be proved.

Irish law is obsessed with the idea of a nuclear family, expressly ensuring that there are a maximum of two candidates for legal parenthood in all domestic ART cases. This has given rise to the unknown donor requirement in the transitional measures of the Children and Family Relationships Act 2015 but can also be

154 Ibid.
155 Ibid, s. 3.
156 E.g. Working Family Payment, Child Benefit, One-parent Family Payment.
157 Parent's Leave and Benefit Act 2019 s. 2.

seen in the Heads of Bill scheme for surrogacy where applications for parental orders are expressly limited to a maximum of two parents.[158] This is indicative of Irish laws' characterisation of the status of legal parenthood as a prize for committed parents engaging in ART rather than the appropriate, child-centred imposition of life-long legal obligations towards the children created.

Irish law also relies on the essentialist premise that there is always one candidate for legal motherhood and second parent candidates should be considered based on their relationship to her. This structure focuses on adult commitments to each other, rather than measuring commitment to children more directly when this is possible. The traditional rules of legal parenthood are mother-centric as a matter of practicality, the gestational mother historically being the only identifiable person at birth with a clear connection to the child, but this direct focus on gestation is questionable in modern times. In situations where children are created through ART, in a State-controlled environment, and where adult intentions are clear before birth, the mother-centric nature of the Children and Family Relationships Act 2015 makes less sense. It is obviously very important that a woman receiving fertility treatment understands and consents to what is happening to her body, but the primacy of the gestational mother's personal consent to fertility treatment should not be elided with her claim to legal parenthood. Legal recognition of the second parent should not be extrapolated from their marital commitment to the mother, but on their direct commitment to the child measured by their consent to parenthood. This approach would take the legal primacy out of motherhood for children conceived through tightly controlled ART processes, making things easier for LGBT+ families. It would also allow parenthood to be degendered, avoiding the need to address domestic surrogacy separately and removing the legal requirement to misgender trans parents who engage in ART.

There is an incoherent approach to protecting the child's right to identity in Irish law also. For children born through DAHR processes, the protection of the right to identifying information is of central importance. For children born through other forms of ART, this right is not protected and, moreover, the social reality of their family situation cannot be recognised through legal parenthood. The traditional rules of parenthood can actively hide correct information about biological parentage from children where parents rely on presumptions based on marriage. While it is an offence under the Civil Registration Act 2004[159] to knowingly give false or misleading information to a State registrar, this is very far from requiring parents to declare correct information about their child's birth. Yet when the court makes a declaration of parentage for a child who is

[158] General Scheme for an Assisted Human Reproduction Bill, Head 47.
[159] Civil Registration Act 2004 s. 69(3).

not conceived through DAHR discretion, it is now considered to always be in the child's best interests to know his or her genetic identity.[160] For adopted children, there is currently no legal right to identifying information, although the Birth Information and Tracing Bill 2022 promises a full and clear right of access to birth certificates, birth and early life information for all persons who were adopted, boarded out, the subject of an illegal birth registration or who otherwise have questions in relation to their origins.

In the Children and Family Relationships Act 2015, legal parenthood is used as a carrot to entice parents to comply with procedures to ensure that children have access to identifying information about their biological parents. If they fail to do so, there is no remedial mechanism to resolve the situation which leaves children without proper legal recognition of their parent–child dependencies. O'Mahony argues that denying the second parent legal recognition where ART does not comply with the requirements of the Act is a proportional means to protect the rights of identity of donor-conceived children because it deters parents from using non-clinical procedures which do not preserve such information.[161] He justifies this position because of the availability of guardianship and adoption as functional 'work-arounds' but, as has been examined, these are inadequate mechanisms for most LGBT+ families. Bracken's study shows that parents are now opting for DAHR procedures, whereas before the implementation of the Act, 31 per cent had used services abroad, most commonly in the UK.[162] It is suggested that the assurance of automatic recognition as legal parents is incentive enough for parents to use the Irish statutory scheme without the need to preclude remedial options.

It also seems heavy-handed to place such emphasis on preserving genetic truth here, when other parts of Irish law take a different approach. While case law from the ECHR has focused primarily on the right to identity in terms of the right to access information about biological family,[163] a broader understanding of children's right to identity which includes legal recognition of the child's family reality should be taken in Irish law.

The denial of parental status disproportionally affects LGBT+ parents who cannot rely on the traditional presumptions of Irish law, presumptions that do

160 Children and Family Relationships Bill 2015, *Explanatory Memorandum*, p. 21, available at: <https://data.oireachtas.ie/ie/oireachtas/bill/2015/14/eng/memo/b1415d-memo.pdf>, last accessed 29.07.2022.

161 C. O'Mahony, *A Review of Children's Rights and Best Interests in the Context of Donor-Assisted Human Reproduction and Surrogacy in Irish Law*, 2020, p. 12.

162 L. Bracken, *LGBTI+ Parent Families in Ireland: Legal Recognition of Parent-Child Relationships*, University of Limerick, 2021, pp. 25–26, available at: <https://www.ul.ie/research/lgbti-parent-families-ireland-legal-recognition-parent-child-relationships>, last accessed 08.03.2022 (although the lack of international mobility could also be attributable to COVID-19 restrictions).

163 Ibid, at pp. 25–27.

not protect the right to identity of children at all. A limited remedial option for children born through any form of ART (in Ireland or elsewhere) that would allow a court to assess individual situations, ensure that children's rights to identity are protected on the facts and award legal parenthood on a best interests basis would not undermine the scheme and would allow all LGBT+ families to be recognised. It would also allow the court to recognise the rules of parenthood from other jurisdictions.

ITALY

ITALY'S 2021 FAMILY LAW REFORM

A Missed Opportunity to Harness Artificial Intelligence for the Benefit of Minors

Isabella FERRARI

Résumé

Le présent article évalue la récente réforme du droit italien de la famille, prévue par la loi n° 206 du 26 novembre 2021, qui entrera en vigueur le 31 décembre 2024.

Outre la création d'un tribunal unique de la famille, compétent pour toutes les questions relatives aux enfants, à la séparation, au divorce et à la protection des personnes vulnérables, le législateur a modifié radicalement les règles de procédure civile, afin de faciliter la gestion du contentieux familial et d'encourager une collaboration efficace entre les parties et leurs avocats.

Les objectifs, le calendrier et les outils de la réforme italienne sont comparés aux différentes solutions adoptées à l'étranger en matière de droit de la famille, et en particulier aux systèmes d'intelligence artificielle prédictifs et analytiques déjà utilisés dans les systèmes de common law, qui se sont révélés particulièrement adaptés pour résoudre des questions récurrentes et évaluables numériquement comme la détermination du montant de la pension alimentaire due à l'ex-conjoint et aux enfants, la détermination du calendrier du droit de visite et d'hébergement et le partage des biens et autres actifs au moment de la rupture.

1. THE CONTEXT OF THE REFORM, BETWEEN THE ATAVIST SLOWNESS OF THE SYSTEM AND THE NEED FOR LEGAL CERTAINTY

With Law No. 206 of 26 November 2021, the Italian Parliament delegated to the executive the obligation to make the civil legal process more efficient, in order to fix the extreme slowness of domestic litigation. The aim of the legislation is to streamline and reorganise civil procedure, and to enhance respect for the important principle of the reasonable duration of the trial, formally recognised at the domestic level[1] and European level.[2]

Official statistics attest a slow decrease in the numbers of civil litigation as of 2019,[3] thus demonstrating the effectiveness of the dispute resolution procedures introduced since 2010.[4]

---

1 See Art. 111, para. 2 Italian Constitution: 'The law … ensures the reasonable duration [of the trial]'.

2 See Art. 6(1) ECHR: 'Everyone has the right to a fair and public hearing within a reasonable time, before an independent and impartial tribunal pre-established by law'.

3 ISTAT, *Annuario Statistico Italiano 2021*, 2021, pp. 215, 239, available at: <https://www.istat.it/it/archivio/264305>.

4 See G. Autorino, D. Noviello and C. Troisi, *Mediazione e conciliazione. Nelle controversie civili e commerciali*, Maggioli Editore, 2013, discussing how the launch of mediation and assisted negotiation in Italy has been rather troubled. In fact, although it was introduced for the first time by Legislative Decree No. 28 of 4 March 2010 ('Implementation of Article 60 of Law No. 69 of 18 June 2009, regarding mediation aimed at the conciliation of civil and commercial disputes'), it was suspended due to its declared unconstitutionality and finally reintroduced on an experimental and temporary basis by Legislative Decree No. 69 of 21 June 2013 (converted into law). More recently, with Law No. 96/2017, compulsory mediation has acquired the character of a structural and permanent element of Italian civil

By expanding the scope of mandatory mediation, the 2021 Italian reform aims to further encourage the use of alternative dispute resolution, thereby reducing litigation, promoting growth and investment, and improving the overall quality of life. There can be no doubt that a long-pending judgment affects personal and professional lives and has a negative impact on overall national economic development.[5]

Italy stands out within the European Union for its high numbers of lawyers[6] and of pending cases[7] (with an obvious connection between these two parameters), which inevitably leads to the extreme length of judicial proceedings: in fact, compared to the average European duration of a civil case at first instance of 194 days, Italy stands at 527 days (with significant disparities at a regional level), and even holds the negative European record of maximum duration on the three levels of judgment with an average of 1,266 days against a European average of 207.4 days for a decision in cassation.[8] Within this framework, the new Italian Law No. 206/2021, together with the economic development interventions included in the national recovery and resilience plan, aims to contribute to boosting the economy in the post-pandemic era.

In order to encourage strategic investment and stimulate economic recovery by attracting internal and external financing, it is necessary to eliminate the backlog of civil and corporate litigation, which is currently congesting Italian courts and causing them to be substantially overloaded. Therefore, the 2021 reform of the Italian civil process aims to simplify, rationalise and speed up litigation procedures by reorganising their structure. In particular, the reform touches three specific areas: the procedure for mediation and assisted negotiation

---

justice, but exclusively within the limits of the topics specifically identified by law (real estate; inheritance; lease; medical and health care liability; defamation by the press or other means of advertising; insurance, banking and financial contracts).

5 See European Commission, *EU Justice Evaluation Scoreboard 2021*, 8 July 2021, available at: <https://ec.europa.eu/commission/presscorner/detail/en/IP_21_3523> (holding that efficiency, quality and independence are the main parameters of an efficient judicial system).

6 See European Commission for the Efficiency of Justice, *CEPEJ Overview 2020*, 2020, available at: <https://public.tableau.com/app/profile/cepej/viz/CEPEJ-Overviewv20201_0EN/Overview> (noting that there are 388.3 lawyers per 100,000 inhabitants in Italy, compared to a European average of 120.4 lawyers per 100,000 inhabitants: more than three times the national average).

7 Ibid (based on data provided by CEPEJ in 2017, Italy had the highest number of cases pending at first instance in Europe).

8 ISTAT, above n. 3. See also M. Azzalini, 'Il ristoro del pregiudizio da eccessiva durata del processo nell'orizzonte della responsabilità civile' in D. Barbierato (ed.), *Il risarcimento del danno e le sue funzioni*, Jovene, 2012, pp. 1–54; and P. Bondonio, 'La storica insostenibile lentezza della giustizia civile italiana: analisi di un tentativo per ridurla' in G. Romagnoli (ed.), *L'Economia Liberale. Saggi per Francesco Forte*, Franco Angeli, 2018, p. 138 (addressing fair compensation for the excessive duration of trial). See also A. Keidel, 'Gascogne Sack Deutschland, Groupe Gascogne, and Kendrion: Excessive length of cartel proceedings' (2014) 5(3) *Journal of European Competition Law & Practice* 142 (slow justice is a widespread problem, as the *Gascogne* case demonstrates).

(to be simplified and reorganised within the so-called TUSC),[9] family law, and foreclosure and executive procedures. Ancillary interventions are also envisaged in related disciplines (legal deontology, tax matters, appeals, auxiliaries, etc.). The final objective, announced by the legislator itself in Article 1 of Law No. 206/2021, is 'the formal and substantive reorganisation of the civil process' with a view to its 'simplification, rapidity and rationalisation'.

1.1. FOCUS ON FAMILY LAW

This contribution focuses exclusively on the area of family law, which is governed by Articles 23–31 of Law No. 206/2021. The recent reform initiates a gradual change in civil law, to be completed with the decree laws expected by 24 December 2022 and the final entry into force of the reform as a whole on 31 December 2024. Therefore, the current phase represents a first step towards a broader change for the future of civil and family law in Italy. However, it is necessary to evaluate and take stock of the reform implemented so far, in order to check its adequacy and effectiveness in practice, and to assess possible corrective actions.

1.2. DYSFUNCTIONS OF THE CURRENT SYSTEM

The fragmented management of Italian family justice has often caused delays and confusion, to the point of frequently giving rise to opposing decisions between the same parties. In fact, Italy has a double track for family proceedings. On the one hand, there is the juvenile court, with civil, criminal and administrative jurisdiction over minors, which operates with a mixed composition (two ordinary and two honorary judges) and has very broad competences (ascertainment of the state of abandonment or danger of the child, deprivation of parental authority, custody and adoption provisions, etc.). On the other hand, there is the ordinary civil court, which, within its family section, deals with separations and divorces, and also, since 2013,[10] addresses economic issues concerning children born out of wedlock.

---

9 TUSC stands for Unified Text for Complementary Tools to the Jurisdiction. Art. 1(4)(b) of the law under review here, Law No. 206/2021, charges the executive with responsibility for reforming mediation and assisted negotiation procedures: 'the legislative decree or decrees on amendments to the disciplines of the mediation procedure and assisted negotiation shall be adopted in compliance with the following guiding principles and criteria: … to harmonise, at the outcome of the monitoring to be carried out on the area of application of compulsory mediation, the regulations on out-of-court dispute resolution procedures provided for by law and, for this purpose, to collect all the disciplines in a single text of complementary instruments to jurisdiction (TUSC), as well as with appropriate valorisation of the individual competences by reason of the matters in which said procedures may intervene'.

10 See Decree-Law No. 154 of 28 December 2013.

Moreover, the Italian system grants the judiciary, in its various compositions and functions, additional competences in regard to minors: the guardian judge must authorise parents intending to subject the child's assets to acts that go beyond ordinary administration (e.g. sale or mortgage, acceptance or waiver of inheritances or donations, transactions in the interest of the minor, etc.), while the supervisory magistrate monitors those who have committed a crime as juveniles, up to the age of 25, and the court of reconsideration and the execution judge are competent for appeals and ancillary proceedings. The social services also deal with minors, in the context of at-risk or troubled families. In essence, the system branches into various bodies, which often do not communicate with each other:[11] this results in unfair decisions, as in the event that a perpetrator of femicide, who has been convicted in criminal court, retains in civil court parental responsibility, together with the visitation rights for or even custody of any offspring, as well as the right to manage the victim's assets on behalf of the offspring.

Within this general framework, there are also grey areas, which can be dealt with by either the juvenile or civil court. This is clearly a chaotic and complex system, totally unsuited to the context of family law, which needs clarity and speed more than any other area of justice, to protect not only the weak parties involved in its judgments, but the community as a whole.

2. THE COURT FOR INDIVIDUALS, YOUTH AND FAMILIES

The 2021 Italian reform unifies the courts and methods of recourse for family disputes, streamlining access to justice in the interest, above all, of the minors involved.[12] A single court with overall jurisdiction in family matters is established, the so-called Court for Individuals, Youth and Families, with the simultaneous suppression of the juvenile court, the reorganisation of the courts of first and second instance (which are also changing their names, as explained below), and the introduction of a single claim form for all family disputes.

These structural and procedural changes, currently only sketched out by the reform, will completely revolutionise the judicial handling of family matters.

Hitherto, in fact, family matters have been handled separately by the juvenile courts and ordinary civil courts, with a gradual expansion of civil

---

11 See G. Magno, *Elementi di Diritto Minorile*, Giuffrè, 2019, pp. 57–135, 229–270 (giving an overview of the position of the minor in the Italian civil and criminal proceedings); see also G. Autorino, *Manuale di Diritto di Famiglia*, Giappichelli, 2016; and G. Ferrando, *Manuale di Diritto della Famiglia*, Laterza, 2005.

12 See G. Autorino, 'I figli nella crisi della famiglia: esperienze europee a confronto' (1998) 39(2) *Rassegna di Teologia: Digest cattolico* 239 (offering a comparative analysis of the offspring after parental separation, divorce and break-up, the author calls for the simplification of the Italian family system in line with European standards).

court jurisdiction aimed at ensuring equal treatment of natural and legitimate offspring. Law No. 206/2021 further promotes this equalisation by completely unifying the various pre-existing family procedures. This is a momentous change, which pursues multiple objectives:

- simplifying access to the courts, overcoming the frequent uncertainties in identifying the competent forum;[13]
- ensuring uniform protection for children born in and out of wedlock; and
- promoting the centring, appropriateness and timeliness of judicial decisions, including through the introduction of a career-path restriction for family judges, resulting in their increased specialisation.[14]

In addition, the Court for Individuals, Youth and Families will be organised into circuit courts (located within each trial court) and district courts (part of the appellate courts): the former will be responsible for the day-to-day management of family crises, while the juvenile court's current jurisdiction over adoption, foster care and juvenile offences will be transferred to the district courts.

2.1. INTRODUCTORY CLAIM FORM AND THE NEW FAMILY PROCESS

The 2021 reform also affects the introductory claim form. Overcoming the current dichotomy between writ and petition,[15] it provides for a single claim form to be used before the Court for Individuals, Youth and Families. Moreover, Law No. 206/2021 requires the parties' introductory documents to be as complete and exhaustive as possible (also with regard to the evidence produced or the probative inquiry requested), in order to allow the judge to have an immediate view of the overall situation, to ensure the most appropriate provisional and urgent decisions.

At the same time, however, the new Italian law expressly requires clarity and conciseness, both from the parties and from the judge.[16] The timetable of family trials is also changing, due to new interim deadlines (to amend claims, and request court investigations), the structural use of online hearings (resulting

13 The forum discussion often leads to the shift of the judicial focus on technical issues (i.e. content, or territorial jurisdiction), to the detriment of the examination on the merits.

14 In addition to specific expertise in family matters, family judges will be assigned exclusively to family courts, with the abolition of the ten-year limit on assignment in their function. This will create a separation of careers in the judiciary, enhancing sectoral specialisation.

15 One to be used for the civil court (*atto di citazione*) and the other for the juvenile court (*ricorso*).

16 As will be better explained in the forthcoming decree of the Minister of Justice, after hearing the opinion of the Superior Council of the Magistracy and the National Forensic Council.

from the COVID-19 pandemic),[17] and the replacement of the final hearing with written handlings. In addition to all of this, each family judge will be required to schedule all proceedings from the first hearing, for greater organisation and speed in the system as a whole.

2.2. COURT OF APPEALS AND COURT OF CASSATION

The reform also affects the appellate level, introducing the reasonable likelihood of success as a basic requirement for an appeal; in addition, in the event of manifestly unfounded appeals, a fine of €250–10,000 may be issued, with a clear deterrent intent.

The filter section of the Supreme Court of Cassation, which currently decides on the admissibility of the petitions lodged, will also be abolished, and each family judge will have the power to make a preliminary referral to the Supreme Court for new, recurring, relevant and serious hermeneutical questions of law. This transformation is aimed at facilitating the rapid adaptation of jurisprudence to changes in society, anticipating the nomophylactic intervention of the Court of Cassation[18] when an interpretative question of law arises, without having to wait to finally receive the judgment of the court of third instance.

2.3. TOOLS FOR DEFLECTING LITIGATION

The 2021 reform has also introduced new tax incentives and legal aid to further boost the use of mediation and assisted negotiation in family disputes[19]

---

17 See R. Susskind and D. Susskind, *The Future of the Professions: How Technology Will Transform the Work of Human Experts*, Oxford University Press, 2015, p. 70 (discussing how COVID-19's only positive contribution was to overcome any discussion of the appropriateness of online legal services and remote hearings).

18 Nomophylactic function refers to the task of ensuring the exact observance and uniform interpretation of the law. This task is assigned to the Court of Cassation by virtue of Art. 65 of the Law on the Italian Judiciary, and is divided into two specific activities: on the one hand, to ensure the implementation of the law in the concrete case, and on the other hand, to provide uniform interpretive guidelines in order to maintain, as far as possible, the unity of the legal system, through a substantial standardisation of jurisprudence to ensure legal certainty. In order to avoid continuous interpretative drifts, with Legislative Decree No. 40/2006, particular relevance was attributed to the pronouncements of the United Sections of the Supreme Court, with express prohibition for the simple sections to deviate from them, except by reasonably referring the problematic issue to a new pronouncement of the United Sections.

19 A. Busani et al., *Procedura civile e ADR*, IPSOA, 2021, pp. 923–926, 1017–1026 (for an in-depth analysis of the relationship between rights protection and the cost of justice, see S. Holmes and C.R. Sunstein, *The Cost of Rights: Why Liberty Depends on Taxes*, W.W. Norton, 2000).

(also authorising the judicial production of evidence gathered during ADR, overcoming the past secrecy of the same).

This measure aims at reducing the workload of judges, through the use of extrajudicial rather than judicial procedures, with a prospective decrease in the number of disputes discussed in court and consequently in the average duration of judicial proceedings.

3. ASSESSMENT OF THE REFORM

As mentioned, Law No. 206 of 26 November 2021 must be implemented with the necessary decree laws, which will make it possible to verify whether the measures that have so far only been sketched out will have a positive impact on family justice.

The new legislation has some glaring anomalies, partly attributable to its genesis. First, it should be noted that the reform was promoted by an enlarged parliamentary committee, with the support of external consultants, mostly from the Milan Bar Association. There is no doubt that the malfunctioning and incomplete formulation of the reform, which introduces legal tools drawn from foreign systems, omitting, however, the prior hermeneutic and comparative study that is indispensable for their adaptation to a different legal context,[20] is due to the incomplete expertise of the parliamentary committee, mostly restricted to practitioners of domestic law, lacking in international and comparative skills and knowledge.[21]

---

20 B. Pozzo, 'Multilingualism, Legal Terminology and Problems of Harmonizing European Private Law' in B. Pozzo and V. Jacometti (eds.), *Multilingualism and the Harmonization of European Law*, Kluwer Law International, 2006; see also A. Watson, *Legal Transplants: An Approach to Comparative Law*, Georgia University Press, 1993; and P.G. Monateri, 'The Weak Law: Contaminations and Legal Cultures' (2003) 13 *Transnational Law and Contemporary Problems* 591; L. Antoniolli, 'Of law and numbers: the challenges of quantification for transnational law and European private law' (2019) III(2) *Católica Law Review* 31 (arguing that globalisation has increased the proliferation of 'transnational legal spaces', in which legal pluralism of sources permeates both legal norms and their practical application, fostering the creation of 'legal hybrids, composite legal materials produced by a dynamic process of interaction').

21 See E. Calzolaio, 'The (Mis)use of Overruling in the Italian Case Law: Comparative Remarks' (2018) 5 *The Law Quarterly Review* 1 (noting that reasons for comparative law to be used as a tool for the study, investigation and preparation of any legal reform, are summarised in the definition that 'comparative law itself is "strange", in the sense that, unlike other fields of legal studies, it is not a body of rules, but a way of legal learning'); and A. Somma, *L'Uso Giurisprudenziale della Comparazione nel Diritto Interno e Comunitario*, Giuffrè, 2001, p. 259 (arguing that the Italian inattention to legal comparisons is examined and criticised in an interesting volume, which also tries to suggest a balanced use of comparative law in the field of 'personal and family law, often affected by developments that make it indispensable to search for models from which to obtain new solutions').

Extrapolating a legal instrument from the foreign context of reference in which it was born, developed and perfected over time, in order to impose it authoritatively and without any adjustment in a different legal system, inevitably leads to erroneous outcomes.[22] To copy virtuous examples from abroad without any understanding of their origins and foundations is an approach destined to produce dysfunctional results, as demonstrated by some of the innovations introduced by the Italian reform in Law No. 206/2021, which appear ill-conceived even from their initial profiling (see below on the reform's call for court decisions' conciseness in relation to legal certainty).

3.1. CLARITY AND CONCISENESS REQUIREMENTS

Common law systems have always pursued clarity in legal drafting to facilitate the search for binding precedents among a myriad of similar cases. The advent of digital legal databases[23] has simplified and expedited legal research, as online databases can quickly review and skim thousands of previous decisions. But this in no way eliminates the need for maximum clarity and accuracy of legal texts, which is essential for the proper functioning of artificial intelligence legal services.

Indeed, common law doctrine has long debated how to combine clarity and precision in practice: see the *Journal of Technical Writing and Communication* (JTWC), published for over 40 years, the *Guidelines for Drafting and Editing Court Rules*, the *Dictionary of Modern Legal Usage*, etc.[24] Thus, lexical simplification in common law systems has not been implemented *sic et simpliciter*, but was rather researched, reasoned and implemented gradually and uniformly.

On the contrary, the recent Italian reform authoritatively and immediately imposes a change that is indeed necessary, but which should have been adequately prepared over time.

Law No. 206/2021's call for clarity and conciseness in the parties' briefs and court decisions in family matters is correct. However, in order to respect the rule of law, avoiding excessive formalities that would impede free access to justice,

---

22 An imported law should be developed so as to match demand, as correctly pointed out by D. Berkowitz, K. Pistor and J.F. Richard, 'The Transplant Effect' (2003) 51 *The American Journal of Comparative Law* 163. On legal transplants and legal globalisation, see also M. Bussani, 'Deglobalizing Rule of Law and Democracy: Hunting Down Rhetoric Through Comparative Law' (2019) 67 *The American Journal of Comparative Law* 701.

23 Such as HeinOnline, Westlaw, LexisNexis, DeJure, et al., collecting case law and court reports.

24 B. Garner, *Guidelines for Drafting and Editing Court Rules*, Administrative Office of the United States Courts, 1996; B. Garner, *Dictionary of Modern Legal Usage*, 2nd ed., Oxford University Press, 1995; J. Kimble, 'Guiding Principles for Restyling the Federal Rules of Civil Procedure', (2005) 84 (Sept/Oct) *Michigan Bar Journal*. See also *The Clarity Journal*, published by the International Association Promoting Plain Legal Language, Michigan, on the back of the pressing and widespread demand for simplification of the legal vocabulary.

an explicit reference to Article 6(1) ECHR would have been necessary. In fact, the limitations imposed by the reform must not be disproportionate to the proper administration of justice (as the ECHR requires), so as not to undermine legal certainty.[25]

It is indisputable that Italy often produces an excessive and overabundant number of detailed rules, which slow down the functioning of its bureaucratic judicial apparatus.[26] It is therefore necessary that the decree laws to be adopted after the 2021 reform be clear and precise in defining the need for clarity and conciseness in family proceedings, without imposing disproportionate or unnecessary constraints. In this regard, it would be preferable to opt for requirements of 'clarity and precision' with reference to family legal writing, rather than aligning with the 'clarity and conciseness' required by Law No. 206/2021, which is not always manageable in practice.

3.2. THE NOMOPHYLACTIC FUNCTION OF THE COURT OF CASSATION

The Italian reform of 2021, in addition to making all decisions of the family courts appealable, introduces the possibility for any family judge to file a preliminary appeal to the Court of Cassation to request its timely intervention as part of its nomophylactic function.[27]

This is likely to have a significant impact on the development of Italian family law, allowing for a more rapid and timely adaptation to the needs dictated by the constant changes in contemporary society. However, it is necessary to better specify when, in practice, the family judge may stay the decision and order a referral to the Supreme Court, since the criteria of 'relevance in law' and 'recurrence in practice' set by Law No. 206/2021 are excessively vague and general.

The comparative-historical examination of law shows that the lack of precise rules increases the litigiousness of the parties, with consequent lengthening of the time to reach a final judgment.[28] Thus, the omission of specific criteria for

---

25 See T.E. Frosini et al., 'The Rule of Law: A Fundamental Safeguard or an Instrument of Plunder' (2011) 3(1) *Italian Journal of Public Law* 170 (analysing the intrinsic relationship between rule of law, supremacy of law, and limits on the exercise of discretionary powers).

26 *Absit iniuria verbis*, at least for the fact that the author is Italian. On the current over-production of norms affecting contemporary societies and compromising the efficiency of the related legal systems, V. Zeno Zencovich, 'A normative metastasis' (2020) 7 *European Journal of Comparative Law and Governance* 43.

27 See above n. 18.

28 M. Feteris, 'Roadmap on Comparative Law in the Case-Law and Practice of the Supreme Courts of the EU' (2021) 17(1) *Utrecht Law Review* 6; M. Bobek, *Comparative reasoning in European supreme courts*, Oxford University Press, 2013; M. Andenas and D. Fairgrieve, *Courts and Comparative Law*, Oxford University Press, 2015.

preliminary referral to the Supreme Court in family law matters could cripple the Court itself, committing it to examining the admissibility of petitions rather than sifting through the underlying legal issues, all to the detriment of the nomophylactic interpretation and development of family law.

A similar issue has already been addressed and resolved for some time in the United States, where the Supreme Court receives approximately 7,000 requests for certiorari per year. To avoid a stalemate in the court, it is common for law clerks (who work as assistants to the justices) to screen grantable writs, thus making the justices' tasks easier and allowing them to focus on the cases to be decided.

Italian law clerks, on the other hand, have completely different functions and competences from their American counterparts, since they do not necessarily hold a law degree and deal exclusively with the bureaucratic and administrative management of litigation: case numbering, paper or digital filing, transcription and recording of hearings, etc. This comparison suggests that the apparatus that surrounds the Italian cassation judges needs to be adjusted. The addition of technically competent officials who can examine and screen the appeals received by the court will allow the judges to concentrate exclusively on their decision-making tasks, to the benefit of the overall speed and justice of the system.

3.3. ALTERNATIVE DISPUTE RESOLUTION

The common law origins of alternative dispute resolution techniques are well known and need no further explanation.[29] However, it is necessary to dwell briefly on the requirements for professional mediators and negotiators.

In Italy, since 2010, mediators or negotiators have been required to attend training courses (with an average duration of 42–54 hours in total, reduced to only 15 hours for lawyers), without any final examination. This is a fairly ridiculous requirement, especially as opposed to the much more comprehensive training required in the United States. Furthermore, in Italy family mediators are not part of any regulated profession; there is no register or professional order nor any minimum legal requirement for them. In the vast majority of cases, lawyers, psychologists and social workers also practise as mediators.

In contrast, in the United States, some states impose complex educational requirements for mediators, including extensive training in law, psychology,

---

29 A. Miranda, 'The Origins of Mediation and the A.D.R. tools' in A. Miranda (ed.), *Searching for mediation's common standards at the cross road of different legal culture*, Aracne, 2014, pp. 9–26. See also P. Rescigno, 'Interessi e conflitti nella famiglia: l'istituto della mediazione familiare' (1995) IV *Giurisprudenza Italiana* 73; C. Irti, 'Gestione condivisa della crisi familiare: dalla mediazione familiare alla negoziazione assistita' (2016) XLV *Diritto di Famiglia e delle Persone* 665.

and economics, lasting one to two years, and most states have mandatory requirements to be certified and listed on the official registry of court-appointed mediators. There are also numerous Bachelor's and Master's degree programmes that train well-rounded competent mediators, professionals who can work constructively with parties to resolve their conflicts outside of court. The enormous disparity in the specialised training of Italian mediators compared to American ones is confirmed by the negative Italian outcome of ADR procedures: successful conciliations do not even reach an average of 15 per cent of total cases.[30]

Italian ADR procedures,[31] entrusted to professionals with only a few hours of training (clearly insufficient to acquire complex skills and knowledge), are intended to be a useful tool to solve the serious overload problem of the courts of justice, but may turn instead into an expedient process that is rather poor in practice, due to the lack of educational foundation to allow them to function properly.

3.4. ROLE OF THE EXPERT WITNESS

The expert witness is appointed by the family judge to evaluate the family as a whole in order to assess potential problems, personality disorders, relationship deficiencies, and the conditions and needs of the children.[32] However, it is common practice in Italy for experts to overstep their official duties, making detailed and clear recommendations to the judge regarding child custody and placement, visitation schedules, and so forth. In doing so, the judicial role is partly entrusted to an independent and autonomous third party, who does not follow the rules and checks of the judicial system. Thus, expert opinions frequently undergo changes in scope and objective: starting from evaluative and cognitive purposes, they often turn into a tentative resolution between the parties, by the sole decision of the expert, and even go so far as to establish binding rules that the family must follow in the future. Such excesses in the expert's functions stem from the lack of sufficient personnel in the family judiciary, as well as from the long delay in updating civil procedure. These two negative factors

---

30 Data released by the Italian Ministry of Justice, as well as by Camera di Mediazione Nazionale, Camera Arbitrale di Milano, et al.

31 V. Varano and N. Andrews, *L'altra giustizia: i metodi alternativi di soluzione delle controversie nel diritto comparato*, Giuffrè, 2007.

32 See A.G. Danovi, 'L'avvocato, la consulenza e la valutazione psicologica. I mutamenti intervenuti nella legislazione del diritto di famiglia: maggiore necessità di un protocollo' in G. Gulotta et al. (eds.), *La Scienza Psicosociale nell'affidamento dei Figli*, Giuffrè, 2016, pp. 51–71 (detailing the role of the expert witness in Italian family litigation); T. Magro and M. Lutzu, 'Le relazioni familiari nella separazione e nel divorzio: alcuni strumenti per la valutazione psicoforense' in *La Scienza Psicosociale nell'affidamento dei Figli*, ibid, pp. 115–129; A. Scolaro, *La consulenza tecnica nel conflitto genitoriale*, Giappichelli, 2014.

have unfortunately persisted for decades in the Italian legal system, leaving the judiciary no choice but to give space to its auxiliaries (i.e. expert witness, social worker, counsellor, etc.), making them de facto participants in the final judicial decision.

The 2021 reform addressed this problem, but instead of diminishing the duties of expert witnesses, and restoring their original function (of pure evaluation of the case), it legitimised the transformative nature of their opinions with a clear overreach of constitutional limits. Suffice it to say that Article 23, paragraph (ee) of Law No. 206/2021 expressly provides for the right for the judge 'to appoint a professional chosen from among those registered in the list of professional expert witnesses, or even outside the list if requested by both parties', with the task of intervening in the family unit 'to overcome conflicts between the parties, to provide help to minors and for the recovery or improvement of relationships between parents and children.' Therefore, instead of forcing experts to abdicate the decision-making role that should not be theirs, due to an absence of the necessary legal training, the reform makes the problem of their excessive power structural, despite the formal complaints that have long been raised.

The Italian reform would certainly have been more effective if, instead of looking at (and confirming) old domestic practices, the legislature had broadened its horizons to assess the adoptability of foreign solutions. In the Netherlands, for example, the role and importance of expert witnesses has been strengthened, but without transferring any decision-making power to them. 'No Kids in the Middle' is a Dutch pilot project that involves expert witnesses in their specific field of expertise:[33] through a multi-family intervention, which does not aim at reconciliation of the original family unit, but rather at helping the parties to identify the behavioural, emotional and cognitive factors that cause their conflict, the experts promote strategies of de-escalation of the conflict.[34] The sphere of action of the experts is thus widened, but exclusively within the limits of their professional role and their technical competences. It is not at all like the questionable solution adopted by Italy, with a partial transfer of judicial power from judges to expert witnesses, of dubious constitutional legitimacy.

---

33 J. Van Lawick, 'Vechtscheidende ouders en hun kinderen' (2012) 24(3) *Systeemtherapie* 129; M. Visser and J. van Lawick, *Group Therapy for High-Conflict Divorce: The 'No Kids in the Middle' Intervention Programme*, Taylor & Francis, 2021 (as part of the so-called 'Family Ties Project', the National Centre for Children and Families in the UK has also promoted therapy based on the multifamily group approach, thus following van Lawick and Visser's pilot project that was first started in the Netherlands and Belgium).

34 Approximately six to eight families are initiated into group work, within three dialogically safe, separate and parallel therapeutic spaces: one for the parents, one for the children, and one for the network of involved people around them. In each group there is a facilitating therapist, whose task is not to judge the individual participants, but on the contrary to help the group as a whole to develop pro-child parental collaboration on the one hand, and a harmonious recovery of quality of life on the other, regardless of the ascertainment of blame. The overall work aims to foster dialogue, spontaneity and the creativity of each participant.

4. GENERICNESS OF THE REFORM

The recent reform sometimes dwells in detail on specific interventions, while at other times it uses a general and superficial approach. Suffice it to mention Article 23 of Law No. 206/2021, which, although in paragraph (a) generically referring to new provisions to be adopted at a later date to introduce the Unified Court for Individuals, Youth and Families, in paragraphs (b) and (c) instead minutely details the new powers and obligations of family judges.[35] And so on throughout the legislative text, alternating between generic provisions and the detailed definition of new institutions or procedures, with disconcerting inconsistency, partly due to the formulation of the reform.

In fact, the legislator has combined speed and precision with an arduous balancing act between the needs expressed by family lawyers, forensic psychologists, associations protecting victims of domestic violence and politicians. Thus, by combining different demands and priorities, an uneven and non-linear text has emerged, certainly in need of corrections and subsequent additions.

5. COMPARATIVE LAW AND NEW TECHNOLOGIES

The establishment of a unified court to handle separations, divorces, child custody and all family matters is undoubtedly a positive addition to Italian family law, which will eliminate fragmentation of jurisdiction, duplication of judgments and contrary decisions. However, the 2021 reform does not fully address the needs of the thousands of families who turn to the family courts each year,[36] appearing rather as a trivial time-saving gimmick, ill suited to the post-pandemic families of the twenty-first century.

The simultaneous filing of separation and divorce proceedings or judgments on parental custody and loss of parental responsibility before different courts should be avoided. A single point of collection and review for all family matters should be created that is highly specialised and competent to render its own decisions, with the elimination of unnecessary and misleading duplication.

If this is achieved in practice, the number of cases will decrease and the average time for a first instance decision will be considerably reduced (statistics even hint at a possible 40 per cent reduction in the average duration of family

---

35 E.g. the obligation for the magistrate to hear directly the child who refuses to meet a parent, with a prohibition on delegating this task to third parties or expert witnesses.

36 ISTAT, above n. 3. See P. Cendon and T. Puntillo, *Separazione e Divorzio*, Giuffrè, 2015; M. Dogliotti and A. Figone, *Separazione e Divorzio: I Presupposti. Profili nazionali, internazionali, comunitari*, Giuffrè, 2012; F. Danovi and P. Schlesinger, *Il processo di separazione e divorzio*, Giuffrè, 2015.

litigation). But in addition to all this, in the promulgation of decree laws, a different approach is required, one that is comparative and interdisciplinary, capable of drawing on foreign experience to point the way forward. Only by opening up to the technologically advanced legal tools already in use abroad will it be possible to achieve a reform of family law that is not merely cosmetic, but structural, effective and possibly lasting.

5.1. A MISSED OPPORTUNITY FOR ARTIFICIAL INTELLIGENCE IN THE CONTEXT OF ITALIAN FAMILY LAW

Artificial intelligence systems offer incredible advantages even in the legal field.[37] WestLaw, LexisNexis, HeinOnline and the Italian DeJure, are not simple databases for routine legal searches, but rather complex tools that can refine their search methods over time in order to provide the user with the most appropriate and specific result possible. Machine learning techniques allow search platforms to generate statistical codes that return the correct result according to a recognised pattern based on previous examples.[38] Therefore, the accuracy of the final result depends on the quality and quantity of data made available to the system.

The more coherent and well-assembled the body of underlying data is, the more accurate the information artificial intelligence systems can provide. The key, then, to the effective use of artificial intelligence lies not just in a set of algorithms, but rather in the dataset, i.e. the collection of data made available to the software. In other words, artificial intelligence is all the more effective the more repetition or recurrence there is in the source data.

It is therefore necessary to ask whether the field of family law is suitable for the introduction of artificial intelligence tools, which will interact with judges to increase the speed and accuracy of the system.[39] Are there areas of family law

---

37 M. Taruffo, 'Judicial Decisions and Artificial Intelligence' (1998) 6 *Artificial Intelligence and Law*, 311. See also A. Santosuosso, 'A general theory of law and technology or a general reconsideration of law?' in E. Palmerini and E. Stradella (eds.) *Law and Technology: The Challenge of Regulating Technological Development*, RoboLaw Series Vol. 1, Pisa University Press, 2013, pp. 145–166 (examining the possibilities of mutual exchange between new technologies and legal disciplines, with an analysis that is at the forefront of the research on the topic). See also E. Francesconi, 'Intelligenza Artificiale e Diritto: tra scienza e fantascienza' in S. Dorigo (ed.), *Il ragionamento giuridico nell'era dell'intelligenza artificiale*, Pacini Giuridica, 2020, pp. 1–11 (giving an overview of historical developments in the legal approach to the use of artificial intelligence).

38 See U. Ruffolo, 'La responsabilità da artificial intelligence, algoritmo e smart product: per i fondamenti di un diritto dell'intelligenza artificiale self-learning' in U. Ruffolo (ed.), *Intelligenza artificiale. Il diritto, i diritti, l'etica*, Giuffrè, 2020, p. 94 (discussing machine learning, deep learning and neural nets).

39 E. Francesconi, 'The winter, the summer and the summer dream of artificial intelligence in law' (2022) 1 *Artificial Intelligence and Law* 30, 147–161 (offering interesting insights into

characterised by repetitiveness and recurrence, or that can be decided in purely numerical terms? Experience leads us to answer this question positively, subject to the considerations and reflections in the following section.

5.2. PREDICTIVE ARTIFICIAL INTELLIGENCE AND ANALYTIC ARTIFICIAL INTELLIGENCE

In common law systems, predictive artificial intelligence and analytical artificial intelligence systems have long been used to identify the likely outcome of litigation.[40] Using machine learning techniques, these systems process large amounts of data to understand and identify recurring patterns, and extract relevant features from prior decisions. As more data is processed (i.e. more cases are examined), there is a proportional increase in the accuracy of the results. In addition, if artificial intelligence systems work in arrays sharing data from multiple systems operating separately and simultaneously, the increase in the accuracy of the result is exponential.[41]

Translated into legal terms, this means that a legal artificial intelligence tool is able to advise its user whether it is advantageous for him to litigate in court or settle, or within what limits to negotiate, in light of the statistical probability of victory that emerges from comparison with previous cases.[42] Predictive analytics

---

the opportunities offered by the development of intelligent systems in the legal sector, using a technical engineering approach); See also E. Gabellini, 'La "comodità nel giudicare": la decisione robotica' (2019) *Rivista Trimestrale di Diritto e Procedura Civile* 1305. AI has extended to family law, as critically investigated by F. Bell, 'Family Law, Access to Justice and Automation' (2019) 19 *Macquarie Law Journal* 103. Of a different opinion on the use of AI in family law, see N. Semple, 'A Third Revolution in Family Dispute Resolution: Accessible Legal Professionalism' (2017) 34(1) *Windsor Yearbook of Access to Justice* 130.

40 L. Vagni, 'The Role of Human Judge in Judicial Decisions. Preliminary Remarks on Legal Interpretation in the Age of Artificial Intelligence' in E. Calzolaio (ed.), *La decisione nel prisma dell'intelligenza artificiale*, Cedam, 2020, pp. 185–202. See also D. Walton, 'Similarity, precedent and argument from analogy' (2010) 18(3) *Artificial Intelligence and Law* 217 (providing an interesting guide on the logical structure and application of analogy in case law, and on the classification and operation of the rule of precedent for the specific use of engineers programming legal software).

41 In essence, human cognitive processes can be technologically replicated in a very short time, to the point of reproducing the activities performed over decades by hundreds of individuals in a matter of minutes, thus allowing software to accumulate immeasurable amounts of experience. See D. Katz, M. Bommarito II and J. Blackman, 'A General Approach for Predicting the Behavior of the Supreme Court of the United States' (2016) 12 *PLOS ONE* 10 (building on developments in machine learning and prior work in the science of judicial prediction, the authors designed a model to predict the behaviour of the Supreme Court of the United States, achieving over 70% accuracy in outcome as compared to real decisions).

42 On predictive analytics, see V. Zambrano, 'Algoritmi e giustizia predittiva: tra esigenze di certezza e responsabilità' in G. Comandè and M. Graziadei et al. (eds.), *Annuario di Diritto Comparato e di Studi Legislativi*, Edizioni Scientifiche Italiane, 2020, pp. 611–646. See also on predicting legal outcomes, K.D. Ashley, *Artificial Intelligence and Legal Analytics: New Tools for Law Practice in the Digital Age*, Cambridge University Press, 2017, pp. 107–125.

AI software can even be more refined, estimating the win rate based on a specific opponent, opposing counsel or judge, and may even be able to recommend defensive or argumentative strategies to increase success in the case.

Ultimately, algorithms can help refine defensive strategies, reducing the time needed to study each case and identify binding precedents on similar issues, to the advantage of the lawyer and the judge.[43] There are also online forms and chat bots that use algorithms to divide real estate and financial assets between ex-spouses in light of the time spent together, each spouse's contribution to joint income and expenses, etc., or software that calculates alimony and custody contributions based on parental financial resources and equalisation criteria, or legal tools to draft deeds and decisions when the specifics of the case are typed in.

As a result of the ongoing financial crisis, further exacerbated by the COVID-19 pandemic, online legal services (cheaper and faster than a real lawyer) have become increasingly popular in the US, Australia and the UK, turning into fearsome competitors for small claims, family law disputes, leases and drafting wills.[44] In fact, in these areas, predictive artificial intelligence tools can be used on multiple fronts:

- by the client, to decide whether or not to be assisted by a lawyer, in light of the real chances of success identified by the system; or to define the goals to be pursued, in so far as they are achievable according to artificial intelligence;
- from the lawyer, to streamline legal strategies and write legal documents; or
- by the magistrate, to quickly frame the case and discover binding precedents.

Technological advances make it possible to design and create software that learns as it works: the predetermined data package required to start a specific artificial intelligence tool grows exponentially as the tool works, storing more and more new information.

---

43 On the opportunities and risks provided by the use of AI in the legal field, see A. De Franceschi and R. Schulze, 'Digital Revolution – New Challenges for Law: Introduction' in A. Franceschi, R. Schulze, M. Graziadei, O. Pollicino, F. Riente, S. Sica and P. Sirena (eds.), *Digital Revolution – New Challenges for Law*, C.H. Beck, 2019, p. 10.

44 In addition, online dispute resolution (ODR) systems have also developed, targeting disputes arising from e-commerce transactions (e.g. eBay and PayPal). Companies using ODR usually do not have an exceptionally large number of disputes, but they want to maximise the number of successful transactions by providing quick resolutions, to enhance their professional reputation. See also S. Casabona, 'Intermediazione digitale e composizione delle controversie: dall'alternative dispute resolution all'alien dispute resolution' (2017) 32(3) *Il diritto dell'informazione e dell'informatica* 497; L. Mingardo, 'Online Dispute Resolution' in P. Moro and C. Sarra (eds.), *Tecnodiritto*, Franco Angeli, 2017, p. 121; G.N. Giudice, 'Mediazione Online' in I.S.I. Pisano, G. Buccarella and F. Fimmano (eds.), *Giustizia Digitale. Processi Telematici e Udienza Da Remoto*, Giuffrè, 2021, pp. 280–281.

The only limitation of artificial intelligence seems to be the human factor, due to the widespread reluctance to use such systems in some professional contexts. Proof of this is the Italian family law reform of 2021. Historically, the Italian lawyer helps his or her client to solve a legal issue after the problem has already arisen, mostly intervening in the pathological phase of the relationship[45] (whether personal, professional or business). The fiduciary bond between the client and his lawyer is therefore very strong and strictly personal: thus, it can hardly be replaced by chat bots or similar digital software.[46]

However, the fact that the 2021 reform did not even integrate artificial intelligence into the judicial system is completely incomprehensible. The judiciary could have benefited greatly from the use of artificial intelligence, in terms of optimising resources, reducing the duration of proceedings, and ensuring the circularity of jurisprudence between the first and second instance and uniformity of judgment throughout the country.

Without doubting the specificity and uniqueness of each family, child and case, it is certain that among all family matters there are recurring themes and topics: allowances to ex-spouses and children, visitation schedules, extra expenses, school authorisations, authorisations for study trips and summer camps, sports activities, etc. Currently, each individual matter must be decided by the assigned judge after reviewing records, documents and evidence.

It would be sufficient to delegate to a software program at least the initial examination of the file (i.e. the verification of the complete and correct production of the documents) and the managing of the timetable (setting and postponement of judicial hearings, notifications to the parties and auxiliaries, and similar merely managerial tasks), in order to relieve the magistrates of an ordinary but considerable workload, without risk to the rule of law and legal certainty.[47]

---

45 E.g. prenuptial agreements are forbidden in Italy. See G. Giaimo, 'Riflessioni sparse, in chiave comparatistica, sugli accordi prematrimoniali' (2021) 1 *Diritto di Famiglia e delle Persone* 261.

46 A clear example of the typical reluctance of Italian lawyers to make use of artificial intelligence systems in their professional field is offered by a curious and interesting article between law, computer science and music, in which the author interviews the famous Italian singer-songwriter Paolo Conte: G. Resta, 'Dialogo su Diritto e Musica' (2021) 6 *Diritto dell'Informazione e Dell'Informatica* 930. Distrust of AI legal tools extends far beyond Italian borders: S. Chesterman, 'Through a Glass, Darkly: Artificial Intelligence and the Problem of Opacity' (2021) 69(2) *The American Journal of Comparative Law* 271. On generational hesitation in welcoming ODR in family disputes, see C. Rule, 'Online Dispute Resolution: Technology is disrupting the law – and this disruption may generate significant opportunities for those attorneys willing to embrace change and evolve their practices' (2019) Fall. *Family Lawyer Magazine* 6.

47 See D. Ward, 'Lo studio sicuro nell'era del legal tech' in G. Ziccardi (ed.), *Lo Studio Legale Sicuro*, Giuffrè, 2021, pp. 263–264 (legal tech does not mean integral replacement of lawyers or judges in favour of computerised and automated processes, but rather reorganising the tasks of these professionals, to let them focus on items of greater economic and intellectual

This is not to mention the possibility of entrusting artificial intelligence software with decisions on the merits.[48] As foreign experiences show (see the US, Australia, the UK, etc.), it is possible to develop sophisticated software that is capable of correctly dividing assets between ex-spouses or calculating the appropriate amount of alimony due,[49] or of assisting with co-parenting on a daily basis, through applications (e.g. OurFamilyWizard) that allow parents to exchange information, requests and payment receipts, upload timetables and calendars of their children's school and extracurricular activities, etc. – all under the supervision of the court, and without the possibility of deleting any data that would become usable as documentary evidence in the event of litigation.

For a complete analysis of the topic, it must be specified that two possible dangers are inherent in the use of AI systems instead of a physical judge:

- AI systems can commit gender and/or racial discrimination;[50] and
- AI systems can drift towards formal justice, without adapting to the fairness of the actual case.[51]

Regarding the danger of discrimination, an easy practical example can be offered: given that in most cases it is the father who has to pay child support, an AI tool could infer that fathers are always obligated to pay child support, regardless of placement decisions and financial resources. This is because, based on statistical processing, the system incorporates a cognitive bias (fathers usually pay child support, so in AI reasoning they are always obliged to do so, regardless of the

value); see also T.E. Frosini, *Apocalittici o integrati*, STEM Mucchi Editore, 2021 (on the contribution of modern digital technologies to the development of civil liberty).

48 Very interesting is the distinction between supportive technology, replacement technology and disruptive technology for the legal sector, examined in E. Calzolaio, 'Intelligenza Artificiale ed Autonomia della Decisione: Problemi e Sfide' in E. Calzolaio (ed.), *La decisione nel prisma dell'intelligenza artificiale*, Cedam, 2020, pp. 3–4.

49 E. Al Mureden and R. Rovatti, *Gli assegni di mantenimento tra disciplina legale e intelligenza artificiale*, Giappichelli, 2020 (using an interdisciplinary approach, the authors highlight the usefulness of computational methods based on artificial intelligence as tools for the use of family law).

50 On AI's 'disparate treatment', G. Sartor and F. Lagioia, 'Le decisioni algoritmiche tra etica e diritto' in U. Ruffolo (ed.), *Intelligenza artificiale. Il diritto, i diritti, l'etica*, Giuffrè, 2020, p. 77. On possible algorithm bias, see G. Smorto and M.C. Cavallaro, 'Decisione pubblica e responsabilità dell'amministrazione nella società dell'algoritmo' (2019) 16 *Federalismi.it* 1; D.L. Chen, 'Machine Learning and the Rule of Law' (2019) *Revista Forumul Judecatorilor* 19; J. Dressel and H. Farid, 'The Accuracy, Fairness, and Limits of Predicting Recidivism' (2018) 4 *Science Advances* 1.

51 See D.K. Citron, 'Technological Due Process' (2008) 85 *Washington University Law Review* 1249 (discussing the difference between rules and standards, and their different goals (in that 'rules establish basic instructions for behavior and facilitate predictability', while 'standards permit decision makers to tailor an outcome to the facts, increasing the likelihood of an "ideal" ruling' and suggesting how to navigate between automation and discretion to avoid succumbing to efficiency).

placement of offspring and parental income) that, if identified and corrected, becomes unrepeatable (in other words, once a cognitive bias is detected and corrected by the software designer, it is avoided for good).

Regarding the other danger (a shift towards formal justice to the detriment of fairness), artificial intelligence tends to prefer a numerical standard of justice over the equity of a particular actual case.

For financial calculations, such as child or spousal support, many jurisdictions provide for judicially or legislatively adopted formulas that incorporate equations that take objective factors such as the parents' respective incomes and custodial time into account. These formulas are mechanistic, but transparent in their calculations, thus it is always possible to check them and any departure from the prescribed outcomes must be justified in writing by the judge.

On the other hand, we have decisions on the placement of the offspring, visitation rights and parental responsibility. AI systems that incorporate machine learning prescribe outcomes based on previous patterns. For example, an AI program may see from past cases that mothers are more likely to receive the majority of custodial time and are less likely to have demanding jobs. The program may therefore conclude that fathers have less flexibility in picking up children from school, and therefore award fathers more custodial time during the weekends and mothers more time during the week. The program uses assumptions that produce biased outcomes in circumstances where the biases may not always be apparent. This stems not so much from a problem of software opacity (which is nevertheless often objected to), but rather from the composition of the dataset. In other words, the AI reproduces exactly the same errors contained in the decisions with which the software is fed: the discriminatory approaches of previous judgments, even if not manifested in the *obiter dicta*, are nonetheless taken up by the AI system and elevated to a binding rule. Any discrimination or biased outcome committed by the AI must therefore be blamed on those (individual judges) who took the previous decisions. The only way to avoid such bias in the future is to carefully select the dataset, to purify its contents. What is needed, therefore, is the joint effort and collaboration of experts in all the fields involved, from legal to technical engineering, from IT to psychology and sociology, to provide clean and neutral datasets to enhance fairness and equity.

6. CONCLUSIONS

Substituting artificial intelligence for human judges is a very extreme solution, which does not correspond at all with the purpose of this chapter. On the contrary, the goal is to suggest, through a comparative and interdisciplinary analysis, solutions that can relieve magistrates of routine, or merely managerial and bureaucratic, tasks, in order to allow them to focus instead on matters of law, which certainly require their irreplaceable expertise and technical skills.

Without putting families at the mercy of the automated and inscrutable decisions of technological processors, as in Huxley's *Brave New World*, it is desirable to harness the potential of artificial intelligence, so long as it does not undermine the rule of law. Family law proceedings may be the perfect scenario in which to introduce artificial intelligence legal tools in Italy, through software that organises the complete calendar of each family proceeding, updating itself and all parties involved as needed; or software that checks the correctness and completeness of the parties' filings, similar to those in use in M&A due diligence; or software that divides assets between ex-spouses and determines alimony and child support obligations; or a co-parenting tool to facilitate conflict de-escalation.

Artificial intelligence offers tremendous opportunities to streamline family proceedings without jeopardising rights and protections. While the 2021 family law reform has been highly praised for its reorganisation of the courts and unification of family jurisdiction, it now needs to go a step further to embrace modern technology. The hope is that in drafting implementing legislation, the necessary attention will be paid to comparative law and law and technology to achieve a truly effective reform worthy of the current times.

NORWAY

LEGAL CAPACITY IN FAMILY LAW MATTERS

Implementing Article 12 of the CRPD in Norway

Katrine K. Fredwall

Résumé

Cet article évalue la mise en œuvre norvégienne du droit à l'autodétermination – suite à la Convention des Nations Unies relative aux droits des personnes handicapées et à d'autres traités relatifs aux droits de l'homme. Le droit international semble considérer la privation de la capacité juridique comme une atteinte grave au droit au respect de la vie privée et familiale ainsi qu'au droit à l'autodétermination. Ainsi, l'article conclut que la privation doit être remplacée par des mesures de soutien. Néanmoins, la privation peut toujours être un recours légal lorsqu'elle est utilisée en dernier recours et si elle offre un juste équilibre entre la prévention des abus et la garantie des droits, de la volonté et des préférences. Le droit international exige également que l'ingérence soit proportionnée, adaptée aux circonstances du requérant et soumise à l'examen d'instances compétentes, indépendantes et impartiales.

Cet article décrit également comment la Norvège, par le biais de réformes en cours, a tenté de mettre en œuvre le droit à l'autodétermination et comment la capacité juridique est réglementée dans les affaires pertinentes du droit de la famille – telles que le mariage, la cohabitation, le divorce et la parentalité. La nécessité d'un développement et d'une coopération plus poussés avec les personnes handicapées et leurs organisations est soulignée comme la voie à suivre pour assurer un changement de paradigme durable.

1. INTRODUCTION

Disability law is family law. Most of us will lose ability and will need support at some stage in life. Persons with disabilities live in families; they grow up; they may live independently; they buy and sell; they may marry and perhaps divorce; and they will hopefully become elderly in the end. Most people will need different kinds of support during their lives in order to be legal actors exercising legal capacity. This chapter will describe and assess the Norwegian implementation of some core obligations of the United Nations Convention on the Rights of Persons with Disabilities (CRPD).

The CRPD was adopted in 2006[1] and came into force in 2008. The process leading to the adoption of the CRPD was 'long and winding'.[2] Since then, countries all over the world have undergone perhaps their most intensive period of disability law reform.[3] These reforms were accelerated and strengthened by the first General Comment of the CRPD Committee and the work of the

1 The United Nations Convention on the Rights of Persons with Disabilities (CRPD) was adopted on 13 December 2006 in New York, USA.

2 C. De Bhailís and E. Flynn, 'Recognising legal capacity: Commentary and analysis of Article 12 CRPD' (2017) *International Journal of Law in Context* 6, 7–8, describing the process which led to a new Convention.

3 See e.g. X. Li and J. Zuo, 'China. The Adult Guardianship System in the Civil Code Era of China' in M. Brinig, *International Survey of Family Law*, Intersentia, 2021, pp. 135–154. The chapter illustrates that these are questions to be dealt with worldwide.

UN Special Rapporteur on the rights of persons with disabilities.[4] It has been remarkable to observe the work taking place across a range of different states with different legal systems and to follow academic debates over the meaning of the CRPD and discussions around the options for implementation.[5] Seldom has the entire world been more dedicated to looking for solutions to implement a human rights convention.[6] The main challenge has been, and will continue to be, how to implement the CRPD such that it balances rights, secures autonomy and ensures non-discrimination in a form acceptable to both those concerned and the CRPD Committee. As with other international human rights treaties, the CRPD is in many ways a statement of general principles. Seldom does it define key terms or delve into the practicalities of how to achieve the rights set out. Although this approach is, to some extent, necessary for a global human rights convention, it still creates obstacles and confusion for states trying to implement it.[7] Experience has also revealed that the CRPD is partly controversial by nature, which is clearly illustrated by the long list of reservations, declarations and understandings states have made in relation to ratification.[8]

2. AUTONOMY, RIGHTS AND NON-DISCRIMINATION: A CONTRADICTION IN TERMS? SOME EXAMPLES

The CRPD is fast becoming one of our core human rights conventions, with 184 members. It is an exciting move, creating and clarifying rights. The CRPD

---

4 The rapporteurs have visited a number of countries giving specific advice. The mission to Norway took place in autumn 2019, with a final report published in 2020: Report of the Special Rapporteur on the rights of persons with disabilities on her visit to Norway, 14 January 2020, A/HRC/43/41/Add.3.

5 The author had the opportunity to observe the developments and challenges during the period 2000–2021 as a civil servant in the Ministry of Justice; during meetings of the Committee of Experts on Family Law (CJ-FA) by the Council of Europe from 2000 and onwards; as a visitor to the EU High Level Group on Disability; and during meetings with the UN Special Rapporteur on the rights of persons with disabilities and with the CRPD Committee in Geneva 2019. The author has also been involved in numerous meetings with organisations and stakeholders in Norway advocating the need for disability law reform. Since 2021, the author has been participating in FL-EUR, a European academic network which works specifically on the topic of empowerment and protection of vulnerable adults.

6 See a summary of the ongoing work in a number of states and organisations in Council of Europe, *A Study on the Equal Recognition Before the Law. Contribution Towards the Council of Europe Strategy on the Rights of Persons with Disabilities*, Council of Europe Publishing, 2017.

7 C. De Bhailís and E. Flynn, above n. 2, at p. 9.

8 While 184 states and organisations of states (European Union) are parties to the CRPD, as many as 37 members have set out reservations, declarations or understandings (for instance, Australia, Belgium, Canada, France, Ireland, Japan, the Netherlands, Norway, Singapore and Thailand). A central finding is that many states oppose the idea that substitute decision-making should be denied in all circumstances. Most states are of the opinion that such

challenges traditional thinking and urges states to find new ways of securing human rights for all persons in line with others – including those with disabilities. The core obligations outlined in the CRPD are to secure self-determination (autonomy), rights following from national and international law, and non-discrimination. From a more political or societal point of view, most states might find it obvious that states should be obliged to ensure the central human rights like the rights to life, health, housing and freedom from discrimination; nevertheless, when these rights are combined with the right to self-determination, most states have encountered difficulties in finding practical ways of implementing the CRPD. Hardly any state has found solutions that are deemed fully acceptable by the CRPD Committee. The heart of the problem seems to be that it is difficult for the lawmaker to secure legitimate political expectations related to securing the rights mentioned above without reducing the right to self-determination directly or indirectly.

Some examples inspired by Norwegian court cases and administrative cases may illustrate the relevant legal dilemmas.

> Person A is living independently in society but has reduced cognitive abilities. A gets a boyfriend and is very happy about her new situation. Every time she receives her social security money, the boyfriend visits. They go out shopping for expensive gifts for him and generally have a good time. However, for the rest of the month, she is lonely and more or less without money for the bare necessities. Should the State be entitled to interfere or not? She is happy spending time with her boyfriend, but it leaves her extremely poor for the rest of the month. Is the boyfriend's exploitation discrimination based on her disability? If so, does the State have a duty to end this discrimination?

> Person B has only minor reduced cognitive abilities. He wants, as do we all, to live independently and to have an apartment, sufficient food and a social life. B is also addicted to gambling[9] and cannot resist the urge to gamble. B has a support person, his brother D, who tries to persuade him to pay his bills and reduce his gambling habit. Even if this is in line with B's longer-term desires, he often follows his preferences in the moment and spends too much money on gambling. When B does so, he cannot afford to pay his rent and other necessities such as electricity, food, etc. In this situation, autonomy is secured, but B is at risk of losing access to important human rights, such as the right to housing, food, welfare, health, etc. Should the State intervene?

> Person C is elderly and has dementia. He was previously headmaster of a grammar school and is used to being in charge. He receives letters from Nigeria persuading him

decision-making may be necessary in appropriate circumstances and in accordance with the law. For details, see: <https://treaties.un.org/Pages/ViewDetails.aspx?src=TREATY&mtdsg_no=IV-15&chapter=4&clang=_en>, last accessed 28.01.2022.

9 A further question, which is not dealt with here, is whether or not different kinds of addictions should be seen as disabilities.

to send money to a home for abandoned children there. His wife and adult children try to explain that this is fraud and that no abandoned children will receive his money. He does not believe so and sends all his money to 'Nigeria'. He even wants to sell his (and his wife's) home to be able to send even more money. Should the State intervene?

In these three examples, interference by the State or others might reduce the person's autonomy, while non-interference may readily lead to loss of rights or discrimination on the grounds of disability. In a legal context, it will from time to time be necessary to balance autonomy, rights and non-discrimination. The question is how Norway and other states should *balance* these rights in an acceptable manner according to international human rights law.

3. ARTICLE 12 OF THE CRPD AND THE CRPD COMMITTEE'S INTERPRETATION

3.1. THE OBLIGATIONS

The recognition of legal capacity has been a core human rights obligation over time and is based on a number of human rights instruments. In addition to Article 12 of the CRPD, Article 16 of the International Covenant on Civil and Political Rights (ICCPR),[10] Article 15 of the Convention on the Elimination of All Forms of Discrimination against Women (CEDAW)[11] and Article 8 (on 'private life') of the European Convention on Human Rights (ECHR), all have at their core the recognition of legal capacity.[12] Interpretations of these instruments might be relevant in exploring the rights of a person, including the right of autonomy. However, Article 12 of the CRPD remains central. It states:

1. States Parties reaffirm that persons with disabilities have the right to recognition everywhere as persons before the law.
2. States Parties shall recognize that persons with disabilities enjoy legal capacity on an equal basis with others in all aspects of life.

---

10 UN General Assembly, International Covenant on Civil and Political Rights, 16 December 1966, UN Treaty Series, vol. 999, p. 17. Adopted and opened for signature, ratification and accession by General Assembly resolution 2200A (XXI) of 16 December 1966; entry into force 23 March 1976, in accordance with Art. 49.

11 UN General Assembly, Convention on the Elimination of All Forms of Discrimination Against Women (CEDAW), 18 December 1979, UN Treaty Series, vol. 1249, p. 13. CEDAW is often described as an international bill of rights for women.

12 V. Della Fina, R. Cera and G. Palmisano, *The United Nations Convention on the Rights of Persons with Disabilities: A Commentary*, Springer, 2017, p. 273 (hereafter, *CRPD Handbook*).

3. States Parties shall take appropriate measures to provide access by persons with disabilities to the support they may require in exercising their legal capacity.
4. States Parties shall ensure that all measures that relate to the exercise of legal capacity provide for appropriate and effective safeguards to prevent abuse in accordance with international human rights law. Such safeguards shall ensure that measures relating to the exercise of legal capacity respect the rights, will and preferences of the person, are free of conflict of interest and undue influence, are proportional and tailored to the person's circumstances, apply for the shortest time possible and are subject to regular review by a competent, independent and impartial authority or judicial body. The safeguards shall be proportional to the degree to which such measures affect the person's rights and interests.
5. Subject to the provisions of this article, States Parties shall take all appropriate and effective measures to ensure the equal right of persons with disabilities to own or inherit property, to control their own financial affairs and to have equal access to bank loans, mortgages and other forms of financial credit, and shall ensure that persons with disabilities are not arbitrarily deprived of their property.

Article 12(1) reaffirms the right to recognition everywhere as *persons before the law*. Paragraph (2) insists that all persons shall enjoy *legal capacity* on an equal basis with others. Paragraph (3) underlines furthermore the states' obligation to secure access by persons with disabilities to the *support* they may require in exercising their legal capacity. Paragraph (4) underlines the states' duty to secure *effective safeguards* to prevent abuse related to the given support. And in paragraph (5), the states' obligations are described as a duty to 'take all appropriate and effective measures to ensure the equal right of persons with disabilities.'

3.2. THE INTERPRETATION OF THE CRPD GENERAL COMMENT NO. 1

Although the CRPD is a binding instrument of law for the 184 parties to the Convention, in Norway, as in most countries, the CRPD Committee's interpretations are not legally binding. Nevertheless, the Norwegian courts will normally give due weight to comments from a United Nations committee set up under an agreed convention.[13] However, national courts will often consider a number of relevant sources of law, which means that in a given case other sources of law may prevail.

---

13 T.A. Hellerslia, 'Uttalelser fra FN-komiteene – en strukturell analyse', (2018) 53 *Jussens Venner* 71.

In General Comment No. 1 (2014), the Committee provided valuable interpretations and clarifications of Article 12 CRPD.

The CRPD Committee highlighted the fact that legal capacity in line with Article 12(2) includes the capacity to be both a holder of rights and an actor under the law.[14] Being an actor under the law means having the legal agency to act on one's rights and 'to have those actions recognized by the law'.[15] Another crucial statement made by the Committee is that cognitive or psychosocial disability shall not lead to the removal of legal capacity, but to support in the exercise of that legal capacity.[16]

The Committee has not been entirely satisfied with states parties' implementation of the CRPD. Some of the interpretations provided by the Committee are far reaching and difficult to reconcile with states' other human rights obligations under this Convention and other human rights conventions. The CRPD Committee has stated, for example, in General Comment No. 1 to Article 12(3):[17]

> Support in the exercise of legal capacity must respect the rights, will and preferences of persons with disabilities and should *never* amount to substitute decision-making. Article 12, paragraph 3, does not specify what form the support should take. 'Support' is a broad term that encompasses both informal and formal support arrangements, of varying types and intensity [emphasis added].

The fact that support in the exercise of legal capacity must respect the rights, will and preferences of persons with disabilities is today widely accepted. From a state's point of view, however, the question is to what extent the phrase 'should never amount to substitute decision-making' should be seen as a necessary interpretation of the Convention, or should be viewed as the Committee's non-binding opinion: often relevant, but not always.

On 23 February 1999, the Committee of Ministers of the Council of Europe adopted Recommendation No. R (99) 4 on principles concerning the legal protection of incapable adults.[18] Principle 3 of this Recommendation on *the maximum preservation of capacity* may also strengthen such interpretation. However, this instrument dates from a time prior to CRPD General Comment No. 1 (2014). It would have been helpful if the CRPD Committee had reflected on this important source of law in its 2014 General Comment.

---

14 Committee on the Rights of Persons with Disabilities, General Comment No. 1, *Article 12: Equal recognition before the law*, 19 May 2014, CRPD/C/GC/1 (2014), para. 12.

15 Ibid, at para. 14.

16 Ibid, at para. 15.

17 Ibid, at para. 17.

18 Council of Europe, Recommendation No. R (99) 4 on principles concerning the legal protection of incapable adults, adopted by the Committee of Ministers on 23 February 1999 at the 660th meeting of the Ministers' Deputies.

In December 2014, six months after CRPD General Comment No. 1 was published, the UN Human Rights Committee published a General Comment on Article 9 of the ICCPR. It stated:

> The existence of a disability shall not in itself justify a deprivation of liberty but rather any deprivation of liberty must be necessary and proportionate, for the purpose of protecting the individual in question from serious harm or preventing injury to others. It must be applied only as a measure of *last resort* and for the *shortest appropriate period of time*, and must be accompanied by *adequate procedural and substantive safeguards* established by law. The procedures should ensure *respect for the views of the individual* and ensure that any representative genuinely represents and defends the *wishes and interests of the individual* [emphasis added].[19]

The European Court of Human Rights (ECtHR) has, step by step, confirmed the need for stronger procedural safeguards on the imposition of legal incapacity and has drastically reduced the circumstances under which such incapacities can be legally imposed. However, it has not accepted the CRPD Committee's 'never substituted' doctrine.[20] The Court stated in *Shtukaturov* that:

> The applicant claimed that full incapacitation had been an inadequate response to the problems he experienced. Indeed, under Article 8 the authorities must strike a fair balance between the interests of a person of unsound mind and the other legitimate interests concerned. However, as a rule, in such a complex matter as determining somebody's mental capacity, the authorities should enjoy a wide margin of appreciation.[21]

In *Shtukaturov*, the ECtHR seems to recognise the deprivation of legal capacity both as a lawful remedy and as a serious intrusion into the right to respect for

---

19 Human Rights Committee, General Comment No. 35, *Article 9: Liberty and security of person*, 16 December 2014, CCPR/C/GC/35, para. 19 (parts of).

20 See relevant ECtHR decisions. The fact that the removal of legal capacity can constitute a violation of Art. 8 ECHR was affirmed by the Court in *Sýkora v. Czech Republic* (Application No. 23419/07) [2012] ECtHR, pp. 7–8. See also the development in the ECtHR's views in: *Glor v. Switzerland* (Application No. 13444/04) [2009]; *Stanev v. Bulgaria* (Application No. 36760/06) [2012]; *Salontaji-Drobnjak v. Serbia* (Application No. 36500/05) [2009]; *X & Y v. Croatia* (Application No. 5193/09) [2011]; *DD v. Lithuania* (Application No. 13469/06) [2012]; and *N v. Romania (No. 2)* (Application No. 38048/18) [2021]. In the last case, the court underlined in para 68 that:

> 'This complaint is, in essence, directed at the fact that the applicant had no say in the proceedings leading to the appointment of a new guardian. The Court observes that the applicant, on account of his legal incapacitation, was ultimately prevented from deciding for himself about who would protect his interests and exercise his rights. There has accordingly been interference with the applicant's right to respect for his private life under Article 8 of the Convention [see, *mutatis mutandis*, *A.-M.V. v. Finland*, (Application No. 53251/13), §77, 23 March 2017].'

21 *Shtukaturov v. Russia* (Application No.44009/05) [2008] ECtHR para. 87.

private and family life protected by Article 8 ECHR. The ECtHR underlined that such intrusion is a tailored response necessary in striking a fair balance.[22] The Council of Europe Commissioner for Human Rights indicated in 2009 that the ECtHR's interpretation in *Shtukaturov* was in line with the CRPD.[23]

In light of the CRPD Committee's 2014-failure to consider the bearing of other human rights instruments in interpreting the CRPD, it is interesting to follow the ECtHR's further reasoning in 2017 on Article 8 ECHR. ECtHR seems here to point at a more nuanced interpretation of the right to self-determination than formulated by the CRPD Committee.[24] In *A-MV v. Finland* the ECtHR took into account relevant international instruments and reports in order to interpret the guarantees of the ECHR and establish whether there was a common standard in the field concerned; also CRPD was held to be a relevant instrument.[25] In *A-MV v. Finland*, the ECtHR stated:

> The Court is mindful of the need for the domestic authorities to reach, in each particular case, a balance between the respect for the dignity and self-determination of the individual and the need to protect the individual and safeguard his or her interests, especially under circumstances where his or her individual qualities or situation place the person in a particularly vulnerable position. The Court considers that a proper balance was struck in the present case: there were effective safeguards in the domestic proceedings to prevent abuse, as required by the standards of international human rights law, ensuring that the applicant's rights, will and preferences were taken into account. The applicant was involved at all stages of the proceedings: he was heard in person and he could put forward his wishes. The interference was proportional and tailored to the applicant's circumstances, and was subject to review by competent, independent and impartial domestic courts. The measure taken was also consonant with the legitimate aim of protecting the applicant's health, in a broader sense of his well-being.[26]

The Court stated in the same judgment that a 'margin of appreciation must, inevitably, be left to the national authorities, who by reason of their direct and continuous contact with the vital forces of their countries are in principle better placed than an international court to evaluate local needs and conditions.'[27] However, the Court underlined that this margin would vary and would 'tend to be narrower where the right at stake is crucial to the individual's effective

---

22 *CRPD Handbook*, above n. 12, at p. 274.

23 *A-MV v. Finland* (Application No. 53251/13) [2017] ECtHR para. 74.

24 Council of Europe, above n. 6, at p. 21: 'the jurisprudence of the European Court of Human Rights which allows for certain forms of substitute decision-making under certain controlled circumstances.'

25 *A-MV v. Finland*, above n. 23, at para. 74.

26 Ibid, at para. 90.

27 Ibid, at para. 83.

enjoyment of intimate or key rights.'[28] Further, it would be 'reduced where a particularly vulnerable group is subjected to differential treatment on grounds that are not specifically linked to relevant individual circumstances.'[29]

Furthermore, in its strategy for 2017–2023, *Human rights: A reality for all*, the Council of Europe stated that:

> States are required … *as far as possible* to replace substituted decision-making with systems of supported decision-making. Possible limitations on decision-making should be considered on an individual basis, be proportional and be restricted to the extent to which it is absolutely necessary. Limitations should not take place when less interfering means are sufficient in light of the situation, and accessible and effective legal safeguards must be provided to ensure that such measures are not abused [emphasis added].[30]

To sum up, none of the UN Human Rights Committee, the Council of Europe or the ECtHR interpret the human rights guarantees on self-determination as strictly as the CRPD Committee. The ECtHR insists that domestic authorities must reach a balance between respect for the individual's self-determination and the need to protect the individual and safeguard his or her interests.

Where the individual's capacities or situation place him or her in a particularly vulnerable position, the ECtHR has emphasised the importance of existing procedural safeguards.[31] In the same case, the Court observed that there had been effective safeguards in the domestic proceedings to prevent abuse, as required by the standards of international human rights law. The Court also insisted that the person's 'rights, will and preferences were taken into account.' The person was 'involved at all stages of the proceedings: he was heard in person and he could put forward his wishes.'[32] The interference by the State was seen as 'proportional and tailored to the applicant's circumstances, and was subject to review by competent, independent and impartial domestic courts.'[33] Thus, despite the fact that the authorities did not satisfy the person's wishes (due to legitimate interests in protecting his health and well-being), they were not found to have breached Article 8 ECHR.[34]

These interpretations of the reach of the right to self-determination suggest that the CRPD Committee's comment that support should *never* amount to substitute decision-making is not reflected in the judgments or comments of

[28] Ibid.

[29] Ibid.

[30] Council of Europe, *Human rights: A reality for all – Council of Europe Disability Strategy 2017–2023*, Council of Europe Publishing, 2017, para. 63.

[31] *A-MV v. Finland*, above n. 23, at paras. 82–84, 90.

[32] Ibid, at para. 90.

[33] Ibid.

[34] See European Court of Human Rights, *Guide on Article 8 of the Convention – Right to respect for*, Council of Europe Publishing, 2018 (last updated 31 August 2021).

other relevant human rights bodies. However, the essential comment from the CRPD Committee, that support in the exercise of legal capacity must respect the rights, will and preferences of persons with disabilities, seems widely accepted and respected.

4. ADJUSTING TO A MOVING TARGET: AMENDMENTS STEP BY STEP

Norway ratified the CRPD in the summer of 2013. At the same time, a major law reform came into force as part of the process of implementing the Convention. The law reform was based on four pillars:

1. Legislative reform: the existing Acts on guardianship and deprival of legal capacity were repealed and a modern Guardianship Act based primarily on supported decision-making was adopted (Vergemålsloven 2010).[35]
2. Organisational reform: the tasks involved were professionalised and the county governor became the new authority in this field.
3. Competence reform: it was decided that persons employed will normally have a Master's degree and support persons should receive training, guidance and supervision from the competent authority (i.e. the county governor).
4. Attitudinal reform: an attitudinal reform was included to ensure the CRPD paradigm shift in practice.

However, despite the best of intentions, it proved difficult to change attitudes and the social mindset overnight. In addition, as the interpretation of the CRPD developed, several adjustments were needed. A number of law reforms have followed since 2010.[36] In addition, the Civil Law Authority has, since 2013, worked intensely on training and developing digital and pedagogic systems and techniques to improve and ensure supported decision-making in practical life.

In 2018 and 2020, further amendments were proposed following public hearings.[37] The proposed amendments to sections 20, 33 and 59 of the 2010 Act on supported decision-making, self-determination and reasonable accommodation, are likely to be followed up in 2022.

---

35 Acts repealed: Act of 28 November 1898 (Umyndiggjørelsesloven) LOV-1993-06-04-55; Act of 22 April 1927 no. 3 (Vergemålsloven) LOV-1927-04-22-3. Act adopted: Act of 26 March 2010 no. 9 (Vergemålsloven) LOV-2010-03-26-9.

36 The original law reform proposals: Ot.prp. nr. 110 (2009–2010); Prop. 4L (2009–2010); later amendments: Prop. 46 L (2012–2013); Prop. 36 L (2015–2016); Prop. 39 L (2017–2018).

37 Ministry of Justice: Høringsnotat november 2018 (18/5852); Høringsnotat juni 2020 (20/2965).

Further amendments to the 2010 Act to secure implementation of the CRPD linked to rules where criticism has been received are to be expected.[38] It is likely, due to comments received from the CRPD Committee, that there will be discussion about the terminology of the Act, the use of diagnostic criteria and the need to create and test new tools or arrangements for supported decision-making.[39]

According to the CRPD Committee, all law reform processes concerning legal capacity must be 'deliberate, well planned and include the consultation and meaningful participation of people with disabilities and their organizations.'[40] In Norway, the dialogue with persons with disabilities, their organisations and other stakeholders has enriched the ongoing work on amendments. The dialogue has been tremendously important in the efforts to find ways to implement the CRPD which serve the persons at its core. During the legislative process, 'dialogue meetings' and 'working group meetings' have been held that have been particularly valuable when seeking to implement the CRPD obligations.[41] This continuous dialogue has also been particularly valuable to strengthening the regulation of supported decision-making rights and the right to reasonable accommodation.

5. CAPACITY AND LEGAL CAPACITY IN NORWAY: FAMILY LAW MATTERS

5.1. FROM A TRADITIONAL SYSTEM TO A CRPD-REVISED SYSTEM

Norway, like many other countries worldwide, had (up until recently) a traditional understanding of legal capacity. According to this obsolete tradition, all persons had the ability to be holders of rights and duties, but not all adults had the legal ability to act.

---

38 Innst. 285 (S) 2020–2021, Dokument 8: 77 (2020–2021).

39 Committee on the Rights of Persons with Disabilities, *Concluding observations on the initial report of Norway*, 7 May 2019, CRPD/C/NOR/CO/1, at para. 20 a and b where Norway has received criticism in connection with legal rules which the Committee still understands as forms of substituted decision-making or deprivation of legal capacity. The Committee has stated: '20 (a) Consider systemic change by replacing guardianship and all other forms of substituted decision-making with supported decision-making for all persons with disabilities, regardless of their support requirements; (b) Repeal the Guardianship Act, which allows for the deprivation of legal capacity based on impairment, ensure that no person is placed under guardianship and increase training on the recognition of the full legal capacity of all persons with disabilities'.

40 CRPD/C/GC/1, above n. 14, at para. 30.

41 These are the author's own reflections as the person in charge of such processes on behalf of the Ministry of Justice in Norway from 2018 to 2021.

When the Norwegian Guardianship Act was revised, one important aim was to amend the legislation to implement the CRPD. Article 12(2) of the CRPD states: 'States Parties shall recognize that persons with disabilities enjoy legal capacity on an equal basis with others in all aspects of life.' The starting point, according to the CRPD, is that all persons, including all persons with disabilities, enjoy legal capacity on an 'equal basis' with others.

5.2. ADULTS WITH LEGAL CAPACITY

When the modernised Norwegian Guardianship Act was amended in 2010, the Parliament adopted rules with the intention to secure legal capacity from the age of 18, no matter the person's physical or psychological health or cognitive abilities.[42] Today, it follows from section 2 of the 2010 Act that all adults have full majority and full legal capacity under Norwegian law, unless their legal capacity is otherwise restricted in limited cases (see sections 5.3 and 5.4 below).

According to the CRPD Committee, legal capacity and mental capacity are distinct concepts.[43] In line with this understanding, the former legal link between *legal* capacity and (factual) *mental* capacity has been severed to create two distinct concepts in Norwegian law. While decision-making skills may vary from one person to another – and may be different for a given person depending on many factors, including environmental or societal factors – the person will still, according to Norwegian law, have legal capacity as an adult human being.

Today, an adult under Norwegian law may be both a holder of rights and duties and a legal actor regardless of his or her possible lack of mental ability to act. The person maintains the *legal* capacity to act even if (or when) the person is receiving different kinds of support. The fact that a power of attorney has been granted by the person, with the effect of having an attorney acting on his or her behalf, neither interferes with, nor restricts, the person's legal capacity. Furthermore, legal capacity as such is not affected, even if the county governor establishes a modern, voluntary guardianship to support the person or if another support arrangement is put in place (see section 2(3) of the 2010 Act).

An important consequence of this regulation is that the individual, the individual's attorney and/or a (modern) guardian within their mandate or power will all have parallel competence. If, for instance, a guardian is appointed to support the acquisition or sale of an individual's home, the individual will still maintain competence as a legal actor. This regulated 'double competence' may lead to challenges if, for instance, the home is sold both by the individual and

---

[42] 2010 Act (Lov 26. mars 2010 nr. 9 om vergemål) s. 2(3), in force 1 July 2013, last amended 1 July 2021.

[43] CRPD/C/GC/1, above n. 14, at para. 12.

by his or her support person to different buyers. In section 21 of the 2010 Act, it is specified that, when a guardian is appointed, the individual (still) can take legal action and dispose of his or her own funds. He or she may also revoke a disposition made by the (modern) guardian.[44] The legal risks following from this approach to competence were discussed in the preparatory work, but the Ministry of Justice was willing to accept a certain number of disadvantages in order to achieve the greater good, implying that the benefits related to preserving autonomy would likely outweigh the negative impacts of such regulation.[45] An argument in favour of this assessment is that the support person/modern guardian is obliged by law to discuss any major disposition with the individual concerned (see section 33(1) of the 2010 Act). It also follows from section 33(2) that 'the guardian cannot make the disposition if the person who has been placed under guardianship objects.'[46] Assuming a well-functioning dialogue between the person and the support person/modern guardian, the risk related to duplicated dispositions should be limited.

To summarise, all adults in Norway have legal capacity in the sense that they can be holders of rights and duties as well as legal actors. If the person is represented by a lasting power of attorney, a guardian or other forms of support, the person nonetheless retains his or her unlimited legal capacity. However, this capacity can be somewhat limited by a court decision or based on customary law (see sections 5.3 and 5.4 below).

5.3. RESTRICTIONS ON LEGAL CAPACITY

Although the system of legal capacity in Norway was fundamentally changed by the 2010 law reform and when the rules on incapacitation were abolished, there are still some legislative remnants that hark back to substitute decision-making. According to section 22 of the 2010 Act, legal capacity can be limited by court order when this is *necessary* to protect the person against his or her own conduct or misuse by others.[47] The restrictions on legal capacity have to be limited to the level of protection required and should never have effect for a longer period than necessary.[48] Under Norwegian law, such restrictions are seen as coercive and must be decided by the courts. In Norway, courts have made decisions on guardianship with such limitations on legal capacity

44 2010 Act, above n. 42, at s. 21 (author's own translation).
45 Ot.prp. nr. 110 (2008–2009), p. 42, 179. The Ministry of Justice states, for instance, that 'the consideration of the right to self-determination as a starting point should outweigh the consideration of third parties' (author's own translation).
46 2010 Act, above n. 42, at s. 33(2) (author's own translation).
47 Ibid, at s. 22.
48 Ibid, at s. 21(3).

for approximately 280 individuals of the 42,000 or so individuals receiving support measures.[49] This means that restrictions are made for approximately 0.6 per cent of persons who need support following decision-making difficulties. Based on experience from the county governors, about half the court orders seem to involve elements of a voluntary request for limitation, while the other half will be involuntary. A person with reduced cognitive abilities and a gambling addiction may, for instance, wish to give his brother competence to pay his bills and other necessities and the right to control how much money he can dispose of each month. Based on a court order, the brother in this example can be given the competence to limit the person's legal actions within the specific mandate following from the court order.

The Norwegian Supreme Court has made important clarifications as to how such restrictions should be limited.[50] In a ground-breaking 2017 case, a 25-year-old adult, 'A', had reduced cognitive ability and reduced impulse control. He had received some treatment for his gambling addiction, but was still considered addicted. A was renting an apartment, but he was in apparent danger of eviction since he was months behind on the rent, due in particular to his gambling habit. The county governor suggested limitations to his legal capacity to manage his own finances in the economic area to safeguard his independent living conditions. The Supreme Court took as its starting point 'the principle of least intervention' enshrined in law. The Court considered that the guardianship should not be made more comprehensive than necessary and should be tailored to the person's circumstances.[51] The first voting judge of the Supreme Court also stated:

> [I]t is, from overriding considerations, particularly related to the desire to limit interventions as much as possible and to provide strong protection for personal matters. In my view, this is precisely what is followed up when A is only deprived of the right to enter into, change or terminate the tenancy agreement on his own. He retains his right to self-determination as far as possible. Furthermore, I find it clear that the legislator's clear instruction to look at the person's motivation in case of doubt cannot be disregarded.[52]

As a result of this court decision, A retained full legal competence in personal matters, including the right to decide where he wanted to live. Competence to manage his own finances was limited, depriving A of his right to enter into,

49 Since the measures must never have effect for a longer period than necessary, there will constantly be minor changes in the numbers, but we have not seen major changes in the last years.
50 HR-2017-275-A.
51 Ibid, premise 30 (author's own translation).
52 Ibid, premise 58 (author's own translation).

change or terminate the lease on his own. The limitation of legal capacity to manage his own finances was construed as narrowly as possible in light of the need to protect A's autonomy as well as his right to an adequate standard of living. In this way, the Supreme Court not only interpreted strictly internal law, but indirectly also balanced A's rights to autonomy and self-determination under international human rights law against his rights to adequate living conditions.[53]

The question remains, however, whether such rules would be acceptable under prevailing international human rights obligations – without any specific interpretative declarations from the State.

The CRPD Committee has, both in the comments to the states and in General Comment No. 1, been very clear that blanket substitute decision-making is not permitted. The CRPD Committee has repeatedly stated that state parties must take action to replace systems of substitute decision-making with supported decision-making that respects the will and preferences of the individual concerned.[54]

Based on the initial reports from the various state parties, the CRPD Committee stated:

> [T]here is a general misunderstanding of the exact scope of the obligations of States parties under article 12 of the Convention. Indeed, there has been a general failure to understand that the human rights-based model of disability implies a shift from the substitute decision-making paradigm to one that is based on supported decision-making.[55]

However, the Committee has also underlined that the CRPD does not provide for derogations from existing international law.[56] With this in mind, it is interesting to link back to the key findings under section 3 above, including the assessments of the Human Rights Committee published in General Comment No. 35 on Article 9 of the ICCPR, which states:

> The existence of a disability shall not in itself justify a deprivation of liberty but rather any deprivation of liberty must be necessary and proportionate, for the purpose of protecting the individual in question from serious harm or preventing injury to others. It must be applied only as a measure of last resort and for the shortest appropriate period of time, and must be accompanied by adequate procedural and substantive safeguards established by law. The procedures should ensure respect for

---

53 Art. 1 (autonomy) and Art. 11 (adequate living conditions, including housing, etc.) of the International Covenant on Economic, Social and Cultural Rights, 16 December 1966, and in addition the rights following from Art. 12 of the CRPD (on self-determination).

54 See, for instance, CRPD/C/GC/1, above n. 14, at para. 17.

55 Ibid, at para. 3.

56 Ibid, at para. 5.

> the views of the individual and ensure that any representative genuinely represents and defends the wishes and interests of the individual.[57]

The Subcommittee on the Prevention of Torture and Other Cruel, Inhuman or Degrading Treatment or Punishment has adopted a similar position.[58]

Based on the CRPD Committee statement that the CRPD does not provide derogation from international law and the assessments from the Human Rights Committee and the Subcommittee mentioned above, substitute decision-making measures should be evaluated on the basis of disability and should 'not in [themselves] justify a deprivation of liberty.'[59] Moreover, 'any deprivation of liberty must be necessary and proportionate, for the purpose of protecting the individual in question from serious harm or preventing injury to others.'[60] In addition, such measures must be applied only as a 'last resort and for the shortest appropriate period of time, and must be accompanied by adequate procedural and substantive safeguards established by law.'[61] Finally, the procedures should ensure respect for the views of the individual and ensure that any representative genuinely represents and defends the wishes and interests of the individual. Additionally the ECtHR referred to Article 8 ECHR in *Shtukaturov* to further underline that 'the authorities must strike a fair balance between the interests of a person of unsound mind and the other legitimate interests concerned.'[62] In 2017 the ECtHR distinguished the case further and instructed the states 'to reach, in each particular case, a balance between the respect for the dignity and self-determination of the individual and the need to protect the individual and safeguard his or her interests.'[63]

Amendments or clarifications of the remnants of the Norwegian substitute regime might still be required, but a broader analysis of sources of international law does not necessarily require an abolition of all substitute measures.

It can be argued that the committees and courts mentioned above are in fact providing the states parties with at least a vague 'recipe' on how to construe legal rules that seek to balance rights and autonomy and avoid discrimination.

The ongoing Norwegian amendment project makes amendments or clarifications likely with regard to these rules.[64] Thus, the above-mentioned 'recipe' handed down by the Human Rights Committee and others should be valuable to this project.

---

57 CCPR/C/GC/35, above n. 19, at para. 16.

58 See comments in G. Szmukler, '"Capacity", "best interests", "will and preferences" and the UN Convention on the Rights of Persons with Disabilities' (2019) 18 *World Psychiatry* 34.

59 CCPR/C/GC/35, above n. 19, at para. 16.

60 Ibid, at para. 16.

61 Ibid, at para. 16.

62 See above n. 21.

63 See above n. 23, at para. 90 first sentence.

64 Innst. 285 (S) 2020–2021, Dokument 8: 77 (2020–2021).

5.4. INVALID LEGAL DISPOSITION UNDER CUSTOMARY LAW

According to customary law, a legal disposition may be considered invalid for various reasons linked to the motivation or content of the disposition. According to this rule, the focus is not on the individual's abilities. The crucial question, according to Norwegian court practice, is whether a serious mental illness has affected the disposition in a way that makes it unreasonable to consider the disposition legally binding.[65] It is thus not sufficient that the person has a serious mental illness; the disorder must have affected the legal disposition in such a way that it is unreasonable to consider the disposition legally binding.

5.5. LEGAL CAPACITY IN FAMILY MATTERS

5.5.1. Consent at the Heart of Family Law Dispositions

Valid consent often lies at the heart of family law dispositions. Dispositions related to family law are often of immense importance to an individual's degree of autonomy. Under Norwegian law, the starting point is that the person must individually give consent to a typical family law disposition.

Particularly personal legal dispositions cannot be included in a lasting power of attorney or any form of guardianship, unless this is specified in an Act.[66] A ruling of the Supreme Court indicates that an objective, rather than a subjective, norm must be used in order to interpret whether or not the matter is particularly personal.[67] Section 21(4) of the 2010 Act specifies that competence to vote in an election, to enter into marriage, to consent to fatherhood, to consent to the use of coercion or to organ donation, to make or alter a will and any other particularly personal dispositions must be agreed to by the person him- or herself. Other matters may be considered to be 'particularly personal' only if they are objectively comparable to the examples given in section 21.

5.5.2. Entering into Marriage and Cohabitation

The right to cohabitate is closely linked to the right to live independently.[68] While the right to live independently is important in itself, it is also a prerequisite for establishing a cohabitation relationship. The Norwegian Supreme Court has demonstrated that the threshold for restricting a person's personal right to

---

65 Rt. 1995 s. 1540.

66 2010 Act, above n. 42, at s. 21(4).

67 See, in particular, HR-2019-1758-A, para. 47, with reference to the preparatory work (Ot.prp. nr. 110 (2008–2009)) and to some extent HR-2017-275-A, paras. 56–58.

68 Cf. CRPD Art.19.

decide where (and with whom) to live is high.[69] The author is not aware of any Norwegian court order denying cohabitation. However, it is likely that some groups of disabled persons are more likely to experience family members or care workers, etc., who wish to hinder or avoid cohabitation in more informal ways. At any rate, the threshold for a possible *legal* denial is high.

To enter into marriage, both persons must be present and voluntarily consent. Under Norwegian law, a person must consent to marry on his or her own behalf even when a guardian is appointed or an attorney chosen to handle other matters. The person him- or herself will be the legal actor in nearly all situations involving marriage. However, a guardian may, according to section 2 of the Marriage Act, be given the explicit right to consent to marriage *in addition* to the future spouse in rare situations. If the guardian refuses to consent to an individual's marriage, the county governor may nevertheless give permission for marriage if there is no reasonable ground for such refusal. The author is aware of only *one* administrative case since 2013 where consent was denied, in that case to hinder a forced marriage. An attorney cannot be given the ability to consent to a marriage over the objections of the intended spouse.

5.5.3. Consent to Separation and Divorce

Any married person has the right to initiate a divorce. Matrimonial proceedings brought before the courts shall always be instituted by or against a spouse personally even if he or she is a minor or a person whose legal capacity has been restricted pursuant to section 22 of the 2010 Act. The person will be treated as a person before the law, and therefore as the relevant actor in any family law proceedings. When proceedings are instituted, a guardian may assist this spouse. The guardian shall be notified about the case by the county governor. If the case is brought before the courts, the writ must also be served on the guardian. A guardian may, on rare occasions, bring proceedings *on behalf of* a spouse whose legal capacity is restricted if this is *essentially* in the interests of the said spouse. This will typically be the case where a spouse is abused, otherwise harmed by the other spouse or particularly vulnerable to exploitation. These cases are dealt with by the courts, who decide whether there are grounds for legal action. If a spouse has a voluntary guardianship and it is part of the guardian's mandate to act in or to bring proceedings for separation or divorce or matrimonial proceedings, the provisions of section 28(1) and (2) of the Marriage Act apply correspondingly to that guardian. These rules are intended to avoid exploitation.[70]

---

69 HR-2017-275-A, para. 58.

70 According to the Marriage Act s. 28 the measures shall be used only if there is an urgent need to protect the spouse. This is also underlined in the preparatory works, NOU 1986: 2, comment to §5-2 (Marriage Act s. 28).

5.5.4. *Pre- and Post-Nuptial Agreements*

In Norwegian law, both pre- and post-nuptial agreements are valid and enforceable. Creating a pre- or post-nuptial agreement is likely to be considered a 'particularly personal' legal disposition or transaction under section 21 of the 2010 Act. Indeed, it is likely that creating such marriage agreements will be treated in the same way as making a will, which means that the documents must be completed by the person him- or herself (section 21 of the 2010 Act). According to section 54(2) of the Marriage Act, the person must be mature and fully in control of his or her senses and recollections to create pre- and post-nuptial agreements. Anyone aged 18 and above is considered mature and as having the overall legal capacity to enter into pre- and post-nuptial agreements. The question is whether the person is judged to have the mental capacity to enter into the actual agreement. Capacity is assessed on a case-by-case basis and never as a general matter. The test is whether the person understands the nature and quality of the relevant legal disposition. This means that the person's soundness of mind or mental age is of relevance, but the degree of reasonable accommodation offered in the relevant situation and the complexity of the agreement will also play an important part in the decision. A reasonable agreement of little complexity is more likely to be seen as valid over a complex and unbalanced agreement.

5.5.5. *Parenthood: Health-Related Matters*

Many intrusive dispositions are regulated by health legislation and seldom lead to assessments based on the 'particularly personal' doctrine. Section 4 of the Sterilisation Act and section 4 of the Abortion Act are notable examples.[71]

6. CONCLUDING REMARKS: THE NEED FOR FURTHER IMPLEMENTATION

This chapter describes important changes in Norwegian disability law that are relevant to the CRPD. However, there remains a need for legal clarifications, further research and more experimental activities to try to develop future support measures tailored to protecting the human rights of the disabled in the Nordic welfare systems.

Brennan and Traustadóttir have examined implementation of the CRPD in the Nordic states and argue that it has revealed a 'disaccord between some

[71] Sterilisation Act (Steriliseringsloven) LOV-1977-06-03-57, s. 4; Abortion Act (Abortloven) LOV-1975-06-13-50, s. 4.

of the key aspects of the human rights approach and the culture of the Nordic welfare services.'[72] Such findings are not necessarily surprising. In a situation where there are conflicting interests in balancing rights, non-discrimination and autonomy, this balancing activity will be more challenging in states where disability gives rise to comprehensive welfare rights. In these societies, a lack of mental capacity combined with autonomy will more easily lead to the loss of rights or discrimination. Given this context, hesitancy towards awarding 'too much autonomy' in Nordic welfare services is not an unlikely finding.

The findings set out in this chapter could give rise to arguments that there is a need for support measures tailored not only to the person, but also to the Nordic welfare systems, in order to avoid the loss of rights. Such measures are unlikely to be developed, however, without comprehensive contributions from persons with disabilities and their organisations. Is development of a future disability-neutral basis for intervention in order to protect the human rights of people at risk of discrimination, loss of rights, abuse, exploitation or neglect possible? The answer lies in the future. It is likely that most countries can make important steps in the direction of increased autonomy. Norway still has stairs to climb. Perhaps our most important expectation is that states should be willing to move, evaluate and explore the different routes forward.[73] In the *CRPD Handbook*, the authors urge:

> Creative ideas and practical examples must be actively shared in an effort to find innovative solutions to challenges like mental and emotional distress beset by inequality in law and practice. This is not an easy task and will only be achieved when the views of those most affected are instrumental in driving the legal and policy changes with the express support of States Parties and others. The advantages to society would be significant.[74]

Creative cooperation between persons with disabilities, their organisations and the State seems to be the only way to ensure a lasting paradigm shift. That would also be the case for Norway.

72 C. Brennan and R. Traustadóttir, 'Implementing Article 19 of the CRPD in Nordic Welfare States: The Culture of Welfare and the CRPD' in E.J. Kakoullis and K. Johnson (eds.) *Recognising Human Rights in Different Cultural Contexts:* Palgrave Macmillan, 2020, pp. 257–268.

73 A. Arstein-Kerslake, J. Watson, M. Browning et al., 'Future direction in supported decision making' (2017) 37 *Disability Studies Quarterly*, available at: <http://dsq-sds.org/article/view/5070/4549>, last accessed 18.02.2022. This article underlines the need to explore ways to enable supported decision-making in real life.

74 *CRPD Handbook*, above n. 12, at p. 277.

POLAND

LEGAL EFFECTS OF INCAPACITATION IN POLISH FAMILY LAW

Małgorzata BALWICKA-SZCZYRBA and Anna SYLWESTRZAK

Résumé

Le droit polonais de la famille contient des dispositions relatives aux conséquences juridiques des mesures d'incapacité qui interfèrent de manière excessive avec l'autonomie de la volonté personnelle, le droit à la liberté et le respect de la vie privée. En outre, il manque également d'adaptabilité aux besoins individuels spécifiques. L'incapacité légale est une institution du droit polonais dont la portée et les principaux effets juridiques sont régis par le Code civil polonais (CCP). Le Code civil polonais différencie l'incapacité légale en deux groupes: l'incapacité légale totale (article 13) et l'incapacité légale partielle (article 16). Le Code polonais de procédure civile (PCCP) réglemente la procédure judiciaire relative à la mise en œuvre de l'incapacité en son article 554. Parallèlement, d'autres lois, telle que la loi polonaise sur la famille et la tutelle (Polish Family and Guardianship Law – PFGC), précisent d'autres effets juridiques de l'incapacité, de manière directe ou indirecte. Dans le présent article, les conséquences d'une mesure d'incapacité légale sur les droits intéressant la famille sont évaluées au regard de ces lois. Une analyse détaillée de la compatibilité des dispositions de la PFGC avec les droits de l'Homme et avec les principes fondamentaux du droit civil polonais est également effectuée en tenant compte du cadre fixé par la Convention des Nations Unies relative aux droits des personnes handicapées. Il en ressort que ces normes sont en contradiction avec les obligations découlant du droit international applicable, y compris la Convention des Nations Unies relative aux droits des personnes handicapées, et ne sont pas non plus conformes aux principes fondamentaux du droit civil polonais. Cependant, les conséquences juridiques des mesures d'incapacité en droit de la famille ont été imaginées de manière plus appropriée que dans d'autres domaines. Elles n'interfèrent donc pas de manière déraisonnable avec les droits civils de la personne handicapée en matière de mariage ou quant à la fondation d'une famille. Ces questions sont développées plus en détail dans le présent article.

1. INTRODUCTION

Legal incapacitation is an institution of Polish law, the substance, scope and primary legal effects of which are governed by the Polish Civil Code (PCC). The PCC distinguishes between two types of incapacitation: full legal incapacitation (Article 13 of the PCC) and partial legal incapacitation (Article 16 of the PCC). The Polish Code of Civil Procedure (PCCP), specifically Article 554 et seq., sets forth the judicial procedure for incapacitation. Simultaneously, other laws, such as the Polish Family and Guardianship Code (PFGC), directly or indirectly elaborate on further legal effects of incapacitation. These laws will be the primary focus of this chapter. While the effects of incapacitation may be contemplated from the standpoint of various legal relations, it seems that family law relations play a particularly important role, as they most affect the incapacitated person in terms of marriage and family. The quality of life, sense of security and, by extension, progress in therapy of the person concerned are all affected by the way in which he or she functions in these relations.

This chapter will consider the PFGC provisions that set forth the legal effects of full and partial legal incapacitation, especially with respect to the provisions' compliance with human rights, including those set out in the UN Convention on the Rights of Persons with Disabilities,[1] as well as their conformity with the basic principles of Polish civil law. The assumption is thereby made that the legislature's interference with legal relations, especially where this affects the individual's private life, should occur only to a reasonable extent and within necessary limits. In keeping with the present-day approach to disability, a person in need of support should not be treated as a 'recipient

---

1 The Convention was drafted in New York on 13 December 2006, signed by Poland on 30 March 2007 and ratified into law on 6 September 2012, Journal of Laws of 25 October 2012, item 1169.

of help' but as a 'user of help'[2] who is given access to flexible tools that can be adapted to the specific needs of a particular person.

Polish family law features norms concerning the legal effects of incapacitation that excessively interfere with an individual's personal autonomy of the will and his or her right to freedom and respect for private life,[3] while also lacking adaptability to specific individual needs (a case in point being the regulations on impediments to marriage or the legal effects of appointment of a guardian). In this sense, these norms are in conflict with the obligations arising from international law applicable to Poland, including the UN Convention on the Rights of Persons with Disabilities, while also failing to ensure full compliance with the fundamental principles of Polish civil law. However, in other areas (such as protection against the adverse effects of the statute of limitations for filing the petition to disestablish paternity), the legal consequences of incapacitation under family law have been properly constituted and therefore do not unreasonably interfere with the incapacitated individual's civil rights associated with marriage or starting a family. These questions will be elaborated in more detail in the later sections of this chapter.

2. THE SUBSTANCE OF INCAPACITATION UNDER POLISH LAW

The purpose of incapacitation is to provide individuals suffering from mental impairments with protection regarding their property and non-property interests,[4] including personal rights, such as health. However, incapacitation is not a status designed to safeguard the public interest and cannot be used instrumentally as a means to enforce specific state policies.[5] According to well-established judicial practice, incapacitation may be applied only when motivated by the good of the person concerned, and not by the interests of the

---

2 See ruling of the Polish Supreme Court of 18 March 2021, V CSKP 235/21, LEX No. 3150202.

3 The need to honour the right of individuals to have their private life respected, in the context of the Constitution of the Republic of Poland, is particularly emphasised by P. Mostowik, 'Kilka uwag o ochronie małżeń na tle Konstytucji' in J. Łukasiewicz, A. Arkuszewska, A. Kościółek (eds.), *Wokół problematyki małżeństwa w aspekcie materialnym i procesowym*, Wydawnictwo Adam Marszałek, 2017, p. 55.

4 Thus in S. Dmowski and R. Trzaskowski in J. Gudowski (ed.), *Kodeks cywilny. Komentarz, Księga pierwsza. Część ogólna*, Wolters Kluwer, 2014, LEX electronic legal information system. Thus also in M. Balwicka-Szczyrba and A. Sylwestrzak, 'Instytucja ubezwłasnowolnienia w perspektywie unormowań Konstytucji RP oraz Konstytucji ONZ o prawach osób niepełnosprawnych' (2018) XL *Gdańskie Studia Prawnicze*163.

5 On the subject of incapacitation serving a public purpose, cf. A. Bladowski and A. Gola, *Ubezwłasnowolnienie. Opieka i kuratela*, Wydawnictwo Prawnicze, 1989, p. 14; L. Ludwiczak, *Ubezwłasnowolnienie w polskim systemie prawnym*, LexisNexis, 2012, p. 29.

applicant or any other third party.[6] The word 'may' in the provisions setting forth the prerequisites of incapacitation (Articles 13 and 16 of the PCC) should be construed as excluding any possibility of them applying automatically, thus obliging the court to examine on a case-by-case basis whether or not incapacitation is advisable. Therefore, compliance with statutory prerequisites for incapacitation is insufficient for the court to decide that it is advisable.[7]

Pursuant to Article 13 of the PCC, *full legal incapacitation* can be applied to a person who is at least 13 years of age and who is unable to control his or her behaviour as a result of mental illness, mental retardation or other mental impairment, including alcoholism or drug addiction. Therefore, the measure of incapacitation is conditioned by age (13 years of age or more) and inability to manage one's own affairs as a result of mental impairment.[8] The types of disorders set out in these provisions are examples only. A circumstance warranting incapacitation but not explicitly listed in Article 13 of the PCC is old-age dementia.[9]

In Poland, incapacitation is ordered under non-contentious proceedings by a district court composed of a bench of three professional judges (Article 554 of the PCCP). The court order continues indefinitely unless the order is rescinded upon showing that circumstances have changed.

Full legal incapacitation has serious legal consequences. An incapacitated person has no capacity for legal acts and therefore cannot effectively enter into transactions under civil law. This can be equated with 'civil death', as expressed in Article 14 of the PCC, which invalidates any legal act by a person who lacks proper capacity. The law allows an exception for ratification of such an act where minor day-to-day matters are concerned. Under Article 14(2) of the PCC, a contract executed by a person with no capacity for legal acts, concerning a minor day-to-day matter, becomes effective at the time it is performed, unless it causes serious harm to the incapacitated person. The effect of these Polish regulations makes an incapacitated person equal to a juvenile aged 0–13, who is subject to a similar lack of legal capacity.

---

6 See rulings of the Polish Supreme Court of 18 April 2018, IV CSK 587/17, LEX No. 2515716.

7 For more detail, see Balwicka-Szczyrba and Sylwestrzak, above n. 4, at p. 163.

8 For case law, see the ruling of the Polish Supreme Court of 14 January 1983, I CR 480/82, OSNC 1983/10/158; ruling of the Polish Supreme Court of 18 May 1972, II CR 138/72, LEX No. 1436; ruling of the Polish Supreme Court of 5 February 1965, I CR 356/64, LEX No. 291; ruling of the Polish Supreme Court of 19 August 1971, I CR 297/71, OSNC 1972/3/53; ruling of the Polish Supreme Court of 6 September 2017, I CSK 331/17, LEX No. 2382434.

9 Thus in M. Tomaszewska, 'Oblicza starości osób ubezwłasnowolnionych a wykluczenie społeczne' in W. Wilk and M. Gołowkin-Hudała (eds.), *Prawne aspekty starości*, Difin, 2014, p. 123; M. Balwicka-Szczyrba, 'Sytuacja osoby starszej w prawie rodzinnym i opiekuńczym' in J. Łukasiewicz and M. Załucki (eds.) *Prawo rodzinne i spadkowe wobec współczesnych zjawisk technologicznych i społecznych*, Wydawnictwo Adam Marszałek, 2018, pp. 209–223.

As mentioned earlier, the effects of full legal incapacitation are also governed by other legislation. As will be explained in more details later on, the PFGC covers in particular the inability of a fully incapacitated person to enter into marital relations (Article 11(1) of the PFGC), separation of assets arising from operation of the law between a fully incapacitated person and his or her spouse (Article 53(1) of the PFGC), as well as guardianship and curatorship of the incapacitated person (Article 145 et seq. of the PFGC).[10]

The grounds for *partial legal incapacitation* are similar to those for full legal incapacitation. Under Article 16 of the PCC, a person who has attained the age of majority may be fully incapacitated due to mental illness, mental retardation or other mental impairments, including alcoholism or drug addiction, but if such person's condition only requires assistance in the management of the person's affairs, then full legal incapacitation is not justified. Partial incapacitation is defined by age (majority) and the need for assisted living as a result of mental illness, mental retardation or other disorders, where the person's condition does not warrant full legal incapacitation.

Partial legal incapacitation does not produce effects as pervasive as full legal incapacitation. Under Article 15 of the PCC, a partially incapacitated person has limited capacity for legal acts and his or her legal status is equal to that of a minor aged 13–18. In line with the general principle set out in Article 17 of the PCC, and without prejudice to any exceptions provided for in the law, a legal transaction through which a person with limited capacity for legal acts contracts an obligation or exercises a right is null and void unless ratified by the statutory representative. Derogations from this rule are codified in Articles 20, 21 and 22 of the PCC, as well as in other specific legislative acts.

Both forms of incapacitation have indeterminate duration, i.e. they remain effective until repealed or modified, as the court cannot foresee in advance how long they should last. In addition, the effects of incapacitation are comprehensive, as their scope is specified by law and they cannot be applied solely to a certain category of affairs or a limited time-frame.

3. DISCUSSION ON THE ABOLITION OF INCAPACITATION IN POLAND

Due to its far-reaching legal consequences, incapacitation is currently the subject of debate in Polish academic circles. It is debated whether the institution should be maintained and, if so, to what extent it should be modified. The most radical elements call for a complete abolition of incapacitation and its replacement with other remedies, consistent with a trend observable in other European

10 For more detail, see Balwicka-Szczyrba and Sylwestrzak, above n. 4, at p. 162.

legislatures towards eliminating the institution altogether. For instance, the 1992 amendment of guardianship laws in Germany abolished incapacitation. The same happened in Austria and France.[11] The trend of shifting away from incapacitation is also evident in the former Eastern Bloc, including Georgia.[12]

In Poland, calls for abandoning incapacitation materialised for the first time in the 2015 draft amendment to the PCC.[13] However, the project was discontinued for political reasons following the dissolution of the Civil Law Codification Commission. The Commission was working to move away from incapacitation and towards modern solutions compatible with global trends. This was consistent with a growing number of criticisms about outdated statutory solutions being out of step with international standards. In this debate, it is clearly necessary to support solutions that waive incapacitation, as it no longer meets modern standards of care for persons with disabilities.[14] Protection for people with mental impairments should be ensured through a more flexible medium. This medium could be a suitably reformed institution of care, which should allow for temporary implementation and for a scope tailored to the needs of a particular case. Support for vulnerable persons, such as people with mental disabilities and the elderly, should reflect the model of *supported decision-making*,[15] rather than a system of exclusion combined with legal representation by a guardian. The growing number of demands and reform proposals are paving the way for future changes, which are necessary to comply with current human rights standards.

4. THE STATUS OF A REPRESENTATIVE AND THE INCAPACITATED PERSON'S SCOPE OF AUTONOMY

Under existing law, a fully incapacitated person has a guardian appointed for him or her, as long as this person does not remain under parental authority. The appointment of a guardian is necessary, as full incapacitation means the loss of capacity to enter into legal transactions (Article 12 of the PCC) and capacity to perform acts in court proceedings (Article 65(1) of the PCPC). The appointed

---

11 These legislative acts are indicated by L. Kociucki, *Zdolność do czynności prawnych osób dorosłych*, C.H. Beck, 2011, p. 185 et seq.

12 See M. Szwed, 'Likwidacja konstrukcji ubezwłasnowolnienia w Gruzji po wyroku Sądu konstytucyjnego z 8 października 2014 r' (2017) No. 1 *Przegląd Legislacyjny* 71.

13 For more detail, see P. Machnikowski, 'Pełnomocnictwo opiekuńcze w pracach Komisji Kodyfikacyjnej Prawa Cywilnego w latach 2012–2015' (2016) No. 5 *Rejent* 59.

14 See Balwicka-Szczyrba and Sylwestrzak, above n. 4, at p. 166.

15 See M. Domański, 'Ubezwłasnowolnienie w prawie polskim a wybrane standardów międzynarodowej ochrony praw człowieka' (2017) No. 17 *Prawo w Działaniu* 11; Balwicka-Szczyrba and Sylwestrzak, above n. 4, at p. 166; U. Ernst, 'Ubezwłasnowolnienie' (2010) No. 4 *Transformacje Prawa Prywatnego* 31.

guardian becomes by law the statutory representative of the incapacitated person, responsible for caring for the person, managing their property and representing them in legal transactions. Consequently, incapacitation has a far-reaching effect on the legal condition of a person, excluding him or her from participation in civil law transactions. In such a case, he or she will be able to participate only through a legal guardian.

Polish legislation prevents a fully incapacitated person from performing any independent legal acts whatsoever, even if these acts were to fall within a court-ordered category of exemptions. The only exception to this rule is the ratification mechanism applicable to the day-to-day matters, as discussed above (Article 14(2) of the PCC). As a result, incapacitation transfers civil law autonomy from the incapacitated to their appointed legal guardians.

The situation is different for a partially incapacitated person for whom a curator is appointed. In such a case, the incapacitated person has only limited capacity for legal acts (Article 15 of the PCC), and the curator's task is to provide assistance. However, the scope of assistance is quite broad, for the curator exercises control through his or her power to grant or refuse permission for the ward to assume contractual obligations or make dispositions.[16] This power is always vested in the curator, regardless of the scope of authority granted to him or her by the guardianship court.[17] The guardianship court may not exclude any activities from the competences of the guardian. In Polish law, the guardian is responsible for all legal activities. Additionally, if the guardianship court empowers the curator to represent the incapacitated person, the curator may perform legal acts in lieu of the incapacitated person. Under Article 181(1) of the PFGC, the guardianship court may also entrust the curator with the administration of the property of the partially incapacitated person. A person who is of age, partially legally incapacitated and has had a curator appointed 'to manage their day-to-day, including official, affairs' has no capacity for acts in court proceedings or in civil litigation and may only act through a curator.[18] However, the fact remains that the scope of the autonomy of the will of a partially incapacitated person is much broader than that of a fully incapacitated person, and the curator mainly has a supporting role. The guardianship court is therefore able to modify the curator's powers to some extent (with respect to legal representation and administration of property), as opposed to in full incapacitation, the legal effects of which, including the powers of the guardian, cannot be adjusted in any way.

---

16 See the ruling of the Polish Supreme Court of 25 March 1968, II CR 57/68, 167655.

17 Thus, in the ruling of the Polish Supreme Court of 30 September 1977, III CRN 132/77, LEX No. 2249.

18 Thus, in the ruling of the Court of Appeals in Katowice of 12 July 2016, ref. No. III AUa 958/15, LEX No. 2309530.

5. EFFECTS OF LEGAL INCAPACITATION ON THE CAPACITY TO ENTER INTO MARITAL RELATIONS AND ON THE LEGAL EFFECTS OF MARRIAGE

Marriage, as a legal union between two people, can only arise as authorised by law. The impediments that accompany incapacitation accordingly affect the ability to enter into a valid marriage. These impediments constitute grounds precluding the celebration of marriage and may form the basis for the annulment of a marriage celebrated despite their existence. Impediments to marriage are therefore specific circumstances that legally curtail the freedom of one or both prospective spouses to enter into marital relations.[19] The existence of impediments is investigated by the Chief Registrar who – pursuant to Article 4^1 of the PFGC – issues a certificate of no impediments. Consequently, marriage may be celebrated in the absence of impediments, but their existence precludes a lawful marriage. By extension, celebration of marriage despite impediments is a ground for annulment of the marriage.[20]

The catalogue of marriage impediments listed in the PFGC is close-ended.[21] Full legal incapacitation is an impediment to marriage (Article 11 of the PFGC), but partial legal incapacitation is not.[22] As a result, full legal incapacitation interferes considerably with an individual's autonomy, preventing him or her from getting married even where both prospective spouses agree to such a relationship knowing that one of them is legally incapacitated.

Notably, a fully incapacitated person has no access to a mechanism to override an impediment to marriage through a court order, a remedy available to persons suffering from mental impairments but not otherwise legally incapacitated. Under Article 12(1) of the PFGC (last sentence), the court may allow a person suffering from a mental illness or mental retardation to enter into marital relations, unless the person's health jeopardises the marriage or the health of any future offspring. In the case of a fully legally incapacitated person, marriage can be celebrated only if the court legally reverses the incapacitation order or changes full to partial incapacitation. As long as incapacitation is effective, neither the court nor any other authority may re-examine the incapacitated person's ability to marry or live in a married relationship, particularly with regard to any possible beneficial effect of marriage on the person's protection.

This examination of Article 11 of the PFGC, which establishes marriage impediments for fully legally incapacitated persons, calls for considering the

---

19 See T. Sokołowski, *Prawo rodzinne. Zarys wykładu*, Ars boni et aequi, 2013, p. 41.

20 In the context of Art. 11(2) of the Polish Civil Code, an annulment may be requested by either spouse. The public prosecutor has independent legal standing.

21 See the ruling of the Appellate Division, Court of Appeals, U IACr 464/92 OSA 1993, No. 6, item 44.

22 See the ruling of the Supreme Court of 7 April 1967, I CR 559/66, LEX No. 6135.

trend towards abolishing or reducing marriage restrictions for persons with mental disorders. The trend can be seen in Article 23(1) of the UN Convention on the Rights of Persons with Disabilities. The impediment discussed in Article 11 of the PFGC operates automatically, allowing no consideration of individual cases, and seems therefore to be excessive compared to the standards of protection offered by human rights conventions, particularly those relating to legally incapacitated persons with disabilities. It should also be noted that old-age dementia is not infrequently the cause of incapacitation, and preventing such persons from marrying affects their quality of life.[23] It should be kept in mind that marriage can fulfil numerous social functions, which can be carried out properly even if one of the spouses is fully incapacitated. This is evidenced by the fact that where incapacitation was declared in the course of marriage, it does not constitute a ground for the dissolution of marriage or divorce as long as the spouses continue to live together. The legal system therefore protects the durability of marriage, seeing it as having social and personal value. Why, then, should marriages of fully legally incapacitated people be disallowed from the outset, when it is not impossible that such a union could function properly in a specific case, as a source of assistance, support and protection for the person with mental illness, while also in all probability stabilising their factual and legal situation and benefiting their therapy? For the above reasons, it would be necessary to amend Article 11 of the PFGC in such a way as to enable courts to permit fully legally incapacitated persons to marry. Of course, it would be necessary to ensure that a person seeking to enter into marriage does so with sufficient discernment and awareness of the legal consequences to ensure that the consent given is voluntary, and not under any duress. These issues would have to be examined by the court making the decision to allow the marriage.

The impact of incapacitation on the rights and obligations of spouses depends to a large extent on the choice of representative for the incapacitated person. Pursuant to Article 176 of the PFGC, the guardian/curator of an incapacitated person should be that person's spouse, unless this is against that person's best interests. In the case of a functional marriage, it is natural for the court to appoint the spouse, who by acting as a guardian or curator also fulfils the marital duty of assistance (Article 23 of the PFGC). The fulfilment of spousal duties by acting as a guardian or curator then becomes a new element of cohabitation in the personal sphere (intensified care for the incapacitated person may foster spiritual community and an associated sense of attachment and trust) and in the material spheres (running a joint household and joint residence). This creates an advantage for the guardian spouse, whose sphere of decision-making extends into the previously inaccessible sphere of the incapacitated spouse's independence. For example, the guardian spouse may prohibit the ward from

[23] See Balwicka-Szczyrba, above n. 9, at pp. 210–212.

leaving the house,[24] which would not have been allowed before the incapacitation was declared. Incapacitation therefore entails a statutory derogation from the symmetrical distribution of marital rights and obligations between the spouses in line with the principle of equity. To the extent that a spouse can be expected to make an extra effort to act as a guardian/curator (this expectation being formulated by the principles of community life and the marital duty of assistance), the assistance is provided free of charge. However, the circumstances of the case, and in particular the significant burden on the spouse, particularly where it has a detrimental impact on his or her earning capacity, may sometimes justify the court awarding the spouse, at his or her request, a fee for exercising guardianship or curatorship over the spouse.[25]

On the other hand, if the marriage has broken down, it is not advisable for the court to appoint the spouse as a guardian.[26] As a rule, pursuant to Article 176 of the PFGC, the court shall appoint the incapacitated person's parent, and if such appointment is impossible, another close person or even a stranger.[27] Incidentally, it should be noted that a study of jurisprudential practice has revealed a number of irregularities in this regard, including failure to examine the ward's preferences as to the choice of a representative.[28] Appointment of a person other than the ward's spouse as a guardian or curator necessarily leads to legalisation of third-party interference with spousal relations. Depending on his or her powers, the representative may take over the management of the incapacitated person's assets, while also taking control of his or her income, which in turn determines the method of performance of marital obligations. If the payments made by the incapacitated spouse to meet the needs of the family go beyond minor day-to-day matters (as the ward retains legal capacity in that respect), they are controlled by the guardian or curator.[29] However, the

---

24 L. Ludwiczak, *Ubezwłasnowolnienie w polskim systemie prawnym*, LexisNexis, 2012, p. 76.

25 The performance of marital duties does not justify unlimited unpaid effort for the benefit of the spouse – for more detail, see M. Jadczak-Żebrowska, *Prawa i obowiązki małżonków*, Wolters Kluwer, 2017, pp. 124–129.

26 L. Kociucki, *Zdolność do czynności prawnych osób dorosłych i jej ograniczenia*, C.H. Beck, 2011, p. 215. Studies of court practice have shown that courts base their knowledge of the state of the spouses' marriage only on the declaration of the spouse volunteering to be a guardian, a practice which deserves criticism – thus in I. Kleniewska, 'Praktyka sądowa w zakresie ustanowienia i nadzoru opieki dla osoby ubezwłasnowolnionej całkowicie' (2008) No. 4 *Prawo w działaniu* 111–112.

27 Further criteria concerning the choice of a guardian/curator are set out in Art. 149 of the PFGC. The interpretation of these provisions suggests that a stranger can be chosen only if there is no suitable candidate among the incapacitated person's next of kin or other relatives.

28 Jankowska's research has shown that in only 57% of cases was any effort made to find out the preferences of the person for whom curatorship was sought; such preferences were given any consideration only in 10% of cases: M. Jankowska, *Kuratela nad osobą ubezwłasnowolnioną częściowo, Instytut Wymiaru Sprawiedliwości* 2018, pp. 22 and 29.

29 In the event of a dispute concerning alimony obligations designed to meet the needs of the family, and in particular of the children, the court will award maintenance under Art. 27 of the PFGC.

guardian/curator cannot act arbitrarily and is obliged to obtain the authorisation of the guardianship court in all major matters concerning the ward (Article 156 of the PFGC).

A grant of incapacitation does not relieve spouses of non-financial marital obligations, such as living together, marital assistance (including in personal matters) and fidelity. One of the spouses having a mental illness of makes him or her vulnerable, requiring a higher level of care from the other spouse in areas such as health, recovery and treatment.[30] On the other hand, the incapacitated person's abnormal behaviour caused by mental impairments, as well as communication problems, may cause conflicts between the spouses and lead to marital breakdown, and consequently cause one of the parties to apply for divorce or request the court to award separation. It should be stressed that acts committed by the incapacitated person in a state of diminished accountability as a result of a mental impairment cannot justify assigning fault in divorce proceedings.[31] In addition, the judicial assessment of the other spouse's compliance with marital obligations must take into account the totality of the circumstances, including unlawful and provocative behaviour of the unaccountable spouse, which may justify separation from the spouse and may clear the applicant spouse of any fault for ending the marriage. In such situations, the termination of cohabitation is often perceived as a defensive action by the spouse who cannot bear to live under constant stress and a sense of danger from the incapacitated person.[32]

The determination of incapacitation (full or partial) means that, under Article 53 of the PFGC, a mandatory marital regime of property separation is established at the time that the judgment becomes final and binding. The mandatory character of the regime means that it cannot be changed or revoked by the spouses and remains effective towards third parties. This particular solution addresses potential problems that could arise under a community property regime as a result of the incapacitated spouse's lack of or diminished capacity for legal acts. The property separation regime is based on a simple separation of assets of the spouses, eliminating the need for cooperation, and minimising the risk of mutual violation of property interests.[33] Besides, a mentally disabled spouse could by his or her irresponsible actions cause damage to the joint property, and therefore the dissolution of the community of property protects the other spouse's interests.[34] However, as mentioned before, if the other spouse has been appointed as the incapacitated spouse's guardian or curator, he or she

30 See T. Smyczyński in T. Smyczyński (ed.), *System Prawa Prywatnego. T. 12. Prawo rodzinne i opiekuńcze*, C.H. Beck, 2003, p. 821.

31 Z. Krzemiński, *Separacja*, Wydawnictwo Zakamycze, 2002, pp. 36–37.

32 See the ruling of the Polish Supreme Court of 18 March 1999, I CKN 1050/97, Orzecznictwo Sądu Najwyższego. Izba Cywilna OSNC 1999/10/177.

33 M. Nazar in J. Ignatowicz and M. Nazar, *Prawo rodzinne*, LexisNexis, 2016, p. 333.

34 M. Sychowicz, 'Przymusowy małżeński ustrój majątkowy' (2006) No. 1 *Przegląd Sądowy* 24.

is able to influence the ward's property affairs by taking over the management of his or her assets or by exercising control over his or her actions performed. This situation is potentially threatening to the incapacitated spouse's property interests, as he or she is dependent on the actions of the spouse. This threat is to be counteracted by supervision of the guardianship court over the exercise of guardianship or curatorship, allowing the court to intervene to protect the interests of the incapacitated spouse by issuing appropriate orders, and in extreme cases, by dismissing the guardian or curator on the basis of Article 169(2) of the PCC. However, there is no doubt that the other spouse can exert greater influence on the financial situation of the incapacitated spouse than was the case before incapacitation, which, in the event of a conflict of interests, – may result in abuses that are very difficult to discover, if only because of the high degree of interconnectedness of joint affairs (shared household, raising children, holidays together, etc.), of which the court often remains unaware.

It is noteworthy that incapacitation does not result in inability to inherit, nor does it modify the rules of succession between spouses. An incapacitated spouse whose condition prevents him or her from engaging in paid work may additionally count on a higher amount of inheritance from the deceased spouse (Article 991(1) of the PCC).[35] Even if the incapacitated spouse has committed, in a state of insanity, a breach of family obligations or rules of social conduct, it is not possible for the other spouse to disinherit him or her in the will by depriving him or her of the right to his or her statutory share (*legitim*).[36]

In sum, it should be emphasised that the assistance provided by a guardian or a curator may constitute a basic tool to protect the interests of an incapacitated person, provided that this function is performed by a person who is strongly committed to and guided by the interests of the incapacitated person. If a guardianship relationship of this kind is established between spouses, its proper functioning is directly affected by the degree to which the marriage functions properly. The more conflicts or other signs of marital breakdown between spouses there are, the lower the level of legal security provided to the incapacitated person by the spouse acting as a representative. In this case, the court should use such a solution with caution, and if it does, it should apply increased supervision (e.g. through periodic community interviews by a probation officer, rather than through the system of guardian/curator reports often used in practice, consisting of the representative's declarations, the credibility of which depends on the confidence in the representative's reliability). It should be noted that too

---

35 A person who is permanently incapacitated is entitled to a reserved share equal to two-thirds of the value of the share of the estate which would be due to that person in the event of statutory succession. This is an exception to the rule according to which the statutory share (*legitim*) is half of the value of that share.

36 G. Wolak, 'Glosa do wyroku Sądu Apelacyjneg z dn. 15.04.2015, I ACa 985/14' (2015) No. 9 *Rejent* 118.

little flexibility is available in terms of the legal effects of guardianship, including limited scope for the court to define the representative's powers. These limits make it difficult for the courts to adequately safeguard the interests of the ward. Another problem is how to properly choose a representative when the choice of a spouse, who is the first candidate for this function under Article 176 of the PFGC, raises concerns, due to, for example, conflicts between spouses. If such spouses are still cohabiting, appointing a third party as a guardian/curator is problematic, because of the potential for outside interference with the sphere of marital cohabitation, marital maintenance obligations and management of the household. Such an appointment could therefore lead to an escalation of conflicts, a breakdown of marital relations and further deterioration of the incapacitated spouse's situation. If it were possible to adapt the representative's powers to the specific case or to appoint a representative for a limited period of time instead of the current rigid system, which in the case of full legal incapacitation adopts an 'all-or-nothing' approach, the protection of mentally disabled people would be strengthened, especially when none of the guardian candidates appears to be satisfactory and the decision taken by the court is in fact a choice of the lesser evil.

6. EFFECTS OF GUARDIANSHIP ON THE RELATIONSHIP BETWEEN PARENTS AND CHILDREN

In filiation law, a severe mental impairment underlying full legal incapacitation is a factor that modifies the running of the time limit for bringing an action in three categories of civil cases: actions to disestablish maternity, actions by the mother's husband to disestablish paternity, and actions to establish the nullity of an acknowledgment of paternity. Article 64 of the PFGC, which is applicable *mutatis mutandis* in the other cases mentioned above, provides that if the husband of the mother suffered from a mental impairment during the time limit for bringing an action to disestablish paternity,[37] the action may be brought by his legal representative within one year from the date it is established, or – should the legal representative learn that the child is not the mother's husband's offspring after the expiry of that time limit – one year from the day on which he or she learned of it. Bringing an action regarding the child's origin is a 'matter of primary importance' concerning the ward; therefore, the guardian must

[37] The doctrine rightly postulates its broader interpretation justified by the aim of the legislation: protection should also cover cases in which a person entitled to bring an action was completely incapacitated before he or she learned about the birth of the child. Thus in K. Piasecki in K. Piasecki (ed.), *Kodeks rodzinny i opiekuńczy. Komentarz*, LexisNexis, 2011, p. 666.

obtain the court's permission to do so (Article 156 of the PFGC).[38] Because the guardian of the mother's incapacitated husband will not always use his or her entitlement to bring an action, especially when the husband's guardian happens to be his wife, who may not be interested in denying the paternity of the child borne by her, section 2 of the provision in question allows the action to proceed at the husband's request within a year from the repeal of the guardianship, and if the husband learns that the child is not his biological offspring after the expiry of that period, a year from the day when he learned thereof.[39] It should be emphasised that the protection of the right to correct determination of marital status provided for in the above-mentioned regulations is effective only if the person entitled to bring an action suffers from a severe mental impairment, warranting total legal incapacitation. The remedy is not available to a partially incapacitated spouse. A partially incapacitated person retains the right to bring an action in the cases discussed above (Article 453^1 of the PCCP) and is not represented by a guardian[40] in this area.

The legal effects of (full and partial) incapacitation include the creation of a legal impediment to the exercise of those familial and custodial roles that require full legal capacity. When the decision on incapacitation becomes final and binding, the parental authority of the incapacitated person ceases, and if there is no other parent with parental authority over the child, the guardianship court establishes custody of the child (Article 94 of the PFGC). However, this effect does not exclude the exercise of the right to contact the child, which, in a situation where the family continues to live together, is exercised naturally or, where they have separate residences, is determined by the decision of the guardianship court. Article 96(2) of the PFGC allows a parent who does not have full legal capacity to participate in the day-to-day care and upbringing of the child, unless the guardianship court decides otherwise for the sake of the child's welfare.[41] If a guardian is appointed for the child, the guardian is required to inform the parents about decisions in important matters concerning the minor (Article 158 of the PFGC), to avoid conflicting actions on the part of the parent and of the guardian. However, the type of mental impairment the parent has and its negative impact on the child may become the basis for limiting or even

---

38 More broadly in M. Domański in K. Osajda (ed.), *Kodeks rodzinny i opiekuńczy. Komentarz*, C.H. Beck, 2017, pp. 962–963. The freedom of a guardian to bring an action to disestablish paternity without seeking permission from the court is advocated by H. Haak and A. Haak-Trzuskawska, *Pokrewieństwo i powinowactwo*, C.H. Beck, 2019, p. 75.

39 If a person entitled to bring an action has not been fully legally incapacitated despite the existence of grounds to do so, he or she may bring an action within one year from the date when his or her mental disorder ceases (Art. 65 of the PFGC).

40 See M. Domański, above n. 38, at p. 666.

41 This was legislated in the PFGC in 2009, primarily with a view to strengthening the position of underage mothers who do not have parental authority but who in fact raise their children. As we can see, this regulation also serves to legalise the exercise of custody over children by incapacitated parents.

prohibiting contact with the incapacitated parent, based on a court decision (Article 113–113[23] of the PFGC), but this can be changed or repealed when the circumstances change. It should be added that incapacitated persons cannot act as guardians, curators or foster parents, nor can they apply for adoption, because they do not meet the requirement of having full legal capacity.

The opposite situation, in which an underage child under parental authority becomes legally incapacitated, may occur only with regard to children who are at least 13 years of age. The scope of parental authority is then reduced by operation of law, since the limitations to which the guardian is subject apply (Article 108 of the PFGC). What we are dealing with here is a statutory departure from the principle of family autonomy, according to which the functioning of the family is not subject, in principle, to supervision by the public authorities. As a result of the child's incapacitation, the exercise of parental authority is subject to the supervision of the court and the scope of parental independence shrinks, as parents have to obtain permission from the guardianship court in every important matter concerning the child. These restrictions are justified by the need to protect the welfare of the child, whose incapacitation removes the possibility of acquiring limited capacity for legal acts, making his or her affairs almost entirely subject to the authority of the parents.[42] These restrictions are designed to prevent the excessive extension of the parents' authority as a result of the child's incapacitation, causing the parents to acquire the powers of a guardian.[43]

If the parents do not have parental authority, another person is appointed the guardian of the child, with consideration given to the priority criteria set out in Article 149 of the PFGC. However, the lack of parental authority does not automatically affect visitation rights, meaning that parents are entitled (and at the same time obliged) to exercise visitation rights with the child, as provided for in the agreement executed between the parents and the guardian, and in the absence of such an agreement, as decided by the guardianship court and in cooperation with the child's guardian.[44] However, the legal effects of full legal incapacitation on the child's relationship with his or her parents change when the child reaches the age of majority. In a resolution of 17 May 2018, the Polish Supreme Court ruled that the parents of an adult child who is fully legally incapacitated due to mental disability and for whom a guardian has been appointed are not entitled to demand that the guardianship court decide on the

---

42 H. Dolecki in H. Dolecki and T. Sokołowski (eds.), *Kodeks rodzinny i opiekuńczy. Komentarz*, Wolters Kluwer, 2013, pp. 723–724.

43 The advisability of introducing these restrictions is questioned by J. Słyk in K.Osajda (ed.) *Kodeks rodzinny i opiekuńczy. Commentary*, C.H. Beck, 2017, p. 1287.

44 Pursuant to Art. 113[1](2) of the PFGC, the PFGC provisions on the establishment of visitation rights with children apply *mutatis mutandis* where the child is in the care of a third party.

method of exercising visitation rights.[45] Forced regulation of visitation rights by a court decision cannot be applied to an adult who has the personal right to freely form his or her family relationships. The literature, however, rightly points out that if an incapacitated person who is interested in visiting his or her family members were to be obstructed by a guardian acting arbitrarily, the guardianship court could intervene considering the ward's welfare, by issuing an order under Article 168 of the PFGC to regulate the method of exercising visitation rights.[46]

7. CONCLUSION

The institution of incapacitation, founded on noble motives of supporting and safeguarding the interests of people with mental impairments, is today increasingly seen as a means of oppression of these people. However, there is no denying the need for an institution that can be a mechanism for representation, support and assistance for people suffering from severe mental impairments. Such an institution should be flexible in the sense that the scope of its operation should be determined by the court on a case-by-case basis in line with individual needs. It should also meet other criteria specified in Article 12 of the UN Convention on the Rights of Persons with Disabilities, which the current institution of incapacitation fails to do. Specifically, it should respect the will of the disabled person, be applied for the shortest possible period of time, and be reviewed regularly by the court. Therefore, we advocate either for a thorough overhaul of the institution of incapacitation or its replacement with a new legal construct (e.g. an institution of care). Such a reform should consider the existing family ties of the person with disabilities in order to strengthen and protect these ties, while also – subject to a careful consideration of his or her mental condition – allowing marriage, as long as a proper grasp and understanding of the legal consequences is demonstrated. Placing people with mental impairments in a position of family responsibility should be part of their recovery plan, and the expected new regulations should facilitate that.

---

45 III CZP 11/18, Orzecznictwo Sądów Polskich, 2019, Nos. 7–8, item 70.

46 T. Justyński, 'Glosa do uchw. SN of 17.05.2018, III CZP 11/18', Orzecznictwo Sądów Polskich, 2019, Nos. 7–8, item 70.

SEYCHELLES

GROUND(S) FOR DIVORCE IN SEYCHELLES

Jamil Ddamulira Mujuzi*

Résumé

Aux Seychelles, le divorce est régi par la Partie II du Matrimonial Causes Act. Le 4 janvier 2021, le Code civil des Seychelles (le « Code civil ») est entré en vigueur. La Partie II du Matrimonial Causes Act a été codifiée aux articles 230 à 237 du Code civil, bien que celui-ci n'abroge pas le Matrimonial Causes Act. Avant janvier 2021, la Cour suprême s'appuyait sur le Matrimonial Causes Act pour traiter des demandes de divorce. Depuis janvier 2021, la Cour suprême se fonde désormais

* I am grateful to Judge Samia Andre (Supreme Court of Seychelles) and to Ms Sylvia Kamanja (Senior Legal Researcher, Supreme Court and Court of Appeal of Seychelles) for the comments on the earlier draft of this chapter. I am also grateful to Judge Andre for sending me some of the cases I relied on to write the chapter. The usual caveats apply.

sur le Code civil ou le Matrimonial Causes Act. Dans cet article, l'auteur analyse la jurisprudence de la Cour suprême pour montrer comment celle-ci interprète les causes de divorce et l'obligation de conciliation préalable avant dissolution du mariage. L'auteur démontre, notamment, que la Cour suprême n'est pas cohérente dans son interprétation de certaines causes de divorce. Dans certaines affaires, la cause de divorce qui fonde la dissolution du mariage n'est pas claire et la Cour n'est guère plus cohérente au sujet de l'obligation des parties de se soumettre à une tentative de conciliation préalable au divorce.

1. INTRODUCTION

In Seychelles, divorce is governed by Part II of the Matrimonial Causes Act. On 4 January 2021, the Civil Code of Seychelles Act (Civil Code) came into force. Part II of the Matrimonial Causes Act was reproduced verbatim as Articles 230–237 of the Civil Code although the Civil Code does not repeal the Matrimonial Causes Act.[1] Before January 2021, the Supreme Court relied on the Matrimonial Causes Act to deal with divorce petitions. Since January 2021, the Supreme Court has relied on the Civil Code. The cases which were decided under the Matrimonial Causes Act are applicable when the Court is applying the Civil Code. Part II of the Matrimonial Causes Act and Articles 230–237 of the Civil Code provide for applications for divorce, reconciliation, grant of divorce, rescission of a conditional order of divorce, supplemental provisions regarding evidence of breakdown, protection of the respondent in cases of filing for divorce in certain circumstances, relief for the respondent in divorce proceedings and the prohibition of appeals in case of an absolute order of divorce. The purpose of this chapter is to illustrate how the Supreme Court in Seychelles, the only court with the jurisdiction to grant a divorce, has interpreted the conditions which must be met before a divorce is granted. The author also deals with the issue of reconciliation. A study of the case law from the Supreme Court shows, inter alia, that in some cases the Court has granted divorce when it lacked the jurisdiction to do so (the petitioners were neither domiciled nor habitually resident in Seychelles), that in most cases the Court does not require petitioners to prove that they attempted reconciliation before filing for divorce, and that in some cases the ground on which a divorce was granted is not clear.

1 It is anticipated that the Matrimonial Causes Act will ultimately be repealed.

2. GROUND(S) FOR DIVORCE

Section 4 of the Matrimonial Causes Act[2] provides that:

> (1) Subject to this Act, a party to a marriage may petition the court for divorce on the ground that the marriage has irretrievably broken down because –
> (a) the respondent has committed adultery and the petitioner finds it intolerable to live with the respondent;
> (b) the respondent has behaved in a way that the petitioner cannot reasonably be expected to live with the respondent;
> (c) the respondent has deserted the petitioner for a continuous period of at least 2 years immediately preceding the presentation of the petition; or
> (d) the petitioner and the respondent have lived apart for a continuous period of at least 1 year immediately preceding the presentation of the petition and the respondent consents to the grant of the divorce.
>
> (2) Subject to subsection (3), a party to a marriage may not petition for divorce within one year of the date of the marriage.
>
> (3) The Court may, on an application, grant leave for a petition for divorce within the one year referred to in subsection (2) if the court is satisfied that the petitioner has suffered exceptional hardship or the respondent is exceptionally depraved.

Section 4 of the Matrimonial Causes Act is reproduced verbatim in Article 230 of the Civil Code.[3] However, the Civil Code adds another ground for divorce under Article 230(1)(e) to the effect that 'the petitioner and the respondent have lived apart for a continuous period of five years or more.' Since there is no contradiction between the two provisions, section 4 is not affected by the coming into force of the Civil Code.[4] It also implies that should the Matrimonial Causes Act be repealed, case law developed under section 4 will be equally relevant under Article 230 of the Civil Code.[5] Since January 2021, the Supreme Court has relied either on the Civil Code[6] or on both the Civil Code and Matrimonial

2 Matrimonial Causes Act Chapter 124 (1 September 1992).

3 Civil Code of Seychelles Act, Act 1 of 2021.

4 Section 4 of the Civil Code provides that '[u]nless otherwise provided expressly or by necessary implication, where there is an inconsistency between a provision of the Code and a provision in any other enactment, the provision in the Code prevails.'

5 It appears that in the future 'all civil related issues' will be included in the Civil Code. It is therefore likely that the Matrimonial Causes Act will be repealed sooner than later. See Civil Code of Seychelles Bill, Bill No. 13 of 2018 (objects and reasons).

6 *Germain Christian Francoise v. Cyrillia Francoise* (DC 133/2021) [2021] SCSC 879; *Ketty Annabel Tirant v. Gerard Edward Tirant* (DC 153/2021) [2022] SCSC 205 (10 March 2022); *Damoo v. Damoo* (DC 160/22) [2022] SCSC 172 (1 March 2022) (the Court relied on the Civil Code only to dissolve the marriages on the ground of adultery); *May Paule Dubel nee Marguerite v. Daniel Dubel* (DC 123/2021) [2022] SCSC 161 (25 February 2022) (ground of separation); *Marie-Helene Bernadette Hoareau (born Mousbe) v. Shawn Hugton Emmanuel Hoareau* (DC 169/2021) [2021] SCSC 184.

Causes Act[7] when dealing with divorce petitions. This chapter discusses cases decided under both the Matrimonial Causes Act and the Civil Code and makes the following observations about section 4 (the arguments made here also apply with equal force to Article 230 of the Civil Code). Firstly, the Supreme Court is divided on how many grounds for divorce section 4 recognises. In some cases, it held that there is only one ground for divorce – the marriage has irretrievably broken down. However, that ground could be proved by one of the four factors mentioned under section 4(1)(a)–(d).[8] In other cases, it has held that section 4 provides for different grounds of divorce, each of which leads to the irretrievable breakdown of the marriage.[9] The first interpretation – that there is one ground for divorce (irretrievable breakdown of the marriage) which has to be proved by one of the facts enumerated in section (4)(1)(a)–(d) – has been followed in other jurisdictions with similar legislation.[10] A divorce petition which does not disclose any of the grounds under section 4(1) will be dismissed.[11] As a general rule, before any person petitions for divorce, he or she should have been married for at least one year. However, a court will grant a divorce if the marriage is less than one year old if 'the petitioner has suffered exceptional hardship or the respondent is exceptionally depraved.' Section 4 is applicable to marriages contracted abroad as long as the parties are domiciled or resident in Seychelles.[12] Section 4 has to be read with section 3, which provides for the jurisdiction of the Supreme Court in divorce matters. It is to the effect that:

> (1) Subject to subsection (2), the Supreme Court shall have jurisdiction in relation to matrimonial causes on an application of a party to a marriage who, at the date when proceedings are begun –
> (a) is domiciled in Seychelles; or
> (b) has been habitually resident in Seychelles throughout the period of one year ending with the date when proceedings are begun.

7 See e.g. in *Gabriel v. Gabriel* (DC 27/2021) [2021] SCSC 853 the Court refers to both Acts but the petition is decided on the basis of the Matrimonial Causes Act.

8 *JM (nee A) v. NM* (DV 148/2016) [2018] SCSC 503 (28 May 2018), para. 4; *Gabriel v. Gabriel* (DC 27/2021) [2021] SCSC 853, para. 30.

9 *Ernesta v. Ernesta* (DS 119/2018) [2020] SCSC 161 (28 February 2020), para. 1.

10 See e.g. *Donnelly v. Donnelly* [2002] NIFam 16 (26 June 2002) (High Court of Justice in Northern Ireland Family Division); *CKF v. LHL* [2016] HKFC 128; FCMC 17031/2014 (28 October 2016) (Family Court, Hong Kong); *Anthony Morgan v. Violet Morgan* [2013] ECarSC 172 (28 June 2013) (Eastern Caribbean Supreme Court); *Price & Underwood* (Divorce Appeal) [2009] FamCAFC 127 (14 July 2009) (Family Court of Australia).

11 *DL v. EL* (DS 163/2016) [2017] SCSC 17 (18 January 2017); *Tania Beverly Banane nee Sicobo v. Giovani Hugh Banane* (85 of 2011) [2011] SCSC 97 (1 December 2011); *Gabriel v. Gabriel* (DC 27/2021) [2021] SCSC 853.

12 *Ragedonge v. Ragedonge* (103 of 2007) [2008] SCSC 70 (25 March 2008) (the marriage was contracted in the United Kingdom); *IP v. LP* (145 of 2005) [2006] SCSC 55 (26 July 2006) (the marriage was contracted in Germany); *Albert v. Albert* (MA 39/2019 (arising in DV 97/2018)) [2020] SCSC 618 (1 September 2020) (Mauritius); *Capet v. Capet nee Betoko-Doo* (69 of 2004) [2004] SCSC 20 (2 July 2004) (France).

(2) The Supreme Court shall have jurisdiction in respect of proceedings –
  (a) under section 25 if a party to the marriage –
    (i) is domiciled in Seychelles; or
    (ii) is resident in Seychelles at the date when proceedings are begun;
  (b) for nullity, if a party to the marriage –
    (i) is domiciled in Seychelles; or
    (ii) has been habitually resident in Seychelles throughout the period of the year ending with the date when proceedings are begun;
  (c) in relation to a relevant child, if the child is in Seychelles at the date when proceedings are begun.

In simple terms, for the Court to have jurisdiction over the matter, the petitioner has to be either domiciled or habitually resident in Seychelles. Since the Act does not define the two concepts, the Supreme Court has explained in detail what they mean.[13] Article 10 of the Civil Code has defined the two concepts.[14] The Court held that where the petitioner fails to provide evidence to show that Seychelles is his or her country of domicile or habitual residence, the application will be dismissed.[15] What matters is that the petitioner is domiciled or habitually resides in Seychelles, even if the respondent is domiciled and habitually resides in a foreign country.[16]

Although in most cases the Supreme Court will only deal with a divorce matter after highlighting that either the petitioners or both parties are domiciled or are habitually resident in Seychelles, in a few cases the Court appears to have dissolved marriages even though the facts showed that neither party was domiciled nor habitually resident in Seychelles. In *Stepanov v. Drahuradova*,[17] the parties celebrated their marriage in Seychelles but at the time of the divorce petition, which was filed by the petitioner's lawyer on her behalf, the parties

---

13 See generally *Dituro v. Dituro* (DC 136/2014) [2016] SCSC 169 (3 March 2016), para. 6, the Court referred to s. 3 of the Act and held that '[i]n order for the Court to entertain the present Petition therefore, the Petitioner must satisfy the Court that he is either domiciled in Seychelles or has been habitually resident in Seychelles throughout the year preceding the filing of the Petition.'

14 Article 10 of the Civil Code of Seychelles Act defines these two concepts. It is to the effect that '(1) "Domicile" means the country of habitual residence of a person. (2) Habitual residence is a matter of fact determined by an assessment of all the relevant circumstances. (3) Without limiting its meaning, "relevant circumstances" includes (a) the place which is the centre of the person's interests; (b) the place of usual residence of the person; (c) whether the purpose of residence in the country is temporary or settled; (d) the length of time a person has been physically present in the country; (e) how well the person has integrated into the particular country, taking into account factors such as whether the person has social contacts in that country, is adapted to the local culture, or speaks the local language. (4) Every person has one habitual residence. (5) Loss of habitual residence occurs only after a new habitual residence has been acquired. (6) It is presumed that the habitual residence of a ward is that of the guardian.' See *Gabriel v. Gabriel* (DC 27/2021) [2021] SCSC 853, paras. 25–26.

15 *Dituro v. Dituro* (DC 136/2014) [2016] SCSC 169 (3 March 2016).

16 *LES v. Born S* (136 of 2010) [2010] SCSC 113 (9 November 2010). See also *Singh (nee Lukas) v. Singh* [2022] SCSC 242.

17 *Stepanov v. Drahuradova* (86 of 2007) [2008] SCSC 60 (3 February 2008).

were 'both employed, domiciled and resident in Bratislava, Slovak Republic' and had 'lived apart for a continuous period of at least one year immediately preceding the presentation of this petition.'[18] The Court did not refer to section 3 but dissolved the marriage. It appears that the Court based its decision on the fact that the marriage was celebrated in Seychelles. In another case, the Court dissolved the marriage even though it noted that the petitioner, a Seychellois, 'was domiciled and presently residing in Italy' but the respondent was residing in Seychelles.[19] The Court also did not refer to section 3 of the Act. It appears that, in this case, the Court assumed jurisdiction on the basis that the petitioner was a Seychellois. In another case, the Court, before dissolving the marriage, observed that the petitioner was a foreign national 'and a temporary resident of Seychelles', whereas the respondent was a Seychellois who was domiciled and resided in Seychelles.[20] The Court will waive the residence requirement if there are compelling reasons.[21] A divorce petition may be heard *ex parte* if the respondent consents to the divorce[22] or refuses to come to court.[23] What follows is a discussion of each of the factors under section 4(1).

2.1. ADULTERY

Under section 4(1)(a), the Court will grant a divorce if 'the respondent has committed adultery and the petitioner finds it intolerable to live with the respondent.' In this case, the petitioner has to prove two facts: (1) that the respondent committed adultery and (2) that the petitioner finds it intolerable to live with him or her. In other words, the mere fact that the petitioner has committed adultery is not enough for the Court to grant a divorce. In addition to proving adultery, the petitioner should also prove that he or she finds it intolerable to live with the respondent. This approach is different from that followed in some African countries, such as Namibia,[24] Kenya[25] and

18 Ibid, at p. 1.

19 *Michel v. Michel* (DC 118/2014) [2014] SCSC 367 (25 September 2014), para. 2 (divorce on the ground of separation).

20 *WNK v. BAAK Nee I* (150 of 2006) [2006] SCSC 84 (30 November 2006), p. 1.

21 See e.g. in *Nancy (Born Adela) v. Nancy* (31 of 2007) [2007] SCSC 34 (12 August 2007), the petitioner was based in Italy and she could not travel to Seychelles because she had overstayed in Italy. In *Humphrey v. Humphrey* (139 of 2004) [2005] SCSC 27 (25 January 2005) the parties were domiciled in Seychelles but lived in England.

22 *JWH v. RH nee C* (2 of 2005) [2005] SCSC 45 (31 July 2005) (in this case the respondent was outside Seychelles and informed her lawyer that she had consented to the divorce under s. 4(1)(b)).

23 *L (nee R) v. L* (133 of 2004) [2005] SCSC 37 (8 June 2005).

24 S. 59(1) of the Recognition of Certain Marriages Act, 1991 (Act 18 of 1991) provides that '[e]ither spouse may seek the divorce on the grounds of adultery committed by the other spouse.'

25 Marriage Act, No. 4 of 2014 ss. 65(a) (Christian marriage), 66(2)(a) (civil marriage), 69(1)(a) (customary marriage) and 70(d) (Hindu marriage).

Tanzania,[26] where adultery on its own is a ground of divorce. Section 4(1)(a) has to be read with section 8(1) of the Act, which provides that 'for the purposes of Section 4(1)(a)' of the Act:

(a) a party to a marriage may not rely on the adultery of the other party if, after the adultery became known to that party, the parties have lived together for a period of, or periods which together amount to, more than 6 months;
(b) the court shall, in determining whether the petitioner finds it intolerable to live with the respondent, disregard the fact that the parties to the marriage have lived together for not more than 6 months after the party came to know of the adultery of the other party.

A combined reading of sections 4(1)(a) and 8(1)(a) shows that for a person to rely on adultery, he or she has to initiate the divorce proceedings in not more than six months of becoming aware of that fact, if both parties live together. However, the use of the word 'may' instead of 'shall' implies that even in cases where the petitioner has lived with the respondent for more than six months after becoming aware of the adultery, he or she may still initiate divorce proceedings on the basis of adultery. In this case, he or she may be required to explain the basis for the delay. Otherwise, the delay could be interpreted to mean that the person found it 'tolerable' to live with the respondent after becoming aware of the adultery. In other words, there is a presumption that he or she has found it tolerable to live with respondent after becoming aware of the adultery. However, if the divorce proceedings are initiated when the parties have lived together for less than six months after the petitioner became aware of the adultery, he or she is presumed to have found it intolerable to live with the respondent because of the adultery. In this case, he or she is not required to explain why he or she continued living with the respondent after becoming aware of the adultery. This is so because he or she is still in the 'grace period' of six months in which to file a divorce.

There are cases in which divorce has been granted on the basis of adultery. These have included instances where the respondent 'left the matrimonial home and is now living with adultery with another man',[27] where the respondent gave birth to a child out of wedlock,[28] and where the petitioner left the matrimonial

26 S. 107(2)(a) of the Law of Marriage Act (Chapter 29) provides that a court may grant a decree of divorce in the case of 'adultery committed by the respondent, particularly when more than one act of adultery has been committed or when adulterous association is continued despite protest.'

27 *Jean-Paul Leon v. Marie-Eve Leon* (DC 189/2014) [2015] SCSC 45, para. 2.

28 *Fa Lin v. Xiao Shan Zhuang* (DC 140/2014) [2015] SCSC 490; *Margarette Lucie Almage (Nee Camille) v. Steve Atoine Almage* (DC 135/2015) [2015] SCSC 566; *Terry Maxime Marie v. Marie Sabrina Marie* (DC 118/2015) [2015] SCSC 24; *Damoo v. Damoo* (DC 160/22) [2022] SCSC 172 (1 March 2022).

home and the respondent is living there with another woman in an adulterous relationship.[29] A marriage can be dissolved on the ground of adultery even if the adulterous act was committed outside Seychelles.[30] A divorce can be granted on the ground of adultery if one of the parties admits that he or she is having an extramarital affair.[31]

In some cases, the petitions are not clear on what ground the divorce was granted. For example, in *Fa Lin v. Xiao Shan Zhuang*,[32] the petitioner submitted that the marriage had irretrievably broken down because 'they have live[d] apart for a continuous period of more than 3 years and also the respondent has deserted the matrimonial home since 2012 … [and] the Respondent has committed adultery with another man and has given birth to a child.'[33] The Court dissolved the marriage without clarifying which of the above four grounds was relied on.[34] The Court has followed a similar approach in other cases.[35] It can be inferred from these cases that the marriage was either dissolved on the basis of adultery or on another ground such as desertion or on both grounds. In other words, a marriage can be dissolved on more than one ground. For example, in *Lindy Achille Laporte Nee Dine v. Arsen Benjamin Laporte*[36] the Court dissolved the marriage because the respondent admitted that he had committed adultery and also because of his misbehaviour (cruelty towards the petitioner).[37] In some instances, the Court will dissolve a marriage on the basis of adultery even if the respondent disputes the allegations of adultery and argues that he or she still loves the petitioner. What matters is that the Court finds the petitioner to be a reliable witness.[38]

As mentioned above, for a person to succeed on the ground of adultery, he or she must also plead or prove that he or she finds it intolerable to live with the respondent. Failure to do so will lead to the dismissal of the petition by the court.[39] The Court does not often ask the petitioner to explain why he or she finds it intolerable to live with the respondent. However, this can be inferred

---

29 *Argette Denise Gobine v. Joseph Thomas Gobine* (DC 40/2015) [2015] SCSC 153.

30 See *Fa Lin v. Xiao Shan Zhuang* (DC 140/2014) [2015] SCSC 490 (the adulterous acts were committed in China).

31 *Lindy Achille Laporte Nee Dine v. Arsen Benjamin Laporte* (DC 108/2014) [2016] SCSC 340; *JM (*nee *A) v. NM* (DV 148/2016) [2018] SCSC 503 (28 May 2018), para. 9.

32 See *Fa Lin v. Xiao Shan Zhuang* (DC 140/2014) [2015] SCSC 490.

33 Ibid, at para. 2.

34 Ibid, at paras. 3–4.

35 *Margarette Lucie Almage (Nee Camille) v. Steve Atoine Almage* (DC 135/2015) [2015] SCSC 566; *Terry Maxime Marie v. Marie Sabrina Marie* (DC 118/2015) [2015] SCSC 24.

36 *Lindy Achille Laporte Nee Dine v. Arsen Benjamin Laporte* (DC 108/2014) [2016] SCSC 340.

37 See also *Mr Francois Hoareau v. Mrs Maribel Hoareau Bualan (Nee Anog)* (DC 25/2016) [2016] SCSC 706 (the marriage was dissolved because of misbehaviour, adultery and separation).

38 *Phyllis Marie Lena Confait (Nee Henriette) v. Patrick Hensley Confait* (DC 124/2015) [2016] SCSC 127.

39 *Gabriel v. Gabriel* (DC 27/2021) [2021] SCSC 853, para. 34.

from the facts of the case, for example if the petitioner informs the Court that he or she stopped having sexual intercourse with the respondent after becoming aware of the adulterous conduct,[40] or if the petitioner cannot tolerate the respondent playing an active role in the life of the child who was born out of wedlock and always being in the company of the woman with whom he was having an adulterous relationship.[41]

2.2. MISBEHAVIOUR

Under section 4(1)(b), a court can grant divorce if 'the respondent has behaved in a way that the petitioner cannot reasonably be expected to live with the respondent.' Section 4(1)(b) has to be read with section 8(2), which provides that:

> For the purposes of Section 4(1)(b), the court shall, in determining whether the petitioner cannot reasonably be expected to live with the respondent disregard the fact that the parties to a marriage have lived together for a period of, or periods which together amount to, not more than 6 months after the date of the occurrence of the last incident relied on by the petitioner and held by the court to support the petitioner's petition.

The following observations should be made about the combined reading of sections 4(1)(b) and 8(2). First, it is for the Court to determine whether or not the respondent's behaviour supports the petitioner's argument that the respondent 'behaved in a way that the petitioner cannot reasonably be expected' to live with him or her. If the Court is not satisfied that the incident complained about meets that threshold, it will dismiss the application. Second, if the parties in the marriage have lived together for a period of six months or less after the last incident relied on by the petitioner for the divorce under section 4(1)(b), the Court is obliged to exclude it as a factor in determining whether or not petitioner 'cannot reasonably be expected to live with the respondent'. In other words, the fact that the petitioner lived with the respondent for a period of not more than six months after the incident being relied on for a divorce cannot be invoked as a ground to argue that the petitioner is presumed to be reasonably expected to live with the respondent. Thirdly and related to the foregoing, in determining whether the petitioner cannot reasonably be expected to live with the respondent, the Court cannot ignore the fact that the petitioner lived

---

40 *Emmeline Therse Slyvanna (Dugasse Nee Denys) v. Ted Georges Dugasse* (DC 86/2021) [2021] SCSC 724, para. 9; *Germain Christian Francoise v. Cyrillia Francoise* (DC 133/2021) [2021] SCSC 879, para. 11 (the marriages were dissolved on only one ground – adultery).

41 *Damoo v. Damoo* (DC 160/22) [2022] SCSC 172 (1 March 2022).

together with respondent for a period exceeding six months after the date of the occurrence of the last incident relied for the divorce. Put differently, if the petitioner has lived with the respondent for a period exceeding six months after the last incident being relied on for divorce, he or she is presumed to be reasonably expected to live with the respondent irrespective of the incident. Otherwise, he or she should convince the Court to the contrary.

The Supreme Court has held that for it to grant a divorce on the basis of section 4(1)(b), the petitioner must, on a balance of probabilities, prove two 'elements', that is, 'the behaviour of the other party and that he [or she] cannot reasonably be expected to live with her [or him].'[42] The Court will dismiss a divorce petition under section 4(1)(b) unless the petitioner has 'grave and weighty' reasons.[43] For section 4(1)(b) to apply, the misbehaviour in question has to be that of the respondent and not of the petitioner. For example, in *JM (nee A) v. NM*[44] the petitioner filed for a divorce under section 4(1)(b) on the grounds that:

> she had been committing adultery for the duration of the marriage, and that she has been living with another man for the past two years. She … [added] that she does not love the Respondent and gave evidence that they last had sexual relations three to four years ago.[45]

In the light of the above submissions:

> The Court acknowledges that the Respondent, under the circumstances, would have had grounds to petition for a divorce, namely the fact of adultery. However, he has not brought the Petition for the divorce before the Court, nor has he consented to the same.[46]

Against that background, the Court dismissed the petition. In *JWH v. RH nee C*,[47] the Court granted a divorce under section 4(1)(b) on the basis of petitioner's evidence that the respondent 'consistently argued with him over money matters; was a spenthrift [sic] and generally made life unbearable for him to live with her.'[48] The Court has also granted divorce where the respondent threatened to harm

---

42 *JM (nee A) v. NM* (DV 148/2016) [2018] SCSC 503 (28 May 2018), para. 7. See also *JM v. JM nee D* (47 of 2006) [2007] SCSC 21 (27 February 2007); *Gabriel v. Gabriel* (DC 27/2021) [2021] SCSC 853, paras. 35–36.

43 See *JM v. JM nee D* (47 of 2006) [2007] SCSC 21 (27 February 2007), in this case the application was dismissed as the petitioner could not prove that the respondent had denied him sexual intercourse. He had applied for divorce to be able to live with another woman.

44 See *JM (nee A) v. NM* (DV 148/2016) [2018] SCSC 503 (28 May 2018).

45 Ibid, at para. 8.

46 Ibid, at para. 9.

47 *JWH v. RH nee C* (2 of 2005) [2005] SCSC 45 (31 July 2005).

48 Ibid, at p. 2.

the petitioner with a machete and also did not take action against her children when they assaulted the petitioner.[49] This implies that the act in question does not have to be exclusively committed by the respondent personally. It suffices if it is attributable to him or her through the actions of people under his or her control. The Court has followed a similar approach in another case.[50] In *Majah v. Majah*,[51] the parties had been married for 24 years and in the last three years preceding the divorce petition, the petitioner mistreated her as follows:

> The respondent has been treating the petitioner with persistent cruelty and neglect causing her mental torture and hardship. The respondent did not even allow her to sleep on the mattress. He took the mattress away from the bedroom and forced her to sleep on the floor. He also stopped giving her maintenance and refused to provide even important things a woman needs for her personal use including sanitary towels. He also used to hide everything from the bathroom such as toothpaste and body soap. He never gave money for her to buy things for her personal use. He was always telling her to go out of the matrimonial home so that he could bring his other wife … into the house to replace the petitioner. He used to insult her in front of the children, who were also afraid of his violent behaviour and attitude … [T]he respondent even asked her to go out and sell her body for money to buy things in order to meet her personal needs … [H]e neglected the family and failed to provide maintenance for the petitioner and for the children … [He] used to tell her that … he had a right to have sex whenever he wants: for four, five or even six times in a day. Whenever the petitioner refused to accommodate his sexual desires, the respondent got wild and used to threaten her with violence … [T]he respondent used to snore very loudly at night and she could not sleep in the same room with the respondent. As a result of the ill-treatment, the petitioner became hypertensive, fell sick and could not even sleep at night. Consequently, the petitioner was forced to leave the matrimonial home and is now living with her parents.[52]

Based on the above factors, the Court granted a divorce under section 4(1)(b). Other acts which fall in the ambit of section 4(1)(b) have included adultery and desertion,[53] insults both at home and in public (for example, calling the

---

49 *Lafortune v. Lafortune* (29 of 2003) [2006] SCSC 14 (24 May 2006).

50 *Meriton v. Meriton* (1 of 2006) [2007] SCSC 96 (23 September 2007) at p. 2, the evidence showed that '[w]hen beaten and also threatened with a knife by their children, the petitioner had to return to his mother's house where he had for quite some time been washing his clothes, having meals and spending most of his time … [T]hroughout the latter part of the marriage the respondent has been violent, aggressive and frequently abuses the petitioner. That she connives with, instigates and incites their children to harass and beat up the petitioner. The petitioner cited one incident at night when the children returned from a party, knocked down his door, beat him up as the respondent looked on yet given her immense influence over all the children she was in a position to stop or avert the attack.'

51 *Majah v. Majah* (DC 127/2008) [2010] SCSC 65 (6 October 2010).

52 Ibid, at pp. 1–2.

53 *Cafrine nee Andre v. Cafrine* (159 of 2003) [2004] SCSC 24 (28 October 2004).

petitioner a pig) and threating to kill the petitioner,[54] that 'the Respondent has an aggressive attitude and has been violent towards the Respondent',[55] 'unreasonable behaviour on the part of the Respondent',[56] adultery and violence,[57] cruelty and assault,[58] and that the respondent 'abandoned the Petitioner and has left the matrimonial home and the jurisdiction without any notice, warning or explanation' and did not offer her any financial assistance.[59] Other factors have included the adulterous conduct of the respondent, her refusal to share a bed with the petitioner and her absence from the matrimonial home without valid reasons.[60] They have also included the respondent's drug addiction, theft of household items and refusal to work to make a financial contribution to the household expenses.[61]

Although the standard of proof is one of a balance of probabilities, the Supreme Court has taken two approaches in deciding whether the petitioner has discharged the evidential burden to prove misbehaviour as a ground of divorce. In most cases, the Court relies on the petitioner's testimony to grant a divorce. This could be characterised as the 'less strict' approach. There are also cases in which the Court requires the petitioner to call witnesses to court and support his or her allegations. This could be classified as the 'strict' approach. For example, in *Seraphine nee Youpa v. Seraphine*[62] the petitioner filed for divorce under section 4(1)(b) and gave the following reasons why it was no longer reasonably possible for her to live with the respondent:

> [W]hen she walked on the road she encountered a lot of harassment and … the Respondent harassed her even when she slept at night. She added that the Respondent even came to her place of work where she is a Supervisor …, sat in a chair and stared at her and that made her colleagues to ask as to what was the problem. She also deposed that the Respondent would come to her at the Counter [at her place of work] asking her if she still loved him. When asked by the Petitioner why he acted like that, the Respondent said that because of his love that he has for her. The Petitioner further testified that she has been having an extra marital affair.[63]

54 *LP v. AP* (80 of 2010) [2011] SCSC 3 (9 January 2011).

55 *Payet v. Payet* (51 of 2004) [2008] SCSC 71 (26 March 2008), p. 1; *Thomas v. Thomas* (34 of 2005) [2008] SCSC 74 (30 March 2008) (however, the Court does not explain the specific aggressive acts).

56 *Hertel v. Hertel* (DC 161/2014) [2015] SCSC 33 (4 February 2015), para. 3 (the Court does not explain the unreasonable behaviour in question).

57 *Loze nee Marie v. Loze* (24 of 2007) [2007] SCSC 122 (4 December 2007).

58 *Marcel v. Marcel* (DC 44/2014) [2014] SCSC 271 (24 July 2014).

59 *Mrs RPB nee D v. Mr FAB* (97 of 2006) [2006] SCSC 67 (11 October 2006), p. 1.

60 *Ricky Rosalie v. Leonida Georgette Rosalie* (DC 96/2021) [2021] SCSC 685.

61 *Marie-Helene Bernadette Hoareau born Mousbe v. Shawn Hugton Emmanuel Hoareau* (DC 169/2021) [2021] SCSC 184.

62 *Seraphine nee Youpa v. Seraphine* (47 of 2004) [2005] SCSC 42 (5 July 2005).

63 Ibid, at p. 2.

The Court held that the petitioner 'failed to specify when or during what period the Respondent harassed her, or what form such harassment took'.[64] The Court concluded that:

> In this case I have observed the demeanour of the Petitioner when she was testifying and I find that she had not been forthright and truthful to the Court. She is living with her husband and their children in her parent's house up to now. Had her parents find [sic] the Respondent to be what the Petitioner wanted this Court to believe, they would have at least not tolerated his presence in their home up to now and moreover they would have at least come forward to testify about the misbehaviour of the Respondent. If indeed the Respondent really misbehaved at the Petitioner's place of work, the least that was expected of her was to support her testimony by at least one of her work colleagues. Had the Respondent misbehaved to the point that the Petitioner invited Police to her home, the Police would have at least taken certain measures against the Respondent. It is only after [being] questioned by the Court that the Petitioner admitted that she had been having extra-marital affairs ... I believe that this is the principal reason why this marriage is in peril and this is being caused by the marital misbehaviour of the Petitioner who is now only seeking the stamp of approval of this Court for her to deal the final blow to this marriage so that she would be at liberty to pursue her chosen course much to the detriment of her family and her children. This Court being one of the pillars of State is bound to uphold the constitutional provision enshrined in Article 32 of our Constitution, hence it recognizes that the family is the natural and fundamental element of our society and as such the Court should be promoting and protecting the family and not to so lightly approve its break up, unless for proven and serious reasons. It is incumbent upon the Petitioner to adduce sufficient evidence to satisfy the Court that such harassment was unbearable in the circumstances.[65]

Against that background, the Court dismissed the application. Sometimes the Court dissolves a marriage on the ground of misbehaviour but it does not expressly say so. For example, in *Belle v. Joubert*[66] the petitioner filed for divorce on the grounds that:

> [T]he respondent has committed adultery; the respondent has deserted the Petitioner for a continuous period of about four years; the parties do not share the same religion and the Respondent is opposing to the Petitioner practicing her religion; and the Respondent treated her with mental cruelty in that he used to persecute, insult and criticise the Petitioner regarding her religious believes [sic].[67]

---

64 Ibid, at p. 3.

65 Ibid, at p. 4.

66 *Belle v. Joubert* (DC 09/2014) [2015] SCSC 133 (7 May 2015).

67 Ibid, at para. 1.

The respondent opposed the petition on the ground that the petitioner did not have a valid ground of divorce.[68] Without explaining on which ground it dissolved the marriage, the Court held that the evidence before it showed that 'the marriage between the parties has irretrievably broken down' and that 'there is no possibility of reconciliation'.[69] Since the petitioner did not adduce evidence to prove adultery and the respondent did not consent to the divorce, it can be inferred that this marriage was dissolved on the ground of either misbehaviour or desertion. However, since the respondent opposed the divorce, it could be argued that he had no intention to desert the petitioner. Therefore, it is very likely that the applicable ground was misbehaviour. The Court dissolved the marriage on the basis of section 4(1)(b), but the facts are silent on the exact act or omission attributable to the respondent as misbehaviour.[70]

2.3. DESERTION

Under section 4(1)(c), a court may grant a divorce if 'the respondent has deserted the petitioner for a continuous period of at least 2 years immediately preceding the presentation of the petition.' Section 4(1)(c) should be read with section 8(3), which states that:

> (a) the court may treat a period of desertion as having continued at a time when the deserting party was incapable of continuing the necessary intention if the evidence before the court is such that, had the party not been so incapable, the court would have inferred that his desertion continued at that time;
> (b) the court shall not take into account any period of, or periods which together amount to, not more than 6 months during which the petitioner and the respondent have resumed living together but such period or periods shall not be counted as part of the period of desertion.

For a divorce to be granted under section 4(1)(c), the minimum period of desertion is two years. It should also be continuous. The petitioner has to prove physical separation and the respondent's intention to desert him or her. For a person to be taken to have formed the intention to desert, he or she should have the mental capacity to do so. However, if the deserting party suffers from mental incapacity to form the requisite intention, the Court can, depending on the circumstances of the case, still presume that the deserting party would have continued with the intention to desert. Under section 8(3)(b), if the intention to desert and physical separation are in place but the parties resume cohabitation for a brief period (not more than six months) before the continuous period

68 Ibid, at para. 2.
69 Ibid, at para. 7.
70 *Frederic v. Frederic* (37 of 2007) [2007] SCSC 106 (11 October 2007).

of two years is reached, that brief cohabitation will not be presumed to have interrupted the continuous period of two years. However, that brief period is not considered as part of the continuous two-year period.[71] In other words, none of the parties benefits from the brief resumption of cohabitation. The 'deserter' would have to wait for another six months (or the duration of the brief stay) to complete the two-year period and the 'deserted' cannot use that period to argue that it interrupted the continuous two-year period. The Court has granted divorce where the petitioner deserted the respondent for periods such as seven years,[72] ten years,[73] and 11 years.[74] In some cases, although the divorce is granted on the basis of desertion, the facts are silent on the period of desertion.[75] The intention to desert can be inferred from the respondent's absence from Seychelles for the minimum period of two years without the intention to return.[76]

In cases where desertion is the strongest basis on which a divorce is to be granted, the Court will rely on it even if another ground is alleged. For example, in *L (nee R) v. L*[77] the petitioner filed for divorce

> [b]ecause her marriage has irretrievably broken down on the ground that she and the Respondent have been living separate and apart for a continuous period of one year immediately preceding the presentation of his Petition and secondly, that the Respondent has deserted the matrimonial home for a continuous period of over two years immediately preceding this Petition.[78]

It is thus evident that she sought the divorce on two grounds. However, in granting the divorce, the Court observed that:

> The Petitioner ... testified that the marriage has now irretrievably broken down for the reason that the Respondent deserted the matrimonial home for a continuous period of over two years immediately preceding this Petition and that there is no possibility of reconciliation. She testified that in fact the Respondent left her over 10 years ago following an argument between them when he left.[79]

Although the Court does not expressly state that the divorce was granted on the basis of desertion, this can be inferred from the fact that the respondent did not

71 *'Onesi v. 'Onesi* [2021] TOSC 104; FD 59 of 2021 (10 June 2021), para. 26 (the Supreme Court of Tonga interpreting a similarly worded provision).

72 *Leon v. Ssebanakitta* (DC 116/2015) [2016] SCSC 126 (17 February 2016).

73 *Amande v. Amande* (DC 78/2018) [2018] SCSC 382 (11 May 2018).

74 *WJM v. AFA* (62 of 1998) [2007] SCSC 31 (4 July 2007). See also *Chang-Time (nee Louis) v. Chang-Time* [2022] SCSC 575 (18 years).

75 *Celestine v. Celestine* (55 of 2006) [2007] SCSC 113 (14 November 2007).

76 *Leon v. Ssebanakitta* (DC 116/2015) [2016] SCSC 126 (17 February 2016) (the respondent returned to his home country Uganda). See also *L'estrange v. Habaragodage* [2022] SCSC 381 (the respondent returned to his home country Sri Lanka).

77 *L (nee R) v. L* (133 of 2004) [2005] SCSC 37 (8 June 2005).

78 Ibid, at p. 1.

79 Ibid, at p. 2.

give consent to the divorce, which is a requirement for a divorce on the basis of separation under section 4(1)(d).

2.4. SEPARATION

A court may grant a divorce under section 4(1)(d) if 'the petitioner and the respondent have lived apart for a continuous period of at least 1 year immediately preceding the presentation of the petition and the respondent consents to the grant of the divorce.' Section 4(1)(d) should be read with section 8(4), which states that:

> (a) the court shall not take into account any period of, or periods which together amount to, not more than 6 months during which the petitioner and the respondent have resumed living together but any such period or periods shall not be counted as part of the period during which the parties have lived apart;
> (b) the petitioner and the respondent shall be treated as living apart unless they are living with each other in the same household;
> (c) the consent of the respondent shall not be valid unless given by the respondent –
> (i) in court in the course of the proceedings for the divorce; or
> (ii) in the prescribed form.

The observations above on section 8(3)(b) are applicable to section 8(4) with the necessary modifications. Unlike in the case of divorce under section 4(1)(a)–(c) where the respondent's consent is not needed, in the case of divorce under section 4(1)(d) that consent is a prerequisite. Without that consent, the application will be dismissed.[80] The consent can be given in court (orally)[81] or in writing (in a prescribed form).[82] When a petitioner appears in court and informs the Court that he or she is not contesting the divorce, the Court considers that to be oral consent.[83] There are instances where the respondent gives

[80] *Morgan nee Nur v. Morgan* (DC 109/2018) [2018] SCSC 809 (6 September 2018), para. 10 (in this case, the petitioner informed court that the respondent, who had in Egypt, had undertaken 'to make one available to' the respondent). See also *Ernesta v. Ernesta* (DS 119/2018) [2020] SCSC 161 (28 February 2020) (the respondent opposed the petition).

[81] *Agathine v. Agathine* (DC 104/2014) [2014] SCSC 407 (1 October 2014), para. 4 (the respondent came to court and stated that they had no objection to the grant of divorce).

[82] In these cases the petitioners signed the form: *Ragedonge v. Ragedonge* (103 of 2007) [2008] SCSC 70 (25 March 2008); *IP v. LP* (145 of 2005) [2006] SCSC 55 (26 July 2006); *Noel v. Noel* (80 of 2005) [2005] SCSC 61 (11 December 2005); *Holey nee Adrienne v. Holey* (139 of 2006) [2006] SCSC 34 (7 November 2006); *Nancy (Born Adela) v. Nancy* (31 of 2007) [2007] SCSC 34 (12 August 2007); *Capet v. Capet nee Betoko-Doo* (69 of 2004) [2004] SCSC 20 (2 July 2004); *Ragedonge v. Ragedonge* (103 of 2007) [2008] SCSC 70 (25 March 2008); *Leste v. Leste* (DC 157/2014) [2015] SCSC 17 (21 January 2015) (letter of consent); *Ketty Annabel Tirant v. Gerard Edward Tirant* (DC 153/2021) [2022] SCSC 205 (10 March 2022).

[83] *Bristol v. Bristol* (DC 110/2014) [2014] SCSC 403 (15 October 2014), para. 2; *Leopold v. Leopold* (Civil Side: DC 116/2014) [2014] SCSC 406 (22 October 2014), para. 1.

written consent to the divorce and also comes to court and confirms the same under oath.[84] In some cases, the judgments are silent on the form in which the consent was given.[85] In one case, the Court dissolved the marriage on, inter alia, the basis of separation even though the respondent opposed the petition.[86] However, if the respondent is based abroad, consent can be given in a legal document, for example 'in a document notarially executed before a notary.'[87] A respondent based abroad can also give consent through their proxy in Seychelles.[88] In at least one case, the divorce petition was seemingly based on section 4(1)(d), but the facts are silent on whether or not the respondent consented to the divorce.[89]

In most of the cases where marriages were dissolved on the basis of section 4(1)(d), the parties were not living under the same roof. However, section 8(4)(b) provides that 'the petitioner and the respondent shall be treated as living apart unless they are living with each other in the same household.' Put differently, a divorce will not be granted on the basis of section 4(1)(d) if the parties live together in the same household. However, a marriage will be dissolved if the parties live under the same roof but are 'operating separate household[s]' for over a year.[90] Sections 4(1)(d) and 8(3)(b) should be read in tandem with section 9 of the Act, which provides for protection of the respondent.[91] Section 4(1)(d) is applicable even in cases where the parties are

---

84 *Briat v. Briat* (DC 122/2014) [2014] SCSC 345 (18 September 2014); *Constance v. Constance* (DC 2/2015) [2015] SCSC 37 (12 February 2015); *May Paule Dubel nee Marguerite v. Daniel Dubel* (DC 123/2021) [2022] SCSC 161 (25 February 2022).

85 *HJ v. LJ* (143 of 2010) [2010] SCSC 117 (18 November 2010); *Larue v. Esparon* (144 of 2010) [2011] SCSC 19 (17 February 2011); *Barbe v. Barbe* (DC 154/2014) [2015] SCSC 35 (4 February 2015); *Basset v. Basset nee Gertrude* (76 of 2005) [2005] SCSC 59 (11 December 2005); *LES v. Born S* (136 of 2010) [2010] SCSC 113 (9 November 2010); *Esparon v. Esparon* (144 of 2007) [2008] SCSC 54 (15 January 2008); *Murray v. Murray* (129 of 2007) [2007] SCSC 123 (4 December 2007); *Poudret v. Poudret* (DC 107/2014) [2014] SCSC 410 (15 October 2014).

86 *Mr Francois Hoareau v. Mrs Maribel Hoareau Bualan (Nee Anog)* (DC 25/2016) [2016] SCSC 706.

87 *Humphrey v. Humphrey* (139 of 2004) [2005] SCSC 27 (25 January 2005), p. 2 (the respondent and petitioner were based in England); *Stepanov v. Drahuradova* (86 of 2007) [2008] SCSC 60 (3 February 2008) (Slovak Republic).

88 *Alves v. Alves* (DC 24/2014) [2014] SCSC 175 (19 May 2014).

89 *Kilindo v. Nduta* (20 of 2010) [2010] SCSC 120 (8 December 2010).

90 *Georges Thomas Kilindo v. Marie Yvonete Rebecca Kilindo (Nee Michel)* (DC 43/2021) [2021] SCSC 725, para. 8.

91 S. 9 provides that '(1) Where the court has granted a conditional order of divorce based on section 4(1)(d) and the respondent has, at any time before the order is made absolute, applied to the court, the court (a) may rescind the order where the respondent alleges and the court is satisfied that the petitioner misled the respondent, whether intentionally or otherwise, about any matter which the respondent took into account in deciding to consent to the grant of the divorce; or (b) shall, subject to subsection (2), not make the order absolute unless, after considering all the circumstances, including the age, health, conduct, earning capacity, financial resources and financial obligation of the parties, and the financial position of the

based abroad. In other words, the separation for over a year took place abroad.[92] It is also applicable in cases where the separation is based on the fact that the respondent has lived abroad for more than a year provided he or she consents to the divorce.[93] The periods of separation have included just over one year, two years,[94] five years,[95] nine years,[96] 15 years,[97] and 32 years.[98] In the event that the petitioner is, for whatever reason, unable to get the respondent's consent for the divorce under section 4(1)(d), he or she may have to invoke another applicable ground in the Act. As mentioned above, Article 230(1)(e) of the Civil Code provides that a party to a marriage may petition for a divorce because 'the petitioner and the respondent have lived apart for a continuous period of five years or more.' In this case, the respondent's consent is not needed. In computing the period of separation, the Court also considers the period the petitioner spent abroad, as long as there is evidence that during that period he or she intended to terminate the marriage.[99]

In some cases, the Court appears to blur the distinction between a divorce on the basis of desertion (under section 4(1)(c)) on the one hand and separation (under section 4(1)(d)) on the other. For example, in *Kilindo v. Nduta*[100] the court granted a divorce on the ground that:

> The Petitioner averred that the marriage has irretrievably broken down on the ground that the Respondent deserted the Petitioner [for] the last more than one

---

respondent as, having regard to the divorce, it is likely to be after the death of the petitioner should the petitioner die first, the court is satisfied that – (i) the petitioner should not be required to make any financial provision for the respondent; or (ii) the financial provision made by the petitioner for the respondent is reasonable and fair or the best that can be made in the circumstances. (2) Notwithstanding subsection (1)(b), the court may, if it thinks fit, make a conditional order of divorce absolute if (a) it appears that there are circumstances making it desirable that the order should be made absolute without delay; and (b) the court has obtained a satisfactory undertaking from the petitioner that the petitioner will make such financial provision for the respondent as the court may approve.'

92 *Humphrey v. Humphrey* (139 of 2004) [2005] SCSC 27 (25 January 2005) (the respondent and petitioner were based in England).

93 *Alves v. Alves* (DC 24/2014) [2014] SCSC 175 (19 May 2014) (the respondent lived in Portugal).

94 *Ketty Annabel Tirant v. Gerard Edward Tirant* (DC 153/2021) [2022] SCSC 205 (10 March 2022).

95 See *Alves v. Alves* (DC 24/2014) [2014] SCSC 175 (19 May 2014); *Amade v. Amade (nee Paulin)* [2022] SCSC 131.

96 *Michel v. Michel* (DC 118/2014) [2014] SCSC 367 (25 September 2014) (the petitioner in Italy and the respondent in Seychelles).

97 *Georges Thomas Kilindo v. Marie Yvonete Rebecca Kilindo (Nee Michel)* (DC 43/2021) [2021] SCSC 725, para. 8. See also *Adrienne (nee Arissol) v. Adrienne* [2022] SCSC 51; *Suleman v. Suleman (nee Florine)* [2022] SCSC 624.

98 *RPB v. DB Nee J* (42 of 2006) [2006] SCSC 63 (1 October 2006) (both parties residing in Seychelles). See also *Adonis v. Simeon* [2022] SCSC 451 (40 years).

99 *Julia Fatima Volcere v. Elvis Daniel Octave* (DC 154/2021) [2022] SCSC 185 (3 March 2022).

100 *Kilindo v. Nduta* (20 of 2010) [2010] SCSC 120 (8 December 2010).

> year and the Petitioner and the Respondent have lived since separate and apart for a continuous period of over one year immediately preceding the presentation of this petition. The Petitioner testified that all their attempts at reconciliation have not proved successful and there is now no possibility of reconciliation.[101]

In the above case, the facts are silent on whether the respondent consented to the divorce. The blurring of the distinction between the divorce under section 4(1)(c) and (d) could be explained by the fact that the Court does not mention the exact statutory provision on which the divorce is based. In some instances, it is not clear what is required of a party to prove separation as a ground of divorce. For example, in *DL v. EL*[102] the petitioner filed for divorce in November 2016 and argued that the marriage had irretrievably broken down because 'the parties stopped living together as husband and wife [in] February, 2012' and that '[f]or the last few years the parties faced certain irreconcilable differences and in February, 2012, the parties separated.'[103] However, the Court dismissed the petition on the basis, inter alia, that the petition did not disclose any ground under section 4(1) of the Act.[104] This was the case even though, at the time of the petition, the parties had separated close to four years earlier.

There are also instances where the facts are not clear on which ground the divorce was granted. For example, in *Basset v. Basset nee Gertrude*,[105] the facts show that the petitioner sought divorce on two grounds: 'the Respondent has behaved in such a way that he cannot reasonably be expected to live with her' and 'the parties had been living apart for a period of more than two years'.[106] The facts are silent on the respondent's alleged misbehaviour. However, the divorce was granted because, inter alia, the respondent consented to the same. This implies that this was a divorce under section 4(1)(d) as opposed to section 4(1)(b).[107] In another case, the petitioner alleged both separation and misbehaviour. The Court does not explain the ground on which divorce was granted. However, since the facts of the case are silent on the respondent's consent, it can be assumed that the divorce was based on misbehaviour, although the Court does not explain how the petitioner could not reasonably be expected to live with the respondent.[108] Section 4(1)(d) is applicable in cases

---

101 Ibid, at p. 1.

102 *DL v. EL* (DS 163/2016) [2017] SCSC 17 (18 January 2017).

103 Ibid, at para. 2.

104 Ibid, at para. 4.

105 *Basset v. Basset nee Gertrude* (76 of 2005) [2005] SCSC 59 (11 December 2005).

106 Ibid.

107 See also *Freminot v. Freminot* (80 of 2008) [2008] SCSC 94 (22 July 2008) (where the respondent had deserted the matrimonial home for over five years but the divorce was granted on the basis of his consent, which implies separation as the ground).

108 *Khan v. Khan* (123 of 2005) [2007] SCSC 112 (8 November 2007) (the relevant facts were that 'the respondent has behaved in such a way that the Petitioner and Respondent cannot

when the one-year continuous period of living apart is spent abroad[109] or in Seychelles.

2.5. EXCEPTIONAL HARDSHIP AND MINIMUM DURATION OF MARRIAGE BEFORE DIVORCE

The Act imposes a minimum duration of marriage before any of the parties can petition for divorce. Section 4 provides that:

> (2) Subject to subsection (3), a party to a marriage may not petition for divorce within one year of the date of the marriage.
> (3) The Court may, on an application, grant leave for a petition for divorce within the one year referred to in subsection (2) if the court is satisfied that the petitioner has suffered exceptional hardship or the respondent is exceptionally depraved.

Section 4(2) and (3) has been reproduced as Article 230(2) and (3) of the Civil Code. In terms of section 4(2) and (3), the general rule is that the minimum duration for which a party should be married before petitioning for a divorce is one year.[110] This is perhaps meant to combat sham marriages or marriages of convenience.[111] The Court of Appeal explains some of the factors which may be considered in assessing whether or not the marriage is one of convenience.[112] However, there are two exceptions in which a divorce may be permitted under section 4(2)–(3): if the petitioner has suffered exceptional hardship or if the respondent is exceptionally depraved. In *Lesperance v. Jaosily*[113] the petitioner and the respondent got married in December 2006.

---

be reasonably expected to live together … [T]hat since the celebration of their marriage the Respondent has never lived in the same house with him for a period of more than five days').

109 *LES v. Born S* (136 of 2010) [2010] SCSC 113 (9 November 2010) (the respondent was based in Bahrain); *Marshall v. Marshall* (154 of 2005) [2007] SCSC 111 (28 October 2007) (the respondent was in the United Kingdom).

110 In *Tania Beverly Banane nee Sicobo v. Giovani Hugh Banane* (85 of 2011) [2011] SCSC 97 (1 December 2011), the Court criticised the lawyer for the petitioner for filing a misleading divorce affidavit (stating that parties had separated for over a year yet the marriage had lasted for less than ten months).

111 In some cases, the Court has emphasised the fact that petitioners and respondents did not collude to initiate a divorce. This implies that the Court was aware of instances of sham marriages which are accompanied by divorces shortly afterwards. See for example *Thomas v. Thomas* (34 of 2005) [2008] SCSC 74 (30 March 2008); *Morgan nee Nur v. Morgan* (DC 109/2018) [2018] SCSC 809 (6 September 2018) (the petitioner (a Seychellois) and the respondent (a foreign national) got married and cohabited for a week before the respondent travelled to his country, never to return).

112 *Bacco & Anor v. Bacco* (SCA 46/2018 arising in CS 72/2018, SCSC 700) [2021] SCCA 25 (9 July 2021), paras. 15–19.

113 *Lesperance v. Jaosily* (82 of 2007) [2007] SCSC 28 (14 June 2007).

In May 2007, the petitioner filed for divorce under section 4(3) of the Act on the grounds that:

> The Respondent failed to show love to the Petitioner. The Respondent failed to care for and do her wifely duties. The Respondent was a persistent nagger through her cohabitation after the celebration of the marriage. The Respondent stole SR50,000 from the Petitioner before her departure to Madagascar. The Respondent left for Madagascar without informing the Petitioner. The Respondent misappropriated a motor vehicle worth SR38,000 which the Petitioner purchased in Madagascar for business. The Respondent stole 45 million-franc Malgache. The Respondent left Seychelles in January 2007 never to return save for writing a letter ending relationship dated 10th February 2007. No address, no contact or other particulars for contact were given. The Petitioner has tried in vain to locate the Respondent for 4 months but to no avail. The Respondent has informed the Petitioner in her letter that she wanted a divorce but has left no contact or mailing address.[114]

The petitioner argued that in the light of the above, he 'suffered exceptional hardship during the short-lived marriage.'[115] The Court agreed with the petitioner 'that the marriage has broken-down irretrievably and that now there is no hope of reconciliation.'[116] As discussed below, for the Court to grant a divorce under section 4(3), there is no requirement that the parties have attempted reconciliation.

3. RECONCILIATION

Before a court grants a divorce under section 4(1), evidence has to show that an attempt was made to reconcile the parties and that that attempt was unsuccessful. Section 5 of the Act provides that:

> (1) Subject to this Act, the court shall not grant a divorce on a petition under section 4(1) unless it is satisfied that –
> (a) [an] attempt has been made to reconcile the petitioner and the respondent;
> (b) after inquiring into the evidence presented by the parties to the proceedings, there is no reasonable possibility of reconciliation between the parties; and
> (c) the marriage has irretrievably broken down as provided in section 4(1).
>
> (2) The court shall, if it appears to the court at any stage of the proceedings for divorce that there is a reasonable possibility of reconciliation between the parties, adjourn the proceedings for such period as the court thinks fit to enable attempt at reconciliation to be made.

[114] Ibid, at p. 1.
[115] Ibid.
[116] Ibid, at p. 2.

Section 5 of the Act has been reproduced substantially as Article 231 of the Civil Code of Seychelles. Under the Matrimonial Causes Act, reconciliation is only applicable to a divorce petition under section 4(1). In other words, the attempt to reconcile the parties is not applicable to a divorce under section 4(2) and (3), that is, if the parties have been married for less than a year and the marriage is dissolved because 'the petitioner has suffered exceptional hardship or the respondent is exceptionally depraved.' However, under Article 231 of the Civil Code, reconciliation is applicable to all marriages. For example, in *Lesperance v. Jaosily*[117] the Court, when granting a divorce under section 4(3) of the Matrimonial Causes Act, never mentioned any reconciliation attempts between the parties as this is not a requirement for a divorce under section 4(3).

In a case where the parties have reconciled, the divorce petition will be set aside and the file closed.[118] The Court held that '[i]n accordance with Section 5 of the Act, the Court must be satisfied on the evidence presented that reconciliation has been explored and has failed.'[119] It is the duty of the petitioner to convince the Court that before filing for a divorce, reconciliation was attempted but was unsuccessful. The Court has followed different approaches in dealing with the issue of whether or not reconciliation attempts have been unsuccessful and that there is no possibility of reconciliation between the parties.

There are cases in which the Court's description of the facts of the case do not disclose the exact reconciliation initiatives/attempts taken by the parties. All that is mentioned is that the reconciliation attempts were unsuccessful.[120] In some cases, the Supreme Court has dissolved the marriage because the petitioner alleged that there was no possibility or hope of reconciliation. This is the case even though the Court's recitation of the facts is silent on the exact reason(s) why the possibility of reconciliation does not exist and on whether or not any effort was made by the parties to reconcile.[121] There are cases in which

117 Ibid.

118 *Jeannevol v. Jeannevol* (DC 129/2009) [2014] SCSC 92 (13 March 2014).

119 *JM (nee A) v. NM* (DV 148/2016) [2018] SCSC 503 (28 May 2018) para. 12.

120 *Larue v. Esparon* (144 of 2010) [2011] SCSC 19 (17 February 2011); *IP v. LP* (145 of 2005) [2006] SCSC 55 (26 July 2006); *Agathine v. Agathine* (DC 104/2014) [2014] SCSC 407 (1 October 2014); *Capet v. Capet nee Betoko-Doo* (69 of 2004) [2004] SCSC 20 (2 July 2004); *HJ v. LJ* (143 of 2010) [2010] SCSC 117 (18 November 2010); *Esparon v. Esparon* (144 of 2007) [2008] SCSC 54 (15 January 2008); *Ragedonge v. Ragedonge* (103 of 2007) [2008] SCSC 70 (25 March 2008); *Murray v. Murray* (129 of 2007) [2007] SCSC 123 (4 December 2007); *Marie-Helene Bernadette Hoareau born Mousbe v. Shawn Hugton Emmanuel Hoareau* (DC 169/2021) [2021] SCSC 184 (reconciliation attempts over a period of four years failed).

121 *IP v. LP* (145 of 2005) [2006] SCSC 55 (26 July 2006) (divorce under s. 4(1)(d)); *Noel v. Noel* (80 of 2005) [2005] SCSC 61 (11 December 2005) (divorce under s. 4(1)(d)); *L (nee R) v. L* (133 of 2004) [2005] SCSC 37 (8 June 2005) (desertion); *Holey nee Adrienne v. Holey* (139 of 2006) [2006] SCSC 34 (7 November 2006) (separation); *Nancy (Born Adela) v. Nancy* (31 of 2007) [2007] SCSC 34 (12 August 2007) (separation); *Briat v. Briat* (DC 122/2014) [2014] SCSC 345 (18 September 2014) (separation); *Barbe v. Barbe* (DC 154/2014) [2015] SCSC 35 (4 February 2015) (separation); *Basset v. Basset nee Gertrude* (76 of 2005) [2005] SCSC 59

the Court dissolved the marriage 'after enquiring into the uncontroverted evidence' that there is no possibility of reconciliation.[122] However, the Court's recitation of the facts is silent on which specific attempts were made. In some cases, the facts are silent on whether any reconciliation attempt was made at all.[123]

There are also cases in which the parties notify the Court of the person or government office which tried to reconcile them.[124] Both parties can also 'admit' before the Court 'that there is no chance of reconciliation'.[125] In this case, they do not have to adduce evidence of attempted reconciliation efforts. However, there are also instances in which the Court has required the parties to make genuine reconciliation attempts. For example, in *Seraphine nee Youpa v. Seraphine*[126] the petitioner filed for divorce under section 4(1)(b) and the respondent informed the Court that he 'wanted a reconciliation'.[127] On the basis of that submission, 'the Court referred the matter to the Probation Services'. Subsequently, the probation officer reported to the Court that the 'reconciliation attempt' was unsuccessful.[128] It is on this ground that the petition was heard *ex parte* as the respondent declined to go to court. In rejecting the probation officer's report, the Court held that:

> I find that the report of the Probation Officer is not helpful in the sense that this Court is not informed as to whether reconciliation really took place or there was only an attempt and that such attempt did not lead, for example, to the meeting of the parties to try and reconcile them. This is a requirement under Section 5(1)(a) of the Matrimonial Causes Act, 1992 ... It is now becoming apparent to this Court that petition for divorce is being taken too lightly. It is high time that a clear message is sent out that the Court is there, to bury dead marriage, so to speak, and not to assist in killing it ... So often, a party seeking divorce would simply stay away from the other for one year and thereafter seek a divorce. It is to be reiterated, that the granting of divorce is conditioned on the parties having tried to reconcile themselves

---

(11 December 2005) (separation); *Poudret v. Poudret* (DC 107/2014) [2014] SCSC 410 (15 October 2014) (separation); *Ragedonge v. Ragedonge* (103 of 2007) [2008] SCSC 70 (25 March 2008), p. 2; *Pool v. Pool* (DC 113/2014) [2014] SCSC 416 (22 October 2014); *Leste v. Leste* (DC 157/2014) [2015] SCSC 17 (21 January 2015), para. 2; *Damoo v. Damoo* (DC 160/22) [2022] SCSC 172 (1 March 2022), para. 14.

122 *May Paule Dubel nee Marguerite v. Daniel Dubel* (DC 123/2021) [2022] SCSC 161 (25 February 2022), para. 14.

123 *Lafortune v. Lafortune* (29 of 2003) [2006] SCSC 14 (24 May 2006) (divorce on the ground of intolerable behaviour).

124 *Meriton v. Meriton* (1 of 2006) [2007] SCSC 96 (23 September 2007) (Department of Social Services); *Phyllis Marie Lena Confait (Nee Henriette) v. Patrick Hensley Confait* (DC 124/2015) [2016] SCSC 127 (probation officer).

125 *LP v. AP* (80 of 2010) [2011] SCSC 3 (9 January 2011), p. 1.

126 *Seraphine nee Youpa v. Seraphine* (47 of 2004) [2005] SCSC 42 (5 July 2005).

127 Ibid, at p. 1.

128 Ibid.

> in the first instance. I believe that such reconciliation process should be undertaken by professional person or institution proficient in such matters, and, such person or institution will have to report to the Court fully on the process undertaken.[129]

The above holding ensures that parties are compelled to attempt reconciliation. In other words, steps toward reconciliation have to be taken. There are instances where the Court has referred the parties to social services for possible reconciliation.[130] However, attempting reconciliation does not guarantee that it will succeed. Case law shows that a party determined to end the marriage may attend the reconciliation sessions just for the sake of attending.[131] Requiring such reconciliation sessions to be conducted by professionals is likely to undermine the role of family members, especially elders, and religious leaders in settling marriage disputes.[132]

In the author's opinion, the most important consideration should be whether or not reconciliation attempts were made. Subsequent case law shows that the Court has not emphasised the above requirements (set in *Seraphine nee Youpa v. Seraphine*) in all cases. In many cases decided after this decision, judges have not required the involvement of probation officers in the reconciliation process. In fact, there are cases in which the facts are silent on any reconciliation attempts taken and why they failed.[133] This means that the prevailing view is that probation officers do not have to be involved in the reconciliation attempts.

As mentioned above, section 5 requires that Court to establish whether reconciliation attempts have been made before it dissolves a marriage. However, in one case, the Supreme Court appears to have introduced another factor – settlement. In *Chetty v. Chetty*,[134] the Court dissolved the marriage because, inter alia, it was 'satisfied that there is no possibility of settlement or reconciliation between the parties'.[135] It is not clear whether settlement is the same thing as

---

129 Ibid, at pp. 3–4.

130 *Belle v. Joubert* (DC 09/2014) [2015] SCSC 133 (7 May 2015), para. 3.

131 For example, in *Ricky Rosalie v. Leonida Georgette Rosalie* (DC 96/2021) [2021] SCSC 685, para. 10, before granting a divorce, the Court held observed that '[t]he Petitioner testified, that all attempts at reconciliation have been unsuccessful because the Respondent had shown no interest in reconciliation, instead, maintaining her adulterous relationship.' See also *Emmeline Thersse Slyvanna (Dugasse Nee Denys) v. Ted Georges Dugasse* (DC 86/2021) [2021] SCSC 724, para. 10.

132 For example, in *Majah v. Majah* (DC 127/2008) [2010] SCSC 65 (6 October 2010), p. 2, the petitioner explains how the Muslim religious leader unsuccessfully tried to reconcile the parties. In *Lindy Achille Laporte Nee Dine v. Arsen Benjamin Laporte* (DC 108/2014) [2016] SCSC 340, the parties explain how a pastor unsuccessfully tried to reconcile them. In *Dubel v. Duble* [2022] SCSC 492 (family members, amongst others, tried to reconcile the parties).

133 *Barbe v. Barbe* (DC 154/2014) [2015] SCSC 35 (4 February 2015); *Constance v. Constance* (DC 2/2015) [2015] SCSC 37 (12 February 2015).

134 *Chetty v. Chetty* (DC 76/2014) [2014] SCSC 342 (18 September 2014).

135 Ibid, at para. 3.

reconciliation. A court will grant a divorce if there is 'absolutely no hope of reconciliation'.[136]

It has been illustrated above that section 5 provides that the 'court shall not grant a divorce on a petition under Section 4(1) unless it is satisfied that' reconciliation attempts have been made. Although in a few cases the Court has required proof of attempted reconciliation before granting a divorce, in the majority of cases it has not required such proof. This creates room for the argument that the Court is not fully complying with section 5. The use of the word 'shall' instead of 'may' under section 5 implies that the Court must ensure that reconciliation attempts have been made before it grants a divorce. In other words, parties must prove that these attempts happened to the satisfaction of the court. The facts of the case must disclose those attempts if they were indeed made. The Court of Appeal has held that the use of the word 'shall' in a statute means that the act or function stated therein must be done.[137] Put differently, the use of '"shall" is imperative and takes away any discretion' from the court.[138] Although there are circumstances in which the use of the word 'shall' can be permissive (as opposed to being mandatory),[139] in the absence of a compelling reason from the Supreme Court why 'shall' under section 5 should be interpreted as permissive, it should be given its natural meaning. That is, it should be mandatory.

4. CONCLUSION

In this chapter, the author has illustrated that in Seychelles there is one ground of divorce – the marriage has irretrievably broken down. This ground can be proved by one of the factors under section 4 of the Matrimonial Causes Act or Article 230 of the Civil Code. The discussion has shown that in many cases the Court does not specify the ground on which a divorce has been granted. It is very important that in each case the Court should specify the basis for divorce so that the validity or otherwise of the divorce is not in doubt. For divorces under section 4(1), the Court should also insist on proof that the parties have attempted reconciliation. Those attempts should be included in the judgment so that there is no doubt that indeed section 5 of the Act was complied with. This is because the word 'shall' instead of 'may' is used.

---

136 *LP v. AP* (80 of 2010) [2011] SCSC 3 (9 January 2011), at p. 2.

137 See e.g. *Marie Hunt v. Jane Hunt* (SCA 07/2010) [2012] SCCA 19 (31 August 2012); *DJS Capital Ltd & Ors v. FIU* (SCA 01/2014) [2016] SCCA 3 (22 April 2016), para. 42.

138 *Agnes v. The Republic* (SCA 20/2019) [2020] SCCA 39 (18 December 2020), para. 36.

139 *Allisop v. FIU* (SCA 39/2013) [2016] SCCA 1 (22 April 2016).

SLOVENIA
THE IMPACT OF COVID-19 ON FAMILY RELATIONS IN SLOVENIA

Suzana KRALJIĆ*

Résumé

En mars 2020, la Slovénie a introduit des mesures visant à réduire la propagation du COVID-19. La pandémie de COVID-19 a eu des répercussions immédiates et profondes sur tous les domaines de notre vie (par exemple l'économie, la mobilité humaine, l'éducation et la santé). Il ne fait aucun doute que le COVID-19 a également eu une incidence sur les relations familiales. Cet article analyse les mesures législatives et les décisions judiciaires adoptées pendant la pandémie de COVID-19 en Slovénie. Une attention toute particulière est accordée aux relations parents-enfants, à l'adoption et au mariage.

1. INTRODUCTION

Infectious diseases and related epidemics or pandemics[1] have left an indelible mark on history. They have caused widespread fear, suffering and death. All of

* suzana.kraljic@um.si.

[1] Endemic means the normal and usual occurrence of a disease in a given population. If a disease crosses a certain threshold (for example, for influenza, this threshold is 10% of the population) and spreads rapidly, we speak of an epidemic. In an epidemic, although the outbreak is rapid and crosses a critical threshold in terms of magnitude, the disease is still confined to a specific area. However, if the disease crosses national borders or even spreads

these have impacted individuals, countries and, of course, family life. The current COVID-19 pandemic, which appeared in Europe in early 2020, has also had an immediate and profound impact on our established lives.[2] The consequences immediately spread to almost all areas of our lives (for example, the economy, human mobility, education and health care). There is no doubt that COVID-19 has also impacted family relationships in all respects. As a particularly social and vulnerable group, children were or are still exposed to the impact and consequences of COVID-19. They faced the extinction of public life, the loss of friends and the death of relatives, schooling moved online, sports and cultural clubs did not function, etc. Restrictions on movement and curfews limited the dynamics of their lives mainly to the family environment, which did have its advantages. On the other hand, children became even more exposed to domestic violence and increased distress and fear, as many did not understand the new situation, which thus affected family relationships. Despite the multifaceted nature of the issues raised by the COVID-19 pandemic, this chapter focuses only on the impact and consequences in the area of family relations.

2. THE IMPACT OF COVID-19 ON PARTNER RELATIONSHIPS

In 2016, the Civil Union Act[3] (CUA) was adopted, which made the status of same-sex partners in a civil union equal to that of married couples. Following the CUA, in 2017 the new Family Code[4] (FC) was adopted. In Slovenia, four types of partnership are regulated by the law: marriage, extra-marital union, civil union, and de facto civil union. The first two are intended only for heterosexual partners, i.e. men and women. At the same time, a civil union and de facto civil union are possible only between same-sex partners, i.e. between two men or two women. At the same time, the CUA did not grant same-sex partners rights that are certainly among the most desirable, namely the right to marry and the right to joint adoption of a child in Slovenia. Nor do they have the right to IVF in Slovenia.

---

to other continents, we speak of a pandemic (S. Kraljić, 'Historische Aspekte ausgewählter rechtlicher Maßnahmen zur Verhinderung der Ausbreitung von Infektionskrankheiten', in: E.C. Herger, B. Holcman and M. Steppan (eds.), *Festschrift Gernot Kocher zum 80. Geburtstag: für den Interpreten der Bildsprache*, Leykam, 2022, p. 207.

2 Slovenia declared an epidemic at 6 pm on 12 March 2020 based on Article 7 of the Communicable Diseases Act (*Zakon o nalezljivih boleznih*): Uradni list RS, št. 33/06 – official consolidated version, 49/20 – ZIUZEOP, 142/20, 175/20 – ZIUOPDVE, 15/21 – ZDUOP, 82/21, 178/21 – odl. US.

3 Civil Union Act (*Zakon o partnerski zvezi*): Uradni list RS, št. 33/16, 94/22- odl. US.

4 Family Code (*Družinski zakonik*): Uradni list RS, št. 15/17, 21/18 – ZNOrg, 22/19, 67/19 – ZMatR-C, 200/20 – ZOOMTVI, 94/22- odl. US.

However, on 8 July 2022, the Constitutional Court of the Republic of Slovenia (CCRS)[5] ruled that legislation stipulating that only two people of different sexes can marry and that same-sex partners living in a formal partnership cannot adopt a child jointly is unconstitutional. The CCRS annulled the first sentence of Article 2(3) of the CUA and the first indent of Article 22 of the FC. It further found that Article 3(3)(1) of the FC ('marriage is the union of husband and wife'), is incompatible with the Slovene Constitution. Articles 213(1) and 223 of the FC are also incompatible with the Constitution. Therefore, the National Assembly has six months to rectify the unconstitutionality. Marriage is considered a living union between two persons, regardless of gender, and same-sex partners living in a civil partnership may jointly adopt a child under the same conditions as spouses.

COVID-19 and related measures to curb its spread led to fewer marriages than usual in 2020. In 2020, there were 5,214 marriages in Slovenia, or 1,458 (21.9 per cent) fewer than in 2019. The marriage rate, or the number of marriages per 1,000 inhabitants, was 2.5 in 2020, the lowest since the number of marriages has been tracked statistically in Slovenia (i.e. since 1954).[6]

The lowest number of marriages was recorded in April 2020, with 95.9 per cent fewer marriages contracted than the average number of marriages in April from 2015 to 2019. This is due to the adoption of measures to curb the spread of COVID-19, which severely affected and limited family life and, by extension, partnership life. The subsequent relaxation of the measures in turn led to an increase in marriages. In August 2020, 1,009 marriages were contracted, which is 9.3 per cent higher than the average for August 2015–2019. The epidemic was re-declared in October, and when the related measures were put back in place, the number of marriages contracted fell again. In November and December 2020, there were 71 and 42.7 per cent fewer marriages respectively than the average for November and December in 2015–2019.[7]

In 2020, there were also registered 47 civil unions (same-sex partnerships) in Slovenia, 21 for men and 26 for women. In Slovenia, however, there are no statistics on extra-marital unions and de facto civil unions, as no formality is required for their creation, making it impossible to keep statistics.

There were also fewer divorces in 2020, with 1,774 (or 28 per cent) fewer than in 2019. Marriages that ended in divorce in 2020 had lasted on average 14.2 years. In 2020, 941 (or 53 per cent) were marriages with no minor dependent children. The remaining 833 (or 47 per cent) had a total of 1,389 dependent minor children at the time of divorce. Most of the dependent minor children

5 U-I-486/20-14, 8 July 2022.

6 SURS, 'V letu 2020 manj porok in manj razvez kot v 2019', 2021, available at: <https://www.stat.si/StatWeb/News/Index/9580>, last accessed 24.02.2022.

7 Ibid.

(63.6 per cent) were assigned to their mothers at the time of divorce, 4.9 per cent of children were assigned to fathers, and 29.1 per cent to both parents.[8]

One of the new FC's most significant modifications and innovations in 2017[9] was related to notaries. The FC also introduced the option of contractual property regulation between spouses, allowing them to opt out of the legal property regime and govern and adapt their property relations according to their wants and expectations. Article 85 of the FC regulates the so-called 'contract on the regulation of property relations between the spouses' (in Slovene: *pogodba o ureditvi premoženjskopravnih razmerij med zakoncema*; hereinafter: contract) or the contractual property regime as an alternative to the statutory matrimonial property regime. The autonomy of the spouses is reflected in their decision to enter into a contract and thereby change the statutory matrimonial property regime. It is for the future spouses to decide whether they will use such a contract and change the statutory matrimonial property regime or not. That reflects the spouses' autonomy.[10] The contract shall be in the form of a notarial deed. According to the Register of Contracts on the Arrangement of Property Relations,[11] administered by the Chamber of Notaries of Slovenia, in the first year of the FC (April–December 2019), 96 couples chose to use the contract. In 2020 and 2021, which have been marked by COVID-19, there were 108 contracts in 2020 and 98 in 2021. In the light of these statistics, and given that this is an innovation that only allows contracts to be concluded from April 2019, it is difficult to draw any concrete conclusions on the impact of COVID-19 on this property law relationship.

Partnerships also felt the impact of COVID-19 in the case of prisoners, whose visits were immediately stopped or severely restricted when the epidemic was declared in Slovenia, which meant that they may have lost genuine contact with their partners (and children), even though they had so-called online contact.[12] The restriction on visits has applied to all visitors. However, Slovenian prisons have been very quick to address this issue. By respecting safety requirements (e.g. disinfection, masks, glass walls), visits were restored to immediate family, especially spouses, parents and, initially, adult children, but later also minors.

---

8 Ibid.

9 The FC was adopted on 21 March 2017, published in the Slovene Official Journal (Uradni list) on 31 March 2017 and came into force on 15 March 2017. Due to preparations for the changes and innovations, its application was postponed for two years. The FC has thus been applicable since 15 April 2019.

10 See e.g. S. Kraljić, 'Slovenia. The role of the Slovene Public Notary in property relations between partners under the (new) Family Code' in M.F. Brinig (ed.), *International Survey of Family Law*, Intersentia, 2021, p. 436.

11 The Register is a computerised database maintained by the Chamber of Notaries of Slovenia.

12 Before COVID-19, Slovenian prisons were facing overcrowding. As a result, on 1 January 2000 there were 1,449 prisoners in Slovenia, which represented 108.9% of the prison capacity. On 15 April 2020, i.e. a good month after the declaration of the COVID-19 epidemic in

3. THE IMPACT OF COVID-19 ON PARENT–CHILD RELATIONS

Since the declaration of the epidemic in Slovenia (12 March 2020), to limit the spread of COVID-19 we have all been subject to various restrictions in our professional and private lives. Social isolation, school/child care closures and job insecurity have given rise to unprecedented conditions for families raising children at home.[13] The same has held true in Slovenia. COVID-19 has not affected all families equally. It has inflicted more harm on the children of low-income and less educated parents, who tend to have lower academic and socio-emotional skills compared to higher-income or more educated parents.[14]

During the first and second waves of COVID-19, the European Union Member States generally allowed smooth and safe travel for professional reasons. Recognising the importance of family ties, countries also allowed cross-border travel for personal reasons. At the same time, the COVID-19 crisis has often led to the separation of family members located in different Member States. This, of course, made an essential contribution to the fight against the COVID-19, but family life naturally suffered as a result. Member States have thus made it possible to reunite families safely, with exceptions to travel restrictions.[15] Slovenia also included family reunification among the exceptions that allowed movement between municipalities during the curfew and also cross-border travel.

The COVID-19 pandemic has also left its mark on the field of parent–child relationships, where divorced parents, in particular, have been suddenly confronted with a whole new set of circumstances, hitherto unknown. The child's contact with the parent with whom the child does not live is usually arranged directly, often overnight and over the weekend. Thus in the ordinary course of contact, children move from one parent's household to the other. Article 141(1) of the FC provides that a child has the right to contact with both parents and both parents have the right to contact with the child. The right of

Slovenia, the number of prisoners was reduced to 1,122, which was 84.4% of the available capacity, as a result of the measures taken to contain the spread of the disease.

13 See for more A.C. Gadermann, K.C. Thomson, C.G. Richardson et al., 'Examining the impacts of the COVID-19 pandemic on family mental health in Canada: findings from a national cross-sectional study' (2021) 11 *BMJ Open* 1, doi:10.1136/bmjopen-2020-042871.

14 A. Kalil, S. Mayer and R. Shah, 'Working Paper No. 2020 – 143 Impact of the COVID-19 Crisis on Family Dynamics in Economically Vulnerable Households', October 2020, p. 3, available at: <https://bfi.uchicago.edu/wp-content/uploads/2020/10/BFI_WP_2020143.pdf>, last accessed 01.03.2022.

15 European Commission, Communication from the Commission: COVID-19 – Towards a phased and coordinated approach for restoring freedom of movement and lifting internal border controls, OJ C 169/30, 15.05.2020, p. 7.

contact may be restricted or withdrawn if the contact endangers the child, and their best interests can be protected only in this way. Contact enables the child to maintain a parent–child relationship, which has a significant impact on the child's growth and development. A child's right to contact is a personal, inalienable, non-transferable right linked to the child's immediate family relationship. The right to contact is expressed in real life through visits, the right to participate in the child's upbringing, and the right to take the child on holidays. In exercising the contact, the parent must ensure the child's safety and health and exercise supervision.[16]

The restrictions have particularly affected how contact between parents and children is conducted. Contact between a child and a parent who live separately cause complications in everyday life, even in the absence of a pandemic.[17] The COVID-19 pandemic has created many new problems or deepened existing ones.

As already mentioned, the declaration of an epidemic in Slovenia also brought with it strict measures, with many restrictions (for example curfews) and many (health-related) recommendations. Following the instructions given at that time by the authorities, children should not be passed between families, as this would allow infection to be transferred from one environment to another. These instructions caused confusion and distress for parents who do not live with their children, since the measures restricted the movement between municipalities. Therefore, on 6 April 2020 the Supreme Court of the Republic of Slovenia intervened and published the following clarifications on its website:

> The resulting emergency situation causes severe distress for separated parents and their children, and often a desire to avoid direct contact with the parent with whom the child is no longer living for the duration of the epidemic. We believe that, in the absence of any risk circumstances on the part of the parents or the child or other close family members living in the same household, there are generally no grounds for such a measure, which would place them in a particularly vulnerable group.[18]

The Court emphasised that, in the context of the COVID-19 pandemic, the absence of contact should not be an excuse for not exercising it or for it to be withdrawn.[19] Contact had to be coordinated and adapted in a way that

---

16 See S. Kraljić, *Družinski zakonik: [s komentarjem]*, Poslovna založba MB, 1st ed., 2019, pp. 455–456.

17 O. Szeibert, 'Human Rights During the COVID-19 Pandemic in Hungary with Special Regard to the Right to Have Contact' (2021) 14(2) *Medicine, Law & Society* 411.

18 It was announced on 6 April 2020 on the website of the Supreme Court of the Republic of Slovenia (www.sodisce.si), but is no longer available.

19 *VSL sklep IV Cp 897/2020* (ECLI:SI:VSLJ:2020:IV.CP.897.2020), 17 June 2020.

minimised the possibility of spreading infection but still kept children and parents who were living apart connected. For this reason, an exception to the prohibition on crossing municipal borders was allowed, as it was also written in the announcement of the Ljubljana District Court on 6 April 2020. Contact between parents and children who did not live in the same municipality was possible, since, according to the published position of the Ministry of the Interior, the measure prohibiting movement outside the place of permanent or temporary residence did not apply to the maintenance of contact between parents and children which had been arranged by a court settlement or a court decision.[20]

As already mentioned, COVID-19 and these restrictions quickly made their way into court decisions on the implementation of parent–child contact. Thus, the Supreme Court's position was evident when it stated in its decision that if parents adhere to the prescribed precautions and follow the position of the Ministry of Justice, personal contacts should be carried out if possible despite the crisis period of the pandemic.[21] The Ministry of Justice also suggested that if contact could not be provided or implemented due to the risk of spreading COVID-19, parents should use technology, telephones or possibly videoconferencing to provide contact aimed at maintaining a relationship with the other parent. If the parents cannot reach an agreement, the court will decide on these issues.

The court has also held that the COVID-19 pandemic is not a reason not to have contact if there is no risk to the parents, the child or other close relatives living in the same household.[22] When contact takes place, it is necessary to assess whether there are risk factors involved. The primary goal is for the parents to agree on the continuation of contact, even during a pandemic.[23] The parents themselves know best the family dynamics, the needs of the child and their capacity to provide contact. If the parents cannot reach an agreement on contact themselves, the Social Work Centre and mediators can help. If the parents themselves, even with the help of the Social Work Centre and the mediator, cannot reach a contact agreement, the court will decide on contact. The court may restrict or withdraw the right to contact from one or both parents and determine that face-to-face contact should not occur if this is the only way to protect the child's best interests.[24] Through contact, the child maintains or gains

---

20 S. Ahlin-Doljak, 'Otrok ima pravico do stikov tudi v času epidemije' (2021) 11 *Pravna praksa* 11; Odvetništvo Pipuš, 'Problematika stikov otroka s tistim od staršev, kateremu otrok ni zaupan v varstvo in vzgojo v času epidemije bolezni COVID-19 (t. i. Koronavirus)', n.d., available at: <https://www.pipus.si/stiki-z-otroki-koronavirus>, last accessed 23.02.2022.

21 *VSL sklep IV Cp 897/2020* (ECLI:SI:VSLJ:2020:IV.CP.897.2020), 17 June 2020.

22 *VSL sklep IV Cp 1978/2020* (ECLI:SI:VSLJ:2020:IV.CP.1978.2020), 2 December 2020.

23 Republika Slovenija, 'Izvajanje stikov med starši in otroki v času epidemije, 6. april 2020', 2020, available at: <http://www.sodisce.si/vsrs/objave/2020040610490634/>, last accessed 02.10.2020.

24 Kraljić, above n. 16, pp. 299–300.

a sense of emotional attachment, belonging and connectedness to the parent he or she does not live with. The emergency situation and the potential risk of infection are not in themselves grounds for interfering with a court decision already made nor for further restricting the child's already reduced contact with the non-custodial parent. The court stated that living with the COVID-19 virus is becoming a reality, and the solution lies not in limiting contact but in taking responsibility for implementing protective measures to prevent infection.[25]

The custodial parent can provide for the child's emotional, educational and protective needs during the contact, especially in an area where the other parent is not skilled or is unable to do so. Even if the measures are only for one or two months, this could feel like an eternity to a youngster who does not see his non-custodial parent.[26] Even if the child was sick and in a health care institution, contact can be made during a pandemic if the child's health status allows, taking into account the instructions for preventing infection with COVID-19.[27]

In another case, the court rejected the mother's excessive and unreasonable request that the father should prove by taking a test that he was not infected with COVID-19. Since the mother, as the custodial parent, does not need to be tested, the father, as the non-custodial parent, does not need to prove that he is not infected to have contact with his daughter.[28]

As mentioned above, the child's right to contact may also be restricted or withdrawn if the exercise of contact would not be in the child's best interests (Article 173 of the FC). The court issued such an opinion in a case where the petitioner was employed in Italy and worked at various construction sites. The court considered that it was a well-known fact that Italy was (at that time) a country in which the morbidity caused by COVID-19 was very high. Therefore, the reasons justifying the court's decision not to have the child continue personal contact during a declared epidemic, when strict measures were in force, were to protect the best interests of the child, and were convincing.[29] The restriction or withdrawal of the right to contact must always be in accordance with the principle of proportionality.[30]

---

25 *VSL sklep IV Cp 1046/2020* (ECLI:SI:VSLJ:2020:IV.CP.1046.2020), 21 July 2020.

26 *VSC sklep I Ip 135/2020* (ECLI:SI:VSCE:2020:I.IP.135.2020), 6 April 2020.

27 *VSL sklep IV Cp 66/2021* (ECLI:SI:VSLJ:2021:IV.CP.66.2021), 2 February 2021.

28 *VSL sklep IV Cp 931/2020* (ECLI:SI:VSLJ:2020:IV.CP.931.2020), 16 June 2020.

29 *VSL sklep IV Cp 929/2020* (ECLI:SI:VSLJ:2020:IV.CP.929.2020), 9. July 2020.

30 More about the principle of proportionality see S. Kraljić and K. Drnovšek, 'Zaštita najboljeg interesa djeteta kod posvojenja i utjecaj načela razmjernosti' in A. Huseinbegović (ed.), *Aktuelna problematika porodičnopravne teorije i prakse: zbornik radova*, Deveti međunarodni naučni skup Dani porodičnog prava, Mostar, Pravni fakultet Univerziteta 'Džemal Bijedić', 2021, pp. 264–276.

In another court decision, the court noted that Slovenia and other parts of Europe were in a state of emergency due to the COVID-19 pandemic, which prevented travel and border crossings. Therefore, the court decided that the petitioner could not be faulted for not travelling from Germany to Slovenia and making the court-ordered personal contact. Thus, the court stressed that it was more important that both parties to the proceedings (father and mother) should make arrangements for video contact to occur. This is the task of the petitioner and the respondent, as such contact can only take place with their cooperation.[31]

During the COVID-19 pandemic, the family courts have also addressed applications for interim injunctions under the Domestic Violence Act[32] (DVA) and applications for measures to protect the child's best interests under the FC. In applications for interim measures, the courts shall not carry out procedural and enforcement actions requiring personal contact between the enforcers, participants and other persons involved in these proceedings unless the performance of these actions is necessary to avert a threat to the life and health of persons or property of significant value.[33] All orders, meetings and hearings shall be conducted by videoconference, provided that the technical and spatial conditions are met. If this is not possible, the judge will assess, taking into account the circumstances of the individual case, which procedural steps to take and in what manner and will justify this in the decision issued. There is a need to involve a family law lawyer in such cases.[34]

The Supreme Court of the Republic of Slovenia has taken a different view on supervised contact. Supervised contact is ordinarily carried out at the competent Social Work Centres, but during the pandemic, the Centres have direct contact with clients only in emergency cases. As a rule, therefore, ordinary supervised contact is not carried out at Social Work Centres. In cases where supervised contact is provided, in the event of a prolonged pandemic the court, taking into account the circumstances of the individual case, will have to find an alternative solution to the parents' proposal and resolve it by means of an interim order in the best interests of the child. A family law lawyer must make the application for a change of contact.[35]

Courts have also ruled on the impact of COVID-19 on the maintenance obligation of the parent as the maintenance obligor. In one case, the parent claimed that his ability to support his child had been affected by the COVID-19 pandemic. The court found that the parent's allegations of the impact of

---

31 *VSL sklep IV Cp 895/2020* (ECLI:SI:VSLJ:2020:IV.CP.895.2020), 16 June 2020.

32 Domestic Violence Act (*Zakon o preprečevanju nasilja v družini*): Uradni list RS, št. 16/08, 68/16, 54/17 – ZSV-H, 196/21 – ZDOsk.

33 Odvetništvo Pipuš, above n. 20.

34 Ibid.

35 Ibid.

COVID-19 on his ability to work were merely vague. In particular, the parent did not specifically explain why, despite having a two-year time limit which he claims expired in August 2020, he did not complete additional training by passing a professional examination, which ultimately resulted in the amicable termination of his employment contract and the beginning of a new part-time contract, and hence a lower monthly income. Therefore, the court concluded that the applicant had not explained in the proceedings how the COVID-19 pandemic had affected his training or the fulfilment of the conditions of his employment contract, or how much funding was required for the latter. The mere assertion of these reasons, which were not fully explained, could not affect the court's decision.[36]

In another maintenance case, the court argued that despite the COVID-19 pandemic leading to the lockdowns and restrictions, the pandemic by itself could not be dispositive as to whether the petitioner had lower costs during her graduation year as a result. A needs assessment is never a precise mathematical calculation, which would be practically impossible in the court's view. The cost of living for necessities can also vary considerably from month to month (both in type and amount), which is a well-known fact of life. The monthly estimate is therefore an approximation of an average.[37]

4. THE IMPACT OF COVID-19 ON ADOPTION

The FC provides for only one form of adoption – full adoption (*adoptio plena*). According to Article 218(1) of the FC, a child may only be put up for adoption if the parents, after the child's birth, have consented to the adoption before the Social Work Centre or the court. Consent for adoption must be confirmed after the child is eight weeks old. Otherwise, the consent has no legal effect. However, if one of the parents has been deprived of child care responsibilities or is permanently unable to express his or her wishes, his or her consent is not required.

COVID-19 also impacted adoption in Slovenia. There were fewer adoptions in 2020 compared to the years before the COVID-19 pandemic. In 2020, only 21 child adoptions were recorded in Slovenia, compared to 47 in 2019. Of the 21 children adopted, 14 were adopted by couples (in 2019, 21 children were adopted by couples), i.e. by spouses or cohabiting couples. In seven adoptions in 2020, the adopter was the spouse/partner of the child's biological parent,

---

36 *VSM sklep III Cp 289/2021* (ECLI:SI:VSMB:2021:III.CP.289.2021), 18 May 2021.

37 *VSL sklep IV Cp 1605/2021* (ECLI:SI:VSLJ:2021:IV.CP.1605.2021), 29 October 2021.

while in 2019 this was the case for 22 children. In this situation, unlike when neither adoptor is related to the child, the couple can also be same-sex partners from a civil union or de facto civil union. In 2020, there were no adoptions by individuals, while in 2019 four children were adopted by individuals.[38]

5. CONCLUSION

COVID-19 has been influencing our lives in all areas for two years now, but especially our family lives. As a social group, children have been impacted and affected by the pandemic in many areas. Social contact is of great importance for a child's development. The closure of educational institutions has undoubtedly had an impact, and we will certainly be discussing the long-term consequences for many years to come. COVID-19 has, of course, also had an impact on partner relationships, as well as on parent–child relationships. In Slovenia, we saw a sharp decline in marriage in 2020 as a result of COVID-19. The reasons for this are certainly the various restrictions and measures that have been taken to curb the spread of COVID-19. There has also been a decrease in the number of adoptions, mainly influenced by restrictions on travel abroad and by restrictions on the activities of State bodies. In particular, the courts have been affected by restrictions on movement in the exercise of contact. It must be said that the interests and welfare of children have always been the priority The courts have been aware that it is precisely during this public health crisis that children must continue to have contact with the parent with whom he or she does not live, subject, of course, to measures to contain the spread of COVID-19.

[38] SURS, 'Priznanja in ugotovitve očetovstva, posvojitve otrok, Slovenija – 2020', 2021, available at: <https://www.stat.si/StatWeb/News/Index/9653>, last accessed 06.03.2022.

SOUTH AFRICA

HOMOSEXUAL MUSLIMS IN SOUTH AFRICA

Some Legal Implications, Including Constitutional, Marriage and Succession

Najma MOOSA and Zaahirah AMERICA*

* nmoosa@uwc.ac.za. The chapter is a revised version of a 2021 research paper submitted by Ms. America in the Muslim Personal Law (MPL) module taught by the primary author. It was completely reworked for publication by Professor Moosa (with some collaboration from Ms. America). Unless otherwise indicated, the information in this chapter pertaining to Imam Muhsin Hendricks was gleaned from personal communications between him and the primary author of this chapter from February to April 2022.

Résumé

Les ouvrages ont tendance à traiter séparément de la succession et de l'homosexualité dans l'Islam, et ne mettent pas l'accent sur la liberté testamentaire et les droits de succession des homosexuels masculins (gays) et féminins (lesbiennes). Cet article montre que l'homosexualité, *i.e.* le fait d'avoir un rapport sexuel gay ou de consentir à un mariage homosexuel, au-delà de l'identification de l'orientation sexuelle, est interdite dans l'Islam en ce qu'elle constitue une zina (généralement l'adultère entre personnes hétérosexuelles). Les homosexuels ne correspondent pas tout à fait à cette définition, et le terme « homosexualité » ne figure pas dans le Coran (livre saint de l'islam). La zina est interdite dans le Coran, qui la considère également comme un crime hadd (crime contre Dieu qui entraîne une punition spécifique). Bien que l'homosexualité en elle-même ne soit pas traitée comme un obstacle à l'héritage en raison de la nature hétéronormative de la loi islamique sur la succession, les érudits religieux (oulémas) ont une croyance dominante (conservatrice) selon laquelle, lorsque les homosexuels défendent ouvertement des points de vue alternatifs (progressistes) en désaccord avec la position islamique, par exemple en les exprimant ou en écrivant à ce sujet, cela constitue une apostasie (ridda). L'apostasie, comme la zina, est un crime hadd. De plus, les apostats (murtads) ont quitté le cadre de l'islam. Ainsi, un imam gay sud-africain (clerc musulman) et son organisation gay inclusive ont tous deux été exclus de l'islam par un corps d'ulémas de la province du Cap occidental. Contrairement à la zina, l'apostasie est un motif de déchéance, et donc d'exclusion, de l'héritage. Ainsi, elle a un impact à la fois sur les droits des bénéficiaires « musulmans » homosexuels à recevoir un héritage et sur la liberté des testateurs « musulmans » homosexuels à léguer un héritage. Les droits des testateurs et des bénéficiaires hétérosexuels sont garantis par la Constitution de la République d'Afrique du Sud (1996). Les homosexuels pratiquant leur homosexualité, notamment lorsqu'ils sont mariés avec une personne de même sexe, sont protégés par d'autres lois et par la jurisprudence de la Cour constitutionnelle. Cet article analyse les implications constitutionnelles, non encore vérifiées judiciairement, d'une éventuelle exhérédation par les testateurs musulmans des bénéficiaires homosexuels en raison de leur orientation sexuelle, de leur homosexualité ou de leurs convictions religieuses (apostasie).

1. INTRODUCTION

This chapter focuses on the succession rights and testamentary freedom of male (gay) and female (lesbian) homosexuals in Islam and in South Africa.

It highlights that the practice of male homosexuality, through an act of gay sex or entering into a same-sex marriage (*nikah*), rather than mere identification with the status of being homosexual (sexual orientation), are prohibited in Islam. However, Muslim scholars and religious authorities (*ulama*),[1] in South Africa and elsewhere, hold opposing conservative (default) and progressive views in this regard. Some progressive scholars and *ulama* are gay, gay imams or gay converts to Islam, and some have entered into same-sex *nikahs* and long-term same-sex partnerships. Contrary to the default Islamic law position, and in line with progressive views, the controlling law in South Africa, the Constitution of the Republic of South Africa, 1996 (Constitution, 1996 Constitution or final Constitution) protects gays and lesbians from unfair discrimination on grounds of sexual orientation and religion. Although the term 'sexual orientation' encompasses both heterosexual (opposite-sex attracted) and homosexual (same-sex attracted) persons, and by implication the rights of everyone falling under the umbrella of LGBTQ+,[2] the focus of this chapter is restricted to homosexual persons. The term 'gay' is sometimes used as a synonym for homosexuals of both sexes, and 'queer' as a synonym for LGBTQ+ persons in general.

Apart from the Constitution, through the intervention of the judiciary, including the apex Constitutional Court (CC), male sodomy has been decriminalised, legislation permits same-sex civil marriage, and succession laws have been amended to protect from unfair discrimination against persons in unrecognised permanent same-sex partnerships and opposite-sex Muslim marriages (*nikahs*). South African Muslims are able to, and some do, enter into all these types of marriages and relationships, including same-sex *nikahs*.

This chapter contends that a homosexual orientation, homosexuality and same-sex marriages may not be treated as impediments to inheritance because of the heteronormative nature of the Islamic law of succession. However, it is a dominantly held (conservative) belief of religious scholars (*ulama*) that when homosexuals publicly (for example, by voicing or writing about them)

---

1 In this chapter the Arabic term '*ulama*' (singular '*alim*') is used to refer to Muslim religious authorities and includes clerics, such as 'imam', '*shaykh*' (also spelt '*sheikh*'), '*moulana*' or '*mufti*'.

2 This acronym translates as lesbian, gay, bisexual, transgender, queer (or sometimes questioning) and further identities represented by the 'plus' symbol. See K. Cherry, 'What Does LGBTQ+ Mean?', *Verywell Mind*, available at: <https://www.verywellmind.com/what-does-lgbtq-mean-5069804>, last accessed 05.05.2022.

advocate alternative (progressive) views disagreeing with the default Islamic position, the act of claiming an Islamic basis for their views is regarded as unbelief and therefore such persons are deemed to be apostates (*murtads*). An *ulama* body in the Western Cape Province has issued an Islamic legal opinion (*fatwa*, plural *fatawas*) to this effect and declared a gay imam (Muslim cleric) to be beyond the fold of Islam on these grounds. This is problematic because apostasy (*ridda*), usually limited to a voluntary or deliberate renunciation of Islam, is a ground for disqualification, and therefore exclusion, from inheritance. It would accordingly have an impact on both the rights of homosexual 'Muslim' beneficiaries to receive an inheritance and the freedom of homosexual 'Muslim' testators to bequeath an inheritance. The religious-based Muslim personal or family law (MPL), which is regulated by the prescriptions of *Shari'a*, includes marriage and succession. Since the *ulama* body provides guidance and assistance in such matters (which may end up in court and be enforced in South Africa), this chapter analyses the possible implications for this role of the *ulama* body's stated positions on homosexuality and same-sex marriage.

Since the rights of heterosexual testators and homosexual beneficiaries are also guaranteed by the Constitution, this chapter analyses the as-yet judicially untested constitutional implications of a potential disqualification by Muslim testators of homosexual beneficiaries on the basis of their sexual orientation, homosexuality or religious conviction (apostasy).

In addition to this introduction (section 1) and the conclusion (section 7), which proposes some recommendations for the way forward, the chapter is divided into a further five sections as follows. Section 2 briefly refers to the discourse on homosexuality in Islam to highlight that it forms the basis of opposing views held by Muslim academics and *ulama*. Section 3 briefly elaborates on the position of homosexual sexual orientation, homosexuality and same-sex marriage in terms of South African law. Section 4 briefly elaborates on opposing views on homosexuality in South Africa and among *ulama*. Section 5 briefly focuses on the implications of apostasy and elaborates on some of the differences between the South African and Islamic laws of succession. Section 5 also examines how the *ulama* body in question, given its stated position on homosexuality, will respond to a homosexual Muslim testator seeking its services, and how impartial and unbiased its advice to testators and lawyers can be expected to be. Section 6 examines whether excluding homosexuals from inheriting on the basis of apostasy, and the different treatment of such persons on the basis of their sex and gender, would amount to unfair discrimination on the basis of religion and sexual orientation in South Africa, and would not pass constitutional muster if challenged on these grounds.

2. HOMOSEXUAL SEXUAL ORIENTATION AND HOMOSEXUALITY IN ISLAM[3] AND THE OPPOSING VIEWS OF MUSLIM SCHOLARS AND *ULAMA*

Progressive and conservative Muslim scholars and *ulama* in South Africa and elsewhere advocate divergent or opposing views on whether homosexuality and same-sex marriage are prohibited in Islam based on the same two primary sources, namely, the Quran[4] (holy book of Islam) and the *Sunna* (traditions) of Prophet Muhammad (on whom be peace) and the Islamic law (*Shari'a*) interpretations thereof. Two further subsidiary 'sources' of Islam or legal techniques are also used for resolving these issues. These are *qiyas* (analogical deductions or logical reasoning based on the primary sources) and *ijma* (consensus of opinions of either *ulama* or Muslim communities in any particular age on any matter of *Shari'a* or juridical rule based on the primary sources).

Much has been written on the default Islamic position. That default position may elicit future constitutional challenges, focusing greater attention on the less well-known progressive alternative. This latter position will accordingly be discussed in detail.

Although the Quran may allude to both male and female homosexuality,[5] it does not refer to, or contain, explicit words that mean 'homosexual' (lesbian and gay), 'homosexuality' or 'heterosexuality'. All these words are recent (nineteenth century) constructs coined after the advent of Islam (seventh century) and equivalent Arabic terms had to be invented.[6]

The Quran was revealed to Muhammad over a period of 23 years. Hence his traditions (things he did or said or tacitly consented to) also serve as a magnifying glass through which Quranic verses have been interpreted.

---

3 Unless otherwise indicated, definitions and explanatory information pertaining to the sources of Islam and Islamic law detailed in this section were summarised from N. Moosa, *Unveiling the Mind: The Legal Position of Women in Islam – A South African Context*, Juta, 2nd ed., 2011, pp. xxxv, xxxvi, xxxviii, xxxix, 21, 27, 30–31, 56 and 68–70.

4 Quranic references in this chapter are given in the format: Q.1:2. The first number is the number of the chapter or *surah*. The number following the separating colon indicates the verse or *ayat*. Due to space constraints, unless otherwise indicated, the content of Quranic verses can be found in the English translation of the Quran by Yusuf Ali. See Y. Ali, *The Holy Qur'an: Text, Translation and Commentary*, Islamic Education Centre, 1946.

5 See e.g. Q.4:15, Q.4:16 (read with Q.24:2), and Q.24:31.

6 See S.S.A. Kugle, 'Sexuality, Diversity, and Ethics in the Agenda of Progressive Muslims' in O. Safi (ed.), *Progressive Muslims: On Justice, Gender and Pluralism*, Oneworld, 2003, pp. 200–201; H. Oosterhuis, 'Sexual Modernity in the Works of Richard von Krafft-Ebing and Albert Moll' (2012) 56(2) *Medical History* 144; and G.D. Newby, *'Lûṭ'*, *A Concise Encyclopedia of Islam*, Oneworld, 2004, p. 132.

Although Muhammad was not keen that this occur during his lifetime, lest they overshadow the Quran, these traditions were nonetheless embodied in a body of texts contained in books called *hadith* (plural *ahadith*), compiled some 200 years after his death. This chapter focuses on the collections of *ahadith* compiled by Imam Al-Bukhari and Imam Muslim (imams of traditions as distinguished from the imams of Islamic jurisprudence referred to below), as these are the two most authoritative and reliable (*sahih* or authentic) collections.[7]

Shari'a is used in this chapter to refer to the classical Islamic law or jurisprudence developed in the eighth century through the formation by jurists of essentially four different Sunni (orthodox) schools of thought (*madhahib*, singular *madhhab*), namely, Hanafi, Maliki, Shafi'i and Hanbali. These schools were named, in order of precedence, after their founders, namely, Imams Abu Hanifa, Malik, Shafi'i and Hanbal. These jurists interpreted and applied the sources of Islam in different ways and made it clear that they never intended their views on any topic to be a final expression of Islam if its primary sources indicated otherwise.[8]

The practice of homosexuality, rather than a mere homosexual sexual orientation, is regarded as a major sin, and therefore forbidden, in Islam. It is equated with sodomy or anal sex between males only. Since there is no equivalent term in Islam, and although it does not quite fit into this definition, male homosexuality is treated as analogous to, or as a form[9] of, *zina* (usually adultery but defined as pre- or extramarital illicit heterosexual sex)[10] which constitutes the gravest form of sexual misconduct in Islam. Since male homosexuality is treated as *zina*, it incurs *hadd* (plural *huddud*),[11] punishments imposed for the crime of *zina*. Because *hadd* punishments are clearly defined in the Quran, they are mandatory and non-discretionary. Nonetheless, although the act of homosexuality incurs sin and demands specified punishment, the Muslim parties involved are not condemned or expelled from the fold of Islam because of it. However, what is deemed to be problematic, and the actual rationale for such expulsion, is when such persons seek to publicly, by means of various forums (lectures, sermons) and mediums of communication (social media websites and blogs, publications, radio, television, film, etc.), defend and

---

7 Due to space constraints, unless otherwise indicated, English translations of the content of these *ahadith* can be found at <https://www.searchtruth.com/hadith_books.php>, last accessed 05.05.2022.

8 Moosa, above n. 3, pp. 58–59 and 137.

9 C. Adang, 'Ibn Hazam on Homosexuality' (2003) 24 *Al Qantara* 8.

10 Z. Mir-Hosseini and V. Hamzić, *Control and Sexuality: The Revival of Zina Laws in Muslim Contexts*, Women Living Under Muslim Laws (WLUML), 2010, p. 21.

11 Kugle, above n. 6, at pp. 190–234 (a *hadd* crime, or a crime against God, 'is a crime that is explicitly defined in the Qur'an and for which specific punishment is demanded in the Qur'an.' A discussion of the punishment for homosexuality, although further elaborated in the *Sunna*, is beyond the scope of this chapter).

justify their homosexuality, or homosexuality in general, on the basis of Islam. Since this is deemed not to be possible because homosexuality is, for example, not even mentioned in the Quran, claiming an Islamic basis for it is regarded as an act of *kufr* (unbelief or apostasy) and will mean such persons are deemed to be apostates (*murtads*). Apostasy is therefore not limited to an actual or voluntary renunciation of Islam, but includes crimes against God for which there is a corresponding *hadd* punishment, such as, apostasy (*ridda*),[12] *zina*,[13] and the slanderous accusation of *zina*.[14] Although *hadd* punishments for these crimes are non-discretionary, they are subject to strict evidentiary requirements being met,[15] and the proof thereof may be difficult, or near impossible, to obtain. For this reason, although local Muslims engage in both *zina*[16] and homosexuality (which fall under the same umbrella), they cannot frivolously be condemned or deemed to be apostates.

The rationale for concluding that only male homosexuality is forbidden in Islam is largely based on literal interpretations of the parable of the people of Lut[17] (Lot) in its primary source, the Quran. The story is found also in the Old Testament of the Christian Bible. Although the Quran does not generally or explicitly refer to women as 'inferior', pre-Islamic patriarchal values and male interpretations of the Quran are still treated as an inherent component of Muslim identity. It is therefore not unsurprising that the homosexual activity of lesbian females is treated differently from that of their male counterparts, even if both past and present authorities justify it on the basis of affording lesbians more favourable treatment as far as punishment for homosexuality is concerned.[18] The rationale for this is that lesbian intercourse (tribadism) does not involve anal sex but mere 'rubbing' of private parts. As a result, the sexual identity and experiences of lesbian Muslims are given hardly any serious attention.[19]

Although there is disagreement on *ahadith* attributed to the Prophet in this regard, both primary sources adopt a very negative position towards male homosexuality and, although to a lesser extent, female homosexuality.[20]

---

12 See e.g. Q.4:89.

13 See e.g. Q.24:2.

14 Adang, above n. 9, 8.

15 J. Rehman and E. Polymenopoulou, 'Is Green a Part of the Rainbow? *Sharia*, Homosexuality and LGBT Rights in the Muslim World' (2013) 37(1) *Fordham International Law Journal* 1, 10 and at n. 33.

16 N. Moosa, 'Polygynous Muslim Marriages in South Africa: Their Potential Impact on the Incidence of HIV/AIDS' (2017) 12(3) *Potchefstroom Electronic Law Journal* 65, 81.

17 Although there are several other chapters and verses referring to the story of Lut in the Quran, we refer only to the following verses in some chapters due to space constraints: Q.7:80–81, Q.15:67–68 and 71, Q.26:165, Q.29:28–29 and Q 54:37.

18 See Rehman and Polymenopoulou, above n. 15, 12.

19 See Adang, above n. 9, 7–8 (further reference to female homosexuality in the primary sources).

20 Ibid, at p. 9 (emphasis added).

Anal sex is also considered to be prohibited among men on the basis of several *ahadith*[21] in which the Prophet Muhammad exhorted men not to have anal intercourse with their wives. However, these *ahadith* emphasise that anal sex can occur among both male homosexuals and heterosexuals. Although many *ahadith* are cited in support of the orthodox position that homosexuality is forbidden in Islam,[22] it appears that the collections of *ahadith* compiled by Imam Al-Bukhari[23] and Imam Muslim may not necessarily support this as they do not appear to contain any references to homosexuality.[24]

The jurist-founders of the four schools of Islamic law essentially agreed that homosexuality, on the basis that it is analogous to *zina*, is forbidden in Islam, although they differed on the type of punishment to be imposed therefor.[25]

Although the Quran may allude to homosexuality, the fact that it makes no direct mention of it has also made it possible for Lut's story to be interpreted in a variety of ways. Some Muslim scholars, on the basis that the Quran is deemed by Muslims to be the literal word of God, adopt a literal reading of it, and therefore espouse the default or conservative view that homosexuality is irreconcilable with Islam. Some progressive scholars, by employing a subsidiary 'source' of Islam called *ijtihad* or 'independent reasoning' to apply the *Shari'a* to contemporary (modern) circumstances, have taken a fresh look at Lut's story, to come to an opposite conclusion. For example, Scott Kugle,[26] an American scholar and gay convert[27] to Islam, who favours the legitimacy of homosexuality from within an Islamic paradigm, argues that a contextual (semantic) reading of the story leads to a different conclusion. However, a study by another American scholar, Mobeen Vaid,[28] challenges the arguments and sources Kugle uses in his publications on sexual diversity and homosexuality in Islam.

Unfortunately, Sunni Muslims closed the gates of *ijtihad* a few centuries ago and declared that scholars must rely on the legal decisions of past authorities instead of on their own academic exertions. Fuelled by conservative

---

[21] See e.g. Book 29 (Divination and Omens) of Sunan Abu-Dawud, Hadith Number 3895.

[22] See M. Hendricks, 'Islamic Texts: A Source for Acceptance of Queer Individuals into Mainstream Muslim Society' (2010) 5 *The Equal Rights Review* 31, 32 and n. 16.

[23] See e.g. Sahih Bukhari, Book Number 72 (Dress), Hadith Number 774 (standing as an example of one such *hadith*, which, although emanating from one of the most reputable sources of *hadith* (Sahih al-Bukhari), occurs in a book pertaining to dress code).

[24] See also Hendricks, above n. 22, 42; and Kugle, above n. 6, at p. 220.

[25] See Hendricks, above n. 22, 33; and Rehman and Polymenopoulou, above n. 15, 11–12.

[26] See Kugle, above n. 6, at pp. 203–215.

[27] S. Henking, 'Coming Out Twice: Sexuality and Gender in Islam', *Religion Dispatches*, 17 April 2012.

[28] M. Vaid, 'Can Islam Accommodate Homosexual Acts? Qur'anic Revisionism and the Case of Scott Kugle' (2017) 34(3) *American Journal of Islamic Social Sciences* 45, 45.

religious rhetoric, section 4 will highlight that it is not uncommon for Muslim homosexuals to still experience discrimination (homophobia) in South Africa.

The default position is that a marriage (*nikah*) between persons of the same sex is deemed to be prohibited in Islam.[29] Quranic verses which encourage marriage[30] have been conservatively interpreted as only legitimising sexual relations between heterosexual persons. Yusuf Ali translates Q.24:32 (one of these verses) as: '*Marry* those among you who are single, or the virtuous ones among yourselves, *male or female*'. This verse could imply that the Quran, because it does not restrict marriage to one gender, may not necessarily disapprove of same-sex marriage.

In 2016 it was reported that '[t]here are 12 gay imams in the world and eight are openly gay'.[31] The following practical examples demonstrate that there are progressive *ulama* (all imams) who do not agree that homosexuality and same-sex and interfaith marriages are prohibited in Islam or that publicising a contrary view makes them apostates. A gay French imam entered into a same-sex *nikah* with a Muslim South African and did so with the blessing of another French imam.[32] He is the author of a book on homosexuality.[33] An American imam, who is very vocal about his views on homosexuality, converted to Islam after he came out as gay. He was in a long-standing relationship with a closeted Christian man.[34] The South African gay imam who will be referred to in section 4 entered into a long-term same-sex partnership and same-sex interfaith *nikah* with a Hindu Indian national. He also authored a journal article on homosexuality which is referenced in this section. While all these imams perform *nikah* ceremonies for homosexual couples, the South African imam is also a registered marriage officer able to perform same-sex civil unions in terms of the Civil Union Act 17 of 2006 (CUA).

---

29 K. Hodkinson, *Muslim Family Law: A Sourcebook*, Croom Helm, 1984, p. 92.

30 See Q.24:32–33, Q.24:33 and Q.24:3.

31 A.T. Singh, 'There are 8 openly gay imams in the world: Daayiee Abdullah', *The Times of India*, 15 June 2016.

32 See L. Pajon, 'Ludovic-Mohamed Zahed : gay et musulman, il garde le prêche' ('Ludovic-Mohamed Zahed: gay and Muslim, he keeps preaching'), *Jeun Afrique*, 19 April 2013, available at <https://www.jeuneafrique.com/137659/societe/ludovic-mohamed-zahed-gay-et-musulman-il-garde-le-pr-che>; and 'Concilier islam et homosexualité, le combat de Ludovic-Mohamed Zahed' ('Reconciling islam and homosexuality, the fight of Ludovic-Mohamed Zahed'), *France24*, 30 March 2012, available at: <https://www.france24.com/fr/20120330-france-mariage-homosexuel-musulmans-gay-religion-imam-coran-corps-livre-ludovic-mohamed-zahed>, last accessed 05.05.2022. (Google translations from French into English).

33 See L.M. Zahed, *Homosexuality, Transidentity, and Islam. A Study of Scripture Confronting the Politics of Gender and Sexuality*, Amsterdam University Press, 2020.

34 See C. Kuruvilla, '6 Questions With A Gay Imam, Daayiee Abdullah', *Huffington Post*, 10 April 2015, available at: <https://www.huffpost.com/entry/gay-imam-daayiee-abdullah_n_7043502>, last accessed 05.05.2022.

3. HOMOSEXUAL SEXUAL ORIENTATION, HOMOSEXUALITY AND SAME-SEX MARRIAGE IN TERMS OF SOUTH AFRICAN LAW

Since politically motivated racial segregation (apartheid) only ended in 1994, the main aim of the 1996 Constitution and the Equality Act, fully titled the Promotion of Equality and Prevention of Unfair Discrimination Act (PEPUDA),[35] enacted in 2000 on the basis of section 9 (equality clause) of the final Constitution, is to avoid the injustices of the past generated in South Africa by colonialism, apartheid and patriarchy.

In 1993 South Africa promulgated its first democratic Constitution (interim Constitution).[36] When the interim Constitution[37] directly included a prohibition of unfair discrimination on the basis of sexual orientation in a Bill of Fundamental Rights (Chapter 3), South Africa became the first country in the world to do so. This prohibition was retained in the Bill of Rights (Chapter 2) of the final Constitution.[38]

Although until democratic rule in South Africa, most laws had only catered for the needs of heterosexual persons, the equality clause of the final Constitution and the Equality Act explicitly recognise and protect the rights and identities of both male and female homosexual persons, under the term 'sexual orientation', regardless of religion.

The government has also amended existing laws to ensure that sexual minorities like homosexuals are protected from unfair discrimination. In most of these instances the judiciary, including the apex Constitutional Court, prompted these changes. They include the decriminalisation of sodomy (consensual anal sex between adult men) in 1998;[39] the recognition of same-sex marriages or partnerships with the passing of the CUA[40] in 2006; and amendments to the existing intestate and testate succession laws, namely, the Intestate Succession Act (ISA)[41] and the Wills Act.[42] Although not detailed in this chapter due to

35 Promotion of Equality and Prevention of Unfair Discrimination Act 4 of 2000.

36 Constitution of the Republic of South Africa Act 200 of 1993.

37 See ibid, s. 8(2).

38 Ibid, s. 9(3). See also D. Bilchitz, 'Constitutional Change and Participation of LGBTI Groups: A Case Study of South Africa', International Institute for Democracy and Electoral Assistance (International IDEA), 2015, pp. 4 and 17.

39 See *National Coalition for Gay and Lesbian Equality and Another v. Minister of Justice and Others* 1999 (1) SA 6 (CC).

40 Civil Union Act 17 of 2006 (the CUA came into being as a direct result of the decision of the CC in *Minister of Home Affairs and Another v. Fourie and Another* 2006 (1) SA 524 (CC) (1 December 2005)).

41 Intestate Succession Act 81 of 1987.

42 Wills Act 7 of 1953.

space constraints, some of these amendments include affording protection to persons in permanent or life-long same-sex partnerships and in heterosexual Muslim marriages (*nikahs*), even though these partnerships and *nikahs* are not formally, legally recognised.

4. OPPOSITION IN SOUTH AFRICA TO HOMOSEXUALITY AND TO SAME-SEX MARRIAGE

Historically, South Africa experienced periods of both Dutch and British colonialism, starting with Dutch colonialism in the mid-seventeenth century and terminating with British colonialism at the end of the nineteenth century. During the period of Dutch rule, Islam was introduced in South Africa, initially at the Cape (now the Western Cape Province) by Muslims who hailed from the Malay-Indonesian Archipelago (East Indies) and therefore mainly subscribed to the Shafi'i school of Islamic jurisprudence. Subsequently, during the period of British rule, Muslims arrived from the Indian sub-continent and settled in the Cape Colony as well as in the Natal region (now KwaZulu-Natal Province), and they primarily subscribed to the Hanafi school of law.[43]

While it is difficult to give accurate estimates, especially since the number of Muslims would have increased since then, according to the latest General Household Survey conducted in 2015,[44] Muslims are estimated to be a small fraction (over one million) of the total population (currently over 60 million[45]). They nonetheless constitute the largest of several religious minorities in a predominantly Christian South Africa.

---

43 See e.g. Y. Da Costa, 'Muslims in Greater Cape Town: A Problem of Identity' (1994) 45(2) *The British Journal of Sociology* 235; E.M. Mahida, *History of Muslims in South Africa: A Chronology*, Arabic Study Circle, 1993, pp. 22 and 26; N. Moosa, *The Mystery of the Apostasy of Shaykh Yusuf of Makassar's alleged Grandchildren: The Children of the Rajah of Tambora*, Shaykh Shahid Esau, 2021, pp. 15 and 28; and Moosa above n. 3, at p. 151.

44 See Statistics South Africa, 'Statistical Release P0318 – General Household Survey 2015', pp. 3 and 27, available at: <https://www.statssa.gov.za/publications/P0318/P03182015.pdf>, last accessed 05.05.2022 (religious affiliation has not formed part of published population censuses in South Africa since 2001 so there is, unfortunately, no official population census data from which to accurately gauge the number of Muslims currently living in South Africa. Relying on statistics contained in the latest (2015) General Household Survey, Christians were estimated to constitute 86% of a then total population of some 54 million, while Muslims were estimated to constitute merely 1.9% (or roughly 1 million). Hindus were estimated to constitute 0.9% of the population and Jews 0.2%. These statistics also highlight that Muslims constituted the largest religious minority group and that the largest number of Muslims were located in the Western Cape Province).

45 See Statistics South Africa, 'Statistical Release P0302 – Mid-year population estimates 2021', *Statistics South Africa Media Release*, 31 July 2021 (the current (2021) mid-year population of South Africa is 60.14 million).

Many local Muslims rely for guidance on *usul al-fiqh*, the jurisprudential opinions of the Sunni jurists as championed by religious leaders and given effect in religious tribunal bodies located all over South Africa. The Muslim Judicial Council (SA) (MJC-SA),[46] established in 1945, is one of the oldest such tribunals and is based in the Western Cape Province where Muslims are predominantly located. The *fatawas* (Islamic legal rulings and opinions) issued by the MJC-SA are primarily based on the Shafi'i school of law but do not preclude the views of other schools being followed when deemed appropriate, or even a deviation from all schools when deemed necessary.[47]

The MJC-SA advocates the conservative view that same-sex marriage and homosexuality are forbidden in Islam. In 2006 it formally opposed the proposed introduction of the CUA on the ground that '[t]he institution of marriage is the voluntary union of a man and a woman only'.[48] In 2007 it issued a *fatwa*[49] on homosexuality on behalf of the *ulama* in the Western Cape Province which declared that the practice of homosexuality is irreconcilable with Islam. The *fatwa* further declared that 'any Muslim' who differs or deviates from this point of view is deemed to be an apostate (*murtad*) who has left the fold of Islam. On this basis, the MJC-SA declared South Africa's only openly gay imam, Muhsin Hendricks, who also hails from the Western Cape Province, to be an apostate, not because of any change of religion on his part or because of his sexual orientation (he came out as gay in 1996), but because he had changed a previously held personal belief or opinion that homosexuality was contrary to Islam and had made that publicly known. The *fatwa* was issued in response to his participation, in the same year, in a programme on homosexuality hosted by a local Muslim radio station and the release of an international film documenting the lives of gay and lesbian Muslims, in which he featured.[50] In both these forums, he expressed and supported the position that the Quran does not ban homosexuality.

46 See 'History of the MJC', available at: <https://mjc.org.za/about-mjc/history/>, last accessed 05.05.2022.

47 A copy of a letter from the MJC-SA (dated 19 July 2017) confirming this is on file with the primary author.

48 See A.F. Carr, 'Submission on Civil Union Bill B26-2006 – The Muslim Judicial Council objects to the proposed Civil Unions Bill', 2006, available at: <https://static.pmg.org.za/docs/2006/061016mjc.pdf>, last accessed 05.05.2022.

49 See D. Terblanche, *Islam and Individual Predisposition to Homosexuality*, unpublished MA thesis, University of South Africa, 2009. The *fatwa* is referred to on p. 43 of this thesis and is available as an Annexure at pp. 84–85.

50 Ibid, at pp. 43, 85–86 and 93.

Recently, on 4 July 2022, and following the release of another such documentary in which Muhsin Hendricks also features, the MJC-SA issued a further *fatwa* in which it briefly clarifies and reiterates its position on homosexuality.[51]

Although there are gay and lesbian Muslims who may have voluntarily left the fold of Islam, there are also others who, having reconciled their homosexuality with their understanding of the practice of Islam, have not abandoned Islam. While some have decided to remain closeted[52] for personal reasons, because of a fear of being ostracised or because of social stigma and cultural concerns, there are also a growing number of homosexual Muslims in South Africa who are openly gay.[53] However, it appears that the Muslim community and the population in general are opposed to homosexuality.

A study conducted in 2016 highlights that 'almost three quarters (72 percent) of the South African population' believe that 'same-sex sexual activity is morally wrong'.[54] The study further highlights that only a small minority of the South African population identified their sexual orientation to include being homosexual.[55] A large percentage of South African Muslims believe that Islam approves only of heterosexuality as a sexual orientation and disapproves of homosexuality.

A 2014 study highlights that '86 percent of Muslims surveyed across South Africa reported believing that homosexuality is a *choice* … Over 80 percent … cite the story of Lut or *hadith* as the reasons for their belief that queer sexuality is incompatible with Islam'.[56]

---

51 The *fatwa*, especially given it was met with widespread criticism, cannot be found on the website of the MJC-SA but is available at: <https://www.al-ghurbaah.org.za/wp-content/uploads/2022/07/MJC-Fatwa-6th-July-2022.pdf>, last accessed 27.07.2022.

52 See P. Hendricks (ed.), *Hijab: Unveiling Queer Muslim Lives*, African Minds, 2009 (examples of anonymous stories regarding Islam and homosexuality).

53 See R. Davis and M.H. Dawjee, 'Lut's People: The struggle to be gay & Muslim in Southern Africa', *Daily Maverick*, 13 June 2018; and C. Collison, 'The Muslims who will not choose between their God and being gay', *Mail & Guardian*, 18 April 2019; and N. Maesela, 'Gay, proud and Muslim', *City Press*, 7 May 2020.

54 See The Other Foundation and The Human Sciences Research Council, 'Progressive Prudes, A survey of attitudes towards homosexuality & gender non-conformity in South Africa', 2016, p. 3.

55 Ibid.

56 See A. Kamrudin, 'Bringing queer into Muslim spaces: Community-based pedagogy in Cape Town' (2018) 34 *Journal of Feminist Studies in Religion* 143, 143–144 (emphasis added). For the full report see M. Tofa, *The Narrative of Islam and Sexual Diversity: An Anatomy of Attitudes, Challenges, Opportunities and Trends in the South African Context: A Research Report by The Inner Circle*, Inner Circle (TIC), 2014.

5. MUSLIM HOMOSEXUALS AND APOSTATES AS HEIRS AND TESTATORS: SOUTH AFRICAN LAW AND ISLAMIC LAW[57]

While the Islamic law of succession basically remains unchanged due to its divine origin, the South African law of succession has undergone many changes since the advent of democratic rule. These changes were largely based on judicial challenges, and some have been beneficial to Muslims and women in particular.

The option of drafting a will is available to all South Africans, including Muslims, because the colonial common law (a mixture of Roman-Dutch law and English law) principle of freedom of testation is entrenched in South African law.[58] While both the South African and Islamic legal systems may have some aspects in common, there are fundamental differences between them. For example, a South African testator has complete freedom of testation and it is not uncommon for him or her to dispose of their entire estate via a validly executed will in terms of the provisions of the Wills Act. There is, furthermore, no limit to the value of a legacy that a testator may leave in a will to a legatee (of his or her choice, and which may therefore exclude a spouse, child or close relative). Since legatees are paid before heirs, if nothing remains of an estate after legacies are paid out, then heirs get no inheritance. This cannot happen in terms of Islamic law, because a testator's freedom of testation is limited to one-third of his or her estate and the rest of the estate devolves 'intestate' according to Quranic (divine) prescription, over which the testator has no discretion.[59] In South Africa it is technically incorrect to refer to a will as an Islamic will if it is validly executed in terms of South African law and contains the testator's wish to have his or her estate distributed in terms of the Islamic law of succession. If, however, the testator also exercised his one-third testamentary prerogative in the same will, then it could be argued that it is an Islamic will within a South African will. Intestacy as understood in South African law is used as a 'term of convenience' to describe the Islamic law of inheritance, since technically the heirs of the deceased under Islamic law are only determined at the time of his or her death. While there are about 35 Quranic verses dealing with succession,

---

57 Unless otherwise stated or updated, the comparative information pertaining to the two systems is summarised from N. Moosa, *A comparative study of the South African and Islamic law of succession and matrimonial property with special attention to the implications for the Muslim woman*, LLM dissertation, University of the Western Cape, 1990, pp. 39, 42, 48 and 52–55.

58 See M. Abduroaf and N. Moosa, 'Islamic Law Mode of Estate Distribution in South Africa', in B. Atkin (ed.), *The International Survey of Family Law*, Jordan Publishing, 2016, p. 458.

59 Q.33:36.

only about three (Q.4:11–12 and 176) provide specific details of inheritance shares, the precise details of which have been worked out on the basis of the *Sunna* of Muhammad, his Companions, interpretation and analogy. Muslim jurists also differ in their opinions regarding certain aspects of succession, but these are usually of a minor nature.[60] A fundamental principle of the Islamic law of succession is that the female always inherits half the share of the male. Although the male inherits double the share of the female, and there are exceptional[61] cases where the female may be excluded, the female is generally not excluded.

In terms of South African law, a person dies intestate with respect to any property's succession which he or she has not regulated by a valid will. Thus, when a Muslim fails to draft a will which indicates an intent to have the Islamic law apply, and thereafter dies, certain rules which are codified in the ISA automatically kick into operation to determine how the deceased's property must be distributed.

While nothing would preclude a Muslim testator, if he or she so wishes, from distributing all his or her assets only in terms of South African law or from gifting it during his or her lifetime, which is allowed in terms of both South African law and Islamic law,[62] a testator may also draft a will or have a will drafted for him or her conforming to the provisions of the South African Wills Act that also comply with the *Shari'a* to ensure that his or her estate be distributed entirely in terms of the Islamic law of succession upon his or her demise. In such a will, a testator can stipulate how or to whom they wish to distribute one-third of their estate (the extent which is allowed in terms of the Islamic law of testate succession) and further indicate in the will that the provisions of the Islamic law of (intestate) succession are to apply to the residue (the remaining two-thirds) of their net estate, or dispose of their entire estate if they have not elected to make use of the one-third option. Given that the testator may not be knowledgeable of the intricacies of the Islamic law of 'intestate' succession, he or she would simply add, without further elaboration, '[a] clause in his or her will [that] would state that an Islamic law expert or Islamic institution should draft an Islamic distribution certificate listing his or her beneficiaries and their shares in terms of the Islamic law of succession'.[63]

---

60 See A. Hussain, *The Islamic Law of Succession*, Darussalam, 2005, p. 29.

61 See e.g. Abduroaf and Moosa, above n. 58, at pp. 474–475 (discussing an example of how a male residuary beneficiary inherits to the exclusion of his female counterpart).

62 See Moosa, above n. 57, at p. 152.

63 M. Abduroaf, 'A constitutional analysis of an Islamic will within the South African context' (2019) *De Jure Law Journal* 257, 258; see also N. Gabru, 'The applicability of the Islamic law of succession in South Africa' (2005) 26(2) *Obiter* 340, 354.

In the Western Cape Province, the MJC-SA, as is evident from its website,[64] has a dedicated Fatwa Department manned by a Mufti (expert on Islamic law) and a Fatwa Panel comprised of 'seven learned scholars of Shariah'. The Fatwa Department is responsible for drafting 'Shariah-compliant wills' and the issuing of 'distribution certificates' (which it defines as 'a document listing the heirs of a deceased and the portions each one receives according to the Islamic Laws of Inheritance').[65] As part of the service that it offers to the community and the legal fraternity, the Fatwa Department assists Muslims with the drafting of wills, and families and lawyers with the winding up of deceased estates. For example, in a recent case, *Moosa NO and Others v. Harnaker and Others*,[66] the deceased had left a will in which he indicated that his estate be devolved according to Islamic law and that a certificate from the MJC-SA or similar authority would be final and binding on his executors. As a consequence, the MJC-SA had issued a distribution certificate listing his beneficiaries and their shares as per the Islamic law of succession (see paragraph 7). This certificate was submitted by the executor to the Master of the High Court, who had accepted it for the purposes of administering the estate (at paragraph 9). This highlights the recognition of the enforcement of an Islamic will in South Africa on the basis of freedom of testation. On the other hand, in an earlier case, *Faro v. Bingham NO and Others*,[67] the Western Cape Division of the High Court overruled a final decision of the MJC-SA that a marriage between parties was already terminated at the time the husband had died, and accordingly declared the wife to be a spouse for the purposes of the ISA (see paragraphs 5, 6 and 47(a) of this judgment).

We contend that being a sexually active homosexual Muslim is not necessarily incompatible with the Islamic law of succession because it is heteronormative in nature and makes no reference to homosexuality. This means that it is based purely on the physical or biological sex (male or female) of a testator or beneficiary regardless of his or her heterosexual or homosexual sexual orientation. While heteronormativity may suggest that heterosexuality is the norm and the only valid form of sexual orientation, this does not automatically exclude gender and sexual diversity. The assumption that everyone is heterosexual is therefore not only incorrect but can also lead to discrimination against other sexualities and gender identities. The authors therefore contend that the Islamic law of 'intestate' succession, especially given its 'default' and non-discretionary

64 See MJC-SA, 'Fatwa', available at: <https://mjc.org.za/departments/fatwa/>, last accessed 05.05.2022.

65 Ibid.

66 *Moosa NO and Others v. Harnaker and Others* 2017 (6) SA 425 (WCC) (14 September 2017).

67 *Faro v. Bingham NO and Others* (4466/2013) [2013] ZAWCHC 159 (25 October 2013).

nature, does not prevent heterosexual Muslim testators from leaving property to homosexual beneficiaries. However, although *ulama* may therefore not unfairly discriminate against such beneficiaries on the basis that homosexuality is prohibited in Islam, they may do so on the basis that the disqualification is based on a difference, or change, in religion, which is a ground for such exclusion. The MJC *fatwa* declaring a person to be out of the fold of Islam does not serve as a blanket ruling and has to be determined on a person-to-person basis.

The religion of an individual as regards inheritance is his or her religion at the time of the death of the testator. The general rule is that there are no ties of inheritance between Muslims and non-Muslims, the difference in religion being the factor which would deprive heirs of an inheritance. This appears to be based on an authentic *hadith* (recorded in both Sahih al-Bukhari[68] and Sahih Muslim[69]) to the effect that 'a Muslim cannot be the heir of a disbeliever, nor can a disbeliever be the heir of a Muslim'.[70]

Apostasy by one of the spouses is deemed to constitute a 'civil death' and therefore terminates a *nikah* and results in the deceased's prospective Muslim heirs being unable to inherit.[71] The South African gay imam, declared an apostate by the MJC-SA, is of Indonesian descent and therefore a follower of the Shafi'i school of thought. He has three biological children from a first heterosexual *nikah*. To remedy the situation, he can, for example, utilise his freedom of testation in terms of the South African law to leave them part of, or the entirety of, his estate. The beneficiaries have the option to either adiate (accept) or repudiate in terms of South African law.

We now distinguish between an apostate as heir and as testator.[72] As regards the apostate as an heir, if a Muslim testator dies and leaves behind a non-Muslim son or daughter, such son or daughter would not inherit anything.

As regards inheriting from an apostate, and in accordance with the principle that a Muslim does not inherit from a non-Muslim, according to three (Maliki, Shafi'i and Hanbali) of the four main schools of Islamic law, the entire estate of an apostate goes to an Islamic State or Public Treasury (*Baytul Mal*). This means

---

68 See Sahih Bukhari, Book Number 80 (Laws of Inheritance (Al-Faraaid)), Hadith Number 756.

69 See Sahih Muslim, Book Number 11 (Pertaining to the Rules of Inheritance (Kitab Al-Farai'd)), Hadith Number 3928.

70 Hussain, above n. 60, at p. 58.

71 See N. Moosa, *An Analysis of the Human Rights and Gender Consequences of the New South African Constitution and Bill of Rights with Regard to the Recognition and Implementation of Muslim Personal Law (MPL)*, unpublished LLD dissertation, University of the Western Cape, 1996, p. 138.

72 Unless otherwise indicated, the information in this section pertaining to an apostate as an heir and as a testator was obtained and summarised from Hussain, above n. 60, at pp. 59–61.

that the Muslim relatives, including the spouse of an apostate, are not entitled to inherit from him or her. However, in terms of the Hanafi school of law, the Muslim relatives of an apostate are able to inherit from him or her. Nonetheless, Imam Abu Hanifa draws a distinction between a male and a female apostate. In the case of a male apostate, the portion of his estate acquired whilst still Muslim will be inherited by his heirs while the property acquired after he had apostatised will go to an Islamic State Treasury. In the case of a female apostate, the whole of her estate will be inherited by her Muslim heirs with no further strings attached. As is the case with female homosexuality, female apostates are also treated differently and more favourably, and this may have constitutional implications in South Africa, as detailed in the next section.

6. TREATMENT OF MUSLIM HOMOSEXUAL BENEFICIARIES: THE CONSTITUTION, FREEDOM OF TESTATION AND FREEDOM OF RELIGION

A validly executed will excluding a beneficiary or providing for unequal treatment on the basis of a homosexual sexual orientation, homosexuality, same-sex marriage or religious conviction (apostasy) has as yet not been challenged on constitutional grounds in a South African court.

Section 15(1) (freedom of conscience, religion, thought, belief and opinion) of the Constitution guarantees the right to freedom of religion to all South Africans, including Muslims and other religious minorities. Although section 15 is narrowly constructed and makes no formal reference to the profession of any faith, the CC[73] has interpreted the right to religious freedom to include within its ambit the right to manifest and practise religious beliefs. However, the fundamental rights protected in the Bill of Rights, including freedom of religion (section 15), are not absolute and their manifestation may be restricted in terms of section 36(1) (limitation clause) of the Constitution to promote the public interest or to protect other equally guaranteed human rights like the freedom of testation included in section 25 (property clause), which is linked to the rights to dignity (section 10) and privacy (section 14).

It is understandable that the common law (on the basis of, for example, public policy considerations) and legislation may legitimately restrict the testator's freedom of testation based in general on socio-economic considerations in

[73] *S v. Lawrence; S v. Negal; S v. Solberg* [1997] (10) BCLR 1348 (CC); *Christian Education South Africa v. Minister of Education* 2000 (10) BCLR 1051 (18 August 2000), paras. 18–19; and *Prince v. President of the Law Society of the Cape of Good Hope* 2002 (3) BCLR 231 (25 January 2002), paras. 38–39.

the light of section 36 (limitation clause) of the Constitution.[74] However, what happens in cases where the testator's rights to property or freedom of testation (section 25), religious freedom (section 15), dignity (section 10) and privacy (section 14) clash with other equally guaranteed human rights in the Constitution, such as a beneficiary's right to equality (section 9) and dignity (section 10)? Section 39(2) of the Constitution encourages us to strive for the achievement of an effective and meaningful development of the common law. This implies an engagement with succession law (private law) within the ambit of human rights law (public law).

Even if restricted, some sort of balance has to be sought between the above-indicated conflicting rights to ensure equal or fair treatment in terms of section 9 (equality clause), which prohibits all unfair discrimination on the basis of sexual orientation. Section 9(3) has a vertical operation (between 'the State' and 'anyone'). Section 9(4) has horizontal operation between individuals ('person' and 'anyone') and, read with the immutable considerations of section 9(3), provides that no person may directly or indirectly discriminate unfairly against anyone on the basis of immutable considerations, such as 'race, *gender*, *sex*, pregnancy, *marital status*, ethnic or social origin, colour, *sexual orientation*, age, disability, *religion*, *conscience*, *belief*, *culture*, language and *birth*' (emphasis added). Section 6 of the Equality Act, the PEPUDA ('prevention and general prohibition of unfair discrimination' clause), also has both vertical and horizontal application.

Nothing in South African law precludes a Muslim testator, who envisages a different or discriminatory distribution of his or her assets that excludes homosexual persons, from disposing of them according to his or her own wishes whilst alive (*inter vivos*) by employing the Islamic law pertaining to gifts (*hiba*)[75] or the property clause of the Constitution. This begs the question whether, in the light of the immutable considerations mentioned in section 9(3), a Muslim testator, in executing a valid will, who either disposes of assets according to Islamic law or indicates that his or her estate devolve in terms of Islamic law can disinherit a beneficiary (for example, a son or daughter) or conditionally include a beneficiary on the basis of a homosexual sexual orientation, homosexuality, same-sex marital status or religious conviction. The testator could also include such a beneficiary in a valid will subject to a condition that could be connected to a section 9(3) consideration. If the testator subscribes to the mainstream Islamic law view that both homosexuality and same-sex marriage are forbidden in Islam, does his or her exercising of the rights to religious freedom and testation outweigh the right to equality of the excluded or conditionally included beneficiary?

---

74 See M.J. De Waal and M.C. Schoeman Malan, *Law of Succession*, Juta, 5th ed., 2015, p. 4.

75 See Moosa, above n. 57, at pp. 152–154.

Section 9(5) provides that the '[d]iscrimination on one or more of the grounds listed in subsection (3) is unfair unless it is established that the discrimination is fair.' The constitutionality of a will in which a testator disinherits a close relation on the basis of immutable section 9(3) considerations has as yet not been raised in a South African court. Succession law experts[76] have opined that in such cases of disinheritance the testator's right to freedom of testation should be given preference or priority as it would outweigh the right to equality of the excluded beneficiary. Furthermore, should the beneficiary challenge a will on constitutional grounds, he or she would in all likelihood not meet with success. Included among the reasons proffered by these experts in support of this view is that '[a]n opposite conclusion would lead to almost insurmountable practical difficulties'.[77]

Unfortunately for the Muslim testator, the Islamic law of 'intestate' succession is heteronormative and shares are prescribed and divinely allocated to beneficiaries regardless of a homosexual status. We therefore contend that a South African court, in cases contesting the exclusion of Muslim beneficiaries on the basis of a homosexual sexual orientation, may not necessarily be faced with the same 'insurmountable' difficulties that other such South African beneficiaries would generally face. For example, the MJC-SA or other experts can easily assist with the calculation and re-calculation of Islamic shares as they do in Islamic distribution certificates required in terms of validly executed wills. In the case of the conditionally included beneficiary, should the testator, for example, indicate that a beneficiary must become 'straight' or divorce a same-sex partner, then it is more likely than not that such conditions, if linked to an immutable section 9(3) consideration, would probably also be found to be invalid on constitutional grounds if challenged.[78] However, we concede that the question of a professed apostasy (where a 'Muslim' beneficiary may be excluded by a testator on the basis of his or her religious conviction that Islam does not condone homosexuality, or conditionally excludes such a beneficiary until his or her 'reversion' back into the fold of Islam by accepting its default position on homosexuality as correct) may be more difficult, but still not insurmountable, to deal with.

The South African common law contains a rule called 'the doctrine of religious entanglement', which requires that courts not interfere or question doctrinal practices of religions. This has been reiterated by the Supreme Court of Appeal (SCA): 'A court should only become involved in a dispute of this kind

76 See De Waal and Schoeman Malan, above n. 74, at pp. 5–6.
77 Ibid, at p. 6.
78 Ibid, at pp. 6–7 (including more detail on testamentary conditions).

where it is strictly necessary for it to do so. Even then it should refrain from determining doctrinal issues in order to avoid entanglement.'[79]

Although judges may therefore refrain from getting involved in doctrinal matters of a religious nature, this has not prevented them from making rulings on religious law both prior and subsequent to the enactment of the Constitution.

In 1965, many years prior to the MJC-SA's *fatwa* on homosexuality, which referred to apostasy, the MJC-SA had issued another *fatwa* pertaining to apostasy, which ended up being judicially challenged on doctrinal grounds. In this *fatwa*, it declared *Ahmadiyyas*, who essentially believe in all the tenets of the Islamic faith but deny that its Prophet Muhammad was the last of the prophets, to be apostates and condemned the *Ahmadiyya* movement, to which they belonged as members, to be un-Islamic. Since the MJC-SA had acted as both judge and jury in the matter, it was futile for members of this movement to approach the MJC-SA to request a review of its decision. This left them with little option but to approach the secular courts. Several cases ensued from 1982 and concluded in 1995 (during a time that the interim Constitution was still in operation) to resolve the matter on the basis of freedom of religion.[80] In the light of the human rights provisions of the Constitution, we contend that the courts ought not to adopt, as it did with the apostasy question in the *Ahmadiyya* cases, a hands-off approach by declining to decide fundamental questions pertaining to freedom of religion.

The Western Cape High Court has since 1996 also dealt with a doctrinal matter involving MPL.[81] When it comes to denying a homosexual Muslim succession rights, given especially that it involves a complex balancing of several constitutionally guaranteed rights, it would appear that the courts would justifiably have to become doctrinally entangled in matters of a religious nature, especially when faced with a constitutional challenge.

Contrary to the views espoused by the succession experts De Waal and Schoeman Malan in 2015 in their textbook on succession,[82] there are two precedent-setting recent (2021) CC cases which make serious inroads into testamentary freedom and provide authority for the view that discrimination on the basis of such immutable section 9(3) considerations may yet be deemed to be unfair and therefore unlawful.

---

79 See *De Lange v. Presiding Bishop of the Methodist Church of Southern Africa for the time being and Another* [2015] 1 All SA 121 (SCA) (29 September 2014), para. 39 (while the CC is the highest court for constitutional matters, the SCA is the highest court for criminal and civil cases).

80 See Moosa, above n. 71, at pp. 305–309 (further elaboration of the *fatwa* and these cases).

81 See *Ryland v. Edros* 1997 (2) SA 690 (C).

82 See De Waal and Schoeman Malan, above n. 74.

At the time (2015) that the succession law experts espoused the view that freedom of testation should and will prevail if a challenge is brought against such a disinheritance, there was no real case law available, particularly as regards the disinheritance of beneficiaries or potential beneficiaries on the basis of some of the immutable characteristics as defined in section 9(3) of the Constitution. Although the CC has yet to decide whether such cases would be justified or amount to unfair discrimination, in the two cases *King v. De Jager*[83] and *Wilkinson v. Crawford*,[84] the CC went as far as to encroach on a testator's freedom of testation when it decided to confer, respectively, benefits on adopted children not included in a testator's will, and on females specifically excluded from a will. Unfortunately, neither case deals with same-sex relationships or homosexuality.

While we have these two recent judgments, all succession experts may still not necessarily agree with their outcomes.[85] Although some of these experts may believe that to strike down disinheritances goes to the heart of freedom of testation and while some may have certain fundamental difficulties with these latest judgments, these CC decisions do constitute the positive law and therefore obviously provide authority, and very potent authority, for the point of view that a testator's freedom of testation does not extend as far as excluding or disinheriting (even in a private bequest) beneficiaries on the basis of the immutable characteristics as defined in section 9 of the Constitution. Incidentally, in the *Wilkinson* case, the CC had much to say about freedom of testation.[86]

In the *King* case, Jafta A.J., writing for the majority, said that although freedom of testation is protected by law, this did not preclude testators from acting within the framework of the law:

> I do not think that freedom of testation empowers a testator to violate the rights of members of his or her family by *unfairly discriminating* against them. Lest I be misunderstood, *the Constitution does not require the testator to treat his or her family equally* when gifting them with his or her property. Nor does it oblige him or her to leave any of his or her assets to them. They too have no entitlement to his or her property. But *what the Constitution prohibits is unfair discrimination on the part of the testator when disposing of his or her property.*[87]

83 *King NO and Others v. De Jager and Others* 2021 (4) SA 1 (CC) (19 February 2021).

84 *Wilkinson and Another v. Crawford NO and Others* 2021 (4) SA 323 (CC) (16 April 2021).

85 For a forthcoming article wherein the three co-authors examine a balance of views ranging from strong support to strong dissent on the outcome of the *King* case see F. du Toit, M. Harding and A. Humm, 'King N.O. v De Jager: Three Perspectives' (2022) *Stellenbosch Law Review*, forthcoming.

86 *Wilkinson*, above n. 84, at paras. 118–143.

87 *King*, above n. 83, para. 153 (emphasis added).

The very fact that women and adopted children are, or can be, included by a Muslim testator implies that if a will is challenged purely on the basis that these heirs are not treated equally, such challenge may not be successful. Whether or not a Muslim female (including a lesbian) or an adopted child will be successful in a contestation of a diminished inheritance in terms of the Islamic law of succession (the half share of the female or the one-third bequest for an adopted child) remains to be seen. The outcome of the *King* case implies that while a person may not be unlawfully excluded from a will on the basis of status, it does not mean an entitlement to an increased share.

Section 8 of the PEPUDA (the 'prohibition of unfair discrimination on ground of gender' clause) provides that '[s]ubject to section 6, no person may unfairly discriminate against any person on the ground of gender, including – .... (*c*) *the system of preventing women from inheriting family property*' (emphasis added). It has been recommended by an expert in the Islamic law of succession, who is also a member of the MJC-SA, that one sure way of avoiding a constitutional challenge and achieving the same results would be for the testator to have the consequences of Islamic law of succession incorporated into a valid will without any reference to the Islamic law ('system').[88]

In doing so, the female Muslim heir, although she gets a decreased share, nonetheless gets a share and moreover is not excluded on the basis of religion. In other words, should a challenge arise on the basis of the unequal treatment of male and female heirs, it would be unlikely to succeed because it would be based on the right to freedom of testation and not the right to religious freedom. However, we contend that, although practically doable, this may be problematic, since 'intestate' beneficiaries are only determined at the time of the testator's death. The fact that there is no reference to the Islamic law also effectively rules out the option of obtaining a distribution certificate. Therefore, to ensure that their wishes are carried out, Muslim testators would have to be proactive and, before they die, do some preparatory homework either by themselves calculating the shares of their 'intestate' beneficiaries or seeking the assistance of Islamic law experts. However, in doing so they still run the risk of their will not being *Shari'a* compliant. For example, a legitimate beneficiary may be excluded if, unbeknown to the testator, his wife was pregnant at the time of his death. However, if a Muslim testator in such a scenario excluded a beneficiary from a valid will purely on the basis of his or her sexual orientation or homosexuality, this may be a different matter. Apart from the fact that the Islamic law of 'intestate' (default) succession is heteronormative and therefore does not exclude such a beneficiary, the Constitution itself limits a testator's freedom by prohibiting unfair discrimination on the basis of sexual orientation. We therefore contend

88 Abduroaf, above n. 63, 261 and 266.

that in such a case a constitutional challenge will succeed (and equally so if no mention is made of Islamic law as suggested by the expert above) on the basis of such unfair discrimination.

While conservative or restrictive interpretations of Islamic law could rely on the conscience of a Muslim to deny him or her such a choice, no person or organisation can prevent Muslims who subscribe to progressive (alternate) interpretations from regulating their personal affairs according to their understanding of religious law. Support for this is to be found in section 31(1) of the Constitution, which guarantees the right of persons to practise their religion individually and as part of a religious group, subject to the limitation that the right is not exercised in a manner that is inconsistent with any provision of the Bill of Rights (section 31(2)). The CC has interpreted this section 31 limitation as ensuring that 'religion cannot be used to shield practices which offend the Bill of Rights'.[89] This would by implication include the right to sexual and gender equality,[90] and should extend to sexual diversity (which includes sexual orientation under this plurality).

7. SOME CONCLUSIONARY REMARKS AND RECOMMENDATIONS FOR THE WAY FORWARD

South African homosexual Muslims face dual discrimination – they are a numerical minority within a religious minority. Muslim women, because they live in a still largely patriarchal religious society, generally face gender discrimination on the basis of their sex. However, lesbian women have to contend with additional discrimination because their sexual identity is essentially ignored by the distinction drawn by Islamic scholars between male and female homosexuality; but this may not necessarily have much, if any, impact on their succession rights.

South Africa is a secular democracy. What distinguishes its supreme law, the Constitution, from others is the fact that it explicitly recognised and protected the rights of homosexual persons at a time when sexual orientation and gender identity were relatively new concepts and no clear direction was to be found within the framework of international human rights law. Today, there still is no dedicated United Nations human rights instrument protecting same-sex sexual orientation or homosexuality. With no clear direction in the primary source of

89 *Christian Education South Africa v. Minister of Education* 2000 (4) SA 757 (CC), para. 26.

90 See W. Amien, N. Moosa and C. Rautenbach, 'Chapter 4: Religious, Personal, and Family Law systems in South Africa' in C. Rautenbach (ed.), *Introduction to Legal Pluralism in South Africa*, LexisNexis, 6th ed., 2021, pp. 72–73, 75 and 78–79; see also M. Paleker, 'Chapter 2: Intestate Succession' in J. Jamneck and C. Rautenbach et al. (eds.), *The Law of Succession in South Africa*, Oxford University Press, 3rd ed., 2017, pp. 25–45, 31 and n. 11.

Islam, progressive Muslim scholars and gay *ulama* have employed independent reasoning (*ijtihad*) to do the same with the novel topics of homosexuality and same-sex marriage.

The South African Constitution guarantees both heterosexual and homosexual Muslims the right to the safe exercise of their rights to freedom of religion, expression, association and peaceful assembly without being discriminated against on the basis of their sexual orientation and gender identity. The fact that the rights of LGBTQ+ persons are contained in a Bill of Rights and not singled out as special rights also highlights that they are basic human rights to which all South Africans are entitled. Although the MJC-SA *ulama*, appointed to serve the community as custodians of MPL, are also bound by the Bill of Rights provisions, it appears that their expressed views on these topics may be viewed as influencing and encouraging homophobic attitudes in the Muslim community.[91]

The schools of Islamic law encourage, and the MJC-SA acknowledges, a deviation from the views of these schools when circumstances necessitate it. We contend that the time may have arrived to consider doing so. Gay Muslims entering into recognised same-sex civil unions and unrecognised long-term same-sex partnerships are afforded protection in South Africa because of judicial intervention. We contend that it is only a matter of time before a judicial challenge seeking similar protection for same-sex *nikahs* will rear its head. There are separate law reform and policy processes currently underway which are considering the legal recognition of permanent same-sex partnerships and heterosexual *nikahs* in South Africa. However, same-sex *nikahs* are not included in these mandates. Whether a judicial challenge by homosexual Muslims in same-sex *nikahs* will yield further amendments to the ISA and the Wills Act also remains to be seen.

Further, given alternative progressive and conservative positions on homosexuality and same-sex marriage, the judiciary may have to enter the doctrinal fray. By accepting and giving 'legal force' to the pronouncements of the MJC-SA, it may indirectly also be recognising MPL issues pertaining to succession.

We contend that homosexuals and homosexual *ulama* should not be marginalised and labelled as apostates by mainstream *ulama* when they practise an atypical form of progressive *ijtihad*, which for them means keeping an open and critical mind when dealing with texts, and understanding them in context, since this will also impact on their succession rights as testators and beneficiaries.

The 2014 research report that highlighted the fact that local Muslims are 'still largely orthodox and homophobic' advises that '[e]ducation, advocacy

---

91 See Tofa, above n. 56, at p. 18.

and awareness campaigns are … the most powerful tools to change attitudes [on homosexuality] in the Muslim community.'[92] In 2012, a progressive South African Muslim theologian and activist, Moulana Farid Esack, who also hails from the Western Cape Province, is reported as being optimistic that this homophobia can be allayed: 'Muslims tend to be far more socially tolerant than they are in public religious discourses, allowing for the potential of a gradual shift in attitudes towards homosexuality.'[93] However, a 2009 study highlights that when it comes to close family, the position may be different in the Western Cape Province, where it appears to be common practice for '[m]any [Muslim] families [to] distance themselves from their relatives who are homosexuals'.[94] Esack confirmed in an interview conducted with him in 2017 that when he was appointed as a gender equity commissioner in the first democratic government, 'he campaigned for the rights of women and homosexuals' and that '[h]e rejects all forms of discrimination – including those based on sexual orientation'.[95]

However, it appears from a 2016 study that his campaigning, while laudable, at the time may not have been very effective in, or adequately filtered down to, the grassroots Muslim community, since the reality is that many citizens, including Muslims, may be oblivious of the constitutional clause protecting sexual orientation: 'it is clear that there is a need for more information and engagement, not only about sexual orientation and gender identity, but also about the Constitution itself. More than half of respondents indicated that they had never heard of the constitutional protection clause and/or did not understand it. Only 1 in 5 South Africans report understanding it very well.'[96]

This confirms that it is not enough to have one of the most progressive constitutions in the world and that this lacuna needs to be more adequately addressed and remedied by human rights and social justice actors before one can expect any real change in homophobic attitudes at the grassroots level.

While a deceased person has neither constitutional rights nor constitutional duties, the South African law protects the deceased's former assets in the interests and rights of his or her heirs.[97] While testators may themselves not have personal reasons to defend a homosexual sexual orientation and homosexuality, they may have immediate family and close relatives who may be homosexual or

---

92 Ibid, at pp. 65 and 66.

93 See A. Okeowo, 'South Africa's Gay Imam and His Disciples', Alicia Patterson Foundation, 2012, updated 7 August 2013 (emphasis added).

94 Terblanche, above n. 49, at p. 45.

95 D. Bax, 'Muslim theologian Farid Esack: More than just an "Israel critic"', *Qantara.de*, 6 March 2017.

96 See The Other Foundation and The Human Sciences Research Council above n. 54, at p. 49.

97 J. Heaton, *The South African Law of Persons*, LexisNexis, 6th ed., 2021, p. 27.

practise homosexuality. Islam, like the Constitution, embraces all of humanity with dignity[98] and does not require or expect that parents and families abandon their children and relations simply because of diversities of sexualities and gender, or deprive them of an inheritance on this basis. Ultimately, shunning homosexuals and banning homosexuality and same-sex marriage does more harm than good to both homosexuals and others.

98 Q.17:70 ('We have honoured (all) the children of Adam with innate dignity').

SOUTH KOREA

GRANDCHILD ADOPTION IN SOUTH KOREA

Dongjin Lee

Résumé

Il y a onze ans, la Cour suprême de Corée a rendu sa première décision sur l'adoption des petits-enfants. L'affaire portait sur une requête en adoption plénière et la Cour était sceptique à l'égard ce type d'adoption. Toutefois, dans une décision d'Assemblée plénière rendue l'an dernier, elle a déclaré que l'adoption des petits-enfants devrait être acceptée par principe. L'affaire portait sur une demande d'adoption simple et n'a pas remis en cause le précédent qui portait sur une adoption plénière.

Du point de vue du droit comparé, on observe que les juridictions traitent différemment l'adoption des petits-enfants. Par exemple, les États-Unis semblent être favorables à l'adoption des petits-enfants, contrairement à l'Allemagne et à la France. Au Japon, l'adoption plénière des petits-enfants n'est en principe pas accordée, alors que l'adoption simple des petits-enfants est acceptée sans aucun contrôle.

La Cour suprême coréenne s'est beaucoup appuyée, dans sa décision d'Assemblée plénière précédemment évoquée, sur l'accord entre le parent adoptif et l'enfant adoptif quant à l'adoption et sur l'autonomie familiale. Ce n'est pourtant guère convainquant. L'adoption d'un petit-enfant est typiquement une adoption de mineur dans laquelle le consentement à l'adoption doit être donné, non pas par l'adopté, mais par son représentant légal, *i.e.* le parent biologique. Il n'y a pas d'autonomie familiale pour l'adopté dans ce cas, et le tribunal ne peut présupposer la validité d'un tel l'accord. Le tribunal de la famille doit examiner si la demande d'adoption est pleinement conforme à l'intérêt supérieur de l'enfant. À cet égard, l'adoption de petits-enfants est rarement dans l'intérêt supérieur de l'enfant, surtout lorsque la motivation principale de la requête est de donner au parent biologique une chance de se remarier sans enfant.

1. INTRODUCTION

Grandchild adoption refers to an adoption of a minor grandchild by one or, more frequently, both grandparents.[1] Until recently, issues surrounding grandchild adoption have attracted little interest in South Korea, possibly due to the small number of cases of such adoptions.[2] The fact that family court control over adoptions was introduced to the South Korean legal system only eight to nine years ago may also contribute to the lack of interest in this issue.

Eleven years ago, the Supreme Court rendered its first decision on grandchild adoption in South Korea. As is shown below in detail, the initial position of the Korean Supreme Court was somewhat sceptical of grandchild adoption, and the lower instance courts (i.e. family court practice) appear to follow that line of reasoning. However, in an *en banc* decision rendered late 2021, the Supreme Court of Korea declared a new position, seemingly more favourable to grandchild adoption. This decision is expected to attract academic interest on this issue in South Korea.

---

1 All the grandchild adoptions discussed in this chapter are the adoption of a minor grandchild by the child's grandparent(s).

2 The Korean national statistics on adoption deliver little detailed information on adoption in South Korea. They provide only the numbers of total adoptions, domestic and foreign adoptions, and male and female adoptees and do not provide the number of kinship adoptions. However, they do show that the number of total adoption cases has dropped rapidly to a couple of hundred cases a year. About half these cases are foreign adoptions, and many of the others are agency adoptions, neither of which include kinship adoptions.

This chapter aims to illuminate the problem of grandchild adoption in South Korea in two parts. First, it will explain how grandchild adoption is addressed in different jurisdictions and why it matters; this explanation is mainly for Korean readers. Second, it will describe the development of Korean case law on this issue. The latter part, written for foreign readers who are interested in an Asian country's family law, analyses and critiques the recent *en banc* decision in light of comparative viewpoints, which the author hopes will be useful to both Korean and international readers.

2. GRANDCHILD ADOPTION IN OTHER JURISDICTIONS

2.1. THE UNITED STATES

Adoption law is not part of the English common law. American adoption law is an invention of state legislatures. Notably, the purpose of adoption in the United States was, and still is, the facilitation of child welfare or the best interests of the child.[3]

Although state adoption laws differ from each other in many respects, they share some basic features. First, adoption is not a matter of contract; it is effectuated by court decree, with, of course, the birth parent's (mostly anonymous) consent or relinquishment of custody.[4] More importantly, the court must review whether adoption is the best alternative in the interest of the child and whether the prospective adopter is the best adoptive parent for the prospective adoptee.[5] Thus, it is possible in the United States for more than two people to compete in an adoption proceeding to be the adoptive parent of the same child. In addition, US courts recognise only full adoption, which creates a new parent–child relationship while terminating the existing parent–child relationship between the birth parent and the child.[6]

There is no provision in state adoption statutes to exclude grandchild adoption in the United States. Thus, grandchild adoption is considered an option.[7] Although the blood relationship between the prospective adoptive

3 C. Hawkins DeBose, *Mastering Adoption Law and Policy*, Carolina Academic Press, 2015, pp. 5 f.

4 See §§3-101 ff. Uniform Adoption Act (1994) (a model law proposed by the United States Uniform Law Commission. Although the Uniform Adoption Act was adopted only in one state, Vermont, and has been criticised for unduly restricting adoptees from accessing information on their biological parents, it still preserves the core features of the US adoption laws).

5 §3-703(a) Uniform Adoption Act (1994).

6 §3-505 Uniform Adoption Act (1994).

7 2 Am. Jur. 2d Adoption §24, November 2021 Update.

parent and the adoptee does not per se create a preference in determining whether the adopter is suitable,[8] grandparents or other relatives may be preferred in adoption proceedings under certain circumstances. First, unlike non-relatives, a relative, including a grandparent, with whom a prospective adoptee has been placed by the parent or guardian is exempt from the requirement of a pre-placement evaluation of their suitability to be an adoptive parent. The relative's suitability as an adoptive parent is evaluated during the pendency of the adoption proceedings.[9] Second, in some states, state agencies must give preference to relatives in adoption placements for the child in their custody,[10] even though it is sometimes subordinate to the preference for a foster caregiver.

Of course, although this preference is subordinate to the best interests of the child, it is undeniable that US courts do not disfavour grandchild adoption. In *Napoleon S v. Walker*,[11] the Circuit Court of Kanawha County made an order to affirm the decision of the West Virginia Department of Health and Human Resources Board of Review (DHHR) determining that grandparents could not become the adoptive parents of their grandson because the grandparents continuously denied the fact that their son, the birth father, intentionally harmed their grandson. The grandparents appealed, contending that the lower court erred in failing to apply a statutory[12] and DHHR policy

---

8 *In re Adoption of LEKM*, 70 P.3d 1097 (Alaska 2003); *In re Estate of Quackenbush*, 926 N.E.2d 127 (Ind.TaxCt. 2010). Also see *Mullins v. State of Oregon*, 57 F.3d 789 (9th Cir. 1995) (a biological connection alone does not give a grandparent a 'constitutionally protected liberty interest' in the adoption of grandchild).

9 §2-201(c) Uniform Adoption Act (1994). Also see C. Hawkins DeBose, *Mastering Adoption Law and Policy*, Carolina Academic Press, 2015, pp. 151 f. (explaining that approximately 31 states follow this line in their own adoption statutes as of 2010).

10 See e.g. §8710(a) California Family Code (holding that '[i]f a child is being considered for adoption, the department, county adoption agency, or licensed adoption agency shall first consider adoptive placement in the home of a relative or, in the case of an Indian child, according to the placement preferences and standards set out in subdivisions (c), (d), (e), (f), (g), (h), and (i) of Section 361.31 of the Welfare and Institutions Code'). See also C. Hawkins DeBose, *Mastering Adoption Law and Policy*, Carolina Academic Press, 2015, p. 151 (further listing Arkansas, Illinois, Minnesota, Nebraska, Ohio and Wisconsin as states that maintain this preference).

11 *Napoleon S v. Walker*, 617 S.E.2d 801 (W.Va. 2005).

12 W. Va. Code §49-3-1(a)(3) (2005) (holding that '[f]or purposes of any placement of a child for adoption by the department, the department shall first consider the suitability and willingness of any known grandparent or grandparents to adopt the child. Once any such grandparents who are interested in adopting the child have been identified, the department shall conduct a home study evaluation, including home visits and individual interviews by a licensed social worker. If the department determines, based on the home study evaluation, that the grandparents would be suitable adoptive parents, it shall assure that the grandparents are offered the placement of the child prior to the consideration of any other prospective adoptive parents').

preference for grandparent adoption. The Supreme Court of Appeals of West Virginia reversed the lower court order and remanded for entry of an order requiring the grandchild to be placed with the grandparents for adoption but also prohibiting contact between the birth father and the grandson.[13] In *Matter of Welfare of DL*,[14] both the foster parents, who had lived with DL since four days after her birth, and DL's maternal grandparents filed petitions to adopt her. The trial court granted the grandparents' petition, based on the preference for family adoption of a minor in the Minnesota statute.[15] The foster parents' appeal was unsuccessful, despite the finding that breaking the bond between the foster parents and DL was expected to cause some trauma to the child. The Supreme Court of Minnesota reaffirmed the ruling in *In re Welfare of MM*[16] that '[i]t has long been a familial phenomenon that the absence, inability, or incapacity of the natural parents to provide and care for their children had prompted other relatives to step forward to assume the benefits and responsibilities of that role and that a body of common law had developed according to a custodial preference to near relatives.'[17]

One must not be misled into concluding that a petition for grandchild adoption would be granted as a matter of course in the United States. There are cases where petitions for grandparent adoption were denied because adoption by other people, especially foster parents, would be in the best interests of the child. For example, in *In re Adoption of LMR*,[18] the Indiana Court of Appeals reasoned that one of the purposes of adoption is to assure the complete severance of family ties by adoption to protect the new family unit that the law had created. Further, the court objected to the grandparents in that case because they had regularly allowed the birth parents to be around the child despite their undisputable inadequacy as parents.

---

13 *Napoleon S v. Walker*, 217 W.Va. 254, 263, 617 S.E.2d 801, 810 (2005) (Maynard J. dissenting) (in this decision, Justice Maynard's dissenting opinion condemned the majority opinion for unintentionally disregarding the grandson's best interests).

14 *Matter of Welfare of DL*, 486 N.W.2d 375 (Minn. 1992).

15 §259.28, subd. 2 of the Minnesota Statutes (1990): 'In the adoption of a child of minority racial or minority ethnic heritage, in reviewing adoptive placement, the court shall consider preference, and in determining appropriate adoption, the court shall give preference, in the absence of good cause to the contrary, to (a) a relative or relatives of the child, or, if that would be detrimental to the child or a relative is not available, to (b) a family with the same racial or ethnic heritage as the child'.

16 *In re Welfare of MM*, 452 N.W.2d 236, 238 (Minn. 1990).

17 Although DL was a daughter of an African American mother, the Supreme Court of Minnesota did not rely on §259.28, subd. 2 of the Minnesota Statutes (1990) because the appellants challenged the constitutionality of the said provision. It rather concluded that a strong family preference exists for all child placement, without regard to race or ethnic heritage.

18 *In re Adoption of LMR* 884 N.E.2d 931 (Ind. App. 2008).

2.2. GERMANY

The German Civil Code (*Bürgerliches Gesetzbuch*) recognises only full adoption.[19] The old contract adoption system was repealed in 1976,[20] and the new decree adoption system has been well established.[21] Under this system, the consent of the minor child[22] and the birth parents[23] cannot be anonymous. The consents are directed to a particular adoption petition, even when the identity of the adoptive parent is not known to either the minor child or the birth parents at the time the consent is given.[24]

There is no provision to exclude kinship adoption in the German Civil Code. On the contrary, §1756(1) of the German Civil Code presupposes the acknowledgment of kinship adoption, stipulating that if the adoptive parents are related by blood or by marriage to the child in the second or third degree, only the relationships of the child and his or her descendants to the parents of the child, and the rights and duties arising from this relationship, are extinguished.[25] It preserves the original kinship between the adopter and adoptee in kinship adoption, which leads to multiple kinships (*mehrfache Verwandtschaft*).[26]

However, §1756(1) of the German Civil Code does not suggest the general or presumptive admissibility of grandchild adoption in Germany. Although the paramount criterion for adjudicating adoption cases in Germany is the best interests of the child, there is an additional requirement for adoption: the expectation to build a parent–child relationship. The first sentence of §1741(1) of the German Civil Code stipulates that adoption is admissible if it serves the best interests of the child and if a parent–child relationship is expected to arise between the adoptive parent and the child. German courts rejected grandchild

---

19 Bürgerliches Gesetzbuch (BGB, Civil Code) §§1754, 1755 and 1756(1) and (2).

20 T. Helms in *Staudinger Kommentar zum BGB*, Sellier de Gruyter, Neubearbeitung, 2019, §1752, Rz. 1 (in German).

21 BGB §1752(1) (holding that '[t]he adoption is pronounced by the family court, on the application of the adoptive parent').

22 BGB §1746.

23 BGB §1747. See also T. Helms in *Staudinger Kommentar zum BGB*, Sellier de Gruyter, Neubearbeitung, 2019, §1747, Rz. 5 (in German).

24 BGB §1747(2) (holding that '[t]he consent may not be given until the child is eight weeks old. It is effective even if the person consenting does not know the adoptive parents, who have already been decided on.' This kind of adoption is often called incognito adoption (*Inkognitoadoption*), as distinguished from anonymous adoption (*Blanketadoption*)). For example, the consent can be given to the intended adoption by the adopter number XX on the list held by the local government agency.

25 T. Helms in *Staudinger Kommentar zum BGB*, Sellier de Gruyter, Neubearbeitung, 2019, §1756, Rz. 9 ff. (in German) explains that this provision applies to the adoption by grandparents, great-grandparents, siblings, uncles, aunts or their spouses.

26 This answers the criticism of A. Lüderitz, *Adoption, Vorschläge zur Auslegung und Änderung des Rechts der Annahme an Kindes Statt*, C.F. Müller, 1972, pp. 78 ff. (in German), although his original proposal was only to exchange the parents' positions.

adoption on the ground not that only is it not in the best interests of the child,[27] but also that a true parent–child relationship was not expected to arise between the adopting grandparent and the adopted grandchild.[28]

For example, a 3 November 1995 decision of the Oldenburg Higher State Court[29] addressed the grandparents' petition to adopt their grandchild born out of wedlock. The court upheld the first instance court's decision to reject the grandchild adoption. Notably, the court relied on the abstract argument that grandchild adoption should be subject to strict conditions because kinship adoption necessarily establishes an artificial relationship, rather than a natural one. Therefore, a potential for conflict also inevitably arises, which can be reconciled with the well-being of the child only in exceptional cases. The court also stressed that the development of circumstances around and relationships among all those involved, including the birth parents and the grandchild, is completely open and that the emergence of a true parent–child relationship between the birth parents and the grandchild can be expected. The birth parents' consent to the adoption does not matter in this regard. To protect the grandchild under these circumstances, guardianship would be sufficient. In justifying its 6 December 1996 decision to uphold a lower court decision rejecting a grandchild adoption, the Bavaria Higher State Court[30] also emphasised the massive confusion in family relationships the grandchild adoption would cause. While grandchild adoption is not categorically excluded in Germany, it is rarely accepted.

2.3. FRANCE

The French Civil Code (*Code civil*) provides for two modes of adoption: full adoption (*adoption plénière*) and simple adoption (*adoption simple*). While the former establishes a parent–child relationship between the adoptee and adopter and sever the parent–child relationship between the birth parent and the child,[31] the latter only establishes a new parent–child relationship while preserving the existing parent–child relationship between the birth parent and the child.[32] France also follows the decree system, and the paramount

---

27 OLG Koblenz *FamRZ* 2016, 1690; BayObLG *FamRZ* 1997, 839; OLG Oldenburg *FamRZ* 1996, 895 = *JuS* 1996, 1033 mit Anmerkung von Hohloch; OLG Hamm *FamRZ* 1968, 110; AG Hannover FamRZ 1966, 45.

28 OLG Oldenburg *FamRZ* 1996, 895 = *JuS* 1996, 1033 mit Anmerkung von Hohloch; OLG Hamm *FamRZ* 1968, 110; AG Hannover FamRZ 1966, 45.

29 OLG Oldenburg *FamRZ* 1996, 895 = *JuS* 1996, 1033 mit Anmerkung von Hohloch.

30 BayObLG *FamRZ* 1997, 839.

31 Code Civil (C. Civ., Civil Code) Art. 356.

32 C. Civ. Arts. 364 and 365.

concern in the adjudication of adoption cases is the best interests of the child.[33] Although the birth parents' and the child's consent are required, these consents can be given anonymously.[34]

The French Civil Code also presupposes the possibility of kinship adoption.[35] However, that does not mean that French courts accept grandchild adoption readily. Scholars point out that kinship adoption in general and grandchild adoption in particular are said to be contrary to the aim of adoption – to provide a family for a child who does not have one – and might lead to a change in family relationships and an upheaval in the genealogical registration of the adoptee. It also generates a risk of confusion among the generations.[36] Some authors even argue against kinship adoption altogether,[37] asserting in particular that kinship full adoption, which severs the existing legal relationship between the birth parent and the child, should be allowed only in very exceptional cases.[38] The French courts also rarely grant full kinship adoption unless both birth parents are dead.[39]

2.4. JAPAN

The Japanese Civil Code (*Minpō*) also has two modes of adoption: full adoption and simple adoption. With regard to simple adoption, grandchild adoption has been utilised and it is understood as a way to lessen the burden of estate tax and, as such, is allowed.[40] This might be partly because simple adoption in the Japanese Civil Code employs the contract system, so there is no court review of the adequacy of the application for adoption in the registry.[41] With this

---

33 C. Civ. Arts. 351, 353, 361 and 362.

34 C. Civ. Art. 348-4.

35 C. Civ. Art. 348-5 (stating that '[e]xcept where there is a relationship or alliance up to and including the sixth degree between the adopter and the adoptee, consent to the adoption of children under two years of age is valid only if the child has actually been handed over to the child welfare service or to a body authorised for adoption').

36 F. Eudier, 'Adoption', *Rép.dr.civ.*, octobre 2008, n° 269 (in French).

37 See A. Batteur, 'L'interdit de l'inceste' (2000) *RTDCiv.* 759, and D. Fenouillet, 'L'adoption de l'enfant incestueux par le demi-frère de sa mère, ou comment l'intérêt prétendu de l'enfant tient lieu de seule règle de droit' (2003) *Dr. fam.* Chron. 29, n° 30 (in French) (contending that kinship adoption should be limited to exceptional circumstances).

38 F. Eudier, 'Adoption', *Rép.dr.civ.*, octobre 2008, n° 270. See also M. Schmitt, 'L'adoption de l'enfant par ses grands-parents' (2002) *AJ fam.* 91.

39 Besançon, 1 February 1994, *JCP* 1994, IV, 564, *RTDCiv.* 1995, 344; Cass. 1re civ., 6 March 2013, *F-P+B*, n° 12-17.183 (adoption simple).

40 Tokyo High Court, He2(Ra)748, 26 April 1990. See also Y. Nakagawa, *Annotation on the Japanese Civil Code*, Yuhigaku, New Edition, Vol. 24, 1994, pp. 166 f.

41 Minpō Art. 800 (Japan). An adoption of a minor is subject to the court's permission, while an adoption of one's own descendant is exempted from the court's permission requirement. Minpō Art. 798 (Japan).

motivation taken into account, most cases are likely to be simple adoptions of adult grandchildren.

Conversely, full adoption in the Japanese Civil Code is conducted under the decree system[42] and can be granted only when (1) parental child-rearing is substantially difficult or inadequate due to exceptional circumstances and (2) the adoption is necessary for the interests of the child.[43] This additional condition makes grandchild full adoption proceedings in Japanese courts extremely rare.[44]

3. SOUTH KOREA

3.1. LEGAL RAMIFICATIONS

The Korean Civil Code (*Minbôb*) also recognises both full adoption (*chin-yangja*) and simple adoption (*yangja*).[45] The original Code provides for only simple adoption under the contract system. In 2005, the legislature introduced full adoption under the decree system, which requires the adoptee to be a minor[46] and a family court decree to grant full adoption. The family court may dismiss a petition for full adoption if it deems the full adoption incompatible with the well-being of the adoptee when factors such as the child-rearing environment, the reason for the full adoption and the prospective parent's child-rearing capability are taken into account.[47] In addition, the legislature revised the Korean Civil Code in 2012 to modify the requirements and procedure for simple adoption. From then on, simple adoption of a minor child cannot be registered without the family court's permission.[48] Again, the family court can refuse to grant permission for simple adoption when it considers simple adoption inadequate in terms of the well-being of the adoptee.[49]

Simple adoption in the Korean Civil Code still seems to adhere to the contract system.[50] Formally speaking, the first requirement for simple adoption

---

42 Minpō Art. 817-2 (Japan).

43 Minpō Art. 817-7 (Japan).

44 Osaka High Court, Hei2(Ra)76, 9 April 1990; Dakamatsu High Court, Sho63(Ra)90, 20 February 1989.

45 Another law regarding adoption in South Korea, the Act on Specific Cases of Adoption, deals with agency adoption and allows anonymous consent of the birth parents for the adoption. However, the effect of adoption under the Act on Specific Cases of Adoption is the same as full adoption under the Civil Code, so that it operates as a full adoption. Moreover, agency adoption has little to do with kinship or grandchild adoption.

46 Minbôb (Civil Code) Art. 908-2(1) no. 2.

47 Minbôb Art. 908-2(3).

48 Minbôb Art. 867(1).

49 Minbôb Art. 867(2).

50 J. Yune and S. Hyun, *Annotation of the Revised Civil Code in 2013*, Ministry of Justice, 2013, pp. 201 f. (arguing that this also corresponds to the understanding of the drafters).

is a meeting of minds on adoption between the parties, the adoptee and the prospective adoptive parent. The adopter makes an offer to adopt, and the adoptee makes an acceptance.[51] If there is no agreement on simple adoption between the parties, the simple adoption is null and void.[52] When the parties are in agreement, they should obtain permission from the family court. However, permission is only a prerequisite;[53] it does not effectuate the simple adoption, which is done by filing with the adoption registry.[54] Moreover, simple adoption of an adult requires only the agreement on adoption, not the family court's permission, and can be resolved by agreement between the adoptee and the adopter.[55] By contrast, full adoption is effectuated by the family court's decree and not by filing with the adoption registry. Full adoption can be resolved only by a family court decision rather than by agreement.[56]

No provision either prohibits kinship adoption or explicitly recognises or prioritises kinship adoption in the Korean Civil Code. However, Article 877 of the Korean Civil Code, which prohibits the adoption of an ascendant or elder, might have some significance for this issue. Article 877 suggests that the adoption of a descendant is allowed, and, as one cannot adopt one's own child, this appears to include grandchild adoption.[57] Most scholars also implicitly consider kinship adoption registrable in principle.[58] However, there is a view that, at least, grandchild adoption violates public order (*ordre public*) and morality,[59] prescribed in Article 103 of the Korean Civil Code.[60] While there is little justification for this view, it suggests disapproval regarding confusion of the family order.

Although grandchild adoption can be recognised in principle, it must meet all the requirements of an adoption of a minor. First, as simple adoption adheres to the contract system, a meeting of minds to adopt is required. For example, when an adoption registration is obtained only to avoid a criminal charge, with no intention of forming a living relationship as a parent and a child, the adoption

51 Minbôb Art. 869.

52 Minbôb Art. 883 no. 1 (holding that '[a]n adoption is null and void: 1. When there is no agreement on adoption between the parties').

53 Minbôb Art. 881.

54 Minbôb Art. 878.

55 Minbôb Art. 898 (it is notable that the same provision does not allow the resolution of adoption by agreement in case of the minor or ward adoption).

56 Minbôb Arts. 908-5 and 908-6.

57 See Minbôb Art. 877 (however, no scholar has paid attention to Art. 877 of the Korean Civil Code in the context of grandchild adoption problem thus far).

58 J. Kim and S. Kim, *Family and Inheritance Law*, Pakyoungsa, 14th ed., 2017, pp. 357 f.

59 D. Park, *Family and Inheritance Law*, Pakyoungsa, 4th ed., 2013, p. 306.

60 Minbôb Art. 103 (stating that '[a] juridical act (*Rechtsgeschäfts*) against public order (*ordre public*) and morality shall be null and void').

is null and void.[61] Likewise, when an adoption registration is obtained only to facilitate another family registration, without any intention of forming a living relationship as a parent and a child, the adoption is again null and void.[62] Thus, grandchild adoption can be null and void if the grandparent and grandchild have no intention of forming a genuine parent–child relationship. In addition, since grandchild adoption in most cases is an adoption of a minor, the Korean Civil Code requires that the adoption is in the best interests of the child, irrespective of whether it is full adoption or simple adoption. Thus, grandchild adoption can be rejected if it is not in the best interests of the child. One author argues that the age difference should be considered in determining the admissibility of a petition for full adoption of a grandchild as it pertains to the best interests of the child.[63] Another argues that the crucial criterion should be whether the adoption is expected to create a genuine parent–child relationship; in this regard, the family court should take a flexible and functional approach that takes into consideration family diversity.[64]

3.2. COURT CASES

3.2.1. Grandchild Full Adoption

In a decision on 16 September 2010,[65] the Ulsan District Court gave rise to the first appellate case to reject full adoption of a grandchild. In this case, the granddaughter was born in 2006 to the appellants' daughter and her cohabitant. The cohabitation broke up shortly after the granddaughter's birth, and, since then, the granddaughter had been raised by the grandparents for about five years. According to the birth mother, her elder sister and the grandparents, the granddaughter considered the grandparents to be her parents and referred to them as such, and the birth mother then resided with the grandparents and the granddaughter. The grandparents were under the age of 60, healthy and financially secure. The purported motives in pursuing full grandchild adoption were that the birth mother lacked the financial capability to rear the grandchild by herself, that she was unlikely to remarry and start a new family if she were to rear the grandchild, that the grandchild had been reared for five years as if

61 Supreme Court, 94Mu1553, 1560, 29 September 1995. The courts have frequently inferred the lack of intention to form a parent–child relationship from the motivation to avoid some legal sanction. The validity of this inference is doubtful.

62 Supreme Court, 2003Mu2411, 9 April 2000.

63 E.-H. Cho, 'The Full Adoption for the Interest of the Child' (2013) 23(2) *Seoul Law Review* 16.

64 K. Kim, 'Adoption of a Child by Grandparents from the Perspective of Comparative Law' (2010) 3(2) *KHU Global Business Law Review* 19.

65 Ulsan District Court, 2010Bu21, 16 September 2010.

she were already the child of the grandparents, and that listing her as their child would be helpful as she would soon enter elementary school.

Although the court admitted that the petition met all the formal requirements of full adoption prescribed in Articles 908-2(1) and 877 of the Korean Civil Code and that the petitioners were found to be capable of rearing the granddaughter, the court upheld the first instance court's decision to reject the petition for full adoption of the grandchild. In its opinion, the appellate court set forth three reasons that granting full adoption in this case was not in the best interests of the child:

> First, it would complicate the familial order. This is not a case where the birth mother died or the contact with the birth mother has been already severed. Rather, the birth mother lived together with the grandchild and the grandparents. Thus, the full adoption would make the maternal grandparents the child's (adoptive) parents and the birth mother her (adoptive) elder sister, which would necessarily substantially complicate familial order and kinship. Although the grandchild does not know their biological relationship at the moment, the undeniable existence of biological kinship among all the family members might create an artificial and unnatural relationship, with a likelihood of influencing the grandchild's emotional stability. When the grandchild later becomes aware of the facts regarding her birth, the court reasoned, it would necessarily cause irreparable confusion of the family relationship and an identity crisis.
>
> Second, there could be motivations for full adoption other than the foremost motivation: the well-being of the child. In this case, the main motivation to adopt the grandchild seems to be to make the existence of the grandchild and her relationship with her birth mother disappear on the family registry, to help the birth mother, the grandparents' daughter, make a new family. The grandparents declared at the hearing that they would have no choice but to place their grandchild in a third-party adoption if their petition was rejected. Thus, the main motivation of the petition is not in the interest of the child but of the birth mother.
>
> Last, the grandchild has already been reared by her grandparents for five years. A full adoption would not change the environment or the condition of her rearing and would modify only the family registry. The grandparents seem able to rear their grandchild without legal parental status. If the grandparents truly want legal custody instead of de facto custody, it would be more logical for the birth mother to relinquish her legal custody to the grandparents as guardians with legal custody.

Thus, the court concluded, the petition for full adoption of the grandchild was not in the best interests of the grandchild.

The grandparents re-appealed. In a 24 December 2010 decision,[66] the Supreme Court upheld the Ulsan District Court's decision that the paramount

[66] Supreme Court, 2010Su151, 24 December 2010.

consideration in adjudicating the petition for full adoption should be the best interests of the child, including the motivation and need for the full adoption and its likely influence on the familial relationship, and that the appellate court properly applied these criteria.

The Supreme Court reaffirmed this opinion in a decision on 27 March 2017,[67] upholding the appellate court's decision to reject the petition for grandchild full adoption. Since then, the lower instance courts appear to follow this line of reasoning.[68]

3.2.2. Grandchild Simple Adoption

In an *en banc* decision on 23 December 2021,[69] the Supreme Court first addressed the permissibility of simple adoption of a grandchild. In this case, the grandchild was born in 2014 to the birth mother and father. The birth mother left the grandchild in the care of her parents when the grandchild was seven months old. Since then, the grandchild had been raised by the grandparents. A couple of years later, the grandparents filed a petition for simple adoption of the grandchild, with the birth parents' consent. The petitioners argued that the grandchild had no contact with the birth parents and believed that the petitioners were the parents. The second instance court,[70] upholding the first instance court's decree to dismiss this petition, reasoned as follows. First, via grandchild adoption, the maternal grandparents would become both maternal grandparents and adoptive parents, and the birth mother would be not only the birth mother but an adoptive sister, causing serious confusion in the internal order of the family and kinship. Second, the petitioners faced little difficulty rearing their grandchild without adoption; any problems could be addressed by guardianship of the minor grandchild. Third, in the future, the grandchild might become aware of their true family relationship, causing significant trauma, such that it would be better to inform the grandchild of the truth rather than to remain silent. Thus, it seems not to be in the best interests of the child to exempt the birth parents from this burden via the adoption.

The petitioners re-appealed. The Supreme Court's divided decision, with ten justices siding with the majority and three dissenting, reversed and remanded the case to the second instance court. The dissenting opinion advocated for upholding the second instance court decision.

---

67 Supreme Court, 2016Su138, 27 March 2017.
68 See e.g. Pusan Family Court, 2017Nudan1124, 24 April 2017.
69 Supreme Court, 2018Su5, 23 December 2021.
70 Ulsan District Court, 2017Bu10, 18 December 2017.

The majority opinion made five important points. First, it addressed the permissibility of grandchild adoption. The court held that grandchild adoption is not categorically prohibited. No statutory provision prohibits kinship adoption, and Korean traditional customary law also allows grandchild adoption. From a comparative law perspective, both US and German law allow grandchild adoption, and many American states even give a preference to grandparent(s) for adoption.

Second, the court considered the intention and motivation of the adoption. Although grandchild adoption is possible, it can also be inappropriate; therefore, all the requirements of adoption should be reviewed carefully. The first requirement for valid grandchild simple adoption is the intent and reason of the adoption. If the grandparent files a petition for adoption merely to have legal custody, without any intention to form a living relationship as a parent and child, the intent to adopt can be denied. However, when the grandparent has an intent to form a new living relationship, the intent to adopt cannot be denied. In this regard, the grandparent's choice not to inform the grandchild about his or her birth parents or adoption must not negate the intent to adopt the grandchild. Although some practitioners and scholars advocate for open adoption to inform the adoptee of his or her adopted status, whether, when, and how to inform the child depends on various factors, such as the conditions of the adoptive family, the age and character of the adoptee and other relevant circumstances. The family court can advise on informing the adoptee about the adoption in the future when it becomes appropriate during the evaluation process, but it cannot reject the petition simply because it is for a closed adoption. The family court should also investigate the main purpose of a grandchild adoption because grandparents might be motivated to adopt their grandchild to facilitate the birth parent's remarriage or other reasons not directly related to the child's best interests.

Third, the court considered the birth parents' informed consent and the hearing of the grandchild's opinion. The birth parents must give consent, and, more importantly, that consent should be based on consultation and information on the support for the birth parents' child rearing, the legal effect of adoption and the process of adoption.[71] The prospective adoptee's opinion should be heard as well.[72]

---

71 No provision in the Korean Civil Code mandates this. However, Art. 13(3) of the Act on Specific Cases of Adoption and Art. 21(a) of the Convention on the Rights of the Child require the birth parent to be consulted and provided with information on adoption. The Supreme Court announced in this case that the same holds true for simple adoption under the Korean Civil Code without explicit statutes, as far as grandchild adoption is concerned.

72 No provision in the Korean Civil Code requires that the court hear the opinion of a prospective adoptee under the age of 13. However, Art. 12 of the Convention on the Rights of the Child mandates this hearing. The Supreme Court announced in this case that the family court should hear the opinion of a prospective adoptee under the age of 13 as far as possible.

Fourth, the court addressed the best interests of the child. It might be difficult to transform a grandparent–grandchild relationship into a parent–child relationship when the prospective adoptee is old enough to go to school and has been raised as a grandchild up to that point. In that case, grandchild adoption might cause emotional confusion; therefore, it is necessary to review whether the grandchild understands the meaning of adoption, whether the grandchild has a positive attitude toward the adoption, and whether other family members are cooperative. When the birth parent lives together with the grandparent and the grandchild or has frequent contact with them, the grandchild might suffer emotional confusion due to the co-existence of the birth parent and adoptive parent or the reaction of other family members who might have difficulty accepting the adoptive parent–child relationship. The family court should carefully investigate the family's interactions and evaluate their influence on the well-being of the child. However, that does not mean that grandchild adoption is always against the best interests of the child. If neither birth parent rears the grandchild, grandchild adoption can establish a stable environment for rearing based on a parent–child relationship. If the grandparent has already established a de facto parent–child relationship with the grandchild, grandchild adoption would create a legal relationship that corresponds to the reality. All these factors would suggest that grandchild adoption is in the best interests of the child. Taking into account the tendency toward more diverse, less stereotypical family relationships, it is necessary to respect individual and family autonomy.[73] Consequently, the family court can deny permission to adopt only when it finds concrete circumstances under which grandchild adoption would endanger the well-being of the child. It is beyond the reasonable discretion of the family court to deny permission based on the obscure presumption that the change of family relationship might create confusion in the family or emotional trauma from the perspective of the traditional familial community. The argument that a complex relationship might be revealed on the family registry does not challenge the validity of this conclusion because the family register law can and should be amended.

Fifth, the court mentioned the relationship between adoption and guardianship. One might think it is better for the grandparent to be appointed as a guardian and to step back whenever the birth parent becomes willing and able to rear the grandchild. However, that mere possibility is too vague and abstract for the family court to reject the adoption outright.

The dissenting opinion, joined by Justices Jaeyeon Cho, Yusuk Min and Dongwon Lee, criticises the majority opinion, making six points. First, the

73 The Supreme Court cited here Supreme Court *en banc* decision of 23 October 2019, 2016Mu2510 and Supreme Court decision of 8 June 2020, 2020Su575.

dissent reflects the majority opinion in the Supreme Court decisions of 24 October 2010[74] and of 17 March 2017,[75] which appear to reject grandchild adoption because it would cause confusion in the family order and the kinship relationship. This reasoning is flawed in that the Supreme Court weighed outmoded notions instead of the well-being of the minor, the paramount consideration in an adoption case. However, the dissenting opinion does not consider the courts' conclusions and family court practice following that line of cases flawed. The dissenting opinion also points out that the acceptance of grandchild adoption in traditional customary law is not pertinent to this decision because the modern purpose of adoption is quite different from its purpose in traditional society or law. The dissent also argues that it is improper to consider the fact that some countries allow kinship adoption because different cultures have different points of view. Moreover, it notes that Germany allows grandchild adoption only in very exceptional cases.

Second, concerning the adoption of a minor, both simple adoption and full adoption require the family court's permission. The family court, which has discretion in adjudicating adoption cases, should investigate *ex officio* and decide whether adoption would be in the best interests of the child. By contrast, the majority opinion is satisfied with the agreement of the parties and the consent of the birth parent and mandates the family court to respect the intention of the parties unless a compelling public interest justifies court intervention; this is contrary to the protective role of the family court in adoption proceedings.

Third, because grandchild adoption is unnatural, the rationale or purpose of adoption should be examined carefully.

Fourth, the intent to adopt is undeniably an intent to form an adoptive parent–child relationship. Regarding simple adoption, this intent presupposes the existence and continuation of the parent–child relationship between the birth parent and the child. However, the existence of the parent–child relationship between the birth parent and the child or the fact of adoption tends to be hidden in many grandchild adoptions. In this case, the petitioners insisted that they would not inform the grandchild about the adoption. The family court may grant an adoption when it is expected that a parent–child relationship would arise naturally between the adopter and the adoptee, presupposing that all parties are aware that that relationship is adoptive. It is difficult to expect a natural parent–child relationship to form when all the parties involved hide the fact of adoption from the adoptee. In such instances, a closed adoption might cause an identity crisis later on.

---

74 Supreme Court, 2010Su151, 24 October 2010.

75 Supreme Court, 2016Su138, 17 March 2017.

Fifth, the child should be raised by their birth parents and remain in the care of their family of origin.[76] The law governing guardianship of a minor has been revised to support the principle of preference for the family of origin.[77] Thus, commencing proceedings to appoint a grandparent as guardian is recommended instead of granting grandchild adoption. The birth parent in most grandchild adoption cases is relatively young and does not have financial capability. Because he or she cannot help but consent to the adoption, this consent has little significance. Because the birth parent is relatively young, he or she may grow psychologically and financially and want to rear his or her own child. However, adoption, unlike guardianship, cannot be revoked once completed.

Last but not least, Justice Yusuk Min supplemented the dissenting opinion with one more point. Because simple adoption does not change the family name of the adoptee, the family name of the adopted grandchild remains different from that of the adopting grandfather if he is the maternal grandfather.[78] Thus, it is impossible to make the adopted grandchild appear to be the birth child on the family register. Of course, the grandparents can petition to change the family name of the grandchild, and the family court can permit a change of family name if it is necessary for promoting the well-being of the child.[79] If the court allows this petition, however, it would open a back door for de facto full adoption, which courts have rarely admitted for grandchild adoption.

3.3. ANALYSIS

3.3.1. *Scope of Applicability of the New Ruling*

The 2021 *en banc* decision makes clear that grandchild adoption can be granted under the Korean Civil Code if it is in the best interests of the child. When the court denies grandchild adoption, the reason should be that it would compromise the well-being of the child, not that it would complicate family

---

76 The Supreme Court cited Art. 7 of the Convention on the Rights of the Child and the Convention of 29 May 1993 on Protection of Children and Co-operation in Respect of Intercountry Adoption, as well as the Act on Child Welfare, which declares the principle of preference of family of origin.

77 The law on parental authority and guardianship of minors in the Korean Civil Code was substantially changed by the 2011 and 2014 revisions. The gist of these revision is to enable the partial limitation of parental authority and partial commencement of guardianship for a minor and to appoint the best person in the case as a guardian for the minor.

78 South Korea follows the principle that the child has the father's family name and the wife does not change her family name to take her husband's family name by marriage.

79 Minbôb Art. 781(6).

order. Thus, the decision did not adopt the view that grandchild adoption is categorically prohibited as being against public order (*ordre public*) and morality.[80] Both the majority and dissenting opinions agreed on this point.

However, the decision leaves many important points unresolved. First, the scope of the ruling is not clear. The *en banc* decision did not formally overrule any precedents, perhaps because all the precedents address grandchild full adoption, while the 2021 Supreme Court case only dealt with simple adoption. Nonetheless, the majority opinion condemned 'the existing (family court) practice' of rejecting grandchild adoption, which must refer to grandchild full adoption.[81] Furthermore, the reasoning of the majority opinion did not manifestly distinguish between full and simple grandchild adoptions. The majority suggests that the new ruling shall apply not only to grandchild simple adoption but also to grandchild full adoption. This opinion stresses that the court should respect the intent of the parties unless it is established that it would contradict the best interests of the child. However, simple adoption in the Korean Civil Code uses the contract system, not the decree system, even in the adoption of minors,[82] and it is conceivable that the court's argument presupposes contractual adoption. Therefore, it would not apply to grandchild full adoptions effectuated by family court decree. Justice Yusuk Min's dissenting supplemental opinion also suggested that the family court would not liberally grant grandchild full adoption, even accounting for the new ruling.

This new ruling cannot extend to grandchild full adoption without some modification, insofar as it relies on the meeting of minds between the adoptee and the adopter to adoption as a counterbalance against consideration of the best interests of the child. Undeniably, the standard of the best interests of the child in adjudications of grandchild full adoptions can be very similar to that in the adjudication of grandchild simple adoptions,[83] but it cannot be identical, as they have different legal effects. Moreover, the meeting of minds of the adoptee and the adopter is missing entirely in full adoption. The prospective adopter commences the proceeding for full adoption, and the family court decides whether it is in the best interests of the child.[84] Although the consent of the child is necessary, it is only a prerequisite for the decision; it does not constitute an acceptance of an agreement to adopt. The majority opinion heavily relied on

---

80 D. Park, *Family and Inheritance Law*, Pakyoungsa, 4th ed., 2013, p. 306.

81 Above nn. 74, 75 (the dissenting opinion shared this point of the majority opinion, citing the precedents about grandchild full adoption).

82 The dissenting opinion neglects this fact, by arguing that not only full adoption of a minor but also simple adoption of a minor presupposes the court's permission.

83 J. Yune and S. Hyun, *Annotation of the Revised Civil Code in 2013*, Ministry of Justice, 2013, p. 203 (manifestly affirming that the best interests of the child standard for simple adoption of a minor in Art. 867(2) of the Korean Civil Code is the same as that for full adoption in Art. 908-2(3) of the Korean Civil Code).

84 Minbôb Art. 908-2(1).

the agreement of the parties, which does not apply in the context of grandchild full adoption.

3.3.2. *Intent to Adopt the Grandchild*

The dissenting opinion also questioned the adoption agreement, or rather the intent to adopt. It noted that simple adoption does not sever the existing parent–child relationship between the birth parent and the child. It therefore inferred from the notion of simple adoption that the intent of simple adoption should presuppose the existence and continuance of the existing relationship so that the intent to adopt for simple adoption should be an intent to specifically form an *adoptive* parent–child relationship, not just a parent–child relationship. Consequently, it advocates for open adoption and rejects closed adoption.[85] However, the majority opinion did not share this conclusion. The majority opinion also acknowledges the value of open adoption but considers open adoption as neither a legal mandate nor what the best interests of the child always requires.

The majority opinion is in agreement with statutory law. Although the Korean Civil Code distinguishes full adoption from simple adoption, it does not relate to the requirement of intent to adopt but to the legal effect of adoption. If one were to petition for a simple adoption that would exclude a legal relationship between the birth parent and the child, it would constitute an ambiguous intent or a simultaneous or sham adoption and therefore be void. However, closed adoption does not contradict the notion of simple adoption. Since the consent of a minor adoptee without capacity is not a requirement for adoption, it does not matter whether the minor adoptee is aware that he or she has another birth parent. Whether to reveal the fact of the adoption may matter in terms of the best interests of the child, but is not a prerequisite for establishing an intent of simple adoption.

3.3.3. *The Best Interests of the Child Standard in the Context of Grandchild Adoption*

The application of the best interests of the child standard to grandchild adoption is paramount. Both the majority and dissenting opinions concede that grandchild adoption can cause problems by complicating and creating an unnatural relationship in the family. In the case of grandchild simple adoption, the grandparents of the adoptee become the parents of the adoptee as well as

[85] In fact, the reasoning of the dissenting opinion is somewhat confusing, so it is uncertain whether the dissenting opinion problematises closed adoption in regard to the best interests of the child standard or to the intent to adopt.

the birth parent, and the mother of the adoptee becomes the brother or sister of the adoptee. The situation is not much different in grandchild full adoption, which can sever the legal relationship but cannot negate the factual or blood relationship. Because the birth parent has access to the grandchild, every other family member would be conscious of that complicated relationship, posing a threat to the development of a true parent–child relationship. In that situation, there is a high chance that the adopted grandchild will become aware of the fact of their adoption in the future and that this will give rise to an identity crisis in the adoptee. Grandchild adoption has a unique but serious potential to work against the child's best interests.

To mitigate these potential negative outcomes of grandchild adoption, the majority opinion relies on the agreement to adopt, that is, the meeting of the minds between the adoptee and the adopter. The majority reinforced its argument by pointing out that there is no longer a stereotypical family relationship; therefore, the court should respect individual or family autonomy. This argument, although correct in principle, is misplaced.[86] Even if simple adoption in the Korean Civil Code adopts the contract system, we cannot say there is a genuine agreement or exercise of individual or family autonomy in grandchild adoption. The adoptee's acceptance is made not by the adoptee but by its legal representative, the birth parent.[87] The legal representative's consent, although necessary, does not account for the kind of atypical parent–child relationship the adoptee intended, since forming a parent–child relationship is intensely personal. The minor adoptee is unable to exercise his or her individual or family autonomy. Further, unilateral imposition of an atypical parent–child relationship by the adopter lacks the suggestive validity of a true contract. The family court's review should fill this gap in justifying the adoption in terms of the best interests of the child. Neither the intent of the parties nor individual or family autonomy supports a less stringent review even in grandchild simple adoption.

The last argument in support of grandchild adoption, despite all the potential for negative outcomes, is that a blood grandparent may be a more trustworthy and responsible candidate for an adoptive parent and may have already played a role as a foster parent. Although this might be true, grandchild adoption is not necessarily in the best interests of the child. Unlike other typical minor adoption

---

86 The autonomy argument is appropriate when it concerns the marital relationship, the adoption of an adult or any other genuine contractual relationship. The Supreme Court *en banc* decision of 23 October 2019, 2016Mu2510, the first case the majority opinion cited here as a reference, is about whether the paternity presumption is applied in the case of artificial insemination by a donor, where the agreement between the husband of the mother and the sperm donor or the family autonomy of the couple matters.

87 See Minbôb Art. 869(2) (mandating that the acceptance of the adoptee should be made by his or her legal representative when the adoptee is under 13 years of age).

cases, the grandchild has not only birth parents but also grandparents, who are usually willing and able to support the birth parents in child-rearing. Even when the birth parents are not ready or able to rear the grandchild themselves, it cannot be conclusively said that grandchild adoption would significantly promote the well-being of the child. Considering the existing natural grandparent–grandchild relationship, guardianship can confer a steady, effective legal arrangement in which to rear the grandchild on behalf of the birth parent. Compared with guardianship, grandchild adoption has many potential negative effects, without providing a significantly greater benefit. Thus, in such cases, adoption per se might not be in the best interests of the child. Grandchild adoption should be permitted in exceptional cases, such as when the birth parents are dead or missing, or when there is no possibility of further contact.

4. CONCLUSION

Different jurisdictions have managed grandchild adoption in various ways. In the United States, some states give preference to grandparents as prospective adopters, while this form of adoption has been regarded with suspicion and is thus rarely accepted in Germany and France. Notably, reported opinions in the United States are more likely to arise in the context of contested adoptions involving allegations of abuse or violence against the birth parents, which deprive the birth parent of his or her custody and necessitate adoption. This does not seem to be the typical case in Germany and France. Japan rarely permits grandchild full adoption but it generally accepts grandchild simple adoption, perhaps because simple adoption in the Japanese Civil Code is essentially contractual.

The first Korean case regarding grandchild adoption, rendered 11 years ago, rejected the petition for grandchild full adoption and has dominated Korean family court practice since then. At the end of last year, the Supreme Court of Korea, sitting *en banc*, handed down a new ruling, this time about grandchild simple adoption. The Supreme Court's decision was divided, with the majority arguing that grandchild adoption should be allowed unless there is a concrete reason to reject it. Its line of reasoning, although not clear, heavily relies on the agreement to adopt and accept an atypical parent–child relationship, including grandchild adoption. The dissenting opinion advocated for more stringent review based on the best interests of the child, problematised the intent to adopt by requiring that the truth of the adoption be told to the adoptee, and simultaneously suggested that the scope of the new ruling is limited to simple adoption and does not extend to full adoption. The review of whether adoption of a minor is in the best interests of the child should not be carried out more superficially even in grandchild simple adoption. There are several reasons to have suspicions about grandchild adoption, and guardianship is as effective as and safer than grandchild adoption in most cases. The argument of the majority opinion of the Supreme Court of Korea, based on the agreement to adopt, is not persuasive.

The majority opinion also declared that the consent of the birth parent should be based on consultation and information and that the prospective adoptee's own opinion should be heard, even though there is no statutory mandate. Although it is *obiter dictum* and therefore non-binding, it is of great importance for the development of family court practice on child adoption generally.

SWEDEN

HARMONISING FAMILY LAW ACROSS BORDERS IN EUROPE

Elizabeth S. Perry*

* elizabeth.s.perry@jur.uu.se.

Résumé

On observe une « européanisation » croissante du droit de la famille, qui coexiste avec les tensions existantes entre l'Union Européenne et les États membres. Cette tendance réduit les difficultés juridiques pour les individus et les acteurs étatiques en Suède et dans toute l'Union Européenne dans le contexte actuel plus général de mondialisation juridique, économique et culturelle. Le droit de la famille, qui n'est plus relégué au second plan par rapport aux autres domaines juridiques de l'Union européenne, joue aujourd'hui un rôle extrêmement important. Cet article offre aux experts en droit de la famille du monde entier un aperçu de cette évolution et une mise à jour des dernières évolutions du « droit européen de la famille » découlant du droit de l'Union Européenne qui s'applique verticalement. Il a pour but d'offrir un aperçu des tensions actuelles (et toujours présentes) entre l'autonomie et l'uniformisation au sein de l'Union Européenne et d'initier les chercheurs non européens à ce domaine juridique croissant et assez complexe, en analysant une sélection de plusieurs changements récents notables et leurs répercussions sur la Suède, en contribuant à l'importante littérature existante sur l'état actuel et les possibilités futures du « droit européen de la famille », y compris dans le contexte suédois. Ce chapitre se concentre spécifiquement sur les règles de conflit de lois permettant de résoudre les litiges familiaux transfrontaliers dans l'UE et plus particulièrement celles relatives à la responsabilité parentale, à la dissolution du mariage et à la répartition des biens lors d'une succession. Sont étudiées les évolutions juridiques du droit de l'UE intéressant les relations familiales transfrontalières au sein des 27 États membres, qui ont été principalement introduites par une importante nouvelle législation européenne et par des décisions récentes de la Cour de justice de l'Union Européenne. Les conséquences de ces évolutions européenne sur le droit national de la famille, tant substantiel que procédural, et sur l'autonomie nationale et personnelle (des parties) sont examinées à l'aide de rapports publiés portant sur des expériences menées dans l'ensemble de l'UE et spécifiquement en Suède. L'expérience de la Suède constitue un exemple de la manière dont le droit de la famille (principalement celui du « droit international privé » ou « DIP », sous-domaine du droit de l'UE), est discuté et mis en œuvre à la fois entre les États membres et au sein de ceux-ci.

1. INTRODUCTION

A steadily increasing 'Europeanisation' of family law is occurring, co-existing with the tensions between the EU and its Member States. This trend is reducing legal difficulties for individuals and State actors in Sweden and throughout the EU within a broader context of ongoing legal, economic and cultural globalisation. Family law, no longer taking a back seat to other European Union legal areas, is today playing a remarkably prominent role. This chapter provides family law experts worldwide with a glimpse into this evolution and an update on the latest changes in top-down, EU-law-derived 'European family law'.[1] It aims to overview ongoing (and indeed ever-present) tensions between autonomy and uniformity interests within the EU and to introduce non-EU scholars to this growing, rather complex legal area by analysing a selection of several notable recent changes and their impacts on Sweden, contributing to the significant existing literature on the present state of and future possibilities for 'European family law', including in the Swedish context.[2] The chapter focuses specifically on conflict-of-law rules for resolving EU cross-border family law cases, most notably those regarding responsibility for children, marital dissolution and distribution of assets after death. Examined are EU-level legal developments affecting cross-border family relationships within the 27 nations of the European Union[3] that have been introduced

1 For a general introduction to the EU legal sources and hierarchical relationship among them see K. Bradley, 'Legislating in the European Union' in C. Barnard (ed.), *European Union Law*, Oxford University Press, 3rd ed., 2020, pp. 101–153.

2 See e.g. J.M. Scherpe (ed.), *European Family Law Volume IV: The Present and Future of European Family Law*, Elgar Publishing, 2016 (which takes up these topics in overview and more specifically, citing inter alia many valuable chapters within the first three volumes of the book series of which it is part) and M. Jänterä-Jareborg, 'The Nordic Input on the EU's Cooperation in Family and Succession Law – Exporting Union Law through "Nordic Exceptions"' in B. Hess, M. Bergström and E. Storskrubb (eds.), *EU Civil Justice: Current Issues and Future Outlook*, Hart Publishing, 2016, pp. 143–60.

3 Norway, Switzerland, Iceland, Ukraine, Russia and (now) the United Kingdom are among the approximately 22 *non*-EU-member countries in Europe, but the majority of countries in Europe are Member States. Five additional 'candidate' countries have qualified for EU membership and are in the process of transposing EU legislation into national law prior to acceding to the Union. See Joining the Union, available at: <https://european-union.europa.eu/principles-countries-history/joining-eu_en>, last accessed 28.06.2022.

primarily through significant new EU legislation and by recent case decisions by the Court of Justice of the European Union (CJEU).[4] The changes' impacts at the national level on substantive and procedural family law and on national and personal (party) autonomy are examined using published reports on experiences across the EU and specifically in Sweden. Sweden's experience is described as an example of how EU-level, increasingly harmonised family law (primarily that in the 'private international law' or 'PIL' sub-field of EU law) is being negotiated and implemented, both between and within EU Member States.[5]

Section 2 overviews important EU and EU PIL topics. Section 3 describes prominent EU family law changes in light of their impacts on autonomy and uniformity concerns. Section 4 focuses on national and specifically Swedish experiences with the Succession Regulation and with the Brussels II *ter* Regulation to date. Finally, section 5 returns the discussion of these developments to the European and global levels.

2. THE SIGNIFICANCE OF EU PRIVATE INTERNATIONAL FAMILY LAW AS A SUBSET OF 'EUROPEAN FAMILY LAW'

'European family law' can be described as including multiple institutions' influences, and even to be converging (becoming more uniform) due to more organic and worldwide societal developments.[6] Institutions contributing quite

---

4 Virtually all EU national courts and tribunals must apply these laws to cases that have connection to more than one of the currently 27 EU Member States, and to some cases with connections to a third-party state (a non-EU country). In cases involving Denmark, one must consult the instruments as well as Danish law, as Denmark has opted out of some of the EU conflict-of-laws instruments (including the Brussels II *ter*, per its recital 96 and more formally per TEU Protocol No. 22, Arts. 1 and 2). In cases involving the UK, now a former EU Member State, one must consult the appropriate national laws of England and Wales or of Scotland.

5 Swedish family law experience with some of these EU-level changes will continue to develop rapidly over the coming months, given the new rules on cross-border divorce and parental responsibility matters that come into effect on 1 August 2022 with the recast Brussels II Regulation, Council Regulation (EU) 2019/1111 of 25 June 2019 on jurisdiction, the recognition and enforcement of decisions in matrimonial matters and the matters of parental responsibility, and on international child abduction, OJ L 178/1 (Brussels II *ter* or the Recast) (see section 3.1.1). More can already be observed regarding changes that went into effect earlier, such as those brought on by the Succession Regulation, Regulation (EU) 650/2012 of the European Parliament and of the Council on jurisdiction, applicable law, recognition and enforcement of decisions and acceptance and enforcement of authentic instruments in matters of succession and on the creation of a European Certificate of Succession, OJ L 359/30 of 16 December 2014 (also known as Brussels IV), fully effective as of 17 August 2015.

6 Cf. SCHERPE, above n. 2, at pp. 2–5 (discussing European family law of roughly these types as 'institutional' and 'organic').

significantly to the legal norms comprising 'European family law' – beyond the EU legal acts and case decisions in focus for this chapter – are for example the European Convention on Human Rights and the European Court of Human Rights (ECtHR) that interprets it; the Hague Conference on Private International Law through its relevant conventions, protocols and soft law instruments; and the International Commission on Civil Status with its various relevant conventions on legal status and recognition issues.[7]

While this chapter refers to the whole curiously engineered machine called 'European family law', it focuses on just one particular component: the norms affecting family law created by explicitly EU legal sources, particularly the private international law rules in both EU legislation and case decisions that affect family law's creation and use within the EU Member States.[8] This 'European family law' can change the results of family law cases with cross-border elements, mainly by determining which EU Member State national court(s) will have *jurisdiction* to decide a given family law issue, or all issues in the case; which national law will be the *applicable law* used to decide a given issue; and to what extent the resulting court, agency or party settlement decision will be granted *recognition* or be *enforceable* for various purposes in another EU Member State.

2.1. CROSS-BORDER VERSUS PURELY NATIONAL ('INTERNAL') FAMILY LAW CASES

The limitation of EU PIL rules to 'cases with cross-border elements' is important, and is best understood in the broader context of all of 'European family law' alongside national (domestic, Member State) family law. The remainder of this second section therefore introduces in more depth the family law in force within the EU Member States and how particularly EU legislation and case law decisions affect it. This clarifies what I term the 'autonomy versus uniformity tensions'

7 Some further, also contributing institutions: the Council of Europe with its relevant conventions and recommendations; the Commission on European Family Law with its model law Principles of European Family Law; and the various national legislatures, universities and research centres where family law expertise is developed and used to promote legal development in the field. The norms created bind different combinations of nations and individuals, to different degrees, but are beyond the scope of this chapter.

8 'Private international law' is also known as 'conflict of laws'. The EU PIL focused on family law has also been called, among other things, 'European international family law'. See D. Martiny, 'European Family Law (PIL)' in *The Max Planck Encyclopedia of European Private Law*, 2012, available at: <max-eup2012.mpipriv.de>, last accessed 04.04.2022. EU competence to adopt harmonising measures concerning conflict of laws and jurisdiction is conferred by Art. 81(2)(c) Treaty on the Functioning of the European Union (TFEU). On the other hand, EU law does not apply to situations purely internal to one Member State, however narrowly the Court of Justice of the EU may construe what is 'purely internal' within a Union guaranteeing free movement rights to its citizens. See e.g. Art. 20 TFEU.

between the EU and its Member States as individual, sovereign nations, while later sections address how recent changes increasingly harmonise family law rules, or at least require mutual recognition of family-related legal relationships and rights determined in any of the Member States.

What defines the 'cross-border' versus 'purely internal' type of EU family law case? Consider a typical family law situation within an EU country. Two Swedish spouses now divorcing and deciding issues of child custody, for example,[9] will settle all issues between them by mediating, seeking administrative agency decisions about these issues or litigating their differences in Swedish courts competent to hear these issues. Such a case is, in other words, simply a matter to be decided by purely 'national law', in the three different respects relevant to the EU-wide legal changes in focus for this chapter that were mentioned earlier:

- Jurisdiction: first, if all parties to a family law dispute are from one EU country, have lived there throughout the relevant relationship and are living in that country at the time of the dispute, then the courts (or relevant agencies) of that country have *jurisdiction* to hear and render decisions that bind the parties.[10]
- Applicable law: second, there would arise no conflict concerning *applicable law* governing their case, and Swedish national law would exclusively be applied by all concerned, to both procedural and substantive questions.[11]
- Recognition: finally, once the case was resolved, *recognition* of the legal validity of and *enforcement* of the resulting legal rights (expressed in a private settlement contract, court judgment, administrative agency decision

[9] Or two Swedish heirs to a newly deceased Swedish resident with an estate consisting of property exclusively in Sweden. Inheritance law is included as an area within family law for the purposes of EU PIL rules and in some Member States, including Sweden. See section 2.2.2.

[10] Within EU law, retention of national-level competence over family law is confirmed by Art. 5(2) of the Treaty on European Union (TEU) ('Under the principle of conferral, the Union shall act only within the limits of the competences conferred upon it by the Member States in the Treaties to attain the objectives set out therein. Competences not conferred upon the Union in the Treaties remain with the Member States') and Art. 81(3) TFEU requiring unanimity among Member States in 'family law' matters, yet then providing for a procedure by which 'ordinary legislative procedure' detailed in Art. 294 TFEU can instead, in theory, be used. For discussion of this *passerelle*, an 'exception to the family law exception', see e.g. A. Fiorini, 'Which Legal Basis for Family Law? The Way Forward', European Parliament Directorate-General for Internal Policies Policy Dept. C: Citizen's Rights and Constitutional Affairs, Legal Affairs Note, 2012, available at: <https://www.europarl.europa.eu/thinktank/en/document/IPOL-JURI_NT(2012)462498>, last accessed 04.08.2022.

[11] This is controlled by national law, in Sweden for example by Section 10:1 of the Swedish Code of Judicial Procedure (Rättegångsbalken). Per Art. 19(1) TEU, EU Member States also 'shall provide remedies sufficient to ensure effective legal protection in the fields covered by Union law', and thus both national and EU law rights must be protected by Member State authorities without differences, deliberate or inadvertent, that give a stronger protection to rights arising from national law.

> or similar instrument), purely inside Sweden, would not require EU or other legal systems' rules to be considered, only the Swedish national laws on validity and enforcement of legal instruments. When one party later moves to another EU Member State during the children's minority, the originally purely national case can, as an enforcement or modification of orders action, become one with a cross-border element, but if modified custody orders were sought merely because a move was anticipated, the case would most likely stay purely national.

These purely national cases, which seem to have nothing to do with EU-level PIL or broader 'European family law', are much more common than cross-border cases, and yet it is arguably cross-border cases that are most rapidly changing Member State lawmakers' understanding of what is legally permissible and not permissible and wise or less wise to introduce into or retain in national family law.

2.1.1. Purely National Family Law Cases in the EU: But Are They?

To have an accurate, forest-level perspective on the state of family law in Europe, it is helpful to recognise two realities qualifying the term 'purely national' as applied to EU family law matters seemingly confined within one Member State.

First, usually no question about using non-national (e.g. non-Swedish) rules arises in a purely domestic matter because family law remains largely regulated at the national level. This is because the EU lacks competence to legislate in the 'family law' area[12] or to operate to enforce rights in cases not involving any element triggering EU jurisdiction over a given question, such as sufficient cross-border impact on other Member States or on the EU as a whole.[13] Legal professionals thus correctly turn exclusively to national sources of law in these

---

12 See e.g. Art. 81(3) TFEU, further discussed in section 2.2.2. The Member States involved in negotiating the EU Treaties originally did not cede control over this area, among others. EU law is nonetheless quite powerful. Pursuant to Art. 2(2) TFEU, for example, EU-level regulation in an area of 'shared' competence, as some aspects of EU family-*related* law (but not family law itself) can be classified, pre-empts national regulation that would conflict with existing or subsequent EU rules on that subject: 'When the Treaties confer on the Union a competence shared with the Member States in a specific area, the Union and the Member States may legislate and adopt legally binding acts in that area. The Member States shall exercise their competence to the extent that the Union has not exercised its competence.' Further, in certain other areas under certain Treaty-specified conditions, 'the Union shall have competence to carry out actions to support, coordinate or supplement the actions of the Member States, without thereby superseding their competence in these areas' (Art. 2(5) TFEU). The Union also has enumerated exclusive competences, listed at Art. 3 TFEU, and there are a number of ways it can act in other areas as well, rendering this list misleadingly narrow.

13 These vertical division of power questions are taken up in section 2.2.1.

cases lacking any across-EU-borders component, and even in some international cases where the cross-border component might be a connection with a foreign nation that is not also within the EU.[14]

Second, however, often domestic family law practitioners and other experts may not realise that the source of many wordings and rules found in the domestic law are identical to wordings and rules in international or EU law sources. National law norms today very often 'are' European-level family law as defined in this chapter, harmonised across many nations' national systems, although now enacted into national law, verbatim or otherwise.[15] Even in 'purely national' cases – and in cross-border cases where for example Swedish courts and national substantive law are chosen by the relevant EU PIL rules – national Swedish family law already conforms to international obligations, even if the Swedish lawmaker has taken a unique approach. A national law provision or its application in specific cases could be challenged in European courts or by the EU's institutions that monitor EU law compliance if it did not conform.[16] National law in Member States thus is drafted (or reviewed and modified) as needed to conform to various EU and international treaty obligations on an ongoing basis, as they arise via EU legislation,[17] new treaty ratifications and sometimes case decisions by European courts, including those protecting fundamental human rights.[18]

---

14 Limits exist in the EU Treaties, however, permitting only the EU as a whole and not individual Member States from entering new international agreements with third-party nations in areas of exercised EU competence, limiting for example Sweden from certain inter-Nordic agreements that were possible prior to recent expansions of EU law's reach. See e.g. P. Leino and L. Leppävirta, 'Does staying together mean playing together? The influence of EU law on co-operation between EU and non-EU states: the Nordic example' (2018) 43(3) *European Law Review* 295, 310 and section 4.3 below.

15 For comments relevant to this phenomenon within Swedish family law see E.S. Perry, *Child Support Law in California and Sweden: A Comparison Across Welfare State Models*, Umeå Studies in Law Vol. 43, Umeå University, 2019, pp. 518–523.

16 See e.g. I.O. Eriksson and H. Pettersson, Report to the European Parliament, 'Obstacles to the right of free movement and residence for EU citizens and their families: Country report for Sweden', 2016, available at: <https://www.europarl.europa.eu/cmsdata/109224/pe%20556%20966%20en_All_Online_Sweden.pdf>, last accessed 01.07.2022.

17 See e.g. Proposition 2021/22:189 of 17 March 2022, The Swedish Government's Proposal to the Swedish Parliament for Legislative Reforms: Increased Legal Certainty and More Rapid Enforcement in International Family Law Cases (presenting for legislative approval the changes to national Swedish law as required by the Brussels II *ter* Regulation, which would go into effect on 1 August 2022).

18 Such rights are set forth in instruments including the European Convention on Human Rights, the Charter of Fundamental Rights, the TEU and the TFEU. In Sweden such sources of human rights law are important sources of law, along with the Swedish national constitutional law on various fundamental human rights, although the hierarchy between them is complicated, in some respects controversial and beyond the scope of this chapter. For our purposes, it suffices to say that a national family law that is held to violate one of these legal sources may need to give way.

2.1.2. *Cases with Cross-Border Elements: Society and Law's Europeanisation as Supported by EU Law*

An increasing percentage of EU citizens at any one time are living in another Member State than that of their national citizenship (namely 3.3 per cent of 20 to 64-year-olds in 2020 compared to 2.4 per cent in 2010).[19] Therefore there is an increasing number of cross-border matters experienced by individuals whose families, like very many in our era, include members with different habitual residences, different citizenships and, quite often, different expectations from family law due to these and other factors.[20]

In summary, when parties to a family law matter are not presently living in the same country, or are living in the same country but that country differs from the one (or more) where they are nationals or lived together previously (and in similar cross-border situations), PIL rules like the EU Succession and Brussels II *ter* Regulations[21] must be applied. Within most of Europe, the matter becomes one requiring the use of what this chapter defines in a narrower sense as 'European family law': EU law and particularly EU PIL applicable in family law matters.

2.2. THE SCOPE OF EU-LEVEL FAMILY LAW

Defining the term 'European family law' broadly is tricky business; its sources, as we have seen, include a closely interacting mix of international, EU and national sources developed by the legislatures and courts in all three contexts.[22]

---

19 Eurostat (Statistical Office of the EU), 'Eurostat Statistics Explained: EU citizens living in another Member State – statistical overview (data extracted August 2021)', available at: <https://ec.europa.eu/eurostat/statistics-explained/index.php?title=EU_citizens_living_in_another_Member_State_-_statistical_overview#:~:text=Among%20the%20EU%20citizens%20of%20working%20age%20(20%2D64),of%20their%20citizenship%20in%202020>, last accessed 01.07.2022. Meanwhile '23.7 million people (5.3%) of the 447.2 million people living in the EU on 1 January 2021 were non-EU citizens.' Eurostat, 'Eurostat Statistics Explained: Migration and migrant population statistics (data extracted March 2022)', available at: <https://ec.europa.eu/eurostat/statistics-explained/index.php?title=Migration_and_migrant_population_statistics#Acquisitions_of_citizenship:_EU_Member_States_granted_citizenship_to_729_000_persons_in_2020>, last accessed 01.06.2022.

20 For a broad and insightful introduction to families and law in a globalising world see D. Hacker, *Legalized Families in the Era of Bordered Globalization*, Cambridge University Press, 2017, including at pp. 17–44 (ch. 1, 'Our Era'). See also section 5 below on EU-level family law in light of ongoing Europeanisation and globalisation.

21 These EU Regulations, in focus below, have supremacy over national law in most Member States, including Sweden. See e.g. Proposition 2021/22:189, above n. 17.

22 See G. DeBaere and K. Gutman, 'The impact of the European Union and the European Court of Justice on European family law' in J.M. Scherpe (ed.), *European Family Law Volume 1: The Impacts of Institutions and Organisations on European Family Law*, Elgar Publishing, 2016, pp. 8–11 (discussing broad and narrower senses of 'European family law' before examining EU legislative and case law impacts upon it). Regarding PIL aspects,

This chapter therefore merely touches upon a broad definition then focuses on the recent EU-level PIL sources that (almost) uniformly apply across EU Member States in cross-border family law cases.

Two final short discussions are nonetheless necessary to help primarily international family law experts from outside of Europe understand the scope of EU-level 'European family law' and the ongoing academic and political discourses concerning it, fulfilling this chapter's aim to overview this complex area for non-EU scholars.

One discussion addresses *constitutionally* the scope of 'family law' (traditionally decided at the national level in EU Member States), now that the EU Treaties provide a supranational constitutional law framework creating an EU legal level of enumerated competences: does the EU have competence to regulate 'family law', or may only each Member State at the national level do that?[23] This topic is covered in section 2.2.1. The other discussion addresses this law's scope *substantively*: which substantive sub-areas of law does 'family law' for EU law purposes include, and specifically does it include succession law, otherwise known as inheritance law? Section 2.2.2 addresses this question.

2.2.1. *'European Family Law' from a Vertical-Division-of-Powers Perspective Impacting Uniformity and Autonomy Interests*

When does the EU have the power to regulate family law? This is in essence a question which requires some understanding of the vertical division of powers created by the constitutional Treaties entered into to create the EU. The EU Treaties set forth aims and impose duties on both Member States and the EU institutions, all of which are bound by this constitutional, primary EU law to act in pursuit of those specified aims[24] while in practice continuing politically to negotiate 'how far is too far' for EU law's uniformity to be taken, at the cost of Member States' autonomy to decide various issues as independent, sovereign states.

---

see D. Martiny, 'The impact of the EU private international law instruments on European family laws' in J.M. Scherpe (ed.), *European Family Law Volume 1: The Impacts of Institutions and Organisations on European Family Law*, Elgar Publishing, 2016, pp. 261–293.

23 See DeBaere and Gutman, above n. 22, at pp. 12–22 (describing an 'in principle' lack of EU power to regulate substantive family law and yet significant indirect effects of EU law on such law). Compare J. NeJaime, 'The constitution of parenthood' (2020) 72 *Stanford Law Review* 261 (extensively examining 'the dialogic relationship between family law and constitutional law' in the US context).

24 'Primary' a.k.a. higher-order law establishing the EU and its competences in relation to those remaining with its Member States consists of three instruments: the TEU, the TFEU and the Charter of Fundamental Rights of the European Union. See Art. 6 TEU. In turn, EU-level PIL rules enter into force as 'secondary' EU law, enacted as EU legislative acts permitted and envisioned by the EU's constitutional Treaties. See Arts. 288–289 TFEU.

The aim of 'Europeanisation', deliberately seeking more uniformity, has a long history. As recorded in the Preamble to 1957's Treaty Establishing the European Community, later to become the European Union, early Member States were 'determined to lay the foundations of an ever closer union among the peoples of Europe'.[25] The Preamble to the Treaty on European Union, entered into in 1992 and currently in force, re-affirmed a resolve among the Member States 'to continue the process of creating an ever closer union among the peoples of Europe'; its Article 1 further clarifies the EU project's ambition:[26]

> This Treaty marks a new stage in the process of creating an ever closer union among the peoples of Europe, in which decisions are taken as openly as possible and as closely as possible to the citizen.

In light of the EU's explicit purposes, then, positive integration of the various Member States' national laws through enactment of the recent EU regulations analysed below in this chapter is not surprising. Europeanisation among EU Member States is an explicit goal, to be achieved in part via EU-level promulgation of new legislative acts and court decisions over time.[27] The question in focus for the rest of this chapter then becomes how family law in particular is affecting and being affected by ongoing Europeanisation in the form of recent EU legislation and court decisions.

EU legislative acts, including the two in closest focus within this chapter, are drafted via multi-stage EU legislative processes involving representatives from every Member State.[28] The EU institutions such as the Commission, the Council and the Parliament draft and pass these acts into EU law, which is then directly applicable[29] across the EU, in large part to resolve jurisdictional, conflict-of-laws, recognition and enforcement questions for cases with cross-border elements by harmonising (replacing with one shared new system of rules)

---

25 Treaty Establishing the European Economic Community (TEEC), signed 25 March 1957, at 11 (Preamble), available in the French official language version at: <https://eur-lex.europa.eu/legal-content/FR/TXT/PDF/?uri=CELEX:11957E/TXT&from=EN>, last accessed 10.06.2022.

26 Art. 1(2) TEU, available at: <https://eur-lex.europa.eu/resource.html?uri=cellar:2bf140bf-a3f8-4ab2-b506-fd71826e6da6.0023.02/DOC_1&format=PDF>, last accessed 10.06.2022.

27 There are simultaneously reasonable arguments to be made against this premise, and there are strong political actors even within the EU institutions working to slow or reverse the extent of current and planned integration. See e.g. N. Brack, 'The roles of Eurosceptic Members of the European Parliament and their implications for the EU' (2015) 36(3) *International Political Science Review* 337. The Member States themselves sometimes take positions challenging whether the EU Treaties support, for example, Court of Justice of the European Union (CJEU) decisions that further integrate them. See e.g. Case C-105/03, *Pupino*, ECLI:EU:C:2005:386, decided 16 June 2005.

28 Art. 289 TFEU.

29 Art. 288 TFEU.

the varying national law rules for deciding these cross-border questions. During the legislative drafting process, EU lawmakers justify the adoption of each new EU-level measure as contributing positively to the achievement of one or more of the EU's aims. This legally justifies the measure's adoption from a constitutional perspective, despite some corresponding loss of national lawmakers' autonomy, once it wins sufficient support to pass into law according to appropriate legislative procedure rules assigned to EU action for measures of this measure's type.

For example, the creation of an 'Area of Freedom, Security and Justice'[30] is a central aim set forth in the EU constitutional Treaties. Proper pursuit of this aim is used to justify the adoption of certain EU measures that facilitate the exercise of EU citizens' free movement rights. Such new EU laws include measures aimed at improving access to justice in the Member States via, for example, guaranteed and simple cross-border mutual recognition of legal instruments such as divorce judgments and child custody orders.[31] When an individual moves to a new Member State, it is per EU PIL generally prohibited for the new Member State to require that a complicated procedure (of the sort that might be considered necessary if someone was moving there from a non-EU country) be used to establish key facts about them for public administration purposes.

Pursuing this aim of achieving an EU-wide 'Area of Freedom, Security and Justice' is a proper purpose for EU action, justifying for example legislative proposals in the 'family law PIL' realm, but for such proposals to be legally adopted nonetheless also requires that the EU has a legal basis to legislate in the manner proposed. Required in other words is a power (competence) among the competences granted to the EU by the Member States under the EU Treaties, to regulate in a particular legal area of EU competence or otherwise towards a proper general aim, and such a power must then be exercised in a particular manner specified in EU law.[32] This brings us into the second discussion.

---

30 See Title V TFEU.

31 See Fiorini, above n. 10, at p. 10 (discussing further general and policy 'integrationist' aims focusing on citizens' needs, interests and opportunities in a globalising world and 'traditional' PIL aims like improved legal certainty, removal of barriers, reduced forum shopping and avoidance of 'limping situations').

32 The EU may decide to exercise another of its competences, for example its competence to conclude international agreements with non-EU countries, 'as an alternative to the often-difficult process of developing its own internal legal framework'. DeBaere and Gutman, above n. 22, at p. 27. This means it may sign onto an agreement with third-party countries that binds all of the EU to follow certain family law rules in cross-border situations, without itself needing to write and pass the rules as EU legislation under another Treaty-based competence. This occurred, for example, with respect to the 2007 Hague Protocol on the Law Applicable to Maintenance Obligations. Ibid.

2.2.2. *EU Family Law Substantively: With or Without Succession Law?*

Which legal areas or issues does the scope of the 'family law' include for EU law purposes? Specifically, is succession law, comprising testate and intestate rules for transferring estates of deceased natural persons, included among the more universally recognised family law sub-areas such as marriage and divorce requirements, parental status or child custody and support?

The somewhat surprising answer is 'sometimes'. When the EU wants to adopt rules in the succession law PIL area, it prefers that succession law not be included as 'family law', to make it easier to legislate, yet on the other hand succession law PIL is seldom excluded from academic or practitioner discussions of EU PIL in the 'family law' realm, and within some Member States (including Sweden) law school teaching and research in succession law is without doubt considered squarely within 'family law', inside and outside of the PIL cross-border case area.[33]

This chameleon-like flexibility for succession law is possible because, although the term 'family law' appears in the Treaties as an area over which the EU has relatively little regulatory control, its substantive scope is not specified there.[34] Article 81(1) TFEU provides, regarding EU PIL competence, that '[t]he Union shall develop judicial cooperation in civil matters having cross-border implications, based on the principle of mutual recognition of judgments and of decisions in extrajudicial cases,' and that it 'may' adopt measures harmonising the Member States' laws to accomplish this. Per Article 81(2), the EU can use 'the ordinary legislative procedure' (OLP)[35] for eight different proper purposes, yet per Article 81(3) such measures concerning 'those aspects of family law with cross-border implications' instead must virtually always be adopted under a 'special legislative procedure' (SLP) requiring, as the sub-article details, unanimous agreement within the Council of Ministers (comprised of ministers from each Member State).

In short, it is possible for the Commission to propose to regulate 'succession law' using the OLP available for non-family-law acts, and it was desirable to do

---

33 For a comparative analysis of the substantive scope of Swedish and US 'family law' see E.S. Perry, 'Family Law Pedagogy in Sweden Today: What is Asked of Us, and What is Happening?' in M. Derlén, L. Landström and N. Nilsson Rådeström (eds.), *Vänbok till Ulf Israelsson [An Anthology in Honor of Ulf Israelsson]*, Umeå University, 2020, pp. 237–260. In the US, succession law a.k.a. inheritance law (or sometimes wills and trusts) is one of many areas considered outside of family law and yet having 'significant distributive impacts' on family members. L.T. Kessler, 'Family Law by the Numbers' (2020) 62 *Arizona Law Review* 903, 917–918.

34 European family law experts recognise that family law's scope is potentially controversial between EU Member States, due to national legal system traditions but also political interests, thus may not be surprised by this.

35 The more forgiving 'ordinary legislative procedure' is detailed in Art. 294 TFEU.

so to increase the chance that the proposed Succession Regulation, introduced in depth in section 3, would be passed into law. The proposal could succeed if a significant enough percentage of those involved in the legislative process agreed that 'succession law' was properly classified as *outside* of the 'family law', or did not mind voting in support of the Regulation *regardless* of its position on this detail.

The Succession Regulation's drafters had reason to propose a *narrow* scope for the definition of EU 'family law', perhaps because the proposal was not sure to have unanimous support,[36] and this is what they did. The Commission Proposal for the Succession Regulation described its position on the legal basis for EU competence over succession issues as follows:

> It should first be emphasized that the vast majority of Member States, *with the exception of the Nordic countries*, classify the law of succession as a matter distinct from family law on account of the fact that it mainly covers property. Even at the level of substantive law, there are significant differences between the two matters. *The main aim of the law of succession* is to define the rules for passing on the inheritance and for regulating the transfer of the inheritance itself. Unlike inheritance law, *the objective of family law* is to govern above all the legal relationships linked to marriage and partnerships, filiation and the civil status of persons. Its basic social function is to protect family ties. Moreover, in contrast to family law, where the wishes of individuals play a very minor role and the vast majority of ties are governed by public policy, the law of succession remains a matter where the wishes of the entitled party play an important role. There is therefore sufficient autonomy within these two branches of civil law for these matters to be treated separately from each other [emphasis added].[37]

Deeper discussion of the European Commission's rather non-Nordic and perhaps even non-European position, including regarding how much public policy and party choice exist in these two legal areas, is not possible within this chapter.[38] Suffice it to say that the Succession Regulation was indeed ultimately adopted on the basis of Article 81(2) TFEU (assigning use of the OLP

36 As becomes clear in section 3 below, the Succession Regulation contains some controversial provisions.

37 Commission Proposal for the Succession Regulation, COM (2009) 154 final, p. 3, available at: <https://eur-lex.europa.eu/legal-content/EN/TXT/PDF/?uri=CELEX:52009PC0154&from=EN>, last accessed 03.04.2022.

38 For a historical and cultural analysis of this topic suggesting the gap between Anglo-American and continental European legal cultures may be narrowing in some respects see M.J. De Waal, 'Comparative Succession Law' in M. Reimann and R. Zimmermann (eds.), *The Oxford Handbook of Comparative Law*, Oxford University Press, 2019, pp. 1058–1087. Reimann also (not unlike this chapter) highlights social and economic changes, questions of harmonisation as well as constitutional and human rights instruments' effects as important for future succession law research and development. Ibid, at pp. 1084–1086. See also below n. 41.

for measures concerning judicial cooperation in civil matters *not* comprising 'family law'). In contrast, other, more undeniably 'family law' PIL EU regulations, including Brussels II *bis* and *ter* on matrimonial matters and matters of parental responsibility and including the Maintenance Regulation on support matters,[39] have successfully been adopted using the Article 81(3) SLP.[40]

This chapter considers inheritance (succession) law as fitting comfortably under the general umbrella concept of 'family law'. Succession law should be analysed as part of 'family law' from an EU perspective, in the sense that EU law and policy is often focused on removing barriers to the free movement of individuals within the EU by reducing legal differences between Member States that might negatively affect 'free mover' individuals' private family lives, and differences in succession law are included. As one example, the explicit objective of the Succession Regulation legislative proposal quoted above was 'to enable people living in the European Union to organise their succession in advance and effectively to guarantee the rights of heirs and/or legatees and of other persons linked to the deceased, as well as creditors of the succession.'[41]

3. THE LATEST EU PIL REGULATIONS CONCERNING FAMILY LAW MATTERS

The latest EU Regulations increasingly harmonising PIL across the EU Member States' legal systems in the 'family law' area include the Brussels II *bis* Regulation recast known as Brussels II *ter* (effective 2022)[42] and the Succession Regulation (fully effective 2015), discussed more deeply in this section.[43]

---

39 Council Regulation (EC) 4/2009 of 18 December 2008 on jurisdiction, applicable law, recognition and enforcement of decisions and cooperation in matters relating to maintenance obligations (consolidated version 31 December 2018) (Maintenance Regulation).

40 Fiorini, above n. 10, at p. 8; see also the title page of each regulation. Additional legal bases used when the EU wishes to adopt further European family law applicable to at least cross-border cases include 'enhanced cooperation' between Member States (see Art. 20 TEU and Arts. 326–334 TFEU) and the EU's competence to enter into international agreements with third countries (see Art. 216 TFEU and above n. 12). Enhanced cooperation procedure is useful in the EU family law area for Member States when only some support harmonised rules in a given area, and thus such proposed rules would not survive an Art. 81(3) TFEU vote of the Council of Ministers. Precisely because the family law area can be contentious, with differing national views preventing unanimous agreement, the availability of a 'side agreement' type solution where some Member States can agree just between themselves and others can join the legislative scheme later on, if desired, can be useful.

41 Commission Proposal, above n. 37, at p. 2. In many European countries, a forced share to be inherited by the vertical heirs of a decedent (as opposed to by a spouse) is of relatively high importance from the comparative law perspective. See De Waal, above n. 38.

42 See Brussels II *ter*, above n. 5.

43 See Succession Regulation, above n. 5.

They also include the Rome III Regulation on choice of law (fully effective in 2012),[44] 'the twin regulations', meaning the Matrimonial Property Regulation[45] and the Registered Partnership Property Regulation[46] (both effective as of January 2019 and virtually identical but for the type of relationship concerned), as well as the somewhat older Maintenance Regulation (effective 2009),[47] among others.

The following sections will address just Brussels II *ter* and the Succession Regulation,[48] but readers should keep in mind how PIL instruments often work together to resolve for example one moderately complex divorce case involving change of status from married to divorced, property division and use of the family home, child support, child custody and so on, and how this might affect public opinion and EU politics, fanning or dampening any smouldering pro-Member-State-autonomy sentiments that might slow the EU's progress in achieving its mandates. This area of law seeks to simplify cross-border family law throughout Europe, and in one sense it does increase uniformity and foreseeability. On the other hand, the existence of so many EU PIL regulations means that for various ordinary family law matters, rules found in diverse and recent EU regulations will actually need to be applied.[49]

Practically, a divorcing couple in a case with cross-border elements will be more likely than a couple in a purely domestic case to need professional legal assistance, and by one or more family law professionals with relatively rare

---

44 Council Regulation (EU) 1259/2010 of 20 December 2010 implementing enhanced cooperation in the area of the law applicable to divorce and legal separation (effective since 21 June 2012) (Rome III Regulation).

45 Council Regulation (EU) 2016/1103 of 24 June 2016 implementing enhanced cooperation in the area of jurisdiction, applicable law and the recognition and enforcement of decisions in matters of matrimonial property regimes (effective since 29 January 2019) (Matrimonial Property Regulation). Per its recital 18, its scope includes 'all civil-law aspects of matrimonial property regimes, both the daily management of matrimonial property and the liquidation of the regime, in particular as a result of the couple's separation or the death of one of the spouses.'

46 Regulation (EU) 2016/1104 of 24 June 2016 implementing enhanced cooperation in the area of jurisdiction, applicable law and the recognition and enforcement of decisions in matters of the property consequences of registered partnerships (effective since 29 January 2019) (Registered Partnership Property Regulation).

47 See above n. 39.

48 These were chosen for deeper discussion mainly as one affects children's developing rights and one is much discussed for significantly changing succession law, including for retirees who move away from their 'home' EU Member State and for the administrators of their estates. They are also more universally binding across the EU, compared with regulations entered into via 'enhanced cooperation' between only some Member States.

49 Compounding this is 'the continental approach of separating the financial consequences of divorce, such as property division and post-divorce maintenance', which 'endangers the domestic common law concept [of the UK, no longer in the EU] according to which these issues shall be decided together.' Martiny, above n. 22, at p. 292. My personal experience as a comparative family law scholar in the EU has been that there is awareness of the need to consider both topics when reforming spousal support or property division, but whether they are resolved within one court action may vary.

and up-to-date PIL practice experience, who will need to explain to them that 'getting divorced' according to one country's divorce law is not always such a simple matter in cross-border cases.[50] Professionals may themselves as a result feel somewhat frustrated with EU law and aims, at least before they have accrued sufficient experience in this legal area, and may oppose juridification of family law generally.[51]

3.1. IN DIVORCE AND PARENTAL RESPONSIBILITY MATTERS

3.1.1. *The Brussels II Regulation Recast Effective 2022 and its Legal Effects*

By establishing uniform PIL jurisdiction, recognition of decisions, procedural rights and diverse related rules affecting a wide range of cross-border cases[52] involving wide-ranging issues of 'parental responsibility', dissolution of marriage

---

50 A typical article to be parsed by a lawyer researching these issues reads, for example, like Art. 13 of Brussels II *ter* on jurisdiction and enforcement (but not choice of applicable law) in matrimonial and parental responsibility (but not spousal or child support or property) sub-matters: 'Maintenance obligations are excluded from the scope of this Regulation, as those obligations are already covered by [the Maintenance Regulation]. In addition to the courts for the place where the defendant, or the creditor, is habitually resident, the courts having jurisdiction under this Regulation in matrimonial matters should generally have jurisdiction to decide on ancillary spousal or post-marital maintenance obligations by application of point (c) of Article 3 of that Regulation. The courts having jurisdiction under this Regulation in matters of parental responsibility generally have jurisdiction to decide on ancillary child maintenance obligations by application of point (d) of Article 3 of that Regulation.' The provisions do, however, attempt to promote efficiency via resolution by one court of multiple matters … 'generally'. The balance between appropriateness in diverse factual situations and simplicity when possible is delicate.

51 Juridification of national-level family law in the Nordic countries can also be said to be occurring and is predicted to continue, in part influenced by internationalising forces such as those this chapter examines. See e.g. T. Sverdrup, 'The changing concept of "family" and challenges for family law in the Nordic countries' in J.M. Scherpe (ed.), *European Family Law Volume II: The Changing Concept of 'Family' and Challenges for Domestic Family Law*, Elgar Publishing, 2016, pp. 208–209. In Sweden relatively few family law matters require or are resolved with professional help or in court, but the percentage seems slowly to be increasing. See Perry, above n. 15, at pp. 245–250 (comparing the Swedish family law legal culture with California's in terms of views on juridification, especially the importance of State oversight in family law matters, illustrating an ideal of private resolutions not involving any lawyer or court).

52 These are called 'civil matters' within the Regulation, a term to be interpreted 'autonomously, in accordance with the established case-law of the [CJEU]', primarily in light of the Regulation's 'objectives and scheme' and secondarily in light of general principles stemming from the national laws of the Member States collectively. 'Civil matters' is to encompass court proceedings, decisions made in such cases, 'applications, measures or decisions as well as authentic instruments and certain extra-judicial agreements' that should be deemed matters of 'parental responsibility' or closely related to it, regardless of whether these matters are classified as of private or public law nature in national law. Brussels II *ter* Regulation, above n. 5, at recitals 4–5.

and 'matrimonial matters' more generally, the new Brussels II *ter* Regulation, first in effect on 1 August 2022,[53] further coordinates and develops EU PIL.

In the 'parental responsibility' area it is applicable in all cross-border cases, for example both in civil disputes, such as those over child custody with or without a related divorce action, and in those cases in public law, such as foster care placement and guardianship, where some cross-border component might require the PIL rules it provides. There are other areas, like adoption, establishment of a parent–child relationship and disputes regarding the name given to a child, that are already subject to other parts of the EU PIL framework and therefore explicitly excluded from the scope of Brussels II *ter*.[54]

It becomes clear while closely analysing this Regulation that PIL rules made by the EU and binding on all Member States (except Denmark) are not limited to, for example, deciding to which court an action within its scope must be presented, but extend to more far-reaching aspects of the conflict-resolution process. Per the Recast's Article 25, for example, a national court 'shall invite the parties to consider whether they are willing to engage in mediation or other means of alternative dispute resolution, unless this is contrary to the best interests of the child, it is not appropriate in the particular case or would unduly delay the proceedings', meaning that national court rules in these regards are to a large extent superseded for cases within the Regulation's scope, or at least held to a minimal floor decided by the Member States during the EU legislative process. The idea that EU family law is slowly being harmonised is not a far-fetched one.[55]

The Recast adds or modifies several provisions of the earlier Brussels II *bis*. One change expands the mandatory recognition, without a 'declaration of enforceability or the registration for enforcement', of decisions between Member States in matters of parental responsibility.[56] The category of more easily

---

53 The full list of topics it addresses in the 'parental responsibility' area includes which court(s) have jurisdiction in matters of child custody and visitation, guardianship, child protection by placement in foster care, protection of a child's property and aspects of rules concerning parental abduction of children (between two EU Member States). See Arts. 1–2 of Brussels II *ter* and related recitals in the preamble preceding them. The only other main topic within the Recast's scope is jurisdiction in specifically divorce, legal separation and marriage annulment cases, per its Art. 1(a). This requires an extensive number of provisions given issues falling under that umbrella, including for example emergency relief, transfers of jurisdiction between courts, *lis pendens* issues, settlements and recognition of orders on these topics.

54 Brussels II *ter*, above n. 5, at Art. 1(4).

55 The Regulation cites 'the principle of mutual trust' between Member State authorities as the basis upon which recognition and enforcement decisions should be made regarding legal instruments from another Member State. Brussels II *ter*, above n. 5, at Art. 55.

56 Brussels II *ter*, above n. 5, at recital 58. See also Art. 30(1) ('A decision given in a Member State shall be recognised in the other Member States without any special procedure being required'). This requires for example Member States where an individual moves to enter the record of their prior divorce into their national civil-status records without any special procedure. National courts making the original decisions must themselves issue a harmonised form

enforceable foreign judgments, orders and other decisions has been expanded from a small subset of such decisions ('certain decisions granting rights of access and certain decisions entailing the return of a child') to 'all decisions', meaning explicitly that 'a decision given by the court of any other Member State should be treated as if it had been given in the Member State of enforcement.'[57] Private settlement agreements that have not been at minimum registered with an appropriate State authority under national law, however, are disfavoured:[58]

> This Regulation should not allow free circulation of mere private agreements. However, agreements which are neither a decision nor an authentic instrument, but have been registered by a public authority competent to do so, should circulate. Such public authorities might include notaries registering agreements, even where they are exercising a liberal profession.

Many commentators have found the most notable of the changes to be the change which strengthens children's rights to be heard and to have their views considered in 'parental responsibility' matters, including in child abduction request-for-return proceedings brought in Member State courts, the subject of several international instruments.[59] The connection between the best interests of a child as protected under the United Nations Convention on the Rights

---

certificate to assist with mutual recognition and enforcement. See Brussels II *ter*, above n. 5, at Art. 36 (specifying at what Annex to the Regulation blank forms for each type of matter it controls are found). There is a multi-page blank form for national courts' use in reporting the details of their parental responsibility case decisions, for example, attached to the Regulation as Annex IX ('Certificate Concerning an Authentic Instrument or Agreement in Matters of Parental Responsibility'). This Certificate 'must not be issued if there are indications that the content of the authentic instrument or agreement is against the best interests of the child', per its first page, in accordance with the Regulation's aim to strengthen children's protections in cases within its scope. See also Art. 39 ('Grounds for refusal of recognition of decisions in matters of parental responsibility').

57 Ibid, at recital 58.

58 Brussels II *ter*, above n. 5, at recital 14.

59 Brussels II *ter*, above n. 5, at recital 39, states a clear legislative intention regarding a child's right to be heard: 'Proceedings in matters of parental responsibility under this Regulation as well as return proceedings under the 1980 Hague Convention should, as a basic principle, provide the child who is subject to those proceedings and who is capable of forming his or her own views, in accordance with the case law of the Court of Justice, with a genuine and effective opportunity to express his or her views and when assessing the child's best interests, due weight should be given to those views. The opportunity of the child to express his or her views freely in accordance with Article 24(1) of the Charter and in the light of Article 12 of the UN Convention on the Rights of the Child plays an important role in the application of this Regulation. The Regulation should, however, leave the question of who will hear the child and how the child is heard to be determined by national law and procedure of the Member States. Consequently, it should not be the purpose of this Regulation to set out whether the child should be heard by the judge in person or by a specially trained expert reporting to the court afterwards, or whether the child should be heard in the courtroom or in another place or through other means. In addition, while remaining a right of the child, hearing the child cannot constitute an absolute obligation, but must be assessed taking into account the best interests of the child, for example, in cases involving agreements between the parties.'

of the Child (UNCRC), the EU Charter of Fundamental Human Rights and the EU Regulation's own provisions is made stronger in the Recast, in part simply by mentioning the UNCRC, as the prior version of the Regulation had not. Significant research has been done recently in Europe regarding judicial decision-making with respect to the child's right to be heard in international child abduction cases, concluding in part that Brussels II *ter* should in practice resolve the confusion of differing standards on when a child can be heard previously found in Brussels II *bis* and the UNCRC, which should then strengthen children's rights in this regard.[60]

Strengthened children's rights are a relatively uncontroversial and prominent policy goal in many Member States currently, especially in the Nordic countries, thus in this way the new Brussels II *ter* Regulation represents a victory for child law at the EU, cross-border level.

3.1.2. Recent CJEU Case Law on the Regulation

While EU legislators have occupied themselves with recasting the Brussels II Regulation, the CJEU has issued several judgments interpreting the Regulation in ways that will continue to have impact. The 'recasting' of the Brussels II *bis* Regulation, now Brussels II *ter*, does not change the legal effect of various case law decisions and other sources of law that interpreted its provisions prior to the recast,[61] although it may strengthen or weaken the likelihood that case law decided now will confirm or overturn previous decisions, depending on any relevant changes to the Regulation's wording.

In 2018 the CJEU decided, in answer to a preliminary ruling request from a Greek court, that the scope of the Brussels II *bis* Regulation extends even to issues related to two parents' joint request to denounce an inheritance on their child's behalf, deeming these questions of parental responsibility and not succession, thus covered by the Regulation and now by its Recast, despite its scope explicitly at Article 1(3)(f) (now Article1(4)(f)) excluding succession law matters.[62]

---

60 T. Van Hof, S. Lembrechts and F. Maoli et al., 'To Hear or Not to Hear: Reasoning of Judges Regarding the Hearing of the Child in International Child Abduction Proceedings' (2020) 53 *Family Law Quarterly* 327 (reporting the results from an empirical study of approximately 1,000 judgments in child abduction (non)return proceedings gathering during the EU-funded VOICE project (2018–19), JUST/2016/JCOO/AG/CIVI/764206, aiming to 'understand if and how judges across Europe give substance to the notion of the child's best interests' when ruling in such proceedings where the child is guaranteed a right to be heard per Brussels II *bis* Art. 11(2), the Hague Convention on Child Abduction (HCCA) Art. 13(2) and the UNCRC Art. 12 and concluding in part, at 350, that Brussels II *ter* will resolve differing standards on when a child can be heard previously found in the above-named articles of Brussels II *bis* and the UNCRC).

61 Brussels II *ter* Regulation, above n. 5, at recital 90.

62 See Case C-565/10, *Saponaro*, ECLI:EU:C:2018:265, decided 19 April 2018 (also confirming that Brussels II *bis* required courts to make a best interest of the child analysis in connection with certain decisions on jurisdiction).

In the case of *OE v. VY*,[63] decided in February 2022, thus also before Brussels II *ter*, the CJEU held that EU lawmakers having made nationality a supplemental 'connecting factor' under Article 3(a) of the Brussels II *bis* Regulation,[64] and thus allowing a Member State's own citizen to secure the jurisdiction of its courts more quickly than could a non-national resident, does not violate the 'principal prohibition of discrimination' on grounds of nationality at Article 18 TFEU. Nonetheless, EU PIL instruments tend to disfavour nationality as a primary connection factor, as '[c]onsiderations of equal treatment, non-discrimination and social integration of mobile European citizens and third country nationals in their host societies prevail over the concept of cultural identity reflected by the spouse's nationality.'[65]

In early 2021 a notable case decision was *SS v. MCP*.[66] The CJEU ruled that what is now Article 9 of Brussels II *ter* (formerly Article 10 of Brussels II *bis*) does not create indefinite continuing jurisdiction in a Member State 'where a child, formerly habitually resident in a Member State, is abducted to and becomes resident in a third State' but rather jurisdiction follows the new habitual residence of the child under other international conventions or under Article 14 of the Regulation.[67] The CJEU went against its Advocate General's opinion in the case, in part on the basis that the legislative intent in adopting the Regulation clearly was to control PIL questions in cases between Member States,[68] and not

---

63 Case C-522/20, *OE v. VY*, ECLI:EU:C:2022:87, decided 10 February 2022.

64 In Brussels II *ter* this is Art. 3(a)(vi). Art. 3 reads: 'In matters relating to divorce, legal separation or marriage annulment, jurisdiction shall lie with the courts of the Member State: (a) in whose territory … (v) the applicant is habitually resident if he or she resided there for at least a year immediately before the application was made, or (vi) the applicant is habitually resident if he or she resided there for at least six months immediately before the application was made and is either a national of the Member State in question'.

65 S. Corneloup, 'Introduction' in S. Corneloup (ed.), *The Rome III Regulation: A Commentary on the Law Applicable to Divorce and Legal Separation*, Elgar Publishing, 2020, p. 20. Connecting factors in PIL are an engaging and important topic largely beyond the scope of this chapter.

66 Case C-603/20 PPU, *SS v. MCP*, ECLI:EU:C:2021:231, decided 24 March 2021.

67 N. Lowe, 'The Application of Art. 10 of Brussels II-Bis to Children Abducted Out of the EU: The Last UK Reference on Family Law?' (2021) 6(1) *European Papers* 219, 219 (summarising that the case comment considers 'the impact of this decision first, for EU Member States both under Brussels II-bis and its successor, Brussels II-ter, and secondly, for the UK now that it has become a third State' and concludes 'that from all perspectives, the CJEU decision is a sound and welcome one', including for the best interests of children affected).

68 In very practical terms this will affect which instruments of 'European family law' control – the EU PIL one being replaced by the applicable Hague Conventions – where a child has been abducted from the EU to the UK post-Brexit, a not insignificant change given that approximately 67% of Convention-based applications received for return of children from England and Wales were from EU Member States in 2015, according to one statistical study. Ibid, at 228 n. 38 (internal citation omitted).

with regards to abductions to a third country.[69] Due to a change increasing party autonomy introduced in the Recast, however, parties may now privately agree to jurisdiction in a court in an EU Member State with a 'substantial connection' to the child, including if the child is a citizen there, but only in so far as it is in the child's interests.[70]

The Brussels II *ter* Regulation will continue to cause changes at the national level in many Member States in the coming months and years. Member States reviewed its text thoroughly, of course, first during the drafting and adoption process, so most unanticipated aspects will be unforeseen arising from how the provisions work in practice.

3.2. IN SUCCESSION MATTERS

3.2.1. The Succession Regulation Effective 2016 and its Legal Effects

Because the area of succession was never harmonised to the extent and in the ways introduced by the Succession Regulation, surveying all of its provisions here that were new to EU PIL in the family law area is beyond the scope of this chapter.[71] A few of the largest changes made to EU family law for cases with cross-border aspects by the Succession Regulation are highlighted here.

One was the replacement of the general rule previously common in cross-border succession (defined to include 'all forms of transfer of assets, rights and obligations by reason of death' for individuals dying testate or intestate),[72] that such matters would be decided in the courts and under the law of the deceased's *nationality*. Instead, the general rule became that the courts and applicable law to be used, 'on the succession as a whole', would instead be those of the state in which the deceased was *habitually resident* at the time of death, regardless of whether that state was in the EU.[73]

69 These situations were already controlled in all Member States by the 1980 and 1996 Hague Conventions at the time of the Brussels II *bis* legislative proposal, and the Court concluded that applying the Regulation to third-country abductions from the EU by conferring indefinite jurisdiction on the Member State of origin would require national courts under EU law to depart from their existing international treaty obligations in a manner neither intended nor desirable from a best interests of the child perspective (jurisdiction where the child is now habitually resident being best in most cases, under Brussels II and the Hague Conventions). Ibid, at 223–225. See also what is now Art. 53(3) of Brussels II *ter*.

70 Ibid, at 226.

71 See instead any of a number of commentaries on the Regulation, from various national perspectives or from an external one, or – and I highly recommend this – read the Regulation's text including the recitals included as a preamble.

72 Succession Regulation, above n. 5, at Art. 3(1)(a).

73 Succession Regulation, above n. 5, at Arts. 4 and 21(1). This reduces the frequency in Sweden of courts needing to apply foreign law for immigrants to Sweden who retain foreign nationality, but is qualified by Art. 21(2).

The Regulation requires use of this controlling 'habitual residence' connecting factor unless the individual chooses instead in writing which law will govern: only the law of any state where he or she is a national, or alternatively the law of the state where he or she is habitually resident at the time of the choice or is determined to be resident at the time of death, may be specified.[74]

Such personal autonomy is granted, per the Regulation, but was made subject, in the recitals preceding the Regulation, to national courts' 'mechanisms designed to tackle the evasion of the law'.[75] Recital 50 similarly protects the interests of presumed heirs but also the testator's autonomy to a certain extent, in that if an individual has left a writing with regard to succession, the law governing it under the Regulation 'should be [interpreted by a national court] without prejudice to the rights of any person who, under the law applicable to the succession, has a right to a reserved share or another right of which he cannot be deprived by the person whose estate is involved.' Together these caveats and certain other provisions (for example those on lifetime gifts) were meant to alleviate concerns that a new nationality, habitual residence, will or mutual will could be arranged by an individual to avoid particularly the forced share of the estate that national law guaranteed to the deceased's closest heirs.[76]

In exceptional cases, if a court determines that the deceased at the time of death had an 'obviously' closer connection with the country of his or her nationality, that law can instead be applied rather than the one of his or her last habitual residence.[77] The Regulation makes clear however that this exception will not mean that unclear factual circumstances making difficult a determination of where a decedent was habitually resident at the time of death, or cases where a decedent was more closely connected to a foreign culture or religion, can be resolved under this exception.[78]

This change immediately had implications for individuals planning for the future distribution of their assets, even before a dispute could arise, although the Succession Regulation's application was phased in to a certain extent and a presumption included: pre-existing writings (wills) made under the law that a decedent *could* have chosen under the Regulation would be deemed a valid

---

74 This latter is the default rule in the absence of a valid choice. See Succession Regulation, above n. 5, at Art. 22. Art. 23 provides a list clarifying in particular all the aspects that the chosen law will govern, including 'the causes, time and place of the opening of the succession', the determination of beneficiaries and their respective shares, and so on.

75 Succession Regulation, above n. 5, at recital 26.

76 See D. Wiedemann, 'Understanding and Interpreting the Succession Regulation through its National Origins' in J.M. Scherpe and E. Bargelli (eds.), *The Interaction between Family Law, Succession Law and Private International Law*, Intersentia, 2021, pp. 144–150.

77 Succession Regulation, above n. 5, at Art. 21(2).

78 See Succession Regulation, above n. 5, at recital 25 and M. Bogdan, 'Den nya EU-förordningen om internationell successionsrätt' (2012) *Svensk juridisk tidning* 745, 746–747.

choice of that applicable law.[79] Those whose testamentary planning instruments had already been prepared according to the law of their nationality did not need to act to change this, lessening the problem of retirees dying without realising the Regulation had changed the law applicable to their estate.

A Swedish retiree, per these new rules, *now* moving to and ultimately dying in Spain would however have his or her estate settled pursuant to Spanish jurisdiction and substantive law, if he or she does not make prior arrangements properly in accordance with the new Regulation to choose an available alternate jurisdiction's law.[80] A failure to plan ahead could indeed surprise the deceased's presumed heirs, often residents of, in this example, Sweden and most familiar with the typical results of its inheritance law, and not Spain's. This is relevant in many Member States, particularly because all EU jurisdictions provide for some kind of forced share to the deceased's near relatives, though who those interested parties may be varies among the national legal systems.[81]

The Succession Regulation also introduced a European Certificate of Succession,[82] in practical terms a standard form required to be issued by and mutually recognised by all Member States (except Denmark) in order to simplify cross-border settlement of estates. The Certificate, while it brings ease to the cross-border interaction of national-level officials and individuals working with cross-border succession matters, has led to an unanticipated headache attributable to a CJEU interpretation of the Regulation that seems to have altered what its drafters had carefully negotiated. The case law decision is introduced next, and discussion continues in section 4 regarding reception of the Regulation.

3.2.2. *Recent CJEU Case Law on the Regulation*

One case decision by the CJEU[83] complicated the smooth roll-out of the Succession Regulation, particularly in connection to the fairness concerns between Member States that they considered already resolved during the drafting process.

---

79 Succession Regulation, above n. 5, at Art. 83(4).

80 See e.g. Bogdan, above n. 78, at 745 ('The ordinance entails for Swedish several items of important news, including a transition from the nationality to the domicile principle, a certain acceptance of the testator's right to choose the applicable law and the introduction of a European Certificate of Succession to be used by heirs and executors who need to prove their status or exercise their powers in another Member State') (translation mine).

81 Wiedemann, above n. 76, at p. 144 (detailing some of the differences, such as that German law protects children, parents and a spouse, while English law does not generally protect adult children).

82 Succession Regulation, above n. 5, at Art. 62 et seq.

83 Case C-658/17, *WB v. Notariusz Przemysława Bac*, ECLI:EU:C:2019:444, decided 23 May 2019.

Because the national succession law of some Member States (including Finland, Lithuania and others) permits notaries to issue final, binding legal decisions in succession cases, other Member States where only a traditional court has that power were concerned during the drafting of the Succession Regulation about the definition of the term 'court' and whether all State official actors in all Member States would be bound to respect each other's ongoing succession cases, or if notaries might be able to act regardless of *lis pendens* rules.[84] The result was Article 3(2) of the Regulation, a functional definition defining 'court' to include all authorities and legal professionals with competence in these matters, so long as their decisions protected rights of procedural due process by including guarantees of impartiality, rights to be heard for all parties, rights to appeal or be reviewed by a judicial authority, and a resulting force and effect similar to a court decision.

The CJEU does not, however, resort to evidence of legislative intent when interpreting the wording of a regulation; it 'pursues an autonomous and uniform interpretation' of its provisions in their final form, as enacted. It therefore, as could have been predicted, considered the plain meaning of Article 3(2) when questions of whether notaries were 'courts' first arose in practice.[85] The Court ruled that a Polish notary did not qualify as a 'court' because per the provision as enacted it needed to 'exercise judicial functions' *and* meet the Article 3(2) criteria. If a notary requires a unanimous request of the heirs to issue a certificate of succession, it does not 'exercise judicial functions' in the Court's reasoning, even if the notary meets the conditions set forth in Article 3(2) of the Regulation, and therefore such a notary is not bound by the Regulation's *lis pendens* rules. The Member States who had sought uniformly protective *lis pendens* rules, not to disadvantage their citizens in a 'race to the court', were left without the benefit of their negotiations.

Similar interpretive questions continue to be decided by the CJEU. In this light, and in light of the fact that the Regulation must be understood by millions of individuals across Europe with different assumptions as to how succession law is designed, the drafters' verbosity[86] as reflected in this and other EU PIL instruments may be more sympathetically understood.

---

84 For a thorough discussion of this decision's aftermath and the legislative process leading to the Regulation, see WIEDEMANN, above n. 76. See also E. GOOSSENS, 'The Impact of the European Certificate of Succession on National Law: A Trojan Horse or Much Ado about Nothing?' in J.M. SCHERPE and E. BARGELLI (eds.), *The Interaction between Family Law, Succession Law and Private International Law*, Intersentia, 2021, pp. 157–180 (going into more depth on case law following the Succession Regulation's entry into force).

85 Ibid, at pp. 150–151.

86 Discussed further, from a Swedish perspective, in section 4.2.

4. EVOLVING EU CONFLICT-OF-LAW RULES' INFLUENCE ON NATIONAL FAMILY LAW AND PRACTICE

How have specifically the Succession Regulation and the new Brussels II *ter* Regulation influenced family law rules and practice in the Member States, and particularly in Sweden?

Scholars have used various colourful analogies and examples to answer these or similar questions. European family law has been called a '"Sleeping Beauty", now awakened in full splendour amidst a flurry of initiatives, measures and case law at the European level, not to mention the ongoing scholarly research'.[87] Meanwhile scholars have felt 'tempted to refer to the two states [Sweden and Finland] as "backseat drivers", who have not been entrusted with the driving of the vehicle called "the EU's cooperation in family and succession law" but who feel a need to intervene, often irritating the driver.'[88] Even creative examples have been used to describe Sweden and Finland's orientations towards the development of more harmonised EU family law.[89]

More concretely expressed, there have been some unique effects of these Regulations in these specific national contexts, while more generally these uniform Union laws have had, as anticipated by their drafters, more uniform and on balance positive effects across the EU as a whole.[90]

This section first focuses on the emerging national-level response after five years with the Succession Regulation, with Sweden as an example to illustrate the general and more specific-to-Sweden effects thus far observed. Given the newness of Brussels II *ter*, a shorter analysis regarding Brussels II *ter*, commenting on Sweden's view of and influence on Brussels II's earlier versions, follows.

---

87 DeBaere and Gutman, above n. 22, at p. 6.

88 Jänterä-Jareborg, above n. 2, at p. 1 (aiming 'to analyse whether the interventions by Sweden and Finland have prevented the EU from finding and taking the optimal course or whether, on the contrary, their contributions have enabled the vehicle to stay on the road/on course and to reach the destination in a more stable manner' and concluding the latter).

89 See M. Jänterä-Jareborg, 'Den internationella familjerätten i Europa' (2014) *Svensk juridisk tidning* 226 (retelling in detail the tale of film star Ingrid Bergman's many marriages, divorces and parental responsibility orders over international borders to describe the international family law of Europe and to criticise it from a Swedish family law perspective), for example.

90 For example the new rules providing for more automatic recognition of 'foreign' (non-national) judgments and similar binding decisions to be enforced in other EU Member States and creating new EU-wide documents (like the Certificates discussed above, created by both major Regulations discussed) have promptly much cooperation across the EU to implement the Regulations and in the process make progress towards greater family law dispute resolution efficiency and greater compliance with existing EU rule of law and authenticity safeguards.

4.1. NATIONAL-LEVEL IMPACT: ONGOING RECEPTION OF THE SUCCESSION REGULATION

Six years of experience with the new Succession Regulation across the EU and in Sweden have now accrued, and the general sense among family law, private international law and European law scholars seems to be that the Regulation has been mainly well received by Member State courts and other State legal actors,[91] in part due to the clear training materials the EU has provided to aid national judges as they began to apply the Regulation.[92]

There had been concerns early on among Swedish scholars that the Regulation's provisions, although largely positive, would be difficult to apply due to their complexity[93] and particularly that Swedish retired people habitually resident in the southern EU Member States would have their succession law matters determined under the substantive law of a place in which earlier research had shown that the majority of foreign retirees did not feel culturally integrated.[94] These worries have been mitigated by the various carefully negotiated provisions introduced above, however. After the enactment, a number of electronic and other resources, by or co-funded by the EU, have also been made available that help national experts learn what is required in a given different Member State in order to, for example, record succession property with the proper Swedish officials in accordance with the Regulation.[95]

In addition, an inter-Nordic exception was granted by which, in estate situations over Nordic borders, the Nordic states may continue to distinguish between procedural and substantive aspects of the case, therefore apply their preferred *lex fori* rules even while applying other substantive law to a succession

---

91 See e.g. Goossens, above n. 84.

92 See e.g. G. Palao Moreno, 'Highlights and Pitfalls of the Succession Regulation after Five Years' Experience', a detailed e-presentation filmed at the ERA's Annual Conference in European Succession Law 2020, available at: <https://www.youtube.com/watch?v=EtgA2QdmyAw>, last accessed 30.03.2022.

93 See Bogdan, above n. 78, at 744–745 (concluding nonetheless that 'recognition and enforceability of enforcement titles and the creation of European Certificates of succession can be considered as very significant progress' in European PIL harmonisation but also that the scope, detail level and pace of expansion of EU PIL law are problematic) (translation mine).

94 Jänterä-Jareborg, above n. 89, at 243 (internal citations omitted) (also recognising that the Succession Regulation's Art. 21 left 'habitual residence' deliberately undefined, although with recitals 23 and 24 as guidance for national courts, and that in exceptional cases per Art. 21(2) a totality of the circumstances review could permit a court to substitute another Member State's law for the one of the deceased's habitual residence at death, but concerned that the Regulation's 'party autonomy' safeguard, the right to choose the law of one's citizenship, could only be helpful if every free mover who might die a resident of another Member State knew of the safeguard and acted on that knowledge).

95 See e.g. European Land Registry Association, 'Registration of certificate of inheritance – Sweden', available at: <https://www.elra.eu/contact-point-contribution/sweden/registration-of-certificate-of-inheritance-13/>, last accessed 03.07.2022.

case, and also their own rules on mutual recognition and enforcement, which in turn agree to give priority to the Succession Regulation's rules on substantive issues while retaining only the procedural aspects of their differing inter-Nordic agreement.[96] Such tailored solutions within what is otherwise an extensive expansion of EU-level, harmonised rules does not significantly compromise the benefits of increased harmony and legal certainty sought with the Regulation. These steps along the road to smooth use of the Regulation across the EU illustrate the legal development dialogues that are extensive and ongoing between the national and EU levels' courts and legislatures.

Criticism of the use of 'habitual residence' as the Regulation's most important connecting factor, introduced above, has continued to be common at the national level. The connecting factor is very commonplace in EU PIL generally, yet because the law of succession, like other areas of family law, deals with individuals' long-held assumptions and expectations of what it means to be part of a family and how their interests are recognised and protected by the law,[97] this is a particularly sensitive topic of interest to many individuals not ordinarily or often in contact with family law. When PIL instruments determine not only which courts will have jurisdiction over a dispute concerning an inheritance but also which substantive law will be applied to all but certain public law aspects, as the Succession Regulation does, putting at risk close relatives' interests in the succession (like forced shares secured under national substantive law), a defensive posture and lingering resistance can to some extent be expected.

On the other hand, the Succession Regulation was drafted and adopted by the EU institutions in consultation with and in many cases representing various Member States' interests in preserving the autonomy of their national substantive family and succession laws. Because the Regulation functions to preserve shares of an inheritance guaranteed under national law in several ways, and also the continued force of wills written prior to the Regulations as a presumed choice of applicable law (all discussed in section 3.2.1), citizens of the various Member States – often but not always adult children and grandchildren of the deceased, or a surviving partner – most often do have their expectations realised, even in cross-border cases.

The lack of an explicit definition of 'habitual residence' in the Succession Regulation itself has been criticised, above and beyond the choice of habitual

96 Jänterä-Jareborg, above n. 2, at p. 12 ('This demonstrates a highly pragmatic approach on behalf of Sweden and Finland and a loyalty towards the EU's visions, accepted as necessary by the other Nordic countries'). See also the Swedish Official Report on international legal relations concerning inheritance, SOU 2014:25 (Internationella rättsförhållanden rörande arv) and the resulting legislative Proposition 2014/15:105 (Arv i internationella situationer) modifying Swedish law as required by the Succession Regulation.

97 For a comprehensive vertical comparison of succession laws see L. Garb and R. Norridge (eds.), *International Succession*, Oxford University Press, 5th ed., 2022 (overviews succession law in 55 jurisdictions within its 1,072 pages).

residence as the primary connecting factor previously mentioned.[98] Another true problem arose concerning the Regulation's creation of the mandatorily recognised Succession Certificate, as introduced above, where again a CJEU interpretation of the Regulation surprised its drafters and caused non-uniformity in practice, the impact of which has been analysed on an EU level.[99]

Specifically addressing Sweden's reception of the Regulation, Swedish scholars have kept abreast of EU family law development and the interactions of the various new instruments in the PIL area, reporting them to the academic and practitioner communities at both the time of proposal and after entry into force, sometimes with and sometimes without a focus on normative critique of the new laws from a national perspective. Because of the pre-planning done as the Regulation was drafted, which led to provisions friendly to Sweden, including the granting of the Nordic exception for inter-Nordic succession cases discussed above, the reaction specifically in Sweden to the changes it introduced seems not to have been dramatic.

4.2. NATIONAL-LEVEL IMPACT: EARLY RECEPTION OF BRUSSELS II *TER*

The legislative bill introducing the changes to Swedish law necessitated by Brussels II *ter* confirmed that the government was in support of the legislative changes it required.[100] Most of the Swedish resistance to the Regulation's scheme had been resolved, to the extent it could be, at earlier stages in the development of the Brussels II *ter* instrument's predecessors.

Historically, Swedish officials entering the stage shortly after Sweden's 1995 accession to the EU reportedly had success in influencing how liberal the Brussels II Regulation rules were regarding for example impediments to easily obtained divorce:[101]

> The combination of options regarding jurisdiction and guarantees against a reconsideration of a divorce judgment was of utmost importance for Sweden and Finland. Otherwise, they would have risked that their 'free-moving' citizens could

---

98 See e.g. Palao Moreno, above n. 92.

99 See e.g. Goossens, above n. 84, at pp. 157–180.

100 See Proposition 2021/22:189, above n. 17, at p. 1 (summarising approvingly the changes included with the Recast: 'The new regulation strengthens the legal security of children and parents. A general obligation is introduced for the court to allow a child to express their opinions and to have considered those opinions in relation to the child's age and maturity. All decisions on parental responsibility are made directly enforceable in other EU countries. In addition, the new regulation partially harmonises Member States enforcement rules. Furthermore, the exchange of information between authorities of the Member States is improved, which facilitates and improves their grounds for decision-making') (translation mine).

101 Jänterä-Jareborg, above n. 89, at 233 (translation from Swedish mine).

> have been forced to file [a lawsuit requesting divorce] in an EU state where a divorce can only be granted after several years of separation. ... Even worse would have been if Swedish or Finnish divorce judgments could have been categorically refused recognition in some EU states, when the judgment came at the request of only one of the spouses ... The fear was concrete during the negotiations, as many of the EU member states considered 'our' rules to be too liberal at the expense of family stability.

From Swedish scholars' point of view, then, the emerging EU PIL instruments in the family law area in general and the Brussels II jurisdiction and recognition rules in particular have from the start been regarded with a reasonable dose of suspicion, on cultural and policy grounds but even due to some differences in what I have called in other contexts 'legal culture', meaning how law is expected to be expressed and to work in practice.[102] Law in Sweden is relatively simply stated and construed; the economy of words and the efficiency and private resolution of family law disputes between usually unrepresented parties (or parties only served by professional lawyers for a very limited number of hours) is an aspect of the national legal culture valued by its legal community. Swedish law professor Maarit Jänterä-Jareborg's expression of dissatisfaction with EU regulations including Brussels II in this 'legal cultural' regard is illustrative:[103]

> The number of provisions in each regulation significantly exceeds what has ever been needed in national law or in international convention cooperation. Furthermore, each regulation begins with a large number of indicative introductory points in respect of which each word is said to have been weighed with a 'gold scale'. The language is clumsy, and it is not a given that the Swedish-language version correctly reproduces what is intended. I am therefore not surprised that so far I have not met a single practising lawyer who admits to fully understanding the content of any of the regulations. In the light of Swedish case law, our courts may also miss the fact that a situation falls under a binding EU family law regulation.

---

102 See e.g. Perry, above n. 15, at pp. 476–486.

103 Jänterä-Jareborg, above n. 89, at 239 (translation from Swedish mine) (internal citations omitted). Michael Bogdan is of a similar view, writing for example that '[t]he Succession Regulation fills 28 pages in the EU's Official Journal, while the current Swedish IDL [Swedish PIL on international succession which the Regulation replaced] does not correspond in scope to more than perhaps 5 such pages.' Bogdan, above n. 78, at 745. Personally, I feel much more at home with the style of the Regulation than with Swedish national law, which leaves a great deal, in my view, unsaid and often undecided, but expect I would feel differently if I had been initially trained within Swedish legal culture. As a comparatist but perhaps even more as an Anglo-American, I nonetheless prefer all of the Regulation's detail. As a former family law specialist in practice, I see a great deal of similarity between the EU and California forms-based, thorough, detailed family law regulatory schemes that provide practitioners and scholars with a nuanced understanding of all the aims, balances of interests and caveats necessary to provide a usable legal instrument across so many cultural borders and diverse factual situations. This view is qualified by the admission that I have not to date used the Regulation in practice with clients instead of with law students learning EU PIL from a Swedish perspective.

The complexity is explained by the years of negotiation that occur between Member States, the European Parliament and the European Commission prior to such a regulation's adoption. According to Jänterä-Jareborg, Swedish ministry staff who might otherwise have been available during the first decade of Sweden's membership in the EU to draft potential reforms to Swedish national family law were instead required to make the large investment of time necessary for the EU work.[104]

There are a number of Swedish scholars working to keep abreast of the constantly evolving current rules and their interactions with Swedish and the remaining inter-Nordic agreements on subjects now harmonised by EU or other international law whose work cannot be extensively presented here.[105]

4.3. TWO POINTS OF TENSION BETWEEN SWEDISH NATIONAL AUTONOMY AND THE BENEFITS OF EU-LEVEL HARMONISATION IN FAMILY LAW-RELATED MATTERS

As was established above, EU-level legal measures in the family law area are limited to those with cross-border implications between Member States and are further restrained by the special legislative procedures usually required to implement them if they are to go into force uniformly across the EU.[106] However, as also previously introduced, there are multiple avenues by which not only European legislation but also case law from European (EU and human rights) courts may and are currently erecting new barriers to national substantive family law diversity or, seen from another perspective, are succeeding in bringing the various national laws into a more uniform and well-coordinated EU-level system.

Sweden has had a number of concerns with recent changes to EU PIL laws, including regarding family law areas; two commonly named points of tension are summarised here.

The first, as has already been mentioned, concerned the fact that inter-Nordic cooperation has been pre-empted by the EU, thus frustrating the ability for the

[104] Jänterä-Jareborg, ibid, at 240.

[105] For one extensive, complex publication kept current by two prominent Swedish scholars see M. Bodgan and M. Hellner, *Svensk internationell privat- och processrätt*, Nordstedts Juridik, 9th ed., 2020 (presenting the full interworkings of PIL in Swedish family law matters as well as in other civil matters, for use in legal education and in professional legal practice).

[106] It still requires the use of a special legislative procedure where the Council acts unanimously after consulting the European Parliament, per Art. 81(3) TFEU, allowing one or more Member States opposed to an EU legislative act to almost certainly block its adoption, frustrating European family law development by preventing it or diluting the acts that can win unanimity in the Council.

Nordic countries inside and outside of the EU to enter new agreements or to modify existing agreements with each other, and thus to favour citizens with nationality from other EU Nordic nations in ways not extended to all citizens of all EU Member States.[107] Only the EU itself may now bind an EU Member State to new international obligations with third states, including by pre-approving certain inter-Nordic agreement proposals as compatible with EU law[108] and by granting requests by Sweden and Finland for 'Nordic exceptions' to new PIL rules (to allow for the continued uniform use of inter-Nordic agreements between them and the other Nordic, non-EU nations).[109] Nordic cooperation agreements, even if in areas outside of EU competence, may nonetheless not give preferential treatment to Nordic-country citizens over EU citizens from non-Nordic EU states in any EU Member State; recognising foreign social welfare benefit rights or foreign-earned professional qualifications on an inter-Nordic but not fully inter-EU basis violates EU law prohibiting discrimination on the basis of nationality, for example.[110]

---

107 See LEINO and LEPPÄVIRTA, above n. 14.

108 LEINO and LEPPÄVIRTA, above n. 14, at 310 ('Of particular interest for Nordic arrangements is the EU Regulation establishing a prior approval procedure for the negotiation and conclusion of agreements between Member States and third countries in the field of family law ... which partly covers pre-existing Nordic agreements. If these Nordic agreements required amendment, the Regulation stipulates that the Nordic EU Member States would need to obtain authorisation for the issues within the scope of exclusive Union external competence'). See also P. LEINO and L. LEPPÄVIRTA, 'Is there room for legal pluralism in EU relations with third states? A study of Nordic approaches to European integration' in G. DAVIES and M. AVBELJ (eds.), *Research Handbook on Legal Pluralism and EU Law*, Elgar Publishing, 2018, p. 292 ('With the development of EU membership obligations, the traditional objective of finding distinct Nordic solutions to common challenges has had to give way to the legal necessities flowing from EU law').

109 The EU usually grants these with a narrower scope than the Nordic requesting countries had hoped for, but they continue to request the exceptions, in part because they are of the view that existing Nordic rules are at least partially superior to the EU regulations that would otherwise take their place. JÄNTERÄ-JAREBORG, above n. 89, at 236. Where an opportunity is missed to request an exception, due to for example Sweden and Finland not anticipating that Brussels II 'parental responsibility' matters would be interpreted to include 'public law' matters, Sweden's ability to continue to use inter-Nordic rules can inadvertently be forfeited. Ibid, at 240 ('An insight or mere suspicion of such an interpretation [by the CJEU] would, perhaps, have led the countries to request an exemption in favour of the continued application of harmonized inter-Nordic rules on the recognition and enforcement of administrative decisions on the care and placement of children, based on a 1970 Nordic convention').

110 LEINO and LEPPÄVIRTA, above n. 14, at 296 (citing for more detail A.H. STOOR, 'Får Norden vara bättre? – Den nordiska biståndskonventionen och EU-rätten' (2015) 2 *Nordisk Administrativt Tidskrift* 5). For a compelling argument that these 'Nordic exceptions have, contrary to some criticism, helped expand the EU project by exporting several rules to three states that would not otherwise have them (Denmark, Iceland and Norway), see JÄNTERÄ-JAREBORG, above n. 2, at p. 6. In a complementary fashion, the EU instruments have encouraged modernisation of inter-Nordic instruments, in order to be in line with EU law and non-discriminatory and therefore qualify for the granting of exceptions from pre-emption. Ibid, at p. 10.

The second tension concerns EU PIL with respect to choice of law to be applied in cross-border matters. This issue is not controlled by Brussels II *ter*, which regulates which Member State(s) will have jurisdiction to resolve a given cross-border case, but due to mainly southern as opposed to northern European Member States entering into 'enhanced cooperation' on the issue, it has now been addressed and harmonised, as between participating Member States only, by the Rome III Regulation effective since mid-2012.[111]

Presently 17 of the 27 current Member States are bound by the Rome III Regulation. Sweden is not among them, and indeed formally tried to block Rome III out of concern for assuring the liberal availability of divorce to individuals seeking it,[112] thus wanting to avoid applicable law being used from a Member State with more preconditions to be satisfied prior to a divorce being granted than Swedish law includes.[113] Which court takes jurisdiction pursuant to Brussels II rules nonetheless often affects which substantive and procedural law will be applied, often in favour of the forum that takes jurisdiction,[114] but public policy concerns of the forum with jurisdiction, in this example Sweden, may continue to lead that forum to resist harmonisation of choice-of-law rules to the extent that such harmonisation would restrict or define when it could

111 See above at n. 44.

112 Radical reforms implemented in 1974 'to liberate Swedish family law from all "inherited moral perceptions"' removed not only impediments to divorce but also the ability to obtain an annulment, as opposed to a divorce, in Sweden, as it was seen as superfluous when free divorce, free of moral judgment, was available. 'Rules on legal separation were also scrapped.' Jänterä-Jareborg, above n. 89, at 231 (describing this as cultural expression and a result of the social and political atmosphere in Sweden from the late 1960s through the early 1970s) (translation from Swedish is my own).

113 See Corneloup, above n. 65, at pp. 9–11. Per the Swedish Marriage Code, Swedish law requires no grounds for divorce or waiting period (in cases of mutual agreement on the divorce and where no children under 16 live with the parties or one of them). It is considered one of the most liberal Member States and indeed in the world, with its policy intent to keep divorce accessible to individuals and free of State-imposed impediments or other non-neutrality with respect to individuals' choices of cohabitation forms. See e.g. C. Sörgjerd, 'Marriage in a European Perspective' in J.M. Scherpe (ed.), *European Family Law Volume III: Family Law in a European Perspective*, Elgar Publishing, 2016, pp. 12–21 (also noting quite rightly at p. 23 n. 84 that Sweden's law applying quasi-marriage-like obligations automatically on cohabiting partners paradoxically 'can be seen as increasing the level of official participation in the private sphere.').

114 See section 5 below, at n. 120. See also Jänterä-Jareborg, above n. 89, at 235 (criticising the drafting process in that 'the fundamental importance that Swedish and Finnish law attach to each spouse's right to freely dissolve a marriage was disregarded' and reporting that 'Finland found reason to issue a special statement deploring the deepening of cooperation without regard to differences in the legal traditions of the Member States') (translation from Swedish mine). Jänterä-Jareborg concludes that the criticism Sweden receives about blocking Rome III is undeserved, since for example Germans and the French receive benefits from the Regulation compared to relying on national PIL, as Sweden does today, regarding choice of law, and Denmark and (formerly) the UK are even more culpable holdouts when it comes to EU family law harmonisation.

apply its substantive law to a cross-border case for public policy reasons, such as not wishing to enforce law treating women's access to divorce differently than men's, or preferring not to recognise certain agreements or aspects of religious law that would apply if the law of another jurisdiction were used to decide the case.

5. EUROPEANISATION, GLOBALISATION AND FAMILY LAW'S NEXT STEPS

European family law is expanding in many directions, and EU law has been a major contributor to the trend. Looking broadly, what can be concluded about the tensions from a legal and socio-legal normative perspective?

Largely it seems that legislative cooperation, a rights-based trend in judicial decision-making and the benefits of EU PIL family law in practice are supporting a rapid uniformity expansion in this legal area and in Europe, outpacing more conservative Member States and others from reversing the trend in defence of their autonomy interests.[115] The CJEU (and, separately, the ECtHR) have made a number of rulings which then bind other courts and tribunals throughout the Member States, in more 'directly' family law matters, as section 3 introduced with respect to those involving the Brussels II *bis* and *ter* Regulations, but also in a huge range of other EU law matters than incidentally touch upon family law. This tends to increase personal autonomy to an extent, and also to decrease Member States' autonomy to enact law varying from what EU law requires to be uniform or minimally compliant with all binding EU and international rights obligations as they are dynamically interpreted with the passage of time.

Recent case decisions in the European family law realm include, in addition to those discussed above, those resolving family-related claims regarding rights of migration (free movement within the EU),[116] employee benefits, and

---

115 Wide margins of appreciation for Member States that for example do not provide a right to same-sex marriage or to confirmation of one's gender identity remain, defended as appropriate under the law, although many scholars suspect that eventually the scales will tip in favour of more uniform enforcement of EU non-discrimination ideals. See e.g. Scherpe, above n. 2, at pp. 38–39, and Martiny, above n. 22, at pp. 290–292 (concluding at p. 292 that 'taking everything into account it can be said that certain domestic traditional family law rules … face increasing pressure to justify themselves, and at the same time, the recognition rules of both the fundamental freedoms and the [EU PIL Regulations] favour an ongoing and gradual liberalisation').

116 An example of these non-PIL EU family law cases is Case C-490/20, *VMA v. Stolichna obshtina, rayon 'Pancharevo'*, ECLI:EU:C:2021:1008, decided 14 December 2021, where the CJEU held for the first time that a parentage relationship established by one EU Member State, at least where the parent is a primary caregiver to an EU citizen minor child, must be recognised by other Member States for the purposes of issuing identity documents needed for the Union citizen child to move and reside freely within the EU, regardless of the second Member State's stance in its national law on whether the same family relationship would be

anti-discrimination, especially where LGBTQ+ people's family members have been denied recognition and family-tie-related rights protected by the European Convention on Human Rights, the Charter of Fundamental Rights and other instruments discussed above.[117]

Because national family law governs in strictly internal situations, which remain the sizable (if shrinking) majority of situations, some specialists in family law across the EU – academics and graduating law students at the masters and doctoral levels included, in this author's experience – consider European-level family law a distant and fairly foreign phenomenon of which they need not often take notice.[118] Given that the text of or harmonising effects of EU and other international law are integrated directly into national law on an ongoing basis, this may be less of a concern than it could be, specifically for what appear to be 'purely national' cases.

Meanwhile the lack of full harmonisation over family law conflict-of-law (and procedural and substantive) rules within the EU continues to cause stress and uncertainty for litigants (and attorneys) involved in cross-border family

---

legally recognised. Thus, a child to a Bulgarian mother (listed as 'mother A' on the child's Spanish birth certificate) was entitled (under the TEU and Charter of Fundamental Rights of the EU) to be considered a 'direct descendent' of the mother under Art. 2 of the EU Free Movement Directive, Directive 2004/38/EC of the European Parliament and of the Council of 29 April 2004 on the right of citizens of the Union and their family members to move and reside freely within the territory of the Member States, and thus to receive a Bulgarian identity document, even where the other parent, listed as 'mother' on the birth certificate, was not a Bulgarian citizen (she was from a non-EU country, the UK), it was unclear to Bulgaria which woman had a biological tie to the child, and Bulgaria to date is given a 'margin of discretion' permitting it under national law not to recognise such a parentage tie. This was held not to violate Bulgaria's right to have the EU respect its national identity, set forth in Art. 4(2) TEU, because it required no change in national law, recognition of legal parentage for EU law purposes. A previous but also recent case, Case C-673/16, *Coman and Others v. Inspectoratul General pentru Imigrări and Others*, ECLI:EU:C:2018:385, decided 5 June 2018, had held that a same-sex spouse needed to be recognised as a 'spouse' under Art. 2 of the Directive, also for free movement purposes (subject to Art. 7 of the Directive equally for all 'spouses') and regardless of national law prohibiting same-sex marriage. Romania could not refuse a right of residence to the husband of a male Romanian citizen who had lived in another Member State, married there, and wished to move to Romania with his husband.

117 For a detailed discussion of the EU courts' influence and the 'European "Federal Common Law" in Family Law' up to the date of its publication, see DEBAERE and GUTMAN, above n. 22, at pp. 30–46. Footnote 88 presents several newer cases decided by the CJEU recently regarding the Free Movement Directive.

118 Other Swedish research has made similar findings. See JÄNTERÄ-JAREBORG, above n. 89, at 242 ('An attitude I often encounter in Sweden is that the current rules are nothing to worry about or that they at least only concern a few people. This ignorance, especially among lawyers, worries me. As part of EU law, the rules are binding on Sweden in all respects. It follows that our courts and authorities are obliged to apply them and lawyers must learn to use them. The statement that only a few are affected, I find astonishing … [In actuality two to three] million individuals with strong Swedish (and foreign) connections are affected by EU family law regulations, often without the slightest knowledge of what this may mean for their rights') (translation from Swedish mine).

law matters. This is true for example with respect to the failure of Member States to reach unanimous agreement on Rome III or another regulation to harmonise the choice-of-law rules that their courts apply in cross-border matters:[119]

> The inability of the Member States to agree on [harmonised rules for choice of law in cross-border matters] has resulted in a situation of 'variable geometry' in the European legal landscape. Eleven out of 28 [sic] Member States apply their own choice of law rules on divorce and legal separation. Some apply a *lex fori* approach, others rely on nationality as the main connecting factor, while still others refer to the habitual residence of the spouses. Under such circumstances, one can hardly speak of a clear legal framework providing citizens with predictable outcomes. Party autonomy, in particular, is generally not allowed in private international law of [Rome III] nonparticipating Member States.

As these researchers also point out, divorcing spouses who agree on the law applicable to their divorce under the right to choose provided by the Rome III Regulation often have no guarantee that the court seized with jurisdiction will enforce their choice.[120] On the other hand, there now exist a variety of conflict-of-law rules increasing the likelihood – at least in the EU cross-border divorce or legal separation proceedings covered by Rome III for those Member States that have acceded to it, but even in the full range of EU 'parental responsibility' and divorce matters covered by Brussels II *ter* – that cases will be decided under the substantive law of the national court which is determined to have jurisdiction over them per Brussels II *ter*.[121]

---

119 Corneloup, above n. 65, at p. 11 (internal citations removed). Note that choice of substantive law to be applied differs from choice of which legal system will have jurisdiction to consider the matter; as discussed above, jurisdictional questions and mutual recognition of decisions questions are already more harmonised.

120 Ibid. Inclusion of a requirement for EU courts in cross-border matters to allow choice of court jurisdiction agreements 'could have brought the necessary legal certainty, but neither the … Brussels II bis Regulation nor its 2019 recast provides for them.' Ibid.

121 This is in part because applying Brussels II to jurisdictional questions and then the Rome III Regulation to choice of law (for those Member States participating in it) frequently results in the applicability of the *lex fori*, thus using substantively and procedurally that same court's national law. Meanwhile the connecting factors controlling which courts will have jurisdiction in a given case, primarily those in Art. 3 of Brussels II that binds more Member States than Rome III, are quite similar to those in Art. 8 of Rome III (choosing a particular forum's applicable law) and thus often point to the same courts in similar factual situations. Often cases using Brussels II but not Rome III then will be in practice both using the same forum and also its law, as has been recognised in prior scholarship. It is the cases where a Member State or party wishes to have flexibility not to use a given substantive law that can lead to a different result. Corneloup, above n. 65, at p. 11 (discussing cases to which Rome III applies; however, these reasons for local law to be applied can also often be found in national choice-of-law rules, including Sweden's).

This can be argued to be more or less desirable from a uniformity versus autonomy standpoint, as when for example Sweden, due to its own public policy concerns, can in cases where it has jurisdiction apply its substantive law instead of the law that would otherwise be used. If the political and historical differences between Member States continue on average to lessen in intensity over time – as diversity within societies and more shared, global family norms about acceptable rights-based bounds continue to emerge – it seems likely that uniformity of European family law, at least in cross-border cases, might continue to increase.

UNITED STATES OF AMERICA

THE SURPRISING CONTINUING LACK OF CONSENSUS UNDER US LAW FOR THE AWARD OF SPOUSAL SUPPORT AFTER DIVORCE

J. Thomas OLDHAM

Résumé

Les trois conséquences patrimoniales potentielles d'un divorce sont en droit américain: le partage des biens, la pension alimentaire pour les enfants (s'il y a des enfants mineurs) et la pension pour un époux. Les règles régissant le divorce étant promulguées au niveau des États, elles varient évidemment à certains égards. Il existe toutefois un accord de principe sur les normes relatives au partage des biens et à l'octroi d'une pension alimentaire pour les enfants. Le consensus sur diverses questions relatives à l'attribution d'une pension pour un époux est, en revanche, loin d'être atteint. Dans cet article, j'analyserai les domaines qui semblent faire l'objet d'un accord général ainsi que ceux qui sont plus conflictuels.

1. INTRODUCTION

The three potential economic remedies at divorce under US law are property division, child support (if there are minor children) and spousal support. Because divorce rules are promulgated at the state level, they obviously vary in some ways. But there is general agreement regarding standards for the division of property and the award of child support.[1] There is much less agreement about various issues relating to the award of spousal support.[2] In this chapter I will note those areas where there appear to be general agreement as well as the other matters where there is more conflict.

2. VARIOUS ISSUES THAT ARE PRESENTED BY THE CONCEPT OF POST-DIVORCE SPOUSAL SUPPORT

2.1. TYPES OF POST-DIVORCE SUPPORT POSSIBLE

There are three main types of spousal support available in a number of states. The first is 'rehabilitative support', which is support given for a fixed period so that the recipient can obtain career training to better prepare them to obtain employment. The second is 'reimbursement support', which is support given to one spouse who has financially supported the other during marriage so that he or she could obtain education or training. The third type is a more 'general support' where one spouse is ordered to pay the other spouse after divorce a certain amount of money (normally every month) for a certain period of time due to substantial differences between the post-divorce earning capacities of the parties. This chapter will focus on the last type of support.

---

1 See generally H. Krause, L. Elrod and J.T. Oldham, *Family Law: Cases, Comments, and Questions*, West Academic Publishing, 8th ed., 2016, chapters 15, 17.

2 See generally J.T. Oldham, 'A Survey of Lawyers' Observations about the Principles Governing the Award of Spousal Support throughout the United States' (2017) 51 *Family Law Quarterly* 1.

2.2. ENTITLEMENT TO SUPPORT

2.2.1. *Marriages of Short Duration*

It is rare for a spouse to receive 'general support' when parties are divorcing after a relatively brief marriage.[3] Some states have enacted statutes to this effect. For example, in Texas it is not possible to receive spousal support if the marriage did not last at least ten years, unless there has been recent domestic violence or the claimant spouse is disabled or caring for a disabled child.[4] Maine has also enacted a statute providing that there is a rebuttable presumption that general support should not be awarded if the parties have been married for fewer than ten years.[5]

2.2.2. *Marriages of Longer Duration*

2.2.2.1. Factors a Court is Instructed to Consider

In many states, courts are instructed, when making a decision whether to award spousal support, to consider various factors, such as the duration of the marriage, the parties' health, ages, needs, debts and earning capacities.[6] Some permit the court to consider which spouse was 'at fault' in causing the divorce.[7] In a few states, spousal support is forbidden if the claimant spouse is found to be at fault.[8]

As stated above, spousal support is rarely awarded in short-duration marriages. Half of all divorcing couples have been married seven years or less.[9] Spousal support is awarded only if one of the spouses can afford to pay it. Professor Marsha Garrison in her study of divorcing couples found that many barely earned enough to support themselves and that courts did not ordinarily award support if it would impoverish the payor spouse, even where a substantial difference in income existed.[10] Therefore, perhaps it is not surprising that

---

3 Of course, rehabilitative support and reimbursement support might be more common in marriages of short duration.

4 See Tex. Fam. Code §8.051.

5 See Me. Rev. Stat. Ann. Tit. 19-A §951.

6 See generally R. Kirkman Collins, 'The Theory of Marital Residuals: Applying an Income Adjustment Calculus to the Enigma of Alimony' (2001) 24 *Harvard Women's Law Journal* 23, 33.

7 See I.M. Ellman, 'The Place of Fault in Modern Divorce Law' (1996) 28 *Arizonan State Law Journal* 773.

8 See Ga. Code §19-16-1; La. Civ. Code Ann. Art. 112; N.C. Gen. Stat. §50-16.3A; and Va. Code Ann. §20-107.1.

9 See A. Cherlin, *Marriage, Divorce, Remarriage*, Harvard University Press, rev. ed., 1992, p. 24.

10 See generally M. Garrison, 'Good Intentions Gone Awry: The Impact of New York's Equitable Distribution Law on Divorce Outcomes' (1991) 52 *Brooklyn Law Journal* 621, 707.

spousal support appears to be awarded in no more than approximately 10–20 per cent of all divorces.[11]

2.2.2.2. A Note about Career Enhancement and Marital Property Division

In a US divorce, in most states the court will divide all 'property' accumulated by either party during marriage (other than a gift or an inheritance received by one spouse).[12] However, the concept of property does not include an increase (or decrease) in the earning capacity of either party during the marriage. The value of any property acquired during marriage, or savings accrued, is divided approximately equally at divorce.

But the spouses could be leaving the marriage with very different career prospects, and those different career prospects are not addressed via the division of the marital estate. Spousal support can be used to address these income differences where the jurisdiction provides that this is an appropriate purpose for spousal support, raising the question of what circumstances are necessary to justify such a spousal support award.

The spouses might have different career prospects for many different reasons. First, they might have chosen careers with very different probable salaries for reasons unrelated to the marriage. Second, one spouse might have become ill or injured during marriage. Third, one spouse might have stopped working outside the home for a substantial period to care for the parties' children, thereby suffering 'career damage' when he or she attempts to restart that career after divorce. For purposes of entitlement to spousal support, should all three situations be treated the same?

In many states, the answer to this question is not clear. One prominent commentator regarding spousal support law, Professor Ira Ellman, has argued that the purpose of spousal support should be to compensate a spouse for career damage incurred as a result of a role assumed during the marriage.[13] The American Law Institute, in its Principles of the Law of Family Dissolution, provides that, in connection with the decision to award spousal support, the focus should be on (1) the extent to which the claimant spouse suffered career damage due to a role assumed during the marriage, and (2) in longer-duration marriages, the extent to which the claimant spouse will suffer a lower standard of living.[14]

---

11 See J. McMullen and D. Oswald, 'Why Do We Need a Lawyer? An Empirical Study of Divorce Cases' (2010) 12 *Journal of Law & Family Studies* 57, 75.

12 See generally J.T. Oldham, *Divorce, Separation and the Distribution of Property*, Law Journal Press, 2021.

13 See I.M. Ellman, 'Inventing Family Law' (1999) 32 *UC Davis Law Review* 855, 879 n. 54.

14 American Law Institute, *Principles of the Law of Family Dissolution: Analysis and Recommendations*, 2002, §§5.04, 5.05.

2.2.2.3. The Prevailing Standard for Determining Whether to Award General Spousal Support

It was stated above that general spousal support is rarely awarded in short-duration marriages. In longer-duration marriages, many courts do not currently appear to apply the approach suggested by Professor Ellman referred to in the preceding paragraph. US courts have a tendency to award support if one spouse can 'afford' it and the other 'needs' it. A few states, like Texas, have enacted a standard that support should be awarded only if the claimant spouse cannot otherwise meet his or her 'minimum reasonable needs'.[15] This language suggests that, to qualify for support in Texas, the claimant spouse must show that he or she will be close to destitute without support. In contrast, almost all states have enacted as a standard that the claimant spouse must show that he or she cannot otherwise meet his or her 'reasonable' needs.

Most courts have interpreted this to mean, at least in longer-duration marriages where the higher earner's career was substantially enhanced during the marriage, that the claimant spouse cannot maintain something approximating the marital standard of living.[16] This standard suggests that spousal support might be an indirect way to allow the spouses to share in one spouse's career enhancement during the marriage. But the claim to spousal support is certainly not treated as an ownership interest of the claimant spouse. For example, the right to spousal support is generally lost when the claimant spouse dies, remarries or cohabits.

If the court determines that spousal support is warranted, the court then invites the claimant spouse to submit a budget summarising what amount of support is needed at divorce, after considering any other income of the recipient, to maintain the standard of living during the marriage.[17] The obligor spouse frequently challenges the submitted budget as excessive.[18]

So, in order to calculate the amount of support, the most common approach is to focus on the claimant spouse's 'needs'.[19] This generally requires the obligor spouse to pay a percentage of his or her post-divorce income to the claimant. Note that, even in a marriage of very long duration, it is extremely rare for a court to fashion a spousal support award that would result in equal post-divorce income-sharing. Even after the spousal support award is subtracted from the obligor's income, generally the obligor's income is significantly higher than that of the claimant spouse.

---

15 See Tex. Fam. Code §8.051.

16 See *Rainwater v. Rainwater*, 869 P.2d 176 (Ariz. App. 1993).

17 See *Naramore v. Naramore*, 611 S.W.3d 281 (Ky. App. 2020).

18 See *Sulkin v. Sulkin*, 619 S.W.3d 155 (Mo. App. 2021).

19 See *Wold v. Wold*, 744 N.W.2d 541 (N.D. 2008); *In re Marriage of Gust*, 858 N.W.2d 402 (Iowa 2015); and *Young v. Young*, 81 N.E.3d 1165 (Mass. 2017).

2.2.2.4. Determining the Amount of Support

As set forth above, the manner in which the amount of support is calculated in most states is based on the difference between the income of the claimant spouse and his or her 'reasonable' expenses. Some contend that there should be some sort of cap on the amount of spousal support that can be awarded. For example, in Texas the maximum spousal support award cannot exceed the lesser of (1) 20 per cent of the obligor's income or (2) $5,000.[20]

The Texas statute presents two different issues. First, should there be a maximum percentage of income that the obligor can be ordered to pay as support to the other spouse? Second, should there be a maximum amount? These issues arise when the parties enjoyed a high standard of living during marriage due to the career success of one of the spouses. To allow the other spouse to maintain that high standard of living after divorce in these situations, the spousal support award would need to be quite large. Some argue that such awards would go beyond meeting the recipient spouse's reasonable needs and amount to a distribution of the higher earner's career assets.

In a number of jurisdictions, where spouses have been married for long time, and the parties enjoyed a high standard of living due to one spouse's high income, the spousal support award can be quite large. For example, in a recent Massachusetts case, the husband's income exceeded $7 million annually in the last two years of the marriage.[21] The trial court awarded the wife general spousal support of 33 per cent of the husband's gross annual income.[22] The Massachusetts Supreme Court reversed the award expressed as a percentage of annual income and remanded the matter to the trial court to determine a fixed annual amount, but the court did not state that the award was excessive.[23]

In other recent cases, courts endorsed a finding that the claimant spouse has substantial reasonable financial needs. For example, a Tennessee case found that a spouse's needs were $15,000 per month.[24] A Connecticut case similarly affirmed a monthly award of $15,000 in support.[25] A recent New Jersey case affirmed an annual award of $450,000 in support.[26]

While these awards might be considered substantial, they generally do not attempt to share post-divorce income equally. For example, in a recent Iowa case, the spouses were divorcing after 28 years of marriage.[27] The husband's

20 See Tex. Fam. Code §8.055.
21 *Young v. Young*, 478 Mass. 1 (2017).
22 Ibid.
23 Ibid.
24 *Stratienko v. Stratienko*, 529 S.W.3d 389 (Tenn. App. 2017).
25 *Dan v. Dan*, 105 A.3d 118 (Conn. 2014).
26 *SW v. GW*, No. A-4063-14T3, 2018 WL 944074 (N.J. Super. Ct. App. Div. Feb. 20, 2018).
27 *In re Marriage of Mauer*, 874 N.W.2d 103 (Iowa 2016).

monthly income exceeded $80,000, and the wife's earning capacity was approximately $2,000 per month.[28] The wife was awarded $12,600 in monthly support.[29] Similarly, a Hawaiian couple divorced after 18 years of marriage.[30] The husband's monthly income was approximately $25,000. The wife did not have a job but the court awarded her investment property that generated income of about $4,500 per month.[31] The trial court found that her reasonable expenses were $6,237 per month.[32] The court of appeals ruled that the wife should receive $4,000 in monthly alimony (so the wife's total monthly income would have been $8,500).[33] The Hawaiian Supreme Court held that, without more specific findings why such an award was reasonable, it was an abuse of discretion to award the wife an amount of alimony that, when considering her other income, exceeded her monthly needs[34] (note that, even with the award of $4,000 per month, the husband's household income would be $21,000 compared to the wife's monthly income of $8,500).

Awards of general spousal support can be later modified if there is a substantial change in either of the parties' circumstances, if the change in circumstances was not anticipated when the original order was made.[35]

When determining whether a spouse petitioning for support 'needs' support, it can be relevant whether the spouse is receiving substantial property in the divorce. Should the claimant spouse be required to use the property division assets for his or her support? Many statutes require that, to qualify for support, the claimant must show that, based on his or her available income and property, including property received in the divorce, he or she cannot provide adequate support.[36] This language suggests that the property division assets should be considered when deciding upon whether to grant a spousal support award. This would seem to be a sensible rule.

In one recent case, the wife received $800,000 in liquid assets in the divorce. The court assumed that the wife could receive a 4 per cent return on these assets, generating $32,000 in investment income each year. When analysing how much spousal support the wife needed after divorce, the court compared her reasonable expenses to the sum of her wages and the estimated investment income.[37]

---

28 Ibid.

29 Ibid.

30 See *Jacoby v. Jacoby*, 498 P.3d 689 (Haw. 2021), *reconsideration denied*, 2021 WL 5505503 (Haw. Nov. 24, 2021).

31 Ibid.

32 Ibid.

33 Ibid.

34 Ibid.

35 See *Banks v. Banks*, 980 N.E.2d 423 (Ind. App. 2012).

36 See Colo. Rev. Stat. Ann. §14-10-114 (3) (d).

37 See *In re Marriage of Mauer*, 874 N.W.2d 103 (Iowa 2016).

Perhaps the result in the divorce of actor John Cleese in California will then be surprising. Cleese had been married to a psychotherapist for 16 years. They did not have children and accumulated a great deal of wealth during the marriage. In California the community property estate must be divided equally, so the wife received property worth $17 million in the divorce. In addition, Cleese (who was 70 years old at the time) was also ordered to pay his former wife approximately $1,000,000 per year in spousal support for seven years.[38] This really is a quite stunning result in light of the size of the property settlement, the fact that the Cleese's spouse did not appear to have suffered any career damage as a result of the marriage, and the fact his career was established before the marriage began.

2.2.2.5. The Duration of the Support Award

Perhaps the most hotly debated issue in the US pertaining to spousal support awards relates to the duration of such awards. In a few states, there is a maximum duration for spousal support awards. For example, in Texas, if the marriage lasted fewer than 30 years, a spousal support award cannot exceed seven years in duration, unless the claimant spouse is disabled or is caring for a disabled child.[39] In Indiana, spousal support generally cannot exceed three years in duration.[40] In Delaware, spousal support cannot exceed 50 per cent of the marital duration.[41] In Utah, absent extenuating circumstances, the spousal support award cannot exceed the length of the marriage.[42] But most states give courts discretion to choose the appropriate duration of a spousal support award.

In cases involving divorces of 'medium' duration (10–15 years), some courts have recently awarded support for a term resembling the duration of the marriage. For example, when a New Jersey couple was divorcing after ten years of marriage with minor children, the appellate court affirmed a spousal support award lasting ten years; the support ended when the youngest child would be 18.[43] In an Arkansas case, where the parties were divorcing after 12 years of marriage with small children, the claimant spouse was awarded support for ten years.[44] A South Dakota court awarded support for eight years when the parties were divorcing after seven years of marriage.[45]

---

38 See A. Pierce, 'John Cleese in £12 Million Divorce Settlement', *The Telegraph*, 18 August 2009, available at: <https://www.telegraph.co.uk/news/celebritynews/6043628/John-Cleese-in-12-million-divorce-settlement.html>.

39 Tex. Fam. Code §8.054.

40 Ind. Code Ann. §31-15-7-2.

41 Del. Code Ann. Tit. 13 §1512 (d).

42 Utah Code Ann. §30-3-5 (8).

43 *JEV v. KV*, 45 A.3d 1001 (N.J. Super. App. Div. 2012).

44 *Foster v. Foster*, 506 S.W.3d 808 (Ark. 2016).

45 *Urbaniak v. Urbaniak*, 807 N.W.2d 621 (S.D. 2011).

An Illinois case involved spouses who were both medical doctors who were divorcing with minor children after 16 years of marriage. The wife was working part-time at the time of the divorce, earning $100,000 annually. The husband was earning more than $1,700,000 annually. The appellate court affirmed an award of $18,000 in monthly child support and $8,500 in monthly spousal support for 102 months. The court noted that the spousal support award duration amounted to an award of 60 per cent of the marital duration.[46]

Perhaps the most controversial issue relating to spousal support duration is how long a support award should continue when spouses are divorcing after a 'long' (more than 20-year) marriage, the spouses have very different career prospects and it is unlikely that the spouse with the lower income can generate a substantial post-divorce career. When a number of US states were adopting 'equitable distribution' divorce statutes in the 1970s and 1980s and women were entering the workforce in increasing numbers, there was a hope that a dependent spouse's financial needs after divorce could be addressed through the property division. There also was a hope that the spouse could develop a career by obtaining training for a period after the divorce. So, in the 1970s and 1980s it was not uncommon for a dependent spouse divorcing after a long-duration marriage to receive support for only a few years.[47]

However, it gradually became apparent that many spouses at divorce did not have much property to divide, and that many dependent spouses divorcing after a long marriage could not create any meaningful career after many years of being out of the workforce fulfilling the role of a wife and mother. This resulted in what has been referred to as the 'second wave' of alimony reform in the US.[48] These new laws encouraged judges, when considering a spousal support award, to be more realistic about the extent to which a spouse could become self-supporting after many years out of the workforce. As a result, it has become more common in a number of states, when spouses are divorcing after a long marriage where the wife has been out of the workforce for a substantial period raising children, for a dependent spouse to receive an award of spousal support for an indefinite duration, with the support ending upon (1) the death of the payor spouse or (2) the death, remarriage or cohabitation of the recipient spouse.

But of course, such an award can tie the parties economically for a very long time after the divorce. In what situations is it appropriate? Maryland has tried to clarify this issue. In Maryland, fixed-term support is the norm.[49] However,

46 *In re Marriage of Jones*, 2016 IL App. (5th) 150212-U.

47 See *Otis v. Otis*, 299 N.W.2d 114 (Minn. 1980).

48 See generally M.K. Kisthardt, 'Rethinking Alimony: The AAML's Considerations for Calculating Alimony, Spousal Support or Maintenance' (2008) 21 *Journal of the American Academy of Matrimonial Lawyers* 61.

49 See *St. Cyr v. St. Cyr*, 137 A.3d 332 (Md. App. 2016).

indefinite alimony is possible in exceptional circumstances where the 'standard of living of one spouse will be so inferior … to the standard of living of the other to be morally unacceptable and shocking to the court.'[50] This had been referred to as the 'unconscionable disparity' standard.[51]

But what is an 'unconscionable disparity'? In long marriages, courts have compared the claimant's income to the payor spouse's income. In a few recent cases, where the claimant's income amounted to 2–4 per cent of the payor spouse's income, perhaps it was not surprising that the Maryland court found that an unconscionable disparity existed.[52] It is more surprising that courts have found that an unconscionable disparity existed when the claimant's income amounted to 43 per cent and 46 per cent of the payor's income.[53]

States have disagreed in defining what is a 'long' duration marriage that should qualify for support for an indefinite duration. A Florida case has stated that there is a rebuttable presumption that indefinite-term support should be awarded when spouses divorce after a long marriage.[54] A Florida statute defines a long marriage as one of 17 years or more.[55] The guidelines adopted by Colorado, Illinois and Massachusetts (to be discussed in more detail in section 3.3 below) provide that indefinite-term support can be awarded if the marriage duration exceeded 20 years.[56]

Courts have been reluctant to establish rules of thumb regarding indefinite-term support. For example, in a New Jersey case involving a couple divorcing after 15 years of marriage, the trial court stated that indefinite-term support should be awarded only if the marital duration exceeded 25 years. The court of appeals reversed, stating that indefinite-term alimony should generally be awarded when the marital duration exceeded 15 years. The New Jersey Supreme Court rejected these attempts to tie indefinite-term alimony to a specific marital duration.[57]

Should indefinite-term alimony continue until the payor dies or the recipient dies or remarries? Massachusetts has enacted a rule that spousal support should stop when the obligor reaches 'normal retirement age'.[58] To the extent that spousal support is perceived as a way to allow the recipient spouse to share in the payor's post-divorce income, it makes sense that it should terminate when the

50 *Karmand v. Karmand*, 802 A.2d 1106 (Md. App. 2002).

51 *Kaplan v. Kaplan*, 241 A.3d 960 (Md. Spec. App. 2020).

52 See *Kaplan v. Kaplan*, 241 A.3d 960 (Md. Spec. App. 2020); and *KB v. DB*, 227 A.3d 705 (Md. 2020).

53 See *Broseus v. Broseus*, 570 A.2d 874 (Md. 1990); and *Caldwell v. Caldwell*, 653 A.2d 994 (Md. 1995).

54 See *Fichtel v. Fichtel*, 141 So.3d 593, 595 (Fla. App. 2014).

55 See Fla. Stat. Ann. §61.08 (4).

56 See Colo. Rev. Stat. Ann. §14-10-114 (3) (b) (II) (A); and 750 Ill. Comp. Stat. Ann. §5/504 (b-1) (1) (B); and Mass. Gen. Laws Ann. ch. 208 §49 (c).

57 See *Gnall v. Gnall*, 119 A.3d 891 (N.J. 2015).

58 See Mass. Gen. Laws Ann. ch. 208, §49 (f).

payor spouse retires. In addition, to the extent the pension benefits were earned by the employee during marriage, it would be customary for a divorce court to equally divide those pension benefits between the spouses, so that the non-employee spouse would share some of the pension benefits after the employee retires as part of the property settlement.[59]

I mentioned above that indefinite-term support is most commonly limited to cases when spouses are divorcing after a 'long' marriage. This is not true in some states. For example, some Missouri decisions state that 'there is a judicial preference for awards of unlimited duration'.[60] This clearly is a minority view.

3. ARE GUIDELINES THE ANSWER?

3.1. GENERAL DISCUSSION

Judicial discretion in some areas of US divorce law, such as property division and child support, has been significantly reduced with recent changes in family law. It is odd that the standards for the award of spousal support continue to be unclear in a number of states. The award of spousal support at divorce can significantly affect the divorce's financial outcome for the parties. It would seem sensible if more guidance could be provided to judges, lawyers and their clients regarding the rules for the award of spousal support.

I have attempted to describe above the general norms for spousal support awards in the US today. However, a significant number of family lawyers report anecdotally that in any given case it frequently is unclear what standards a judge will apply when deciding an alimony claim. Some contend that the current amount of discretion given judges in many states today leads to arbitrary and unpredictable results.

Some studies have found that lawyers believe the standards for the award of spousal support are unclear. For example, a committee formed by the Iowa Supreme Court to study standards for the award of spousal support found exactly that – responding lawyers frequently stated that the standards were unclear.[61] A survey of Ohio judges asking them to predict the award of spousal support in various situations found that there were substantial differences in the approaches of the judges surveyed.[62] A Nevada trial court judge has written that

---

59 J.T. Oldham, *Divorce, Separation and the Distribution of Property*, Law Journal Press, 2021, section 7.10.

60 See *Parciak v. Parciak*, 553 S.W.3d 446, 453 (Mo. App. E. Dist. 2018).

61 See *Report of the Iowa Supreme Court Family Law Case Processing Task Force*, Spousal Support Work Group Report, Appendix D 20 (22 March 2010) (79% of respondents stated that the standards for the award of spousal support were inconsistent where they practised).

62 See L. Herndon Spillane, 'Spousal Support: The Other Ohio Lottery' (1998) 24 *Ohio Northern University Law Review* 282.

'Nevada decisional and statutory law provide support for almost any conceivable alimony decision.'[63] Similarly, a prominent Nevada divorce lawyer has written that the standards for the award of spousal support in Nevada are 'muddled, vague, contradictory and inadequate'.[64]

Presumably due to the concerns mentioned in the preceding paragraph, a handful of states during the past decade have adopted guidelines for the award of spousal support. As the term 'guidelines' suggests, these are not fixed formulas that have to be rigidly applied. However, they do attempt to provide a clearer potential framework for the award of spousal support. These guidelines do not guide the court in its determination regarding whether spousal support should be awarded. If the court does decide to award support, the guidelines provide general principles for determining the amount and duration for an award.

3.2. CALCULATING THE AMOUNT OF SUPPORT UNDER VARIOUS GUIDELINES

One question that needs to be addressed when formulating a support guideline is whether the amount of post-divorce income-sharing should increase as the marital duration increases. Most guidelines do not address this issue. However, under the Maricopa County, Arizona guidelines, the amount of support varies with the marital duration.[65] The guideline applies to spouses who have been married for more than five years where the income of the spouse with the lower income is no more than 75 per cent of the other spouse's income.[66] The support amount is determined by first calculating the difference in the net incomes of the parties at divorce.[67] Then the difference is multiplied by 1.5 per cent times the number of years of marriage.[68] So, for parties ending a ten-year marriage, the support amount would be 15 per cent of the net income difference, while the support amount would be 30 per cent of the difference if the marriage has lasted 20 years.[69] The Vermont guidelines also increase income-sharing with marital duration.[70]

---

63 D.A. Hardy, 'Nevada Alimony: An Important Policy in Need of a Coherent Policy Purpose' (2009) 9 *Nevada Law Journal* 325, 343.

64 See M.S. Wilick, 'A Universal Approach to Alimony: How Alimony Should Be Calculated and Why' (2014) 27 *Journal of the American Academy of Matrimonial Lawyers* 153, 171.

65 See Superior Court of Arizona, Maricopa County, Family Court Department, 'Spousal Maintenance Guidelines' (October 2002). For a judicial discussion of the guidelines, see *Collum v. Collum*, 160 P.3d 231 (Ariz. App. 2007).

66 Ibid.

67 Ibid.

68 Ibid.

69 Ibid.

70 See Vt. Stat. Ann. Tit. 15 §752 (b) (8).

Under the guidelines that have been adopted in Colorado, Illinois and New York, the duration of marriage does not affect the amount of support. Instead, the support amount is determined by a calculation based on the difference in the net incomes of the parties.[71] The Massachusetts guideline suggest that the amount of a support award should not exceed 30–35 per cent of the difference between the gross incomes of the parties.[72]

3.3. DETERMINING THE AWARD DURATION UNDER THE GUIDELINES

All guidelines now arrive at an award duration, as opposed to amount, based on the marital duration. Under the New York guidelines, the award duration should be 15–30 per cent of the marital duration if the marriage lasted 15 years or less.[73] For marriages that lasted 20 years or more, the award duration should be 35–50 per cent of the marital duration.[74] In Vermont, for marriages that lasted 10–15 years, the award should be 40–60 per cent of the marital duration.[75] If the marriage lasted 15–20 years, the duration should be 50–70 per cent of the marital duration.[76]

Similarly, under the guidelines adopted in Colorado, Illinois and Massachusetts, support duration is also a function of the duration of the marriage. In Colorado, for marriages that did not last 20 years, the suggested maximum duration is 50 per cent of the marital duration.[77] Delaware and Maine have adopted a similar standard for support duration.[78] In Massachusetts, the maximum duration of an award is 50 per cent of the marital duration if the marriage lasted five years or less.[79] The percentage gradually then increases with marital duration, so the suggested maximum support term for marriages that lasted 15–20 years is 80 per cent of the marital duration.[80] In Colorado, Illinois and Massachusetts indefinite-duration support is possible if the marital duration exceeds 20 years.

---

71 See Colo. Rev. Stat. Ann. §14-10-114 (3) (b) (I) (A); and 750 Ill. Comp. Stat. Ann. §5/504 (b-1) (A).

72 See Mass. Gen. Laws Ann. ch. 208 §53 (b).

73 See N.Y. Dom. Rel. L. §236.

74 Ibid. See also E. Karabatos and E. Tepper, 'New York Spousal Maintenance Guidelines' (2017) 51 *Family Law Quarterly* 51.

75 See Vt. Stat. Ann. Tit. 15 §752 (b) (8).

76 Ibid.

77 See Colo. Rev. Stat. Ann. §14-10-114 (3) (b) (II) (B).

78 See Del. Code Ann. Tit. 13 §1512 (d); and Me. Stat. Tit. 19A §951-A.

79 See Mass. Gen. Laws Ann. ch. 208 §49.

80 Ibid.

4. CONCLUSION

In many states today, divorce judges have a great deal of discretion regarding issues relating to the entitlement, amount and duration of a spousal support award. Lawyers report that the result in any given case often is unpredictable. This perceived lack of standards has caused some states to adopt spousal support guidelines. The adoption of guidelines could provide more uniformity, at least regarding the amount and duration of awards. However, it appears that many judges do not now support spousal support guidelines.

It is unclear whether the 'high-discretion' approach toward spousal support currently practised in a number of states today can long endure. In American equitable distribution law, a fundamental principle is that a spouse's post-divorce earnings should not be divided. When an award of spousal support is made, this creates a substantial exception to this fundamental principle of US divorce law. It seems extremely unwise to create such a significant remedy at divorce and then give judges very little guidance about how spousal support claims should be evaluated. In many states, some mechanism needs to be adopted soon to provide more guidance to judges, lawyers and their clients regarding this very important aspect of US divorce law.

INDEX

www.ingramcontent.com/pod-product-compliance
Ingram Content Group UK Ltd.
Pitfield, Milton Keynes, MK11 3LW, UK
UKHW051918100926
8556IPUK00021B/1251

9 781839 7026